Studies in Celtic History XXIV

ST DAVID OF WALES

CULT, CHURCH AND NATION

The cult of St David has been an enduring symbol of Welsh identity across more than a millennium. This volume, published to commemorate the fourteenth centenary of the death of the saint, traces the evidence for the cult of St David through archaeological, historical, hagiographical, liturgical, and toponymic evidence, and considers the role of the cult and church of St David in the history of Welsh society, politics, and landscape. The collection includes a new edition and translation of the *Life* of St David by Rhygyfarch, based on the text in British Library MS Cotton Vespasian A.xiv, as well as new evidence concerning the relics of the saint enshrined in St Davids Cathedral.

J. WYN EVANS is the Dean of St Davids Cathedral.
JONATHAN M. WOODING is Director of the Centre for the Study of Religion in Celtic Societies at University of Wales Lampeter.

STUDIES IN CELTIC HISTORY

ISSN 0261–9865

General editors
Dauvit Broun
Máire Ní Mhaonaigh
Huw Pryce

Studies in Celtic History aims to provide a forum for new research into all aspects of the history of Celtic-speaking peoples throughout the whole of the medieval period. The term 'history' is inderstood broadly: any study, regardless of discipline, which advances our knowledge and understanding of the history of Celtic-speaking peoples will be considered. Studies of primary sources, and of new methods of exploiting such sources, are encouraged.

Founded by Professor David Dumville, the series was relaunched under new editorship in 1997. Proposals or queries may be sent directly to the editors at the addresses given below; all submissions will receive prompt and informed consideration before being sent to expert readers.

Dr Dauvit Broun, Department of History (Scottish), University of Glasgow, 9 University Gardens, Glasgow G12 8QH

Dr Máire Ní Mhaonaigh, St John's College, Cambridge, CB2 1TP

Dr Huw Pryce, Department of History and Welsh History, University of Wales, Bangor, Bangor, Gwynedd LL57 2DG

For titles already published in this series
see the end of this volume

ST DAVID OF WALES

CULT, CHURCH AND NATION

Edited by

J. WYN EVANS
JONATHAN M. WOODING

THE BOYDELL PRESS

First published 2007
The Boydell Press, Woodbridge

ISBN 978–1–84383–322–2

The Boydell Press is an imprint of Boydell & Brewer Ltd
PO Box 9, Woodbridge, Suffolk IP12 3DF, UK
and of Boydell & Brewer Inc.
668 Mt Hope Avenue, Rochester, NY 14620, USA
website: www.boydellandbrewer.com

A catalogue record of this publication is available
from the British Library

This publication is printed on acid-free paper

Printed and bound in Great Britain by
Antony Rowe Ltd, Chippenham, Wiltshire

CONTENTS

ILLUSTRATIONS

List of Illustrations

Figures

Tables

PREFACE

This volume in the long-established and distinguished series Studies in Celtic History is the fruit of a collaboration between two institutions linked by nearly two centuries of history: the Cathedral of St David and the University of Wales Lampeter (founded in 1822 as St David's College Lampeter, by Thomas Burgess, bishop of St Davids). To mark 175 years since the opening of the college, in 1827, and to commemorate the fourteenth centenary of the death of St David, a slightly less-securely dated event, the Centre for the Study of Religion in Celtic Societies (CSRCS) hosted a four-day conference in Lampeter, with a day excursion to St Davids.

The idea for the present volume arose from that conference, though only twelve of the chapters of this volume were presentations on the occasion. The intent of the editors, respectively the Dean of St Davids and the Director of CSRCS, was to produce a volume which brought together studies of the key questions for research that emerged from that conference. These had been, in particular, the need for renewed attention to be paid to the Vespasian recension of the *Vita S. Dauid* by Rhygyfarch, which it was suspected was closer to the author's original work than the shorter recension edited by J.W. James; new evidence which had emerged concerning the relics of St David preserved in the cathedral; a wealth of recent research into aspects of the cult of St David pursued in particular through the study of dedications, liturgical texts, and other neglected sources. The kind offer by Professor Richard Sharpe and Dr John Reuben Davies, to whom we are deeply indebted for their labours, to produce a new edition of the *Vita S. Dauid* provided a focal point for a volume that we hope will serve to stimulate a renewed interest in the cult of a saint in whom the interest of the Welsh people has rarely waned, but for whom there appears to have been fairly limited academic interest for some decades.

It remains to conclude with acknowledgements of the contributions of a number of individuals. It is invidious to single out a few among many, but for their assistance with the conference and the volume we would particularly like to thank the support staff of University of Wales Lampeter, who worked hard to organise the accommodation, meals, transport and other aspects of the conference. The Dean and Chapter, vergers and lay staff of St Davids Cathedral and the Cartref Restaurant in St Davids also warrant special mention. Professor Thomas O'Loughlin, Dean of the Faculty at Lampeter, contributed both his administrative and intellectual support to the conference and this volume. Professor D.P. Davies provided unending support, though finally was prevented by illness from delivering his planned keynote lecture. Professor Len Nokes and Professor Bernard Knight provided vital support for the session on the relics. Mrs Pat Jones, PA to the CSRCS Director, assisted in the final production of the text. The editorial staff at Boydell, especially Caroline Palmer and Anna Morton, and the series editors also warrant especial thanks.

The more recent element of the conference proceedings had as its main focus the work of Rice Rees, the first professor of Welsh at Lampeter, whose *An Essay on the Welsh Saints or the Primitive Christians usually considered to be the founders of churches in Wales* of 1836 remains a formative work in the study of Celtic hagiography, and whose family, Rees of Tonn, contributed so much to the vision of learning in Lampeter and the Diocese of St Davids. This volume is happily dedicated to this pioneer in our field whose work we are proud to continue.

Jonathan M. Wooding
Director, Centre for the Study of Religion in Celtic Societies, University of Wales Lampeter

J. Wyn Evans
Dean of St Davids Cathedral

CONTRIBUTORS

Dr Julia Barrow, School of History, University of Nottingham

Professor Christopher Bronk Ramsey, Research Laboratory for Archaeology & the History of Art, University of Oxford

Dr Jane Cartwright, Department of Welsh, University of Wales, Lampeter

Dr Fred Cowley, formerly University of Wales, Swansea

Dr John Reuben Davies, School of History, Classics and Archaeology, University of Edinburgh

Professor Owain Tudor Edwards, Norwegian Academy of Music, Oslo

The Very Rev. J. Wyn Evans, St Davids Cathedral, Pembrokeshire

Dr Tom Higham, Research Laboratory for Archaeology & the History of Art, University of Oxford

Dr David Howlett, Faculty of Classics, University of Oxford

Daniel Huws, National Library of Wales, Aberystwyth

Dr Graham Isaac, National University of Ireland, Galway

Heather James, formerly Cambria Archaeology, Llandeilo, Carmarthenshire

Dr John Morgan-Guy, Dept of Theology and Religious Studies, University of Wales, Lampeter

Professor L.D.M. Nokes, School of Engineering, Cardiff University

Professor Huw Pryce, School of History, Welsh History and Archaeology, University of Wales, Bangor

Dr Mark Redknap, Amgueddfa Cymru–National Museums and Galleries of Wales, Cardiff

Professor Richard Sharpe, Faculty of History, University of Oxford

Professor Bernard Tanguy, Centre de Recherche Bretonne et Celtique, Université de Bretagne Occidentale

†Professor Sir Glanmor Williams, formerly Department of History, University of Wales, Swansea

Dr Jonathan M. Wooding, Centre for the Study of Religion in Celtic Societies, University of Wales, Lampeter

Professor W. Nigel Yates, Department of Theology and Religious Studies, University of Wales, Lampeter

ABBREVIATIONS

AC	*Annales Cambriae*, ed. J. Williams (Ab Ithel) (London 1860).
AC (A)	The A-text of *Annales Cambriae*: annals, kept at St Davids in the ninth and tenth centuries, and found in an eleventh-century manuscript, London, British Library, MS Harley, 3859, fols 189v–193v. Ed. Phillimore, 'The *Annales Cambriæ*', at 152–69, reprinted in J. Morris, *Arthurian Sources*, V.11–55.
AC (B)	The B-text of *Annales Cambriae*: a continuation of the A-text, also kept at St Davids, and found on the fly-leaves of the Breviate Domesday Book, London, PRO, MS E. 164/1 (*saec.* XIII). Ed. in *AC*.
AC (C)	The C-text of *Annales Cambriae*: another continuation of the A-text, but independent of B, found in London, British Library, MS Cotton Domitian A.i (*saec.* XIII[ex]). For 682–954, parallel edition and translation by Dumville of all three versions. For 1039–1093, the B- and C-texts in Lloyd, 'Wales and the coming of the Normans', at 166–79. Other years, ed. Williams (ab Ithel).
Arch. Camb.	*Archaeologia Cambrensis*
ASC	Anglo-Saxon Chronicle: *The Anglo-Saxon Chronicle*, gen. edd. Dumville and Keynes: MS A: ed. Janet M. Bately, vol. 3 (Cambridge 1986) MS B: ed. Simon Taylor, vol. 4 (Cambridge 1983) MS D: ed. G.P. Cubbin, vol. 6 (Woodbridge 1996).
AWR	*The Acts of Welsh Rulers, 1120–1283*, ed. H. Pryce with the assistance of C. Insley (Cardiff 2005).
BBCS	*Bulletin of the Board of Celtic Studies.*
BL	British Library
ByS	*Brenhinedd y Saesson*: ed. and transl. T. Jones (Cardiff 1971).
ByT (Pen. 20)	*Brut y Tywysogyon, or, The Chronicle of the Princes, Peniarth MS. 20 Version*, transl. Thomas Jones (Cardiff 1952).
ByT (RB)	*Brut y Tywysogyon, or, The Chronicle of the Princes, Red Book of Hergest Version*, ed. Thomas Jones, 2nd edn (Cardiff 1973).
CMCS	*Cambridge Medieval Celtic Studies* 1–25 (1982–1993); *Cambrian Medieval Celtic Studies* 26– (1994–).
CPR	*Calendar of the Patent Rolls preserved in the Public Record Office* (London 1891–).
DMLBS	*Dictionary of Medieval Latin from British Sources.*
DWB	*Dictionary of Welsh Biography.*
ECMW	*The Early Christian Monuments of Wales.*
EWGT	*Early Welsh Genealogical Tracts*, ed. P.C. Bartrum.
JWEH	*Jnl of Welsh Ecclesiastical History.*
NLW	National Library of Wales.
NLWJ	*National Library of Wales Jnl.*

ODNB	*Oxford Dictionary of National Biography*, ed. Matthew and Harrison.
PNP	*Place-names of Pembrokeshire*, ed. B.G. Charles.
Taxatio	1291 *Taxatio* of Nicholas IV, ed. Ayscough and Caley.
VCH	*Victoria County History.*
VSBG	*Vitae Sanctorum Britanniae et Genealogiae*, ed. A.W. Wade-Evans.
WHR	*Welsh History Review.*

1

THE FIGURE OF DAVID

Jonathan M. Wooding

It is around fourteen hundred years since the death of St David (Dewi Sant), notable early holy man, monastic founder and patron saint of Wales. The fourteenth centenary was marked by commemorations at Lampeter and St Davids which, in default of a more certain date, were held to coincide with the 175th anniversary of the opening of St David's College Lampeter; these in turn inspired the present volume.[1] Our calibrations of St David's *obit* lack certainty to the extent that we might have celebrated the fourteenth centenary in 1989 or 2001, or, if we move beyond the witness of the annals, one of a number of other calculations.[2] In fact the most that we can say with certainty is that St David's death occurred in some year fairly adjacent to AD 600. We are on surer ground in holding that his death occurred on 1 March. The Bollandists hold that feast days of saints, notwithstanding the actual year, tend to be enduring 'co-ordinates' in tradition.[3] If 1 March might still seem a suspiciously 'tidy' date, hyperscepticism can be countered by the observation that people are as likely to die on the first of the month as any other day.

Such questions concerning the co-ordinates of a historical St David are not a central concern in most of the contributions to this volume, which reflect the trend in studies of Celtic saints toward concentration upon the more substantial evidence of the *cults* of early saints, away from the less historically substantial figures that they celebrate.[4] This fairly recent trend, while on the one hand placing the focus of attention on the more substantial evidence, also, on the other, arguably, acknowledges the theological dimension of sainthood. Sainthood is a generally posthumous affair. Post-mortem miracles characterise the cults of saints – though their relative absence from early hagiography in Wales and Brittany has sometimes been claimed.[5] In ecclesiastical and secular politics it is axiomatic that dead holy persons were, through the appropriation of their names or their corporeal remains, brought to affirm territorial claims and attract endowments to major churches. In such matters

---

1   A conference on St David was held at University of Wales Lampeter on 23–27 June 2002, with a session and public lecture in St Davids. A public lecture was held on 1 March. The chapters in this volume by Julia Barrow, Jane Cartwright, John Davies, Wyn Evans, Tom Higham, David Howlett, Graham Isaac, Huw Pryce, Richard Sharpe, Nigel Yates, the writer, and the late Glanmor Williams develop papers or symposium discussions from the conference.
2   Baring-Gould, *Lives*, 305–6; Wade-Evans, 'The death-years', 63–4. For discussion see: Miller, 'Date-guessing', 41–50; Dumville, *Saint David*, 4, n. 10.
3   Delehaye, *Cinq leçons*, 13–14.
4   See, for example, the comments in reviews of Jankulak's *The Medieval Cult of St Petroc* by Stacey, 181; and Brett, 108. By contrast, in the context of Anglo-Saxon studies, a recent volume by Wilson concerning St John of Beverley (*The Life and After-life*, 2) espouses belief that the recovery of the historical saint from later hagiography is still a worthwhile enterprise.
5   Smith, 'Oral and written', 321–2, 340.

the facts of the actual life of the patronal figure were often little more than a distraction – sometimes a definite obstacle – to the business at hand.

The contributions in this collection are almost exclusively concerned with events occurring more than three centuries after the death of the saint. This is partly a matter of circumstance, with four contributions to the conference that were concerned with the period before A.D. 1100 being unavailable for this volume.[6] Nonetheless, this circumstance only serves to sharpen what is already a fairly pronounced distinction between saint and cult in the historiography of St David. In this introductory chapter, in surveying some of the themes of this collection, I will therefore take the opportunity to review some of the evidence for the 'missing years' and reflect on whether *such* a separation of the cult from its patron is really warranted in the case of St David.

St David and his cult

Most of the facts recorded of the saints of the sixth century were assembled after their lifetimes, with all the benefits of hindsight. Accounts of insular saints, as the late John Morris put it, sometimes appear to have been 'written long after the events they concern by men who had no understanding of the past and no wish to understand it'.[7] These striking words reflect the frustration of a positivist historian in the face of mostly later literary evidence.[8] A more inclusive assessment of the literary evidence would also note that the work of the tenth-century and later promoters of St David is dramatic, elegant and imaginative; it is worthy of treatment as more than simply a quarry for events which occurred centuries previous to its time of writing. As Graham Isaac observes of the tenth-century poem *Armes Prydain Fawr*,

> The fact that we know St David to have been a man of flesh and blood is of no more significance than the fact that we know that Myrddin, cited as an authority for the content of the poem in line 17, was not. They are both symbols, utilised by the poet in his political rhetoric to bolster and propagate his case.[9]

We should also consider the perspective of the medieval author. For him, the moment of death of his patron was, as Adomnán wrote of St Columba, only 'the beginning of his rewards ... joined with the apostles and prophets, he is enrolled in the number of thousands of white-robed saints'.[10] From either perspective, the saint was an efficacious figure in the present day; either through the propaganda of his followers or

---

6   Máire Herbert's paper on St David and the cults of Irish saints, Thomas Charles-Edwards's paper on Asser and Einhard, Nancy Edwards on the field monuments and sculpture of St Davids and Thomas Clancy on the education of Sulien. Dr Edwards's conclusions are published in the *Festschrift* for Rosemary Cramp ('Monuments'), while Professor Charles-Edwards's contribution was based on a section in his forthcoming volume of the *History of Wales*.

7   J. Morris, 'The dates', 342.

8   Morris's most enduring work was, after all, as a continuator of Theodor Mommsen: see Jones, Martindale and Morris, *Prosopography*. In this project, which completed Mommsen's project 'Prosopographicum Inscriptionem Romanorum', commenced in 1877, Morris famously retrieved Mommsen's card index by driving to East Berlin. On Mommsen and positivism see Collingwood, *The Idea*, 126–33.

9   Isaac, '*Armes Prydain Fawr* and St David', below, 162.

10   *Ista meritorum exordia ... apostolis et profetis consertus, numero aggregatus albatorum milium agnino in sanguine suas sanctorum*: *Vita S. Columbae* III.23 (ed. Anderson, *Adomnán's Life*, 232, trans. Sharpe, *Adomnán*, 232); cf. *Vita S. Antonii* § 60.

through his own agency, which did not cease with his death. How much this agency depended on the detail of his earthly existence is arguable.

We will return to the problem of the historical St David below. Before doing so, however, it is appropriate to reflect on the substantial monuments to the cult of the saint which are the focus of the present collection. Two sets of papers in this volume, arising from two symposia held at our 2002 conference, might be seen to form focal points for this collection. The first symposium concerned the writing of the *Vita S. Dauid* at the end of the eleventh century.[11] The second symposium concerned the re-discovery of the relics of St David in the thirteenth century.[12] These two symposia focused on events which were benchmarks from which leading figures of post-conquest Wales, in one case a native episcopal family, in the other an incoming Norman episcopate, created figures of St David appropriate to their own needs. Both these events initiated processes that were worked out in detail in subsequent sources and events examined in the contributions to this volume.

Vita S. Dauid, a literary masterpiece, was written at a time of confrontation and change in the Welsh church by Rhygyfarch ap Sulien (*ob.* 1099), a brilliant member of an accomplished family.[13] The contributions by Richard Sharpe and John R. Davies consider the textual problems presented by the different recensions.[14] Their analysis of the text presents a detailed case as to why we should regard the longer (Vespasian) recension, existing in a single copy, as the superior witness to Rhygyfarch's original. They reject J.W. James's widely accepted case for the priority of the shorter ('Nero-Digby') recension. Sharpe and Davies question various assumptions in James's edition, in particular what Sharpe describes as the:

> misapplication of the principle applied in biblical criticism, where the shorter reading represents the more original version than the longer reading; that is, it is a principle to help judge between the original text and a rewritten version, not a text-critical rule to eliminate errors of transcription.[15]

In Sharpe's view the briefer Nero–Digby recension, rather than to be understood as an original text expanded upon by later redactors, is an attempt '… to abbreviate and, according to the common practice of hagiography, to reduce the amount of particular detail that would mean nothing to a non-local audience'.[16] Davies, in his note on the Nero-Digby text, focuses on the issue of the Vespasian recension's Graecisms and specific Latin constructions, concluding:

> If we were to suppose (as seems most likely from the wide dissemination of those recensions) that ND [Nero-Digby] represent versions of the *Life* written for wider circulation – that is, beyond Wales – at the direction of Bishop Bernard in his campaign for the metropolitan status of St Davids, then the editorial actions of the reviser might be understood. First, all obscure, pretentious, or Greek vocabulary and expressions have

---

11 Participants: John R. Davies, David Dumville, David Howlett, Thomas O'Loughlin, Richard Sharpe and Charles Thomas.

12 Participants: Wyn Evans, Tom Higham, Bernard Knight and Len Nokes.

13 In this volume we follow the view of Kenneth Jackson (*Language and History*, 668) and Patrick Sims-Williams (*pers. comm.* to Prof. R. Sharpe) that *Ricemarchus*, the form of his name given by the author of *Vita S. Dauid*, derives its first element from *rö- ('great') not *ri: go- ('king'). Hence Rhygyfarch, not *Rhig-*, as in, for example, the edition of J.W. James.

14 Sharpe, 'Which text', below, 90–105; Sharpe and Davies (edd.), 'Rhygyfarch's *Life* of St David', below, 107–55; Davies, 'Some observations', below, 156–60.

15 Sharpe, 'Which text', below, 95.

16 Sharpe, 'Which text', below, 102.

been expunged. Secondly, all passages with syntax that does not conform to what the editor considered to be sound Latin style have been excluded or paraphrased. Thirdly, all derogatory or critical references to other saints have been removed (in particular, those about Patrick and Gildas), probably from the desire to remove inessential proper nouns.[17]

Both Sharpe and Davies, against a backdrop of evolutionary assumptions inherited from Biblical source criticism, point up the need to consider specific historical circumstances of the production of texts. This critique gives us a new text and translation of Rhygyfarch's *Vita* in the present volume – a major contribution to the study of the cult of St David. It may also inspire a wider reflection upon the influence, in insular studies, of evolutionary models of text edition that have been taken over from New Testament criticism.

The reassessment of the character of Rhygyfarch's text by Sharpe and Davies also has direct implications for some derivative texts. In his review of the English version of the late Simon Evans's edition of the Welsh *Life* of David, David Dumville stated, for example, that,

> The Middle Welsh life of St David has – it is safe to say – no claims to original content or to historical merit; it is a fourteenth-century translation of a literary work already known to us, the Vespasian recension of Rhigyfarch's *Vita S. Dauidis*.[18]

The study of the Welsh text becomes potentially a more important task, whatever its intrinsic interest, where it might bear witness to a recension of Rhygyfarch's original text. Rhygyfarch's narrative of St David was also extended by further *Vitae*, as well as Latin texts of other genres. Wyn Evans, in common with Sharpe, draws our attention again to the specific historical importance of the interpretation of Rhygyfarch's *Vita* by Gerald of Wales (Giraldus Cambrensis) – another text requiring a new edition.[19] The liturgical contributions to the present volume note the influence of this neglected work.[20] A full study of the relations between all these derivatives of Rhygyfarch's *Vita* is an important future project.

The influence of Rhygyfarch's vision of St David is also seen in a wider literary context. Bernard Tanguy and Jane Cartwright explore the Breton tradition of St David (Divi) and its particular development of the cult of St Non (Nonne), the mother of St David. Both highlight in detail the ways in which the Breton writers expanded upon the vision of Rhygyfarch.[21] Cartwright's immensely detailed survey of the dedications to St Non in Wales, Cornwall and Brittany points up the distinctive features of her cult in the context of feminine sainthood in the early medieval Celtic world, in which she is an unusually international figure. We are also particularly fortunate, through the kindness of Professor Tanguy – and of Karen Jankulak, as translator – to be able to print an English version of his seminal study of this cult in its Breton context. John Morgan-Guy, in another section of the volume, provides an interesting sidelight on the reintroduction of this cult to St Davids in the 1930s; a concrete example of the influence of local politics and the cult of relics in the foundation of a new cult site.[22]

---

[17] Davies, 'Some observations', below, 158–9.
[18] Dumville, Review of D.S. Evans, *The Welsh Life*, 99.
[19] See below, 28–32 and 96–8.
[20] See below, 224 and 240.
[21] Cartwright, 'The cult of St Non', below, 182–206; Tanguy, 'The cults', below, 209–11.
[22] Morgan-Guy, 'Shrine and counter-shrine', below, 286–95.

Daniel Huws, Owain Tudor Edwards and David Howlett all show in their contributions how the extent of St David's cult can also be traced through what Huws terms 'the incorporeal element' of the cult of the saint: the liturgies of the saint and his presence in a wider sweep of liturgical commemoration, much of which is directly related to Rhygyfarch's text.[23] These contributions indicate the scale of the important evidence to be explored in the liturgical context. Huws attempts to map out the terrain for future work with an 'up-to-date view of the relevant sources now available, some of them unknown in [Silas] Harris's time'.[24] This survey, with two invaluable appendices, is a work of characteristic generosity to present and future scholarship. If, in Huws's words, 'What survives of liturgy is at best something that might be regarded as its libretto, together, sometimes, with something by way of a score ...', Edwards, *inter alia* of his edition of one short text from a Paris manuscript, provides many thoughtful observations upon the scale and character of these 'libretti' and 'scores' of the saint's cult and more than a few thoughts on the nature of the performance.

The enshrinement of the relics of St David in the thirteenth century presents the second benchmark for the re-invention of the figure of St David after A.D. 1000, in this case in corporeal terms. Fred Cowley and Tom Higham *et al.* demonstrate that the relics preserved in the cathedral as St Davids are not those of its patron, but most likely of a burial in the churchyard made *ca* 1000–1200.[25]

The enshrinement of the relics was in many ways a cruder act of propaganda than Rhygyfarch's finely crafted literary vision of St David. The greater appeal – and, in the case of David's dossier, the greater visibility – of the process of literary creation to the scholar should not, however, distract us from the point that the impact of relics on the minds of the public was much the greater – though one fed off the other. The most remembered fact from St David's dossier in modern Wales is an oral tradition of Rhygyfarch's story of the ground rising under the saint's feet to form the mound upon which the church stands at Llanddewi Brefi. Interestingly, the re-dating of the bones was the only item of interest to the media arising from the 2002 conference.[26] These cases, along with the evidence for performance of the liturgies of St David, serve to remind us that the cult 'outside the text' – often far less readily recoverable – is as significant as that within the literary record.

Cult and church in the landscape

The break between high medieval revival and early medieval survival of the cult of David is a very clean one in the case of the relics: the older relics were lost in the eleventh century, leaving open the possibility of proclaiming new ones. Such a clean break is less to be found on the literary side, though the limited nature of the tradition prior to Rhygyfarch – at least as far as it survives – can permit treatment of the existing literary record as if it were more or less a *tabula rasa*. Bishop Sulien (*ob.* 1091), the father of Rhygyfarch, inherited a church which had endured

---

23 Huws, 'St David in the liturgy', below, 220; Edwards 'The office', below, 245; Howlett, 'A triad of texts', below, 261–2.

24 Huws, 'St David in the liturgy', below, 220.

25 Cowley, 'The relics', below, 227; Higham *et al.*, 'AMS radiocarbon dating', below, 284–5.

26 BBC News, 28 June 2002: 'Bones are "not St David's"', http://news.bbc.co.uk/1/hi/wales/2070072.stm

destructive Viking raids and which faced an uncertain future in the face of Norman settlement. The degree to which its vision and history were open to reconstruction by the intellectual energies of the gifted family of Sulien and by their Norman successors depends on what monuments, literary and architectural, we see them as having inherited. Questions as to the nature and extent of the earlier literary record at *Menevia* are partly intertwined with controversies carried on outside of Wales, as we will see. These wider controversies, and the general scepticism as to the historicity of early historic figures that they can inspire, challenge a great deal of what was formerly held to be certain about the early formation of a diocese and major church of St Davids and its continuity into the present day.

Contributions to this volume by Wyn Evans, Heather James, Huw Pryce and Julia Barrow survey the processes by which St David's cult and church were established in the landscape of medieval West Wales. Wyn Evans shows how Sulien, Gerald (Giraldus Cambrensis, *ob.* 1223), and the Norman bishops of St Davids (1115–) engaged with a church rooted in local traditions of the saint. He illustrates the ways in which the evidence of earlier sources was brought to serve the claims of a new social order – with Gerald's vision possibly pivotal in this transition. Evans is concerned to trace how:

> The survival of the cathedral and its association with the patron saint ... conceals some quite dramatic and revolutionary changes. Some of the ideological and ecclesiological reasons motivating the protagonists of change over the centuries of the existence of the site, cult and buildings call into question the concept of continuity. The attitudes lying behind the various approaches – in particular to the building – have oscillated between conscious attempts to create deliberate discontinuity between past and present, and equally conscious attempts to recover and recreate an ideal past, eliding the intervening dissonance.

The contingency of past events is a contemporary theme in historiography, often leading to overly sensational reception of critiques of basic received wisdoms – in medieval studies as much as modern history. Evans's critique, however, though it enshrines a quite sensational claim as to the identity of the 'real' *Menevia*, is an attempt to appreciate the agency of medieval writers in the transformation of the early- into the high-medieval church, as well as the intensity of the encounters that shaped it. He is critical of the evolutionary teleologies that have seen institutions such as the *clas* judged in negative and anachronistic terms. Evans explores our historiography concerning these matters from its pre-modern roots, highlighting the remoteness in cultural terms of pioneering scholars such as Thomas Burgess and Rice Rees, whose ideas were nonetheless formative of our modern conceptions.

Huw Pryce explores in detail the engagement of the Welsh princes with the church in transition from Welsh to Norman ownership. He observes that the extent of the cult of the saint and his church's claim to lands ensured that this transition could never be a simple matter.[27] Julia Barrow's detailed survey of the cathedral's statutes between 1224 and 1259 extends her previous editorial work on the cathedral *acta* into comparisons between the English and Welsh cathedrals in a way which sheds further light on the cultural encounter set out by Evans and Pryce.[28]

Cultural collision did not end with the middle ages. William Barlow's (*ob.* 1568) opportunistic approach (1536–1548) to a chapter of unusual structure is the subject

---

[27] Pryce, 'The dynasty', below, 306–7.
[28] Barrow, 'The statutes', below, 317–29.

of one of the late Glanmor Williams's many – regrettably to be one of his last – incisive contributions to early modern Welsh history.[29] In survey of another neglected period, Nigel Yates confronts the often negative assessments of the Anglican bishops in the eighteenth and nineteenth centuries in Wales through analysis of visitation records in particular, to conclude that

> the state of the established church in the diocese of St Davids bore comparison with that of the established church in other parts of Britain and Ireland, a little worse in some areas and rather better in others.[30]

Yates places emphasis on the positive efforts made to educate clergy in the face of the obstacles presented by poverty and geography. Like Evans, he is concerned to confront an often ideological historiography that has highlighted only negatives in the impact of foreign bishops upon the diocese.

If the co–ordinates of the life and cult – what the Bollandists term the 'hagiographical dossier' (*dossier hagiographique*) – of St David may have been sufficiently insubstantial to allow scope for imaginative, sometimes ingenious, reconstruction it is worth observing that the *landscape* of St David, the geographical inheritance of the saint's cult in West Wales, emerges out of all these studies as a very substantial presence. Medieval Norman and modern English bishops alike were confronted by a landscape defined by prior claims and inherited structures which they of necessity accommodated in their visions for the diocese. Whether or not the centre of the cult was shifted in the early middle ages – as Wyn Evans and others have suggested[31] – the ability of the cathedral to withstand the 'pull' to a more populous centre is a marked feature of its later history.

Heather James's immensely detailed survey of the archaeological evidence for the medieval cult of St David documents the platform upon which a strong geographical identity of the church of St David is based.[32] As Huw Pryce also demonstrates, the attempts by Norman rulers of the twelfth century to redefine the political landscape of West Wales had only moderate impact upon a religious unity mapped out by the cult of the saint.

When this mapping might have occurred is a more problematical question. In 1836 Rice Rees (1804–1839) was confident in presenting St David as having more or less laid out the diocese that was ruled by his successors.[33] Rees's views were widely formative in the historiography of saints's cults into the late-twentieth century and the 2002 conference that gave rise to this volume was in part a reflection upon his work (also see Wyn Evans, below).[34]

Rees was concerned to explain how, in the absence of martyrdom or a visible early cult of relics, dedications came to be made and cults transmitted in the early middle ages.[35] While reluctant to advance one all-embracing rule for the process of dedication, Rees's reasoned position was that cults primarily spread through

---

29 Williams, 'The crisis', below, 330–8.
30 Yates, 'The diocese', below, 350.
31 Evans, 'Transition', below, 38–9; Dumville, *Saint David*, 28, 31.
32 James, 'The geography', below, 41–82.
33 Rees, *An Essay*, 52–56; 193–201
34 He was amongst the foundation professors of St Davids College Lampeter when it opened for business in 1827, on the feast of its patron.
35 Rees, *An Essay*, 57–76; Davies, 'The saints of South Wales', 362; Jones, 'Comparative research', 229.

the person of the saint him- or herself.[36] Having argued that the early saints had personal agency in the spread of their cults, Rees argued that it would be possible to gain some objective sense of their early spheres of influence by documenting the toponymic and other landscape evidence for their cults. Rees's methodology was developed by John Fisher (a Lampeter student, though long after Rees's time) in the *Lives of the British Saints*, written in collaboration with Sabine Baring-Gould and in a lengthy essay of 1913.[37] Cases such as Llan Guorboe, the proprietary church in Ergyng that acquired the name of its first incumbent as its dedication, were probably too eagerly advanced by Fisher to the status of general principles.[38]

Baring-Gould and Fisher indeed had already taken a critical view of Rees's assertions that the diocese of St Davids was more or less laid out by its patron, though, in the absence of evidence for how the cult was transmitted in the pre-Norman environment, they could offer no improvement on the assumption that St David himself had at least founded monasteries throughout its future extent.[39] We now know from the studies of Julia Smith and Karen Jankulak that there were a number of factors at work to facilitate the post-mortem transmission of cults in the early medieval Celtic world, with and without the mediation of relics;[40] but through the studies of Rees and his school it became axiomatic to many British scholars in the late nineteenth and early twentieth centuries that the early British church was different to other European churches in respect of its processes of cult formation.

It is easy to see Rees and his successors as pursuing a somewhat 'protestant' agenda in focusing on the worldly manifestation of the early British saints.[41] However Rees's focus on the historic persona of the early saint was probably as much a product of a positivist view of evidence as it was of a personal or corporate theology. His approach was taken up by scholars of diverse theological perspectives; including Breton scholars as well as the Anglican ritualist Baring-Gould. Rees's *Essay*, with its focus on philological and especially place-name evidence, was in many ways ahead of its time – just as Edward Lhuyd's *Archaeologia Britannica* had been around a century before. In his enthusiasm for these new data Rees did not see that the geographical element in saints's legends was, as the Bollandist Hyppolyte Delehaye observed, potentially one of its most beguiling elements; its verisimilitude nothing more a reflection of the hagiographer's knowledge of the sites in question, potentially at a much later date than the time of the saint.[42] Where medieval hagiography had already 'joined up the dots' to construct imaginary itineraries for their patrons it was easy to find patterns in the medieval dedications to insular saints. Fisher and Baring-Gould treated the dedications of British saints as veritable road-maps of the travels of the saints (we would now view them as maps of the posthumous dissemination of the saints's cults). The work of Joseph Loth in Brittany, and especially his disciple René Largillière, served to make this vision of cults arising from the charisma of living persons into very much a 'British' (in the wider sense) school of interpretation.[43]

---

[36] Rees, *An Essay*, 57–76.
[37] Baring-Gould and Fisher, *Lives*; Fisher, 'Welsh church dedications', 76–108.
[38] Fisher, 'Welsh church dedications', 77.
[39] Baring-Gould and Fisher, *Lives*, II.308, n. 2; Rees, *An Essay*, 197.
[40] Smith, 'Oral and written'; Jankulak, *The medieval cult*, 111–14.
[41] Burgess, *Tracts*; see Yates, 'The diocese of St David's', below, 345; Evans, 'Transition and survival', below, 23.
[42] Delehaye, *The Legends*, 177.
[43] Loth, *Les noms*; Largillière, *Les saints*. Also see Davies, 'The saints of South Wales', 363.

The generalisations which characterised Rees's *Essay* (a work, it must be remembered, of the early nineteenth century) were not swiftly refined by his successors. Despite the advances in historiography in the late-nineteenth century, only the work of Gilbert H. Doble (1880–1945) had extended this study to the level of a more critical, micro-historical, study by the mid-twentieth century – at least in Britain.[44]

All the foregoing account of Rees's contribution to the methodology of studying saints's cults would be of no more than antiquarian interest but for the fact that Rees's views gained a second life through their adoption by the school of archaeo-geography pioneered by Harold Peake, H.J. Fleure and O.G.S. Crawford.[45] First Crawford and then Emrys George Bowen were inspired to attempt to map the dedications of saints in the belief that they provided evidence of communication routes and of early ecclesiastical units.[46] Owen Chadwick took serious issue with this aspect of the legacy of Rees, mediated through the work of Bowen:

> If we turn to the study of dedications, we find a remarkable assumption of abnormality. The continental Church dedicated its churches to dead men, apostles, martyrs, monks or bishops. It is commonly stated, and widely believed, that the Celtic Church of Wales dedicated its churches to living persons: or, much more soundly, that the churches in Wales were called after their founders. This dogma, if true, is of momentous importance for the study of Welsh Christian origins. For the study of the names of dedications would then give some kind of guide to the activities of the early saints like David, some evidence about the area in which they preached or administered the sacraments. This assumption was used to this historical end as long ago as 1836 in Rees' *Essays on Welsh Saints*: since that time it has experienced much fortune. The older extravagances of the theory are now no longer common. But we can still discern the workings of the theory in so scholarly a historian as Professor Emrys Bowen. Professor Bowen has made a most valuable study of the .geographical grouping of certain dedications: but the presence of the assumption that the origins of these geographical groups date back to the sixth century is evident even in the titles of his papers, *The Travels of the Celtic Saints*, *The Settlements of the Celtic Saints in South Wales*. This same assumption has appeared among the liturgiologists studying Celtic forms for consecrating churches.[47]

Chadwick advanced the view that 'Celtic' churches were not any different to other churches in their process of foundation.[48] Bowen was moved to accept Chadwick's critique as valid:

> if we were able to accept without question that an ancient church bearing the name of a Celtic saint was, in fact, established by the saint in question, or by one of his immediate followers … [a]ll that would then be necessary would be to plot all the churches bearing the saint's name and in this way delimit his 'patria', or sphere of influence, and hence his 'culture area'. We have already noted, however, that such a procedure would be open to a number of serious objections, particularly as it is far from certain that all churches with a Celtic dedication were established during the lifetime of the saint whose name they bear. … to assume that the territorial limits of the medieval diocese of St. David's represents the 'patria' or sphere of influence of the saint during

---

44 Doble, *The Saints of Cornwall*; *idem, The Lives of the Welsh Saints.*

45 Crawford, *Said and Done*, 40–1; Crawford, 'Western Seaways', 181–200; Fleure, 'Archaeological problems', 408–9; Wooding, *Communication*, 3–4; *idem, Saints and the Sea* (forthcoming).

46 What Bowen termed the 'culture areas' of saints, an idea arising from anthropological models: Bowen, *Saints, Seaways*, 28–9.

47 Chadwick, 'The evidence of dedications', 176–77

48 Though see Padel, Local saints', 303–16.

his lifetime (merely because it contains almost all the pre-Reformation dedications in his name found in Wales) would be absurd.[49]

This was, in fact, what Bowen *had* previously assumed and it is worth noting for the benefit of those who have been inspired, but not entirely satisfied, by Bowen's vision that he never subsequently resolved entirely what it was that his maps of dedications *were* tracing. Bowen continued to assert that the territory defined by the pattern of dedications to St David 'possessed a large measure of cultural unity long before the limits of the diocese were determined by the medieval bishops, or further dedications made to St. David', arguing that the medieval extension of St David's cult in the direction of eastern Wales and western England had marked parallels with the distribution of ogham inscriptions in the fifth through seventh centuries:

> Here is a clear indication that the future cathedral area was in cultural contact with the most distant part of the medieval diocese certainly two hundred years before the medieval diocese was delimited on a territorial basis with the coming of the Norman bishops. It is therefore clear that any revival or propagation of the saint's cult in the middle ages ... occurred in an area that had already been culturally associated with the saint long before the medieval diocese emerged.[50]

The circumstantial comparison is insufficient to prove Bowen's point. What would be required would be proof that St David's early cult was promulgated along with the cults of his Irish associates – a complex problem, as we will see below. The cult of St David could have been extended into the south-east of Wales at almost any time in the second half of the first millennium.

It is also fitting, however, that we should reflect on the positive legacy that Rees and his successors, such as Bowen, have left in the enterprise of the study of saints's cults as an artefact in the landscape. Projects such as the 'Trans-national Atlas of Saints' Cults', led by Dr Graham Jones at Leicester University, extend a more critical version of Rees's methodology to toponymic evidence.[51] This enterprise encourages micro-historical study of dedications, individually and in clusters, without any prior assumptions as to the chronology of their distribution. Heather James's detailed analysis of the geography of the cult of David in this volume presents the results of such a micro-historical study. Inevitably this takes us forward in time from the era of the saint himself. What we are studying are later religious landscapes, with stone structures usually post-A.D. 1000 in date, in which only place-names, inscribed monuments and as yet undated cist burials are in any way potential evidence of activity at an earlier date. These data, only some as yet refined in date, should provide a basis for further research – just as Rees's survey of the cult of David did in 1836 – but there is a need to eschew generalisation on the basis of undated patterns.[52]

From local to international saint

These reflections on the legacy of Rice Rees help us contextualise the recent historiography concerning the early cult of the saint. It is striking to note quite how recent

[49] Bowen, *Saints, Seaways*, 81.
[50] Bowen, *Saints, Seaways*, 82–3.
[51] For an account see: Jones, 'Diverse expressions', 1–28.
[52] James, 'The geography', below, 43–7.

has been the retreat from the assumed link between the historic saint and the subsequent cult. This disjunction between an heroic 'age of the saints' and the earliest (mostly twelfth-century or later) narratives describing the figures of this 'age' leaves us with a shortfall between the historic figures and the most substantial expressions of their cults. The historiography of these 'missing years' is characterised by an uncertainty as to basic facts and a tendency to 'tentative phraseology' of the type gently mocked by T. Arwyn Watkins in his review of Simon Evans's comments on the historical David.[53]

In the first millennium A.D., prior to the promotion of St David's cult by Rhygyfarch, St David already can be seen to have enjoyed a significant reputation not only in Wales, but across the Irish Sea. *Dauid Cille Muni* features amongst three Welsh saints whose feasts are recorded in the Latin *Martyrology of Tallaght* and the Irish martyrology *Félire Óengusso* in the early ninth century – both probably the work of the same author, and certainly of the community of the *Céli Dé* of Tallaght.[54] David also appears in another early list of saints, the *Catalogus sanctorum Hiberniae*, where he features amongst the British saints from whom the 'second order' of early Irish saints are held to have accepted their ritual of the mass.[55] His *obit* appears in Irish annal collections, probably entered at some time in during first millennium.[56] These references would appear to speak to the relations between the westernmost part of Wales and its closeness to Ireland – the same relationship, perhaps, as is evinced by *Armes Prydain Fawr*.

The kingdom of Dyfed, the early medieval polity in which the region of the modern St Davids is located, was itself, of course, originally under an Irish dynasty – a fact that appears to have been still known in Rhygyfarch's time[57] – but it would be unwise to place much weight upon this early Irish connection of St Davids. The associations of David's cult with Irish saints are as likely to reflect later as earlier connections between these closely adjacent countries. Most of the dedications to the saint in Ireland can be shown with certainty to have been made under Cambro- or Anglo-Norman patronage.[58] The appearance of David in the Irish martyrologies, however, speaks to exchange of cults between Ireland and Wales before A.D. 800. Irish *uitae* add further detail to this testimony. St David features in the *Vita* of St Molua of Clonfert-Mulloe and in the *Vita* of Ailbe of Emly.[59] In both cases he appears in the versions of these *uitae* that are preserved in the Salmanticensis collection amongst the subset (the 'O'Donohue group') which Richard Sharpe has identified as preserving a putatively eighth-century form.[60]

The arguably early reference in the cult of St Ailbe is thus of especial interest for the fact that Ailbe (Elvis) is a saint with a cult near St Davids.[61] In Rhygyfarch's *Vita S. Dauid* Ailbe is joined by six more Irish saints: SS. Patrick, Brendan, Maedóc, Bairre, Modomnóc and Scoithín. Patrick and Ailbe are given the most significant roles in Rhygyfarch's *Vita*. The role of St Patrick – who has a dedication near St

---

[53] Watkins, Review of Evans, *Welsh Life*, 90.

[54] *Martyrology of Tallaght*, ed. Best and Lawlor, 20; *Félire Óengusso*, ed. Stokes, 80. On the dates of the martyrologies see: Ó Riain, 'The Tallaght martyrologies'; Dumville, '*Félire Óengusso*'.

[55] *Catalogus sanctorum Hiberniae* (ed. Grosjean, 205).

[56] For example, *Annals of Inisfallen*, ed. Mac Airt, 78.

[57] *Vita S. Dauid* § 15 (ed. Sharpe and Davies, below, 120–1).

[58] Cunningham and Gillespie, 'The cult of St. David', 32.

[59] *Vita S. Molua* § 43 (ed. Heist, 140); *Vita S. Albei* § 21 (ed. Heist, 123).

[60] Sharpe, *Medieval Irish Saints' Lives*.

[61] See also *Vita S. Dauid*, ed. Sharpe and Davies, below 117, n. 33.

Davids, at Whitesands Bay – is to be the previous denizen of *Vallis Rosina*, the place that will later be the site of St David's monastery.[62] St Ailbe's role is to baptize David.[63] These roles reflect the significance of these saints in Irish history: Patrick as apostle to the Irish; Ailbe as patron to Munster, whose church was second only in status to Patrick. Pádraig Ó Riain is right to argue that these 'facilitating' roles are intended to establish St Davids's status as superior to that of other major insular churches. They are products of a time when these saints's cults had already achieved their existing status in Ireland, not of the time of the historical David.[64] How early or late this period of exchange of information may be placed is a point of contention by Ó Riain.

The proposition that narrative hagiography was rare even in Ireland prior to the twelfth century is the starting-point for Ó Riain's thesis that early medieval Celtic saints were unstable figures in historical terms – their dossiers subject to duplication and relocation.[65] Ó Riain's hypothesis impacts directly on the case of David, both through his studies of St David's associations with Irish saints and in the general impact of Ó Riain's views on historiography of insular saints's cults. In 1981 Ó Riain advanced the hypothesis that St David's associations with these saints was recorded by Rhygyfarch on the basis of martyrological material comparable to the short parables concerning these saints in the Middle Irish *scholia* to *Félire Óengusso*. These present many similarities to the episodes in the *Vita S. Dauid*, leading Ó Riain to suggest that a copy of a similar martyrology was brought back from Ireland, perhaps by Sulien, whom we know to have studied there.[66]

Ó Riain's initial purpose was to counter the argument of Bowen (see above) that the *Vita*'s references to Irish saints betokens an Irish input into the cult of St David dating back to the period of Irish settlement in Wales – the early- to mid-first millennium A.D.[67] In Ó Riain's view, such Irish saints's cults as had become established in the early period had been so assimilated to Welsh culture as to be unrecognisable to Rhygyfarch even where they were the same saints:

> the pattern of Irish settlement in Wales can have exercised little or no influence on the creation of the considerable Irish narrative element in the Welsh lives of saints. These begin to be written in the late eleventh century at a time when, manifestly, the originally Irish affiliations of local saints had with very few exceptions been forgotten.[68]

Ó Riain's subsequent re-dating of the *scholia* to the period after 1170 has caused him to adopt an even more limited vision of material available.[69] Concurrently, he has also asserted a post-1100 date for the 'O'Donohue Group', against the views of Sharpe and others.[70] This leads him to the view that 'Rhigyfarch would seem to have been the first to give written form to David's associations with Irish saints' and to see no reason to imagine that any such stories existed in oral form previous to the event.[71]

---

62 *Vita S. Dauid* § 3 (ed. Sharpe and Davies, below 110–11).
63 *Vita S. Dauid* § 7 (ed. Sharpe and Davies, below 116–17).
64 Ó Riain, 'Hagiography without frontiers', 42.
65 Ó Riain, 'Towards a methodology'; *idem*, *The Making, passim*.
66 Ó Riain, 'The Irish element', 294.
67 Ó Riain, 'The Irish element', 292.
68 Ó Riain, 'The Irish element', 292.
69 Ó Riain, 'Hagiography without frontiers', 47, n. 13.
70 Pádraig Ó Riain, *pers. comm.*
71 Ó Riain, 'Hagiography without frontiers', 42.

One Irish saint from the *Vita S. Dauid* with a pre-existing cult in Wales is commemorated on a pillar stone from the former Cistercian and early medieval site of Llanllŷr (SN 5434 5588), opposite the village of Talsarn in Ceredigion. The language of the inscription (*ECMW* 124) suggests a date between the seventh and ninth centuries.[72] The inscription reads: TESQUITUS DITOC MADOMNUACO AON FILIUS ASA ITGEN DEDIT ('the little *tesqua* of Ditoc that Aon son of Asa Itgen gave to Modomnuac').[73] Here we have the gift of land named after a man (Ditoc) with a religious name in *-oc* or *-ōc* – perhaps, from his possession of a *tesqua*, to be understood to have been a hermit[74] – to the church of a known saint who, though of Irish origin, has a name assimilated to a Welsh form (*-ōc* > *-auc* [MW *-awg*]). Modomnóc occurs in the ninth-century text of *Félire Óengusso* as a saint who travelled between Wales and Ireland.[75]

With his reference to Modomnóc Rhygyfarch was thus associating David with an Irish saint who had an established cult in Ceredigion.[76] It is hard to see that Rhygyfarch would have been misled by the form *Madomnuac* into holding this saint to be a separate figure. That the hermitage of an Irishman is gifted to the cult is also possibly significant in terms of its cultural associations; possibly speaking to the posthumous association of Irish cults and churchmen – a pattern to be found on the Continent.[77]

Cases such as that of Modomnóc suggest that the considerable disjunction proposed by Ó Riain between two distinct, very early and very late, exchanges of Irish and Welsh cults is unnecessary and, in the particular case, places too much weight upon the Irish education of Sulien as providing the fuel for a re-invention of St David. The *Vita* of St Malo (865×872) by Bili indicates a cult of St Brendan in Wales before A.D. 900;[78] that the cult of another Munster saint mentioned by Rhygyfarch, Ailbe, might also have spread to Wales in this period is therefore also plausible. Ó Riain is right to stress that Rhygyfarch's representations of their relations with his subject tell us everything about the perceptions of its own status of St David's church in the eleventh century and little or nothing of the longer history of their cults. The cult of St David is known in Ireland and Brittany in the ninth century,[79] however, and the possibility that the relations St David's cult with those of other saints were formed and sustained by regular contact is a reasonable one – not dispelled by Ó Riain's concern to remain within the confines of the known testimony of the medieval texts, and to retreat with the progressive re-dating of those texts to the later end of their possible spectrum.

Another case of polemic which impacts on our 'missing years' is that of Asser (*ob.* 909), a potentially very significant figure in our vision of the church of St David

---

[72] Sims-Williams, 'The five languages', 31–2.

[73] Revised reading from Edwards, *A Corpus*, Vol. 2 (forthcoming). I would like to thank Nancy Edwards for kindly sending me the text of her entry in advance of publication and Robert and Loveday Gee for allowing me to inspect the monument, which stands now in their garden.

[74] See Handley, 'Isidore', 26–9.

[75] *Hi curchan mo Domnóc anair tar muir nglédenn dobert, brígach núalann, síl mbúadach mbech n-Erenn* ('in a little boat from the east over the pure-coloured sea, my Domnóc brought – vigorous cry! – the gifted race of Ireland's bees', *Félire Óengusso*, ed. Stokes, 60.

[76] *Vita S. Dauid* §§ 41 and 43 (ed. Sharpe and Davies, 136–7, 138–9).

[77] For example in the cases of St Gall and Péronne – though in those cases living religious travel to cult centres established on the basis of cults, whereas in this case the hermitage of an Irishman is being gifted to, presumably, a church on another site.

[78] *Vita S. Machutis* §§ 4–25 (ed. Lot, *Mélanges*, 355–68).

[79] *Vita S. Pauli* (ed. Cuissard, 421); *Félire Óengusso*, ed. Stokes, 80.

of the period before A.D. 1000. That the church of *Menevia* kept literary records from the late eighth century is evinced by the *Annales Cambriae*;[80] that it might have had a literary vision that transcended such a laconic vision of history would seem to be confirmed by the existence of Asser, the Welsh bishop who came to England under Alfred the Great so that Alfred's literary programme might 'benefit in every respect from the learning of St David' (*adiuuaretur per rudimenta Sancti Degui in omni causa*).[81] Asser's account of his own origins position them securely in the *parochia Sancti Degui*, ruled over by his archiepiscopal kinsmen.[82] His literary accomplishments speak to a *Menevia* that was centre of philological and literary education, was conscious of the traditions of St David, and had knowledge of continental biography – evident in Asser's biography of Alfred the Great. The very existence of a figure such as Asser implicitly speaks against a vision of a West Wales in which saints's cults were potentially unstable of record and in which there was no interest in narratives of great men.[83]

The assaults that have been made upon the existence of the literary accomplishments of Asser are therefore significant for any assumptions we might make concerning the character of education at *Menevia* prior to the time of Sulien, whom we know to have studied abroad. The suggestion that the Welsh Asser did not write the *Vita Ælfredi* has been made more than once, most notably by V.H. Galbraith in 1964,[84] but has recently been reasserted by Alfred Smyth in two substantial volumes.[85] The issues raised by Smyth have been extensively refuted by Simon Keynes and David Dumville – amongst many others – and I will note only a few points of the debate.[86] The most implausible elements of his argument are probably his views on the lengths that the supposed tenth-century forger would appear to have gone to provide Welsh forms of English place-names; and his blindness to the consistency of the Asser's body of reading and thought with the actual century in which he is claimed to have worked.[87]

In Smyth's polemic against the historical Asser the implication that he might not expect so sophisticated a writer to emerge out of a ninth-century Welsh context is only incidental to his argument.[88] As in the case of Ó Riain's hypothesis, however, it gives pause that an appropriate degree of scepticism as to the motives of medieval writers and the faith placed in attributions of date and authorship can so quickly create an historical vacuum and reduce St Davids to a silent and isolated backwater.[89]

The evidence of archaeology may serve to fill some aspects of the vacuum. Finds such as the SATURNBIU memorial from Ramsey Island hint at links with the Anglo-Saxon churches, while other sculptural traditions at St Davids suggest links with Ireland during the eighth through tenth centuries.[90] The annals present a largely

---

80 Hughes, *Celtic Britain*, 68–9.
81 Asser, *Vita Ælfredi regis* § 79 (ed. Stevenson, 65–6; trans. Keynes and Lapidge, 94–6).
82 Asser, *Vita Ælfredi regis* § 79 (ed. Stevenson, 65–6).
83 For assessments of Asser's historical vision see: Scharer, 'The writing of history'; Kirby, 'Asser'.
84 See Galbraith, *An Introduction*, 85–128; and response by Dorothy Whitelock, *The Genuine Asser.*
85 Smyth, *Alfred*; idem, *The Medieval Life.*
86 Keynes, 'On the authenticity'; Dumville, Review of Smyth, *Alfred.*
87 Keynes, 'On the authenticity', 534, 537; Kershaw, 'Illness', 222–4; DeGregorio, 'Texts, *topoi*'.
88 Though see Smyth, *The Medieval Life*, 114.
89 Smyth also favours Hughes's latest possible date for the composition of the annals, after 988: *The Medieval Life*, 116.
90 Okasha, 'A new inscription'; James, 'The geography', below, 50; Edwards, 'Monuments', 58–62.

negative vision of the Viking presence, but the find from Pen-Arthur Farm, discussed by Mark Redknap in his contribution to this volume, hints at a more permanent presence of Scandinavian settlers: the proprietors of the major communication networks of the later first millennium.[91] One is easily reminded here of the discoveries at Whithorn (Dumfries and Galloway) in 1984 – a mid-peninsular British monastery and episcopal seat with more than a few geographical resemblances to St Davids. There the detection, in 1984, of a previously unsuspected Scandinavian settlement of the twelfth century was part of a wider exposition of the ongoing cultural connections of the site throughout the later first millennium and into the second.[92] In the light of the possibility that St Davids may not have been the most important early cult centre of St David it is tempting to note that a similarly negative case was advanced for Whithorn as the early cult centre of St Ninian prior to the discoveries of 1984.[93]

St David – the man himself

This latter point is an important one. The real missing years in the cult of St David may lie most of all between the time of the saint himself – for whom, more than St Ninian, we have good grounds to assert a distinct and real identity – and the cult that, taking the maximal view of the Irish evidence, we might suggest achieved substantial form at least by the eighth century, either at St Davids, or with St Davids later coming to be the major church of his cult.[94]

The evidence for a historical St David is not insubstantial. Four decades ago, John Morris – whose contributions to early medieval British history perhaps above all others exhibit the greatest strengths and greatest weaknesses of the positivist method – argued that the outline of the rule of life of David's community given in Rhygyfarch's *Vita S. Dauid* §§ 21–31 came from a genuinely early source. There must be few historians of early monasticism who have read the relevant chapters of the *Vita* and not suspected that it came from a genuinely early source amongst 'the most ancient of our country':

> and especially of his own monastery ... eaten away along the edges and the spines by the constant devouring of grubs and the ravages of the passing years, and written in the handwriting of our forefathers, they have survived until now.[95]

The failure of this earlier stratum of Welsh literature – by Rhygyfarch's account in a perilous state nine hundred years ago – to survive for our scrutiny today, leaves us free only to treat Rhygyfarch's statement as potentially a *topos*, on the model of cases such as Geoffrey of Monmouth's, unless we can find some external evidence

---

[91] Redknap, 'St Davids and a new link', below, 88–9.

[92] Hill, *Whithorn and St Ninian*, 55–60. As at St Davids (cf. Davies, *Wales in the Early Middle Ages*, 117), Scandinavian settlement was hinted at in place-names, but nothing more.

[93] Simpson, *St Ninian*, 75–8. As Thomas Clancy has observed, however, even though a sixth-century date can now be proved for the earliest phases at Whithorn itself, the case for the site having been occupied by an early 'St Ninian' is still open to doubt: Clancy, 'The "real" St Ninian'.

[94] For the earliest dedications in Ceredigion, at Llanddewi Brefi and Henfynyw, see the detailed account in Bowen, *The St David of History*.

[95] ... *uetustissimis patrię, maxime ipsius ciuitatis ... quę assidua tinearum edacitate ac annosis ęui terebraminibus per oras et cardines corrosa, ac ex antiquo seniorum stilo conscripta, nunc usque supersunt.* *Vita S. Dauid* § 66 (ed. Sharpe and Davies, below, 152).

of sources – the problem encountered above with Ó Riain's hypothesis. Morris, however, observed that several passages in this account present close parallels to the fragments of a letter to Finnian attributed to Gildas. The early date of this letter, from the leading theologian of sixth-century Britain to the acknowledged founding-father of Irish monasticism, is demonstrated by its citation by St Columbanus to Gregory the Great in A.D. 600.[96] Dumville has set out the evidence most fully in his Hughes Memorial Lecture of 2002, so I will not repeat it in detail. The parallels between Gildas's image of monks who 'drag ploughs and dig in the ground with mattocks and plunge spades in ground in presumption and pride' (*Frag.* § 4) and Rhygyfarch's of monks who (§ 22) 'would place the yoke upon their shoulders; they would push spades and shovels into the earth with their unfailing arms' are notable. The broad visions of monks who disdain worldly possessions and live mainly on bread and water also indicate that Gildas's target must at least be more or less identical in rule to David's community as described by Rhygyfarch.

In the words of Dumville, Rhygyfarch's account:

> … embodies phrases which are also found, half a millennium earlier, in Gildas's letter to Uinniau. The only convincing explanation appears to be, as Morris saw, that both authors were quoting from David's Rule, now lost but recoverable in some measure through Rhygyfarch's narrative reporting it.[97]

It is hard not to baulk a little at the certainty of this statement. Gildas does not name David. He may have been describing some other figure; Rhygyfarch may have laid his hands on the rule used by this hypothetical other churchman – or even be reverse-engineering his imagery from Gildas's letter itself. Yet such scepticism seems only to deny the obvious. The holy man David was Gildas's target; the name 'David' likely was in his mind as he wrote.

This very ascetic David was notorious enough to feature in international correspondence. It is interesting to note that when Pope Gregory the Great was reflecting, though the figure of St Benedict, on everything that was right in monastic rule, his model of everything which was *not* may well have been St Columbanus's account of the leadership of David. The figure presented to Gregory was also anonymous – perhaps to the benefit of David's subsequent reputation in Rome – but it may be presumed, even if it cannot be proved, that David was remembered in Wales for his extreme asceticism. This ascetic figure of David does not come to us out of a historical vacuum. That a very influential ascetic tradition existed in South Wales is supported by the *Vita S. Samsonis*, a probably seventh-century work in which, as Richard Sharpe has observed, Samson's career as depicted in the *Vita* 'could be seen as illustrating the trend advocated by Gildas'.[98]

David's asceticism is a fact consistent with what we know of the Wales of his time. It is a characteristic still marked in Rhygyfarch's figure of David. This is significant insofar as we might identify a disjunction between this David and the saint who might have been required by Rhygyfarch to promote the interests of a Welsh ecclesiastical hierarchy. The David of the 'rule' is an extremist whose monks

---

[96] J. Morris, 'The dates', 349–50, 384–5; *Gildas*, ed. Winterbottom, 143–5 and notes, 154–5; Columbanus, *Epistulae* I.7 (ed. G.S.M. Walker, *Opera*, 8–9).

[97] Dumville, *Saint David*, 12.

[98] *Vita S. Samsonis* I.20–1 (ed. Flobert, 178–81); Sharpe, 'Gildas as a father', 199. On the date see Orme, *The Saints*, 7–8; Flobert, *La Vie*, 101–11; Sharpe, 'Marytrs', 85, n. 47; Olson, 'The early hagiography', 123–31.

made silent rebuke of the worldliness of other communities – not, on the face of it, any more positive a trait to eleventh-century reformers than to David's contemporaries. The David of the 'rule' fasts constantly and fails to celebrate the events of Christ's birth and resurrection through the feasts of the liturgical calendar. These characteristics, we might note, are sufficiently similar to those of the *Céli Dé* of Tallaght to perhaps cause his appearance in their martyrologies.

One is tempted to see him as a somewhat awkward presence, a figure who needed to be accommodated and explained, as if Rhygyfarch were not free to simply make of him a portrait of an eleventh-century clergyman. He is not a figure able to be recreated in the image of St Benedict, St Augustine, or the *claswyr.* There could be reasons why Rhygyfarch might have seen value in promoting the cause of this extreme ascetic leader. The *clas* system into which much of the Welsh monastic order had evolved, with laymen often holding the titular abbacies of communities of non-celibate canons, while not the corrupt institution it has sometimes been judged of having been, was transparently open to unfavourable contrast with the incoming reformed orders. In drawing attention to David's individual vision of holiness, Rhygyfarch might have been deliberately trying to elevate David above the worldliness of religious life in his own time. It also may be that the orthodoxy of such a figure so remote in time was less at issue than his basic holiness. St David is presented as a pioneer, compared to the desert fathers (§ 31), with perhaps no fear that his specific theology would require justification in the present climate. Nonetheless, the climactic episode in Rhygyfarch's narrative, the Synod of Brefi, seems to have the function of affirming the orthodoxy of St David in contrast to Pelagianism – with which his views might *conceivably* have been compared – while also making the required bridge between the life of the extreme ascetic and his archiepiscopal role.[99]

We might note in conclusion that, while it might be convenient to present medieval promulgators as able to create history from scratch, as it were, the promoters of David's cult do appear to be taking over a saint whose dossier – in the form of text and, most importantly, landscape – contained irreducible facts and associations. As Graham Isaac observes in Chapter 8 of this volume, in *Armes Prydain Fawr* we can see St David used as a figure to unite peoples or churches in the way that we also subsequently find in Rhygyfarch's *Vita* – albeit the peoples and churches are subtly different.[100] John R. Davies, in his examination of the espiscopal lists from Glasbury,

---

99   Bryan Holmes, while admittedly taking the evidence beyond reasonable limits, would take this argument further, suggesting that the events of the Synod of Brefi can be reconstructed as reflecting David's defence of the orthodoxy of his *own* community – not a matter that it would have been in Rhygyfarch's interest to represent in such terms: Holmes, 'The synod', 9–13. Herren and Brown (*Christ*, 86–7) take this point up more cautiously: 'it is difficult to believe that Rhigyfarch completely invented the details of two councils [Brefi and Victory], especially as they point to the embarrassing presence of heresy in his homeland' (*ibid.*, 87). It remains within the bounds of possibility that a later tradition conflated the work ethic of David's community with a Pelagian theology. Thomas O'Loughlin's discussions of the Patrick dossier (*Celtic Theology*, 25–47; *idem*, 'One island', 4–13; also Charles-Edwards, *Early Christian Ireland*, 215) show how the controversial theologies of another early holy man came to be assimilated in his projection as national saint, rather than simply ignored. We should also note here the fact that Llanddewi Brefi features earlier in the cult of St David than the time of Rhygyfarch, though both the early date of the inscription – no longer intact – and the certainty of the reading of the name *Dauid* in it remain subject to *caveats*: Bowen, *The Historic St David*, 8; Jackson, 'The Idnert inscription', 232–4.

100   Isaac, '*Armes Prydain Fawr* and St David', below, 168.

in Chapter 16 of this volume, sets out a tentative case for an archiepiscopal status for St Davids in the first millennium, providing:

> some glimpses of the archbishopric of St Davids in operation – the morsels of flesh …
> which can be attached to the skeletal frame of an archbishopric otherwise only known
> from the survival of archiepiscopal terminology.[101]

Again, as in the same way as for the 'national' vision of David in *Armes Prydain*, this early medieval archiepiscopal status was no doubt of a very different character to that claimed subsequently for St Davids. These hints, respectively from the end of the first millennium and the beginning of the second, towards an earlier importance of the saint and his church should, however, reveal the *parochia Sancti Degui* of Asser (*ob.* 909) as a substantial landscape – notwithstanding literary – presence from which began its patron's journey from local to national saint.[102]

One of the facts to emerge most strongly from this collection is the degree to which the veneration of St David as more than a local saint is a continuum from the early middle ages into the modern period. The periodic attempts to promote the cult to particular ends all appear to rest on an enduring acceptance that his figure was a key to engagement with a wider British identity. The extent of St David's veneration in liturgy and vernacular poetry are measures of his popular significance.[103] The wearing of the leek on 1 March was to Shakespeare the obvious symbol by which to identify the king with his alternate persona of 'Harry Monmouth':

> FLUELLIN: "Your Majesty takes no scorn to wear the leek on St Tavy's Day"
> KING: "I wear it for a memorable honour;
>   For I am Welsh, you know, good countrymen" (*Henry V*, IV.7).

Williams is probably correct to see Shakespeare's enthusiasm for Henry's Welsh identity as a comment on the Welshness of his Tudor contemporaries as much, if not more, than that of Henry V, but the importance of the cult of St David as a paradigm of Welshness is evident.[104]

The enduring observance of St David's feast-day in some of the most Protestant communities of Wales is notable. Some of this is undoubtedly an intellectual revival, fuelled by confessional histories in which the early British church was able to be seen as distinct from the mainstream of 'Roman' Christianity.[105] Dedications such as Bishop Burgess's establishment of 'St David's College' in Lampeter represent one manifestation of such intellectual promotion of the cult of David. These intellectual efforts, aided by the hagiographical scholarship of the Rees family of Tonn, a native family in service of an ambitious episcopate, like the efforts of the family of Sulien 700 years earlier, nonetheless required a 'grass-roots' devotion to build upon.[106] The papers in this volume reveal hints of an early British church in which St David was a unifying figure in the landscape. They reveal hints of an archiepiscopal status – of whatever sort – for his successors. They track the significance of

---

[101] Davies, 'The archbishopric St Davids and the bishops of *Clas Cynidr*', below, 303.
[102] On the emergence of St David as national saint out of the middle ages and into the modern period see Glanmor Williams, 'The tradition', esp. 119–26.
[103] Williams, 'The tradition', 114–17
[104] Williams, 'The tradition', 117.
[105] Williams, 'The tradition', 119; Williams, 'Some Protestant views'.
[106] On the Rees family of Tonn and Bishop Burgess, see George Eyre Evans, *Lampeter*, 89–101, 151–60; Price, *History of St David's College*, 11–14.

the observance of St David's feast through a wide range of liturgical sources. The St David who is revealed by these studies is a consistently significant figure in the Welsh consciousness, fourteen centuries after his death, as well as in most of the centuries in between.

2

TRANSITION AND SURVIVAL:
ST DAVID AND ST DAVIDS CATHEDRAL

J. Wyn Evans

Introduction

The most eminent saint of Wales ... David, or, as his countrymen call him, Dewi, was the son of Sandde ab Ceredig ab Cunedda, by Non, the daughter of Cynyr of Caer Gawch:[1] To repeat all the fabulous legends invented respecting him, would be to heap together a mass of absurdity and profaneness; for the monks, in the excess of their veneration, have not scrupled to say that his birth was foretold thirty years before the event, and that he was honoured with miracles while yet in the womb. But to pass by these wretched imaginations of a perverted mind, it will be sufficient to notice only those statements of his history which have an appearance of truth. It is said by Giraldus that he was born in a place since called St David's, and that he was baptized at Porth Clais in that neighbourhood by Ælveus, or rather Albeus, bishop of Munster, 'who by divine providence had arrived at that time from Ireland.' The same author adds, that he was brought up at a place, the name of which, meaning the 'old bush,' is in Welsh 'Hen Meneu'[2] and in Latin 'Vetus Menevia.' The locality of Hen-Meneu is uncertain, and a claim has been set up on behalf of Henfynyw in Cardiganshire,[3] which answers to the name, and its church is dedicated to the saint; but it is clear that Giraldus and Ricemarchus, from whom the information is derived, intended to designate some spot near the western promontory of Pembrokeshire, possibly near the Roman station of Menapia, for the latter writer intimates that the 'Old Bush,' as he calls it, was the place where Gistlianus resided before he removed to the valley of Rosina.[4]

---

[1] Neither Rhygyfarch nor Gerald gives us any account of Non's parentage. It is, however, in *Bonedd y Saint,* see Bartrum, *EWGT*, 54.

[2] In a footnote on page 194(*), Rees says that his etymology of the word is borrowed from two languages, *hén* being the Welsh for *old* and *muni*, as he says, is the Irish term for a *bush*.

[3] Rees, in another footnote(†) on page 194, refers the reader to Carlisle's *Topographical Dictionary of Wales, voce* Henfynyw.

[4] Rees, *An Essay*, 193–4. The third footnote on page 194(‡) reads: 'Various readings in Giraldus, in Wharton Vol. II, – see also, page 162 of this essay.' Page 162 deals with Cynyr of Caer Gawch and his descendants; he states that both Non and Gistlianus, Dewi's uncle, under whom he was educated, were born of his second wife, Anna, daughter of Vortimer. He then goes on to remind his readers of the relative positions of *Menevia* and *Old Menevia*: '... Giustlianus, whom was a bishop at Menevia some time before the elevation of St. David to that dignity, whose residence or see, which was perhaps the particular establishment endowed by Gynyr, was situated at some distance from the present cathedral. It was afterwards removed by him to the valley of "Rosina," where the cathedral now stands, at the instance of St. David; ...'. Rees considered that this 'brief narrative, the miraculous part being set aside, is not unlikely to be true; and if, as the same author asserts elsewhere, a monastery had been founded by St Patrick in the valley of the Rosina, thirty years before the birth of St. David,

I have quoted this extract at length out of *pietas*: first of all to the authors named above, Giraldus Cambrensis and Rhygyfarch, as exemplars of all those who had a part in the process which enabled the transition of St David and St Davids from one state of existence to another; and which ensured the survival of both cult and site up to the present. With them I also want to honour Rice Rees (1804–39), who wrote the piece quoted above.[5] Rees was the first professor of Welsh and Librarian at what was then St David's College, Lampeter.[6] He had been brought to Lampeter by a personage who was a predecessor both of mine as dean of St Davids and of the vice chancellor of University of Wales, Lampeter; someone indeed who had taught Rees at Jesus College, Oxford, namely, Llewelyn Lewellin (1798–1878): dean of St Davids from 1840 until his death and principal of St David's College, Lampeter, from 1827 also until his death. He held both offices in plurality – together with the vicariate of Lampeter.[7]

Rees's achievement in his tragically short life (1804–39) – he died of overwork – is much to be lauded in the context of this volume.[8] Without him and without his pioneering book, it would not have been possible to mount the symposium which gave rise to the present volume. We, therefore, salute as pioneers and forerunners both Rees and his work, which was originally either, according to the *Bywgraf-fiadur*, the winning essay at the Eisteddfod at Carmarthen in 1835 or, according to Canon William Price, an extended version of his prize-winning essay at the Cardiff Eisteddfod of 1834.[9] It was printed in 1836 as an exhaustive treatment of the subject – in J.E. Lloyd's words *yn llawn a golau*: 'full and illuminating'.[10] It is, in any case, a convenient starting point for what I want to say about transition and survival in relation to David as a saint culted at St Davids and elsewhere; the site with which he is associated today; and the transitions and changes which that site itself has seen over the centuries.

That Rice Rees was able to speak about Dewi at all in 1836 was tribute to the survival of the fame, if not of the cult, of David. It was, after all, a fame which led to the naming of St David's College, Lampeter; a fame, indeed, which might have been further enhanced, had the original intention of establishing it in Llanddewi Brefi been carried through – a fame, dare I say, which would have gained even greater lustre had anyone ever thought of locating it at St Davids itself. There is no evidence to indicate that anyone did so, nor has it ever been put forward that Llewelyn Lewellin himself suggested a transfer from Lampeter to St Davids. His

---

it would have furnished Gistlianus with a more obvious reason for changing his residence'. In the footnote to this observation Rees states that the residence of St Patrick at *Menevia*, though noticed by Gwynfardd, is at variance with chronology and the most approved histories of his life. Rees also suggests that Ailfyw (Elvis) was a grandson of Cynyr but deriving his name from St Aelbeus who baptized Davud (Rees, *An Essay*, 163).

5 And Professor D.P. Davies, who was unable, on account of illness, to give his planned lecture on Rice Rees to the symposium.

6 Price, *A History of St David's College*, Vol. 1, 36–8; 64. The symposium was held to mark the 175th celebration of St Davids College, Lampeter as well as the fourteenth centenary of one of the dates of Dewi's death. This paper was also designed to furnish a background and introduction to the visit of the participants to St Davids on the following day.

7 Lewellin was the first occupant of both posts: principal of St David's College, Lampeter, 1828–1878; dean of St Davids Cathedral, 1840–1878.

8 He died by the roadside at Newbridge-on-Wye on 29 May, 1839: Price, *A History of St David's College*, 64.

9 As indeed the fly leaf of *Welsh Saints*, bears out, since the essay was dedicated to the Marquis of Bute, as President of the Gwent and Dyfed Royal Eisteddfod held in Cardiff Aug. 20, 21 and 22, 1834.

10 In Jenkins, *Y Bywgraffiadur*, *sub* 'Rice Rees', 779A.

reasons for not doing so may have been either because of the parlous condition of the buildings of the cathedral and close, or because of the continuing existence of the ancient Cathedral Grammar School, which was still producing ordinands.[11] Nevertheless, although the condition of the cathedral may have been parlous, it was still there in Rees' time ('where the cathedral still stands').[12] It had survived many transitions, creating that apparent continuity exemplified today at St Davids by the continued association between Dewi Sant and the site and buildings.

The survival of the cathedral and its association with the patron saint, into Rees's time and beyond, conceals some quite dramatic and revolutionary changes. Some of the ideological and ecclesiological reasons motivating the protagonists of change over the centuries of the existence of the site, cult and buildings call into question the concept of continuity. The attitudes lying behind the various approaches – in particular to the building – have oscillated between conscious attempts to create deliberate discontinuity between past and present, and equally conscious attempts to recover and recreate an ideal past, eliding the intervening dissonance. Thus, not only the survival of the tradition itself but also the continued existence of the site and buildings at St Davids has been nothing short of miraculous.

From Reformation to disestablishment

Most of the changes and transitions involved in securing the survival of cult and site are known and documented. They have left their mark both on the historical record and on the site and buildings at St Davids. Not all changes have, however, done so and this paper will seek to identify some of them. The one major and obvious transition which comes to mind is that process, both abrupt and long drawn-out, which saw St Davids transformed from a significant pilgrimage centre in medieval Wales (and medieval Europe), to become an equally significant powerhouse of the emerging Protestant Anglican Church of England in Wales. This was the period when St Davids was graced by bishops like Richard Davies, precentors like Thomas Huet and musicians like Thomas Tomkins the elder and younger. In the persons of Davies and Huet we find significant figures in furnishing both the Prayer Book and Scriptures in the Welsh language. In this they were more successful in securing the Reformation than William Barlow (bishop, 1536–47), who slighted the shrine of David and destroyed the relics in 1538. Barlow neither appreciated nor foresaw that in a diocese like St Davids – and in a country like Wales, for that matter – his programme of reformation in an urban setting and through the medium of English simply would not work. He was, however, clearly and absolutely determined to create a complete break with the medieval past on theological, ideological and ecclesiological grounds.[13] Davies, by contrast, exemplifies an approach far more positive in its evaluation of Welsh culture and its contribution to the success of the Reformation in Wales, creating the myth of the ancient British Church, primitive,

---

11   It is, however, worth noting that Price states that St Davids in Pembrokeshire 'was considered as a site, but was not considered wholly suitable'. What Bishop Burgess had in mind was the establishment not of a College at St Davids, but something at the other end of a clerical life: 'an Asylum for *Sacerdotes decrepiti viribusque corporis destituti*', Price, *A History*, 12.

12   Rees, *An Essay*, 162.

13   Heal, *Reformation*, 280–1.

Protestant and Welsh-speaking. He was appealing to an ideal religious past, and, for him, the Reformation was not novelty but recovery.[14]

It was, of course, the sixteenth-century Protestant Reformation that gave rise to the somewhat robust views expressed by Rice Rees in the nineteenth century. It is true that he did not actually use the word 'superstition', although 'a mass of absurdity and profaneness' comes close.[15] Bishop William Barlow, however, did use that precise term, *superstition*, in order to justify his destruction of the shrine and his intended removal of his cathedral to an urban and anglicised centre such as Carmarthen or Brecon.[16] That particular physical transition did not take place, though the dwelling place of the bishops was transferred to the former college at Abergwili – Barlow was at least successful in that.[17] His successors did not return to live permanently at St Davids, though the palace was apparently at least partly habitable until the middle of the seventeenth century.[18] In the latter half of that century, Bishop William Thomas attempted not only to secure a licence to demolish the remains of the palace, but also tried to effect, and equally unsuccessfully, the transfer of the cathedral to Carmarthen.[19]

There was much more justification for effecting such a physical – and terminal – transition at that later period, since the cathedral lay in semi-ruin. This was the result of the fervently ideological and vigorously practical Puritanism of the troop of dragoons who came in August 1648 to take 3,000 pounds of lead off the roof,[20] laying bare to the elements both transepts, the choir and chapel aisles and the Lady Chapel.[21] They also vandalised the organ, the bells, tomb brasses and stained glass windows; and gave the *coup de grace* to the manuscripts and books of the cathedral library – such as remained, that is, after Bishop Richard Davies had sent the cream of the collection off to Archbishop Parker.[22]

That particular sixteenth- and seventeenth-century transition was only one of many affecting the cult of the patron saint and St Davids, the site most intimately associated with both saint and cult. It has the advantage of being more accessible to us, since it is nearer in time and is relatively well documented. It was clearly intended by Bishop Barlow to bring not only the story of the cult of David at St Davids to an end but also to remove any trace of the buildings and the cathedral foundation which had housed and nurtured that cult.

A later transition involved a change in attitude to both medieval buildings and

---

[14] See Evans, 'Anglicaniaeth' and Hughes, 'Continuity and conversion', especially 124.

[15] Rees' views were indeed robust. He wrote that the Primitive Welsh church had been 'forced to accept the Catholic computation of Easter, and thereby to join in communion with the church of Rome', Rees, *An Essay*, 305. Further, 'To the descendants of the ancient Britons the Reformation was ... a restitution of blessings', and the possession of the Scriptures in Welsh would have enabled them 'to resist the aggression of Popery with better success', Rees, *An Essay*, 313–14. His views are those which seek to lay sound foundations for the recovery of an ideal past.

[16] Wright, *Three Chapters*, 184. Evans, 'The Reformation'.

[17] James, 'The bishop's palace', 19–44.

[18] Nor have they yet, although the intervening centuries have seen many attempts to secure suitable property in St Davids; and the search is still continuing.

[19] Evans, 'St Davids cathedral', 73–92.

[20] Charles, *A Calendar*, 82.

[21] Though the stone vault did not fall until 1775: Jones and Freeman, *The History*, 174. That of Holy Trinity did not fall at all, though the tracks made by ingress of water following the removal of the lead can still be seen on the south-east fan vault.

[22] It has to be pointed out that the dragoons arrived after the end the end of hostilities, and that the lead seems to have ended up on the roof of either Cardigan or Swansea Market Hall and a private residence. Willis, *A Survey*, 16 and *Errata.*; see also Evans, 'St Davids cathedral', 83.

Gothic architecture in general and St Davids Cathedral in particular. It emerged in the late eighteenth and nineteenth centuries and still flourishes up to the present day. It rests on the perception, which held that churches could only be valid as religious buildings and liturgical spaces when they were built in the Gothic style or restored to their medieval condition. There was, however, a discontinuity between the attitude of the late eighteenth century as regards the use of Gothic Revival styles at St Davids and that of the nineteenth and twentieth centuries. Before turning to those incidents in the history of the restoration and recovery of the Cathedral, it has to be pointed out that the process of recovery began very soon after the Restoration. The transepts were re-roofed and the arches of the presbytery were in-filled in order to make the truncated building weather-tight and useable.[23] Unlike later construction, the work was driven by practical necessity rather than ideological preference for any particular style of architecture.[24]

The first attempt at restoration occurred in the 1780s and 1790s. This too was driven by practical necessity, but its realisation involved the use of an early Gothic Revival style, one which, truth to tell, appears from surviving photographs to have suited the general style of the original late medieval Gothic better than later restorations. Nash's reconstruction of the West Front was intended as the forerunner of a complete restoration of the whole building.[25] Even as this phase of restoration was being completed, however, tastes were changing and a new attitude to Gothic was emerging, that which was expressed in the more academic restorations by William Butterfield in the 1840s, Gilbert Scott in the 1860s and 70s, and his son Oldrid Scott in the 1890s.[26] These were followed by the contributions of W.D. Caroe during the first three decades of the twentieth century, and those of his son Alban and grandson Martin, in the middle and later decades of the same century. Between them, these restorations succeeded in recovering and retaining the building and ensured both its survival and that of the ancillary buildings clustered around it. That campaign of restoration, conservation and recovery is still in train into the present century.[27]

St Davids Cathedral was certainly not in a restored and conserved condition in Rice Rees's day, notwithstanding the work on the Chapter House and the West Front. Indeed, Nash's Chapter House of 1791, set in the western wall of the churchyard by the south gate and on the site of the former Grammar School,[28] had to be taken down in 1829; and the West Front of 1793 was both badly built and aesthetically displeasing to later Goths.[29] Moreover, the impression conveyed by Llewelyn Lewellin, Rice Rees's superior, is that he was not overly concerned with the cathedral building. He did indeed spend a substantial amount on improvements to the interior in the 1840s, but they were largely swept away by Gilbert Scott from 1865 onwards.[30] It has also to be pointed out that the Scott restoration came about not

---

23 Jones and Freeman, *The History*, 173.
24 Evans, 'St Davids cathedral', 73–92.
25 Nash's client drawings survive in two collections: Haverfordwest County Library and the Library of the Society of Antiquaries.
26 See John Carter's views, quoted in Friedman, *The Georgian Parish Church*, 22. Jones and Freeman express their strongly held ideological dissatisfaction with the earlier Gothic of the West Front. Jones and Freeman, *The History*, 52.
27 Under the direction, still, of the Caroe Partnership and the present cathedral architect, Peter Bird.
28 The remains of the basement can still be seen alongside south gate into the cathedral churchyard.
29 See Evans, 'St Davids Cathedral', 92. It would also seem that Rees himself had no interest in the buildings or in the attractions of Gothic, or at least did not intend to pursue it in his study of dedications. Rees, *An Essay*, xiii.
30 It must also be pointed out in Lewellin's favour that he built a new parish church at Lampeter where

because of any initiative on the part of Lewellin. He seems to have been pressured into it, following a public meeting chaired by Connop Thirlwall, who had become bishop in 1840 – the same year as Lewellin became dean – but who had to wait until 1863 to galvanise his dean into action. Indeed there would have been neither transition nor survival for the building or the site as far as Dean Lewellin was concerned. He does not seem to have been much, if at all interested, as far as I can see, in the survival of the cult of David into the modern period, for which the work of his pupil Rice Rees had secured a base through the listing of sites dedicated to Dewi. The cult of the patron saint and those of other early medieval Welsh saints provided a framework for a new ideology and a new self-understanding of the Anglican church in Wales both before and after the trauma of disestablishment and disendowment in 1920.[31]

Disestablishment, together with the disendowment, which accompanied it, was in itself a major disruption to the life of the Anglican church in Wales. It marked a clear transition from one condition of existence to another, which however dreaded in prospect – for the process had been in train for decades – in retrospect did a great deal to create a new self-understanding for Welsh Anglicans. Disestablishment, however, was not as disruptive as the Reformation as far as the survival of St Davids was concerned; it certainly caused less discontinuity and destruction. Disendowment, although it led to the alienation of property and the break-up of estates held by the church for centuries, was certainly less destructive of religious artefacts than the Reformation. The damage caused to the cathedral and the bishops' palace at St Davids remained as mute witness to the latter point for centuries after the Reformation, whereas the decades during which the campaign for disestablishment and disendowment gained momentum were to be those that saw the restoration of the cathedral; and the decades after saw a continuation of that process, however difficult the financial situation. The transition from being part of an Established Church of England to that of a disestablished Church in Wales caused less disruption than had been feared. After disestablishment, the church in Wales remained Anglican, and as an autonomous province, regained control over its organisation and redirected its mission more specifically within a Welsh rather than a British context; nor was it the first in these islands to undergo the process: the Church of Ireland had been disestablished in 1869.[32] Furthermore, the Church in Wales had been aware of the possibility of disestablishment for some time, in contrast to the canons of St Davids in the sixteenth century, who had little inkling of the forces for change unleashed on their cathedral and cult by the Reformation in the persons of Bishops William Barlow and Robert Ferrar and, to a lesser extent, Richard Davies. The latter, at least, had an interest both in the past and its significance for the church

---

he was Vicar (and in whose churchyard he is buried). There is a carved corbel head representing him over the south door at Lampeter parish church. He also spent a considerable amount of money in 1851 on the rebuilding of his Deanery.

[31] Given the discussion in June 2002 about a successor to the See of Canterbury, I could not, and especially in the context of the symposium, forego a feeling of irony, if not superiority if the Disestablished and surviving elder sister in Wales were to furnish an archbishop to her younger and still established sister in England with whose history and polity she was intertwined for so many centuries. In the event, of course, that was what happened with the appointment of Rowan Williams. For the ideology of the past of the Welsh church deployed by both sides in the debate see Evans, 'Anglicaniaeth', 10–25. It is also worth noting that C.A.H. Green did not appeal to such a past but to the wider Catholic and Patristic past in his epic work, *The Setting*.

[32] Acheson, *A History*, 200–64.

whose existence and mission he was attempting to justify to his contemporaries in Wales in the preface to the 1567 New Testament.[33]

Site and cult from Bishop Bernard to Bishop Barlow

Both Reformation and Disestablishment caused significant upheaval, but there were earlier transitions, which were as disruptive and as traumatic as either of them. One of those changes marked the re-absorption of the cult of Dewi into the wider European cultural and ecclesiastical world – just as the Reformation had marked a rupture with that world. It embraced a redistribution of property as traumatic as that at Disestablishment. It was perhaps more significant than either of them, in that it was during that period that both the cult of Dewi and St Davids Cathedral attained their recognisable and maximum development. Without decisions relating to choice and retention of site taken during the eleventh and twelfth centuries, the existence and survival of both site and cult at St Davids today is questionable. For, notwithstanding the convulsion occasioned by the Reformation, the neglect of the eighteenth and early nineteenth centuries (Rice Rees's own day) and both the process and event of Disestablishment, the most eloquent testimony to both the manifestation as well as the survival of the cult of Dewi – the cathedral and its ancillary buildings – still exist on the site which they have occupied for almost nine hundred years.

It is salutary, however, to remember that the particular phase of the cult, which came to such an end so abruptly in 1538, was itself of comparatively recent origin. It began with the building of the present cathedral around 1182.[34] It attained a high point with the construction of the new shrine in 1275 and reached its climax with the completion of the cathedral represented by the remodelling of the Lady Chapel and the construction of Holy Trinity Chapel around the 1520s. When twenty or so years later, Barlow in accordance with Royal Injunctions,[35] brought the practice of pilgrimage to an end, the cult itself was flourishing and the building in good heart.[36]

Building and cult are clearly intertwined, for the success of the cult and the income deriving from it, are expressed in the quality of craftsmanship to be seen in both the cathedral and the buildings ancillary to it within the Close.[37] The nave ceiling in the cathedral, the roof and liturgical arrangements of the presbytery, the choir stalls and misericords all date from this latter period of the medieval cult's existence; as does the exquisite chantry chapel created as his own resting-place and dedicated to the Holy Trinity by Edward Vaughan (bishop, 1509–22). Bishop Gower's magnificent Bishops' Palace,[38] his equally magnificent *pulpitum* and tomb space, his soaring episcopal throne,[39] his ambitious, partly realised scheme for trans-

---

33 Lewis, 'Damcaniaeth eglwys protestannaidd', 116–40.
34 Williams Ab Ithel, *Annales Cambriae*, 55.
35 Wright, *Three Chapters*, 184.
36 A drawing of around 1600 shows the building at its maximum extent before the destruction wrought in 1648. It is the earliest representation of the cathedral known to me. See Charles, *George Owen*, 184.
37 Evans, 'The Reformation', 6–7.
38 See now Turner, 'St Davids bishops palace', 87–194.
39 Modified by John Morgan (bishop, 1496–1504). His own tomb in the nave with its conjunction of mediaeval and Renaissance decorative schemes is itself eloquent testimony to the prosperity, material and spiritual of St Davids in the early Tudor period.

forming the cathedral into a 'hall-church', together with the other fourteenth-century decorative work in the cathedral, reveal a site and cult enjoying considerable prestige and patronage. *The Black Book of St Davids* lists the manors and estates from which the bishops derived much of the wealth, which made possible the realisation of episcopal intentions such as those of Gower.[40] Bishop Houghton's college, chapel and cloister erected at the end of the fourteenth century in an early Perpendicular style make the same point.

None of this activity as expressed – and surviving – in wood and stone would have been possible had it not been for the erection of the new shrine of St David by Bishop Richard de Carew in 1275.[41] The story of the discovery of the putative body of Dewi and its consequent enshrining has been well told by Dr Fred Cowley.[42] It was at this shrine that Edward I came to pray with Queen Eleanor in 1284 and to make gifts to the shrine and its cathedral. He was one among thousands of pilgrims who made the journey to the far west to say their prayers at the shrine of David and Justinian.[43] Whether he then visited some of the other sites in the vicinity, the network of holy wells and small chapels, hallowed as they were by association with Dewi, his family and companions, we do not know. One wonders whether the king or one of his entourage, Archbishop Pecham perhaps, had with them an account of a journey made through Wales about a century before by Baldwin, a previous Archbishop of Canterbury, accompanied by the author of *A Journey through Wales* (*Itinerarium Kambriae*). Again, one wonders whether the royal party had made use of the same author's *Description of Wales* (*Descriptio Kambriae*) to prepare themselves for their excursion, or indeed whether they had to hand a *Life* of the patron saint, and in particular the one written by the same authority as had written the *Itinerary* and *Description*. Had they these three works to hand, they would have been able to make a satisfactory pilgrimage around a sacred landscape of sites ancillary to the shrine and the cathedral.

At this point it becomes necessary to look more closely at a process, which, over at least two centuries, had integrated saint and cult and landscape into the pattern which survives until today. And in looking at the process, we need to try and ascertain who may have been responsible for bringing about that transition. Several people come to mind. The first of them is the most recent, for any discussion of transition and survival relating to St David and St Davids, has perforce to take account of the life, career, literary works and views of Giraldus de Barri (*ca* 1146–1223), the author of the three works mentioned above.

Canon of St Davids Cathedral, Archdeacon of Brecon, unsuccessful candidate for the bishopric of St Davids, pluralist, nepotist, scholar and royal chaplain, Gerald was a not disinterested observer of contemporary life – especially contemporary ecclesiastical life. In his own person, he embodied – both positively and negatively – a response to those forces making for change following Norman incursions into west Wales. He was intimately involved (though not as closely as he would have preferred to have been) in the transition which saw the centre of the cult of St David expressed in the fabric of the building which still in our day (though not in Gerald's) houses the shrine before which Edward I said his prayers. For although Gerald accompanied Archbishop Baldwin on his 'journey around Wales' to elicit support for the Third

---

[40] Willis-Bund, *The Black Book*, and Williams, 'Henry de Gower'.
[41] See Williams Ab Ithel, *Annales Cambriae, s.a.* 1275.
[42] Cowley, 'The relics of St David', below, 274–81.
[43] See Evans, 'St David and St Davids', 10–25; see also Edwards, 'Monuments', 53–5.

Crusade, he did not himself go to the Holy Land. He was released from his vow on grounds of age and weakness – on condition that 'he gave work and aid to the repair (*ad reparacionem*) of the church of Menevia'.[44] Nevertheless, he was associated with, and commented on, the transition of St Davids from native episcopal church to contemporary European cathedral.

Gerald was descended from both the princes of South Wales and the Norman magnates of the Welsh March, that is, from both the losers and winners in the transition from native to Norman Wales. He was thus an informed, if biased, witness to the changes wrought to cult and site in the twelfth and thirteenth centuries. His voluminous writings make clear his views with regard to this process, views that changed both with the passage of time and the waxing and waning of his ambitions. It is in this context, therefore, that we bear in mind what Gerald has to say in the *Itinerary*, the *Description* and his *Life* of St David.[45] It is clear that as we read the *Itinerary*, we are encountering the earlier Gerald, the keen and ambitious young archdeacon. In retrospect, this period marked the high point in his career, this close contact with an archbishop of Canterbury within the context of the allegiance of the Welsh church to Canterbury; at this juncture, there was no hint of anything other than loyalty. Gerald was, not least in his own estimation, clearly a rising star, educated abroad, in touch with continental reforming ideals, running with the tide of reform, and part of that contemporary enterprise, the Crusades – wanting, indeed, to be seen to be taking the Cross. As part of the same enterprise, he also wanted vigorously to reform the Welsh church on continental lines and he criticised the old order vehemently when he came across it as at Llanbadarn Fawr and, as will be seen below, elsewhere. He did of course gain his archdeaconry as a reward for pointing out his predecessor's unreformed and irregular marital state. So, in 1188, he accompanied the Archbishop of Canterbury around Wales, and was present when Archbishop Baldwin celebrated Mass at the High Altar of St Davids Cathedral. Reading and listening to what Gerald says in the *Itinerary*, we have no inkling that there have been any transitions at all in the history of St Davids. The impression given is that the change had been smooth and painless. Clearly these are the views of a winner – the Norman in Gerald's heredity being expressed at the expense of the Native – a winner who expected, moreover, to mop up the glittering prizes, especially the greatest prize of all, the bishopric (archbishopric) of St Davids.

This impression is reinforced when we examine Gerald's version of the *Life* of David. In the extract quoted at the head of this paper, when Rice Rees was referring to Gerald's account of the birth and baptism of Dewi, he was quoting from this '*Life* of St David the Archbishop of Menevia'.[46] That title is itself loaded both with Gerald's personal agenda, as well as the programme which he had in mind for the church in Wales – were it possible to separate the two. Indeed, even in the *Itinerary*, we find the opening words of the second book stating that St Davids was '*urbs olim metropolitana*'. The opening chapter is devoted to the transfer of that status to Menevia by David.[47] This seems to be the only transition with which Gerald was acquainted other than that of the *pallium* to Dol, a transition which he wished

44 Davies, 'Giraldus Cambrensis', 158. Two useful modern studies of Gerald's life and career are Bartlett, *Gerald of Wales* and Richter, *Giraldus Cambrensis.*
45 Richter, 'The Life of St David', 381–7; Bartlett, *Gerald of Wales*, 217.
46 Rees, *An Essay*, 193–4 and *Giraldi Cambrensis Opera*, ed. Brewer *et al.*, III.377–407. See also Richter, 'The Life of St David', 381–6.
47 Ed. Brewer *et al.*, *Opera*, VI.101–3.

reversed, and metropolitan status recovered for St David (and himself). For in the Geraldine version of the *Vita*, the person of the saint is firmly located at the site with which he was associated in Gerald's day and which bears his name today. For Gerald, St Davids[48] and the area around it was the scene not only of Dewi's ministry but of events relating to his birth and the period prior to that.

With the exception of one chapter, Gerald's *Vita* is derivative – he himself entitles it '*vitam … digestam*': a digest of Rhygyfarch's earlier *Life* both in terms of length and content.[49] Gerald's version follows the same pattern as Rhygyfarch's and in largely the same sequence. It is divided into a *proemium* followed by ten lections – rather than the sixty-six chapters of the Vespasian recension – and emphasises the miraculous and providential elements associated with the life and career of the patron saint. In the *Itinerary*, Gerald explicitly states that there were three miraculous events which he considered noteworthy with regard to the patron saint: his origin and conception; the prophecy that he had been chosen thirty years before his birth; and the rising of the ground beneath David's feet at Brefi.[50]

What is relevant to our purposes, however, in Gerald's *Vita*, is the specific topographical detail he inserts. In the very first lection, Sant's lapse from grace in his encounter with Nonnita happens when he had not only entered '*Demeticam regionem*' but when he had reached '*ad partes de Pepidiauc*'. Pebidiog is the *cantref* within which the present St Davids is located.[51] Likewise in the second lection, Patrick, when he returned to his native Britain, came to Ceredigion and thence went to *Demeticam provinciam* and to the *angularem terram* of Pebidiog. Within Pebidiog, he came to *Vallis Rosina*, where he intended spending his life for God. It was not to be: God had reserved *Vallis Rosina* for the as yet unborn David but Patrick is told that he is to evangelise Ireland, which, if he turns his eyes to the West he can miraculously see from the place called in Gerald's day *sedes Patricii*.[52] As he departs, Patrick raises a man called *Dunaudus* from the dead.[53]

Although Gerald is keen to demonstrate his etymological skills in translating *Kaermorva*, the place where Gildas was struck dumb by the presence of the unborn David, as *urbs maritima vel castrum* in *Lectio* II, he does not give its location. Nor does he do so in *Lectio* III, when he deals with David's birth, for although he states that the place where David was born was marked in his day with a church which had in its altar a stone which had been marked by Non's fingers, he does not give a precise location. This is in contrast to the place of David's baptism, which

[48] In Gerald's day, the usual name was *Menevia* see Charles, *The Place-names*, I, 283 ff.

[49] Richter, 'The Life of St David', agrees with James that Gerald's *Life* was derived from an archetype of the Nero MSS but suggests that it was written between 1192 and 1194. Also see Davies, 'Some observations', below, 159–60.

[50] *Itinerarium Kambriae*, ed. Dimock in Brewer, *et al.*, *Opera*, VI.102. Dimock, in contrast to Thorpe's translation, has no mention of an election as archbishop: Thorpe, *The Journey*, 160.

[51] Richards, *Welsh Administrative and Territorial Units*, 170. It was known later as Dewisland and given by Rhys ap Tewdwr, as a marginal note in *Annales Cambriae* makes clear: Williams Ab Ithel, *Annales Cambriae*, 28.

[52] It would indeed need a miracle to see Ireland from the site of the present cathedral, given its low-lying location. *Sedes Patricii* is unknown today though the surviving medieval detail of the entrance to the Treasury has been identified with it. Evans, *The Tŵr Y Felin Guide*, 98.

[53] This differs from Rhygyfarch's account of Patrick's departure in that the person raised from the dead is a certain *Cruimther*; and Dunaud for Rhygyfarch is the stepdaughter of Boia who was killed by her step mother by beheading. Where the blood flowed from the wound, a well called Ffynnon Dunawd flowed which had healing properties and which was clearly known about in Rhygyfarch's day; *Vita S. David* § 18 (ed. Sharpe and Davies, below, 124–5).

is named specifically as Porth Clais. The same lection speaks of the place of his primary education as *Vetus Rubus qui et Kambrice Hen meneu Latine vero Vetus Menevia vocatur*. And Gerald goes on to explain *muni* as 'grove' (*rubus*) and that *Menevia* was 'still today' (*adhuc hodie*) called *Kil Muni* in Irish. David's education was furthered in *Vectam Insulam* under Paulinus, *Germani discipulus*.

Gerald, like Rhygyfarch, tells us that after he had left Paulinus, David is said to have founded twelve monasteries – though only nine are listed, namely, Glastonbury, Bath, Crowland, Repton, Colva, Glascwm, Leominster, Raglan and Llangyfelach.[54] He returned to *Menevia* – the place from which he had departed, where his uncle *Gistlianus* was bishop. An angel however warns David to depart for another place not far away (*non procul hinc locus*) and shows him *Vallis Rosina* 'where a sacred cemetery is extant today'. This would seem to imply that the *Menevia*, which Gerald has in mind, is 'old *Menevia*'; and that *Vallis Rosina* is near to it. It is noteworthy that he does not state that it is the site of the present cathedral – which he does elsewhere. Rees, as we saw above, had drawn attention to the problem regarding the location of *Menevia* and 'old *Menevia*' and their relationship to each other.

When Gerald tells the story of Boia, the location of David's monastery is in *Vallis Rosina* from which the *vir praepotens* can see the smoke rising and challenging his power.[55] Boia's fall allows the *sancta societas*[56] to construct a famous monastery whose location was not blessed with an adequate water supply: Gerald names the River Alun as the culprit. And although he does not locate the well, which David's miraculous powers brought forth, for him, it clearly lay in the Alun valley and can be identified with the one which he mentions in the *Itinerary*. On the other hand, when a certain Terdi requests a well, it is firmly located at Brawdy, four miles distant from St Davids.

Gerald then goes on to recount the miraculous deliverance of the oxen by St Maeddog/Aedan at Solva.[57] Interestingly Gerald in the same lection (V) tells us that St Aedan, when he founded Ferns, followed the rule which he had received from David at *Menevia*.[58]

Lection VI is unique to Gerald's *Vita* and thus worthy of more detailed treatment. It recounts the incident of the 'Unfinished Gospel'. We are told that one day, while Dewi was writing with his own hand the Gospel of John, the bell rang for service. The saint immediately hastened away, leaving 'neither the quire closed, nor the folio completed.' When he returned, he found the unfinished column upon which he had been working completed in letters of gold by an angel. David suppressed the miracle and removed the closed book from human sight, until Gerald's own day – *usque hodie* – when the book was still extant, bound in gold and silver, although its contents were unseen by human eye, for no-one dared to open it. In Gerald's time, however, curiosity was tempting some people to try and see what was inside; but they were dissuaded from doing so.[59] Whether there is confusion here between

---

54 It is interesting that both Gerald and Rhygyfarch give the number of monasteries founded as nine rather than twelve.

55 Gerald calls him *tyrannus*; Rhygyfarch *Scotus. Vita S. Davidis*, ed. Brewer *et al.*, *Opera*, III.367; Rhygyfarch, *Vita S. David* §16 (ed. Sharpe and Davies, below, 120).

56 *Monastica classis* is Rhygyfarch's description: *Vita S. David* §20 (ed. Sharpe and Davies, below, 124).

57 About two miles away from St Davids according to Gerald. It is in reality about three statute miles.

58 Rhygyfarch does not tell us this: did Gerald discover this for himself when he went to Ferns?

59 *Quidam etenim novissimis his diebus id attemptare praesumpserunt; quia semper caritas refrigescit et devotionis de die in diem amplius amor et fidei Deique timor evanescit; sed incontinenti subita*

what was clearly a relic present at St Davids in Gerald's day and the altar brought back from Jerusalem and kept at Llangyfelach – which was also hidden from sight – is not clear.[60] It is also possible that this was the 'worm eaten book covered with silver plate' destroyed by Barlow.[61]

When, in *Lectio* VIII, he gives an account of the synod of Brefi, Gerald, unlike Rhygyfarch, locates it precisely in Ceredigion. Moreover, in his account of the later Synod of Victory whose decrees had been recorded by Dewi in his own hand, Gerald explains their disappearance as a result of depredations by pirates from the Orkneys.[62]

Gerald's last lection (X) deals with the death of David. We learn that David's corpse was buried 'there'[63] by his brethren, 'where until today the Lord shows himself wonderful in his saint with signs and wonders'.[64] It is perhaps strange that neither Gerald, nor Rhygyfarch before him, makes much of the place of the saint's burial nor refers to any shrine that contained his body or any other relic at St Davids.[65]

Thus, in both the *Vita* and the *Itinerary*, Gerald presents us with a success story, not only his own personal (intended) success story, but a success story which saw unbroken continuity between the saint, the site at St Davids and the passage of time – a story which seemed to say that there had been neither disruption nor transition over the previous centuries. The impression Gerald sought to give was that what was present and visible at St Davids – and in the landscape around – had been thus from the time of David onwards. Indeed, we are looking not so much at a transition but at a successful transfiguration of events. That we are not immediately aware of that is a measure of the success of Gerald's achievement; of the package he presented of saint, cult, place, relics, landscape and story; of his identification of *Vallis Rosina* with the Alun valley and with *Menevia*; his distinguishing it from *Vetus Rubus*; and his creation, or highlighting, of a sacred landscape, which was exploited and developed later with the growth of pilgrimage after the thirteenth century and beyond into the modern period. The picture which Gerald presented to his readers is the one which we by and large still present to the modern day visitor and pilgrim. The impression he wished to create at this point was that the church of St Davids was fully integrated into the wider church and engaged in the Crusade – an enterprise of contemporary relevance beyond Wales affecting the whole of Christendom. He further wished to create the impression that the *Menevia* of antiquity and sanctity was associated with the spot where stood the cathedral church. Moreover, he and Bishop Peter de Leia had been put in charge of overseeing the building and repair of the cathedral instead of going on Crusade. In addition, Gerald frequently made clear his conviction that *Menevia* had once been a metropolitan church.

---

divinitus passione percussi, a temerariis ausibus sunt revocait..Vocatur autem a comprovincialibus textus iste evangelium imperfectum; quo usque in hodiernum signis clarus et virtutibus, in maxima non immerito reverentia a cunctius habetur, ed. Brewer *et al.*, *Opera*, III.393.

[60] Although Gerald tells us that the altar was housed in Llangyfelach and that it was famous in his own day, he does not mention that it was hidden; Rhygyfarch, *Vita S. David* § 13 (ed. Sharpe and Davies, below, 120–1).

[61] Wright, *Three Chapters*, 183–7.

[62] Rhygyfarch does not blame Vikings for the loss of records: indeed he flatters himself that he has rescued them from the 'devouring of grubs and the ravages of the passing years': § 66 *Vita S. David* (ed. Sharpe and Davies, below, 152–3).

[63] Rhygyfarch tells us that he was 'laid to rest within his monastery', *Vita S. David* § 65 (ed. Sharpe and Davies, below, 150–1).

[64] *Vita S. Davidis*, ed. Brewer *et al.*, *Opera*, III.404.

[65] See Evans, 'St David and St Davids', 10–25.

But that picture can unravel under closer scrutiny. There is room to be suspicious of the seamless robe Gerald sets before us – to the extent that we want to unpick its seams and to examine the evidence to suggest alternative possibilities. We need to be aware not only that Gerald himself had undergone a transition in his attitude to the Welsh Church but also that he had carried over into his own day an earlier agenda, presumably after the disappointment of his earlier hopes. The picture he presented was not his own but one that he had inherited, though not, as might perhaps be expected, from his uncle David Fitzgerald (bishop, 1148–76). Bishop David was after all descended from those Welsh princes who had endowed St Davids with lands. David Fitzgerald, however, had promised not to espouse any metropolitan claim as part of the arrangement that led to his election as bishop. And there *was* an arrangement: the chapter was split on racial lines and it was the Welsh canons who did not want him as bishop. This hostility clearly lasted throughout David Fitzgerald's episcopate, as the vituperantly hostile – and anonymous – *Vita Davidis II* makes clear[66].

In reality, the immediate origins of the programme implicit in Gerald's *Itinerary* and his composition of the *Vita* of Dewi lay in an unexpected quarter. David Fitzgerald's predecessor, Bernard (bishop, 1115–48) had laboured long and hard to secure metropolitan status and Gerald quite explicitly, though somewhat grudgingly, acknowledges the contribution of Bishop Bernard to the debate about the rights and status of *Menevia*, most particularly the archiepiscopal and metropolitan status of St Davids.[67] For it is, at first sight, quite bizarre that the first Norman bishop of St Davids would have taken on board what was, by all accounts, a lost cause, a hangover from the period before that intrusion into the church in south-west Wales represented by Bernard himself. Nevertheless, it was decisions taken in Bernard's episcopate, and presumably by him, though probably not, as we shall see, by him alone, which led to the survival of both cult and cathedral on the present site, unsatisfactory as that was – and is – for the erection of a massive building.

Before any further examination of the contributions of either Gerald or Bernard is undertaken, we need to remind ourselves that a century before the erection of the present cathedral around 1182 or, indeed, that of its predecessor in 1131, neither the survival of the cult nor the occupation of the site could have been safely prophesied. Disaster and ruin were facing the cult and community of David. In 988, for example, only two centuries before the *Itinerary* of 1188, the place associated with St David suffered only one among many of a series of vicious and effective raids by the Vikings.

The Vikings, however, were not the only attackers: in 982 there was a raid at the hands of the English; and other anonymous raiders attacked the site in 810 and 907.[68] It was the Vikings, however, who were responsible for the raid of 988 and other major churches such as Llanbadarn, Llancarfan, Llanilltud and Llandudoch suffered at their hands in that same year. The Vikings attacked again in 999,[69] but in 1011 it was the Saxons.[70] In 1022 it was a certain Eilaf;[71] in 1073 another Eilaf;[72]

---

[66] Richter, 'A new edition'

[67] Appropriately enough in *De Iure et Statu*, ed. Brewer *et al.*, *Opera*, III.152–3.

[68] Though the attacks are listed from 645: *Annales Cambriae*, ed. Williams Ab Ithel, 7.

[69] *Annales Cambriae*, ed. Williams Ab Ithel, 22.

[70] *Annales Cambriae*, ed. Williams Ab Ithel, 22.

[71] *Annales Cambriae*, ed. Williams Ab Ithel, 23.

[72] Bleiddud died and Sulien assumed the bishopric – to my knowledge *AC* does not use the term *archbishopric* in the text: *Annales Cambriae*, ed. Williams Ab Ithel, 26.

and there was a further attack in 1080.[73] The raids of 999 and 1080 saw the deaths of two bishops of *Menevia*. In 999, Danish pirates killed Bishop Morgeneu and his death had a particular significance in terms of the traditions associated with David. Gerald recounted a vision received by an Irish bishop at the time in which Morgenau pointed to his wounds and said: 'Because I ate flesh; flesh (carrion) I am become.'[74] The implication is that until then the community of David had remained true to the ascetic non-meat-eating tradition established by the patron saint for himself and his original community. The 1080 raid was the one in which Bishop Abraham was killed, an event which led to the recall of Sulien for the second time. In the next year, that descendant of the Vikings, William the Conqueror came to *Menevia, causa orationis*.[75] His advent did not, however, bring Viking raids to an end: in 1091 the men of the Isles destroyed *Menevia*. Nor did it prevent others from raiding: in 1097 the bounds of *Menevia* were ravaged by a certain Gerald, *praefectus* de Penbroc, who was none other than Gerald of Windsor, the grandfather of Archdeacon Gerald de Barri.

Thus, there must, to put it mildly, have been major disruption to the site and community of *Menevia*, a disruption clearly not helped by the theft and despoliation of the shrine and its abandonment, stripped of its gold and silver close to the city (*iuxta civitatem*).[76] Viking rapacity – and that of others – over two centuries, must have made any sort of life – let alone a disciplined, episcopal, communal, religious and pastoral life – almost impossible. And that might well lend credence to the statement made in the life of Caradoc that, because of attacks by pirates from the Orkneys, St Davids was left almost without inhabitant for seven years and it took a visitor almost seven days to get to the tomb of the confessor.[77]

As for the location of the 'tomb of the confessor', its exact whereabouts are unknown. Although Gerald tells us that David was buried 'there' after his death;[78] (and Rhygyfarch tells us that the saint was buried in his own monastery),[79] neither in the *Vita* nor in the *Itinerary* does Gerald mention a shrine, nor does he mention pilgrimage activity, although he draws attention to unspecified miracles associated with David. This raises several questions, not really answered by the discovery of David's body in or just before 1275; it also raises questions as to what was going on at the site after David's death, if indeed David's monastery was on the site of the present cathedral. That in turn raises a more fundamental question: that of geographical transition – a shift both of site and cult from elsewhere.

The episcopate of Bernard is therefore of crucial importance. It is clear that the agenda taken up by Gerald at the end of the twelfth and beginning of the thirteenth centuries seems to have been active – even though it might not have been first formulated – during the years 1115 to 1148. For example, it was in 1131 during Bernard's episcopate that the church of *Menevia* was 'dedicated', presumably as a

---

73 And Abraham was killed: *Annales Cambriae*, ed. Williams Ab Ithel, 27.

74 Ed. Brewer *et al.*, *Opera*, VI.104.

75 *Annales Cambriae*, ed. Williams Ab Ithel, 28.

76 [*Arca Sancti David* MS B.] [*scrinium* MS C alone from *sua* (his) church C].

77 The original life is lost but it survives in John of Tynemouth's epitome (ed. Horstmann, *Nova Legenda Angliae*, 27). The original may well have been composed by Gerald as part of his (unsuccessful) campaign to get Caradog canonised. The saint's body was buried in the aisle of St Stephen proto-martyr, presumably in the 1131 cathedral. His corporeal relics may well be those discovered by Scott in the shrine traditionally associated with Caradog below the North Tower arch and replaced there.

78 *Vita S. Davidis*, ed. Brewer *et al.*, *Opera*, III.404.

79 See Rhygyfarch, *Vita S. David* § 65 (ed. Sharpe and Davies, below, 150–1).

result of the bishop's initiative – and presumably, too, as a setting fit for the relics of Dewi.[80] A plausible context for the building of the new church would have emerged from the period following Pope Calixtus II's advice in the 1120s that pilgrims from England should go to *Menevia* twice rather than to Rome once.[81] The dedication of the church can also be seen as a response to Bishop Urban's enterprise a few years before at Llandaf in creating a new cathedral to house the relics of St Dyfrig. There was one major difference, however. In the case of David, although he had searched long for them, Bernard failed to find any of the saint's corporeal relics.[82] Given that he had failed to find them, it is intriguing that the decision was taken, and again presumably by him, that both the centre of the cult of David and the cathedral should remain in one of the more inaccessible corners of a very large and sparsely populated diocese. He did not, in other words, decide to remove either his cathedral or the centre of the cult from where he found them at St Davids.

Around the same time – as was indeed noted above – Bernard also appears to have bought into the agenda of *Menevia* as a metropolitan church – and hence of the bishop of Menevia as archbishop. Thus his dedication of the new cathedral in 1131 could plausibly be seen as part of the campaign to secure/regain the *pallium*. When he was first appointed, metropolitan status does not seem to have been a major concern.[83] At some point therefore, although the establishment in Britain of metropolitans other than at Canterbury was an issue in the twelfth century,[84] Bernard appears to have 'gone native'. It may be that he had failed to be translated to a wealthier English diocese that he had hoped for, a translation, which perhaps he might have expected on account of his royal service.[85] Thus the quest for metropolitan status may have been a substitute for such advancement – as it may have been for Gerald later.

The evidence for Bernard's support for the metropolitan status of his see is not confined to Gerald's grudging tribute to his efforts.[86] Firstly, there is a series of indignant letters from Bernard's fellow bishops to Pope Eugenius III (1145–53), at the instigation of Archbishop Theobald no doubt, complaining and wondering at the effrontery of the Bishop of St Davids in attempting to deny his subjection to the Archbishop of Canterbury, and arrogating to himself 'the consecration and subjection of the bishops of Wales'.[87] Secondly, there is a letter not from Bernard himself but from the Chapter of St Andrew the apostle and the blessed David – and again to Pope Eugenius III.[88] It survives among the collection of letters and other

---

80 Whether the church of 1131 was the old church of St Andrew is a moot point. See Evans, 'St David and St Davids', 220–21.

81 The evidence is taken from William of Malmesbury writing in the mid-twelfth century. Incidentally Malmesbury also calls David archbishop, William of Malmesbury, *Gesta Regum Anglorum*, V.i (ed. Mynors *et al.*, 779).

82 For a summary of the evidence, see Cowley, 'A note', 47–8; and 'The relics of St David', below, 274–81.

83 See *Episcopal Acts*, ed. Davies, I.239; I.262–64.

84 *St David's Episcopal Acta*, ed. Barrow, 4.

85 He had been Chancellor to queen Matilda, Henry I's first wife (Barrow, *St David's Episcopal Acta*, 2); and as Gerald implies (ed. Brewer *et al.*, *Opera*, III.52), he had been appointed to St Davids by royal favour.

86 *Opera*, ed. Brewer *et al.*, III.152. The whole question of Bernard's claim of metropolitan status for himself and for his diocese has been discussed by Michael Richter through analysis of the contents and the significance of the correspondence between St Davids and the Papacy: Richter, *Giraldus Cambrensis*, 40–5

87 *Episcopal Acts*, ed. Davies, I.263.

88 The body calls itself *capitulum sancti Andreae apostoli sanctique Dauid confessoris*. The letter is

material which Gerald gathered together in *De Invectionibus* to support his great cause.[89] The gist of the letter is that the chapter chose Bernard as metropolitan (*metropolitanum antistem*) for their church, which was the head of the first and greatest province of the whole of Britain; the Welsh bishops were thereby suffragan to St Davids; and they professed obedience to 'our' archbishop. They went on to give the Pope concrete examples of candidates to other Welsh bishoprics promoted to episcopal rank by their archbishops.[90] They make the further point that this had been the practice since the synod of Brefi. However inaccurate the information and confused the chronology and order of events, it has to be pointed out that the latter observation about Brefi harks back to the *Vita S. David* of Rhygyfarch, which is significant both in relation to any attempt to trace the origin of these arguments and the view that the Nero recension of Rhygyfarch's *Vita* was produced for Bernard.[91] This is, at best, ironic since that work was originally written before the arrival of the Normans and perhaps as counter-Norman propaganda. Thus, it would seem that Bernard, or the chapter writing officially as part of his campaign for metropolitan status, was employing an argument relating to the pre-Norman situation relating to Menevia. It is more than likely that they had not sought to carry anything over from any previous regime, in St Davids or anywhere else, as they sought to change the institutions and ethos of the Welsh church in order to bring it in line with contemporary developments on the Continent and in England. The transition that they had in mind was to be abrupt and disjunctive.

The case made by the chapter in the 1140s, thus raises the question as to the origin both of the information contained in the letter and the use made of it, given that it is not an emphasis that might be expected to spring naturally from a reforming churchman such as Bernard. The question is raised more acutely by another letter, purportedly earlier, which was also preserved by Gerald.[92]

The letter was ostensibly written to Pope Honorius II (1124–30), and should thus relate to the earlier years of Bernard's episcopate. The body which sent it called itself not *capitulum* but *conuentus ecclesie Sancti Andree Sanctique Dauid*. Secondly, they make the point that they are of the region of *Demetia* (Dyfed) whence St Samson came. Thirdly, they identify themselves with the Normans (*nostre gentis*). This is in itself confusing, since the arguments they adduce in support of their case are, like the ones noted above, clearly grounded in a sophisticated non- or pre-Norman tradition of history and historiography, citing Fagan, Duuian, Patrick and Samson as well as more recent figures like Wilfrid. At the same time it is less specific as to the more recent past than the later letter to Pope Eugenius. In this it shares the general style, sparse and laconic of the *Annales Cambriae* for the same period.

It has to be pointed out that doubts have been expressed as to the authenticity of this letter, given that it not only appears in material collected by Gerald but also that the hand of Geoffrey of Monmouth has been traced either directly or indirectly

---

usually dated between 1145 and 1148, because of its reference to Bernard who died in the latter year. Richter sees it as dateable possibly to 1145, since it seems to speak of Eugenius's election as a recent event. Richter, *Giraldus Cambrensis*, 45.

[89] That in itself makes both the information contained within the dossier suspect and the way in which it has been shaped and presented.

[90] They state that Joseph had promoted Morclais to Bangor; Sulien had instituted Reuedun also to Bangor and Bleuddud, Melanus to Llanelwy (St Asaph); and Joseph, Herewald to Llandaf.

[91] James, *Rhigyfarch's Life*, vii.

[92] Davies, 'Giraldus Cambrensis', 143–6.

in the nature of the material as well as in the shaping of it.[93] On the other hand, a case for the authenticity of the letter has been argued by Dr John Reuben Davies in relation to other material which also employs the Lucius legend.[94] It is also worth noting that the anonymous *Life* of David Fitz Gerald opens by mentioning letters (*scripta*) from Popes Honorius, Lucius and Innocent still (*adhuc*) in the church of *Menevia*.[95] This, at least, balances any suggestion that Gerald may have created them for the purposes of his own attempts to secure the *pallium*.

What is important about both these letters is not so much the force of the argument or the authenticity of the material but the evidence they contain for the use of, and the transmission from, one political and ecclesiological context to another of arguments designed to defend and justify a situation which should have atrophied after suffering the disapprobation of the Normans. That it did not involves one of the more fascinating and significant transitions, which have affected, indeed guaranteed, the survival of both the cult and site.

Before Bishop Bernard

It also brings us back to the question as to who was the guardian and repository of the material from which the letter writers drew their material in the 1120s, especially if they were Normans. A further question relates to the status and influence possessed by such a source, sufficient to bring back on the agenda the metropolitan question with all its overtones of previous high status for St Davids and its bishops.

The question is also raised as to the origins, identity and composition of this *conventus* of the 1120s, who had been co-opted, or who had volunteered their skills to Bernard and his great enterprise. In the first place they appear to have been the kind of body from which Geoffrey of Monmouth gained the raw – and not so raw – material for the composition of his *Historia*. Secondly, given that this body was calling itself *conventus* and not *capitulum*, it may be the case that they were not a formal secular cathedral chapter but something else. One possibility which suggests itself is that they were the descendants of the clerics whom Bernard discovered at Menevia when he took office in 1115; or indeed that they were that body transmogrified into the new cathedral chapter which Bernard founded; or that they were a significant enough proportion of that new body to influence both the policy and the approach of the bishop in the matter of the *pallium*.

The conventional view of the body of clerics found by Bernard in occupation of the church of Menevia would not see them in as positive a light as this in terms either of learning, regularity or influence and certainly not as suitable candidates to staff the new chapter. According to Gerald the bishop found that his episcopal church was administered by clerics called *glaswir*, *recte Claswyr*. Gerald was very disparaging about them. He saw them as governed by barbarous rites, without order and rule and have 'wickedly taken possession of the church's goods'.[96] On the other

---

93 Barrow, *St David's Episcopal Acta*, 4.
94 Davies, *The Book of Llandaf*, 110.
95 Richter, 'A new edition', 245–9.
96 Ed. Brewer *et al.*, *Opera*, III.153. *Clerici namque loci illius, qui Glaswir id est viri ecclesiastici, vocabantur, barbaris ritibus absque ordine et regula ecclesiae bonis enormiter incumbebant.* Gerald confuses *clas* and *eglwys* as the root of *glaswir* (*recte claswyr*) and, constructing a spectacularly inaccurate etymology, sees them as 'men of the church' rather than 'men of the *clas*'.

hand, it is clear that Bernard had not drawn a line under the previous regime at St Davids by removing native clergy and preventing them from serving in his new chapter. He thus implicitly ensured a transition from the previous situation in physical terms if nothing else.

The Welsh element in the chapter in 1148 was not a cowed remnant. On Bernard's death, and when the chapter came to elect his successor, there were, according to Gerald, a number of Welsh canons who wished to elect a pure Welshman. What they got after – or in spite of – their efforts, was David FitzGerald. Nor do they seem to have been a minority either, for the anonymous *Life* of David Fitzgerald – which gives every appearance of having been written by precisely this constituency – although not identifying the *seniores ecclesie et maior et sanior pars capituli* as the Welsh canons makes it clear that they, the majority, had chosen a candidate other than David FitzGerald. Corruption on David's part gained him the episcopate in despite of the Welsh canons and their candidate.[97] But they survived; and it was probably their literal descendants and successors who, in 1188, approached the Lord Rhys to prevent Archbishop Baldwin from entering the Diocese and from visiting St Davids Cathedral. They saw such an act as a slight to Menevia's claim to metropolitan status. That Gerald was able to note this intervention is a record of a remarkable survival, because by that time such canons should have disappeared from history.[98]

It would thus appear that St Davids was administered by a body of hereditary canons like any other late Mother Church in pre-Norman and native Wales.[99] Moreover, given the distinction of some of the personnel governing or associated with such churches in native Wales in both the pre- and post-Norman periods, it is not surprising to note the depth and sophistication of the arguments employed in defence of Menevia's metropolitan claim by the *conventus* of the 1120s or the *capitulum* of the 1140s. Further, whoever was responsible for drafting the letters to the popes seems to be conveying the same impression and the same agenda with regard to the archiepiscopate as the *Vita S. David,* by Rhygyfarch (*ob.* 1099) son of Sulien, who had been bishop of *Menevia* on two occasions in the later eleventh century. This leads one to ask whether the surviving sons of Sulien, as members of the *conventus/capitulum*, or their supporters and/or followers, were responsible for this claim. After all, Daniel ap Sulien was, according to one source, supposed to have been the successor to Wilfrid not Bernard.[100] And he went on to become Archdeacon in Powys, based, possibly, at Meifod.[101] The further point that suggests itself is that the Nero recension of Rhygyfarch's *Vita* might have been produced by the same constituency acting on behalf of Bernard and his attempt to gain/regain the *pallium.* The question must thus be asked whether there was an agreement or an

---

97 See above and Richter, 'A new edition', 245–9.

98 That they had not is due to clerical marriage. It is noticeable, however, that Gerald does not condemn his own family in his own case. His uncle (who had sons and at least one daughter) made him archdeacon; and he expected to follow his uncle as bishop; and he transferred his archdeaconry to his nephew. See Bartlett, *Gerald of Wales*, 34–3 and *Opera*, ed. Brewer *et al.*, VI.15.

99 See Evans, 'The early church', 61–83 and Evans, 'The survival of the *clas*', 33–40. In the case of Llanbadarn Fawr, Gerald having condemned the lay abbot of 1188 is supportive of the surviving canons of 1212.

100 Lloyd, *A History*, II.453.

101 A possibly similar example is that of Simeon of Clynnog, who wrote in support of Bernard and the archiepiscopal claim; and who was associated with Clynnog Fawr. He became archdeacon in Gwynedd and was present at Gruffydd ap Cynan's death bed.

understanding between the churchmen of the old order – who knew how things had been – to try and accommodate themselves to the new order – not least by carrying over the metropolitan agenda. And we ought to note that Daniel's son Cadifor had a connexion with the Diocese of St. Davids (and the cathedral) when he became archdeacon of Cardigan later in the twelfth century.[102]

There is a further point to consider as to the nature of the body administering *Menevia* when Bernard began his episcopate. When Gerald mentioned the organisation and administration of *Menevia* in 1115, which *clas* or its members was he disparaging? There is one other piece of evidence, which not only illuminates the situation at *Menevia* in 1115, but also suggests that perhaps the contribution of Sulien and his sons was not just to do with the metropolitan question.

In 1081, Gruffydd ap Cynan landed at Porth Clais to be met by Bishop Sulien, and Rhys ap Tewdwr. And having met together, the two kings swore an oath on the relics – (presumably in the church of *Menevia*) – and went off to fight and win the battle of Mynydd Carn. Sulien's role within that context is clearly significant. Not only was he showing involvement in the political scene by supporting and identifying with an exile, Gruffydd ap Cynan, he was also associated with Rhys ap Tewdwr, the dispossessed king of Deheubarth, who had gained the *nawdd* (protection) of *Menevia* and was accompanying Sulien to Porth Clais to meet Gruffydd ap Cynan. In the case of both princes, Sulien was identifying with persons who had reason to be hostile to the prevailing order and were intent on bringing it down. Moreover, by being associated with the swearing on the relics he was offering supernatural assistance to both kings in their associated enterprise. In any case, however, it is the entourage that accompanied Sulien to Porth Clais that is of interest. He went down there accompanied by not one but two *clasau: holl glas yr arglwydd dewi ac un eglwys Fynyw*.[103]

The distinction between these two bodies is not immediately apparent. The Latin version of the *Vita* of Gruffydd ap Cynan speaks of *Menevensis Episcopus, doctores ac chorus universus Sancti Davidis, clerique omnes ecclesiae Menevensis* going down to Porth Cleys which was not far from the archiepiscopal see of Menevia (*non longe a sede archiepiscopali Menevensi*).[104] The Latin at least distinguishes between the group associated with David and the one associated with Menevia. One way to take the distinction between the two groups is to see the *chorus universus* as the entourage of Sulien as bishop/archbishop and the other as the clerks/canons of the church of Menevia – the predecessors of the '*glaswir*' mentioned by Gerald as being at Menevia when Bernard arrived in 1115. Alternatively, what the anonymous author of the *Vita Griffini fili Conani* might have been drawing a distinction between was senior and junior clergy of the episcopal/archiepiscopal church: the clergy/canons – the equivalent perhaps, until 1920, of the distinction between the Upper Chapter of Canons and the Lower Chapter of Vicars Choral, lay and clerical. It might also be the case that the first group represented the episcopate of Dewi in terms of clergy drawn from the many churches 'owned by' Dewi other than Menevia, the church normally associated with him in later centuries.[105]

There is another, more unlikely, possibility, given that some sort of distinction

102   Lloyd, *A History*, II.461.
103   Evans, *Historia Gruffud vab Kenan*, 13. For the Latin text: *Vita Griffini Fili Conani* § 17 (ed. Russell, 68–9). This portion of the *Vita* appears to be original: Dr Paul Russell, *pers. comm.*
104   *Vita Griffini Fili Conani* § 17 (ed. Russell, 68–9).
105   For Dewi 'owning' churches see Owen, 'Canu i Ddewi', 443.

is being drawn between the one group linked to Dewi and the other to the church of Menevia. Support for this contention, lies in the distinction between *Mynyw* (*Menevia*), which is the name commonly used for St Davids in the mediaeval period and the place name Hen Fynyw (*Old Menevia*). For it is in the area of the Aeron and Teifi valleys that the greater number of dedications to David occurs; as a glance at Rice Rees's county lists makes clear, there are far more than in Pembrokeshire.[106] Both Henfynyw and that other major centre of David's cult, Llanddewi Brefi, are located in this area of Ceredigion. We are thus entitled to ask whether there was a shift southward in the centre and the distribution of the cult of Dewi at some unknown period before 1081. The lack of evidence allows us to suggest neither a motive for the movement nor, indeed, who was responsible for the focus on Menevia. We might ask whether it was Sulien who moved the cult of David down to West Wales from Hen Fynyw and, commissioning his son Rhygyfarch to write a *Vita*, thereby justified, indeed created, a new scenario. Further, the endowment bestowed upon the cathedral by the largesse of the princes of South Wales was for an indigent site, as well as out of gratitude for sanctuary and support for his kingship on the part of Rhys ap Tewdwr.[107]

On the other hand, given the upheavals they had suffered, it might also be possible to argue that, when Viking raids became too much to bear, the clergy removed themselves and the relics of Dewi (including his body) to other Dewi churches for safety, including the bones.

Hence, a distinction between *Mynyw* and Hen Fynyw, Old and New/Present Menevia may not have been very old; and the cult may only recently have returned to St Davids and *archescopty Mynyw*. Conversely, the distinction may have been very old indeed. The C text of *Annales Cambriae*, when it treats of David's death under the year 601/602, speaks of him as *David episcopus Moni Iudeorum*.[108] This was emended to *moni desorum* by Loth, thus associating *Menevia* with an area in West Wales settled by the Déisi.[109] It may also lie behind the description of *Mynyw yn y deheu* in the Welsh *Life* of Dewi. There have also been suggestions that *Vetus Rubus* / Hen Fynyw may not be the site in Ceredigion but that it was located a mile or so away from the site of the present cathedral in the valley on the shores of Whitesand Bay where Tŷ Gwyn lies within a large cist cemetery very near Capel Padrig and Ffynnon Faeddog. The dry valley extending back from St Davids Head looks a better candidate for *Vallis Rosina* than the wet marshy valley of the Alun, which makes an excellent context for both *muine* (undergrowth) or *rosina* (marsh/valley). The Alun valley is still known as Merivale (Hoddnant) in the vicinity of the cathedral.

In any case, 1081 brought someone else, whose visit certainly brought about a, if not the major, transition to and at St Davids. William the Conqueror came *causa orationis*. But, as we have seen above, St Davids's capacity for survival meant that the transition was absorbed, as have been all the others, over its long history. The agendas of the past were carried over not just to Gerald's day, but beyond – through to Reformation and Disestablishment and up to the present day.

Transitions, however abrupt or drawn out, and survivals, however fragile or robust, have from the very beginning characterised the phenomenon that we know

---

[106] Note Rees, *An Essay*, 232–352.
[107] Williams Ab Ithel, *Annales Cambriae*, 28.
[108] *Annales Cambriae*, ed. Williams (*Ab Ithel*), 6.
[109] For a full treatment of *Mynyw yn y deheu* and Loth's suggestion, see Evans, *The Welsh Life*, 55.

as St David and St Davids. Over the centuries, the changes and chances of this fleeting world have brought about surprising and quite unexpected transformations, affecting site, saint and cult. At the same time a strong thread of continuity runs through the story from the earliest times to the present day: saint and cult and site are still distinguishable fourteen centuries after the death of Dewi Sant.

3

THE GEOGRAPHY OF THE CULT OF ST DAVID:
A STUDY OF DEDICATION PATTERNS
IN THE MEDIEVAL DIOCESE

Heather James

Introduction: the use of dedications

The works of E.G. Bowen on the distribution of dedications to Celtic saints and the role of the western seaways, despite their many controversial points, have not ceased to inspire scholarship.[1] Indeed, in Cunliffe's recent work, Bowen's 'western seaways' have a new proponent.[2] Bowen himself, especially in his later work, did accept that the surviving pattern of dedications and place-names reflects the latest extent of the cult, rather than (necessarily) the missionary activities of the saint and his followers, though he maintained that from a geographical perspective it was not a crucial distinction. He recognised the phenomenon of 're-culting' of newer and more power-fully patronised saints eclipsing earlier local cults. In a lecture to the Friends of St Davids cathedral, later published as a monograph, Bowen also set out a narrative of St David that remains immensely influential.[3] In this late work, written for a general audience, he presented a case in which, when standard hagiographic incidents and themes were taken out of Rhygyfarch's *Life,* an historically reliable core remained. According to this narrative, David was born in Ceredigion and first educated in the monastic life at Henfynyw (*Vetus Rubus*) under Guistilianus, then by Paulinus, somewhere in Carmarthenshire. From there, he and his followers moved about the countryside in the normal fashion of Celtic monks founding churches. After plot-ting the distribution of churches dedicated to St David, Bowen identified two main groups: a northern and a southern. The northern group he thought indicated expan-sion of the cult from Llanddewibrefi, the southern from St Davids. In this model, the final choice of St Davids as a site was due to its nodal position in sea and land routes. Thereafter, he saw the cult as having developed through pilgrimage along the main routes leading towards St Davids: by coastal routes, from north Wales and south-east Wales and across central Wales, often making use of Roman roads. Thus Bowen presented both a dedication pattern centred on the career of David himself, as well as recognising the role of metropolitan aspirations and diocesan struggles in shaping the eleventh- and twelfth-century documentary sources for the cult. In contrast to Bowen's emphasis on the person of David and the aspirations of his church, J. Wyn Evans has stressed the 'active patronage of the dynasty of Deheu-barth' in the eleventh and twelfth centuries in extending what Asser in the ninth century termed the *parochia Sancti Degui*, often at the expense of other saints and

---

[1]   Bowen, *The Settlements*; Bowen, *Saints, Seaways.*
[2]   Cunliffe, *Facing the Ocean*, 458–465.
[3]   Bowen, *Dewi Sant – Saint David.*

their cult centres. Furthermore, Evans sees the pattern of dedications as a means of establishing and sustaining the largest diocese in medieval Wales.[4]

The new Norman system of dioceses, deaneries and parishes reshaped an earlier pattern of 'mother churches' with their subsidiary 'daughter' churches. Nevertheless, the four territorial dioceses essentially in place across Wales by 1150 broadly correspond to the principal early kingdoms of Wales. It has long been recognised that the new ecclesiastical units of the church in Wales were based on older territorial units: deaneries corresponded to *cantrefi* or *cymydau* (commotes), the new office of archdeacon corresponding to a kingdom or region.[5] Evans has pointed out that the new archdeaconries were often administered from important 'mother churches', sometimes termed *clasau*.[6]

Dedication and consecration of churches are combined in the medieval liturgy, which involved the consecration of an altar or altars and the enclosure of relics within them by a bishop. As yet, frustratingly, there is no archaeological evidence for stone churches in Wales prior to the twelfth century, nor any wooden predecessors. Yet we must assume from documentary evidence that there were churches, as well as monastic foundations, from at least the ninth century onwards.[7] Often the earliest documentary reference to a church will be in the 1291 *Taxatio* of Nicholas IV, which is ordered by medieval deaneries.[8] No dedications, other than those embedded in the place-name, are given there and smaller churches and chapels were not included in the lists. Churches and estates were subject to attack and seizure by Vikings, Welsh princes and Norman lords alike. From the late eleventh century onwards, conquest, and in many areas settlement, by incoming Flemings, Normans and English led to new churches, new dedications and a thorough reorganisation of the Welsh church. Pryce makes the point that the native Welsh rulers themselves, as their patronage of the new religious orders demonstrates, were also proponents of change in church organisation.[9] However, particularly in areas that came late under English control and where Welsh patterns of settlement, law and tenure remained, native patterns of piety persisted. Dedications to native saints may well have continued after the eleventh century; equally dedications to 'Latin' saints like Mary or Michael the Archangel could well predate the Conquest.[10]

I propose therefore in this paper to look again at the location of sites, mainly, though not exclusively, churches and chapels dedicated to St David, in the context of what we know of eleventh- and twelfth-century secular and ecclesiastical territorial and administrative units.[11] Most of these units have earlier origins. Sites will also be considered in relation to the medieval estates of the bishop of St Davids.[12] Use will be made both of Rhygyfarch's *Vita S. David* (*ca* 1095) and Gwynfardd Brycheiniog's *Canu Dewi* (*ca* 1170), the latter containing extremely useful lists of churches

---

[4]   Evans, 'St David and St Davids'.

[5]   Williams, *The Welsh Church*, 16.

[6]   Evans, 'St David and St Davids', 23.

[7]   Pryce, 'Pastoral care', 41–62.

[8]   *Taxatio Ecclesiastica Angliae et Walliae*, ed. Ayscough and Caley. [Henceforth *Taxatio*.]

[9]   Pryce, 'Church and society', 27–47.

[10] Ludlow, 'Spiritual and temporal', 72 esp.; see also his unpublished reports for the Early Medieval Wales Ecclesiastical Sites project, in Cambria Archaeology's Sites and Monuments Record (SMR).

[11] Principal sources for the Digiwatu GIS (see n. 15 below) are Richards, *Welsh Administrative and Territorial Units* and W. Rees's maps: *South Wales and the Borders in the Fourteenth Century*.

[12] There is little evidence on these estates before the 1326 extent: *The Black Book of St Davids*, ed. Willis-Bund.

'owned' by Dewi.[13] One of the features of Bowen's method that sustains interest in his studies was his dynamic use of maps. We work now in an era of electronic cultural atlases of all kinds. There can be no doubt that the potential of Geographical Information Systems in mapping hagiotoponyms in dynamic databases accessible through the Internet will revitalise analyses of the origins and development of saints' cults in geographical terms, on a more critical basis than was possible in the past.[14] The data for this article, especially that shown in map form, are based on a developing GIS database of early Welsh administrative and territorial units in Wales being constructed by Terry James.[15] Much more detailed work on refining boundaries has yet to be done. Parish boundaries used on Maps 2–4 are taken from Kain and Oliver, *Historic Parishes of England and Wales*.[16]

A basic classification has emerged from this preliminary study of the geography of the cult of St David. Church and chapel sites dedicated to the saint and his associates seem to fall into one or more of the following locational categories:

- Monasteries, mother churches and lesser churches which are either *liminally* or *centrally* sited in relation to territorial units.
- 'Daughter' sites, often chapels, attached to former mother churches dedicated to other Welsh saints; these may be later post-Conquest dedications when the parochial and diocesan organisation of St Davids had become firmly established.
- Linear/transmontane – sites located along major routeways, some, but not all, of Roman origin and also churches that are sited either side of cross-upland routes.
- 'Estate' churches and chapels whose siting is best explained in relation to lay founders and secular estates.

Archaeological evidence

Archaeological evidence and archaeological techniques are central to the study of a saint and a cult. The physical remains, the saint's burial place and material objects associated with a saint after all constituted key 'co-ordinates' and relics of a saint's cult. Sacred places and associations with the natural landscape were a dynamic source of folklore and focus of pilgrimage. This article draws on current work on the archaeology of the early Christian church in Wales and uses criteria for identifying early medieval ecclesiastical sites developed by the four Welsh Archaeological Trusts in their Cadw-funded, pan-Wales, survey projects.[17] The article was however written before the publication of Edwards's volume in the *Corpus of Early Medieval*

---

[13] 'Rhygyfarch's Life of St David', ed. Sharpe and Davies, below, 107–55; Owen, 'Prolegomena' 51–79. Owen's translations are used throughout this article.

[14] See Graham Jones on the Europe-wide Trans-national Database and Atlas of Saints' Cults (TASC) in Jones, *Saints of Europe*.

[15] I am grateful to my husband, Terry James, for preparing the maps in this article from data in 'Digiwatu' – a GIS database on medieval Welsh administrative and territorial units.

[16] Acknowledgement is hereby made to the data creators, the History Data Service and the UK Data Archive, University of Essex, Colchester CO4 3SQ.

[17] I am most grateful to my former colleagues in the Welsh Archaeological Trusts, especially Neil Ludlow of Cambria Archaeology, for sight of their unpublished rapid survey reports, gazetteers and overviews. Summaries of their work will be published as proceedings of a 2004 conference at Bangor 'The Archaeology of the Early Medieval Celtic Churches'.

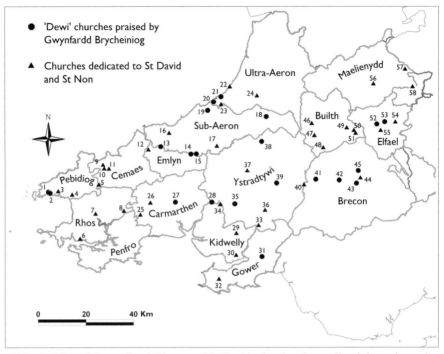

Map 1. Map of the medieval Diocese of St Davids showing the medieval deaneries and numbered churches listed and described in Table 1. (Map by Terry James)

Inscribed Stones and Stone Sculpture in Wales.[18] In an earlier paper, she has reviewed the early medieval physical evidence of cult: tombs, shrines, reliquaries, bells and croziers.[19] Accordingly discussion of such material here has been kept to a minimum. The archaeological criteria used by the Early Medieval Ecclesiastical Sites project (hence EMES) to rank sites most likely to be of early medieval origin are:

- Grade A: pre-(Norman) conquest documentary references; evidence of *clas* or portionary organisation; excavated and radiocarbon dated archaeological evidence, especially cist graves; a saint's grave / *capel-y-bedd*; siting within a Roman fort, villa or town.
- Grade B: multiple churches within the graveyard; church plan form; undated archaeological evidence but of early medieval type; artefacts, especially inscribed and decorated stones likely to be *in situ*; associations with earlier prehistoric ritual, funerary or defensive sites.
- Grade C: churchyard morphology; outer enclosures, Celtic dedication; place-names such as *merthyr* or *eglwys*; associated holy wells; antiquarian references to a site's antiquity.

---

18 Edwards, *Corpus*, Vol. 2. Pending publication of the *Corpus*, references to the early christian monuments and sculpture use the reference numbers in Nash-Williams, *ECMW*. Use has also been made of the on-line database CISP (Celtic Inscribed Stones Project) established and maintained by the Department of History and Institute of Archaeology, University of London. See also Edwards, 'Stones', 15–39; N. Edwards, 'Monuments', 53–77.
19 Edwards, 'Celtic saints', 225–65.

Table 1. Churches and chapels dedicated to St David, St Non and their associates within the medieval diocese of St Davids, ordered by archdeaconries and their component deaneries. The principal source for parochial status is Wade Evans, 1910, 'Parochiale Wallicanum'. Those churches lauded by Gwynfardd Brycheiniog are numbered and named in bold

		Medieval Status	*Archdeaconry*	*Deanery*
1	**Cathedral of St David and St Andrew**	Cathedral	St David's	St David's
2	St Non's Chapel	Chapel of the cathedral		
3	St David, Whitchurch	Chapel of the cathedral		
4	St David, Brawdy	Chapel of the cathedral		
5	St Dogwells, Llanlleddewi	Chapel of deanery		
6	St David, Hubberston	Parish church		Rhos
7	St David, Prendergast	Parish church		
8	St Aidan, Llawhaden	Parish church		
	—	—	—	Penfro
9	St David, Llanllawer	Chapel of Llanychllwydog	Cardigan	Cemais
10	St David, Llanychaer	Chapel of Llanychllwydog		
11	St David, Llanychllwydog	Parish church		
	St David (unlocated)	Chapel of Newport parish church		
12	St David, Bridell	Chapel of Maenordeifi		Emlyn
13	**St David, Maenordeifi**	Parish church		
14	**St David, Bangor Teifi**	Parish church		Sub Aeron
15	**St David, Henllan**	Chapel of Bangor Teifi		
16	St David Blaenporth	Chapel of Llanddewibrefi college		
17	St David, Capel Dewi	Chapel of St Tyssul's, Llandyssul		
18	**St David, Llanddewibrefi**	Parish Church and college		
19	**St David and St Meilig, Llanarth**	Parish church		
20	**St David, Henfynyw**	Parish church		Ultra Aeron
21	St David, Llanddewi Aberarth	Chapel of Henfynyw		
22	St Non, Llanon	Chapel of St Bride's, Llansantffraid		
23	St Non, Llannerch Aeron	Parish Church		
24	St David, Blaenpennal	Chapel of Llanddewibrefi college		
25	St David, Llanddewi Velfrey	Parish church	Carmarthen	Carmarthen
26	St David, Henllan Amgoed	Parish church		
27	**St David, Meidrum**	Parish church		
28	**St David, Abergwili**	Parish church		
29	St Non, Llanon	Chapel of St Illtud's, Pembrey		Kidwelly
30	St David, Capel Dewi, Berwick	Chapel of St Elli, Llanelli		

31	**St David and St Cyfelach, Llangyfelach**	Parish church		Gower
32	St David, Llanddewi in Gower	Parish church		
	St Non, Llan Non	Chapel of St Illtud's, Ilston		
33	St David, Betws	Parish Church		Ystrad Tywi
34	St David, Capel Dewi	Chapel of Llanarthney		
35	St David, Llanarthney	Parish Church		
36	St David, Capel Dewi	Chapel in Llandeilo Fawr parish		
37	St David (?) Abergorlech	Chapel of Llanybydder		
38	**St David, Llanycrwys**	Parish Church		
39	**St David, Llangadog**	Parish Church		
40	St David Dolhowell	Chapel of Myddfai or Llywel	Brecon	Brecon
41	**St Llowel and St David, Llywel**	Parish Church		
42	**St David, Trallong**	Chapel of Llywel		
43	**St David, Llanfaes**	Chapel of Garthbrengy		
44	St David and Holy Trinity, Llanddew	Chapel of Garthbrengy		
45	**St David, Garthbrengy**	Parish Church		
46	St David, Llanddewi Abergwesyn	Chapel of St Cynog's Llangamarch		Builth
47	St David, Llanwrtyd	Chapel of St Cynog's Llangamarch		
48	St David, Llanddewi Llwyn-y-fynwent	Chapel of St Cynog's Llangamarch		
49	St David, Llanynys	Chapel of Maesmynys		
44	St David, Llanddewi Maesmynys	Parish Church		
51	St David, Llanddewi'r cwm	Chapel of Maesmynys		
52	**St David, Cregina**	Parish Church		Elfael
	St Non, Llan Non	Chapel of Gregina		
53	**St David, Glascwm**	Parish Church		
54	St David, Colva	Chapel of Glascwm		
55	St David, Rhiwlen	Chapel of Glascwm		
	St David, Llanddewi Vach	Chapel of Sts Llowes and Meilig, Llowes		
56	**St David, Llanddewi Ystrad Enni**	Chapel of St Cynllo's Llanbister		
57	St David, Llanddewi Heiob (Heyop)	Chapel of St Cynllo's Llangynllo		
58	St David, Llanddewi'n Hwytyn (Whitton)	Chapel of St Cynllo's Llangynllo		

The EMES project team is, of course, well aware that the significance, or indeed occurrence, of these criteria will vary across Wales and have allowed for regional characteristics. However, the benefits of a seamless, uniform grading must surely outweigh the disadvantages of a 'one-fits-all' approach. The conclusion of this article will return to these varied criteria and see whether the evidence presented can indicate at least a relative chronology to the origins and development of the cult of St David.

The seven bishop-houses of Dyfed

Historical evidence suggests that the cult of St David based at Menevia was powerful and extensive in the eighth and ninth centuries. Asser refers to his kinsman, Nobis, as *archiepiscopus*. There is general agreement that in a ninth-century context this rank signified an Armagh-style overlordship over the kingdom of Dyfed. It seems appropriate therefore to begin by examining the text on the seven bishop-houses of Dyfed embedded in later recensions of the Welsh laws and dated by Charles-Edwards to the second half of the ninth century, perhaps early tenth. In a seminal study, Charles-Edwards linked these sites to the seven component *cantrefi* of the fifth- through tenth-century kingdom of Dyfed.[20] He suggested that the *cantrefi* themselves, which were long-lived territorial units, originated as small kingdoms ruled by kings on the Irish model. Dyfed, it is generally accepted, was ruled by an Irish dynasty, the Déisi, between the fifth and eighth centuries. The names of six of these bishop-houses are personal (saints' names) with the *llan-* prefix.[21] Head of the list however is *Mynyw ... penhaf yg Kymry/ Menevia sedes principalis in Cambria*.

It is not the purpose of this article to discuss what kind of institution a bishop-house was. If they had some kind of focal role within their *cantref* the fact is that apart from *Mynyw* itself, they do not continue unchanged into the eleventh and twelfth centuries as important ecclesiastical sites, indeed Llan Geneu disappears. Secondly, their locations are generally 'liminal', that is to say close to the edges or boundaries of the territorial units rather than central. Thirdly, it is clear that in at least some of the *cantrefi* there were other important cult centres. It might be thought that *Mynyw* too is in a liminal location, but it is at a nodal position for sea routes possibly from late prehistoric and Romano-British times as well as early medieval. In short, in every respect, *Mynyw*, cult centre of St David, is exceptional in this list.

Pebidiog

After the Norman conquest, the spiritual power of the bishops of St Davids was accompanied by their secular power as Marcher lords of Pebidiog. The *Annales Cambriae* record that Rhys ap Tewdwr granted Pebidiog to the bishops but we do not know whether this was a confirmation of older royal grants.[22] Gwynfardd

---

[20] Charles-Edwards, 'The seven bishop-houses', 247–62.

[21] In *Llyfr Cyfnerth*, following *Mynyw: Llan Ismael, Llan Degeman, Llan Ussyllt, Llan Teilaw, Llan Teulydawc, Llan Geneu*, Charles-Edwards, 'The seven bishop-houses', 8.

[22] Evans, 'St David and St Davids', n. 4, 23. It is worth noting that Pebidiog is the only one of the seven cantrefi to have a personal name attached to a territorial unit. There are similar commote names to the

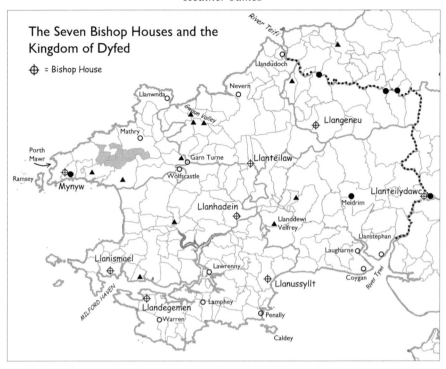

Map 2. The seven bishop-houses and the kingdom of Dyfed. (Map by Terry James)

Brycheiniog in his *Canu Dewi* continues that distinction between St Davids's lordship and overlordship in the world of the late twelfth century: *A'r Deheu ef bieu a Phebidya6c* ('And he it is who possesses Deheubarth and Pebydiog').[23] The parish of St Davids is the largest within the cantref and medieval deanery and probably originally included Whitchurch as well (see Map 2). Tithes of St Davids and Whitchurch parishes jointly supported 'prebendaries cursal' in the cathedral.[24] The joint parishes probably reflect the size of the early patrimony of St David's monastery. The present cathedral close, walled by Bishop Gower by 1344, may wholly or at least in part enclose the area of an earlier monastic enclosure. Before the twelfth century, there was certainly more than one church within that enclosure. Indeed, as Evans has argued, many of the perceived irregularities of alignment and changes in level of the present cathedral (substantially that built by Bishop Peter de Leia 1176–1198) could well be due to that building incorporating remains of its smaller predecessors.[25]

In addition to churches and monastic buildings, the enclosure would have contained a cemetery. In Rhygyfarch's *Vita S. David* there is a strong suggestion that the site of David's monastery was shifted on account of what is explained as

---

east and north – Anhuniog in Ceredigion or Catheiniog in Carmarthenshire. Generally little is known of these eponymous founders; nothing is known of Pebyd although Charles cites similar names in a few Caernarvonshire place-names. Apart from Mynydd Pebyd, there are no other place names, no hagiographic links, no mention in genealogies of the eponymous Pebyd.

23 Owen, 'Prolegomena', lines 34, 67 and 73.
24 Yardley, *Menevia Sacra*, 286.
25 Evans, 'St David and St Davids', n. 2, 19–21.

48

an increased likelihood of salvation through burial in the new site.[26] Gwynfardd Brycheiniog extends this theme to all 'Dewi' churches: *A el y medra6d mynwent Dewi/ Nyd a yn uffern* ('he who goes to the grave in Dewi's cemetery shall not go to hell').[27] Elizabeth O'Brien, drawing on copious Irish evidence, sees a change in burial practice, gathering momentum from the seventh century onwards. Earlier burials, possibly pagan, in circular enclosures or kin burial grounds gave way to burial in consecrated ground, where proximity to a saint's grave or at least holy relics gave better guarantee of salvation.[28] Behind this we have the immensely influential model put forward by Thomas in 1971, namely that of 'undeveloped' and 'developed' cemeteries. The former he termed 'the primary field monuments of insular Christianity'. The latter, by addition of oratories, chapels and churches associated with the relics and cult of a saint, became the medieval parish church within its enclosing, often curvilinear, churchyard.[29] There are a number of cist cemetery sites around St Davids whose origins, abandonment or continuity may be interpreted in the light of such models. It is however important to recognise that most of our knowledge of these sites is from antiquarian references and small-scale excavation. More modern work benefits from radiocarbon dating and this demonstrates the continued use of burial in stone-lined long cists into the post Conquest period.[30] Whilst there may well have been other purposes fulfilled or intended by the erection of Group I early christian monuments [henceforth ECMs] besides that of marking a grave, it is thought that the more numerous cross inscribed Group II monuments were primarily intended as grave markers. Their date range now extends from the seventh to the eleventh centuries. For the purposes of this paper however it is enough to note that those early cemetery sites which 'developed' into chapels dedicated to St David or his associates in the vicinity of St Davids did so in response to, and to foster, the demands of pilgrims. I have explored this more fully in an earlier paper showing how the localisation of hagiographic incidents and the vitality of folklore created an ever-denser 'sacred topography'.[31] Two examples will suffice.

The localisation of St David's birthplace at St Non's chapel seems to have been made in Giraldus's version of the *Vita* of David. Rhygyfarch records only that a rock bearing the imprint of Non's hands made on it during her birth pangs was incorporated into the altar of a church built on the spot. St Non's, a chapel of late-medieval build, is sited within earlier earth-banked enclosures on the coast south of St Davids. A Group II ECM of seventh to ninth-century date (*ECMW* 372) originally located on the outer boundary strongly suggests an earlier cemetery. Possibly the linkage between this ancient burial site and St Non was made at the time of dedication of a chapel which may be no earlier than the twelfth century.

Hagiographic accounts both early and late undoubtedly sought to explain the physical proximity of adjacent dedications by means of personal relationships (saint and disciple, saint and 'confessor') a fact pointed out long ago by E.G. Bowen. The best examples of this in the immediate vicinity of St Davids are the legends, chapel, shrine and dedications associated with St Justinian (Welsh 'Stinan'). On Ramsey Island (Ynys Dewi) there were two chapels, one dedicated to St Justinian, the other to the little-known Dyfanog, both on the east side of the island facing the mainland

---

[26] Rhygyfarch, *Vita S. David* § 14 (ed. Sharpe and Davies, below, 120–1).
[27] Owen, 'Prolegomena', lines 166–7.
[28] O'Brien, 'Pagan and Christian burial', 130–7.
[29] Thomas, *The Early Christian Archaeology*, 50–1.
[30] See for example Ludlow, 'St Cristiolus' Churchyard, Eglwyswrw'.
[31] James, 'The Cult of St David', 105–11.

across the narrow but treacherous Ramsey Sound. Neither chapel has survived but their sites are known and both are close to springs at landing-(or at least watering-) places. No *Vita* has survived for Dyfanog and that of Justinian is a late compilation by John of Tynemouth in the fourteenth century, later published by Capgrave in 1501 in *Nova Legenda Angliae*. It is considered likely that John of Tynemouth, who travelled around Britain gathering materials, derived his account from an earlier source at St Davids.

According to his *Vita*, Justinian's ascetic way of life on the island attracted disciples and so great was his reputation that he became St David's confessor. Justinian's servants hated his strict discipline and killed him and cut off his head. A spring miraculously burst forth on the spot and the murdered saint got up, tucked his head under his arm, and walked across the Sound to Porth Stinan, where he was buried and a chapel built over his tomb. Ruins of a substantial late-medieval chapel survive. Miracles took place there where there was a second holy well dedicated to the saint. The *Vita* ends with the common medieval practice of 'translation' of the saint's remains, in this case by St David himself, for burial in the cathedral. The shrine has not survived, but was recorded by William of Worcestre in the fifteenth century thus: 'St Justinian, Martyr, 5 December on the eve of St Nicholas lies in a chapel in the church of St Davids beneath his tomb, confessor of St David'.[32]

Many of the incidents in the *Vita* are stock hagiographic themes but the numerous topographical details are sound and the narrative thus skilfully explains and links places and place-names traditionally associated with the saint. Porth Stinan is one of the two embarkation points for Ramsey Island and it is clear that this was a pilgrimage destination. The waters of Justinian's well on Ramsey conveyed health to all, according to Tynemouth. Equally convincing was the relationship postulated between David and Justinian. Justinian, however, is not mentioned in Rhygyfarch's *Vita S. David*. The only other dedication to him in Pebidiog is at Llanstinan church located, perhaps significantly, near its eastern borders.

Although no modern excavation, and only scanty antiquarian recording has taken place, it is evident that there was, by analogy with comparable sites on the mainland, an early Christian cemetery on Ramsey. The present farmhouse was built in the late-eighteenth century close to the site of its predecessor and there Richard Fenton was shown 'a burying ground' which workmen had uncovered in digging the foundations for the new house. It is evident from his description that the 'coffins' he described were long cists – slab-lined graves that may have basal slabs, and covering lintel slabs. Further graves were reported in 1860 but the most important discovery was made during building work in 1963 (regrettably without any archaeological supervision). 'Headstones' were reported from the site and graves reported outside the front door on the south side of the farmhouse. These stones were either used for building work or discarded and not until 1967 was a single inscribed stone noted amongst the debris. The stone is a thin slate slab with the inscription S[.]TVRNBIV. Above that single line are drilled terminals to lines of what must have been a sundial, now broken off. It is possible that the stone commemorates an historic person: *Saturnbiu Hail* (the Generous) the first documented bishop of St Davids, whose death was recorded in 831 in the *Annales Cambriae*. The presence of a sundial is in itself, Edwards suggests, diagnostic of a monastic community.[33] The most likely context here is surely that Ramsey functioned as an island retreat for the community at

---

32 William Worcestre, *Itineraries*, ed. Harvey, 75.
33 Edwards, 'Monuments', esp. 58–61 for a full discussion of this stone.

Menevia. Relationships between isolated hermitages, island retreats and monastic houses of this nature have been discussed by Richard Morris.[34]

Over the greater part of Pebidiog however, east of the parishes of St Davids and Whitchurch, dedications to David and his close associates are noticeably absent. As Map 2 shows, there are two other large parishes, Mathry and Llanwnda, which also seem to have had later parishes carved out of them. There, local saints' cults survived which may have predated the establishment of St David's monastery at Menevia. Taking the example of Mathry, its present dedication is to unnamed Holy Martyrs and it is clearly a *merthyr* or 'martyr' place-name. Traditionally there were thought to be seven saints and such group dedications were often linked to the cult of Teilo to the point that in the twelfth century Llandaf actually included Mathry in its claims.[35] Yet the church and its lands seem from an early date to have been attached to St Davids; it was 'the golden prebend'[36] first held by Archdeacon Jordan of Brecon until 1175 when it was held by Giraldus himself. The institution of individual prebends for the newly constituted clergy of the cathedral from what had been communal revenues of the *claswyr* was one of the major changes effected by Bishop Bernard.[37] The church (a nineteenth-century rebuild) and its churchyard in the centre of the village occupy a prominent hilltop position with a radial pattern of roads and tracks extending out from them. Surviving field boundaries and cropmarks indicate an enclosing outer boundary or boundaries. Cist graves have been noted in the churchyard and outside it, but no systematic excavation has been carried out, nor are there any radiocarbon dates. However the presence of the Group I bilingual ECM to the Irish named 'Maccudiccl son of Caticuus' (*ECMW* 346) demonstrates an early (fifth/sixth-century) origin to the cemetery and site. If precursors of fifth- or sixth-century date to St Davids are sought, Mathry must be a strong candidate. In our context, it is surely significant that no attempts at re-culting or promotion of hagiographic links at Mathry other than the simple appropriation of the site and revenues were attempted by St Davids. At Llanwnda, where a local cult to St Degan survived in the parish, the undoubtedly early site contains an extraordinary range of early medieval sculpture. Edwards argues that this is a local group of ninth- to eleventh-century date, with a possibility of Viking influence.[38]

Another noticeable feature of the ecclesiastical geography of Pebidiog are parish churches whose dedications are to obscure saints, personages who may in some instances be lay benefactors. Any hagiographic traditions seem late, intended to explain the dedication name. Examples are Llandeloy, Llanhywel, Llanedren, Llan-rheithan, Llanrhian and Llandrudion.[39] Having defined this group by their dedica-

---

34 Morris, *Churches in the Landscape*, 118–19
35 Davies, *An Early Welsh Microcosm*, charter 127b (16) B 167 where the seven sons of *Cynguaiu* gave their *terra of Marthru* and *Cenarth*, with the consent of King Aergol, to saint Teilo; 'this is a conglomeration of traditions about places in west Wales and has no witness list'. In hagiographic tradition, the seven were none other than the seven 'watermen' of Llanddowror (*Llan Dyfyrwyr*), rescued by Teilo, sent to Llandeilo, then Mathry then Cenarth. See Henken, *Traditions*, 116–17, 132. These rather clumsy attempts to explain place-names seem to ignore the meaning of the epithet 'waterman', *dyfrwr*, attached to St David in the *Life* of St Pol de Leon, indicative of his ascetic habits.
36 '… better endowed than any other in the cathedral'; details from the *Valor Ecclesiasticus* 1535 given in Yardley, *Menevia Sacra*, 232–3.
37 For a full discussion of this and for details of Gerald's trenchant criticisms of Bernard see Evans, 'The bishops of St Davids', 273–5.
38 Edwards, *Corpus*, forthcoming.
39 These interpretations are taken from Charles, *Place-names of Pembrokeshire*.

tion names, it was striking to find that on the ground these churches are in small contiguous parishes in an area inland and east of St Davids. (Their area is shaded in Map 2.) In historic landscape terms the area is characterised by fairly dense but dispersed settlement with numerous *tref* names and relict boundaries of small open field systems which may indicate former hamlets. Few of these churches have many, or indeed any, of the criteria outlined above used by the EMES project. We may tentatively suggest that this group of churches represent relatively late pre- (or even conceivably) post-Conquest foundations but noticeably without dedications to David or his family and associates.

The Europe-wide expansion of population in the twelfth and thirteenth centuries created new settlements and with them new churches. In the cantref of Pebidiog this perhaps began with Flemish settlers along its southern borders in the twelfth century in places like Tancredston and Letterston. It was not a peaceful process. The *Annales Cambriae* record the killing in 1137 of 'Letard Litelking – an enemy of God and of St David' by Anarawd, eldest son of Gruffydd ap Rhys.[40] Some of these new settlements gained parish churches, others did not, but there is a clear and obvious correlation between non-Welsh parish and settlement names and dedications to Latin saints. Many of these new, or reorganised and expanded settlements were possessions of the medieval bishops of St Davids held under English tenure. Giraldus Cambrensis, writing in the late-twelfth century, was highly critical of the actions of Bishop Bernard in the early part of the century. Not only had he redistributed the communal revenues of the *claswyr* to create individual prebends and canonries, but he had reduced their value by appropriating a large slice for his own table and had given up too much land for knights' fees.[41] Nevertheless it seems likely that the native settlement pattern, and with it the pre-Conquest religious topography, was overlain rather than being wholly obscured by twelfth- and thirteenth-century incomers and expansion of settlement and cultivation.

A good example is Letterston itself. A planned village, established by Letard in the early twelfth century, involved a site-shift of the church at *Heneglwys* to the centre of the new settlement. Before 1130 this church, like many others existing or projected in the *cantrefi* of Rhos and Daugleddau, were given by Ivo, son of Letard, to the military order of the Knights Hospitaller at their commandery at Slebech.[42] The new church was dedicated to St Giles who was widely equated in Wales with Silin or Sulien. A 'Ffynnon Shan Shillin' is sited close to the church. Possibly this was the original dedication of Heneglwys. South of Letterston, another church, '*ecclesia de vado Patricii*', was given to Slebech in the same grant. Its dedication to St Lawrence may date to that period. Patricksford was an important crossing point on the upper western Cleddau and the church, perched on high ground above the river may have been formerly dedicated to Patrick. Patrick's role in the *Vita* of St David as the saint's precursor at Mynyw, given Ireland by way of compensation, is well known. A medieval chapel on the shore of Porth Mawr (Whitesands Bay) was also dedicated to him which excavations have shown to be constructed on a cist cemetery site. J. Wyn Evans has suggested that Patrick's may even have been the original cult at Menevia.[43] A close link in the ninth to tenth centuries between St

---

[40] *Episcopal Acts*, ed. Davies, I.257. DIII.

[41] Evans, 'The bishops of St Davids', 274–5.

[42] Kissock, '"God made nature"', 127–9. See also Ludlow, 'Early medieval ecclesiastical sites project: 2. Pembrokeshire: Gazetteer of sites': 'Letterston', prn 2395.

[43] Evans, 'St David and St Davids', 15.

Lawrence church and St Davids is suggested by a disk-headed cross slab (*ECMW* 398) which Edwards has identified as a product of the St Davids school.[44] The location of these two church and chapel/cemetery sites, one possibly, one certainly, dedicated to St Patrick at the 'entry' and 'departure' points of Pebidiog seems more than pure chance.

Other churches dedicated to David or his close associates are also located on or near the bounds of Pebidiog. South of Menevia is the parish church of St David, Brawdy, whose name denotes an earlier attribution to St Bride or Brigit.[45] Brawdy's revenues supported a cathedral prebend, an echo perhaps of a pre-Conquest appropriation and the revenues were directly attached in the thirteenth century to episcopal endowments.[46] A late survival, in the 1326 *Black Book* survey of the bishops' lands, of rents paid to the church as 'procurations' by Welsh tenants holding by Welsh tenure suggests a church originally established by a *gwely* or extended kin group or groups.[47] The present parish church of St Mary, Hayscastle (a zone of Flemish settlement) was a dependent chapelry to Brawdy in the middle ages suggesting a large pre-parish 'territory' all along the southern boundaries of Pebidiog. Brawdy church and churchyard may itself have replaced an earlier high status cemetery within an Iron Age enclosure (Cas Wilia) although this is some distance from the church. At least two Class I ECMs have been found at Cas Wilia. One, inscribed only in ogam, indicates an Irish settler of fifth- or early sixth-century date.[48] Evaluation of the excavated evidence for Romano-British and possibly sixth to seventh-century 'Irish' occupation at the multi-vallate inland promontary fort at Brawdy, excavated by Dark in the early 1990s, awaits full publication of the site.[49] Perhaps the most significant factor however in dedications to David at Brawdy, and indeed Whitchurch to the west, is that they lie on the medieval route to St Davids approaching from Haverfordwest. The suspicion is that this route line is in origin a Roman road whose destination was the embarkation and landing place on the shortest crossing to Ireland from *Porth Mawr* (Whitesands Bay). Any certainty on this point must await aerial reconnaissance and fieldwork to establish the Roman line west from its latest established western point at West Dairy Farm, Wiston (SN01171837).[50] The route line certainly predates the foundation of Haverfordwest as a town.

The development of Fishguard in the middle ages, and the endowment of estates in its hinterland belonging to the monastery of Llandudoch to its sucessor Abbey of St Dogmaels, pulled this parish in the direction of the Lordship of Cemais. Giraldus accused Bishop Bernard of separating Fishguard from Pebidiog; he probably meant the settlement of Lower Town which is on the north side of the Gwaun estuary.[51] In the 1291 *Taxatio*, Fishguard is within the deanery of Pebidiog. Leland, in 1536

---

44 Edwards, *Corpus Vol II*, forthcoming; Dr. Edwards has also pointed out to me that the use of the distinctive Caer Bwdi stone for this monument, that is local to St Davids, could be significant in this context.

45 Charles, *Place-names of Pembrokeshire*, 198; Ó Riain, 'The saints', 390: 'The cult may well have been introduced into Wales by early Irish settlers in Dyfed. These came partly from the Déisi of Munster where Brigit's cult was particularly strong.' Note also early cist burials, a possible multiple church site and later medieval chapel at St Bride's, on the south side of St Bride's Bay, Pembs.

46 Jones and Freeman, *The History*, 314–15.

47 *The Black Book*, ed. Willis-Bund, 69 and 71.

48 *ECMW* 296, ogam only and 298.

49 Dark, *Britain and the End*, 185 and ch. IV for stimulating ideas on 'Irish' cultural identity in Dyfed and the origins of ogam.

50 Driver, 'The road', 60–1.

51 *Episcopal Acts*, ed. Davies, I.270.

noted that 'Gueyn River devidith Pebidiauc from Fisschard in Kemmeisland'.[52]
The boundary shown on William Rees's map, placing Fishguard in Cemais, was
probably established after the Dissolution and the creation of shires and hundreds
in the sixteenth century. There are two interesting incidents in two separate twelfth-
century, locally produced saints' *Vitae* that hint at possible demarcation of saintly
territorial influence in the Gwaun Valley. The *Vita* of St Brynach, patron saint of
the important *clas* church of Nevern, has the saint make his landfall in the harbour
of Milford and, journeying north, pause at *Pons lapideus* (Pontfaen) on the River
Gwaun. Although he freed the place from unclean spirits, Divine Providence directed
him to leave and he continued north to settle upon Nevern.[53] The present church at
Pontfaen is dedicated to Brynach but Nevern was undoubtedly the centre of the
cult. In the second *Vita* of St Carannog, emanating from Llangrannog, the saint's
father is the eponymous Ceredig. Ceredig, as one of the sons of Cunedda, was part
of a family, the *Vita* claims, whose territory extended from the Dee to the River
'Gvoun' or Gwaun.[54]

Llanychllwydog, and two of its former chapels (now parish churches) – Llanllawer
and Llanychaer – in or overlooking the Gwaun Valley near Fishguard are all dedicated to St David. Llanychllwydog is now redundant and excavations preceding
conversion to a private dwelling showed it to be on the site of cist graves one of
which was cut by the wall of the medieval church.[55] A single radiocarbon date was
obtained from a grave on the north side of the church of 747–1067 AD (two sigma
range). The church itself was entirely rebuilt in the nineteenth century when it is
probable that the four Group II cross inscribed ECMs (*ECMW* 338, 339, 340 and
341) which neatly flank four sides of the church were re-positioned. However, whilst
only two seem definitely to be from the churchyard site pre-restoration and thus
associated with the cist cemetery, it is not thought that the others were moved far.
The excavations were small-scale; nevertheless a find of an early Roman bronze
brooch fragment raises interesting questions of a possible association between the
cemetery (and later church) site and nearby Castell Caerwen Iron Age and perhaps
Romano-British defended enclosure. Llanllawer church too was completely rebuilt
in 1860; its churchyard is subrectangular. There are four Group II and III ECMs
probably from the site, although not necessarily in their primary positions (*ECMW*
323 and 324 and two more recently identified). Research by Ludlow for the EMES
project identified a circular outer enclosure to the churchyard from aerial photographs. The bank incorporates a spring now surmounted by a stone well-hood,
reputedly good for sore eyes. Henken has pointed out that healing blindness is a
persistent theme in David's hagiography.[56] Finally Llanychaer, where a Group I
ECM (*ECMW* 335) now lost, but recorded as being in the churchyard, is suggestive
of an early cemetery and certainly there are other early cemetery sites in its close
vicinity. The church itself may have been of new build in the twelfth century when
its parish was formed from a knight's fee. Edwards notes that the cross-decorated
ECMW 337, from Cilrhedyn Isaf farm, with its representation of the crucifixion, is
of a type which may have 'acted as a focus within or on the edge of a cemetery,

52 Ed. Toulmin-Smith, *Leland's Itinerary*, III.65.
53 Wade-Evans, *VSBG*, 7.
54 Wade-Evans, *VSBG*, 149.
55 Murphy, 'Excavations at Llanychllwydog', 77–93.
56 Henken, *Traditions*, 43.

a visible symbol of holy ground, and, if there was no church building, a focus for worship'.[57]

This Gwaun valley group of 'Dewi' churches are thus not only liminally sited on the eastern boundary of Pebidiog but are also all on or near early cemetery sites that are marked by a dense concentration of Group II and III ECMs. Their stylistic affinities, Edwards suggests, are strongly in the Irish Sea traditions and most are of seventh to ninth century date. Early and original dedications to St David, at the time of church building, in an area with long traditions of allegiance to St Davids seems likely.

The monastery of Llandudoch, at modern day St Dogmaels on the south side of the Teifi estuary opposite Cardigan, was contemporary with Asser's *monasterium et parochia Degui*. The topography of the site, its early medieval sculpture and later documentary records of an extensive *noddfa* or sanctuary all point to a major site. It was raided by Vikings in 998. But a worse fate was to follow. To R.R. Davies 'the fate of the ancient *clas* church of Llandudoch epitomizes the attitude of the new Norman lords'.[58] Out of its endowments and on its very site, Robert Fitz Martin, Lord of Cemais, founded a Tironian House to bring reformed Benedictinism to the native church. Fulchard, its first Abbot, was formally enthroned by Bernard, first Norman bishop of St Davids in 1120. Yet the cult of Dogfael/Dogmael or Dogwel as a local saint survived. There is nothing in the hagiography of St David or the sources for Dogfael linking the saints. But on the ground, a dedication and place-name suggests some kind of accommodation between the two cults.

In the south-east corner of Pebidiog, bounded by Cemais to the east and Daugleddau to the south, is the parish of St Dogwells. Possible pre-Conquest links between this church and the community of St Davids may have been reinstated in 1229 when the church was appropriated to the canons of the cathedral. A number of episcopal *acta* from this place suggests some estate focus.[59] Its landed possessions extended into Daugleddau in a tithe-free area called Little Treffgarne attached to St Dogwells. It was here, in 1144, that Bishop Bernard granted a temporary home for the Cistercians of Whitland. It is therefore of considerable interest to note that the 1876 find spot of *ECMW* 390, the bi-lingual Class I 'Hogtivis' stone, was as a gatepost close to Little Treffgarne Farm. There are no archaeological records or place-name suggestions of any cemetery here so we may suggest a possible function as a boundary or territorial marker to this late-fifth- or sixth-century stone. Fenton noted that St Dogwell's name in Welsh was *Llanty Dewi*[60] and there has been speculation on the assumed late descriptor 'Ty-Ddewi' for Menevia. But Charles notes other early forms and prefers *hen lle Dewi,* meaning the old place of Dewi.[61] It seems unlikely that the dedication to St Dogmael is late and it is probable that the church and its surrounding lands were early possession of St Davids, again in a key liminal location which became, in the eleventh and twelfth centuries at least, an unruly frontier area.

Amongst the services owed by tenants of the bishop of St Davids within his Marcher lordship of Pebidiog and, perhaps significantly, from Llawhaden in

---

57 Edwards, 'Stones', 31.
58 Davies, *The Age*, 181.
59 *St Davids Episcopal Acta*, ed. Barrow, 86; Barrow incorrectly here identifies 'St Dogmael de Llan-lledewy' with Llanddewi-Aberarth, but elsewhere (122, 126, 131, 145–6) it is clearly the same as 'St Dogmael's in Pebydiog'.
60 Fenton, *Historical Tour*, 186.
61 Charles, *Place-names of Pembrokeshire*, 323.

Daugleddau, recorded in the 'Black Book' survey of 1326, was the obligation, in time of war, to follow the lord bishop with the relics of the Blessed David. Generally the distance covered was limited by the right to return home the same night. The main purpose of these progresses was to raise funds and amounts are recorded in the *Liber Communis* now in the National Library of Wales.[62] But for a small group of settlements, namely Wolfscastle, Castle Morris and *Vill Camerarii*, the obligation was 'to follow the shrine with the relics of the Blessed David as far as 'Carnetrney'.[63] Garn Turne, an upland area of crags and rocky ground which contains a neolithic chambered tomb, is the point where three *cantrefi* – Pebidiog, Cemais and Daugleddau – meet. Successor administrative boundaries perpetuated this boundary point as an early nineteenth-century stone attests. It is surely significant that the importance and permanence of this boundary should be marked by a progress of St David's relics by those episcopal tenants sited closest to it in what seems to have been, on the evidence of the dedications, an important liminal zone. There are many parallels in early medieval Ireland for processions of portable shrines with relics to reinforce the position of boundaries of lands and churches 'owned' by the saint.

Rhos and Daugleddau

Returning to the list of the seven bishop-houses of Dyfed, the bishop-house for Rhos, *Llan Ismael*, can be certainly identified with St Ishmaels, on the northern side of Milford Haven. In Daugleddau, *Llan Teilaw* is very probably the now ruinous site of Llandeilo Llwydiarth. It appears to have been eclipsed by Llawhaden which is listed in a later redaction. Both *cantrefi* at the time of the *Taxatio* of Nicholas IV in 1291 were within a single deanery – that of Rhos. It is likely that even one hundred and fifty years after the event in the early twelfth century, this reflects the new character of the area as one of Flemish settlement. In the *Itinerarium Kambriae* ('Journey through Wales') written soon after 1188, Giraldus describes St Davids thus: 'it lies between two hostile peoples who are constantly fighting over it, the Flemings and the Welsh'.[64] Toorians highlights this long drawn out hostility.[65] He also discusses the struggle between the monasteries of Worcester and Gloucester for the churches and lands which Wizo the Fleming had originally (*ca* 1112) granted to Worcester but which his descendant granted to the Knights Hospitaller whose extensive Pembrokeshire estates were administered from the Commandery of Slebech. Shortly before his death in 1115, Wilfred, bishop of St Davids had wished to cede many of these churches to the monks of Gloucester provided he could keep the rights and dues. Gerald of Wales accused Wilfred of alienating other church property although he noted that his reasons were to protect St Davids patrimony in troubled times.[66] In view of all this, it is possible that there were churches and lands in Rhos lost to St Davids in the late eleventh and early twelfth centuries. The surviving

---

[62] Rees, *The Medieval Shrines*, 6.

[63] Ed. Willis Bund, 111.

[64] *Itinerarium Kambriae* II i (ed. and transl. Thorpe, 161).

[65] Toorians, 'Wizo Flandrensis', 99–118.

[66] Wilfred's episcopate is fully discussed in Davies, *Episcopal Acts*, I.128–34; see *ibid.*, I.237, D.28, for Gerald's condemnation of Wilfred's alienation of church lands at 'Canarthmaur in Emelyn, Lanrian, Lenreni, Ucceton and several others'. Also see Pryce, 'The dynasty of Deheubarth', below, 312.

pattern of dedications, and indeed episcopal lands, might not fully indicate the earlier extent of native saints' cults and possessions.

Nevertheless, St Ishmael (variously Ismael or Isfael)'s cult was widespread across Rhos. St Ishmaels can therefore be seen as a mother church for the *cantref*. There is a cluster of dedications around Haverfordwest and St Ishmaels itself became a possession of the Augustinian Priory at Haverfordwest. Subsequently however, it was, with Nevern, appropriated to the newly founded St Mary's College at the cathedral. Archaeologically, St Ishmaels displays all the criteria for an important early foundation: accessible from the sea, a large outer enclosure, cist burials and three Group II–III ECMs (*ECMW* 396, 397 and one newly recognised). The Group III fragment of a cross shaft strongly suggests a monastic site of at least tenth- or eleventh-century date. Edwards has identified *ECMW* 396 as a product of the St Davids school on the basis of its geology, probably transported to the site by sea. The others are of local stone. The subordinate position of *Llan Ismael* within the *parochia* of St Davids is perhaps also reflected by the position Rhygyfarch assigns to Ismael in his *Vita S. David* as one of his three most faithful disciples, the others being Aidan and Eliud (Teilo). Apart from this association in a single incident in the *Vita* (lighting the fire on the new site at St Davids) Ishmael features no further whereas in the slightly later and even more propagandist *Vita* of Teilo in the *Book of Llandaf*, he plays a greater role as Teilo's nephew.

The two parish churches dedicated to St David in Rhos are as likely to be in newly founded post-Conquest settlements as they are to be of earlier origins. That at Hubberston on the north shore of Milford Haven was an early appropriation to Pill Priory. Early forms of the place-name (*villa Huberti*) show it to be a Norman-French, not a Viking personal name. The church at Prendergast, also dedicated to St David, was one of 'all my churches of Dugledi' given by Wizo the Fleming to Gloucester Abbey in 1112, a grant which later passed to the Knights Hospitaller in the mid-twelfth century. Wizo's *caput* was at Wiston in the centre of an area that became the barony of Daugleddau. This ancient territorial unit might originally have been defined, as its name suggests, by lying between the Western and Eastern Cleddau rivers and their confluence (the Daugleddau) in the upper reaches of Milford Haven. To the north, the boundary may well have been between enclosed land and open mountain pasture of the Preseli foothills. By the thirteenth century when parish boundaries had become fixed, these natural boundaries had been breached, or defined to accommodate, the extent of the bishop of St Davids estates.

This newer precision left the bishop-house of *Llan Teilaw* (Llandeilo Llwydiarth) just across the border of the northern fringe of Daugleddau in the *cantref*, later Lordship, deanery and hundred of Cemais. The physical characteristics of the site and the presence (probably *in situ*) of two Group I ECMs all argue strongly for early medieval origins.[67] Llandeilo Llwydiarth is a good example of the kind of church site whose former importance is hard to appreciate in its present abandoned state and perceived 'remote' position. The twelfth-century Llandaf claim to all Teilo churches led to its inclusion in Bishop Joseph's list where, interestingly, its liminal position on the borders of two *cantrefi* is stressed: *Llannteliau litgarth. In fin Doucledif ha chemeis. Mainaur*.[68] There was therefore an estate as well as a church. Its status as a bishop-house was eclipsed however by Llawhaden before the tenth century as a later

---

[67] *ECMW* 313 and 314, also 345 at Maenclochog, all sixth century, 313 reinscribed with a cross (seventh–ninth century); all commemorate members of the same family.

[68] *The Text of the Book of Llan Dav*, ed. Evans, 124, line 255.

recension of the list indicates. This area may have been more wooded than it is today because the *Black Book* lists, amongst the bishop's lands, a forest, *Lloydarth*, of 300 acres, which possibly covered the ridge, together with lands held by free Welsh kin groups and demesne intermingled with secular freeholders.[69] These lands were but part of a substantial block of land held by the medieval bishops centring on their towns and manors of New Moat and Llawhaden. Quite clearly, St Davids had gained possession of an estate formerly attached to Teilo's church at Llwydiarth, perhaps in the tenth or eleventh centuries.

Llawhaden is sited on an important administrative boundary between the cantref of Daugleddau and Gwarthaf on the eastern Cleddau at what was, throughout the medieval and early modern period, the lowest bridging point. We now know through recent discoveries in air photography and field work that it was also close to a Roman road which extends west from Carmarthen into Pembrokeshire. The shift by the early medieval period slightly to the south of the Roman line could relate to changes in the river's course and thus a new fording and later bridging point with the church built alongside it. An unusual, and sadly now much eroded, tenth-century Group III cross now built into the church fabric indicates the importance of the site (*ECMW* 343). In the post-Conquest period the church was the focus of an important episcopal manor of the medieval bishopric, with a castle and planted town. Quite evidently the planted town with its burgesses, markets and fairs and its castle which served as the bishop's and court and prison, was a Norman reorganization of a Welsh estate.

Llawhaden church's dedication is undoubtedly to the Irish St Aidan of Ferns, bishop and confessor whose name has several variations including the hypocoristic form Madoc. It was incorporated in the place-name by the ninth century (*Lanhadein*). There are a few other churches dedicated to him: Nolton (St Madog) on the coast of St Bride's Bay and, nearby, Haroldston West. Nolton Haven was possibly a medieval, and was certainly an early modern landing and embarkation point. Further north, a holy well, Ffynnon Faeddog is sited alongside the road from St Davids to *Porth Mawr* (Whitesands Bay) close to the site of St Patrick's Chapel. Aidan, with Ismael and Eliud (Teilo) was one of St Davids three most faithful disciples in Rhygyfarch's *Vita S. David* and thus 'annexed' in a close but subordinate role. Whilst there is but a single mention of Ishmael in the *Vita* there is much on Aidan as disciple and on his journey from St Davids to Ireland to found his own monastery there. In addition to the physical proximity of cult sites noted above, more topographical details were added in later hagiography to explain associations on the ground. In a *Vita* of St Aidan there is a convoluted account of Aidan's journey with a waggon drawn by oxen to the River 'Cledde'. From there he progressed on foot via a straight road to where he had seen David standing and a cross marking the spot. These hagiographic details seem to seek to explain the river crossing at Llawhaden and the Group III cross there, now built into the church.[70] The road through Llawhaden was undoubtedly used by medieval pilgrims to St Davids. Interestingly, night photography by flashlight of the Llawhaden Cross for the forthcoming *Corpus* revealed that its base is covered in small, incised pilgrims' crosses now too faint to be seen by the naked eye.

The church of Llanddewi Velfrey was located centrally in Efelfre, a *cwmwd* of

---

[69] Ed. Willis Bund, 166–9.
[70] Baring-Gould and Fisher, *Lives*, 118–19 and 'Life of St Aidus', in Rees, *Lives of the Cambro-British Saints*, 558–9.

Cantref Gwarthaf. It ranks as a Grade A site in the EMES project.[71] It is sited in close proximity to two major Iron Age forts and may itself be within a larger outer enclosure. There is late sixteenth-century evidence that it was a 'portionary' church, strongly suggestive of early origins. However, there are other now obscure or lost sites within Efelfre with more than a hint of Teilo affiliations. Perhaps, as Efelfre might be considered to be on the western boundaries of the Teilo cult, the waning prestige of distant Llandeilo Fawr might have occasioned the emergence of a mother church or transference to the ambit of Menevia in political circumstances we can barely guess at. This could have been in the tenth or eleventh centuries.

Cemais and Emlyn

Leaving aside the bishop-house of Llandeilo Llwydiarth which more properly belongs to Daugleddau, the two *cantrefi* may have shared the bishop-house of *Llan Genau*. This site has been identified with two farms, Llangenau Fawr and Fach near Clydai. Field work for the EMES project has identified earthworks within an enclosure near Llangenau Fawr which Ludlow suggests might be the site, if not of the bishop-house, then its successor grange chapel belonging to Whitland Abbey.[72] 'Keneu' is listed by Giraldus as an early bishop of St Davids, third in succession to David; there was also a now lost chapel and well dedicated to Ceneu in Brycheiniog. A possible predecessor to Llangenau might have been Clydai itself. Clydai was one of the daughters of Brychan (*Cledei apud Emlyn*) recorded in the *Cognatio Brychan*, a text originating in Brycheiniog and at least of eleventh-century date if not earlier.[73] It is possible that the numerous daughters were a means of explaining church names but if that is so the *Cognatio* still attests a toponymic scope which covers much of Dyfed and Ystrad Tywi. A former churchyard chapel at Clydai (Eglwys Trisant) hints at a multiple church site or the existence of a *capel-y-bedd*. No less than three Group 1 ECMs are thought by Edwards to be associated with the site which suggests a post-Roman cemetery of fifth/sixth-century date (*ECMW* 306, 307, 308). Clydai possesses other characteristics of an early medieval site with a circular churchyard, focal to an irregular boundary system and several springs. It may be significant therefore that Clydai supported a cathedral prebend in the middle ages, a post-Conquest continuation perhaps of an earlier association with St Davids.

There were other cults in both *cantrefi*. George Owen of Henllys, the sixteenth-century historian of Pembrokeshire gives interesting evidence on the late survival of what was evidently a widespread cult of St Meugan.[74] Equally notable was that of St Brynach focussed on the undoubtedly early and important site of Nevern. Not least of the physical attributes indicating its importance is the large size of its parish, even after the Fitzmartins' new borough and parish of Newport was founded. This cult certainly survived the Norman conquest. The *Vita* of Brynach, already alluded to above, was a twelfth-century production from Newport. Whilst not doubting that St Brynach was in a sense the patron saint of Cemais, and Nevern the 'mother church', it is worth noting that his dedications are found south of Cemais and the Preselis in Cantref Gawrthaf (notably at Llanboidy). This 'transmontane' locational pattern

---

[71] Ludlow, unpublished Cambria Archaeology Report (2003/39), prn 46803.
[72] Ludlow, unpublished Cambria Archaeology Report (2003/39), prns 12107, 46783 and 46784.
[73] Wade-Evans, *VSBG*, 315.
[74] Ed. Miles, *The Description*, 301.

either side of a central mountain bloc will be further considered below in relation to St David's cult and Llanddewibrefi.

A smaller cluster, but again with a concentration (but not exclusively so) in a single cantref is that of St Llawddog in Emlyn centring on his church at Cenarth Mawr on the River Teifi, described by Giraldus in 1188.[75] Elsewhere Giraldus had accused Bishop Wilfred of alienating this church with others. It has been assumed that Cenarth had an earlier association with St Teilo and certainly it was claimed by Llandaf on the basis of a spurious charter and the convoluted traditions of the watermen of Llanddowror and Mathry. A charter of Bishop Iorwerth of 1229 granted four churches to the Cathedral Chapter. These were the church of Llawddog (St Leudocus and the nine saints) at Cenarth Mawr, the church of the three saints of Llywel (Brecs.) St Dogwells (noted above) and St Davids, Llanychaer.[76]

Another and substantial group of churches and lands belonging to St Davids are again in liminal positions along the Teifi valley, a major secular and ecclesiastical territorial boundary zone. St Davids, Bridell was a chapel of Manordeifi, itself an important 'Dewi' church, in the medieval deanery of Emlyn. The living at Bridell, even into modern times, was in the patronage of the freeholders of the parish. This type of patronage occurs in a few other places (such as Henllan Amgoed) and is considered to be of early origin relating to native Welsh kin groups. The church itself is undoubtedly on an early site with the present churchyard dominated by a Group 1 ECM, the 'Nettasagrus' stone inscribed only in ogam possibly of fifth- to early sixth-century date with a later cross within a circle (*ECMW* 300). Thomas considers this memorial to be to one of the early Irish settlers in North Pembrokeshire probably a pagan.[77] Associated with the church are a cist cemetery to the west and a well, but no physical evidence in terms of relic boundaries earthworks or cropmarks to indicate an outer enclosing boundary. Bridell is sited alongside what seems to have been a road of at least medieval origins (now the A478) heading southwards from St Dogmaels and Cardigan to cross the Preselis through a wide, high pass at Crymych and thence south to Narberth and Tenby in South Pembrokeshire.

The River Teifi undoubtedly marked a major territorial boundary but as with other major river boundaries such as the Eastern Cleddau and also the River Tywi, the bishops of St Davids, in common with other secular lords, had estates on either side. Three 'Dewi' churches in the Teifi valley were lauded by Gwynfardd: 'And Bangor's refuge and Henllan's great church ... And lowland Maenordeifi'.[78] Some were part of episcopal estates in Welsh tenure in the 1326 *Black Book* survey; other fourteenth-century lands had no connection with cult churches. The name 'Maenordeifi' certainly suggests an estate but it was not one held by the bishop by 1326. Even the patronage of the church was in the hands of the Earls of Pembroke, a circumstance no doubt arising from the Marshalls' division of Emlyn between the Lordship of Cilgerran (Emlyn Is Cych) and Newcastle Emlyn (Emlyn Uch Cych).[79] The likelihood is of a reduced or fractured patrimony in the Teifi valley for St Davids in the post-Conquest period; even so, the medieval bishops held a substantial group of estates mainly on the north bank of the middle Teifi valley (see further, below). This argues for an early association of lands and churches with the cult of St David,

[75] *Itinerarium Kambriae* II i, ed. and transl. Thorpe, 161.
[76] *St Davids Episcopal Acta*, ed. Barrow, 106.
[77] Thomas, *And Shall These Mute Stones*, 69–73.
[78] Owen, 'Prologomena', lines 91–4.
[79] Crouch, *William Marshal*, 78–9.

since it is hard to see how such a bloc of land could have been built up in the late tenth, eleventh or twelfth centuries.

Maenordeifi is sited on the south side of the river; but it appears from modern map evidence, although detailed research would be necessary to substantiate this, that there have been river course changes. Maenordeifi has consequently lost its twelfth-century meadows, referred to by Gwynfardd Brycheiniog. It may have been located at an earlier river crossing point, now replaced by Llechryd Bridge downstream. Across the river, up a small tributary valley, is Llandygwydd, where the medieval bishops had the manor of *Llandogy*. Within this estate was a Ffynnon Dewi. The personal name in the place-name has the hypocoristic prefix **to* or *ty*. The name is obscure and Ó Riain suggests an Irish saint; a lay founder might be another possibility.[80]

Further up-river and now within Ceredigion and the medieval deanery of Sub-Aeron, was another block of churches and land belonging to St Davids. Henllan (old church) as a place-name suggests antiquity and Evans has drawn attention to Gwynfardd's descriptor *bangeibyr* which could imply a wooden church, a term also used for Meidrum.[81] Localisation in Giraldus's version of the *Vita* of David makes *llyn henllan* by the Teifi the place where David's father Sant receives three gifts of a stag, a fish and a hive of bees – indicative of property rights.[82] Henllan church is a nineteenth-century rebuild on the original site close to the River Teifi within a large, circular churchyard. High above, to the east, where the river flows through a gorge, is a strong, multi-vallate Iron Age promontary fort. Some two km. to the east, also on sloping ground above the floodplain of the River Teifi is the church of St David, Bangor Teifi, linked to Henllan in Gwynfardd's praise. Although the place-name 'bangor' has been taken to indicate an early monastic enclosure, no physical attributes of early medieval origin were identified in the EMES survey at Bangor Teifi. Gwynfardd's epithet however suggests a possible area of sanctuary. The church is perched above the Teifi valley and Ludlow notes that it is intervisible with Llangeler, an important mother church on the south side of the river. These lands and churches were valuable possessions of the medieval bishops, still held in Welsh tenure in the *Black Book* survey of 1326 by kin-groups or *gwelyau*, with triennial renders of cattle and other services.

Penfro and Cantref Gwarthaf

The medieval deanery of Penfro and the Marcher Earldom of Pembroke both appear co-terminous with the earlier *cantref*. The Norman Earls Marcher and their knights reshaped the landscape – new settlers and settlements, newer patterns of piety and patronage. Nevertheless, though obscured, the pre-Conquest ecclesiastical landscape can be partly retrieved. The medieval deanery of Carmarthen encompassed the whole area of *Cantref Gwarthaf*. This was much the largest of the seven making up the kingdom of Dyfed and there is evidence for smaller territorial units, *cymydau* (commotes): Amgoed, Efelffre, Elfed, Penrhyn, Peuliniog, Talacharn and Ystlwyf although their original extent is not always easy to trace. In Gwarthaf the post-Conquest political territories were far more fractured than in Penfro and Welsh

---

80 Ó Riain, 'The saints', 395–6.
81 Evans, 'Meidrum', 14.
82 Wade-Evans, *Life of St. David*, 1 and 60–1.

landowners were not wholly dispossessed. Carmarthen itself became a centre of English royal power where kings of England like Henry I were as concerned to curb the powers of their vassal Norman marcher lords as they were to subjugate the Welsh princes. The lordships of Llanstephan, St Clears and of Laugharne had little of the power of Pembroke; nor does there appear to have been organised settlement from England on the scale of that seen in South Pembrokeshire. Welsh tenure and tenurial units, Welsh law and, we may presume native patterns of piety and church organisation persisted. The dominant cult in Penfro was that of Teilo as it was across the south of Cantref Gawrthaf and eastwards into Ystrad Tywi. There were two bishop-houses in Penfro in the ninth/tenth century list. *Llan Ussylt* can be identified with St Issell's near Saundersfoot, some 6 km north-east of Penally. Usyllt seems to have been an obscure local saint 'captured' by the Teilo cult through inclusion in saintly pedigrees as Teilo's father.[83] The second bishop-house in Penfro – *Llan Degeman* – can be located at Rhoscrowther which is sited in the south-east corner of Angle Bay on the south side of Milford Haven in a location not dissimilar to that of *Llan Ismael* in Rhos across the water. A possible large outer enclosure has been suggested from vertical air photographs of the 1950s. There are also a few other elements surviving which might indicate an earlier, more important, status such as St Decuman's Chapel, a possible *capel-y-bedd*, a holy well and another possible dedication at nearby Pwll Crochan. Late hagiographic traditions locate a minor cult in North Somerset. Possibly this site and cult was eclipsed by that of Teilo in south Penfro, at an early date.

The bishop-house *Llan Teulydawc* can with certainty be located in Carmarthen, on the site of the successor Priory of St John and St Teulyddog.[84] Evans has plausibly argued that 'Teulyddog' may be a hypocoristic form of Teilo and that the bishop-house here, located just outside the walled Roman town of *Moridunum,* could have late Roman origins.[85] Certainly though, by the eighth century, the cult was centred at Llandeilo where unique and valuable marginalia in the 'Lichfield' gospels record gifts of estates to the house of Teilo.[86] A 'bishop of Teilo' called Nobis is also recorded there. Yet by the twelfth century and probably much earlier Llandeilo as a monastic and episcopal centre had been eclipsed. The gospel book itself had been lost from the altar of the saint by the year 1000 (Wynsige, bishop of Lichfield's name is inscribed on its first page). Strange has drawn attention to the possible deliberate burial of Llandeilo's high crosses – 'a conscious and forceful removal from sight of its emblematic artefacts'.[87] We see the extent of Teilo's cult of course through the often distorted lens of Bishops Joseph and Urban's campaign to incorporate the whole patrimony of Teilo within their bishopric of Llandaf. The Llandaf charters relating to 'Teilo' estates in South Pembrokeshire around Tenby are late and corrupt. However genuine early material exists and Davies assigns a sixth-century date to some Llandaf charters relating to Teilo's *podum* or monastery at *Penalun* (Penally).[88] Campbell and Lane, in their report on excavations at Longbury Bank (near Penally), a high status secular site of sixth/seventh-century date, have produced a map showing the probable location and bounds of these estates close

---

[83] Baring-Gould and Fisher, *Lives*, 348–9.

[84] For the history and archaeology of this site see James, 'Excavations at the Augustinian priory', 120–61.

[85] Evans, 'Aspects', 239–53, esp. 251.

[86] Jenkins and Owen, 'The Welsh marginalia' (i) 37–66 and (ii) 91–120.

[87] Strange, 'The rise and fall', 1–18.

[88] Davies, *An Early Welsh Microcosm*, 135.

to Penally.[89] The free-standing cross shafts of ninth/tenth-century date from the church site (*ECMW* 363, 364, 365, 366) and a cross-carved stone provide compelling evidence for an important monastic site, but, as Edwards has established, differ in every respect from products of the St Davids school with cultural affiliations quite outside the Irish Sea area.

What this necessarily brief summary of the date and extent of the cult of Teilo shows is how very different it is to that of St David. For Teilo we have clusters of valuable estates in the heartlands of the ancient territorial units of Carmarthenshire and South Pembrokeshire, not the dispersed and liminal patterns suggested so far for David's patrimony. Most of the patrimony of Teilo was finally incorporated into the diocese of St Davids, not Llandaf. It is evident that some of the churches and estates were acquired by the community of Menevia in the ninth or tenth centuries such as the bishop-house of Llandeilo Llwydiarth. There is no doubt that much passed into secular hands and that later the core of the patrimony in Ystrad Tywi was given by the Lord Rhys to the new Premonstratensian foundation of Talley.

Returning to Penfro, Lamphey, site of a palace of the medieval bishops of St Davids and centre of a rich estate, seems to have been in St Davids's hands before the Norman conquests, but perhaps no earlier than the eleventh century. The dedicatee, Tyfei, was claimed as a martyred nephew of St Teilo. West of Lamphey, the medieval bishops of St Davids had a grange and lands at Warren and the presentation of the church, which was dedicated to St Mary. Study of the historic landscape in the Castlemartin peninsula has identified large areas of coaxial field systems and a regularly laid out pattern of routes and boundaries of possibly pre-medieval origin, units readily adopted by later medieval parishes. The 'Celtic' dedications of other churches here are post-Conquest rededications to West Country saints, the home area of many of the post-Conquest incoming settlers. Stackpole however is a 'Teilo' church and it is likely therefore that Warren was also, another 'territorial' gain for the bishops of St Davids – but with no attempt at re-culting.

St Caradog's, Lawrenny is an interesting example of how a new dedication might assert the spiritual power of St Davids in the mixed Welsh and Anglo-Flemish world of the eleventh century. Caradog's life spanned the Norman conquest and his religious life is an extremely interesting, almost unique example of native and Norman-French patterns of piety.[90] It is thought that his final years were spent as a hermit at St Issells (south of Haverfordwest) where he died in 1124. Giraldus (who wrote his *Vita*) notes that he wished to be buried in the Cathedral Church of St David. Despite attempts by Richard fitzTankard of Haverfordwest to retain the body, Giraldus describes a miraculous funerary procession across Newgale sands and burial 'in the left aisle of the church of St Andrew and Saint David, beside the altar of St Stephen the protomartyr'.[91] His shrine seems to have been in its present position in the Cathedral before the construction of a new shrine to David in 1275. It is well known that Bishop Bernard searched in vain for the body of St David. The choice of two local saints – Justinian and Caradog – is a good example of Bernard's abilities to blend old and new, Welsh and Anglo-Norman in his episcopate. The dedication at Lawrenny is unlikely to have been made before 1124; the church and its patronage were in the hands of the lords of the manor, a knight's fee within the Barony of Carew. Gerald of Windsor, Lord of Carew, had after all ravaged the

---

89   Campbell and Lane, 'Excavations at Longbury Bank', 15–77, fig. 9.
90   Lloyd, *A History*, II.591–3.
91   *Itinerarium Kambriae* I ii (ed. and transl. Thorpe, 144–5).

lands of the bishopric of St Davids in 1097. But Lawrenny had before the Norman conquest evidently been in the hands of St Davids since it is one of the churches that Giraldus accused Bishop Wilfred of alienating.[92]

Mother churches of the Cymydau of Cantref Gwarthaf

The commote of Talacharn became the Norman lordship of Laugharne without any change of boundaries. Laugharne and its castle became the *caput* of this lordship. The present parish church, St Martin's, is sited north of the medieval borough. This, together with a fragment of a disc-headed cross shaft of ninth/tenth-century date (*ECMW* 145), suggest that it may have been the mother church of the *cwmwd* at this date at least.[93] An early cemetery is suggested by the now lost Class I ECM recorded by Edward Lhuyd. There was an important fifth/sixth-century high-status secular site at Coygan Camp, south-west of Laugharne, which has Iron Age origins and Roman occupation preceding its final phase.[94] Other later churches in its vicinity which contain Group I ECMs likely to be *in situ* may indicate related high-status burial sites of that date. Of the two such (Llandawke and Eglwys Gymyn) the latter is most interesting. A reused Iron Age enclosure forms the churchyard; the dedication and place-name commemorate St Cynin. He was also culted at Llangynin, where the Afon Cynin forms part of the parish boundary north-west of St Clears.[95] Most unusually however, the Latin and Ogam Group I Eglwys Gymyn ECM (*ECMW* 142) commemorates Avitoria, the daughter of Cunignos, and the latter is thought to be the same person commemorated on a Group I stone from Llanfihangel Croesfeini, in Newchurch parish north-west of Carmarthen (*ECMW* 172). In hagiographic genealogy, his affiliations are with Brychan. It will be suggested below in the section dealing with Brycheiniog that Brychan's associations became linked to St Davids.

Examples have been given of St Davids taking over former Teilo churches and lands. In Talacharn we may have some evidence of the reverse. Llanddowror is often suggested as a pre-Conquest monastic site principally on the basis of the linkage, firmly, and not surprisingly, made in the Book of Llandaf between the watermen of Llanddowror and the cult of Teilo. The confused traditions of the watermen could equally recall the ascetic penitential practices not just of only drinking water but of long periods of immersion which distinguished David *Aquaticus* in an early hagiographic reference.

Across the Taf estuary from Laugharne, a medieval ferry route led to Llansteffan and another ferry point across the River Towy. Pentywyn, on the Llansteffan side of this crossing point was a pre-Conquest possession of *Llan Teulyddog* (later Carmarthen Priory). In hagiographic tradition Ystyffan was a follower of Teilo. Llansteffan church was quite possibly the 'mother church' of the commote of Penrhyn. In Elfed the only possible candidate for a mother church, Cynwyl Elfed, was a chapel of Abernant in the medieval Deanery of Carmarthen, and granted in

[92] *Episcopal Acts*, ed. Davies, 237, D 28. Ludlow suggests that *Ucceton*, the other church with Lanrian, alienated by Wilfred may be located in Churchfield, Upton near the fourteenth-century chapel and Upton castle, both close to Lawrenny, see unpublished Cambria Archaeology Report (2003/39), prn 3450.

[93] Evans, 'Aspects', 241.

[94] Wainwright, *Coygan Camp*; for a more recent re-assessment of the Roman and Dark Age evidence see Campbell 'Coygan Camp', 45–6.

[95] Baring-Gould and Fisher, *Lives*, 261–2.

the twelfth century to Carmarthen Priory. Culted in both Elfed and Caio, Cynwyl's later hagiographic associations were with Deiniol and North Wales.

The commote of *Ystlwyf*'s original boundaries are again uncertain; part became a grange of Whitland Abbey. But it is evident (not least from the large size of its parish and a small detached portion) that Meidrum was the major church of this commote.[96] It is dedicated to St David and is sited on a spur above a bridging point of the River Dewi Fawr. It has long been recognised that the substantial churchyard enclosure is in origin an Iron Age promontary fort. Meidrum is included in the list of churches 'owned' by St David in Gwynfardd Brycheiniog's poem *Canu Dewi* (*ca* 1170):

> A Dewi bieu bangeibyr yssyt
> Meitrym le a'e mynwent i luossyt
>
> (And Dewi owns the great church which is in the place
> Called Meidrum with its cemetery for hosts)[97]

The latter epithet seems probably to refer to the graveyard's status as a sanctuary or *noddfa* although the enclosure is small. It is possible that there may have been some knowledge of the fortified nature of the enclosure.[98] Wyn Evans further suggests that *bangeibyr* may carry the meaning of 'high' church in the sense of a steeply pitched roof and by extension a wooden building, a term Gwynfardd also uses to describe Henllan (Deifi). The medieval bishopric had an estate at Meidrum. There were demesne lands but also rents from four *gwelyau* or kindred groups whose territories later formed the administrative subdivisions of townships in the parish that can still be traced today.[99] A concentration of *sarn* (causeway) place-names led archaeologists to suggest a Roman road line through Meidrum, even though exposure of an eighteenth-century forged itinerary of such a route, enthusiastically espoused by the antiquarians Richard Fenton and Richard Colt-Hoare had cast doubts. In the event, the Roman road line west from Carmarthen (*Moridunum*) has been proven through air-photography, field survey and excavation to lie further south. The route through Meidrum may be another Roman road or it may be an early medieval successor to that route. Strong support for an early medieval use comes in the traditional account in *De Situ Brycheiniog* of a three stage journey by *Marchell* from Brycheiniog to 'Hibernia', via *Lan Semin* (near Llangadog), *Methrum* (Meidrim) and *Porth Mawr* (Whitesands Bay, St Davids).[100]

The post-Conquest Norman lordship of St Clears encompassed the two adjacent *cymydau* of Amgoed and Peuliniog. Control was relatively weak and there is little sign of Anglo-Norman settlements. Native Welsh second-rank lords like Bleddri ap Cadifor seem to have retained their lands and position for some time in the twelfth century. The *caput* of the Lordship, St Clears, contained a small Cluniac Priory, a cell of St Martin-des-Champs, Paris. The major new religious focus for the whole area however was the Cistercian Abbey of Whitland which had several granges within the two *cymydau*, principally donations of the Lord Rhys. Many of these granges occupied earlier ecclesiastical sites some possibly once part of the patri-

---

96   Evans, 'Meidrum', 13–22.
97   Owen, 'Prologemena', lines 89–90.
98   Evans, 'Meidrum', 13–22.
99   Work in progress by Terry James and Muriel Bowen Evans.
100 Wade-Evans, *VSBG*, 313.

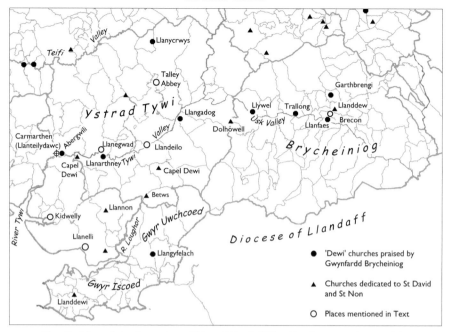

Map 3. Map of the deaneries of Ystrad Tywi, Kidwelly, Gower and part of the archdeaconry of Brecon. (Map by Terry James)

mony of Teilo and of David.[101] Churches therefore belonging to St Davids could well have been early possessions. The principal site is Henllan Amgoed, dedicated to St David, which is on onomastic grounds alone the most likely candidate for a mother church to the commote. Its parish however is small and the dependant chapel (and later small parish) of Eglwys Fair a Churig some distance to the south. Its patronage appears like Bridell to have been in the hands of the freeholders of the parish. Peuliniog presents a problem with no obvious site for a mother church.

Taking Cantref Gwarthaf as a whole, and at the risk of over-simplification, the interpretation which can be put forward on the basis of extant dedications is of a widespread cult of Teilo across the south of the area. Nevertheless it is still possible to discern earlier local cults which may even in some instances have fifth-through seventh-century origins. Their eponyms come not from progenitors in saintly gene-alogies but (admittedly in only one instance) from epigraphy on an Early Christian Monument. Their sanctity, one suspects, comes from local territorial power. Further north there are local cults which clearly persist through the high medieval period to judge from Welsh poetic reference. Yet there are also key churches, perhaps commotal mother churches, several of which are strategically placed along the all important east-west routeways across West Wales. Churches dedicated to St David are in such key positions. These churches 'owned' by Dewi as Gwynfardd expresses it were also in the case of Meidrum the focus of medieval episcopal estates and revenues organised through native patterns of tenure and renders. Their location

---

[101] For example, Parc-y-beddau field name and earthworks, Blaen Pedran Grange, Cilrhedyn parish, holy well and possible chapel, Aberelwyn Grange, Llanglydwen parish and Capel Mair, Maenor Forion Grange, Llangeler parish, all from Williams, *Atlas of Cistercian Lands*, 67.

in the *cymydau* of Ystlwyf and Amgoed is neither liminal, nor within a clustered area of dedications and lands but very much along a major east–west routeway or routeways of Roman and possibly early medieval origin.

Ystrad Tywi

It is evident that the medieval bishops of St Davids finally secured substantial properties and churches in the Tywi valley from the Lord Rhys and his descendants which were in origin part of the patrimony of Teilo's monastery of Llandeilo. Equally, it cannot be doubted that through the Lord Rhys and his descendants' grants, Talley Abbey 'became the inheritor of much of the spiritualities and temporalities of Teilo himself'.[102] This struggle was complicated by Bishop Urban of Llandaf's claims to some of these lands and churches. The key question is whether any of these churches or lands might have belonged to St Davids before the twelfth century or even at the period of Llandeilo's *floruit*.

The church dedicated to St David at Llanycrwys was lauded by Gwynfardd as 'a new monastery' (*lloga6d newyt*). There is no indication that St Davids gained much here other than a dedication at, perhaps, a new stone church. 'Lanecros' was a grange of Talley Abbey, occupying the eastern part of the parish between the rivers Camddwr and Twrch. Originally this had been a much larger estate, Trefwyddog, recorded as a marginal grant of mid-ninth-century date to Llandeilo in the Lichfield Gospels.[103] Its bounds on its north-west side are marked by two standing stones called *Hirfaen Gwyddog* and *Byrfaen Gwyddog*. It is of considerable interest therefore to find a stone mentioned in the section in *Canu Dewi* describing the bounds of the *noddfa* (sanctuary) of Llanddewibrefi, whose large extent was a visible sign of the power and prestige of the church. It seems likely that the stone is *Hirfaen Gwyddog*.

> O Gara6n gan ya6n, gan ehoec,
> Hyd ar Dywi, afon uirein a thec,
> O'r Llyndu, lle'd vu llid gyhydrec,
> Hyd ar T6rch, **teruyn tir a charrec**
>
> (From Caron with its fair rule, with its purple hue,
> From Llyndu, broader was the roused tumult,
> As far as Twrch, where the land is **bounded by a stone**.)
>
> (*Canu Dewi*, lines 144–7, my emphasis)

It is surely significant that a church be dedicated to St David in the upper Twrch valley at Llanycrwys, on the far side of the southern uplands border zone between Llanddewibrefi and Caeo, an area crossed by a Roman road (Sarn Helen).

Churches and possessions definitely once part of Llandeilo's patrimony include Llanegwad in the middle Tywi valley. A small amount of land held by free tenants in Welsh tenure at Llangathen may represent what the bishops could finally secure from a larger estate, once Llandeilo's, lost to lay landowners. The bishops were

---

102 Richards, 'The Carmarthenshire possessions', 121.
103 Jones, 'Post-Roman Wales', 13–316, esp. fig. 44 on Trefwyddog, where the ninth-century bounds are identified and the whole township equated with the commote of Caeo.

never able to exercise rights gained by the accord of 1222[104] to the whole *cwmwd* of Maenordeilo. The episcopal manor of Llandeilo (both *villa* and *patria*) was far smaller and apart from a chapel dedicated to St David in Dinefwr Castle, Teilo's cult, albeit in reduced form, survived at Llandeilo.[105]

Two churches, however, in Ystrad Tywi were praised by Gwynfardd in *Canu Dewi*: Abergwili and Llangadog. St Davids, Abergwili 'which belongs to the gentle one' is only two miles to the east of Carmarthen but is separated by the River Gwili. This is an important boundary area that may have origins in the late Iron Age and Romano-British period. It is thought that as well as the practical aspects of location at the lowest bridging point and highest tidal reach, the Roman choice of Carmarthen, was influenced by the presence of a large Iron Age hillfort at Merlin's Hill east of the town on the north side of the Tywi Valley. Other lesser known hillforts lie on high ground to the south and west. *Moridunum* is the only candidate for the *civitas* capital of the *Demetae*. The identification of the bishop-house *llanteulydawc* with the later Carmarthen priory just outside the eastern defences of the Roman town and south of the Roman road along the Tywi Valley has been noted above. Carmarthen Priory and Abergwili churches were intervisible, separated by the River Gwili. The medieval Priors administered Old Carmarthen (the former Roman town). Certainly Abergwili was an important possession of the medieval bishops where they had a college and a borough. But all of this was the work of Bishop Bek in the thirteenth century. Before then, it is evident that at the time of the accord of 1220 between Bishop Iorwerth and Rhys ap Rhys, lands at Abergwili were 'unjustly held by Guganus Seys, Kedivor filius Enyv and other nobles'. Not until 1270 was the bishop able to grant the remaining half of the church to Carmarthen Priory 'on the death or resignation of Hywel ap Trahaearn *comportionarius*'.[106] Abergwili church and churchyard do not rank highly against the archaeological criteria for early medieval sites. On balance therefore, it is uncertain whether St Davids had any interest there before the eleventh century, but the evidence of portionaries and a large parish with a high number of subordinate chapels suggests an earlier church of some importance. It is of course possible that the 'original' church was at the site of the later college and bishops' palace, and resited, along with a realignment of the former Roman road away from the college, when Bek built both college and town.[107]

On the south side of the River Tywi is Llanarthney. Yates suggests that the personal name 'Arthneu' is that of a founder, not a saint and that the dedication to St David could be early.[108] Edwards now considers that the late Group III cross shaft with its inscription in Latin and Norman-French could well have originally stood in the churchyard. A field name 'Treclas' may simply refer to church land. Our perceptions of this site's location are now conditioned by its position on the B4300, a turnpike road which runs from Llandeilo to Carmarthen on the south side of the river parallelling that of the more ancient road (the A40) on the north side of the river. Before this road, Llanarthney's position, barely 2 km south-east of Llanegwad across the floodplain of the Tywi via an old fording point may be the more relevant, the two being intervisible. Bounds of *cill artyui* (probably Llanarthney) given in a

---

104 *St Davids Episcopal Acta*, ed. Barrow, 176–7. See also, Pryce, 'The dynasty of Deheubarth', below, 313.

105 Strange, 'The rise and fall', 12–14.

106 *St Davids Episcopal Acta*, ed. Barrow, 157–8.

107 James, 'The bishop's palace', 19–43.

108 Yates, 'The "Age of the Saints"', 58.

late (twelfth century) Llandaf pseudo-charter include *pistill deui* which survives today as a farm name at the foot of high ground south-east of Llanarthney.[109] Some five km. west of Llanarthney is Capel Dewi, again easily linked now by the modern B4300. This was a subordinate chapel to Llanarthney, as was Llanlluan.

By the time of the *Black Book* survey of 1326 and the late, but final, English control of Iscennen, Llangadog had been organised as an episcopal town like Llawhaden and Abergwili with 33 burgesses, all of whom were Welsh. A short-lived attempt by Bek to found a college there failed perhaps due to continuing unrest. The morphology of the town shows its origins as a native Welsh nucleated settlement with a possible bond vill at Melindre Sawdde.[110] Tenants of the bishop in the *patria* held by Welsh tenure and rendered Welsh services like the triennial *commortha*. The town was an important economic possession for the medieval bishops. Llangadog is strategically located on the south side of the Tywi valley in a broad tributary valley between the two rivers, Bran and Sawdde close to their confluence with the Tywi. From Llangadog, partly using the Sawdde valley, roads ascend to the Black Mountain and the Brecon Beacons. One in particular, the ancient route known as *Sarn Hir*, crosses Mynydd Talsarn and Mynydd Wysg across the headwaters of the River Usk to descend into the Usk valley and the ancient kingdom of Brycheiniog. It is clear that this route was used by the thirteenth century, if not earlier, in preference to the Roman road line from Llandovery (*Alabum*) to Brecon Gaer (*Cicutio*) across Mynydd Trecastell. The 'Llangadog' route is shown on the fourteenth-century Gough map as the main route into west Wales and on to St Davids. This was the route taken by Edward I from Carmarthenshire to Brecon in 1295.[111] Llangadog prospered because of this route change that was perhaps perhaps forced by river course changes and hence bridging and fording difficulties at Llandovery.

Yates considered that the dedication name was from a lay founder, not St Cadog since the church lay so far distant from St Cadog's cult focus in south-east Wales. Llangadog therefore, he argues, could have been an early possession of St Davids. It is lauded by Gwynfardd in the 1170s in his list of Dewi churches as:

> Llanngada6c, lle breinya6c, ranna6c rihyt
>
> (Llangadog, a privileged place which partakes of glory)
>
> (line 98)

This certainly implies an area of *nawdd* or sanctuary of which the large, formerly circular churchyard of the present church may be a physical reflection.[112] However both Cantref Bychan in which Llangadog is located and the *cymydau* of Gwyr (Gower), Cydweli and Carnwyllion were claimed by Llandaf in the twelfth century, having been part, it was asserted, of the kingdom of Morgannwg. Bishop Herewald of Llandaf claimed to have placed priests in churches in these disputed areas.[113] Despite Yates's assertion regarding Llangadog, the cult of Cadog is also evidenced at Cydweli, likely to have contained the mother church of the *cymwd*. This may have been at Llangadog, close to the Norman borough and Priory church of St Mary, where the place-name Sanctuary Bank also suggests an important church site.

---

109 *The Text of the Book of Llan Dav*, ed. J.G. Evans, 78.
110 Page and Sambrook, 'Dinefwr', 40.
111 Morris, *The Welsh Wars*, 264.
112 James, 'Air photography', fig. 8.14, 76.
113 Davies, *The Book of Llandaf*, 29.

Evans has pointed out that the church of Carnwyllion – i.e the mother church of the *cwmwd* must be Llanelli, a vast parish in the middle ages. The dedicatee, Elli, was linked hagiographically to the cult of Cadog.[114]

Whilst Llandaf did not secure the *cymydau* of Cydweli, or Carnwyllion or indeed Gwyr, it is hard to prove that the cult of St David made much headway in these areas, or indeed Ystrad Tywi until the late ninth/tenth centuries at the very earliest and more probably in the eleventh and twelfth centuries. The earlier period might have seen lay founders dedicating their churches to St David, in a period when Llandeilo's power – and patrimony – was being eclipsed.

The cult of St David was, however, represented in the medieval landscape within the large welshries of the Norman lordships of this area, albeit in subsidiary chapels and holy wells. In the medieval deanery of Kidwelly, Llanon, dedicated to St Non, was a chapelry of St Illtud's Penbre, according to Wade Evans' *Parochiale Walli-canum*. This need not indicate a minor status since parish boundaries and parish churches were probably late to emerge here in an area where Welsh tenure, law and settlement patterns long persisted. It was a focal settlement to *Maenor Llanon* and on an early road line across the Gwendraeth Valleys to a crossing point of the River Loughor at Llandeilo Talybont. It is interesting to note that within this parish of dispersed settlement there are, south of Llanon on the eastern slopes of the Morlais valley, the two substantial farms of Cil-Ddewi uchaf and Cil-Ddewi fawr. Research is underway into their history in what is possibly another example of the St Non-St David pairing in adjacent place-names. Further south, on the west side of the River Loughor close to the ancient Loughor ferry crossing was Capel Dewi at Llwyn-hendy, one of many subordinate chapels of Llanelli.

Perhaps most surprising, at least to modern perceptions, is the incorporation of Gower into the diocese of St Davids, not Llandaf. The most important church here is Llangyfelach centrally placed at the division of this large *cymwd* between *Gwyr Is-Coed* and *Gwyr Uwch-Coed*. This was undoubtedly the mother church in the eleventh and twelfth centuries at least. A manor within the parish, part of the medieval bishops of St Davids estates was called 'The Clase'. It is hard to escape the conclusion that its acquisition by St Davids was late. Llangyfelach is lauded by Gwynfardd following *Mynyw* and *Brefi* and he also mentions 'a fair altar on which man cannot gaze' (line 182). Rhygyfarch gives more details describing the altar as one of the four consecrated gifts to St David from the Patriarch of Jerusalem, on his visit there with Teilo and Padarn. The Patriarch had elevated David to an archbishopric and the consequent location of this altar at David's 'monastery' of Llangyfelach, as Rhygyfarch describes it, could hardly be a more potent symbol of St Davids' metropolitan aspirations and its claim to diocesan territory which was contested by Llandaf. The altar, Rhygyfarch continues, had been concealed from human eyes by coverings of skins since the death of David.[115] Of all types of secondary relics, the fixed or portable altars are most closely connected with the celebration of mass, of consecration and dedication of a church.[116] Llangyfelach is not a church/monastery recorded in any of the Llandaf charters early or late. Within the medieval deanery of Gower, or at least on its boundaries and earlier site may be Llandeilo Talybont,

114   Evans, 'The Anglican Church in Llanelli', 1–29.
115   *Vita S. Dauid* § 45 (ed. Sharpe and Davies, below, 120–1).
116   Thomas, *The Early Christian Archaeology*, esp. ch. 6 'The altar'.

first recorded in a charter Davies dates to *ca* 665.[117] The place-name itself indicates an early bridge at the lowest crossing point of the River Loughor.

In terms of the archaeological criteria selected by the EMES project as diagnostic of early origins, Llangyfelach's ECMs – two cross slabs of ninth-century date (*ECMW* 211 and 213) and the socketted base of a late-ninth/early-tenth-century pillar cross (*ECMW* 212) certainly suggest a site of some importance by the ninth century. Field survey for the EMES project noted an irregular curvilinear shape to the churchyard but no physical evidence of an outer enclosure.[118] The Tithe Map field boundaries however do suggest one. Cyfelach has no convincing hagiographic record and may have been a lay founder. Political circumstances favourable to the kings of Dyfed and later Deheubarth, rather than Morgannwg, must account for St Davids' acquisition of this church and its lands but our sources are too sketchy to allow precise dates. The strategic importance of the site in a later period of definition of dioceses and disputes with Llandaf may have increased its status.

North of Llangyfelach, on mountain land high above the River Amman overlooking its confluence with the River Loughor, is the church of St Davids, Betws, giving its name to Maenor Betws in a border area aptly named 'Stryveland'.[119] Roberts considered *betws* (a borrowing from Old English *bed-hus*, an oratory) to be a relatively late ecclesiastical place-name.[120] Yet field survey for the EMES project by Ludlow has shown clear traces of a larger outer enclosure around the churchyard. Using air photographic and cartographic sources outer enclosures to many churchyards in West Wales were first noted by James. Their morphology was strikingly similar to prehistoric concentric enclosures.[121] These outer enclosures could, James suggested, be termed *bangorau* – more weakly defined (by a hedge or fence) than the inner cemetery. Among several possible functions, that of a *noddfa* or sanctuary is an attractive one. We need only cite the well-known description by Giraldus to be aware that these were still in use in the twelfth centuries.[122] What more likely location for a *refugium* than a site like Betws – late in native Welsh control, on the borders between enclosed land and mountain pasture, notorious for its lawless conditions where a safe resting place for movement of animals was a practical necessity? Therefore, Roberts' suggestion of a late origin on toponymic grounds need not preclude a church site of greater physical extent than at present.

Archdeaconry of Brecon

Archdeacons, new to Wales in the twelfth century, were often Welsh by birth and the seats of their archdeaconries located in important *clas* or mother churches. It is possible that the archdeaconry of Brecon was one of the earliest created in the future diocese of St Davids. Certainly one of its most vigorous and celebrated office holders was Giraldus himself who lived at Llanddew for some period of time. The dedication, to the Holy Trinity, literally means 'God's Church' and is the same as the earlier name of Llandrindod (in the 1291 *Taxatio*).[123] In addition to the Arch-

[117] Davies, *An Early Welsh Microcosm*, LL140, 167.
[118] Evans, 'Early medieval ecclesiastical sites'.
[119] Rees, 'The changing borders', 15–21.
[120] Roberts, 'Welsh ecclesiastical place-names', 41–4.
[121] James, 'Air photography', 41.
[122] *Itinerarium Kambriae* I xviii (ed. and transl. Thorpe, 254).
[123] Morgan and Powell, *A Study*, 93–4.

deacon's house, the medieval bishops had a palace there. The massive thirteenth-century church is likely, on the evidence of *ECMW* 73 (a ring cross stone with an inscription) to have had a pre-Conquest precursor. Yet Llanddew was a chapel of Garthbrengy, and unlike Llywel, Trallong, Garthbrengy and Llanfaes, the only church in this group in the upper Usk valley which was not lauded by Gwynfardd. As his name 'Brycheiniog' suggests, Gwynfardd was a native of the area and may well have known all these churches.

> Nys arueit ryuel Llanuaes, lle uchel,
> Na'r llann yn Llywel gan nep lluyt,
> Garthbryngi, brynn Dewi digewilyt,
> A Thrall6g Kynuyn ker y dolyt,

> (War does not venture to Llanfaes, a lofty site,
> Nor to the church in Llywel with any army,
> Garthbrengi the hill of Dewi, a place without shame
> And Trallwng Cynfyn near the meadows,)

> (*Canu Dewi*, lines 99–102)

The suspicion is that Llanddew may have been a late – even post-Conquest – addition to David's patrimony. However as the *Black Book* survey of 1326 makes clear, Llanddew became the centre of the considerable episcopal estates in Breconshire and Garthbrengy was a component part of that manor. Garthbrengy, the name of both church and parish, has the toponym *garth* meaning mountain ridge or hill, which describes its location on the eastern valley sides of the River Honddu and *Brengi*, a personal name. The latter is either an obscure saint or perhaps a lay founder. Llanfaes was also a chapel of Garthbrengy and it became incorporated in one of the suburban, extra mural areas of the new Norman castle borough of Brecon, founded by Bernard de Neufmarché in the late eleventh/early twelfth century.

Llywel is thought to be a personal name, of a minor saint, attached in Llandaf's hagiographic traditions at least to Dyfrig and Teilo. A grant of 1229 by Bishop Iorwerth, noted above in connection with Cenarth, gave 'the church of the three saints of Llywel' to the Cathedral Chapter. Its dedication therefore to St David seems to have been in addition to at least one local saint. Llywel's medieval parish was very large, divided into sub-divisions suggesting an a territorial unit possibly once a *cymwd*. Llywel is thus a good candidate for a pre-Conquest mother church. Perhaps the triple dedication reflects the divisions (*traians*) of the parish or perhaps we have a multiple church site. It has to be said however that there is little in the present topography to suggest this. Most telling, one of the traians was 'traianglas' indicating a *clas* church status to Llywel.

The Usk valley has been a key route for access to west and central Wales, a fact recognised in the Roman conquest of Wales. At least five routes radiated from the fort at Brecon Gaer (*Cicutio*) west of the Norman choice of site for Brecon. The Roman road west over Mynydd Trecastell to *Alabum* (Llandovery) remained in use for centuries until the valley floor route was constructed in the 1760s. Another route west from the upper Usk valley across the Black Mountain to Llangadog, possibly Roman but also in use in the middle ages, has also been mentioned. Trallong, one of the three chapels of Llywel, was a valuable part of the medieval bishops' Breconshire estates. Although dedicated to St David, Gwynfardd's epithet preserves another personal name, Cynfyn, for Trallong. Without a hagiographic or genealogical record, this name may be that of a lay founder, rather than a saint. Some of the services owed by the fourteenth-century tenants of the bishops reveal close cross-mountain links with Llangadog.[124] Another chapel of Llywel – Dolhowell – a site now lost to forestry if not drowned by the Usk reservoir was located on the Mynydd Trecastell route corridor to the upper Tywi valley. These churches and chapels with their 'Dewi' dedications seem to fall into my 'transmontane' category. Droving services for the triennial commortha render owed by episcopal tenants at both Llangadog and Trallong involved moving animals across the mountain between the two places. Now wholly given over to sheep pastures, it is difficult to recreate the different patterns of seasonal movement when the Black Mountain, like most of upland Wales, was principally grazed by cattle. The importance of meadows for hay and also for rich grazing for fattening cattle cannot be overstressed – meadows attached to David's churches are a constant item of praise for Gwynfardd in his *Canu Dewi.*

This Roman route corridor between the Tywi and Usk valleys was seen by E.G. Bowen as one of the main vectors for the spread of the cult of St David. The discovery of a Roman road into Pembrokeshire west of Carmarthen, whose possible destination is St Davids at first sight reinforces this idea with 'Dewi' churches at Henllan Amgoed and eastwards up the Tywi valley via Abergwili. In addition, we must now consider the question of the origins of the kingdom of Brycheiniog, recently the subject of much work by Thomas. He suggests that 'for the ogam-inscribed, Irish-named, stones in the Usk valley the spacing of those so far discovered might suggest erection of prominent and legible memorials, in each case on the estate or holding of a family whose adult male leader is being signified … with a Christian personal epitaph whose design was commissioned from a local priest'. Several churchyard sites in central Brycheiniog could thus be of sixth-century origin.[125] Thomas has used the twelfth-century 'Brychan' documents, the *De Situ Brecheniauc* and *Cognacio Brychan* (which clearly derive from earlier originals) to propose a detailed historical narrative; others have preferred to see them as origin legends. In such circumstances an early cult of St David in the upper Usk valley would seem likely. It is important however to accept that the demonstration of a fifth/sixth-century Irish presence and an Irish dynasty in Brycheiniog with christian beliefs, traditions of royal burials at churches and continued cultural links westward to the Irish Sea does not, in itself *prove* that the undoubtedly early sites had an equally early association with St David. Furthermore, between the possible 'Dewi' sites west of Carmarthen on the line of a Roman road or roads and those in the Upper Usk valley lie sites along the Roman road along the Tywi valley where we have seen that the cult of Teilo was the earlier and more dominant.

Circumstances permitting a later expansion of the cult of Dewi to churches in Brycheiniog, especially those of the upper Usk Valley west of Brecon, are thus equally plausible. The eclipse of the ruling dynasty of Brycheiniog in the tenth century has now been given dramatic archaeological context by excavations at Llangorse Crannog – likely to have been the site destroyed in 916 in a raid by Aethelflaed, Lady of the Mercians.[126] The route corridor from the upper Usk to the Tywi may well have been equally convenient for Mercian raids, one of which evidently took the 'Chad' gospels back to Lichfield as booty. Such troubled political

---

[124] *The Black Book of St Davids*, ed. Willis Bund, 319.
[125] Thomas, *And Shall These Mute Stones*, esp. chs 8 and 9, 126–7 and fig. 8.8 'Map of Brycheiniog with indications of Demetian settlers'.
[126] For interim reports see Redknap and Lane in *Medieval Archaeology* (1989–1993, 34–37) and *Archaeology in Wales* (1989–1992, 29–32).

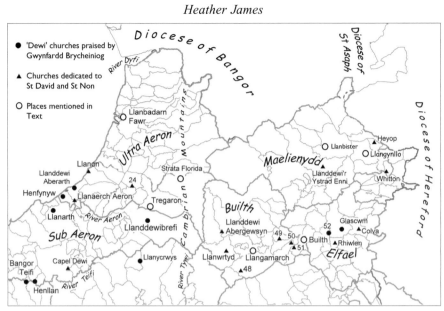

Map 4. Deaneries of Sub- and Ultra-Aeron, Builth, Elfael and Maelienydd.
(Map by Terry James)

circumstances may have contributed to the decline in prestige of the cult centre of
Teilo at Llandeilo. In Brycheiniog, Llandaf endeavoured to take on the mantle of
cults (Illtud and Cadog for example) emanating from monastic centres in south-east
Wales. By the eleventh and early twelfth centuries therefore the large area claimed
as the archdeaconry of Brecon (which included the former kingdoms and regions of
Maelienydd and Elfael now constituted as deaneries) was very much on the 'front-
line' of the struggle to establish diocesan boundaries between St Asaph, Hereford,
Llandaf and St Davids.

The creation of the diocese of St Asaph in the 1140s encompassed most of
northern Powys, leaving the area known as *Rhwng Gwy a Hafren* (between Wye
and Severn), which encompassed older territorial units to St Davids.[127] Yet there
were border disputes and few archdeacons can have been as vigorous as Giraldus
in defence of their diocese. In a celebrated incident in 1175, Giraldus hurried to
the church to St Michael in Kerry for a face-to-face clash with the bishop of St
Asaph on the boundaries of their dioceses and consequently the bishop's right to
conduct a service of dedication. Giraldus ordered the bells to be rung in triples
– part of the rite of excommunication – which caused the bishop and his retinue
to flee.[128] He was supported in this by Cadwallon ap Madog, ruler of *Rhwng Gwy
a Hafren,* who had earlier come to his aid when Giraldus was besieged by local
clergy in Llanbadarn Fawr church near Llandrindod, resentful of his reforming
archidiaconal zeal. This church fell within Maelienydd, again a deanery reflecting
an older minor kingdom with a complex medieval history of conquest and resistance to English rule. In his list of groups of saints assembled at the synod of Brefi

127 For a readily accessible map see Davies, *Age of Conquest*, map 1 and for detail on the area's signifi-
     cance and political history see Remfry, 'Cadwallon ap Madog Rex de Delvain'.
128 Owen, *Gerald the Welshman*, 7–9.

'to accept Dewi with full consent', Gwynfardd includes 'the saints of Maelienydd, the pinnacles of the world'. Morfydd Owen notes that Cadwallon ap Madog ab Idnerth of the Maelienydd line in the 1170s was a cousin to the Lord Rhys, Prince of Deheubarth and active patron of St Davids.[129] Nevertheless, in both the eleventh and twelfth centuries, reflecting shifting political allegiances, there were challenges to St Davids' jurisdiction. Certainly the cult of St David in terms of dedications, is reflected only in chapels attached to major ancient churches of other cults – Llanddewi Ystrad Enni for example, one of six chapels attached to Cynllo's church at Llanbister. Later developing into a parish church, Llanddewi is located along the important north–south valley route of the River Ithon between Llandrindod and Newtown. The two other dedications to St David at Heyop and Whitton were both chapels attached to Llangynllo. Interestingly, these are both in 'liminal' positions close to Offa's dyke and the diocesan boundary. The situation regarding the other component medieval deaneries – Builth and Elfael – of this large archdeaconry of Brecon is complex and discussion of David dedications there are covered below.

Ceredigion

The final section of this article returns via a great circular progress around the medieval diocese of St Davids to Ceredigion, where, arguably, the cult of St David began. There was undoubtedly a strong Irish influence in early medieval Ceredigion, both through fifth/sixth-century settlement and the ongoing cultural influence of the Irish Sea zone. It is instructive therefore to look first at the churches dedicated to St David and his associates within this group along the Ceredigion coast where any immigrant Irish settlement might first have been located. However, as Jenkins has pointed out, until the eighteenth century and construction of harbours, maritime trade and access was through beach landing places with the main villages and hamlets being inland.[130] In the *Black Book* survey of 1326, the bishop held a large tract of land known as Morfa Esgob where a working strip field system survived into modern times.[131] Rhandir Llan-non was granted to Bishop Iorwerth by Rhys ap Gruffydd, some time between 1215 and 1229, presumably a confirmation of earlier grants.[132] The hamlet of Llansanffraid lay to the north of the Morfa with a church dedicated to the Irish St Brigit[133] and to the south, Llanon with a subordinate chapel dedicated to St Non. Llanon has long been characterised as a bond settlement in origin and the settlement's name was also that of one of the nine *gwestfau* into which the commotes of Anhuniog and Mefenydd were divided.[134] It is worth noting that according to south walian lawbooks 'the consecration in a bond township of a church with a serving priest and burial rights was sufficient to make that township free'.[135] It may be that this is why there was only a chapel at Llanon. It

---

[129] Owen, pers. comm.
[130] Jenkins, *Maritime Heritage*, 9.
[131] Davies, 'Field systems', 525–527.
[132] *Episcopal Acts*, ed. Davies, D.473, 357.
[133] '[Her] cult may well have been introduced into Wales by early Irish settlers in Dyfed. These came partly from the Déisi of Munster where Brigit's cult was partiularly strong.' Ó Riain, 'The saints', 390.
[134] Dodgshon defines the *gwestfa* as a territorial unit made up of sharelands.; see his 'Early society', 347–8.
[135] Pryce, *Native Law*, 131.

is certainly possible to argue that the sex, character and history of the eponymous Non in hagiography are attempts to explain a link between the lands and settlement there at Llanon and St Davids. There were however other churches as well as chapels dedicated to St Non. The revenues of Llannerch Aeron, dedicated to St Non, were appropriated to Llanddewibrefi when that church was reorganised by Bek as a college in the thirteenth century.

South of Llanon lies Llanddewi Aberarth (*Gwestfa Llandewi*) at a coastal location where the Arth meets the sea, accessible perhaps for early medieval beach landing vessels but with no harbour.[136] The intertidal areas of beach contain extensive stone fish traps of early medieval origins.[137] Here, by the fourteenth century, the medieval bishops received rents from free Welsh tenants organised in territorial kin-groups or *gwelyau*. The church is sited high on a hill above the village. Its revenues were early appropriated to support a prebend in the Cathedral and it was valued at £4 in the 1291 *Taxatio*. Yet its status was that of a chapel to Henfynyw, despite pre-Norman indication of the importance of the site in the ninth/tenth centuries in the form of fragments of an inscribed decorated cross shaft. Ludlow has noted the similarity in shape and position between the churchyard and an iron age promontary fort.[138]

Henfynyw's topographical location 'near the banks of the Aeron with its clover-filled meadows and acorn loaded trees' is praised by Gwynfardd, along with Llanarth, and the Teifi side churches of Bangor, Henllan and Manordeifi. Henfynyw has many characteristics of an early ecclesiastical site, despite its totally rebuilt church and remodelled churchyard. There are traces of a larger irregular outer enclosure, deemed 'doubtful' by Ludlow.[139] The fragmentary Group I 'Tigernacus' stone (*ECMW* 108), thought to be of sixth-century date, commemorates a Irish individual of a name which also occurs at Jeffreyston in Pembrokeshire. It is considered to be *in situ* and this suggests the site is an example of Thomas's 'developed' cemeteries. There is general agreement that Henfynyw translates into Latin as *Vetus Rubus* the locus for traditions of David's schooling given in Rhygyfarch's *Vita S. David*. However the parish of Henfynyw is small in comparison to other coastal parishes and Llanddewi Aberarth, was, as we have seen a bigger church. In any other circumstances than those of the widely dispersed locations of 'Dewi' churches, it would be perfectly reasonable to propose a site shift from Henfynyw to Llanddewi Aberarth.

Taking a minimalist view, Ó Riain suggests that in writing his *Vita S. David* in the late-eleventh century, Rhygyfarch would have been aware of the churches in Ceredigion dedicated to the saint and would wish to highlight the importance of his native land.[140] This he achieved by making David's parents, with their transparently manufactured names of 'Sanctus' (saint) and 'Nonnita' (nun), come from Ceredigion and Dyfed, and by having the saint educated in Henfynyw before leaving for *Mynyw* Such a narrative left Padarn and his house of Llanbadarn Fawr, seat of Rhygyfarch's learned family, in a kind of partnership. It is Padarn, with Teilo, who accompanies David to Jerusalem. There is no doubt that Ceredigion was an early

---

136 Dr Nancy Edwards has drawn my attention to the Viking hogback grave from the church, which occupies an elevated site and a possible parallel site at Lythe near Whitby overlooking a beach where Viking ships might have been drawn up.

137 Turner, 'Fish weirs and fish traps', 99–100; Fishtraps at Aberarth were granted by Rhys ap Gruffydd in 1184 to Strata Florida Abbey – an example of patronage by the Welsh princes of the newer religious orders at the expense of older communities?

138 Ludlow, unpublished Cambria Archaeology Report 2004/31, 19.

139 Ludlow, prn 49326.

140 Ó Riain, 'The saints', 385.

kingdom, a natural territorial unit with boundaries north and south of rivers, west of the sea and east the mountains as Ieuan ap Sulien observed.[141] There is little doubt either that Llanbadarn was a major ecclesiatical site with traditions of a diocese and a bishop. The *Vita S. Paterni* (*ca* 1200) seeks to define the saint's territorial sway with aspirations to the whole of Seisyllwg.[142] Nevertheless Llanbadarn clearly came within St Davids's sphere of influence and the accommodation is reflected in the dedication patterns with little direct influence of Dewi's cult in north Ceredigion.

Finally, along the Ceredigion coast and coastal plateau is Llanarth, dedicated to St Meilig and St David. Llanarth is a large parish from which the smaller, coast-edge, parish of Llanina (a chapelry) and possibly Llanllwchaern have been carved out. A pioneering study in 1926 identified Llanarth's chapels as part of the parish's component *trefi* or townships.[143] The church is fairly prominently sited on the crest of a steeply sloping valley side to the Afon Lethi and has a cross slab inscribed 'Gurhirt' of ninth/tenth-century date likely to be *in situ*. Its affiliations are with a similar cross slab from Penmon Priory, Anglesey. Ó Riain considers Meilig to be a variant of Maelog, culted, in association with Cybi on Anglesey.[144] Llanarth, then is a good candidate for a mother church and there are indications that the St David dedication may be secondary. However, it is Llanarth, not Llanddewi Aberarth, which is lauded by Gwynfardd. A possible explanation for this might be an early association with Llanddewibrefi. In 1290 Bishop Bek endowed his newly founded collegiate church at Llanddewibrefi with Llanarth and Llanina – perhaps reflecting an earlier link.

Llanddewibrefi is second only to St Davids in terms of the cult. Its role in the hagiography as the location of the synod of Brefi needs no further elaboration here. Owen considers Gwynfardd Brycheiniog's poem *Canu Dewi* to be 'intended for an audience assembled in Llanddewibrefi for a feast day possibly at which the Lord Rhys was present'.[145] The poem both complements and extends the hagiographic record not least in describing one of the chief 'secondary' relics of St David – a golden staff which was one of the gifts given to him by the Patriarch of Jerusalem.[146] This could hardly be more appropriate a symbol of the saint's power in a region where the other principal saint was Padarn whose sole but potent relic was his staff called *cyrwen*. Other attributes praised by Gwynfardd were 'The five altars of Brefi in honour of saints' (line 269). This might well indicate multiple churches on the site, a characteristic of early medieval monastic sites. He also praises Brefi's *braint* (privilege) and *nawdd* (sanctuary). Equally telling evidence on the importance of Llanddewibrefi as an early – if not the earliest – site of the cult of St David comes from the monumental and epigraphic record of the ECMs from the site. Most impor-tant is the now-lost 'Idnert' stone, fragments of which are supposedly built into the fabric of the church. A drawing by the generally reliable antiquarian Edward Lhuyd of late seventeenth-century date gives the inscription as *Hic iacet Idnert filius*

141 Davies, *Patterns*, 20–1.
142 'Vita Sancti Paterni' (ed. Wade-Evans, *VSBG* 252–69). Seisyllwg was a territorial unit of eighth/ ninth century date formed by the union of Ceredigion and Ystrad Tywi, under Seisyll, a supposed descendant of Ceredig.
143 Bevan, 'Notes on Llanarth', 60–70.
144 Ó Riain, 'The saints', 393.
145 Owen, 'Prolegomena', 61.
146 Also see Rhygyfarch, *Vita S. David* § 48 (ed. Sharpe and Davies, below, 140–1); Evans notes that the folk tradition at Llanddewibrefi of naming one of the ECMs *bagl Dewi* (David's Staff) might be a recollection of the original relic. J.Wyn Evans, 'St David and St Davids', n. 24, 22. For croziers see Edwards, 'Celtic saints', 252–4.

Iacobi qui occisus fuit propter predam sancti David, to which Jackson assigned a mid-seventh-century date. If an accurate record, this is the earliest mention of St David and one tied closely to Llanddewibrefi. However, for linguistic reasons, a ninth-century date is preferred in the forthcoming *Corpus*. There also, Edwards translates *predam* as plundering although its meaning has been much debated with 'flock' as one suggestion, but also 'herd' (of cattle) and it may have been used either figuratively or literally.[147] Controversially, Thomas has applied Howlett's work on the Celtic-Latin tradition of biblical style to monumental inscriptions and suggests an elaborately encoded pictorial message and representation to the inscription.[148]

Llanddewi parish is a large one divided into seven townships and three chapelries, second only to Llanbadarn fawr in size in Ceredigion. It has often been noted that it is sited close to the Roman fort of Llanio, probably the Roman *Bremium*, taking its name, like Llanddewi from the River Brefi. But the fort and any possible *vicus* site lie to the west across the River Teifi as does the Roman road line. The true significance of Llanddewibrefi's siting, like Tregaron and indeed the Cistercian Abbey of Strata Florida to the north, is that they are sited above the River Teifi valley, at the mouth of steep narrow tributary valleys. These side valleys provide important routes not only up onto the extensive mountain pastures but also across the southern Cambrian Range into the Irfon and upper Wye valleys. In later centuries, it was the route east from Tregaron through the Abergwesyn Pass that became the principal drovers' route. The older route from Llanddewibrefi however continued to be used and is still traceable (though obscured by forestry and the construction of the Llyn Brianne reservoir). Both routes converge at Abergwesyn where there was a church dedicated to St David. It would of course be anachronistic to suggest any kind of droving type of traffic on this route in the eleventh or twelfth centuries although the origins of the trade are certainly medieval. However it cannot be doubted that the wealth of the uplands was in cattle and that these were subject to raiding, tribute and more regular renders (commorthas) and had to be moved in large numbers for any or all of these purposes. Not only therefore can we suggest that the Llanddewibrefi – Abergwesyn pairing is a good 'transmontane' example but a route line can be followed eastwards beyond Llanddewi Abergwesyn, marked by important 'Dewi' churches which leads to Leominster. The churches include those in the upper Irfon valley, Llanwrtyd and, east of Builth on a cross-upland route through Cregrina, Glascwm and Colva, the latter close to the later diocesan borders and on the marches. This line and others are shown in Moore-Colyer's maps.[149] Its traces need more research than I have yet carried out, but its existence, I believe, is signalled in Gwynfardd's *Canu Dewi*, in the 'structured deposition' of St Davids relics.

Several commentators have drawn attention to the continued vitality of folklore connected to St David in the Llanddewibrefi area, often a localisation or development of incidents alluded to in the poetry. Gwynfardd accounts for the presence of St David's bell, *bangu*, at Glascwm by means of a journey from Llanddewibrefi:

> Deu ychen Dewi, ardderchaóc-oetynt,
> Deu gar a gertynt yn gydpreinyaóc
> Y hebróg anrec yn redecaóc
> Y lasgóm, nyd oet tróm tri urtassaóc;

---

[147] Gruffydd and Owen, 'The earliest mention', 231–2; Jackson 'The Idnert inscription', 232–4.
[148] Thomas, 'The Llanddewi-Brefi Idnert stone', 136–83, but see also McKee, 'Counter arguments'.
[149] Moore-Colyer, *Welsh Cattle Drovers*, maps 2 and 6, 130, 143.

Edewid bangu gu, gadwyna6c,
A'r deu ereill yreisc y Urycheinya6c

(The two oxen of Dewi, two wondrous ones [were they]
They put their backs beneath the cart of Cynog:
The two oxen of Dewi, they were excellent;
Two dear ones who walked beneath the same yoke
In order to take a gift running to Glasgwm – the three dignified objects were
        not heavy
Bangu was left [there, the] dear chained one,
And the two other splendid objects for Brecknock.)   (lines 51–58)

Sir John Rhys discussed the legendary *ychen bannog*, which are here localised both at Llanddewibrefi and attached to David. A large ox horn, known as *Madcorn yr ych Bannog,* was kept in the church and in another local variant oxen were used to cart stones for the building of the church. They were further imprinted on the local landscape when, exhausted, one of the oxen bellowed so loudly that an obstructing hill split in two. This is located at Foelallt, the high crags on the northern side of the narrow Brefi valley route towards the mountains.[150] There are also *clochdy* place-names on Foelallt and, further east along the cross-mountain route. Handbells as relics have been discussed by Edwards and others. Giraldus relates a miracle concerning *bangu* at Glascwm.[151] Amongst several late medieval Welsh poetic references to the clarity and audibility of David's voice at the Synod of Brefi is a comparison made by Ieuan ap Rhydderch *Mal cloch yn Llandudoch deg* ('like a bell in fair Llandudoch').[152]

From Abergwesyn in the medieval deanery of Builth (an echo of its former status as a small kingdom) a route ran south down the Irfon valley to Llanwrtyd and, on the western flanks of Mynydd Eppynt and Mynydd Bwlch y Groes to Llywel, on the upper Usk in Brycheiniog. Llanddewi Abergwesyn, St Davids, Llanwrtyd, and a now lost chapel *Llanddewi Llwyn y Fynwent*, together with a church dedicated to St Bride and a lost chapel to St Madog (Aidan) were all originally subsidiary to the major church of St Cynog at Llangamarch. Gwynfardd's 'cart of Cynog' may be a poetic allusion to this cult centre, Cynog being of course the eldest son of Brychan Brycheiniog in the saintly genealogies and object of a major cult. It is interesting to note that the subsidiary chapel and church dedications of Llangamarch include not only David but the two 'Irish' saints of St Bride and St Madog, closely associated with David in Pebidiog at least 'on the ground' and in the hagiography. Llangamarch became a major part of the endowments made by the medieval bishops of St Davids to their college at Brecon.

At Llanwrtyd the more important eastward route continues down the Irfon, via Llangamarch to Builth on the Wye. There is a small cluster of David dedications around Builth that fit the 'linear' and 'transmontane' patterns proposed in this paper. South-west of Builth is Llanddewi Maesmynys, now a small parish church in the Duhonw valley, to which three churches and chapels were originally subsidiary: St Mary, Builth, St Davids Llanynys and Llanddewi'r Cwm. Both Maesmynys and Llanddewi'r Cwm are at the commencement of southward route (the present B 4520) which crosses over to the Honddu valley flowing south to Brecon itself. Detailed description of drovers' routes fording at the confluence of the Duhonw and the

---

150 Rhys, *Celtic Folklore*, 577–9.
151 *Itinerarium Kambriae* I i (ed. and transl. Thorpe, 79).
152 Henken, *Traditions*, 55.

Wye, crossing Aberedw Hill and proceeding, ultimately, to Leominster via Cregrina, Glascwm and Colva is given by Moore-Colyer.[153] Again, I am not suggesting that these were 'drovers' roads in the early middle ages but that they were direct west-east hill routes, of some antiquity along which animals could be moved.

Gwynfardd's praise of these churches gives a hint of their topography and also suggests sanctuaries attached to them:

> And Glasgwm with its church by the verdant mountains,
> A lofty clearing full of groves, where sanctuary never fails,
> Fair Cregrina here, its mountain is fair and Ystrad Nynnid, whose freedom is available.[154]

The medieval deanery and cantref of Elfael, ruled until the late-twelfth century by a native dynasty within Powys was seized by William de Braose in the late-twelfth century but regained by Llywelyn ap Gruffudd in the thirteenth century. The dedication pattern, which cannot be detailed here, was diverse. Both Cregrina, and most certainly Glascwm were major churches with subsidiary chapels; Cregrina's two dedicated to St Padarn and St Non (a lost site). Rhiwlen and Colva were chapels of Glascwm all with 'Dewi' dedications. In his *Vita S. David*, Rhygyfarch gives a list of twelve monasteries founded by St David: Glastonbury, Bath, Crowland and Repton, Colva and Glascwm, and 'from this place he founded the monastery of Leominster, and next Raglan in the region of Gwent; afterwards the monastery of Llangyfelach, in which he later received the altar sent to him'.[155] Unlike Glascwm, a major church by most criteria, Colva is small – its significance in the list is solely due, in my opinion, to its important liminal location as the first of St David's churches encountered after crossing the border zone between England and Wales from Leominster. It occupies a prominent hill top site. The ancient Priory of Leominster, which became a dependency of Reading Abbey in 1125, had a very large collection of relics described in a thirteenth-century relic list.[156] Bethell has characterised the core of the collection, which later came to Reading as representing 'the piety and interests of the court of King Athelstan'.[157] Irish, West Country, yet very few Welsh saints were represented. Reputedly these included an arm of St David, although this was not included in the list. However there are a series of indulgences to the arm of St David in the Leominster cartulary. In 1229, Bishop Iorwerth granted a twenty one day indulgence 'to all penitents giving gifts to Leominster Priory, which possesses an arm of St David, on the feast of St Peter and Paul ... or on St David's day'.[158] This is not the place for a full discussion of this relic; the suspicion is that it may have been a later rather than early addition to the collection. In the present context, its presence at Leominster reinforces the significant linkages between the cult of St David and an early but long-lived hill route from west to east. There is a noticeable focus on sanctuaries in Gwynfardd's praise of 'Dewi' churches along what we can now see as a routeway. As a final comment, and returning to Gerald's description as we have already noted above for Betws on the upland borders of Ystrad Tywi, the *noddfa* is defined in terms of function and area in terms of a refuge for cattle as much as for men.

---

153 Moore-Colyer, *Welsh Cattle Drovers*, 146.
154 Owen, 'Prologemena', lines 104–8.
155 Rhygyfarch, *Vita S. David* § 13 (ed. Sharpe and Davies, below, 118–21).
156 Doble, 'The Leominster relic list', 58–65.
157 Bethell, 'The making', 61–5.
158 *St Davids Episcopal Acta*, ed. Barrow, 82.

Conclusions

This preliminary study has shown that there are locational patterns in the distribution of churches and chapels dedicated to St David and his close associates within the medieval diocese of St Davids. First it is of course necessary to point out that there are dedications to St David and his close associates in south-east Wales and south-western Britain not covered at all in this analysis. Also there are areas of the medieval diocese where 'Dewi' dedications are wholly or almost wholly absent. Most churches fit more than one of my categories specified at the beginning of this paper. There are, however, differences of emphasis in the relative importance of the categories depending in which deanery the church is situated. The medieval deaneries were formed from older, secular, territorial and administrative boundaries.

There are no dedications across northern Ceredigion, which undoubtedly is due to the strength of the cult of St Padarn at Llanbadarn Fawr. There are good reasons to suggest a ninth- or tenth-century bishopric and diocese based there extending eastwards into Maelienydd. The accommodation reached between Llanbadarn and St Davids in the eleventh century, if not earlier, is epitomised in the roles played by the family of Sulien. In fact there are similarities between the spatial organisation of the cults of Padarn and David in Ceredigion and eastwards across the Cambrian Mountains which throw light on the possible origins of the latter. In brief and perhaps over-simply, both may have original sites eclipsed in importance by later churches. Llangorwen chapel, on the River Clarach north of Aberystwyth, shows archaeological evidence of an early church site and the second element in its name may be that of Padarn's defining relic, the staff *cyrwen* and thus be the origin of the cult.[159] David's relics are more numerous but in Ceredigion, at Llanddewibrefi, he too has a staff, the golden *bagl Dewi*. Henfynyw, in a similar coastal zone location to Llangorwen has the archaeological indications and a strong tradition of an early monastery. Both Llanbadarn Fawr and Llanddewibrefi have large parishes which perpetuate early territories with many indications of sanctuaries and privileges. They focus on major church sites whose monumental and sculptural record amply demonstrates their importance as cult centres in the ninth through to the eleventh centuries. Both have important sites across the Cambrian mountains in my 'transmontane' locations: Llanbadarn Fynydd and Llanbadarn Fawr ym Maelienydd and the churches described above for David en route to Glasgwm and beyond. Generally, as noted within this paper, dedications are thinly dispersed across the diocese. Nevertheless there are clusters which gain added significance when seen against the overall pattern, such as the cluster of sites (19–23) which includes Henfynyw.

There are divergent views on whether the cult of St David originated at what the fourteenth-century Welsh *Life* of David, *Buchedd Dewi*, termed *Mynyw yn y deheu* ('*Mynyw* in the south') in Pebidiog.[160] But it cannot be doubted that the cult was centred there by the late-ninth century and that it had achieved national status. Liminal siting, which has been noted as a characteristic of many Irish monastic sites and indeed characterises several of the ninth/tenth-century 'bishop-houses' of Dyfed is particularly pronounced in Pebidiog. It is important not to impose modern cartographic sensibilities on early medieval concepts of territories. Boundaries changed and may not have been precisely fixed over areas of upland for example. But the topography of Wales with its numerous natural divisions of coastlines, major river

---

[159] Wmffre, *The Place-Names of Cardiganshire*, 1006; Ludlow, unpublished Cambria Archaeology Report (2004/31) prn 50144.
[160] *Buchedd Dewi* 55–6 (ed. Evans, *The Welsh Life*).

valleys, and tributary streams, watersheds and hill and mountain ranges was conducive to 'natural' territorial boundaries. Davies makes it clear that rulers' powers were
'defined in relation to territory' and that 'the spatial extent of these territories was
apparent to those using the terms'.[161] Central, or at least focal, siting in relation to
cymydau does seem to characterise (and therefore define?) 'Dewi' churches like
Llanddewi Velfrey, Henllan Amgoed, Meidrum, Glasgwm, Llangyfelach and Llywel
which can be termed 'mother-churches'. Quite evidently in the case of the last two,
David's was not the original dedication.

It is possible that the location of sites I have termed 'liminal' may, in some
circumstances, have created boundaries rather than respecting them. The incorporation of prehistoric ritual and funerary monuments into boundaries, cannot, necessarily, indicate that such boundaries were ancient. The linking by name of such
monuments to a more recent, though mythic, early medieval past may be more
significant. The extent to which the siting of ECMs and churches may be fruitfully
analysed in such ways can only be suggested here, but clearly, in my view, has
considerable potential.

I have also, not surprisingly, classified most liminal sites as 'linear' or 'transmontane' because they are also sited on or near routeways. Whilst Roman roads
continued function as important channels of communication, they do not, on detailed
examination, have the close association with 'Dewi' sites that Bowen suggested. It
is evident, not least from the recent discovery, or re-discovery, of a Roman road line
west of Carmarthen that more roads and forts await discovery in west Wales. Yet
these were in origin and in use military and administrative means of communication and control, remarkably engineered for wheeled traffic and all-weather use but
only over the area of military infrastructure. They did not, in Wales, develop further.
Quite clearly in some areas they fell out of use – the Roman road from Carmarthen,
for example, eastwards up the Tywi valley continued in use – large sections of that
proceeding westwards did not. Much more detailed local work is needed on the
pre-turnpike roads of Wales to work back to possible medieval and early medieval
routeways. They were however not primarily for wheeled transport but for foot and
horse traffic, and movement of animals. Use was probably seasonal. Within those
constraints they functioned well – the archetypal picture of appalling Welsh roads
and difficulties of communication comes from seventeenth- and eighteenth-century
demands for roads for wheeled transport once again. River crossings were of key
importance and it may well be that with few bridges, routes were also dictated by
fording points. Locations therefore like Llawhaden, or Meidrim, are good examples.

Equally important in terms of the logistics of travel were hill and mountain crossings that would be organised in terms of a day's journey, of significance both in its
starting point and its safe destination or resting place. Such travel may have been
physically feasible but dangerous in terms of security of person, possessions and
beasts. The protection offered by the *refugium* of as powerful a saint as possible at
key locations was perhaps the best that could be hoped for. The route outlined above
from Llanddewibrefi eastwards is one such example.

All that needs to be said here with regard to the EMES archaeological criteria
is that many 'Dewi' churches and chapels seem to have early origins. Only when
other factors are taken into account however can we suggest that they were early or
original *dedications*. The Gwaun valley cluster (9, 10 and 11) may have been, so

---

161 Davies, *Patterns*, 16.

too the coastal cluster around Henfynyw noted above. However, in Ystrad Tywi for example 'Dewi' churches 'scoring' highly against the EMES criteria may originally have been part of the Teilo cult. Clearly, a priority for further research to develop the tentative ideas put forward in this paper is to map and analyse churches dedicated to Teilo as well as other more local cults within the medieval diocese. More detailed mapping too of holy wells and other sacralised natural features is required.

Above all, St David's was a successful cult that survived the transition from native Welsh belief to the more diverse loyalties of the Anglo-Norman world. Continuing study of the nature and location of the churches dedicated to St David in the light of wider parameters than those of this provisional study has, I believe, the potential to further elucidate the reasons for that success.[162]

[162] I am most grateful to the editors, J. Wyn Evans and J. Wooding, for their comments and corrections. Nancy Edwards, Morfydd Owen and Simon Taylor all kindly read drafts of this paper and I am greatly indebted to them for their several suggestions; any remaining errors are mine.

4

ST DAVIDS AND A NEW LINK
WITH THE HIBERNO-NORSE WORLD

Mark Redknap

The most extensive evidence for early medieval activity at St Davids takes two forms. The first is documentary;[1] the second is provided by stone sculpture. The Welsh annals record eleven raids by various groups on St Davids between 907 and 1091, which reflect its position as a centre of wealth and power by this time, and point to a wide recognition of both its prestige and the likelihood that it housed portable wealth in the form of precious objects and potential hostages. Viking raiders are specified ('heathens', 'pagans' or by name) in 982, 988, 999 (when Morgenau, bishop of *Menevia*, was killed by them),[2] 1001, 1022, 1073, 1080 (when bishop Abraham (1078–80) suffered the same fate as Morgenau),[3] 1089, and 1091.[4] These Vikings were principally based in Dublin, though raiders from other Irish ports, as well as the Isle of Man and Western Isles of Scotland, participated at times.[5]

The early medieval sculpture from St Davids and its environs is well known, having been studied by many scholars, including J. Romilly Allen, V.E. Nash-Williams and J.M. Lewis.[6] Most recently, Dr Nancy Edwards's reassessment of this sculpture has illustrated how it sheds interesting light on the different contacts between 'Dewisland' and the world beyond, during this period.[7] The earliest surviving sculpture from St Davids belongs to the ninth century, though the environs contain stones which date from the fifth and sixth centuries. The majority of the sculpture from the Cathedral Close and Pen-Arthur farm, situated a short distance to the north-west, are 'centred on the century or more before the installation in 1115 of the first Norman bishop, Bernard'.[8]

The subject of this short note represents another category of material culture which extends the boundaries of archaeological evidence for contact between the St Davids peninsula and the Hiberno-Norse world beyond: metalwork.

---

1   Records such as the Welsh annals, Asser's *Vita Ælfredi regis* and *Lives* of the Welsh Saints.
2   *ByT* (Pen. 20), 17
3   *Et Abraham a Gentilibus occiditur*; *ByT* (Pen. 20), 155.
4   *ByS*, 29, 45, 47, 49, 55, 79, 81, 83, 85; *ByT* (Pen. 20), 9, 10, 11, 12, 16, 17, 18.
5   Loyn, *The Vikings*; Wendy Davies, *Patterns*; Graham-Campbell, 'The early Viking age'.
6   J. Romilly Allen, 'Catalogue of the early Christian monuments'; Nash-Williams, *The Early Christian Monuments*; J.M. Lewis, 'A survey of the early Christian monuments'.
7   N. Edwards, 'Monuments', 53–77.
8   N. Edwards, 'Monuments', 72.

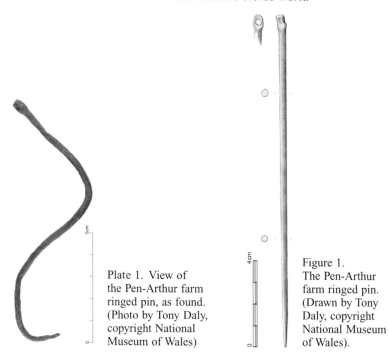

Plate 1. View of
the Pen-Arthur farm
ringed pin, as found.
(Photo by Tony Daly,
copyright National
Museum of Wales)

Figure 1.
The Pen-Arthur
farm ringed pin.
(Drawn by Tony
Daly, copyright
National Museum
of Wales).

The Pen-Arthur farm ringed pin

In 1997, a copper-alloy pin was found with the aid of a metal detector by Mr Roy Lewis in a field to the south of Pen-Arthur Farm, about ¾ mile (1.2km) to the north-north-west of St Davids Cathedral (NGR: SM 7465 2650; Map 5).[9]

Though much of its original surface has been lost through corrosion, the object can be identified as a ringed pin. The shaft has been bent out of shape into an s- configuration by plough damage and its ring is missing, and so classification is reliant on the pin shaft and head. The slightly expanded head (width 4mm) is perforated, and appears to be plain.[10] There are two opposed flattened areas about 20 mm below the head which are the result of blows distorting the shaft. In cross section, the upper half of the shaft is circular, while the lower half is irregular, with some facets. The original length of the pin when straight would have been about 160mm (reconstructed in Fig. 1).

Parallels and date

In form, ringed pins comprised a pin with a loose swivel ring inserted in a looped, perforated or pierced head. They were a form of dress fastener which developed as a result of contact between artisans between the Celtic West and sub-Roman Britain, and prototypes became very popular in Ireland.[11] A wide range of forms, in copper

---

[9] The ringed pin was generously donated by the finder to the National Museum of Wales (now known as Amgueddfa Cymru–National Museum Wales): NMW acc. no. 90.3H.

[10] There is the suggestion of a punched dot on one side, but this appears to be the result of corrosion.

[11] Armstrong, 'Irish bronze pins', 71ff.

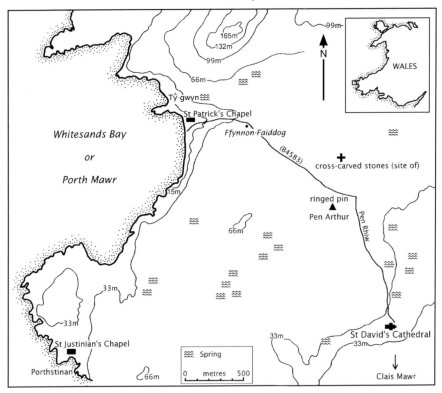

Map 5. Map showing the find-site of the Pen-Arthur farm ringed pin. (Map by Tony Daly).

alloy or iron, with spiral or plain rings, in either baluster or looped pin heads, have been found on crannogs and ringfort sites in Ireland.[12] With Viking settlement in Ireland from the second half of the ninth century, some jewellery types such as the ringed pin were adopted by the Hiberno-Norse during the Viking period.

The form of the Pen-Arthur Farm pin-head does not fall within the five main classes used for the Dublin ringed pins,[13] but is closest to the polyhedral pin-head of cubical form, faceted to create a polyhedron, with a slight collar below the head and 'slight traces of facetting'.[14] According to Fanning, about a third of the corpus of ringed pins known from Europe by 1990 had been found in medieval Dublin.[15]

The number of examples from Wales has until recently remained small, most of which are Insular ringed pins of pre-Viking date (fifth to eighth centuries) such as those from Gateholm Island (National Museum of Wales acc. no. 30.524/12)[16] and Caerwent, Monmouthshire (Newport Museum and Art Gallery acc. no. 84.123, 84.124).[17] A ringed pin of Irish type found on Norton Beach in Swansea Bay has

12 For example, Fanning, 'Some bronze ringed pins', 211–15.
13 Fanning, *Viking Age Ringed Pins*, 7–8.
14 E.g. DRP135; E71:9006; Fanning, *Viking Age Ringed Pins*, 84, fig. 53, right.
15 Fanning, *Viking Age Ringed Pins*, 1.
16 Lethbridge and David, 'Excavation of a house-site', fig. 6.3.
17 Knight, 'Late Roman and post-Roman Caerwent', fig. 7, 4–5.

a pin-head of looped type and is probably of late ninth- or early tenth-century date.[18] The Pen-Arthur Farm example is significant for it clearly belongs to the same class of ringed pin that has recently been discovered at the Viking-age site at Llanbedrgoch, Isle of Anglesey.[19] These share the same head form and similar shaft lengths, and include one with a plain head (found in 1999: SF 2189, length 167mm), one with slight traces of transverse grooves on the head (found in 2000: SF 2362, length 165mm) and another with four punched dots on both faces of the head (found in 1996: SF 929, length 147mm). While some of the ringed pins from Llanbedrgoch have been recovered from ploughsoil and consequently have insecure contexts, others are from contexts associated with the late ninth- or tenth-century phases of activity on the site.

Prior to the National Museum's excavations at Llanbedrgoch, isolated examples dating to the ninth and tenth centuries had been reported from Caerwent and Portskewett in Monmouthshire and Llanfairpwllgwyngyll on the Isle of Anglesey, though these all belong to different classes of ringed pin.[20] The Caerwent example is a Hiberno-Norse multiple-knob ringed pin similar to unprovenanced examples from Ireland and ninth-century parallels from Sogn and Tårnes, Norway.[21] The Portskewett example was found on the foreshore of the Severn Estuary, and is 154.5mm in length.[22] Its flattened lower shaft and ring are decorated with finely incised lines.[23] The Llanfairpwllgwyngyll pin, though missing its ring, has a large polyhedral head of cubical form decorated with a step pattern on the shaft which finds close parallels from the excavations in Dublin, such as several from Fishamble Street, one from a mid-tenth-century context and another dated to the second quarter of the tenth century (Dublin ringed pins 116 and 124 respectively).[24] This form has a wide distribution; findspots include a Norse grave at Tjørnuvík, Faroe Islands.[25]

A total of eleven ringed pin parts have been found at Llanbedrgoch, associated with the late ninth/tenth-century phase of activity at this *caput*, which is situated about 1km from the haven and beach at Red Wharf Bay. This compares with 19 ringed pin parts recorded from the trading centre at Meols on the Wirral (D. Griffiths, *in litt.*). The Pen-Arthur Farm pin is closest in form to the commonest class of the ringed pins from Llanbedrgoch, which can also be paralleled by examples from Chester.[26] On the basis of its form and comparison with examples from elsewhere in Wales and further afield, the Pen-Arthur Farm ringed pin is probably of tenth-century date.

[18] Redknap, 'An early medieval ringed pin', fig. 2.
[19] Excavations undertaken by the Department of Archaeology & Numismatics of the National Museum between 1994 and 2001 and in 2004; Redknap, 'Viking age settlement', fig. 11.
[20] Knight, 'Late Roman and post-Roman Caerwent', fig. 7 no. 7; Fox, 'An Irish bronze pin', 248.
[21] Newport Museum & Art Gallery D2.250; for parallels see Armstrong, 'Irish bronze pins', plate XIII, fig. 2, 3–6; Petersen, *British Antiquities*, 202–3, nos 14 and 14, figs 164–5.
[22] Newport Museum & Art Gallery 92.16; Redknap, *Vikings in Wales*, 82.
[23] For one example with a similar ring, see: Fanning, *Viking Age Ringed Pins*, DRP 14, dated to 'pre-935'.
[24] Fanning, *Viking Age Ringed Pins*, figs 50, 51.
[25] Dahl, 'The Norse settlement', fig. 23.
[26] E.g. Lloyd-Morgan, 'The artefacts', fig. 4.6.

Discussion

While it is frequently assumed that the location of the site of Viking-age *Menevia*, or Rhygyfarch's *Vallis Rosina*, lay under the present Cathedral or in its immediate vicinity, other sites have been proposed for Dewi's monastery, such as Whitesands Bay.[27] Certainly the large number of early medieval inscribed and decorated stones found during restoration of the Cathedral or associated with its Close, favour this location, lying in the pleasant valley (*Hoddnant*), for the site of *Menevia* raided during the tenth and eleventh centuries.

Routes to the west and south of the present site of the Cathedral linked it to White-sands Bay (a popular point of departure for Ireland), Porthstinan and Porth Clais, all of which had medieval chapels, some possibly having pre-Norman origins (St Patrick's Chapel, St Justinian's Chapel,[28] Capel-y-Pistyll, and St Non's Chapel). The findspot for the ringed pin lies between Whitesands Bay and St Davids, along one of these routes to the present Cathedral from the coast. Of relevance to this findspot are the four examples of early medieval stone sculpture published by Nash-Williams from Pen-Arthur Farm, all of which show Irish affinities.[29] One example is recorded on the OS map only about 300m to the north of the findspot of the ringed pin, in 'The Burrows'. One of the stones is inscribed with a Latin cross with bifid terminals, while the three others bear decorated roundels or incised cross with ring attributed to the tenth century. The long accepted association of the stones with *Ffynnon Pen-Arthur* to the east of the farmhouse is incorrect. For *ECMW* 374 and 375, Westwood recorded that they were 'said to have originally been placed upright round a holy well at two fields' distance from Pen Arthur farm-house',[30] while another (*ECMW* 373) was used as a gatepost close to the farm-house. It has recently been shown that two stones (*ECMW* 373 and 374) were found near Parc-y-Berth (two fields north of the farmhouse; SM 7490 2680), marked on the 1964 1:10,560 OS map of the area. It has been argued that they originally came from nearby moorland to the west where a partially buried stone with an inscription and a ring-cross (probably *ECMW* 376) was described by an anonymous sixteenth-century writer (at approx. NGR: SM 747 269).[31] The location of a cemetery between St Patrick's Chapel and cemetery at Whitesands Bay and St Davids itself may be indicated by the suggestion that the bishop of St Davids retained a small parcel of land at 'Arthur's Stone' into the late nineteenth century because it marked an ancient graveyard.[32]

The Pen-Arthur ringed pin is similar in date to three of the Pen-Arthur stones, and similarly reflects contact with Ireland at this period, though it does not neces-sarily constitute evidence for specific events recorded in the Welsh annals. It was discovered some 300m south-east of the site of postulated graveyard, and a number of possible contexts may be proposed for its loss. The first is that the ringed pin could have served as a shroud fastening, as suggested for the Llanfairpwllgwyngyll find, which was found in the parish churchyard during gravedigging. This would raise the possibility that a cemetery operating in the tenth century may once have existed in the vicinity of the original locations of the Pen-Arthur stones (*ECMW*

27 E.g. Dawson, 'The monastery', 1–20; J.Wyn Evans, 'St David and St Davids', 12–13.
28 Boake, 'Report on the excavation', 381f.
29 They now form part of the Cathedral *Lapidarium*.
30 Westwood, *Lapidarium Walliae*, 128.
31 Edwards, 'Monuments in a landscape', 70.
32 Map 5; Edwards, 'Monuments', 70.

374/376), and extended an unknown distance. A second, and more likely, explanation is that it was a casual loss, which may be supported by the bent nature of the pin and the fact that the ring has become detached from its pin. A third possibility is that the pin represents settlement or related activity, for the flattened areas below the pinhead, could be the result of metalworking (recycling). However, this remains unproven in the absence of further supporting evidence. The ringed pin is a significant addition to the small group of tenth-century finds from Pembrokeshire with Hiberno-Norse associations. These include a 'capped' oval weight from Freshwater West, Castlemartin (weight 238.9gm),[33] and a small fragment of another capped lead weight from the vicinity of Milford Haven.[34] A sword pommel of trilobe form from a site near Pembroke, Milford Haven may be slightly later in date.[35] A fragmentary silver penny of Eadred (946–55) from St Davids Head was found at the top of the beach at Whitesands Bay, and was presumed to have fallen from an eroded cliff.[36] Anglo-Saxon coins from Wales are scarce, and the findspot of this coin from northwest England on a beach facing the southern tip of Ireland was seen to support the argument that many of these coins were the product of Viking contact. The closest coin hoard within the distribution from St Davids to Caerwent in the east is that from Laugharne of about 60 reform pennies of Eadgar, deposited *ca* 975.[37] The known distribution of Hiberno-Norse ringed pins similarly mirrors trade routes in the Irish Sea and North Atlantic areas, while the geographical position of St Davids exposed it to sea-borne contacts, both hostile and friendly. The precise circumstances of loss, in most cases, remain speculative, but the Pen-Arthur ringed pin supports growing evidence from Wales for the circulation of Hiberno-Norse material culture around the Irish Sea during the tenth century.[38]

[33] Grimes, 'A leaden tablet', 416–17.
[34] NMW acc. no. 92.12H.
[35] NMW acc. no. 96.17H; Redknap, *The Vikings*, 50, ill. 61 (right).
[36] Found by Ms A. Lewis and A.W. Bartlett in 1985: Blackburn and Bonser, 'Single finds', 68.
[37] Dykes, 'Anglo-Saxon coins', 27.
[38] I would like to express my thanks to the following for their various contributions to this paper: Roy Lewis for promptly reporting the ringed pin and donating it to the national collections; from Amgueddfa Cymru—National Museum Wales, Tony Daly for the illustrations; the Department of Photography for Fig. 1; Edward Besly for information on coin finds.

5

WHICH TEXT IS RHYGYFARCH'S *LIFE* OF ST DAVID?

Richard Sharpe

Rhygyfarch ap Sulien (1056/7–1099) belonged to the family that controlled the *clas* of Llanbadarn in the eleventh century.[1] His father Sulien was bishop of St Davids, and Rhygyfarch's *Life* of St David has always been in some sense a well-known work. He identifies himself as the author in the concluding chapter, where he modestly asks his attentive readers to pray 'for me, who am named Rhygyfarch and who rashly applied my inadequate talent to this subject'. This sentence is included in two versions of the text, however, and at different periods now one, now the other has been accorded precedence as representing most nearly the original work of the author.[2]

From the twelfth century the shorter version was quite widely available in manuscript; an abridged copy was first printed in 1516, and other printed editions of all or part of the work appeared in 1645, 1668, and 1691.[3] The latest of these editions, in *Anglia Sacra*, edited by Henry Wharton (1664–1695), was the first to draw on the longer text preserved uniquely in a manuscript from Brecon priory which by the seventeenth century was bound with other items in the library assembled by the famous book-collector Sir Robert Cotton (1571–1631), where it was shelved under the bust of the Roman Emperor Vespasian with the shelf-mark Vespasian A. xiv. Wharton had taken as his text the version in another of Sir Robert Cotton's manuscripts, Vitellius E. vii, which was a copy of the *Life* as revised by Gerald of

---

[1] Lloyd, 'Bishop Sulien', 1–6; J. Conway Davies, *Episcopal Acts*, 2, 493–506; Lapidge, 'The Welsh-Latin poetry', 68–106.

[2] The editions to which I shall mainly refer are Wade-Evans, 'Rhygyvarch's Life', 1–73; Wade-Evans, *VSBG*; J.W. James, *Rhigyfarch's Life*. The quotation is from § 67. In 1985 in Lapidge and Sharpe, *Bibliography*, 14, I regrettably cited James's edition as the preferred text. I subsequently changed my mind and indicated this in Sharpe, *A Handlist*, 458. The present paper seeks to justify my view that the longer, Vespasian text used by Wade-Evans better represents Rhygyfarch's work than the shorter text edited by James.

[3] The edition of 1516 is a rearrangement of John of Tynemouth's *Sanctilogium Angliae Walliae Scotiae et Hiberniae*, augmented by the addition of a prologue and fifteen further Lives, printed by Wynkyn de Worde as *Noua Legenda Anglie* in 1516 (and also ed. Horstmann); the *Life* of St David is John's abridgement, I.254–62. The other early editions are John Colgan [1592–1658], *Acta Sanctorum Hiberniae* (1645), 425–32 (text of the Irish abridgement, some comparison made with the 1516 edition, and Colgan also knew of Gerald's *Life* and John of Tynemouth's); [The Bollandists], *Acta Sanctorum*, Mar. I (1668), 38–47 (text of the Digby family from an English manuscript then in Utrecht); and Henry Wharton, *Anglia Sacra* (1691), II.628–40 (text as rewritten by Gerald of Wales with selected variants from Vespasian A. xiv as 'Ricemarus'), 645–7 (two lengthy additions from Vespasian A. xiv, §§ 20–31 and 54–8). Note that James (xxiii, xxxviii) mistakenly transfers 1645 as year of publication from Colgan's *Acta* to the Bollandists' *Acta Sanctorum*; at p. xxix he gives 1636 as the date of publication of Colgan's edition and mistakenly names Colgan's expressed source, Bishop David Rothe, as Bishop Richard Routh.

Wales towards the end of the twelfth century.[4] Wharton realised that the Vespasian text was fuller, and he printed extracts from it to complement Gerald's version. In 1853 the complete text from the Vespasian manuscript was put into print by William Jenkins Rees (1772–1855), a graduate of Wadham College, Oxford, who was rector of Cascob in Radnorshire from 1807 until his death and from 1820 also a prebendary of Christ's College, Brecon.[5] This long version of the *Life* was re-edited by Arthur Wade Wade-Evans (1875–1964) in 1913; Wade-Evans included an English translation with his edition of the Latin.[6] The translation was reprinted by the Society for Promoting Christian Knowledge in 1923, and the Latin text was reprinted with other *Lives* of Welsh saints from the Vespasian and other manuscripts in Wade-Evans's volume *Vitae sanctorum Britanniae et genealogiae* in 1944. Wade-Evans's text remained the standard one until 1967, when John Williams James (1889–1983), chancellor of Bangor cathedral (1940–64), brought out a new edition, on which he had worked intermittently since 1930. James was the first to attempt a full investigation of the textual history, so that his edition carried a great deal more academic authority than the earlier editions. He argued that the Vespasian text was a reworking of the *Life*, made at Brecon around the year 1200 but incorporating some changes made a little earlier at St Davids around 1190. He therefore presented instead a text that relied largely on two groups of manuscripts, both of which bore witness to what he called 'the basic mid twelfth-century Latin text'.[7] In so doing he claimed to have recovered the text as revised at St Davids for Bishop Bernard, who held the see from 1115 to 1148. James was elusive on the subject of how far he thought this mid-twelfth-century text differed from the text as composed by Rhygyfarch, but he held that it was not possible to get back nearer to that original. James was conscious that he was going against what had been the general opinion, and he justified this by claiming that he followed the evidence: 'If any long-cherished beliefs will be repelled by my conclusions, I can plead only a convinced acceptance of the evidence of the texts'.[8]

[4] The version by Gerald of Wales has been printed by Brewer: *Opera* III.377–404. Brewer's text was taken from Wharton (including his notes from 'Ricemarus') in the belief that the Vitellius manuscript had been destroyed in the Cotton fire of 1731. Brewer also compared the extracts from Gerald's *Life* quoted by Archbishop James Ussher in *Ecclesiarum Britannicarum Antiquitates*. He seems to have assumed that Ussher's quotations were textually independent, but Ussher was a regular user of Sir Robert Cotton's library and may have quoted from the Vitellius manuscript. This was badly damaged in the fire. A second copy exists in British Library, MS Royal 13 C. I (s. xv), fols 171r–180v; the text here was augmented with miracle-stories extending as late as 1388, and the surviving copy was made in the 1450s for the antiquary William Worcestre. The Royal Library catalogue suggests that this may have been the copy used by Ussher; in his time the Royal manuscripts were kept at St James's Palace, where he could have had access.

[5] Rees, *Lives*, 117–44, with translation, 418–48. The edition was produced by Rees's brother who ran the family's printing business in Llandovery.

[6] There is an account of Wade-Evans's published works by Bachelléry, 'Nécrologie A.W. Wade-Evans', 165–8.

[7] James, *Rhigyfarch's Life*, xxx.

[8] James, *Rhigyfarch's Life*, vii. James's edition appears not to have been widely reviewed, but those reviews that I have found accept his findings. So H.D. Emanuel (40–2) who makes a small number of literal corrections, welcomes James's text as 'a firm textual foundation for further studies'; J.E. Caerwyn Williams (183–5), in the first sentence of his review, says, 'The value of this volume can scarcely be overstated'; and Thomas Jones (156–7) – who had excoriated the deficiences of Wade-Evans's *VSBG*) – accepted all of James's conclusions with the qualification that James's assertion that the textual history could be traced no farther back than ' "two separate copies of an archetype *in the possession of Bernard* ...", although credible on a priori grounds, cannot be other than slightly dogmatic' (Thomas Jones, 'Review of James, *Rhigyfarch's Life*'). Others have also endorsed James's

While I do not dispute that James edited a mid-twelfth-century version of the text that enjoyed some medieval circulation in England and in Normandy, I shall argue that he erred in his judgement of the Vespasian text and that all his reasons for denying its priority were mistaken. When James's assumptions and arguments are cleared away, it becomes evident that Vespasian has preserved for us something very close to Rhygyfarch's text and that its deviations are minor errors of copying that can usually be put right.

James's account of previous scholarship on the text catalogues the stages by which more and more manuscripts were identified.[9] From Wade-Evans's 1913 edition he quotes a few telling points:[10]

> In his Introduction (pp. xi–xiv), following Baring-Gould and Fisher (vol. ii, pp. 285–6), he calls the Vespasian text 'the best ... the fullest, and so far as I know quite unique ... There are at least some slight omissions and alterations', and '... mistakes'. The other Latin texts (excluding the versions of Giraldus Cambrensis and John of Tynemouth) are comprehensively styled 'anonymous Norman-French versions of Rhygyfarch's original work, some as old as, if not older than, the Vespasian MS.' (p. xi); and he then ingenuously admits (p. xii), 'and certainly, all these recensions, and others which are said to exist, have never been collated'.

At the end of his paragraph, James dismissively adds, 'This confession speaks for itself and for the critical worth of his conclusions. Comment is superfluous'. I do not know why James was so condescending about Wade-Evans, but it is clear that this account of his predecessor's work was carefully worded to undermine Wade-Evans's credibility. It implies that Wade-Evans's valuation of the Vespasian text was derivative and came from the popularizers, Sabine Baring-Gould (1834–1924) and John Fisher (1862–1930).[11] It imputes error to the Vespasian text, as if Wade-Evans was admitting that his judgement was ill-founded, and it exhibits Wade-Evans's attitude as dismissive towards the twelfth-century Anglo-Norman manuscripts on which James relied. In particular, Wade-Evans is made 'ingenuously' to confess that he had not bothered to do his homework on these other versions. Elsewhere, James writes:

> Wade-Evans has boldly identified the Vespasian with Rhigyfarch's original, although he admits that none of the various manuscripts has ever been collated and compared with others, nor even with the texts of Giraldus's *Vita*.[12]

In contrast, we are meant to see James as the real scholar whose conclusions, based on laborious examination of the manuscript evidence, command a different order of respect and trust.

James gives a concise overview of the period of his work on the text.[13] He studied the manuscript recently acquired by Cardiff Public Library in 1930–31, when Miss

findings, among them Michael Richter ('The Life of St David' 381), 'The new edition ... has provided a sound basis for all future research in this branch of Welsh hagiography. ... The important conclusion reached by the editor is that the Vespasian recension can no longer be taken as the authoritative version'; and D.S. Evans, *The Welsh Life*, xxxix–xlii, who concisely restates James's views.

9   James, *Rhigyfarch's Life*, xxxviii–xli.
10 James, *Rhigyfarch's Life*, xxxix. The elipses are James's.
11 Baring-Gould and Fisher, *The Lives*, II.285–6. J.W. James, *Rhigyfarch's Life*, xxxix, offers a slighting summary of their work, implying that they could not be bothered to refer to manuscripts specifically and that their judgement between 'amplification' and 'abridgement' was derisory.
12 James, *Rhigyfarch's Life*, xxxii.
13 James, *Rhigyfarch's Life*, viii.

92

E.G. Parker of the Bodleian Library in Oxford collated for him the manuscripts in Oxford and Cambridge. At that date James himself was preparing his dissertation for the degree of Doctor of Divinity of Durham university.[14] At that stage Sir John Edward Lloyd urged James to publish his findings about Rhygyfarch, but circumstances prevented his doing so. After 1946 work resumed on a wider front but was again laid aside. Then in 1959 the bishop of St Davids, John Richards Richards, asked him to lecture on the *Life* of St David, and with the help of Dr Hywel Emanuel from Aberystwyth the work was brought to a conclusion.

By the time the work was finished, James had knowledge of twenty-five Latin manuscripts and four significant early printings of a Latin text. He also refers to ten copies in Welsh, but these are given little discussion.[15] He divided the Latin texts into five 'recensions'. His 'Nero recension' and 'Digby recension' are in reality one and the same, being two family groups of manuscripts witnessing to what is essentially one text, the shorter version which I shall refer to as the Nero–Digby text. His 'Giraldus recension' is the reworking made by Gerald of Wales. His fourth recension is the 'Vespasian recension', that is the longer text previously published by Rees and Wade-Evans, though James added the testimony of two abridgements. Finally his fifth grouping, the 'Irish recension', is an abbreviation of the Nero–Digby text from a well-known Irish collection of Lives of mainly Irish saints.[16] After cataloguing the manuscripts grouped in this way, James offers an analysis of the relationship of the various versions, and it is the reasoning here that most exposes the flaws of his method.

Assumption plays a large part. There is, first, an assumption that the age of the manuscript witnesses provides a guide to the age of the text transmitted. Thus, 'of the five recensions of the *Vita Dauidis* only two, the Nero and the Digby, can be followed back to the mid-twelfth century',[17] 'the Giraldus recension – nearest in age to the Nero and the Digby',[18] and more fully:[19]

> If Giraldus wrote his *Vita* in 1176, using a text of the Nero recension, and palaeographic evidence makes the MS. Digby 112 contemporary with the Nero E. I, then there were three recensions in existence before there is any evidence of the Vespasian text: and all three, well before 1200, are united in challenging the authenticity of one-fifth of the Vespasian text, viz. the 1,600 words of its 7,900 which are not elsewhere recorded.

A prevailing thread in James's reasoning is that the Vespasian text, in a manuscript which he describes as early-thirteenth-century, could not be earlier than the shorter text attested in no fewer than six twelfth-century manuscripts. This assumption is false: it is common for a text to survive only in manuscripts much later than the author's time, and the fact that a related text survives in older copies does not mean that the text itself has to be older. James avoided this error in his consideration of the

---

14 James, 'A history'.
15 James, *Rhigyfarch's Life*, xl, cites anonymously his own paper, James, 'The Welsh version'. For a more up-to-date discussion, consult Evans, *Buched Dewi,* and a revised English edition, *The Welsh Life,* which prints the text from the fourteenth-century Book of the Anchorite of Llanddewibrefi (Oxford, Jesus College, MS 119). D.S. Evans, *The Welsh Life,* lv, has increased the number of known copies to fourteen but discusses only five.
16 The collection in Oxford, Bodleian Library, MS Rawlinson B. 485, is discussed by Sharpe, *Medieval Irish Saints' Lives*, 247–96.
17 James, *Rhigyfarch's Life*, xxx.
18 James, *Rhigyfarch's Life*, xxx.
19 James, *Rhigyfarch's Life*, xxxiii.

Life of St David by Gerald of Wales, which had survived in a single copy made (so James mistakenly thought) in the fifteenth century, from where it was transcribed by Wharton and printed in 1691.[20]

I cannot help wondering whether James was started off on the wrong path by an early influence. Cardiff Public Library in April 1924 bought a collection of saints's Lives from the dispersal of the library of Sir George Wombwell of Newburgh Priory in the North Riding of Yorkshire. The manuscript had no shelf-mark when James used it, but it is now MS 1. 381. We are only concerned with part 2, written (according to Neil Ker) in the first half of the twelfth century and including an early copy of the *Life* of St David.[21] James thought it was hardly later than the copies that he took as the types of the Nero and Digby families; he regarded it as only slightly inferior to the Nero copy. Soon after it was acquired, the Cardiff librarian asked for an opinion on the *Life* of St David from a curator of manuscripts at the British Museum, where Sir Robert Cotton's books, including the Nero and Vespasian texts, were then kept:

> In 1925 the Librarian of the Cardiff Public Library obtained the opinion of the British Museum experts on the text of the *Vita Dauidis* in a manuscript which they had purchased in 1924. Mr J. A. Herbert of the British Museum reported that he considered the Cardiff MS. earlier than the Vespasian A. xiv, but later than the Nero E. i: 'its text was in very close agreement with that of the Nero, but both manuscripts differed considerably from the text of the Vespasian MS. It was possible that the Nero and Cardiff texts represented the original recension, and the Vespasian MS. a later expansion.'[22]

James goes on to say that he himself, 'accepting Mr J.A. Herbert's conclusions, collated the Cardiff text with that of the Vespasian, and sent his collated notes to Dr Hunt, Keeper of the Western Manuscripts at the Bodleian Library, who had them compared with the relevant texts' in Oxford and Cambridge, 'with the result that the overwhelming proportion of the readings in those manuscripts was found in agreement with the Nero–Cardiff texts; and the Vespasian text appeared as a

---

20 James, *Rhigyfarch's Life*, xii. James gives no account of the Vitellius manuscript in his list of copies of Gerald's text; he had presumably accepted that it was destroyed, and I do not know his basis for this date. In my view, it is not correct: three *Lives* were the first items in the manuscript (Gerald's *Life* of St Æthelberht, a *Life* of St Patrick, and Gerald's *Life* of St David), from which a few charred leaves survive; the writing, however, is clear enough to say that these texts were copied around the beginning of the thirteenth century. I note that Ludwig Bieler had hesitated between dating it to late twelfth century and first half of the thirteenth century (Bieler, '*Anecdotum Patricianum*', 220–37).

21 The manuscript was described by Ker, *Medieval Manuscripts*, II.348–9. J.W. James, *Rhigyfarch's Life*, xv, observed that the manuscript may have come from Dover priory, but this rests on a confusion of part 2 (fols 81–146) with part 1 (fols 1–80), a manuscript of somewhat later date that has at the foot of fol. 2r a Dover shelfmark matching BM1. 169 in the catalogue of the library there made in 1389 by Br John Whitfield (Stoneman, *Dover Priory*, 99). The two parts were bound together in England, probably in the early seventeenth century, when both belonged to Sir Robert Cotton. That part 2 was written at Barking is inferred from its beginning with Goscelin's Lives of the saints of Barking (though this inference really only applies to its first booklet, fols 81–96); its remaining at Barking through the middle ages from that fact that a distinctive hand of the early sixteenth century annotated both this book and Cardiff Public Library, MS 3. 833 (Ker, *Medieval Manuscripts*, II.371), which has still decipherable the *ex libris* of Barking abbey. This may disguise complexity, however, for fols. 81–146 are not a palaeographical unity; of the four booklets, the *Life* of St David is the third, self-contained, fols 121–129 (see below, 104).

22 James, *Rhigyfarch's Life*, xl; he cites a work published by Cardiff Public Library soon after it acquired the manuscript: Anon., *Catalogue of Manuscripts*: v–vi (preface signed by Harry Farr) and 3 (Herbert's description of the manuscript).

more or less isolated version'.[23] Implicit here is a second assumption, that the larger number of witnesses reflects the priority or superiority of the Nero–Digby text. But might there be another, less obvious assumption, that the opinion of an expert from the British Museum outweighed the views of dear old Wade-Evans? Mr Herbert perhaps expressed an opinion that it was 'possible' that Vespasian was a later text, not that there was reason to think so. I cannot help wondering whether he was in the first place consulted for his palaeographical opinion on the manuscript so recently acquired in Cardiff or perhaps on its dating relative to other manuscripts containing the *Life* of St David. As an assistant keeper working under Julius Gilson, the keeper of manuscripts who was largely responsible for the outstanding catalogue of the old Royal manuscripts in the British Museum, published in 1921, he would have been trained to make a comparison with other copies in the collection and did so.[24] It is hard to see that he would have been consulted for a considered text-historical judgement on the *Life*, yet James's tendency to confuse manuscript-copy and text led him to treat it as such, turning Herbert's opinion into 'conclusions'. Ironically, there is a question-mark as to whether the conclusions were Herbert's at all: the passage quoted by James is from the preface to the catalogue, signed by the Cardiff librarian, Harry Farr (1874–1968).

James's next assumption came in part from the biblical scholarship of his time. Textual critics who worked on the Bible had long favoured the shorter reading, and James treated this as a rule, applying it to a medieval text where it was certainly not appropriate.[25] His adherence to the 'shorter reading' (his quotation marks designate the supposed rule) emerges only obliquely. It comes out most precisely in his comments on comparing the Nero and Digby groupings of manuscripts. The two families differed in about 61 readings; 'of these the Nero reading is preferred 47 times and the Digby 14 times', and he goes on to say that 'the 47 preferred Nero readings include instances of the "shorter reading", better grammatical forms, and words that yield the better sense'.[26] This is in fact a misapplication of the principle applied in biblical criticism, where the shorter reading represents the more original version than the longer reading; that is, it is a principle to help judge between the original text and a rewritten version, not a text-critical rule to eliminate errors of transcription. James used the principle more appropriately in an overall appraisal of the tradition, though its purpose was obviously to reinforce his rejection of the Vespasian text. He briefly compared the various texts of the *Life* of St David with the *Life* of St Cadog, analysed by Hywel Emanuel as a composite text deriving from

---

23 James, *Rhigyfarch's Life*, xl. There appears to be some confusion. Here and elsewhere (viii) James attributes this phase of delegated collation by Miss Parker to the period 1930–31, but Dr Richard Hunt was not appointed keeper of western manuscripts until 1945; Edmund Craster was keeper until 1931, when he was succeeded by Edgar Lobel. I am grateful to Mr Steven Tomlinson of the Bodleian Library for the following information. Miss Evaline Gertrude Parker was the daughter of George Parker (1838–1906), who was on the staff of the library from 1854 until his death. About that date Miss Parker started doing work for the Library, answering enquiries that involved more time than the regular staff could give, although not apparently on the establishment. This continued until 1911. Over the next twenty years or more, she seems to have acted as an agent for those who wanted transcriptions or similar work, but nothing appears in library records.

24 John Alexander Herbert (1862–1948) is best known for his work on illuminated manuscripts of the high middle ages and on medieval English and French romances.

25 '*Breuior lectio potior*' was the first of fifteen text-critical principles defined by Johann Jakob Griesbach (1745–1812) in relation to the Greek New Testament, though he allowed circumstances in which it was not to be preferred (Metzger, *The Text*, 120). The principle was always more favoured by biblical scholars than others.

26 James, *Rhigyfarch's Life*, xxx.

seven sources.[27] James claimed to detect only three or four elements of composition in the Vespasian text, but he then generalized:

> Such editing was a common feature in the Middle Ages, and scarcely a document, secular or ecclesiastical, has reached us as it left its author's hand. The Book of Llan Dav, in particular, illustrates such a *process of expansion* (my emphasis).[28]

James's approach was very different from Emanuel's, and the composite nature of the *Life* of St Cadog was something he illustrated rather than assumed. James was unable to show that the Vespasian text was composite in anything like the same way, but in the reading of the textual tradition that he had built around Herbert's opinion Vespasian had to be seen as interpolated. Longer meant worse. James's holding to this view even when he could see that all of the later versions of the *Life* were abbreviated rather than expanded may seem perverse, and one suspects that the conclusion dictated the reasoning where the Vespasian text was concerned.

The assumptions so far identified lie in the background to a considerable extent. Failure to distinguish copy from text, allowing manuscript-date to sway one's view of textual history, favouring the shorter over the longer reading whenever a choice is required, are all aspects of James's textual principles, and we might have expected them to influence his work on any text. A particular assumption, however, plays a large part in his explicit reasoning here. I am convinced that here more than anywhere else the stated reasoning did not lead to the conclusion but was rather a contrived route to reach the preconceived answer. I refer to the argument for rejecting the Vespasian text, based on Gerald of Wales's contribution to the evolution of the text.

It appears to be assumed that, if the Vespasian text had existed when Gerald wrote his paraphrase of the Nero–Digby text, he must have known it. He allows no room for the possibility that Gerald, never a diligent antiquary, might not have known the text; still less that the Nero–Digby text might have suited Gerald's needs better:

> How can Giraldus's omissions of all the local traditions peculiar to the Vespasian text be explained? Is it conceivable that with all his Pembrokeshire antecedents, his strong sense of local patriotism, his upbringing in St Davids itself, his obvious acquaintance with the locality and its traditions, his consuming ambition for that see and none other, and his readiness to sell his soul for the success of his enterprise, is it conceivable that he would have knowingly falsified the traditions as recorded in the Vespasian text, substituting for them creations of his own imagination? The only possible conclusion is that Giraldus was totally unacquainted with the Vespasian text, which must have come into being later than 1176, if not after 1184, and that he had written his *Vita* as a young prebendary and archdeacon in 1172–6, soon after his return to Wales from the University of Paris. The matter in his own work would represent the local traditions current in St Davids in 1150–75, whereas that in the Vespasian MS. represents those of 1184–1200. Had he previously known of the latter, there would have been no occasion to reproduce the former in his own work. The only conclusion possible from the evidence is that Giraldus wrote his *Vita* about 1176, when the text of the Vespasian was as yet unknown in St Davids. The only type of text used by Giraldus was a text of the Nero recension.[29]

---

27 Emanuel, 'An analysis', 217–27 (which made use of his unpublished dissertation, 'The Latin Life of St Cadoc').
28 James, *Rhigyfarch's Life*, xii.
29 James, *Rhigyfarch's Life*, xxxii.

The last short sentence is a statement of fact. In spite of the claim to work 'from the evidence', however, the rest of this, with its rhetoric and its repetitions, is no more than special pleading founded on a protested assumption. Gerald wrote a paraphrase of the Nero–Digby version of the *Life* of St David, and he did so, as he explains in his preface, in order to provide a more elegant version. If the rest of James's blustering was valid, it would mean that the passages peculiar to the Vespasian were in some stronger sense pertinent to Gerald's purpose than the four fifths of the text shared by Vespasian and Nero–Digby. If that were so, he might have made the point by citing a few sentences to illustrate. James does not even illustrate what Gerald added to Nero–Digby nor attempt to show in what way it served his metropolitan cause; indeed Gerald's purpose in rewriting the *Life* is assumed. The texts do not support the bluster, and there may be many reasons why Gerald worked from the mid-twelfth-century version rather than the late-eleventh-century original of Rhygyfarch's *Life*.

More revealing is what James does with the dating of Gerald's work. Having confounded the date of the manuscript with the date of the text, the Vespasian text for James took its shape around 1200. Before James, students of Gerald's career had dated his rewriting the Life to the period 1199×1203, when he was most involved with his ambition to be consecrated to the see in circumstances that would confirm its independent metropolitan status. This date was inconvenient for James, since it might mean that Gerald had chosen to use Nero–Digby at a time when at Brecon, his own archdeaconry, there was a copy of the Vespasian text. He therefore redated Gerald's writing the *Life* to a time when he was first nominated to the see in 1176, or rather to the years between his return to Wales around 1172 and his nomination by the chapter of St Davids. This would make the *Life* of St David Gerald's earliest substantial work, predating his first published work by at least a dozen years. The only certainty is that the *Life* was finished before Gerald put together his *Symbolum electorum*, in which around 1199 he collected specimens of his fine writing, including the preface to the *Life* of St David.[30] The probability is that it dates from the 1190s and was not motivated by the metropolitan cause at the turn of the century.[31]

The point of this use of Gerald's *Life* in James's argument is simple. It was the only way James could find to make an argument that Vespasian did not exist significantly earlier than the manuscript in which the text has reached us. It was meant to justify the notion that the shorter text preserved in older copies was the earlier and more authentic version of the *Life*. But what is claimed to rest on evidence, and thereby to vindicate James's 'modern' textual scholarship over Wade-Evans's lazy methods and acceptance of what had become tradition, turns out to depend rather on a series of assumptions. It even seems that James had begun by taking his conclusion from J.A. Herbert.

James offers no coherent discussion of the Vespasian text, still less a reading of how its peculiar passages – additions, as he would have it – change the argument and purpose of the text. He had made up his mind that it was unimportant, in spite of all that local interest that he had assumed would have demanded Gerald's attention.

---

30 Gerald of Wales, *Symbolum electorum*, IV.23. Only Books I–II of this work have been edited by Brewer (*Opera* I.197–364); he gives a synopsis of Books III–IV (*Opera* I.391–5), but the witness of the *Symbolum* to the text of these prefaces has generally not been used by editors.

31 Richter, 'The Life of St David', 381–6.

Ever since its inclusion in W. J. Rees's *Lives of the Cambro-British Saints* (Llandovery, 1853), this version of the *Vita* has been the best known, and it has acquired an importance out of all proportion to its date and critical value, and exaggerated claims have been made for it by enthusiastic students.[32]

A stranger reason is given elsewhere: 'The presence of the Vespasian MS. in the British Museum led to its becoming the most influential of all the texts of Rhigyfarch's *Vita*'. And he goes on:

> But notwithstanding, it cannot be regarded as a primary text. Unlike the Nero E. I, the Cardiff MS., the Rouen U. 141, and the Saint-Omer 716, it is not an independent copy of a vanished archetype. It is only a thirteenth-century copy of a very late twelfth-century copy (*c.* 1190 AD) of a mid-twelfth-century text of the Nero type, of which there are four twelfth-century copies earlier than it – not to mention two twelfth-century copies of the Digby group – all six twelfth-century copies displaying among themselves a considerable degree of agreement in opposition to the characteristic Vespasian readings. Whatever may be said of it, the Vespasian text is only a secondary text, derived from the text of Rouen U. 141.[33]

Apart from the restatement of false inferences based on mistaken assumptions in textual criticism, what case does James make to support his contention that Vespasian has been interpolated at a late date? Two categories of 'late' alteration are discussed.

James's first class of alterations 'comprises the identification of persons and places in Pembrokeshire which differ totally from those of Giraldus'.[34] Nine examples are given. In view of the thrust of what James has said, the reader may suppose that names are changed to alter the localization of the text, perhaps even to reflect a new agenda. Far from it. No alternative names are cited from Gerald's version, and the names concerned are absent from the Nero–Digby text; since that was what Gerald used, he would have had to make up alternative names if he wanted to insert names, but he did not. These names must be either additions in Vespasian where there was no name in Nero–Digby or omissions in Nero–Digby where Vespasian has a name. The latter is typical of hagiographical rewriting. James's mention of 'those of Giraldus' (where 'those' must refer to persons and places imputed to but absent from Gerald's text) is rhetoric to make a trivial reduction of names by a hagiographical abbreviator appear more significant. In three cases the names in question occur in other places in both texts, and their repetition or omission has no effect on the sense. In two examples the name in question is the River Teifi in Ceredigion, not near St Davids. The others are of very minor local interest, and in three cases derive from sections which Nero–Digby had reduced to a single sentence. It is far-fetched to present these changes as significant additions to assert the agenda of the church of St Davids around 1190.

For the one change of this class that matters James gives an incorrect reference, citing for '*Veterem Rubum*' § 13 instead of § 14. He discussed the passage in the context of Gerald's work.[35] St David has returned from founding monasteries in England and Gwent. The Vespasian text reads, *ad locum quo prius proficiscens exulauerat, .i. ad Veterem Rubum, rediit* ('he returned to the place from which he

---

[32] James, *Rhigyfarch's Life*, xxv.
[33] James, *Rhigyfarch's Life*, xxxvii.
[34] James, *Rhigyfarch's Life*, xxxiv.
[35] James, *Rhigyfarch's Life*, xxxi.

had been separated when he set out, namely Vetus Rubus'). He dwelt there for some time, but then chose to move at the prompting of an angel; *ostenditque mihi locum ex quo pauci in infernum intrabunt*; *omnis enim qui in cimiterio illius loci sana fide sepultus fuerit, misericordiam consequetur* ('for [the angel] showed me a place from where few will go to perdition; for everyone who is buried in good faith in the graveyard of that place will obtain forgiveness'). The place to which David and his followers travel is *Rosinam Vallem, quam uulgari nomine Hodnant Brittones uocitant* ('*Vallis Rosina*, which the British call in their common tongue Hoddnant'). This latter is where St Davids now stands. The change of sense introduced by the Nero–Digby version is to omit the place-name of *Vetus Rubus* and to rephrase the angel's direction to include the word 'nearby': *est autem alius prope locus, in cuius cimiterio quicumque salua fide humati fuerint uix eorum unus inferni penas luet* ('there is another place nearby where scarcely one of those buried in the saving faith in its graveyard will pay the pains of perdition'). With Nero–Digby as his source, Gerald's variation was *alius non hinc procul locus* ('another place not far from here'). James, taking Vespasian as the later version, draws the inference that this seemingly small alteration gives rise 'to the false conclusion that St David's *Vetus Rubus* was the Cardiganshire Hen Fynyw near Aberaeron instead of a forgotten site in the vicinity of the present St Davids cathedral'. If this late-twelfth-century interpolator is focused on St Davids, why should he have forgotten the local site and its story and instead looked further afield for a place whose name matched the story? It is surely the reverse: Rhygyfarch was a Llanbadarn man with strong interests in Ceredigion, and the St David of his story moved from *Vetus Rubus*, that is Hen Fynyw, to Hoddnant and St Davids. The name Mynyw (Latinized as *Menevia*) is unusual, deriving from Irish, and it moved with him.[36] The adjectives *Vetus* or *Hen*, that is 'old' or 'former' *Mynyw*, show that Rhygyfarch recognized this move; his loyalty to the site in Ceredigion, however, kept him from using the old name *Mynyw* in reference to the new site, St Davids. Whoever shortened his text to produce the Nero–Digby version may have wanted to avoid any implication that St David himself had connexions elsewhere in west Wales. Or more likely he may simply have thought this was an unnecessary complication and that it was better to remove both place-names and substitute a vague local indicator, 'nearby'.

James's second class of changes is altogether more interesting and raises wider questions. He complained that Wade-Evans's edition of the Lives from the Vespasian manuscript omitted everything connected with the church and see of Llandaf, while noting that the Vespasian Lives do not include the *Life* of St Gildas by Caradog of Llancarfan. He then draws out several phrases shared between the Vespasian text of David's *Life* and other Vespasian Lives, among them *Vita S. Cadoci, Vita S. Iltuti*, and the Llandaf text *Vita S. Dubricii*. The point here is to say that the phrases in the Vespasian text of David's *Life* are not Rhygyfarch's work but reflect alterations made by the Brecon copyist who, he supposed, brought these Lives together for the first time around 1200. The extension of these parallels beyond Lives in the Vespasian manuscript to include two works by Caradog of Llancarfan goes against James's inference: the Brecon copyist did not copy either Caradog's *Vita S. Gildae* or his revision of Lifris's *Vita S. Cadoci*, so the parallels must originate further back. John Davies has shown that these verbal parallels are best explained by seeing several of

---

[36] Gerald of Wales's version glosses *Vetus Rubus*: *Puer autem nutritus est in loco qui Vetus Rubus dicitur, qui et Kambrice Hen Meneu* [Hen Fynyw in modern spelling], *Latine uero Vetus Meneuia uocatur. Sortitus est autem locus hic nomen ab Hybernico Muni quod et rubus sonat* (p. 384).

these Lives as a group composed by Caradog, who must have known Rhygyfarch's *Vita S. Dauid* in the form that has come down to us as the Vespasian text.[37] James had claimed there was no evidence for the existence of the longer text before the date of the Vespasian copy; Caradog's work in effect provides that evidence.

According to James's manner of thought, Caradog's knowledge of the wording of the longer text must have pre-dated the oldest manuscripts of the Nero–Digby text and would therefore have been the older version. As I have said, the date of surviving copies cannot be used in this way.

It is in fact extremely difficult to date the Nero–Digby recension other than that it was made after Rhygyfarch's time and before the earliest witnesses. James suggests that the Nero–Digby reflects:

> Bishop Bernard's attempt to secure for his see independence of Canterbury and primacy in Wales. Papal sympathy was essential to this enterprise, and to win this, Bernard had to gloss over Rhigyfarch's appeal in chapter 46 to the Patriarch of Jerusalem, and also to minimize the role of Padarn and Teilo. The words 'Romana auctoritate' are incompatible with Dewi's promotion to the Archbishopric by the Patriarch; and, despite the angelic injunction to the Patriarch, all mention of Padarn's and Teilo's consecration is suppressed, as is also the description of their gifts from the Patriarch: Dewi must be exalted above them.[38]

How are we to make sense of this? If James were correct in his view that the Nero–Digby text reflects Bernard's version of what Rhygyfarch wrote, whatever Bernard *omitted* from the story must be irrecoverable. What we read about David's consecration by the patriarch is there still in the Nero–Digby text, §§ 44–8; so is his being accompanied by Teilo and Padarn, and the patriarch's preparing for them *tres honoratissimas sedes* ('three seats of the highest honour'). There is no way of recovering whatever might have been omitted, and what James says had to be played down is still there, else neither he nor we could have known of it. Such argument as James offers can only depend on imagination. The story mentions that the patriarch presented David with four gifts: it is imagination to suppose that Rhygyfarch must have also mentioned gifts to Teilo and Padarn. James's other point in this regard is to suggest that § 53 is at variance with the story of consecration by the patriarch in § 46. There the patriarch *ad archiepiscopatum eum* [or *Dauid agium* in Vespasian] *prouehit*, 'he advances him [St David] to the archiepiscopate'. In § 53, however, it is by the consent of all the bishops, kings, princes, nobles, and all ranks that David *totius Brytannicę gentis archiepiscopus constituitur* ('is constituted archbishop of the whole British nation'.) I do not see variance here; the patriarch had consecrated David, the Britons received and installed him as their archbishop, regarding his see as *totius patrię metropolis*, 'metropolitan church of the whole country'. James adds that Christopher Brooke had suspected here a 'suspicious acquaintance with the charters forged in Canterbury during the Canterbury–York primacy dispute'.[39] In Brooke's words, 'these phrases have a sinister ring for anyone who has studied the Canterbury forgeries'.[40] The forgeries, however, are associated with Lanfranc, archbishop of Canterbury, who intended for his see the primacy of all Britain and Ireland. That aspiration and the phrases that express it were evident at Canterbury

---

[37] Davies, *The Book of Llandaf*, esp. 109–31.
[38] James, *Rhigyfarch's Life*, xxx.
[39] James, *Rhigyfarch's Life*, xxx, cites Brooke, 'The archbishops', 214, n. 5.
[40] *Ibid.*

in the 1090s and may have been already widely known.[41] Rhygyfarch himself may have subverted the same phraseology to make David archbishop of the British race – a context might perhaps be found in Bishop Wilfrid's difficulties with Archbishop Anselm around 1095 – though in truth the language is so normal for such titles that I do not think it necessary to suppose any influence from Canterbury. But what of the words *Romana auctoritate*? After the synod at Llanddewibrefi, in § 55 Rhygyfarch introduces a second synod, the Synod of Victory, a name derived from a very early British source;[42] this reaffirms the decisions of the first synod. *Ex his igitur duabus synodis omnes nostre patrie ecclesie modum et regulam Romana auctoritate acceperunt* ('As a result of these two synods all the churches of our country received their pattern and rule by Roman authority'). It is certainly unclear how these local synods could act with Roman authority in any narrow sense, but the phrase is surely intended to convey no more than that the decisions were made in a canonical manner. Again, there is no real conflict with the story of David's consecration by the patriarch. James has adopted a pedantically strict reading in order to find contradictions.

He then touchingly supposes, 'With the exception of passages such as these' (though he did not point to any others), 'there seems no occasion to question the faithfulness to Rhigyfarch of the Basic mid twelfth-century text, or of the manuscripts of the Nero and Digby recensions, so far as they conform to it.'[43] It is perhaps surprising that, after so much insistence on his 'convinced acceptance of the evidence of the texts', James proclaims the authentic Rhygyfarch on such a simple supposition. If he were correct in regarding the mid-twelfth-century text as a reflection of Bishop Bernard's case, it is surely surprising that it does not tally with the account set out by the cathedral chapter in a letter to Pope Honorius II before 1130. The fiction offered there was that David

> communi electione clericalis et laicalis concilii tocius regni occidentalis Britannie assumptus ac deinde a sancto Dubricio antecessore suo et a propria sinodo sicut in eadem mos extiterat ecclesia legitur fuisse archipresul consecratus

> (is said to have been picked out by the common choice of a council of the church and laity of all western Britain and thereafter consecrated archbishop by his predecessor St Dubricius and [according to the custom of the same church] by its proper synod.)[44]

---

[41] Lanfranc's claim is expressed in his 1072 letter to Pope Alexander II (*Epistolae*, ed. Clover and Gibson, 50). Brooke followed Böhmer's dating of the forged decretals to 1070–72 in support of Lanfranc's own interest and identified the forger as one Guerno (Brooke, 'The Canterbury forgeries'); Southern argued for a later dating around 1120–21, associating them with Archbishop Ralph's visit to Rome in 1121 (Southern, 'The Canterbury forgeries', 193–226). Whatever the date of the forgeries, Canterbury pursued the idea of a primacy over the whole of Britain and Ireland throughout this period. Among other sources, Goscelin's Lives of St Augustine and St Lawrence of Canterbury, published in 1099 or soon after, reflect Canterbury's case for such a primacy. The phraseology is used by Anselm as archbishop, for example, in a charter datable to 1101: *A. Cantuariensis archiepiscopus et maioris Britannie atque Hibernie primas*, ed. Dodwell, *The Charters of Norwich*, I.163 (no. 260).

[42] A text survives, probably from the sixth century, recording the decisions of the Synod of the Grove of Victory (ed. Bieler, *The Irish Penitentials*, 68). These bear no relation to what Rhygyfarch says about the Synod of Victory.

[43] James, *Rhigyfarch's Life*, xxx.

[44] The documentation of Bernard's case has been preserved in Book II of Gerald of Wales, *Libellus inuectionum* (ed. Davies, 130–47); the letter of the chapter of St Davids to Honorius II (datable only 1124×1130), II.10, gives this account of David's consecration. The synod is that of the church of western Britain, and the word 'proper' denotes its independent status.

It would appear that no attempt was made to rewrite the argument of the *Life* in Bernard's time by replacing Rhygyfarch's role for the patriarch of Jerusalem with the contemporary interest in Dubricius. That tradition does not enter the *Life* until Gerald of Wales introduced it, and he was able to draw on the letter to Pope Honorius.[45] Rather, the revision sought simply to abbreviate and, according to the common practice of hagiography, to reduce the amount of particular detail that would mean nothing to a non-local audience.

There is one avenue that may help to contextualize the creation of this abbreviated text more closely, but the precise evidence is tenuous. Bishop Bernard did not become interested in metropolitan status for St Davids until around 1125. For the previous six years he had been actively working on behalf of successive archbishops of Canterbury and their primatial claim against Archbishop Thurstan of York. Thurstan's victory meant an end to the notion of a primacy of all Britain and Ireland and for Bernard opened the door to a metropolitan in Wales. Earlier than that, however, there is a possibility that Bernard was already seeking to promote the cult of St David, perhaps in rivalry with his Norman colleague in Wales, Bishop Urban of Llandaf, who twice complained about Bernard to the papacy. Both attended the Council of Reims in 1119, and at that time Urban obtained bulls from Pope Calixtus II (1119–24); Bernard was in Rome in 1123 and obtained a bull for St Davids from the same pope. From this context a false notion grew up that David was canonized by Pope Calixtus; scholars who realise that would be anachronistic have sometimes expressed it rather that the cult was at least approved by the pope, for which there is no direct evidence.[46] In 1120, however, Urban claimed to translate the relics of St Dubricius at Llandaf.[47] Then soon after 1126 William of Malmesbury (eager to preserve Glastonbury's claim to St David's relics) reported that *Bernardum episcopum semel et secundo eum quesisse et multis reclamantibus non inuenisse* ('Bishop Bernard had more than once looked for his body and in the face of many protests could not find it').[48] William also supplies the best evidence that Bernard had sought official recognition for the cult of St David from Pope Calixtus:

---

45 Gerald of Wales, *Vita S. Dauidis*, ed. Brewer, *et al.*, *Opera*, III.401; Rhygyfarch (§ 50) had mentioned Dubricius along with Deiniol as the holy men who brought David to the synod. The discussion of the evolution of accounts of the synod by Richter ('Canterbury's primacy', 184–5), intended to isolate Bernard's contribution in the evolution of the *uita*, is hampered by his acceptance of James's view of the textual history.

46 The notion of canonization is mentioned by Haddan and traced to Francis Godwin (1562–1633), bishop of Llandaf (ed. Haddan and Stubbs, *Councils*, I.316n); it is refuted in some detail by Toynbee, *S. Louis*, 239–40. The review of this by Grosjean (211–13), adds some details, including the observation that Godwin's inference had been rejected already by the Bollandists in 1668. Recent books that have repeated the notion in a qualified form have not cited any evidence (Davies, *Conquest*, 184; Walker, *Medieval Wales*, 72).

47 An account is given of the translation of St Dubricius in the Book of Llandaf (ed. Evans, 84–7). On Friday, 7 May 1120, the body was moved from Bardsey, *uerbo et consensu Radulfi Cantuariensis ecclesie metropolitani*; it was brought into the church at Llandaf on Sunday, 23 May, and on Wednesday, 2 June, the relics were washed before being enshrined. At this point we are told that the church was small and a rebuilding scheme was undertaken, apparently *after* the translation, which is most unusual; but the account goes on to say that on Wednesday, 14 April, in Holy Week, a letter from Archbishop Ralph was received, giving permission to rebuild. The letter is incorporated, p. 87. It may be that this letter was treated as authority for the translation of the saint's body, which was begun just over three weeks later.

48 William of Malmesbury, *Gesta regum Anglorum*, C text, I.25 (ed. Mynors *et al.*, I.810); this is part of a long addition (19.3–29.1) on the history of Glastonbury, added by William in the late 1120s. The passage was expanded a little to describe Bernard as *episcopum Vallis Rosine* in the interpolated text of William's *De antiquitate Glastonie ecclesie* § 16 (ed. Scott, 64).

in his brief notice of the pope's merits, he mentions that he was so far from seeking to exploit pilgrims to Rome *ut Anglos peregrinos magis ad Sanctum Dauid quam Romam pergere ammoneret pro uiae longitudine: ad illum locum bis euntibus idem benedictionis refundendum commodum quod haberent qui semel Romam irent* ('that he encouraged English pilgrims to go to St Davids rather than Rome, because of the length of the journey; those who went twice to St Davids should have the same privileges in the way of benediction as those who went once to Rome').[49] How the pope did this remains unclear, but his favouring St Davids surely reflects the prompting of Bishop Bernard, perhaps when they met in Reims in 1119 but more likely when they met in Rome in 1123. The shorter text of the *Life* was not revised to put forward the new metropolitan arguments of the late 1120s and beyond, nor does it refer to any desire to translate the relics, but it may have been published in the early 1120s in the context of Bernard's first concern to maintain the status of St Davids against the aspirations of Bishop Urban at Llandaf.

If we put away James's assumptions and arguments meant to support what I can only see as a pre-conceived condemnation of the Vespasian text, all difficulties disappear. We need no longer pretend to find early-twelfth-century retouching in comparing the shorter text with an irrecoverable author's archetype. The straight-forward reading of the textual evidence is that Rhygyfarch's text has been best preserved in Wales among the Lives of other Welsh saints in the Vespasian manu-script. Much could be said on the archaism of language and content that we find in the Vespasian text in comparison with the Nero–Digby version.

That there were further copies of this text in Wales is evident from the fact that the Welsh versions depend on the longer text such as we have in the Vespasian manuscript. Two Latin abbreviations are also based on this version. One of these must have been made in the twelfth-century, since the extant copy, now Lincoln Cathedral, MS 149, dates from the latter part of that century.[50] It appears to have been made for Leominster priory in Herefordshire and close to the eastern extremity of the medieval diocese of St Davids.[51] The other is the work of John of Tynemouth, a monk of St Albans who in the first half of the fourteenth century collected legends of local saints from various parts of Britain. From Wales he has no fewer than fourteen *uitae* derived from texts found in the Vespasian collection, and in his case it seems probable that he had used the extant manuscript at Brecon.[52] A further possible trace of the Vespasian text appears at Glastonbury. William of Malmesbury wrote a history of Glastonbury abbey, and the text as preserved certainly shows

---

49 William of Malmesbury, *Gesta regum Anglorum*, V.435 (ed. Mynors *et al.*, I.778–81).

50 Thomson, *Catalogue*, 115. Thomson noted that James had dated the manuscript to the thirteenth century 'with important consequences for his account of the development of the text': I suspect that the dating of the script was rather the consequence of his argument.

51 Ker, *Medieval Manuscripts*, II.934–9, discusses Gloucester cathedral, MS 1 (s. xiii^in), which was the third volume of the same set; the two volumes are connected by cross-references. The Gloucester volume belonged in the seventeenth century to Fulk Walwyn of Hellens, Much Marcle, about twenty miles from Leominster, and the manuscript shows interest in Reading and its relic of St James, which Ker (*Medieval Manuscripts*, II.939) took as indicative of a Leominster provenance. Leominster was a cell of Reading abbey, and a list of books made *ca* 1192 includes a volume at Leominster containing Lives of St Brendan, St Brigit, St David, and St Edward the Martyr (Sharpe *et al.*, *English Benedic-tine Libraries*, 459). The main Reading section of this book-list includes a three-volume legendary which has been identified as perhaps that now divided between Lincoln and Gloucester (*ibid.*, 443). The second volume may well be Lincoln cathedral, MS 150 (s. xii), a manuscript older by about fifty years, but already paired with MS 149 in the first half of the sixteenth century, when both were annotated in the same italic hand.

52 Horstman, *Noua Legenda Anglie*, I.xxiii–xxv; James, *Rhigyfarch's Life*, xxv.

knowledge of Rhygyfarch's text but unfortunately it is not possible to be sure that it was known to William.[53] The only quotation at Glastonbury that might come from the Vespasian text rather than the shorter text does not appear until the *Chronica* of John of Glastonbury, and even then it is likelier that Glastonbury had the more widely known shorter version.[54]

The shorter Nero–Digby recension survived, so far as one can tell from the extant copies, entirely outside Wales. The only copy now in Wales is that purchased by Cardiff Public Library in 1924. This is an interesting book. Although Ker found evidence that the second half formed a single book at Barking in the early sixteenth century, it is made up of four separate booklets from the twelfth century. We cannot be sure when they were bound together, but they speak loud and clear of the early circulation of such texts, not collected together as whole volumes, but in pamphlets of one or two quires. The *Life* of St David forms a booklet of just nine leaves, a witness to the form in which the text was circulated in the mid-twelfth century. James's two prime witnesses are copies added to already existing books. British Library, MS Cotton Nero E. I (s. xi, Worcester cathedral priory), was already a very large collection when David's *Life* was added, along with several others, around 1130–50. Oxford, Bodleian Library, MS Digby 112 (s. xii^{in}, Winchester cathedral priory), was augmented around mid-century with a copy of the *Life* and other texts. The other early copies are all collections of saints' Lives, the sort of book into which it was obviously hoped that the *Life* would be incorporated as it circulated in booklet form. The other early copies of James's Nero family are in Rouen, Bibliothèque municipale, MS U. 141 (s. xii^{med}, Jumièges abbey), and MS U. 19 (s. xii^2, Jumièges abbey), and Cambridge, Corpus Christi College, MS 161 (s. xii/xiii, St Augustine's abbey, Canterbury). The other early representative of his Digby family is now Bodleian Library, MS Bodley 793 (s. xii^{med}, no provenance). None of these manuscripts is from Wales, but their scatter across prominent houses in southern England and Normandy before the middle of the century suggests that this shorter text was circulated quite widely as a booklet and that many churches decided that it was worth recopying. The most likely context of that publication would be through Bishop Bernard's promotion of knowledge of St David outside Wales. Bernard had

---

[53] Two passages on St David in William's *Gesta regum Anglorum*, I.25 and I.36, are found only in a long addition concerning Glastonbury introduced by William in what the editors call the C-text (ed. Mynors, Thomson, and Winterbottom, I, 810, 814); neither passage shows knowledge of Rhygyfarch's text. William's *De antiquitate Glastonie ecclesie* does not survive in an authentic text but only as interpolated by the monks of Glastonbury at a later date. Here we find § 30 is closely based on Rhygyfarch's *Life*, §§ 44–8; the differences between the longer and shorter texts in this passage are slight, but the Glastonbury text shares one reading particularly with James's D3, namely Bodleian Library, MS Bodley 285 (*SC* 2430) (s. xiii, Ramsey), and both name the Irish bishop as 'Belue' rather than 'Helue'. This particular variant was already noted in 1691 by Wharton, 631, from what he called 'Hist. Glaston.', and repeated by (Brewer, *et al.*, *Opera* III.383.

[54] John of Glastonbury, *Cronica siue Antiquitates Glastoniensis ecclesiae*, § 36 (ed. Carley and Townsend, *The Chronicle of Glastonbury Abbey*, 82), *quandam ingreditur ecclesiam in qua sanctus Gildas sermonem faciebat ad populum*, follows § 5 of Rhygyfarch, where Vespasian reads, *quandam ingreditur ecclesiam ad predicationem euangelii audiendam quam predicabat sanctus Gildas*, with the name Gildas; the shorter text omits the name, but John's wording otherwise is closer to the reading of Nero–Digby, *quandam ingreditur ecclesiam in qua quidam doctor uerbum faciebat ad populum*. Gildas is nowhere named in the shorter text, but this name may have entered the text as gloss, so that the passage does not convincingly attest to knowledge of the longer text at Glastonbury. In § 37 John follows the interpolated version of William of Malmesbury using Rhygyfarch, §§ 44–8, most likely in the shorter text; he adds some direct quotation not found in the interpolations in William's work, however, so he must have had direct access to a copy.

been a prominent figure at court since the opening years of the twelfth century, chaplain to Henry I's queen, Matilda, until promoted to the see in 1115, a trusted colleague of Archbishop Ralph after that. He had the contacts to ensure a reception of the text, and Anglo-Norman circulation at his instigation is probably sufficient explanation of its shortened and somewhat delocalized character.

The advice to the reader who wants to study Rhygyfarch and the Welsh tradition of St David must be to use the Vespasian text. It has long been accessible in the two printings by Wade-Evans, and with a degree of effort it could be read in James's edition too by joining up all the passages relegated to the space below his edited Nero–Digby text. The questions are not all resolved. James noted that three manuscripts classified by him as belonging to the Nero family contained readings that approximated more to the Vespasian text, and in this way he traced the latter back to the copy from Jumièges, Rouen, MS U. 141, a startling inference, and only possible if one supposes that the longer text is an expansion of the shorter text. If the textual connexions were correctly observed, I have been unable to confirm it, and I have not resolved what such shared readings might signify. A new examination of the manuscripts may have to consider the possibility of contamination between copies of the Nero family and the Vespasian text, but this will not greatly affect the resulting edition. The chief means to restore the text of the original Vespasian version must be to investigate where the Nero–Digby version has preserved Rhygyfarch's wording at points where the latest copying of the longer text has introduced minor errors. This is attempted in the edition presented in this volume. James's labour shortened the work involved in arriving at this corrected text of the original and longer version, but his argument delayed our getting there.

6

RHYGYFARCH'S *LIFE* OF ST DAVID

Ed. and transl. Richard Sharpe and John Reuben Davies

The text reflects the text-historical argument set out in Chapter 5. It is based on BL MS Cotton Vespasian A. xiv (V), the only complete witness to the original Latin text of Rhygyfarch's *Life*. The text published in J.W. James's edition, referred to as the Nero–Digby version, represented an attempt to restore the reading of a short-ened version prepared, it is argued, for Bishop Bernard in the 1120s. Since this was based on a copy of the complete text far earlier than V, and possibly earlier than the exemplar of V, it provides a means to restore original readings corrupt in V. A choice between V and ND may be taken on its merits, bearing in mind that, where they differ, ND may represent the decision of the reviser while V should offer only accidental error. There ought, therefore, to be a disposition in favour of V over ND where both readings make sense. The agreement of V with N against D, or conversely with D against N, ought to reflect the archetype. Divergences between the various later witnesses classified as relating to N or D will for the most part result from error subsequent to the hyparchetype ND and therefore contribute nothing to the edited text. Passages in V that were cut out or paraphrased in making the shorter ND text are enclosed in partial brackets ⌜ ⌝. In general readings of ND are expressed in terms of the consensus of manuscripts classified under N or D by James; the reporting of more diverse readings derives from his apparatus and uses his suprascript numbers to identify individual witnesses.

Notes to the Latin text are concerned with the readings of the manuscripts, deci-sions as to preferred readings, and the character of the changes introduced to the original by the abbreviator of ND. The brief notes to the English translation are concerned with the understanding of the text; we have not attempted a historical commentary, for which one can still consult the extensive notes by Wade-Evans, *The Life of St David*, 57–116.

VITA SANCTI DAVID

Incipit uita beati Dauid, qui et Dewi, episcopi et confessoris Kal. Martii.[a]

1 DOMINUS noster, quamuis omnes suos ante constitutionem mundi[a] dilexit atque presciuit, nonnullos tamen multis reuelationum ostensionibus prenuntiauit. Iste itaque sanctus, quem tinctio Dauid uulgus autem Dewi clamat, ueriloquis angelorum oraculis ad patrem quidem prius, deinde ad sanctum Patricium terdenis annis priusquam nasceretur non solum prophitatus, uerum etiam misticis donationum muneribus ditatus innotuit. **2** Nam quodam tempore pater eius, meritis et nomine Sanctus, Ceretiçę gentis regali potentia fretus, qua tandem deposita çeleste regnum comparans, angelica in somnis monitus uoce audiuit, 'Crastina die expergefactus uenatum iturus, ceso prope fluuium ceruo, tria ibi munera repperies ⌐iuxta amnem Theibi¬, ceruum scilicet quem persequeris, piscem, apumque examen ⌐in arbore positum, in loco qui uocatur Linhenlann⌐a¬. Ex his itaque tribus reserues fauum scilicet partemque piscis et cerui, quę custodienda filio ex te nascituro transmitte[b] ad Maucanni monasterium,' quod nunc usque Depositi Monasterium uocatur. Quęquidem munera huius uitam prenuntiant; fauus enim mellis eius sapientiam clamat; sicut enim mel in cera, ita spiritualem[c] sensum historico cepit instrumento. Piscis uero aquaticam eius uitam sonat; sicut enim piscis aqua uiuit, ita iste, uinum et siceram et omne quod inebriare potest respuens, beatam Deo uitam in pane tantum et aqua duxit; inde[d] etiam Dauid aquaticę uitę cognominatur. Ceruus autem in antiquo serpente signat dominium, sicut enim ceruus, expoliatis[e] serpentibus pastus, fontem aquę desiderans, acceptis uiribus uelut iuuentute renouatur, sic iste quasi ceruorum pedibus super excelsa statutus, antiquum humani generis serpentem uiribus nocendi contra semetipsum expolians, fontem uite assiduis lacrimarum cursibus adoptans, de die

---

Inscription

[a]   *The manuscripts all have different headings, but this from* V *is well preserved; the earliest witnesses also use the spelling* Dauid, N⁴ Incipit uita sancti Dauid, N² Incipit uita sancti Dauid archiepiscopi. *Significant developments in later copies are the change from indeclinable* Dauid *to genitive* Dauidis, *its replacement with* Dewi, *and preference for the title of archbishop.*
Section numbering
The text was divided into sections by Wade-Evans, whose numbering is included in James's text, though without paragraphing. In this text these established section numbers are still given, but the paragraph breaks follow those of the large coloured initials in V. *These are closely matched by the red initials in* D, *though the paragraphing in that manuscript ends with the red C at the start of § 44. Each paragraph intended to have a coloured initial is here shown with the first word in small capitals.*

§ 1
[a]   mundi constitutionem ND
§ 2
[a]   Linhenlanu V
[b]   transmitte V] transmittes ND, *apparently a false parallel with present subjunctive* reserues.
[c]   spiritualem ND] spiritalem V, *which elsewhere (§§ 46, 50) has the spelling* spiritualis.
[d]   unde ND
[e]   expoliatis ND (*'having grazed on despoiled snakes'*)] expoliatus V. *James, 29n, provides references for this notion from folk-lore.*

THE LIFE OF SAINT DAVID

Here begins the Life of the Blessed David, who is also Dewi, Bishop and Confessor, 1st March.

§ 1. Our Lord, although he loved and foreknew all his people before the foundation of the world,[1] has nevertheless foretold some of them by frequent signs and revelations. And so it was that this holy man, who was baptized David, but whom the common people call Dewi, became known; not just because he was foretold by the truth-telling prophecies of angels, first to his father, and then to St Patrick, thirty years before he was born, but also because he was enriched with mystical gifts and endowments. § 2. One time, his father, Sanctus (by merits and by name),[2] who enjoyed sovereignty over the people of Ceredig[3] (sovereignty he later laid aside to win a heavenly kingdom), heard the voice of an angelic prophecy in a dream:[4] "When you wake up tomorrow, you will go hunting; having killed a stag near the river, you will find there beside the river Teifi three gifts; namely, the stag that you will pursue, a fish, and a swarm of bees situated in a tree, in a place called Llyn Henllan.[5] You should set aside, out of these three, the honeycomb, and a portion of the fish and the stag; and you should deliver them to the monastery of Meugan,[6] keeping them for the son who is going to be born to you." (To this day it is called the Monastery of the Deposit.) These gifts foretell his life. The honeycomb proclaims his wisdom, for just as the honey is in the wax, so he has understood the spiritual meaning in a literal statement. The fish signifies his watery life, for as the fish lives by water, so does he; rejecting wine and liquor and everything that can inebriate,[7] he has led a blessed life for God on just bread and water; because of this he is surnamed David 'of the watery life'. The stag signifies dominion over the ancient serpent,[8] for just as the stag desires a spring of water when it has grazed on despoiled snakes,[9] and having gained strength is renewed as if with youth, so he is established on the heights, as though with stags' feet,[10] despoiling the human race's ancient serpent of his power to harm him. Choosing the fount of life by the constant flow of tears, renewed from day to day,[11] he made progress, so that in the name of the Holy Trinity

---

[1] cf. Jn. 13.1: *cum dilexisset suos qui erant in finem dilexit eos*; Eph. 1.4: *sicut elegit nos in ipso ante mundi constitutionem*.

[2] i.e. 'saint', 'holy man'.

[3] i.e. Ceredigion.

[4] Is there perhaps an allusion here to the story in Tob. 6.1–5, where the angel instructs Tobias to keep three parts from the fish that had jumped out of the river?

[5] Probably the village of Henllan, on the River Teifi, Ceredigion (SN 35 40).

[6] St Meugan, author of *Orationes Moucani* in BL MS Royal 2 A. xx (*saec.* VIII²), fols 42r–45r. He is also attested in an eleventh-century litany from Exeter, Lifris's *Vita S. Cadoci*, and several place-names. Howlett, '*Orationes Moucani*', 55–74.

[7] Lev. 10.9, Num. 6.3, 1 Sam. 1.15; also Lk. 1.15, where a similar phrase occurs within the story of the conception of St John the Baptist, which appears to form the model for § 5.

[8] *antiquus serpens*, 'the ancient serpent', is a quotation from Rev. 12.9 and 20.2.

[9] The parallel in English, Psalm 42.1, 'As a hart longs for flowing streams', is not present in the Latin, *sicut areola praeparata ad inrigationes aquarum*.

[10] Ps. 18.33 (Vulgate 17.34): *coaequans pedes meos ceruis et super excelsa statuens me*, 'Making my feet like stags' feet, and setting me secure on the heights'; this verse is paralleled in 2 Sam. 22.34 and Hab. 3.19.

[11] 2 Cor. 4.16: *renouatur de die in diem*.

in diem renouatus profecit, ut in nomine sanctę Trinitatis salutarem scientiam <et> castioris prandii parcitate[f] dominandi in demones habere potestatem inciperet.[g]

3 DEINDE Patricius, Romanis eruditus disciplinis, comitantibus uirtutum turmis, pontifex effectus, gentem [a]a qua exulauerat petiuit, in qua fructuosi operis lucernam oleo geminę karitatis infatigabili reficiens labore, non sub modio sed super candelabrum imponere uolens ut cunctos, glorificato omnium patre, roraret, Cereticę gentis regionem adiit, in qua per aliquantulum temporis conuersatus Demetica intrat rura, ibique perlustrans tandem ad locum qui Vallis Rosina nominabatur peruenit, et gratum agnoscens locum deuouit Deo ibi fideliter deseruire. Sed cum hęc secum meditando reuolueret, apparuit ei angelus Domini, 'Tibi,' inquit, 'non istum locum Deus disposuit, sed filio qui nondum est natus nec nisi peractis prius[b] triginta annis nascetur.' Audiens autem hec sanctus Patricius merens [c]⌐et stupens iratusque dixit, 'Cur Dominus despexit seruum suum ab infantia sua sibi seruientem cum timore et amore, elegitque alium nondum in hac luce natum sed neque ante .xxx.[ta] annos nascetur?' Parauitque fugere, et Dominum suum Iesum Christum deserere,⌐ dicens, 'Cum ante Domini mei conspectum incassum labor meus redigitur, et mihi qui nondum est natus superponitur[d], uadam et tali labori amodo non subiaceam.' [e]⌐Sed Dominus multum diligebat Patricium, misitque ad eum angelum suum ut illum uerbis familiaribus blandiretur, cui ait, 'Patrici, letare, Dominus enim misit me ad te ut ostendam tibi totam Hiberniam insulam de sede que est in Rosina Valle,' que modo Sedes Patricii nominatur. Aitque angelus ei, 'Exulta, Patrici, tu enim eris apostolus illius totius insule quam cernis, multaque propter nomen Domini Dei tui in ea patieris, sed Dominus erit tecum in omnibus quę facturus sis,⌐ nondum enim uerbum uitę accepit. Ibique[f] prodesse debes, ibi parauit tibi Dominus sedem, ibi signis et uirtutibus radiabis, totamque gentem Deo subiugabis.[g] Sit tibi hoc in

---

[f] parcitate VN] parcitatem D

[g] inciperet V] inciperet percurreret N inciperet limitaret D. *What is the syntax of this sentence? The simplest conjecture would be to follow V and to insert* et *earlier in the clause, but* inciperet *more clearly governs* potestatem habere *than* salutarem scientiam; *a verb may be missing. After* ut *there are two verbs in ND but no conjunction; Rhygyfarch often has two verbs at end of sentence, but the divergence and opacity of the readings of N and D argue for their struggling with the text of their archetype.*

§ 3

[a] a qua VN[2]] qua N[1] quam D quia N[5]. *While an ablative of separation does not require the preposition,* exulare *is usually construed with* ab; *without it ND lost their way, with some copyists conjecturing* qua<m> *or* qu<i>a.

[b] prius *added as a primary correction in V (in same hand as* \\prodes//se *below), but omitted by James*] *om.* ND

[c] stupensque uolutat, deliberans et corde ND, *deliberately removing Patrick's railing against God.*

[d] superponitur ND] preponitur V. *The survival of the stronger reading in ND is persuasive.*

[e] Hęc autem secum cogitans, talibus blandiciis ab angelo uerba consolationis accepit, Non ita fiet, sed Hibernensium insulę principem constituit te Dominus ND

[f] ibique V] ibi ND

[g] Ego ero tecum ND, *rescuing the phrase from the shortened passage above.*

he would begin to have the knowledge of salvation[12] <and> by the frugality of purer food the power of holding dominion against demons.

§ 3. Then Patrick, a man learned in the Roman disciplines and possessed of a multitude of virtues, having been made a bishop, sought the nation from which he had lived in exile, where he might, through untiring labour, refresh the lamp of fruitful work with the oil of twofold love;[13] for he did not want to place the lamp under a bowl, but on a lamp-stand, so that having glorified the father of all, it might shine on everyone.[14] So he came to the region of the people of Ceredig, and having lived there for a short time, he entered the country of Dyfed.[15] Surveying the country, he eventually reached the place that is named *Vallis Rosina*,[16] and recognizing that it was a pleasant location, he vowed that he would faithfully devote himself to God there. But as he turned these things over in his mind, an angel of the Lord appeared to him. "This place is not assigned to you," he said, "but to a son who is not yet born, nor will be born until thirty years have first passed." Hearing this, however, the worthy Saint Patrick, both surprised and angered, said, "Why has the Lord despised his servant who has been in his service from his infancy with fear and love,[17] and has chosen another who has not yet been born into this light but will not be born for another thirty years?"[18] And he got ready to take flight and forsake his Lord Jesus Christ, saying, "Since my labour is rendered useless in the eyes of my Lord, and one not yet born is set above me, I shall go away, and from now on I shall not submit to such work." But the Lord greatly valued Patrick, and sent his angel to him, to soothe him with kindly words. He said to him, "Patrick, rejoice, for the Lord has sent me to you, so that I may show you the whole island of Ireland from the seat that is in *Vallis Rosina*" (which is now named Patrick's Seat). And the angel said to him, "Be glad, Patrick, for you will be apostle to the whole of that island which you behold, and you will suffer many things in it on account of the name of the Lord your God; but the Lord will be with you in everything that you do, for it has not yet received the Word of Life. And there you must do good, where the Lord has prepared you a seat, where you shall shine with signs and miracles,[19] and you shall make the whole nation subject to God. Let this be a sign to you:[20] I shall show you the whole island,

---

[12] Perhaps a reference to Lk. 1.77: *ad dandam scientiam salutis plebi eius*, 'to give knowledge of salvation to his people'.

[13] This twofold love is probably that described by Christ in Lk. 10.27: 'You should love the Lord your God … and your neighbour …'.

[14] Mt. 5.15, 'Nor do men light a lamp and put it under a bushel, but on a stand, and it gives light to all in the house.' The verb *rorare* is evidently used to mean 'shine on' here (and 'shine' in § 6), although it correctly means to sprinkle with dew; Rhygyfarch's usage was very likely fostered by phrases involving sunrise, such as Ovid, *Metamorphoses* XIII 622, 'Sunrise drops dew (*rorat*) on the whole world'.

[15] Patrick was known to be a Briton who lived and worked as a missionary in Ireland, a voluntary exile from his homeland; Rhygyfarch's story of a return to preach in western Britain is not found in any of the Lives of St Patrick.

[16] Literally, 'the Rosy Valley', but it may be a misinterpretation of an original Welsh name, possibly *Nant Rhosan*, 'the valley of the little marsh', in which the cathedral stands. See Wade-Evans, *Life of St. David*, 66–8. Another possibility (not mutually exclusive) is that the author is playing on the Latin noun *ros, roris*, etymologically implied by the verb *roraret* (see n. 14, above).

[17] *seruum suum ab infantia sua* has bibilical overtones: cf. Gen. 46.34, *uiri pastores sumus serui tui ab infantia nostra*, 'Your servants have been keepers of cattle from our youth'.

[18] cf. Ps. 56 (55).13: *ut ambulem coram Deo in luce uiuentium*, 'that I may walk before God in the light of life'.

[19] cf. 2 Esdr. 9.6; Acts 2.22; 2 Cor. 12.12; Heb. 2.4.

[20] Lk. 2.12.

signum: totam tibi insulam ostendam, curuentur montes, humiliabitur pelagus, oculus trans omnia erectus[h] ex loco prospectans uidebit promissum.' His dictis, erectisque oculis ex loco in quo stabat, qui modo Sedes Patricii dicitur, totam prospexit insulam. [i]「Tandem animus Patricii sedatus libenter dimisit locum sanctum Dauid agio; paransque nauem in Portu Magno suscitauit quendam senem nomine Cruimther[j] per .xii. annos iuxta litus illud sepultum; nauigauitque Patricius in Hiberniam habens secum nuper suscitatum, qui postea episcopus factus est.[7] [k]<Cetera autem uitę eius in Hibernensium litteris scripta qui uoluerit reperit.>

4 [a]「PERACTIS autem .xxx. predictis annis, uirtus diuina misit Sanctum regem Cereticę regionis usque ad plebem Demeticę gentis. Inuenitque rex obuiam sibi sanctimonialem, nomine Nonnitam uirginem, puellam pulcram nimis et decoram, quam concupiscens tetigit ui oppressam, et concepit filium suum Dauit agium[7], quę nec antea nec post uirum agnouit, sed in castitate mentis et corporis perseuerans fidelissimam duxit uitam. Nam ab ipso conceptionis tempore[b] pane tantum et aqua uixit. In loco autem in quo oppressa concepit, modicus patet campus, uisu amenus, munere superni roris plenus, in quo campo tempore ipso conceptionis duo grandes lapides apparuerunt, unus ad caput, alter ad pedes, qui antea uisi non fuerant. Nam terra, conceptui eius[c] congaudens, sinum suum aperuit ut et puelle uerecundiam seruaret et prolis soliditatem prenuntiaret.

5 CRESCENTE autem utero, mater ex proprio more ad offerendas pro partu oblationum elemosynas quandam ingreditur ecclesiam [a]「ad predicationem euangelii audiendam, quam predicabat sanctus Gildas, Cau filius, in tempore regis Triphuni et filiorum eius[7]. Ingressa autem matre, subito Gildas[c] obmutescens quasi clauso gutture tacuit. Interrogatus autem a populo cur interrupta predicatione obmutuerat, respondit, 'Ego communi loquela uos alloqui possum, predicare autem non possum; sed uos extra egredientes, me solum remanere facite ut si uel sic possim predicare.' Egressa igitur foras plebe, ipsa mater in angulo se[d] abscondens latuit,

---

[h]   erectus ND] euectus V. *Although both make sense, the phrase* erectisque oculis *a few words later is more likely to pick up the words of the command than to vary them.*

[i]   ac protinus paratis omnibus nauim petit, resuscitatoque mortuo qui ante duodecim annos defunctus fuerat promissam patriam intrat ND

[j]   Cruimther] Cri | umther V *at line-end,* Criumther ND, *a confusion of minims in the archetype rather than a variant on the Irish name.*

[k]   *om.* V, *but it seems more likely to be original than to have been added in the process of abridgement; compare also below,* § 65.

§ 4
[a]   Labentibus autem .xxx. annorum curriculis Sanctus Cereticę gentis rex Demetiam proficiscitur, ibique perlustrans obuia ei facta est puella nomine Nonita, pulchra nimis uirgoque decora, qum rex concupiscens oppressit eam ND, *omitting the reference to David's conception in what seems to be a careless abridgement.*

[b]   tempore conceptionis ND

[c]   eius V *though James reports the reading as* sui] *om.* ND

§ 5
[a]   in qua quidam doctor uerbum faciebat ad populum ND, *omitting the name of Gildas throughout*

[c]   *om.* ND

[d]   se VN[1]D[4578]] *om.* N[2–9] D[1–2]

mountains shall be moved, and the sea shall be calmed; with your eyes lifted over everything, looking from this place, you shall see the promised land."

When he had said these things, he surveyed the whole island, raising his eyes from the place where he was standing, which is now named Patrick's Seat. At length, when Patrick's emotion had settled, he willingly surrendered that holy place to St David. As he was preparing a ship at Porth Mawr, he raised up an old man, named Cruimther, who had been buried near that shore for twelve years.[21] Patrick sailed to Ireland, taking with him the newly resuscitated man, who was later made a bishop. As for the rest of his life, he who wishes may find it written in the writings of the Irish.[22]

§ 4. When the foresaid thirty years had passed, divine providence sent Sanctus, king of the territory of Ceredig, as far as the kingdom of the people of Dyfed.[23] And the king came across a nun named Nonnita, who was a virgin, an exceedingly beautiful girl, and modest.[24] Lusting after her, he raped her, and she conceived his son, the holy David. Neither before nor after did she know a man, but continuing steadfastly in chastity of mind and body, she led her life most devoutly; for, from the very time she conceived, she lived only on bread and water. In the place where she had been raped and had conceived, there lies a small meadow, pleasant to behold, and filled with the gift of heavenly dew. In that field, at the moment she conceived, there appeared two large stones that had not been seen before, one at her head and the other at her feet; for the land, rejoicing at his conception, opened its bosom, that it might both preserve the modesty of the girl, and declare the significance of her offspring.

§ 5. When her womb had grown, the mother, in accordance with enduring custom, went into a church to offer alms and oblations for the unborn child, and to hear the preaching of the gospel, which St Gildas, son of Caw,[25] was preaching in the time of King Tryffin and his sons.[26] But when the mother entered, Gildas suddenly became dumb, as if his throat were closed. Asked by the people why he had interrupted his sermon and become silent, he replied, "I am able to talk to you in normal conversation, but I am not able to preach. You should go outside and leave me alone, to see if I am able to preach that way." So the people went outside, but the mother concealed herself and hid in a corner: she stayed behind not to disobey his word but, with an intense thirst for the Word of Life, to assert the privilege of her great offspring. Then, for a second time, prevented by heaven, the preacher could

21 *Cruimther*, an Irish word for 'priest' (an early loan-word from Latin *presbiter*), is usually used as an epithet in front of a personal name; perhaps a name followed the epithet in an earlier source.

22 Rhygyfarch presumably alludes to one or more of the Latin Lives of St Patrick, known to him from Irish sources but not recognized as ordinarily circulating in Britain.

23 *ad plebem Demeticę gentis*, 'to the kingdom of the people of Dyfed': Charles-Edwards ('The seven bishop-houses', 251) has given reasons to understand the word *plebs* as sometimes meaning 'kingdom'.

24 1 Kgs 1.4, where King David's courtiers seek a maiden to comfort him in his old age, and find Abishag the Shunammite, *puella pulchra nimis*.

25 This story was later borrowed and shortened by Caradog of Llancarfan in his Life of St Gildas, ed. H. Williams, *Gildae de excidio Britanniae*, 390–413 (§ 4). For a form of the story older than Rhygyfarch's, see note on § 7, below.

26 *Triphun* is no doubt the king of Dyfed who is the grandfather of Vortipor in the Harley genealogies (*EWGT*, 4; Vortipor is the 'tyrant of the Demetae' mentioned by Gildas, *De excidio*, § 31). *Tryfun* appears in the Llandaf charters (125b) as father of *Aircol Lauhir*, king of Dyfed.

non quod precepto non obediens, sed ingenti auiditate precepta sitiens uitalia ad demonstrandum tante prolis priuilegium remanebat. Deinde et secundo toto cordis annisu desudans, celitus inhibitus, nichil ualuit. Hinc perteritus, excelsa profatur[27e] uoce, 'Adiuro te[f],' inquit[g], 'siquis me latet, ut [h]⌐te ex latibulo ostendas⌐.' Tunc ipsa respondens, 'Ego,' inquit, 'hic lateo ⌐inter ualuam et parietem⌐.' Ipse uero diuina fretus prouidentia, 'Tu,' inquit[i], 'foras egredere, populus autem ecclesiam ingrediens repedet.' [j]⌐Venitque unusquisque sicut prius fuerat in sede, et predicauit Gildas quasi de buccina clare. Interrogauitque plebs agium Gildam et dixit, 'Cur non potuisti prima uice euangelium Christi predicare nobis uolentibus audire?'. Et respondit Gildas et dixit, 'Vocate huc sanctimonialem, que exiit extra ecclesiam'. Interrogata autem matre, se esse pregnantem confessa est, et ait Nonnita sancta, 'Ecce assum.' At ille dixit, 'Filius, qui est in utero istius sanctimonialis, maiorem gratiam ac potestatem ordinationemque habet quam ego, quia illi dedit Deus priuilegium et monarchiam ac bragminationem \principatus uel dignitas/ omnium sanctorum Brittannię in ęternum ante et post iudicium. Valete, fratres et sorores. Ego non possum hic diutius habitare propter filium huius sanctimonialis, quia sibi tradita est monarchia super omnes homines istius insule, et ad aliam insulam necesse est michi ire, et Brittanniam totam huius filio dimittere.' Vnde cunctis liquido patuit,⌐ quod illa seculo paritura esset, qui honoris priuilegio, sapientię fulgore, sermonis facundia, cunctos Brittannię doctores excelleret.[k]

6 INTEREA quidam ex confinio tyrannus habebatur, qui ex magorum uaticinio audierat[a] filium suis in finibus nasciturum, cuius potestas totam occuparet patriam. Ipse qui solis terrenis intentus summum sibi bonum in his infimis deputabat, magno inuidię liuore cruciabatur. Notato itaque ex magorum oraculis loco, in quo postea filius nascebatur, 'Solus,' inquit[b], 'tot diebus loco supersedeam[c], et quemcunque ibi uel modicum quiescentem[d] inueniam, meo peremptus gladio occumbet.' His ita destinatis, reuolutisque nouem mensibus quis[e] pariendi tempus aderat, mater per ipsam quadam die egrediebatur uiam in qua parturiendi locus aderat, quem ex magorum presagio tirannus seruabat. Vrgente autem partus tempore, mater predictum petiuit locum. Ipsa uero die tanta aeris tempestas inualuit ut nullus uel etiam fores egredi poterat, ingens enim choruscationum fulgur, horridus tonitruo-

---

[e] profatur VND] profatus *Wade-Evans; compare also* § 59.
[f] *om.* ND; *see note h*
[g] inquid V. *The text in V has* inquit *twenty-one times,* inquid *nine times.*
[h] sese ex latibulo ostendens innotescat ND, *presumably to avoid the switch between second-person* te *and third-person* siquis.
[i] inquid V
[j] Hoc facto, lingua soluta ex more predicat. Interrogata autem matre illaque se esse pregnantem confessa, cunctis pro patulo claruit quod ND, *abridging Gildas's role and again removing his name. The word* buccina *is used again in § 52 and again omitted by* ND.
[k] ND *adds* Quod ex subsequentis uitę meritis comprobatur

§ 6
[a] audierat V] audiebat ND
[b] inquid V
[c] supersedeam ND] supersedebo VN⁵. *The future indicative was clearly intended, but present subjunctive for future indicative is a common confusion in early insular Latin; it is more likely that* V *and* N⁵ *have corrected the grammar than that* ND *has made the reverse change.*
[d] requiescentem ND
[e] quis ND, *the contracted form of* quibus] quibus VN⁷⁹ quando N⁵ *om.* N⁴. *Three copies, including* V, *have correctly interpreted the word, but the other two readings show that the more obscure form* quīs *was original.*

do nothing, even though he was striving with all his might. Terrified by this, he spoke out with a raised voice: "I implore you," he said, "if anyone is hiding from me, to come out from your hiding place." Then she replied and said, "I am hiding here between the door and the wall." But now prompted by divine providence, he said, "You should go outside, and let the people re-enter the church." And everyone came and sat in the same seat as before, and Gildas preached loud and clear as a trumpet.[27] And the people questioned the holy Gildas and said, "Why were you not able to preach the gospel of Christ to us the first time when we wanted to hear it?" And Gildas replied and said, "Summon the nun who went outside the church." And when they had questioned the mother, she acknowledged that she was pregnant, and Saint Nonnita said, "Behold, I am here." But he said, "The son who is in the womb of that nun is greater in grace and power and rank than I, for God has given him the privilege, sovereignty, and princely dignity[28] of all the saints of Wales for ever, before and after Judgement Day. Farewell, brothers and sisters. I am not able to live here any longer on account of the son of this nun, for the sovereignty over all the people of this island has passed to him, and it is necessary for me to go to another island, and leave the whole of Britain to her son."[29] For this reason, it was plain to everyone that the child she was about to bring into the world, by the privilege of his honour, the splendour of his wisdom, and the eloquence of his speech, would excel all the teachers of Britain.[30]

§ 6. Meanwhile, there was a tyrant living nearby who had found out, from the divination of seers, that a boy would be born within his borders whose power would take over the whole country.[31] This man, concerned only with earthly things, considered his highest good to be in these lowest concerns, and was tormented by great malice and envy.[32] And so, when the place where the boy was afterwards born had been pointed out by the revelations of the seers, he said, "I shall keep watch there on my own for so many days, and whomever I find resting there – if only for a short time – shall die, slain by my sword." These things having been foretold in this way, when the nine months had come round and the time for the birth drew near, the mother went out one day along that same road which led to the place of the birth, where the tyrant kept watch in accordance with the seers' prophecy. The time for the birth was pressing, so the mother sought the predicted place; but on that very day, such a great storm blew up that no one could even go outside, for there were flashes of lightning, terrifying peals of thunder, and a tremendous downpour of hail and rain;

---

[27] *buccina*: a word known from the Vulgate (Lev. 25.9, Judg. 3.27, 6.34, Ps. 80.4, etc.), but omitted from the text of ND both here and in § 52.

[28] The unusual word *bragminatio*, here with interlinear gloss *principatus uel dignitas*, is picked up again below in § 57 (see note).

[29] Gildas's leaving Britain for Ireland was given its place in the B-version of the *Annales Cambriae*, s.a. 565.

[30] For this story, cf. Lk. 1.8–23.

[31] The following story is modelled on Herod in Mt. 2.1–19.

[32] 'his highest good'; compare the opening words of Isidore's *Sententiae*, 'Summum bonum Deus est.'

rum[f] clangor, nimia grandinum pluuiarumque inundantia affuit. Locus autem, in quo mater parturiens ingemiscebat, tanta lucis serenitate prelucebat ut ueluti sole presente Deo nubibus obducto roraret. Mater uero parturiens quandam iuxta habebat petram, in qua urgente dolore manibus innixa fuerat, [g]quare uestigium ueluti cere impressum petra intuentibus ostendit; que in medium diuisa dolenti matri condoluit, [r]cuius altera pars saltauit desuper caput sanctimonialis [h]tenus pedes eius quando enixa est puerpera[1]; in quo loco ecclesia sita est, in huius uero altaris fundamine hę c petra tecta latet.

7 [a][r]DEINDE, cum baptizaretur ab Helue Muminensium[b] episcopo, in ipso loco ad baptizandi ministerium fons lucidissimę undę erumpens subito apparuit, qui nunquam antea uisus fuerat. Curauit quoque occulos Moui ceci, qui tenuit eum dum baptizaretur; intelligens enim sanctus ille cecus, qui, sicut fertur, ab utero matris sine nare et sine oculis natus fuerat, infantem quem in sinu suo tenebat plenum esse gratia Spiritus Sancti, accepit aquam de qua corpus sancti infantis ter immersum fuerat, sparsitque faciem suam ex ea tribus uicibus et, dicto cicius, claritatem oculorum totamque integritatem faciei suę hilariter sumpsit; cunctique qui aderant glorificauerunt Dominum et Dauid agium in die illa.[1] **8** [a][r]Locus autem, in quo Dauid agius eruditus est, Vetus Rubus uocatur;[1] crescebatque gratia plenus, uisu amabilis; [r]illicque didicit Dauid agius rudimentum, psalmos, lectiones totius anni, et missas, et sinaxin; ibique uiderunt condiscipuli eius columbam cum rostro aureo ad labia eius ludentem, eumque docentem, et ymnos Dei canentem.[1] **9** Sed [a]succedente tempore, crescentibusque uirtutum meritis, uirginem a sponsę complexibus seruans

---

[f]   tonitruorum V] tonitruum ND tonitrui N[23] *The grammar of the original has been corrected in* ND

[g]   quare uestigium ueluti cere impressum petra intuentibus ostendit V *'for which reason the rock shows the trace impressed as on wax to those who look'*] quare uestigium ueluti cera impressum petram intuentibus ostendit ND. *It is tempting to emend* quare *to* quarum, *referring back to* manibus *in the previous phrase, 'hands, whose trace the rock shows. . .'. James's translation reads 'whereby the marks of her hands, as though impressed on wax, have identified that stone for those who have gazed upon it'.*

[h]   tenus pedes V *presumably for* pede tenus

§ 7

[a]   Deinde ab Elue Muniensium episcopo baptizatus Moui ceci oculos qui eum sub unda tenebat respersis aqua oculis ignotum predstando diem aperuit. In ipse uero loco ad baptizandi ministerium fons subito lucidissimę undę erumpens apparuit ND

[b]   Muminensium ND, *though individual copies show a variety of forms, evidence that the word was not recognized*] Meneuensium N[237]D[4] *and the primary reading in* V, *corrected by the copyist to* Muminensium, *was an obvious if misguided alteration.*

§ 8

[a]   ND *paraphrases.*

§ 9

[a]   succedente VN] et succedente D

but the place where the labouring mother was groaning was lit with such serene light that it shone as if God were present, though the sun was obscured by clouds. The mother, in her labour, had a stone near her on which she had leaned with her hands when pressed by her pains, which is why to those who look the rock shows the mark impressed as on wax. It broke in half in sympathy with the mother in her agony; the other part of it jumped over the head of the nun as far as her feet when the mother gave birth. A church has been built in that place, and this stone lies hidden in the base of its altar.

§ 7. Later, when he was baptized by Ailbe, bishop of Munster, at the same place,[33] a spring of very clear water suddenly appeared, springing up for the administration of the baptism, where none had ever been seen before. Furthermore, it healed the eyes of the blind Mobí,[34] who held him while he was being baptised; for that blind holy man, who, as it is said, had been born from his mother's womb without nostrils and without eyes, perceiving that the infant whom he held in his bosom was full of the grace of the Holy Spirit, took the water, in which the body of the infant had been immersed three times, and splashed it on his face three times and, quicker than saying it, he joyfully obtained the sight of his eyes and the whole completeness of his face; and everyone who was there that day glorified the Lord and the holy David. § 8. Now the place where the holy David was educated is called *Vetus Rubus*, the Old Grove;[35] and he grew up full of grace,[36] pleasant to behold; and there the holy David learned the rudiments, the psalms, the readings of the whole year, the masses, and the divine office;[37] and there his fellow pupils saw a dove with a golden beak playing about his lips,[38] and teaching him, and singing the hymns of God.[39] § 9. But as time passed, he grew in virtues and merits, and keeping his flesh innocent of a wife's embraces, he was made a priest, and elevated to the sacerdotal

---

[33] Ailbe's presence in Britain is not explained, but his association with St David is reflected in the dedication of St Elvis (in Welsh Llaneilw), near Solva, discussed by Wade-Evans. In the earliest text of the Life of St Ailbe, § 21 (Heist, *Vitae*, 123), Ailbe takes the place of Gildas in a story similar to that in § 5 above; Ailbe, not yet himself a bishop, was unable to say mass in the presence of David's pregnant mother because of the unborn bishop in her womb. That text dates from the eighth or ninth century, and may reflect a Life of St David from a still earlier date. One may wonder whether Ailbe figured earlier than David's baptism in Rhygyfarch's main source.

[34] St Mobí of Glasnevin, known in Irish as Mobí Cláirainech ('flat-faced') from his having been born without eyes or nose. No Life survives. He is named in the eighth-century Life of St Fintan of Clonenagh, § 3 (Heist, *Vitae*, 146), and in the later but related Life of St Colum of Terryglass, § 13 (Heist, *Vitae*, 228); his story appears in brief in the Middle Irish scholia on the *Féilire Oengusa* (Stokes, 216, 222–5).

[35] Gerald of Wales equates this name with *Hen Fynyw* 'Old Menevia', but the Welsh text merely translates the Latin, *yr Hennllwyn* 'Old Grove', suggesting the location intended was by then no longer understood.

[36] 'full of grace', Lk. 1.28.

[37] This series advances up the scale of religious knowledge, and the meaning of *synaxis* as the final stage is unclear. The word is used in the New Testament for a religious meeting (e.g. Acts 11.26, 14. 27), while in the Rule of St Benedict, § 17, it is used with reference to vespers, 'uespertina synaxis'; Columbanus defines the word, *cursu psalmorum et orationum modo canonico* 'the canonical round of psalms and prayers'. Distinct from the mass, it may refer to the round of daily services that make up the divine office. In Byzantine usage it refers to the service on special occasions such as saints' days.

[38] The phrase *ad labia eius ludentem* 'playing at his lips' may reflect a vernacular idiom, though the Welsh version has simply *yn gware yn y gylch* 'playing around him'; compare Irish *ar bélaib* 'on the lips', an idiom for in front of someone.

[39] A dove would later instil words into David's preaching, § 52.

carnem, presbyter effectus, sacerdotali dignitate sullimatur. **10** [a]'Exinde perrexit ad Paulinum[b] scribam, discipulum sancti Germani episcopi', qui in insula [c]in Wincdilantquendi gratam Deo uitam agebat, [d]'quique eum docuit in tribus partibus lectionis donec fuit scriba. Mansit autem ibi sanctus Dauid multis annis legendo implendoque quod legebat'. **11** [a]'Contigit autem, dum esset Dauid agius apud Paulinum[b] magistrum, illum amisisse lumen oculorum suorum propter nimium dolorem eorum; uocauitque cunctos discipulos suos ex ordine ut inspicerent et benedicerent oculos suos, feceruntque sicut preceperat illis, et a nullo eorum accepit remedium. Tandem inuitauit Dauid agium ad se, et ait illi, 'Dauid agie, considera oculos meos, multum enim me cruciant.' Responditque Dauid agius et dixit, 'Pater mi, ne mihi precipias uultum tuum inspicere, decem enim anni sunt ex quo tecum scripturę operam dedi, et adhuc faciem tuam non aspexi.' Et ait Paulinus[c] nimiam uerecundiam admirans illius, 'Quia ita est, satis erit ut palpando benedicas oculos meos et sanabor'. Statimque ut tetigit eos in ictu oculi sanati sunt, expulsisque oculorum tenebris, sublatam magister accepit lucem. Tunc grates Deo soluuntur, benedixitque Paulinus[d] Dauid agium omnibus benedictionibus, que in ueteri et in nouo testamento scriptę sunt.'

12 NON [a]post multum temporis angelus Paulino[b] apparens[c], 'Tempus est,' inquit[d], 'ut [e]Dauid agius, duplicatis ex commercio talentis, commissum sibi[f] sapientię talentum non terrę fodiens lento desidię torpore pigrescens mandet, sed acceptam Domini sui pecuniam meliore lucri incremento augescat ut intra gaudium Domini constitutus animarum manipulos ad superna ęternę beatitudinis horrea cumulando aggreget.' Nam quantis exortationis ungue exaratis triticeis seminibus insertis aliis quidem centenum aliis sexagesimum[g] aliis tricesimum[h] bonę messis captauit fructum. In boue enim firmę et asino exiguę uirtutis pariter non arans, sed aliis firmum uitę panem aliis pię exortationis lac attribuens, quosdam intra cenobialis claustri septa coartans, quosdam uero latioris uite sequaces diuersa monitos eruditione a secularium uoluptatum lubricis cupiditatibus ablactans, omnibus omnia factus est. **13** Nam duodecim [a]ad laudem Dei monasteria fundauit; primum adueniens Glas-

§ 10
[a] Exin profectus Paulinum Germani discipulum adit doctorem ND
[b] Paulinum ND] Paulentem V, *corrected above the line; in § 49 Paulinus is the reading of all witnesses*
[c] in Wincdilantquendi ND *with a diversity of spellings*] quadam V
[d] *om.* ND
§ 11
[a] ND *paraphrases.*
[b] Paulentem V
[c] Paulens V
[d] Paulens V, *corrected above the line*
§ 12
[a] post multum temporis V] post multum tempus ND, *normalizing the grammar.*
[b] Paulenti V
[c] apparens ND] apparuit, *corrected to* apparens V; *Wade-Evans printed* apparuit.
[d] inquid V
[e] Dauid agius V] Dewi ND
[f] sibi VND] *James incorrectly reports the reading of* V *as* ibi.
[g] sexagenum *Wade-Evans*
[h] tricenum *Wade-Evans*
§ 13
[a] ad laudem Dei V] admodum ND, *except that* D[8] *omits and* N[5] *paraphrases, suggesting that there was some unclarity in the reading.*

rank. § 10. After that he went to the scholar Paulinus, a disciple of the holy bishop Germanus, who, in an island in *Wincdilantquendi*,[40] led a life pleasing to God. He taught him in the three parts of reading until he was a scholar. Saint David remained there many years studying the Bible and following what he studied. § 11. While the holy David was with his teacher Paulinus, it came about that the latter lost the sight of his eyes because of their great pain. He called each of his disciples in turn to inspect and bless his eyes; they did as he had told them, but he did not receive a cure from any of them. At last he summoned the holy David to him and said to him, "Holy David, look closely at my eyes, because they are tormenting me." And the holy David responded and said, "My father, do not ask me to look at your face, because for ten years I have given my attention with you to scripture, and so far I have not looked at your face." And Paulinus, admiring his extreme modesty, said, "Since it is so, it will be sufficient for you to touch my eyes and bless them, and I shall be cured." And as soon as he touched them – in a twinkling – his eyes were cured;[41] the darkness of his eyes having been banished, the teacher received the light that he had lost. Then thanks were rendered to God, and Paulinus blessed the holy David with all the blessings that are written in the Old and the New Testament.

§ 12. Not long afterwards an angel appeared to Paulinus and said, "It is time that the holy David, having doubled his talents by putting them to good use, should not bury in the ground the talent of wisdom entrusted to him and become sluggish with the lingering inactivity of idleness, but should increase the money he had received from his lord with a better growth of profit; so that, established in the joy of the Lord, he might gather in the sheaves of souls to fill up the heavenly storehouse of eternal bliss."[42] For he sowed and ploughed a great quantity of wheat-seed with the plough-share of exhortation, and then gathered in the fruit of a good harvest, in some instances a hundred-fold, in others sixty-fold, and in others thirty-fold.[43] For he did not plough with a powerful ox and a weak ass together,[44] but he provided some with the strong bread of life, and others with the milk of godly encouragement; he gathered some within the cloisters of monastic communities, but counselled others eager for the broader road of life with different advice, in order to wean them from the slippery desires of worldly pleasures. Thus he became all things to all men.[45] § 13. For he founded twelve monasteries to the glory of God. Reaching Glastonbury first,

---

[40] The name is corrupt. *Wincdi* might represent OW *Uuinn-di*, 'Gwyn-dy, White-house'; or *Uuint-di*, 'Gwynt-dy, Windy-house'. *Lantquendi* looks like *Lant=Nant* (cf. Llancarfan for Nantcarfan in Lifris's *Vita S. Cadoci*), and then *-quendi* looks like *Gwyndy* again – or possibly even *Gwendy*. N₅ has *Wincdiland* simply; thus, *-quendi* could be a gloss that has crept into the text. The name is given as *Withland*, i.e. Whitland (Hendy-gwyn), Carmarthenshire (SN 19 16), in N₇, I₁₋₃, ₅, but this may be speculation on the part of the copyist. It could be that the whole phrase is a later gloss that has entered the text, where *in Wincdilant (quendi)* may have been intended as synonymous with *in insula quadam*. Alternatively, V may have replaced gibberish with *quadam* where its exemplar contained a name, and the shortened ND text has unusually preserved the name. (We are grateful to Dr O. J. Padel for help with this note.)

[41] Mt. 9.29; 20.34: *tetigit oculos*.

[42] cf. the parable of the talents, Mt. 25.14–28.

[43] cf. the parable of the sower, Mt. 13, esp. 13.8.

[44] cf. Deut. 22.10. This analogy uses the image of a plough that would have been drawn either by two oxen or two asses, as opposed to one of each at the same time.

[45] 1 Cor. 9.22.

timberi[b], ecclesiam ibi construxit; deinde uenit Badum[c], ibique mortiferam aquam benedictione salutarem efficiens, lauandis corporibus dignam perpetuo donauit calore; postea uenit Croulan et Reptun[d]; ⌜inde ad⌝ Coluan[e] et Glascum[f], ⌜et altare anceps secum habebat⌝; hinc Leuministre monasterium fundauit; postea in regione Guent in loco, qui dicitur Raclam[g], edificauit ecclesiam; deinde monasterium ⌜in loco, qui dicitur⌝ Langemelach, ⌜fundauit in regione Guhir⌝, in quo postea altare missum accepit. Pepiau[h] quoque regem Ercig[i] cecum, restauratis oculorum luminibus, sanauit; ⌜duo quoque sancti Boducat et Martrun in prouincia Cetgueli dederunt sibi manus⌝. **14** His itaque ex more fundatis, dispositisque canonici ordinis utensilibus, ac ordinata cenobialis habitus regula, ad locum, quo prius proficiscens exulauerat, i. ad Veterem Rubum, rediit. Habitabat autem ibi Guistilianus[a] episcopus fratruelis eius; cum autem colloquiis diuinis inter se consolarentur, sanctus ᵇ⌜inquit Dauid, 'Angelus Domini mihi⌝ locutus dixit, Ex loco, in quo deseruire proponis, uix e centum unus ᶜ⌜poterit ad Dei regnum euadere. Ostenditque mihi locum, ex quo pauci in infernum intrabunt, omnis enim qui in cimiterio illius loci sana fide sepultus fuerit, misericordiam consequetur⌝.'

15 QUADAM uero die ᵃDauid et tres eius fidelissimi discipuli, multa condiscipulorum comitante turba, conueniunt, Aidanus, scilicet, Eliud, et Ismael, pariterque una concordes dilectione locum, quem angelus premonuerat, adeunt, ᵇ⌜id est, Rosinam Vallem, quam uulgari nomine Hodnant Brittones uocitant, in qua, primo⌝ accenso in nomine Domini foco, fumus in summis eleuatus, totam, ut apparebat, insulam necnon et Hiberniam circumgirans, implebat. **16** Quidam autem ex uicinia loci propinquus ⌜satrapa magusque⌝, Baia uocatus, ⌜Scottus,⌝ sparsis in mundo solis fulgoribus, arcis menibus residens, uiso tali signo hebetans intremuit; tantaque permotus ira ut nec prandii meminisset totum tristis peregit diem; ad quem ⌜eiusdem⌝ mulier ⌜ueniens

---

b   Glastimberi ND] Glastoniam V, *a Latinized form that had become more widely known in the twelfth century.*

c   Badum ND] Bathoniam V, *another increasingly accessible Latinization.*

d   Reptun ND] Repetun V

e   Coluan ND] Colguan V *The letter* u *in* ND *represents the sound* /v/, gu *in* V *represents* /w/; *on the alternation of these sounds in Middle Welsh, Evans, Grammar, § 10.*

f   Glascum ND] Glascun V

g   Raclam ND] Raglam V

h   Pepiau VD[347]] Proprium ND. *It is hard to explain the split among the readings of the D family. Peibio Claforog (MW Pepiau Clauorauc) appears in the Life of St Dyfrig and several charters in LL as king of Ergyng.*

i   Ercig ND] Erging V

§ 14

a   Guistilianus V] Guistidianus N[37] Guistdianus N[2] Guisdianus N[159]D[1247] *with a variety of still more decadent forms in other manuscripts.*

b   inquiens Dewi, Mecum ait qui comitatur angelus ND

c   ND *paraphrases.*

§ 15

a   Dauid et V] ad eum ND *The reading of V is clear, 'David and three disciples meet', but* ND*'s reading, 'to him three disciples come together', is not merely less clear but goes against the convention of naming the saint in each chapter; and here there is a definite chapter-marker in the phrase 'Quadam uero die'.*

b   *om.* ND, *losing details of the topographical setting of David's career.*

he built a church there; then he came to Bath, and here, making the death-dealing water health-giving by blessing it, he endowed it with perpetual heat, making it suitable for the bathing of bodies. Afterwards he came to Crowland and Repton; from there to Colfa and Glascwm, and he had a double altar with him; from here he founded the monastery of Leominster; afterwards he built a church in a place called Raglan, in the region of Gwent; then he founded a monastery in the place called Llangyfelach, in the region of Gower, in which he later received the altar sent to him. He also cured the blind Peibio, king of Ergyng, by restoring his eyesight;[46] also two holy men in Cydweli, Byddugad and Martrun, helped him. § 14. When he founded these churches according to the usual practice, having distributed to each one the vessels of canonical order, and having laid down the rules of monastic dress, he returned to the place which he had left behind when he first set out, that is *Vetus Rubus*, the Old Grove. His brother's son, Bishop Gwystli, was living there;[47] but when they were comforting each other with godly conversation, Saint David said, "The angel of the Lord has told me, 'From the place where you intend to serve God, scarcely one out of a hundred will be able to ascend to the kingdom of God.' Instead, he showed me a place from where few will go to perdition; for everyone who is buried in good faith in the graveyard of that place will obtain forgiveness."[48]

§ 15. One day, David and his three most faithful disciples – namely Aidan, Eliud and Ishmael[49] – all met together, accompanied by a throng of their fellow disciples.[50] By unanimous choice, they went to the place previously foretold by the angel, that is, the *Vallis Rosina*, which the Welsh are in the habit of calling by the common name of Hoddnant. There, when the first fire had been lit in the name of the Lord, the smoke rose up on high, and it seemed to fill the whole island, also swirling around Ireland too.[51] § 16. A neighbour from the surrounding area, a warlord and seer called Baia, an Irishman, was resting within the ramparts of his castle while the sun's rays were diffused over the earth. On seeing such an omen he trembled and grew faint; and he was moved to such great anger that he did not remember his lunch and spent a

---

[46] This king appears in the Llandaf charters (72a, 72b, 73a, 73b, 75, 76a) and in the Life of St Dyfrig in the Book of Llandaf and Vespasian A. xiv.

[47] *Sanctus Gistlianus episcopus et confessor* appears in the Kalendar of BL MS Cotton Vespasian A. xiv with his feast on 2 March ('The kalendar', ed. Harris, 47).

[48] Burial in the right place was seen as a guarantee of salvation in the traditions of several Irish saints, among them St Finnbarr of Cork (see § 39).

[49] On Aidan, whose name is Irish, see §§ 35–7, 42 below. Eliud (better known under the Welsh hypocoristic form Teilo) appears again, §§ 44, 48. Ishmael does not appear elsewhere in the Life, but his Hebrew name (like David's own) is a distinctive feature of Welsh custom, and he is mentioned in other sources. *Llanismael* 'St Ishmael's' is second (after St Davids) among the seven bishop-houses of Dyfed (Wade-Evans, *Welsh Medieval Law*, 121).

[50] Lk. 6.17: *turba discipulorum eius.*

[51] For the dramatic story of how St Patrick lit his fire in Ireland before the fire was lit in the king's house, and its prophetic implications, see Muirchú's Life of St Patrick, I 15, or in *Vita III S. Patricii*, § 37.

interrogansque⌐ cur insolitum mensę obliuisceretur, 'Quid tam tristior et tam stupe-factus', inquit, 'solus meres ipse?' Ad hęc ille, 'Vidisse me,' inquit, 'doleo fumum ex Rosina Valle surgentem, qui omnem circumibat patriam, certum enim teneo quod eius incensor potestate et gloria cunctos antecellet ⌐in quamcunque partem fumus hostię eius circumiuit usque in finem mundi⌐; nam[a] quasi quodam prenuntio fumus iste eius famam predicit.' Cui coniunx ⌐in insaniam uersa⌐, 'Surge,' inquit, 'accep-taque seruorum turba, ⌐uirum illum et seruos suos ignem accendentes super agros tuos absque precepto tuo⌐, tale ausos facinus, strictis insecutus gladiis, cunctos inte-rime.' [b]⌐Veneruntque Baia satellitesque eius ut occiderent Dauid et discipulos eius, sed febris subito per uiam gradientes tenuit eos, nec potuerunt occidere Dauid aut pueros eius, sed blasphemauerunt Deum et Dauid agium, malaque uerba dixerunt⌐; neque enim nocendi uoluntas deerat, quamuis ęterno prohibita numine operandi facultas exinaniret. Domum inde regressi, obuiam inuenerunt coniugem. 'Pecora' inquit 'nostra [c]⌐et iumenta et oues et omnia animalia mortua sunt.' Et lamentaue-runt Baia et coniunx eius et tota familia eius ualde, et ululauerunt omnes pariter et dixerunt 'Sanctus ille et discipuli eius, quos blasphemauimus, mortificauerunt pecora nostra⌐; reuertamur itaque, flexisque poplitibus misericordiam postulantes, seruum Dei adoremus ut si uel sic et nostri et pecorum misereatur'. Reuertentes-que[d] seruum Dei adeunt, lacrimis et orationibus misericordiam petentes, 'Terra,' inquiunt, 'in qua es, tua in sempiternum fiat'. ⌐Deditque Baia eadem die Dauid agio totam Rosinam Vallem perpetuo possidendam.⌐ Seruus autem Dei, ⌐Dauid,⌐ respondens benigno animo, 'Pecora,' inquit, 'uestra reuiuiscent.' ⌐Inuenitque Baia domum reuersus pecora sua uiua ac sana.⌐

17 ALTERA autem die uxor eius liuoris zelo accensa, conuocatis ancillis, 'Ite,' inquit, '⌐ad flumen quod dicitur Alun,⌐ et nudatis corporibus in conspectu sanctorum ludicra exercentes, impudicis utimini uerbis.' Ancille obediunt, impudicos exercent ludos, concubitus simulant, blandos amoris nexus ostendunt; monachorum mentes quorundam ad libidines pertrahunt, quorundam molestant. [a]⌐Cuncti uero discipuli eius illam intolerabilem iniuriam non ferentes, dixerunt Dauid agio 'Fugiamus de hoc loco quia non possumus hic habitare propter molestiam muliercularum mali-gnantium'.⌐ Sanctus autem pater ⌐Dauid⌐ patientię longanimitate solidus, cuius anima nec prosperis mollita dissolueretur nec aduersis fatigata terreretur, 'Nostis,' inquit, 'quod odit uos mundus, sed tunc[b] scitote quod plebs Israelitica, comitante federis archa, terram repromissionis ingrediens, continuis preliorum periculis cesa[c]

---

§ 16
[a] nam quasi ND] namque quasi V
[b] Hoc facto grande pacti scelus ingenti per uiam gradientes febre correpti eneruauere. Viribus tamen inualidi spurcissimis oppobriorum blasphemiis oppugnant ND
[c] *It is not apparent that this omission was deliberate, in the interests of economy, or accidental, caused by eye-skip.*
[d] Reuertentesque V] Reuerso gressu ND
§ 17
[a] deserere monachi locum conantur ND
[b] tunc ND] *om.* V
[c] cesa VN] cassata D

whole day in gloom. His wife came to him, asking why he should have unusually forgotten his meal. "Why are you so miserable and confused," she said, "feeling sorry for yourself on your own?" To this he replied, "I have been disturbed by the sight of the smoke rising from *Vallis Rosina*, which is encompassing the whole country, for I am certain that he who lit that fire will excel everyone in power and glory wherever the smoke of his sacrifice travels, even to the end of the earth; for, as if by some portent, this smoke predicts his fame." His wife said to him, having turned angry, "Get up and take a troop of slaves and, with your swords drawn, kill that man and his servants, who light a fire on your estates without your permission, for having dared such an offence." And Baia and his attendants came to kill David and his disciples; but walking along the road, a fever suddenly gripped them and they could kill neither David nor his servants; but they blasphemed God and holy David and spoke evil words, for the will to do them injury was not lacking, even if the means to accomplish it was drained from them, having been thwarted by providence. When they were returning home from there, they found his wife coming to meet them. "Our cattle," she said, "and beasts of burden, and sheep and all the animals are dead." And Baia and his wife and his whole household lamented very much, and everyone wailed alike and said, "That saint and his disciples, whom we have blasphemed, have killed our cattle; therefore let us return and ask for mercy on bended knees, and entreat the servant of God that he will thus have mercy both on us and our cattle." And turning back, they came to the servant of God; begging for mercy with tears and prayers, they said, "The land where you are shall be yours for ever." And on that same day Baia gave holy David the whole of *Vallis Rosina* in perpetual possession. And David, the servant of God, responding in good spirit, said, "Your cattle will revive." And when he returned home, Baia found his cattle alive and well.

§ 17. Another day, his wife, inflamed with jealous spite, called her maids and said, "Go to the river called Alun and bare your bodies, playing games and using lewd words in front of the holy men." The maids obeyed, they played immodest games, imitating sexual intercourse and displaying love's seductive embraces. They enticed away the minds of some of the monks to lust; they irritated the minds of others. Indeed, all of his disciples, not willing to suffer that intolerable insult, said to the holy David, "Let us flee from this place because we cannot live here on account of the annoyance of these mischievous little women." But the holy father, David, stead-fast with the long-suffering of patience, whose soul might neither be melted when softened by prosperity, nor be frightened when wearied by adversities, said, "You know that the world hates you,[52] yet understand that the Israelites, accompanied by the Ark of the Covenant, entering the promised land, beaten down by the continuous dangers of battles, yet not defeated, annihilated the uncircumcised people who were

---

[52] Jn. 15.18.

nec tamen uicta, insistentem[d] prope et incircumcisum deleuit populum, quod nostrę uictorię certamen manifesto signat indicio; qui enim supernę patrię promissum querit, necesse est aduersitatibus fatigari nec tamen uinci, sed Christo comite inmundam uitiorum labem tandem superare. Debemus itaque non uinci a malo, sed uincere in bono malum, quia si Christus pro nobis, quis contra nos? Estote ergo fortes insuperabili bello, ne de fuga uestra inimicus uester gaudeat. Nos debemus manere, Baia autem deficere.' His dictis, discipulorum corda roborauit, ⸢et ieiunauit Dauid in illa nocte et discipuli eius usque mane⸣.

18 ⸢ᵃIN ILLA DIE dixit coniunx Baia ad priuignam suam, 'Eamus simul ad uallem Alun, et queramus cucumeros illius ut inueniamus nuces in eis'. Ac illa humiliter suę nouercę respondit dicens, 'En ego prompta assum.' Perrexerunt pariter ad profunditatem uallis predictę; cumque peruenissent illuc, nouerca sedens delicate ait ad priuignam suam, Dunaut nomine, 'Tribue caput tuum in sinu meo, uolo enim cirros tuos leniter inuestigare'; ac illa puella innocens, que ab infantia sua pie ac caste inter pessimas mulierum turmas uixerat, uertit caput innocuum in sinum nouerce sue; illa uero nouerca insan<i>ens cito euaginauit nouaculam suam, amputauitque caput illius felicissimę uirginis; sanguis uero eius in terram fluxit, fonsque lucifluus ab eo loco surrexit, qui multos hominum languores abunde sanauit, quem locum Martirium Dunaut usque in hodiernam diem uulgus uocitat. Illa uero nouerca a Baia fugit, nemoque sub celo nouit quanam morte uitam finiuit; hinc Baia satrapa amariter fleuit, Dauid uero cum pueris suis laudem Deo eterno decantauit.⸣ **19** ⸢ᵃSicque destinauit Baia ut Dauit agium occideret. At filius Paucaut, inimicus suus, Lisci nomine, in arce sua caput eius amputauit; erat enim porta illius diluculo aperta, cum hostis inopinatus de naue uenisset; moxque ignis de celo cecidit totumque edificium suum cito combussit. Nemoque dubitet quod Dominus propter Dauid seruum suum percussit Baiam et uxorem eius;⸣ nam qui uiri Dei mortem sub cede minabatur, dignum est ut ᵇiusta eum cedes persequatur, et qui in seruos Dei immisericors erat, sine misericordia uindicetur.

20 Expulsa igitur Deo propitio inimicorum malitia, monastica in Domino classis in loco, quem angelus premonuerat, insigne construxit monasterium. **21** Perfectisque omnibus, talem cenobialis propositiᵃ feruore rigorem sanctus decreuit pater ut

---

ᵈ   insistentem V] insidentem ND, *a near arbitrary change from pursuit to ambush by the uncircumcised.*

§ 18

ᵃ   *The whole section is tastefully reduced to:* Proxima autem die eadem uxor, occisa prius innocente priuigna, in cuius martyrii sede fons sanitatum redditor emanauit, in insaniam uersa, nusquam comparuit ND

§ 19

ᵃ   Baia autem inopinato percussus hoste interiit; arx uero eius emisso celitus igne combusta euertitur ND

ᵇ   iusta *scripsi*] ista N ixta D¹ ita D² iusta D³⁴⁷ *om.* V *An early confusion is attested in ND, suggesting a lack of clarity in the exemplar;* ista *contributes little or nothing, and* D³⁴ *appear to offer the best sense, though it may well represent a shrewd conjecture at that point in the transmission.*

§ 21

ᵃ   propositi ND] prepositi VN¹³

closely pursuing them. That struggle is an evident token of our victory, for he who seeks the promise of the heavenly country must be wearied by adversities yet not be overcome, but with Christ as his companion, he must eventually prevail over the evil stain of his sins. Therefore we must not be overcome by evil but overcome evil with good,[53] for if Christ is for us, who is against us?[54] Show yourself strong,[55] therefore, with a dogged fight, lest your enemy rejoice in your flight. We must stand fast; it is Baia who must withdraw." Having said these things, he strengthened the hearts of his disciples, and that night David fasted, and his disciples too, until the morning.

§ 18. On that day, Baia's wife said to her stepdaughter, "Let us go together to the Alun valley and look for its earth-nut plants so that we may find nuts in them."[56] She humbly answered her stepmother, saying, "See! I am ready now." They went together to the bottom of the aforesaid valley, and when they arrived there, the stepmother, sitting delicately, said to her stepdaughter, named Dunod, "Place your head in my bosom, because I want gently to examine your locks." That innocent girl, who had lived piously and chastely among multitudes of the worst women since her infancy, turned her innocent head to the bosom of her stepmother, and the barbarous woman quickly unsheathed her razor and cut off the head of that most fortunate virgin. Her blood ran on to the ground, and a clear spring rose up from that place,[57] and it abundantly cured many human diseases.[58] The common people call this place Merthyr Dunod to this very day.[59] The stepmother fled from Baia, and no one under heaven knew by what manner of death she ended her life; therefore the warlord, Baia, wept bitterly, but David and his pupils sang praise to the everlasting God. § 19. So Baia planned to kill the holy David, but his enemy Llysgi, the son of Peugod, cut off his head in his castle, for its gate was open at daybreak when the enemy had come unexpectedly from a ship. Soon after, fire fell from heaven and quickly burned down the whole of his building. No one may doubt that the Lord smote Baia and his wife on account of his servant David; for it was fitting that a just death should catch up with the one who was threatening the man of God with death by the sword, and that he who was unmerciful to the servants of God should be punished without mercy.

§ 20. Now that the malice of its enemies had been cast out by the favour of God, the monastic community built a famous monastery in the Lord's name on the site that the angel had previously shown them. § 21. When everything was complete, the holy father, in his zeal for the monastic vow, decreed such austerity that every monk, sweating away at his daily work, spent his life in the community in manual labour.

---

53 Rom. 12.21.
54 Rom. 8.31.
55 2 Sam. 13.28.
56 Literally, 'look for its cucumbers (*cucumeros*) so that we may find nuts (*nuces*) in them'; the Welsh translation refers only to nuts, 'ac awn yn dwy y Lynn Alun y geissyaw kneu'. Anthony Harvey points out that in a Middle Irish tract on Latin declension (Stokes, *Irish Glosses*, 3–35, at 32, line 1049), *cucumer* is translated *cúlarán* 'pig-nut, earth-nut', cognate with Welsh *cylor*, but the word refers to the 'nut', that is the edible root-tuber, rather than the plant. The genus is *Conopodium Majus*, and is common in British woodland.
57 *fonsque lucifluus*: *lucifluus* is a late Latin adjective that is first used by Juvencus; it is found in Ieuan ap Sulien, *de familia Sulgeni*, line 84: *lucifluum ... regnum* (ed. Lapidge, 'The Welsh-Latin poetry', 84).
58 *qui multos hominum languores abunde sanauit*: cf. Mt. 4.23: *sanans omnem languorem.*
59 Otherwise unknown.

monachorum quisque, cotidiano desudans operi, manuum labore suam in commune transigeret uitam. Qui enim non laborat, ait apostolus, non manducet. Noscens enim quod secura quies uitiorum fomes et mater esset, monachorum humeros diurnis[b] fatigationibus subiugauit; nam qui sub otii quiete tempora mentesque summittunt, instabilem accidię spiritum libidinisque stimulos sine quiete parturiunt. **22** Igitur inpensiori studio, pede manuque laborant; iugum ponunt in humeris; suffossoria[a] uangasque inuicto brachio terrę defigunt[b]; sarculos serrasque ad succidendum sanctis ferunt manibus; cuncta congregationis necessaria propriis expendunt uiribus. Possessiones respuunt, iniquorum dona reprobant, diuitias detestantur; boum nulla ad arandum cura introducitur; quisque sibi et fratribus diuitię, quisque et bos. Acto opere, nullum audiebatur murmur, nullum preter necessarium habebatur collo-quium, sed quisque, aut orando aut recte cogitando, iniunctum peragebat opus. **23** Peracto autem rurali opere, ad monasterii claustra reuertentes, aut legendo aut scribendo aut orando totam ad uesperum peragebant diem. Veniente autem uespere, cum nolę pulsus audiebatur, quisque studium deserebat; si enim in auribus cuius-cunque pulsus resonaret, scripto litterę apice uel etiam dimidia eiusdem litterę figura, citius assurgentes sua sinebant officia, sicque cum silentio sine ulla collo-quii fabulositate ecclesiam petunt. Expletis psalmorum canticis, consona cordis et uocis intentione, genuflexionibus inseruiunt quoadusque sidera celo uisa finitum clauderent diem. Solus autem pater, egressis omnibus, secretam Deo [a]pro ecclesię statu fundebat orationem. **24** Tandem ad mensam conueniunt; quique[a] fessos artus accepte cenę refectione releuant[b], nec tamen[c] ad saturitatem, nimia enim satietas, quamuis solius panis, luxuriam gignit, sed tunc pro impari corporum uel ętatum statu quisque cenam capit. Non diuersorum fercula saporum, non esculentiores pastus apponunt, sed pane et oleribus sale conditis pasti, ardentem sitim temperato potionis genere restingunt. Infirmis tunc uel ętate prouectis uel etiam longo itinere fatigatis, aliqua suauioris cibi oblectamenta procurant, non enim omnibus ęquali mensura pensandum est. **25** Peracta autem gratiarum actione, ecclesiam canonica [a]cum pulsione adeunt, ibique quasi per tres horas uigiliis orationibus genuflexio-nibus insistunt. Quamdiu autem in ecclesia orarent[b], nullus oscitare, nullus sternuta-tionem facere, nullus saliuam foras iacere licenter audebat. **26** His ita gestis, sopori membra componunt. Pullorum uero cantu expergefacti, orationi genuflexioni dediti,

---

[b]   diurnis D] diuinis VN *The stemma argues for* diuinis *'godly exertions', but there is no contextual need for this word; plain sense argues for* diurnis *'daily exertions'; the two words are easily confused, and* diuinis *might have arisen as a mistake with more than one copyist.*

§ 22

[a]   suffossoria VN[239]] suffossorias ND

[b]   defingunt V] figunt ND

§ 23

[a]   pro ecclesię statu VN[269] D[347]] per ecclesię statum N[134]D[12] *It would seem that ND was in error, but it is a simple correction to restore the text, and several ND copies made it.*

[a]   quique VD] quisque N

[b]   releuant V] renouant ND

[c]   tamen VN[5]D[347]] tunc N[23469]D[12] *om.* N[1] *Again it appears that ND read* tunc *but several copies corrected the text.*

§ 25

[a]   cum pulsione V *'with canonical ringing of the bell'*] compulsione ND

[b]   orarent VN] laborarent D

"For he who does not work", says the apostle, "let him not eat."[60] Knowing that carefree leisure was the kindling and the mother of vices, he burdened the shoulders of the monks with godly exertions; for those who, in the tranquillity of leisure, relax their heads and minds, develop an inconstant spirit of sloth and restless urges to lust. § 22. Therefore they would work with their feet and hands with more vehement zeal; they would place the yoke upon their shoulders;[61] they would push spades and shovels into the earth with their unfailing arms; they would carry hoes and saws in their holy hands for cutting, and they would, by their own efforts, provide for all the needs of the community. They despised possessions, they rejected the gifts of the wicked,[62] and they detested riches. There was no bringing in of oxen to do the ploughing; rather, everyone was riches unto himself and the brethren – and ox too. When the work was completed, not a murmur would be heard; no conversation was held beyond what was necessary, but each one performed his appointed task with prayer and proper meditation. § 23. When the work in the fields was completed, returning to the cloisters of the monastery, they would spend the whole of the day until evening in reading or writing or praying. When evening arrived and the ringing of the bell was heard, everyone would abandon what he was doing. Even if the bell resounded in anyone's ears when just the tip of a letter – or even half the shape of that letter – was written, they would quickly get up and leave what they were doing. Thus, in silence, and without any chatter, they would make their way to the church. When the chanting of the psalms had ended, the purpose of their voices and their hearts being in harmony, they would devote themselves on bended knees until the appearance of the stars in the heavens brought the day to a close. After everyone had gone out, the father, alone, would pour out his private prayer to God for the condition of the church. § 24. Eventually they gather at table. Everyone relieves his weary limbs by partaking of dinner, but not to excess – for being filled to excess, even with bread on its own, gives rise to dissipation – rather, everyone receives a meal according to the varying condition of their bodies or their age. They do not serve dishes of different flavours, nor richer types of food, but feeding on bread and herbs seasoned with salt, they quench their burning thirst with a temperate kind of drink. Then, for either the sick, those advanced in age, or likewise those tired by a long journey, they provide some other pleasures of tastier food, for it is not to be dealt out to all in equal measure. § 25. When they have performed the thanksgiving, they go to church at the canonical ringing of the bell, and there they apply themselves to vigils, prayers, and genuflexions for about three hours. While they pray in church, no one freely dares to yawn, no one to sneeze, no one to spit. § 26. After spending the day in this way, they arrange their limbs for sleep. Waking up at cock-crow

---

[60] 2 Thess. 3.10.

[61] An early Irish parallel for monks' pulling the plough themselves can be found in the eighth-century Life of St Fintan of Clonenagh, § 4 (ed. Heist, *Vitae*, 147), which Rhygyfarch may have known (see n. 34).

[62] cf. *Collectio Canonum Hibernensis*, 1. 8: ... *non praesumat dona iniquorum, quae reprobat Altissimus*; 2. 22: *Dona iniquorum, quae reprobantur a Deo, reprobantur a sanctis*; 2. 23: ... *caetera iniquorum reproba, quae reprobat Altissimus* ...

totam deinceps [a]insomnem ad mane usque perducunt noctem; sicque per ceteras noctes inseruiunt.

27 A NOCTE sabbati quousque post diluculum prima diei dominice hora eluxerit, uigiliis orationibus genuflexionibus sese impendunt[a], excepta una tunc hora post sabbati matutinas. **28** Cogitationes patri propalant, patris licentiam etiam uel ad naturę requisita adquirunt. Omnia communia, nichil meum uel tuum, quisquis enim aut 'meum librum' aut aliud aliquid pronuntiaret, protinus durę subderetur penitentię. Vilibus induebantur uestibus, maxime pellinis. Indeficiens obedientia ad patris imperium, nimia perseuerantia in agendis actibus, probitas in omnibus. **29** Nam qui sancti propositi conuersationem desiderans, fratrum inire consortium postularet, prius decem diebus pre foribus monasterii quasi reprobatus, nec non et uerborum opprobriis confutatus remaneret; si autem bene utens patientia ad decimum perstaret diem, acceptus prius sub seniore qui portę preesset constitutus seruiebat; ibique per multum temporis desudans, fractusque[a] multis animi aduersitatibus, tandem fratrum merebatur inire consortium. **30** Nichil habebatur superfluum, uoluntaria diligebatur paupertas; nam quicunque eorum conuersationem cupiebat, nichil eius substantie quam mundo renuntians dimisisset, uel unum, ut ita dicam, denarium in usum monasterii pater acciperet sanctus, sed nudus ueluti e naufragio euadens receptus, nequaquam inter fratres extollens sese eleuaret, uel sua fultus substantia equalem fratribus non iniret laborem; aut religionis habitum apostatans[a] ui extorqueat, quę monasterio reliquit, et fratrum pacientiam commoueat in iram. **31** Ipse autem pater cotidianis lacrimarum fontibus exundans, thurificatis orationum holocaustomatibus redolens, geminę karitatis ardore flagrans, debitam dominici corporis oblationem puris sacrabat manibus, sicque ad angelicum solus post matutinas horas pergebat alloquium. Hinc protinus frigidam petebat aquam, in qua diutius morando rigans omnem carnis ardorem domitabat[a]. Totam deinceps diem docendo, orando, genuflectendo, curam fratrum faciendo, nec non et orphanorum, pupillorum, uiduarum, egentium, debilium, infirmantium, peregrinorum, multitudinem pascendo, immobilis et indefessus ducebat. Sicque incepit, peregit, finiuit. Reliqua autem eius disciplinę rigoris, quamuis ad imitandum necessaria, proposita compendii breuitas uetat nos exponere. Sed Egyptios monachos imitatus, similem eis duxit uitam. **32** Audita itaque boni odoris fama ⌈Dauid agii⌉, reges, principes seculares deserunt sua regna eiusque monasterium petunt. Hinc contigit ut Constantinus, Cornubiensium rex,

---

§ 26

[a] insomnem ad mane ND] diem insomnem a mane V *The two versions differ in their interpretation; while ND takes it that cockcrow is still during the night and that the text concerns the night office, V takes it that cockcrow begins the day and refers to the community spending a sleepless day. The day office is dealt with in § 31.*

§ 27

[a] impendunt VN] impendant D^{12} impendebant D^{347}

§ 29

[a] fractusque N^{69}D^{12347}V^{23}] fractisque VN^{1234} *The agreement of the manuscripts goes against the stemma, but the error that attracts* fractus *to agree with* multis *might occur in more than one context, and the correction is easily made too.*

§ 30

[a] apostatans ND *though some copies have* apostans D^{124} *corrected in* D^{24} apositans N^2] aporians V appretians N^1 *The archetype would appear to have been less than clear, since relatively early copies such as* D^{12}N^1 *already show divergent readings; V's* aporians *'impoverishing' (2 Cor 4:8) is perhaps a rather imaginative guess when faced with* apostans?

§ 31

[a] domitabat VN] domitauit D

and having prayed and genuflected, they spend the rest of the night, until morning, without sleep; and so they devote themselves throughout the other nights.

§ 27. From Friday evening until after daybreak shines at the first hour of Sunday, they devote themselves to vigils, prayers, and genuflexions, except for one hour after matins on Saturday.[63] § 28. They reveal their thoughts to the father, and even obtain his permission for the requirements of nature. All things were in common: nothing was 'mine' or 'yours',[64] for whoever might declare either 'my book' or 'my anything else' would be subjected straightaway to severe penance. They wore clothes of poor quality – mainly skins. There was unfailing obedience to the father's command, their perseverance in the performance of their duties and their upright-ness in all things were beyond measure. § 29. He who desired the way of life of a holy vow – who might ask to enter the fellowship of the brethren – would first remain before the gates of the monastery for ten days as one rejected, and even be put down by reproachful words. If he put his patience to good use, however, and stood there until the tenth day, having first been admitted he would be put to serve under the elder who had charge of the gate. He would exert himself there for a long time, and subdued by the many conflicts of his soul, he would at last be considered worthy to enter the fellowship of the brethren. § 30. Nothing would be kept that was superfluous – voluntary poverty was highly valued – for the holy father would not accept anything for the monastery's use from property that anyone who desired their way of life had given up to the world when he renounced it – not even one penny, so to speak. Rather he was received naked, as though escaping from a shipwreck, lest he should by any means exalt himself among the brethren, praising himself; or lest on grounds of his wealth he should not undertake his equal share of work with the brethren; or lest, renouncing his monastic habit, he should extort by force what he had left to the monastery and excite the patience of the brethren to anger. § 31. But the father himself, brimming with daily well-springs of tears, perfumed with the censed sacrifices of prayers, and ablaze with the fire of twofold love,[65] would consecrate the due oblation of the Lord's Body with pure hands; and in this way, after matins, he would go alone to talk with angels. Immediately afterwards he would seek cold water; by remaining in it long enough and pouring it over himself he would tame every passion of the flesh. After that he would spend the whole day teaching, praying, genuflecting, and caring for the brethren; also in feeding a multi-tude of orphans, wards, widows, needy, feeble, sick, and pilgrims; he did this invari-ably and untiringly. In this way he began, continued, and finished. The intended brevity of this short account, however, prevents us from explaining the remaining aspects of the severity of his discipline, although they are necessary as an example; but he imitated the monks of Egypt and lived a life like theirs. § 32. And so, having heard the report of the good reputation of the holy David, kings and princes of the world would abandon their kingdoms and seek his monastery. Hence it came about that Constantine, king of Cornwall, abandoned his kingdom and submitted the hith-erto untamed neck of his pride in lowly obedience in one of this father's cells; and he lived there for a long time in faithful service.[66] At length he departed for another

---

[63] *A nocte sabbati* 'from the nightfall on Saturday' must here refer to Friday evening; liturgical custom begins the cycle with nocturns in the evening.

[64] Acts 4.32.

[65] See above, note 13.

[66] King Constantine was addressed as ruler of the south-west peninsula by Gildas, *De excidio*, § 28. For later traditions, see Doble, *St Constantine*.

suum desereret regnum, ac indomita ante suę elationis colla humilitatis obedientię in huius patris cella subiugaret; ibique diu fideli conuersatus seruitio, tandem in aliam longinquam patriam monasterium fundauit[a]. Sed quia satis de eius conuersatione locuti sumus, nunc iterum ad eius miracula redeamus.

33 QUADAM die conuenientes in unum fratres conqueruntur, 'Locus iste,' inquiunt, '[a]hyeme habet aquas, sed[b] estate uix tenui riuulo fluuius illabitur.' His auditis, sanctus proficiscens pater ad proximum locum, quo eum angelus alloquebatur, perrexit, ibique sedule ac diutissime deprecans, eleuatis in celum oculis, necessariam petiuit aquam. Cum uoce orantis fons lucidissime[c] affluxit[d] aquę; et quia uineis fructifera[e] non erat patria ad efficiendum dominici corporis ⌜et sanguinis⌝ sacramentum, in uinum uersa est, ⌜ita ut in tempore suo nunquam indiguerit mero. A Domino Deo tali uiro donum fuit dignissimum⌝. Sed et alias dulces aquas a discipulis ad patris imitationem datas hominum utilitati et sanitati proficuas nouimus.

34 QUADAM quoque die quidam rusticus, nomine Terdi, orans et [a]deprecans multum, caritatis petebat officia, 'Terra,' inquiens, 'nostra aqua[b] est exhausta, ⌜quare⌝ laboriosam ad aquandum, quia e longinquo distat fluuius, habemus uiam[c]'. Sanctus autem pater proximorum compatiens necesitati, humilis ingressus est, credens quod supplici petentis postulatione et eius humillima compassione aquam poterat inuenire. Egrediens itaque et[d] aperiens paululum baculi cuspide glebę superficiem, fons emanauit lucidissimus, qui perpetua ebulliens uena frigidissimam caloris tempore donat aquam.

35 ALIO autem tempore dum sanctus Aidanus eius discipulus casu quodam ad firmandum [a]doctrinę acceptum <librum>[a] foris legeret monasterii affuit prepositus imperans ei ut ad deportanda de ualle ligna acceptis duobus bobus abiret[b], erat

§ 32
[a] fundauit V] edificauit ND
§ 33
[a] hyeme habet aquas VN[2]] tepidas habet aquas N[13]D[47] tepide habetur aque N[456]D[123] rapide habetur aque *conj. James The reading of* VN[2] *is clearly preferable, contrasting* hyeme *with* estate, *but the course* ND *has taken is obscure.*
[b] sed et D *Compare* § 9, *where* D *again adds* et *after* sed.
[c] lucidissimę V *'of most clear water'*] dulcissimę ND *'of most sweet water'*
[d] affluxit V] effluit N[1]D[1238] affluit N[234569] effluxit D[4] *The perfect tense is appropriate, but* ND *had favoured a present tense;* D4 *has realised the preferability of the perfect.*
[e] fructifera V] frugifera ND
§ 34
[a] deprecans multum V] multum deprecans ND
[b] aqua V] aquis ND, *perhaps to break the sequence of -a endings.*
[c] uiam VN[236]] uitam N[149]D
[d] et VN] terram D
§ 35
[a] doctrin" acceptum] doctrin" librum apertum N[4] doctrinam acceptum libram D[8] *The word* librum *seems to be a conjecture in both cases, inferable from context but not mentioned in any extant copy until several lines later;* acceptum *however requires a noun to agree with it, and it is probable that the book was mentioned.*
[b] abiret V] iniret ND iret N[5]D[478]

distant land and built a monastery there. But since we have said enough about the way David lived, let us now once more return to his miracles.

§ 33. One day the brethren gathered together and complained. "This place", they said, "has water in winter but in summer the river flows as scarcely even a trickle." When he heard this the holy father set out and went to the place nearby where the angel would talk to him; and earnestly praying there at great length, with his eyes raised to heaven,[67] he asked for the essential water. While he was praying, a spring of the clearest water flowed out; and since that region produced no vines, the water was turned into wine for celebrating the sacrament of the Lord's Body and Blood, so that in his time they would never want for pure wine. This was a most worthy gift to such a man from the Lord God. But we also know of other sweet waters that were provided by his disciples, in imitation of the father, for the use of mankind and the benefits of health.

§ 34. One day, moreover, a peasant named Terddi, appealing and entreating excessively, was pleading for charitable assistance, saying, "Our land is exhausted of water, and so we have a laborious journey to fetch water because the river lies a long way off." But the holy father, sympathizing with the needs of his neighbours and being a humble man, gave it his attention, believing that by the lowly request of the petitioner, and by his own most humble compassion, he would be able to find water. And so he went forth and made a little opening in the surface of the soil with the point of his staff, and the clearest spring flowed out; its stream welled up all the year round, providing the coldest water, even in the hot season.

§ 35. Another time, while his disciple, Saint Aidan, happened to be out of doors reading a book given to him to strengthen his learning, the abbot of the monastery showed up and ordered him to take two oxen and go down to fetch firewood from the valley, for the forest was some distance away.[68] Aidan the disciple, being obedient, as soon as it was said, and not taking care to shut the book, made for the forest. When he had prepared the wood and harnessed the beasts, he started to walk back.

---

[67] Jn. 17.1.

[68] St Aidan, introduced in § 15 as one of David's three most devoted disciples, is nowhere in the Life identified as Irish, though his name is Irish. He is better known in Ireland under the hypocoristic name Maedóc (see § 42 below; Maodhog in Modern Irish, St Mogue). This story appears in a more detailed and exotic form in the Life of St Maedóc (§ 12), which was available to Rhygyfarch, and is also to be found in BL MS Vespasian A. xiv.

enim silua in longinquo posita. Discipulus autem Aidanus citius dicto obediens nec ᶜclaudendi librum moram accipiens siluam petit. Paratis autem lignis iumentisque impositis regrediens uiam carpit. Via autemᵈ ad preruptum gradiebatur precipitium ᵉ<sub quo mare influit. Veniente autem ad precipitium> uehiculo boues precipitati sunt in mare. Ruentibus autem signum imponit crucis, atque ita factum est ut ex undis sanos et incolumes cum uehiculo accipiens boues lętus ingrederetur uiam. Cum autem iter faceret tanta pluuiarum inundantia exoritur ut fossę riuulis fluerent. Perfecto itinere, solutisque e labore bobus, ubi librum reliquerat ingreditur, sicque apertum et a pluuiis illesum repperit ⌜sicut dimisit⌝. Fratribus autem hec audientibus, et patris gratia et discipuli humilitas pariter collaudaturᶠ. Nam patris gratia librum indicabat <a>ᵍ pluuiis intactum obedienti seruatum discipulo, discipuli autem humilitas boues patri custodit incolumes. **36** Sanctus autem Aidanus ad plenum eruditus, uirtutibus pollensᵃ plurimum excoctis ad purum uitiis Hiberniam petit; constructoque ᵇmonasterio ibi quod Hibernensi lingua Guernin uocatur, sanctissimam duxit uitam.

37 Cᴜᴍ autem nocte Paschali orationem impensius assequeretur, apparuit ei angelus, inquiens, 'Nosti quod uenerabili sancto Dauidᵃ uestro scilicet patri crastina die uenenum a quibusdam fratribus ad prandium apponetur?'. Sanctus autem ⌜Aidanus⌝ respondens, 'Nescio,' inquit. Cui angelus, 'Mitte,' ait, 'ex ministris quendam patri ad indicandum.' Respondens autem sanctus Aidanus, 'Nec nauis,' inquitᵇ, 'parata, nec uentus ad nauigandum est directus.' Cui angelus inquitᶜ, 'Condiscipulusᵈ tuus, Scutinus nomine, ad litus pergat maris, ego enim eum illuc transferam.' Discipulus autem obediens litus petit, mare intrat ad genuᵉ. Accipiens autem eum belua transuexit ad ciuitatis confinia. **38** Peractis autem Paschalis festiuitatis solemnibus, sanctus pater ᵃDauid agius refectorium ad prandium una cum fratribus petit. Cui obuius factus est quondam discipulus eius Scutinus. Narratisqueᵇ omnibus quę erga eum gesta fuerant et quę de illo angelus mandauerat, pariter in refectorium discumbunt lęti gratias Deo agentes. Finita oratione, assurgens diaconus, qui patri ministrare consueuerat, panem ueneno confectum mense inponit, cui cocus et economus consenserant. Scutinus autem, qui et Scolanus aliud nomen habens, se erigens, 'Hodie,' inquitᶜ, 'nullum, frater, patri ministerium adhibebis. Ego enim impendamᵈ'.

ᶜ   claudendi librum V] librum claudendi ND
ᵈ   autem <qua> V, *an attempt to restore sense lost through the omission later in the line*
ᵉ   *om.* VN²³⁴⁶⁹ *by eye-skip; the same mistake must have happened at least twice.*
ᶠ   collaudatur N] collaudantur V celebratur D
ᵍ   a ND] *om.* V
§ 36
ᵃ   uirtutibus pollens V] *the word* pollens *is out of place in* ND, *following* uitiis, *and different copies make different attempts to restore sense or resort to omission.*
ᵇ   ibi monasterio ND
§ 37
ᵃ   Dewi ND
ᵇ   infit ND
ᶜ   inquid V
ᵈ   <autem> ND
ᵉ   genu VN] genua D
§ 38
ᵃ   Dauid agius V] Dewi ND
ᵇ   narratisque V] narratis ND
ᶜ   inquid V
ᵈ   impendam VN] ministerium impendam D

Now, the road led to an abrupt precipice, under which the sea flowed. When the cart came to the precipice, the oxen fell into the sea. But he made the sign of the cross over them as they tumbled; and so it came about that he received the oxen and the cart safe and sound from the waves and joyfully proceeded on his way. But as he was travelling, such a rain-storm suddenly blew up, that the ditches flowed with streams of water. When he had completed his journey and released the oxen from their labour, he went to the place where he had left the book, and he found it open, just as he had left it, and not damaged by the rain. When the brethren heard these things, both the father's grace and the disciple's humility were praised in equal measure; for the father's grace showed that the book was preserved untouched by the rain for the obedient disciple; and the disciple's humility preserved the oxen, unharmed, for the father. § 36. Now, Saint Aidan, when he had been fully instructed, excelling in virtue, his vices purged to the highest purity, travelled to Ireland; and he built a monastery there, which in Irish is called *Fernae*, Ferns, and led a most holy life.[69]

§ 37. Now, on Easter Eve, when he was rather earnestly engaged in prayer, an angel appeared to him, saying, "Do you know that tomorrow, at lunch, poison will be served up by some of the brethren for the venerable Saint David, that is, your father?" Saint Aidan answered, "I do not know." The angel said to him, "Send one of your servants to inform the father." And Saint Aidan answered, "There is no ship ready, and the wind is in the wrong direction for sailing." The angel said to him, "Let your fellow disciple Scuithín go down to the seashore, and I will transport him there." The obedient disciple made for the shore and entered the sea up to his knees; and a sea-beast took him and carried him across to the outskirts of the city.[70]
§ 38. When the Easter solemnities had ended, the holy father, Saint David, made his way, along with the brethren, to the refectory for dinner. His former disciple, Scuithín, met him and told him everything that had been done towards him and what the angel had commanded concerning him. They took their places together at table in the refectory, joyfully giving thanks to God. When they had said grace, the servant[71] who had been accustomed to serving the father got up and placed the bread made with poison on the table (the cook and the steward had agreed to this plan). And Scuithín (who also had another name, Scolanus)[72] got up and said, "Today, brother, you shall not wait upon the father: I shall serve." The servant, being conscious of what he had done, withdrew, confused and stupefied with fear.

---

69 St Aidan or Maedóc was the founder of the monastery of *Fernae* (gen. *Fernann*), Ferns in Co. Wexford; as elsewhere Rhygyfarch writes the Irish place-name in a Welsh spelling, Gwernin.

70 There are other stories of holy men who were carried by sea creatures, but Scuithín appears in the *Félire Oengusso*, when St Bairre, travelling by ship, meets him riding on the waves (ed. Stokes, 41).

71 Rhygyfarch uses the Greek word *diaconus* 'servant who waits at table', and hence liturgically 'deacon', but there is no evident connotation of clerical status.

72 Scuithín's alternate name points towards Ysgolan, a figure of Welsh legend who appears in a poem in the Black Book of Carmarthen (Jarman, *Llyfr Du*, 55).

Diaconus autem confusus abscedens, facti conscius, hebetans diriguit. [e][Accepitque Dauid agius panem illud uenenosum, diuidensque in tres partes, unam dedit canicule foris stanti iuxta ostium, statimque ut morsum gustasset misera morte uitam finiuit. Omnes enim pili illius in ictu oculi ceciderunt, ita ut uiscera eius foras erumperent, corio passim infracto, stupueruntque fratres omnes illud uidentes. Misitque Dauid agius alteram partem coruo, qui erat in nido suo in fraxino, quę erat inter refectorium et amnem ad australem plagam, moxque ut rostro tetigit exanimis de arbore cecidit. Tertiam uero partem Dauid agius in manu sua tenuit, et benedixit comeditque eam cum gratiarum actione, inspexeruntque in eum cuncti fratres miro modo stupentes] quasi per tres horas. Ipse autem, nullo mortiferi ueneni signo apparente, intrepidus uitam seruauit incolumem. [Nuntiauitque Dauid agius fratribus suis omnia, que ab illis tribus predictis uiris facta fuerant. Surrexeruntque fratres omnes, et planxerunt, maledixeruntque illos uiros dolosos, economum scilicet et cocum et diaconum, dampnaueruntque eos et successores eorum, ex uno ore dicentes nunquam habituros eos partem regni cęlestis in ęternum.]

39 ALIO quoque tempore cum inextinguibile[a] desiderium ad sanctorum Petri et Pauli apostolorum reliquias uisitandas haberet[a], inter ceteros fidelissimus ille abbas Hibernensium[b], cui nomen Barre, sacratam peregrinandi uiam indefessis carpebat plantis. Perfecto salutari uoto, ad monasterii claustra reuertens[c], sanctum uisitabat uirum, [Dauid agium,] ibique per aliquantulum temporis in diuinis colloquiis ex uoto moratus, prepedita uentorum indigentia naui qua patriam reuisere parauerat, longiori retardabatur mora. Timens autem ne sine abbate in fratribus contentiones, lites, rixe, soluto caritatis uinculo, exorirentur, ueluti apes, rege perempto, fauorum cellas quas tenaci glutino solidauerant, diruunt, euertunt, sollicita perscrutatus mente mirabile inuenit iter. Nam quadam die equum, in quo sanctus pater [Dauid] ad ecclesiasticas utilitates insidere[d] consueuerat, petiuit. Concessum accepit. Accepta patris benedictione, portum petit, mare intrat; fidens patris benedictione ac sustentaculo equi utitur pro naui. Equus enim tumentes fluctuum cumulos ceu planum perarabat campum. **40** Cum autem in mare longius graderetur, apparuit ubi sanctus Brendanus super marinum cetum miram ducebat uitam. Sanctus autem Brendanus, hominem in mare uidens equitantem, stupefactus, ait, 'Mirabilis Deus in sanctis suis.' Eques appropinquabat ubi erat[a], ita ut [b]salutare se inuicem possent. Salutantibus [illis se] mutuo, Brendanus rogat unde esset et a quo uenisset et quomodo in mare equitasset. Cui Barre, narratis suę peregrinationis causis, inquit, 'Cum me prepedita nauis a fratribus suspenderet, sanctus pater Dauid[c] equum, in quo insidere[d]

---

[e] ND *paraphrases.*

§ 39

[a] cum inextinguibile desiderium . . . haberet V] cum inextinguibile Hibernensium desiderium . . . arderet ND *By moving the word* Hibernensium ND *avoids describing Bairre as 'abbot of the Irish', and the associated change of* haberet *to* arderet *creates an impersonal desire among the Irish to visit Rome.*

[b] om. ND *See previous note.*

[c] reuertens V] reuersus ND

[d] insidere VN] insedere D; *compare* §§ 40, 43.

§ 40

[a] erat V] esset ND

[b] salutare se VN] se salutare D³ resalutare D¹²⁴

[c] Dauid V] Dewi ND

And holy David took the poisoned bread: dividing it into three parts, he gave one of them to a little dog that stood just outside the door. Immediately, as it tasted the mouthful, the dog died a miserable death, for all its hair fell out in the twinkling of an eye, its bowels ruptured, and its skin was broken all over. When they saw it, all the brethren were astonished. Holy David sent the second part to a crow that was on its nest in an ash tree between the refectory and the river, on the south side. As soon as it touched it with its beak, the crow fell down dead from the tree. Holy David held the third part in his hand; he blessed it and ate it with thanksgiving.[73] All the brethren looked at him with wonder and amazement for about three hours; but undaunted, he confidently preserved his life unharmed and no sign of the deadly poison appeared.[74] Holy David told the brethren about all the things that had been done by those three men. The brethren all rose up and wailed, and they cursed those deceitful people – the steward, the cook, and the servant – and unanimously condemned them and their successors, saying that they should never have a place in the kingdom of heaven.

§ 39. Another time, affected by an unquenchable desire to visit the shrines of SS. Peter and Paul the apostles, that most faithful abbot of the Irish, named Bairre, among others trod the pilgrims' hallowed route with unwearied footsteps.[75] When he had accomplished his soul-saving vow, he turned back towards his own monastic cloisters and visited the holy David. He wanted to linger there for a while in godly conversation, and prolonged his stay because the ship that was made ready for his return to his own country was delayed by a lack of wind. Fearing that, in their abbot's absence, the bond of charity would be loosened and that disputes, quarrels, and brawls would arise among the brethren – just as the bees, when their sovereign dies, pull apart and break up the honeycomb cells which they had fastened together with firmly binding wax – he anxiously searched and found a wonderful way to return. One day he asked for the horse which the holy father, David, had been accustomed to ride on church business. He obtained permission, and having received the father's blessing, he reached the harbour and entered the sea. Trusting in the father's blessing, he used the horse instead of a ship as support. The horse ploughed its way through the swelling crests of the waves as if through a level field.[76] § 40. When he had travelled further out to sea, he came to where Saint Brendan was leading a wonderful life on the back of a whale.[77] Seeing a man riding a horse on the sea, Saint Brendan was astonished and said, "God is wonderful in his saints."[78] The man on horseback was approaching the place where he was, so that they would be able to greet each other. Having exchanged mutual greetings, Brendan asked from what place he might be, from whom he might have come, and how he rode a horse on the sea. Having related the cause of his journey, Bairre told him, "Since my ship's delay was keeping me away from my brethren, the holy father David gave me the horse on which he was accustomed to ride, so that I might have use of it in my need; and

---

73 cf. *Dauid agius in manu sua tenuit, et benedixit comeditque eam*: cf. Mat. 26.26, *accepit Iesus panem et benedixit ac fregit deditque discipulis suis et ait, 'Accipite et comedite …'*

74 cf. Mk. 16.18: *si mortiferum quid biberint non eos nocebit.*

75 St Bairre or Finnbarr, patron of Cork. The story of his riding St David's horse across the sea appears in the O-text of the Life of St Bairre, quoted by Plummer, *Vitae*, i. 69n.

76 Compare the Irish story of Manannán, in the voyage-tale *Immram Brain*, who rides his chariot over the sea as if over a flowery plain.

77 The story is told in the late-eighth-century *Nauigatio S. Brendani*, ed. Selmer, § 10.

78 Ps. 67.36.

consueuerat, ut eo necessitate fungerer donauit, sicque eius benedictione munitus, talem ingressus sum uiam.' Cui Brendanus, 'Vade,' inquit[e], 'in pace. Ego ueniam et uidebo eum.' Barre autem illeso gressu patriam adiit. Fratribus [f]erga eum que gesta fuerant narrauit[g]. Equum in cellę ministerio [h]usque ad obitum eiusdem[h] tenuerunt. Post obitum uero ad miraculi memoriam depictam equi imaginem formauerunt, quę usque adhuc, auro tecta, in Hibernensium insula habetur, quę etiam signorum copia claret.

41 ALIO quoque tempore alius eius discipulus, Modomnoc[a] nomine, cum fratribus uiam prope ciuitatis confinia in procliuo cauabat, quo ad deferenda necessitatum onera uiantibus facilior fieret accessus. Ipse autem cuidam ex laborantibus inquit 'Quid tu tam desidiose et segniter laboras?' At ille ad loquentis uerba iracundie permotus spiritu, ferrum, quod manu tenebat, id est, bipennem, in altum eleuans, in uertice eum ferire conatus est. Sanctus autem pater ⌐Dauid⌐ hoc a longe aspiciens, facto crucis signo, manum ad illos eleuauit, sicque [b]manus ferientis arida facta est.

42 ⌐VERUM pene tercia pars uel quarta Hibernię seruit Dauid Aquilento, ubi fuit Maidoc, qui et Aidanus ab infantia, cui dedit sanctus Dauid tintinnabulum, quod uocatur Crue din. Sed ille, nauigans ad Hiberniam, oblitus est tintinnabuli sui. Misitque Maidoc nuntium ad Dauid agium ut transmitteret ad se gratum tintinnabulum. Aitque sanctus Dauid, 'Perge puer ad magistrum tuum'. Et factum est, dum reuerteretur legatus ille, et ecce fuit tintinnabulum crastina die iuxta Aidanum clarum, angelo portante trans mare antequam uenisset nuntius eius.⌐

43 POSTQUAM autem [a]predictus sanctus Modomnoc[a] longo annorum uertigine obedientię humilitati deditus fuerat, crescentibus uirtutum meritis, Hiberniam petiit[b] insulam. Nauim ingressum[c] cuncta apum multitudo eum secuta est, secumque in naui, ubi insederat[d], collocauit[e] ⌐in prora nauis⌐. Nam idem[f], apum stationibus inseruiens, cum reliquo fraternitatis opere alueariis ad nutriendos examinum fetus operam dedit[g], quo indigentibus aliqua suauioris cibi oblectamenta procuraret. Ipse

---

[d]   insidere V] insedere ND; *compare §§ 39, 43.*
[e]   inquid V
[f]   erga eum quę VN] quę erga eum D
[g]   narrauit VN] indicauit D
[h]   usque ad obitum eiusdem V] ad eiusdem usque obitum ND usque ad eiusdem obitum D[347]
§ 41
[a]   Modomnoc V] Midimnauc ND, *assimilating the name to Welsh orthography as Myddyfnawg; the form is phonetically correct.*
[b]   manus ferientis arida facta est V] ferientis manus aruit ND
§ 43
[a]   predictus sanctus Modomnoc V] idem discipulus ND
[b]   petiit V] petit ND
[c]   ingressum VN] ingressus D
[d]   insederat VD] insiderat N
[e]   collocauit VN] collocant D
[f]   isdem D
[g]   dabat ND

so fortified by his blessing, I have travelled on such a route as this." Brendan said to him, "Go in peace. I shall come and see him." So Bairre reached his country, his journey unimpaired, and told the brethren what had happened to him. They kept the horse in the service of the monastic house until its death. After its death, they fashioned a likeness of the horse in memory of the miracle. To this day, covered with gold, it is preserved in the island of Ireland, and is famous also for a great number of miracles.[79]

§ 41. On a different occasion, another one of his disciples, named Modomnóc,[80] was digging a road with the brethren on the slope near the boundary of the monastery, so that access should be made easier for travellers to deliver their loads of supplies. He said to one of the workmen, "Why do you work so slothfully and slowly?" The worker, excited by a spirit of wrath at the speaker's words, lifted up the tool that he was holding in his hand (that is, a twin-headed axe), and attempted to strike him on the head. The holy father, David, however, seeing this from a distance, made the sign of the cross, lifted up his hand towards them, and so the hand of the assailant was withered.

§ 42. And nearly a third or a quarter of Ireland served David Aquilentus, where Maedóc was, who was also named Aidan since his infancy. He is the one to whom Saint David gave a little bell,[81] which is called *Crue din*.[82] When he sailed to Ireland, however, he forgot his little bell. So Maedóc sent a messenger to the holy David, so that he might send on to him the pleasing little bell. Saint David said, "Servant, go to your master!" and it happened that, while the messenger was on his way back, behold, the next day the little bell was with the famous Aidan (an angel had carried it across the sea before his messenger could come).

§ 43. The previously mentioned Saint Modomnóc, who had been devoted to obedience and humility over a long course of years while the merits of his virtues increased, afterwards travelled to the island of Ireland. Boarding a ship, a large swarm of bees followed him and settled with him in the prow of the ship where he sat. For he, attending the bee hives in addition to the rest of the work of the community, gave attention to the bee hives in order to nourish the swarms of young bees, so that he might provide the pleasure of some more agreeable food for the needy. He could not, however, endure to be deprived of brotherly communion; he returned

---

79 This reference to a miraculous image in Ireland is a surprise. What is it? Gerald of Wales, in his revision of the text, refers to a horse, cast in metal (*fusilem*), with a man sitting on it, decorated with gold and silver, but small in size and portable; he adds that it was kept in the church at Cork and continued to work miracles. The mention of Cork is inferred from the name of the saint, and there is nothing to suggest that Gerald has more precise information than Rhygyfarch. A reliquary of some sort is no doubt possible, but Irish hagiography took little interest in posthumous *miracula*.

80 St Modomnóc's name is given in Irish spelling in V and in Welsh, modern Myddyfnog, in ND. He is recorded in *Féilire Oengusa* (13 February); his principal church was *Tipra Fachtnai*, Tipperaghney (Co. Kilkenny), in the territory of Osraige. The name is found as MADOMNUAC in an inscription at Llanllyr, Cardiganshire, in which two men with Irish names dedicate land to the saint (Nash-Williams, *ECMW*, 26, 100 (no. 124); Sims-Williams, *The Celtic Inscriptions*, 69, 320). Gerald of Wales calls him 'Dominicus Ossoriensis', telling a story of his introducing bees from Wales to Ireland (*Topographia Hibernie* I 6, ed. Dimock, in Brewer *et al.*, *Opera* v. 29).

81 *tintinnabulum*: a word found in Ex. 28.33–4; 39.24.

82 The name of the bell is Irish, *Cruaidín* 'little hard one' or 'little strict one'; the same name was given to the sword of Cú Chulainn.

autem fraterne communionis fraudem non tolerans, iterum sancti patris presentiam uisitans, repedauit, apum comitatus turba, quęque ad sua uolitant. ⌐Cui benedixit Dauid pro humilitate sua.⌐ Hinc patri fratribusque ualedicens salutatus abiit, sed iterum apes eum sequntur[h], sicque factum est ut, si quando ipse egrediebatur, et ipsę sequerentur. [i]⌐Tertio iterum ille nauigauit aliquandiu, et factum est sicut prius. Secutaque sunt eum examina, reuersusque est ad Dauid tribus uicibus. Tertia uice dimisit Dauid agius Modomnoc nauigare cum apibus, et benedixit eas, inquiens,⌐ 'Terra, ad quam properatis, uestro sit abundans semine, nunquam ex ea uestrum deficiat germen. Nostra autem ciuitas a uobis erit in eternum deserta. Nunquam in ea fetus uester excrescat.' Quod nunc usque seruatum experimento didicimus, nam ad eiusdem patris ciuitatem examina comperimus deportata, sed ibi per aliquantum[j] temporis mansitantes deficiendo[k] deficiunt. Hibernia autem, in qua nunquam usque ad illud tempus apes uiuere poterant, nimia[l] mellis fertilitate ditatur. Itaque sancti patris benedictione Hibernia creuerunt in insula, cum constet[m] eas nequaquam ibi primo uiuere potuisse, nam si Hibernensem[n] humum aut lapidem mediis apibus immitteres, dispersę atque fugaces nimium deuitarent.

44 CRESCENTIBUS autem meritis, crescunt et[a] honorum[b] dignitates. Nam quadam nocte ad eum angelus affuit, cui inquit, 'Crastina die precingens calcia[d] te, Ierusalem usque pergere[e] proficiscens, optatam carpe uiam. Sed et alios duos comites itineris uocabo, Eliud, scilicet,' qui nunc Teliau uulgo uocatur, qui quondam eius monasterio interfuit monachus, 'necnon et Paternum,' cuius conuersatio atque uirtutes in sua continentur hystoria. Sanctus autem pater, admirans imperii preceptum, dixit, 'Quomodo hoc fiet, nam quos promittis comites trium uel eo amplius dierum spatio a nobis uel a semetipsis distant? Nequaquam ergo pariter crastina conueniemus die.' Angelus ad eum nuntiat, 'Ego hac nocte ad quemquam illorum uadam, et ad condictum, quod nunc[f] ostendo, conuenient.' Sanctus autem ⌐Dauid⌐, nichil moratus, dispositis cellulę utilitatibus, accepta fratrum benedictione, primo mane iter incepit. Peruenit ad condictum, repperit ibi promissos fratres, pariter [g]uiam intrant. Equalis commeatus, nullus enim mente alio prior, quique eorum minister, quique dominus, sedula oratio, lacrimis uiam rigant. Quo amplius pes incederet, merces excresceret, una illis[h] anima, una leticia, unus dolor.

---

[h] sequntur V] secuntur ND
[i] ND *paraphrases*
[j] aliquantum V] aliquantulum ND
[k] deficiendo V] decrescendo ND, *presumably to avoid the repetition.*
[l] *om.* V
[m] constet V] constat ND
[n] Hiberniensem V, *though* V *usually has the spelling* Hibernensis.
§ 44
[a] et VN] *om.* D
[b] honorum VD[347]] bonorum ND[12] *It would appear that* ND *shared the error* bonorum *but some of the* D *witnesses were able to correct it.*
[d] calcia VN] et calcians D[128] et caligas D[3] et caligans D[47]
[e] pergere VN] peragere D[12] peregre D[478]
[f] nunc V] tantum N[19] tamen N[2346] tibi modo D
[g] uiam intrant V] intrant uiam ND
[h] illis ND] illius V

again to visit the presence of the holy father, accompanied by the swarm of bees, and every one flew to its hive. David blessed him for his humility. Then he bade farewell to the father and the brethren and departed; but again the bees followed him, and so it came about that whenever he went out they would follow him. He sailed again a third time for a good while, and it happened as before. The swarms followed him, and he returned to David three times. The third time, holy David sent Modomnóc away to sail with the bees, and he blessed them, saying, "May the land to which you are hurrying be abundant with your offspring; may your progeny never be lacking in it. May our monastery always be deserted by you. May your young never increase in it." We have learned by experience that this has remained the case until the present, for we have found out that swarms of bees that have been brought to the father's monastery remained there for just a short time, and when they left, they disappeared. Ireland, however, where bees could never live until that time, is enriched with a great abundance of honey.[83] So, by the holy father's benediction, they have increased in the island of Ireland, since it is well known that there was no way they could live there before; for if you threw Irish earth or stone into the midst of the bees, they would very much avoid it, dispersing and flying away.

§ 44. As his merits increased, so also did his rank and respect. For one night, an angel came to him, and said, "Tomorrow, put your shoes on and set out to travel to Jerusalem and make the journey you have longed for.[84] I shall also call two others to be your companions on the way, namely Eliud" (who is now commonly called Teilo and was formerly a monk of this monastery), "and also Padarn" (whose life and miracles are contained in his own history).[85] The holy father, wondering at the authority of the command, said, "How shall this be done?[86] For those whom you promise to be my companions live three days' distance or more away from us and from each other; therefore we cannot by any means meet tomorrow." The angel said to him, "Tonight, I shall go to each of them, and they will come to the appointed place, which I shall now reveal." Saint David made no delay, but having organized the useful things of his cell, he received the blessing of the brethren and began his journey early in the morning. He reached the appointed place, met the promised brethren there, and they went on their way together. They were equals as fellow-travellers, no one considered himself to be above the other, each one of them was a servant, each one master. Constant in prayers, they watered the road with tears. The further their feet took them, the greater was their gain. They had one mind, one joy, and one sorrow.

---

83 Gerald of Wales, *Topographia Hiberniae* I 6 (ed. Dimock, 29), was aware that 'some tell that St Dominicus of Ossory introduced bees into Ireland', but his source may have been Rhygyfarch. The claim is first found in *Féilire Óengusa* (*ca* 830), ed. Stokes, 60: 'In a little boat Modomnóc, from the east over the bright-hued sea, brought – vigorous cry – the outstanding race of the bees of Ireland.'

84 Cluniac influence having been instrumental in its popularity on the continent. In England around this time we know, for example, of a group of Canterbury pilgrims in 1090 (Haskins, 'A Canterbury monk'); and the Wadham gospels (Oxford, Wadham College, MS 2; first generation after 1066) have a well-informed depiction of the holy sepulchre, likely to be based on a model of the edicule brought back by a pilgrim.

85 The reference is to the extant *Vita S. Paterni*, on which see Thomas and Howlett, *Vita Sancti Paterni*.

86 cf. Lk. 1.34.

45 Cᴜᴍ autem trans mare Brittannicum uecti Gallias adirent ac alienigenas diuersarum gentium linguas audirent, linguarum gratia ceu apostolicus ille cętus ditatus est ⌈pater Dauid⌉, ut ne in extraneis degentes gentibus interprete egerent, et ut aliorum fidem ueritatis uerbo firmarent. **46** Tandem ad optate ciuitatis Ierusalem confinia peruenerunt. Nocte autem illa ante eorum aduentum patriarchę in sompnis apparuit angelus, dicens, 'Tres ab occidentis finibus catholici adueniunt uiri, quos cum gaudio et hospitalitatis gratia suscipies, et mihi in episcopatum benedicendoᵃ consecrabis.' Patriarcha uero tres honoratissimas sedes parauitᵇ. Aduenientibus autem sanctis ad ciuitatem, magno lętatus estᶜ gaudio, eos benigne suscipiens paratis sedibus. Spirituali colloquio freti, grates Deo referunt. Deinde diuina fultus electione, ad archiepiscopatum ⌈Dauid agium⌉ prouehit. **47** His peractis, eos alloquens patriarcha, 'Obedite,' inquit, 'uoci meę, et quę precipio attendite. Iudeorum,' inquit, 'potestas inualescit in christianos. Nos commouent, fidem repellunt. Pareteᵃ itaque et ad predicationem singulis procedite diebus ut eorum uiolentia, confutata, conquiescat, noscens christianam fidem occidentis finibus diuulgatam ac ultimis terrę extremitatibus decantatam.' Obediunt imperio. Predicant singuli per singulos dies. Fit grata predicatio. Plures conuertuntᵇ ad fidem. Alios roborant. **48** Perfectis omnibus, ad patriam conantur redire. Tunc patrem Dauidᵃ ᵇpatriarcha quatuorᵇ muneribus ditauit, altari scilicet consecrato, in quo dominicum sacrabat corpus, quod innumeris uirtutibus pollens, nunquam ab hominibus ab eius pontificis obitu uisum est, sed pelleis uelaminibus tectum, absconditum latet; insigni etiam nola, sed et ipsa uirtutibus claret; baculo; ᶜet auro texta tunicaᶜ. Qui baculus, gloriosis choruscus miraculis, totam insignis predicatur per patriam. 'Sed quia,' inquit patriarcha, 'laboriosa uobis sunt in itinere ad ferendum, ad patriam redeuntes, in pace reuertimini. Ego autem post uos transmittam.' Patri ualedicunt, patriam adueniunt. Quisque autem eorum patriarchę promissum expectantes, per angelos missa sua accipiunt munera, Dauidᵈ quidem in monasterio, cui nomen Langemelachᵉ, Paternus, autem, et Eliud, quisque eorum in suo monasterio. Inde ea uulgus uocat e celo uenientia.

§ 46

ᵃ benedicendo ND] *om.* V
ᵇ sedes parauit V] parauit sedes ND
ᶜ est VN¹⁴⁵] *om.* N²³⁶⁹D

§ 47

ᵃ parete VN⁶⁹D] parate N¹²³⁴ *The agreement of* VD *over* N *is decisive, and it is possible that* N⁶⁹ *are scribal corrections.*
ᵇ conuertunt ND, *where a transitive verb is clearly correct*] conueniunt V

§ 48

ᵃ Dauid V] Dewi ND
ᵇ patriarcha quatuor V] quatuor patriarcha ND
ᶜ et auro texta tunica V] et tunica ex auro texta ND *Perhaps one should read* et ex auro texta tunica *?*
ᵈ Dauid V] Dewi ND
ᵉ Langemelach VN²³⁴] Langemelech N¹D

§ 45. When they had sailed across the British sea[87] and arrived in Gaul, they heard the strange languages of different nations, and father David was endowed with the gift of tongues, just as the apostolic company was, so that when they were staying among foreign peoples they should not lack an interpreter, and also that they should confirm the faith of others by the word of truth.[88] § 46. At length they approached the outskirts of the longed-for city of Jerusalem. On the night before their arrival, an angel appeared to the Patriarch in a dream, saying, "Three catholic men have come from western lands; receive them with joy and the grace of hospitality and consecrate them into the episcopate for me." And the Patriarch prepared three seats of the highest honour. When the saints entered the city, he rejoiced with great gladness,[89] and graciously placed them in the chairs he had prepared. Supported by spiritual conversation, they rendered thanks to God. Then, secured by divine election, he promoted holy David to the archiepiscopate. § 47. When this was done, the Patriarch spoke to them, and said, "Obey my voice, and give heed to what I shall order. The power of the Jews," he said, "is increasing against the Christians. They are disturbing us, and they reject the faith. Obey, therefore, and go out to preach every day, so that, being confuted, their violence may be subdued, knowing that the Christian faith is published in western lands and proclaimed in the farthest ends of the earth."[90] They obeyed the order; each of them preached every day; and their preaching met with success. They converted many to the faith, and they strengthened others.[91] § 48. When everything was done, they planned to return to their country. Then the Patriarch enriched father David with four gifts: namely, a consecrated altar on which he used to consecrate the Lord's Body, and which worked innumerable miracles (it has never been seen by men since the death of its bishop but is hidden with hide coverings); also a remarkable bell, which itself was also famed for its miracles; a staff; and a coat woven from gold. The staff, lustrous with glorious miracles, was famous throughout the country. "But," said the Patriarch, "because it will be laborious for you to carry them on your journey when you return to your country, make your way home in peace, and I shall send these gifts after you." They bade farewell to the father and returned to their country. Each one of them awaited what was promised by the Patriarch, and received his gifts, carried by angels. David, indeed, received his gift in the monastery named Llangyfelach; and Padarn and Eliud each received his gift in his own monastery. Hence the common people claim that the gifts came from heaven.

---

[87] i.e. the English Channel.
[88] cf. Acts 2.6, 8; and 1 Cor. 12.10, 28.
[89] A distinctively biblical usage: cf. 1 Kgs 1.40; 1 Chr. 29.9; Tob. 11.21; Mt. 2.10.
[90] cf. Acts 1.8.
[91] On the tensions between Christians and Jews at this time, see Cohen, *Under Crescent and Cross*, 140–43.

49 Quia uero post sancti Germani secundo auxilia Pelagiana heresis, suę obstinationis neruos, ueluti uenenosi serpentis uirus, intimis patrię compaginibus inserens, reuiuiscebat, uniuersalis cunctorum Britannię episcoporum synodus colligitur. Collectis itaque centum decem et octo episcopis, innumerosa affuit multitudo presbiterorum, abbatum, ceterorum ordinum, regum, principum, laicorum, uirorum, feminarum, ita ut cuncta circumquaque loca grandis nimis exercitus operiret. Episcopi autem inter se musitant, dicentes, 'Nimia adest multitudo et non solum uox sed eciam tubę clangor in cunctorum auribus insonare nequibit. Totus itaque fere populus, a predicatione intactus[a] hereticam secum labem, domum repetens, reportabit[b].' Tali ergo sub conditione populo predicare disponitur, ut erecto uestimentorum cumulo in altum terrę unus desuper stando predicaret; at quicunque tali sermonis gratia ditaretur, ut in cunctorum auribus, qui ex longo distabant, eius insonaret loquela, metropolitanus archiepiscopus omnium fieret consensu. Deinde constituto loco, cui nomen Breui, erecta uestimentorum turre, predicare nituntur, sed quasi obstruso[c] gutture uix ad proximos quosque sermo progreditur. Populus expectat uerbum, sed maxima pars non audit. Alter post alterum disputare conatur, sed nichil ualent. Fit magna [d]angustia. Timent populum, indiscussa heresi, [e]ad sua remeare. 'Predicauimus,' inquiunt, 'et nichil lucramur. Incassum ergo noster redigitur labor.' Assurgens autem episcoporum quidam, Paulinus dictus, cum quo quondam sanctus Dauid[f] pontifex legerat, 'Est,' inquit, 'quidam, qui a patriarcha episcopus factus, nostrę adhuc non affuit synodo, uir facundus, gratia plenus, religione probabilis, cui angelus comes est, uir amabilis, uultu uenustus, forma preclarus, quatuor cubitorum statura erectus. Illum ergo meo inuitate consilio.'

50 Nuntii protinus mittuntur, perueniunt ad sanctum episcopum, nunciant ad quod uenerant. Sanctus autem episcopus renuit, 'Nemo,' inquiens, 'temptet me. Quod ipsi nequeunt, qualis sum ut ego possim? Agnosco humilitatem meam. Ite in pace.' Secundo et tertio legati mittuntur, sed neque sic adquiescit. Tandem sanctissimi uiri ac fidelissimi mittuntur fratres, Daniel et Dubricius. Sanctus autem Dauid[a] episcopus, prophetię spiritu preuidens, inquit[b] ad fratres, 'Hodie, fratres, sanctissimi uiri nos adeunt. Lęto animo eos excipite. Pisces cum pane et aqua adquirite.' Adueniunt fratres, mutuo se salutant, spirituali utuntur colloquio. Prandium apponitur. Firmant nunquam se suo monasterio pransuros, nisi secum ad synodum recurrat. Sanctus autem ad hęc dixit, 'Negare uobis non possum. Prandete. Pariter uisitabimus synodum, sed tunc predicare nequeo. Orationibus tamen quantulumcunque iuuamen feram.'

---

§ 49
[a]   intactus VND] uel extorris *above line* V
[b]   reportabit VN[5]D[67]] reportat N[123469]D[12] reportet D[34]
[c]   obstruso V] obtruso ND *'as if the throat had been swallowed'; cf. § 5 'clauso gutture'.*
[d]   <in episcopis> angustia D
[e]   ad sua VN[23]D[467]] sua *cett. The omission of* ad *appears to have been a mistake often passed on but more than once corrected.*
[f]   Dauid V] Dewi ND
§ 50
[a]   Dauid V] Dewi ND
[b]   inquid V

§ 49. Since the Pelagian heresy was reviving – inserting its obstinate strength in the inmost parts of the country like the poison of a venomous snake, even after Saint Germanus had come to help a second time[92] – a universal synod of all the bishops of Wales was assembled. So one hundred and eighteen bishops were gathered, and an incalculable multitude of presbyters, abbots and other orders, kings, princes, laymen, and women, was present, so that a vast crowd covered the whole of the surrounding area. The bishops were muttering among themselves, saying, "There is such a mass of people here, no lone voice – not even the sound of a trumpet[93] – will be heard by all of them. Nearly all the people, therefore, will be untouched by the preaching, and they will take the heretical blemish away with them when they return home." Hence, it was arranged that they should raise up a heap of clothes on the high ground and that one person should stand upon it to preach to the people; also, that if anyone were endowed with such a gift of speech that his words could be heard by everyone, even those who were far off, he should, by everyone's consent, be made metropolitan archbishop. Then, at an appointed place called Brefi, having raised a tower of clothes, they each endeavoured to preach; but their words – as if swallowed in their throats – scarcely reached the people who were nearest. The people waited for the sermon, but most of them could not hear. One after another attempted to preach, but to no avail. A great dilemma arose: they feared that the people would return home without shaking off the heresy. "We have preached," they said, "but with no profit; therefore our labour is rendered useless." And standing up, one of the bishops, called Paulinus, with whom the holy pontiff, David, had once studied, said, "There is one who was made a bishop by the Patriarch, who has not yet been present at our synod. He is an eloquent man, full of grace, whose religion is proven; he is the companion of angels, an amiable man, good looking, with a splendid figure, and four cubits in height. I therefore advise you to invite him."

§ 50. Messengers were immediately sent. They came to the holy bishop, and told him why they had come. But the holy bishop refused, saying, "Let no one tempt me. What sort of a man am I that I should be able to do what they cannot? I acknowledge my humility. Go in peace." Messengers were sent a second and a third time, but not even then would he comply. At last, those very holy men, the most faithful brethren, Deiniol and Dyfrig, were sent. Saint David, however, foreseeing by the spirit of prophecy, said to his brethren, "Today, brothers, some most holy men are coming to us. Receive them in a joyful spirit. Procure fish in addition to bread and water." The brethren arrived, they greeted each other, and talked about spiritual matters. Dinner was served, but they declared that they would never dine in his monastery unless he came back with them to the synod. To which David said, "I cannot refuse you. Eat your dinner. We shall visit the synod together; but I cannot preach then. I shall give you my help – small as it is – with my prayers."

---

92 A reference to the two visits to Britain of St Germanus of Auxerre as described in the *Vita S. Germani* by Constantius, §§ 12–15, 25–7 (ed. Levison, in *Passiones*, ed. Krusch and Levison, i. 247–83). His British legacy included, in the eyes of Rhygyfarch, a disciple Paulinus (§ 10 above).

93 A biblical cliché: cf. 2 Chr. 15.14; Neh. 4.20; Job 39.24; Is. 18.3; Jer. 42.14; Am. 2.2; Zeph. 1.16.

51 Proficiscentes[a] autem ad proximum synodi locum perueniunt, et ecce iuxta funestum audierunt luctum. Sanctus autem ad socios ait, 'Ego ubi ingens habetur ululatus pergam.' Responderunt autem socii et dixerunt, 'Nos congregationem adibimus[b], ne nostra tarditas expectantes molestat.' Vir uero Dei egrediens, ᶜperrexit ad locum[c], ubi luctus aderat[d], ⌐iuxta amnem Theibi⌐. Et ecce orbata mater corpus extincti pueri[e] seruabat, ᵉ⌐qui Magnus uocabatur⌐. ⌐Beatus uero Dauid,⌐ consolans matrem, monitis subleuauit eam[f] salutaribus. At illa[g], audita eius[h] fama, ante pedes eius corruens, importunis deprecatur clamoribus, ut sui misereretur[i]. Compassus autem ⌐uir Dei⌐ infirmitati humanę, ad corpus extincti accedens, faciem lacrimis rigauit, ⌐atque super defuncti funus corruit, orauitque ad Dominum et dixit, 'Domine, Deus meus, qui in hunc mundum pro nobis peccatoribus de sinu Patris descendisti, ut nos redimeres de faucibus antiqui hostis, miserere istius uiduę, et da uitam unico filio suo, atque inspira in eo spiraculum uitę, ut magnificetur nomen tuum in uniuersa terra.'⌐ Tandem ⌐uero⌐ calefactis membris, redeunte anima, corpus intremuit, tenensque pueri manum, ⌐uiuum et⌐ sanum matri restituit. Mater autem tristes fletus in lętas uertit lacrimas, dicens, 'Michi mortuus filius erat, tibi uero et Deo amodo uiuat.' Accipiens autem sanctus uir puerum, euangelii textum, quod semper in pectore gerebat, eius humeris imposuit, atque secum ad synodum ire fecit, qui[j] postea, uita comite, ⌐multis annis⌐ sanctam duxit conuersationem. ⌐Et omnes, qui uiderunt illud miraculum, laudauerunt Dominum et Dauid agium.⌐

52 Synodum inde ingreditur. Gaudet episcoporum turba. Populus lętatur. Omnis exultat exercitus. Predicare petitur. Concilii sententiam non respuit. Iubent constructum uestibus cumulum[a] conscendere, ᵇ⌐at ille recusauit. Iussit itaque puerum nuper resuscitatum sudarium suum sub pedibus suis exponere. Ipse quidem, super illud stans, euangelium et legem quasi ex buccina exposuit. Coram⌐ autem cunctis niuea celitus emissa columba in eius humeris resedit, quę tamdiu permansit quamdiu ille predicauit. Cum autem clara uoce omnibus et qui in proximo et qui in longinquo erant equaliter predicaret, terra sub ipso accrescens attollitur in collem. Ab omnibus, in summo positus, cernitur, ut in montem excelsum stans quasi tuba exaltaret uocem

---

§ 51
a   proficiscentes VN[156]] proficiscentibus N[2349]D
b   adibimus V] adeamus ND
c   perrexit ad locum V] affuit ND
d   aderat V] adesset ND
e   pueri V] iuuenculi ND
e   qui Magnus uocabatur V] cui barbara imperitia magnum nomen dederat ND
f   eam V] *om.* ND
g   illa <mater> D
h   eius V] illius ND
i   misereretur V] misereatur ND, *correcting the sequence of tenses.*
j   qui ND] quique V
§ 52
a   cumulum V *'heap'*] tumulum ND *'mound' The writing of* t *and* c *in* V *is sometimes misleading (e.g. in § 56* parciuntur *for* partiuntur*), but the intended sense is 'a heap of clothes'.*
b   conscendere. Rogat autem solum sibi sudarium superponere. Videntibus autem cunctis N[23]D conscendere. Coram N[14689] *If the omission were made in the archetype of* ND, *we should need to conjecture contamination from* V; *it is possible that the archetypal reading of* ND *retained the sentence* Rogat …, *omitted by most* N *witnesses, while* D *has replaced* Coram *with* Videntibus.

§ 51. Going forth, they came to a place near the synod, and behold, they heard a woeful mourning near them. And the holy man said to his companions, "I shall go to the place where this great lamentation is." His companions answered and said, "We shall go to the assembly in case our delay annoys those who are waiting." The man of God went on and came to the place of lamentation, near the river Teifi. And behold, a bereaved mother was holding the body of her dead son, who was called Magnus.[94] And the blessed David, consoling the mother, comforted her with salutary advice. But having heard of his fame and throwing herself at his feet, she beseeched him with distressing cries that he should have pity on her. The man of God, sympathetic to human infirmity, approached the body of the dead child and watered its face with tears.[95] Then he fell upon the corpse of the deceased and prayed to the Lord, and said, "O Lord my God, who descended to this world from the bosom of the father for us sinners in order that you might redeem us from the jaws of the ancient enemy; have pity on this widow and give life to her only son,[96] and inspire in him the breath of life,[97] so that your name may be magnified in all the earth."[98] At length the boy's limbs became warm and the body trembled as his soul returned, and taking hold of the boy's hand,[99] he restored him, alive and well, to his mother.[100] And the mother turned her sorrowful weeping into tears of joy, and said, "My son was dead, but through you and through God he lives from now on." And the holy man took the boy, and placed on his shoulders the gospel book that he always carried in his bosom; and he made him go with him to the synod. Afterwards, for many years, he led a holy life for as long as he lived. Everyone who saw the miracle praised the Lord and the holy David.

§ 52. Then he made his way to the synod. The assembly of bishops rejoiced, the people were glad, and the whole gathering exulted. He was asked to preach, and he did not reject the decision of the council. They ordered him to ascend the built-up heap of clothes, but he refused. Instead, he ordered the boy recently raised from the dead to place a handkerchief under his feet. Standing on it, he explained the Gospel and the law as if from a trumpet. Before everyone's eyes a snow-white dove, sent from heaven, settled on his shoulders and remained there as long as he preached.[101] And while he preached, which was with so clear a voice that he was heard by everyone – equally by those who were nearest and those who were farthest off – the earth under him swelled and was raised to a hill. Lifted up in this way, he could be seen by all as though he were standing on a high mountain, and he

---

94 This miracle is an allusion to the raising of the widow's son at Nain in Lk. 7.11–15.
95 cf. Lk. 7.44.
96 *unicus filius*: cf. Lk. 7.12, 8.42, 9.38.
97 *spiraculum uitae*: Gen. 2.7 and 7.22.
98 *magnificetur nomen tuum in uniuersa terra*: cf. Ps. 8.9, *quam grande est nomen tuum in universa terra*, 'O Lord, our Lord, how great is thy name in all the earth!'; 2 Sam. 7.26, 1 Chr. 17.24, *magnificetur nomen tuum*.
99 cf. Mk. 5.41.
100 cf. Lk. 7.15.
101 An allusion to approbation of Christ by the Spirit at his baptism (Mt. 3.16; Mk. 1.10; Lk. 3.22; Jn. 1.32); a dove had also instructed David in his youth, § 8.

suam; in cuius collis cacumine ecclesia sita est. Heresis expellitur. Sanis pectoribus fides roboratur. Omnes consentiunt. Grates Deo sanctoque ᶜDauid soluuntur. **53** Deinde omnium ore benedictus atque magnificatus, cunctorum consensu episcoporum, regum, principum, optimatum, et omnium ordinum tocius Brittannicę gentis archiepiscopus constituitur, nec non ciuitas eius tocius patrię metropolis dedicatur, ita ut quicunque eam regeret, archiepiscopus haberetur. **54** Expulsa igitur heresi, catholicę et ecclesiasticę regulę decreta firmantur, quę crebra atque crudeli hostium irruptione exinanita ac pene obliuioni data, euanueruntᵃ. Ex quibus, quasi graui sompno expergefacti, bella Domini certatim quique peregere. Quę in uetustissimis patris scriptis sua sancta manu mandata ex parte inueniuntur. **55** Deinde succedente temporum serie alia colligitur synodus, cui nomen Victorię, in qua, collecta episcoporum, sacerdotum, abbatum turba, ea quę in priori firmauerant adiectis etiam de aliquantis utilitatibus firmo rigoris examine renouant. Ex his igitur duabus synodis omnes nostrę patrię ecclesię modum et regulam Romana auctoritate acceperunt, quarum decreta, quę ore firmauerat, solus ipse episcopus sua sancta manu litteris mandauit. **56** Per cuncta igitur totius patrię loca monasteria construxere fratres. Passim ecclesiarum signa audiuntur. Passim orationum uoces ad sidera eleuantur. Passim uirtutes ad ecclesię sinum indefessis humeris reportantur. Passim caritatis uota patenti manu egenis partiuntur. Sanctus autem Dauidᵃ, episcopus, ᵇcunctorum summus speculatorᵇ, summus protector, summus predicator, a quo omnes normam atque formam recto uiuendi itinere acceperunt, ⌐effectus est⌐. Ipse cunctis ordo, ipse dedicatio, ipse benedictio, ipse absolutio, correctio, legentibus doctrina, egentibus uita, orphanis nutrimentumᶜ, uiduis fulcimen, patrie caput, monachis regula, secularibus uia, omnibus omnia. Quanta monachorum examina seminauit. Quanta cunctis utilitate profuit. Quanta uirtutum gloria claruit. **57** ⌐Dederuntque uniuersi episcopi manus et monarchiam atque bragminationem Dauid agio, et consenserunt omnes licitum esse refugium eius, ut daret illud omni stuproso et homicidę et peccatori omnique maligno, fugienti de loco ad locum, pre omni sancto ac regibus et hominibus totius Brittannicę insulę in omni regno et in unaquaque regione, in qua sit ager consecratus Dauid agio. Et nulli reges nec seniores neque satrape sed neque episcopi principesue ac sancti audeant pre Dauid agio refugium dare. Ipse uero refu-

---

ᶜ   <episcopo> Dauid D
§ 54
ᵃ   euanuerunt V] eneruauere ND euanuere Nᵍ⁶⁹, *presumably an attempt at correction. It is unclear whether* eneruauere *was a twelfth-century embellishment or an error; the word is usually transitive 'to make weak'.*
§ 56
ᵃ   Dauid V] Dewi ND
ᵇ   cunctorum summus speculator V] summus cunctis inspeculator ND
ᶜ   nutrimentum V] nutrimen ND

raised his voice like a trumpet. A church is situated on the top of that hill now. The heresy was expelled; the faith was confirmed in sound hearts; all were in agreement; thanks were rendered to God and Saint David. § 53. Then, blessed and extolled from everyone's mouth, he was appointed archbishop by the consent of all the bishops, kings, princes, nobles, and all ranks of people of the whole British nation. In the same way, his monastery was dedicated as the metropolitan church of the whole country, so that whoever might govern it should be accounted archbishop. § 54. The heresy therefore having been expelled, the decrees of a catholic and ecclesiastical rule were confirmed.[102] These decrees, made void and nearly consigned to oblivion by the frequent and cruel disruption of enemies, had died away. Through them, as if awakened from a deep sleep,[103] everyone earnestly fought the battles of the Lord. These decrees are found, in part, in very old documents of the father, written by his holy hand. § 55. Afterwards, in the subsequent course of years, another synod was convened, named the Synod of Victory.[104] Here, a large company of bishops, priests, and abbots assembled, and they reaffirmed what was settled in the former synod. They also added a number of useful measures, after close and rigorous scrutiny. As a result of these two synods, therefore, all the churches of our country received their pattern and rule by Roman authority; the decrees of these synods, which he had confirmed with his mouth, he – the bishop alone – committed to writing with his own holy hand. § 56. Throughout every part of the whole country, therefore, the brethren built monasteries. Everywhere, the sound of church bells was heard. Everywhere, the voices of prayers were raised to the heavens. Everywhere, virtues were borne back to the bosom of the church on unwearied shoulders. Everywhere, gifts of charity were freely distributed to the needy. And Saint David, the chief overseer, the principal protector, the consummate preacher, from whom everyone received the pattern and form of living in the right way, was made bishop. To everyone he represented holy orders, he was dedication, he was benediction, absolution, correction; he was learning to students, he was life to the poor, nourishment to orphans, support to widows, a head to the country, a rule to monks, a true way to the secular: he was all things to all men.[105] He planted such great multitudes of monks; he benefited everyone with such great service; he shone with so much glory of miracles. § 57. And the whole episcopate gave power, sovereignty, and princely authority[106] to the holy David; and they all agreed that he should be allowed his privilege of immunity, that he might grant sanctuary to every rapist, murderer, sinner, and every miscreant who was fleeing from place to place, above every holy man, and kings, and the men of the whole of the British island, in every kingdom and in every region in which there may be an estate consecrated to the holy David. And no kings, nor nobles, nor governors, and neither bishops, abbots, nor holy men dared to grant sanctuary above the holy David. Indeed, his privilege has precedence over that of

---

[102] This apparent reference to a Rule of St David is reinforced by the two mentions of ancient manuscript copies in §§ 54, 55.

[103] Gen. 45.26; Sir. 22.8.

[104] The Synod of the Grove of Victory, a set of canons with which the Penitential of David travelled, is undoubtedly British, with its reference to the wickedness of betraying Britons to the marauding Anglo-Saxons (ed. Bieler, *The Irish Penitentials*, 68: *Qui praebent ducatum barbaris ...* [*barbaris* in this context can refer to none other than the Anglo-Saxons]).

[105] See note 32, above.

[106] The word *bragminatio* is found only in this text (§§ 5, 57), and the adjective *bragmaticus* a few lines below. In both contexts, V has an interlinear gloss, *bragminatio* 'principatus uel dignitas' (§ 5), and *bragmaticus* 'princeps' (here). If the words are derived from *bragmannus* 'brahmin', then etymologically they refer to a status of honour and respect.

gium ducit ante unumquemque hominem, et nemo ante ipsum, quia ipse est cephal \i. caput/ et preuius ac bragmaticus \i. princeps/ omnibus Brittonibus. Et statuerunt omnes sancti anathema esse et maledictum quisquis non seruauerit illud decretum, scilicet, refugium sancti Dauid.⌐ **58** Sicque ad senium perductus omnis Brittannicę gentis caput et patrię honor canebatur, quod senium centum quadraginta septem ad modum annis compleuit.

59 CUM autem ad compensanda meritorum premia sacrata immineret dies, .viii. kalendarum Martii fratribus matutinas horas celebrantibus, angelus ad eum locutus clara profatus[a] uoce, 'Desiderata,' inquit, 'dudum dies iam in proximo habetur.' Sanctus autem episcopus, amicam noscens uocem, exultanti animo ad eum dixit, 'Nunc dimitte seruum tuum, Domine, in pace.' Fratres autem sonum tantum auribus capientes nec tamen uerborum discrimen intelligentes, audierant enim eos colloquentes pariter, exterriti ceciderunt in terram. Tunc angelorum concentibus odorisque saporiferi fragrantia tota impletur ciuitas. Sanctus autem episcopus clamans uoce magna erecta in celum mente, loquitur, 'Domine Iesu Christe, accipe spiritum meum'. Angelus iterum conspicua uoce, fratribus intelligentibus, inquit, 'Prepara te et precinge. Kalendis Martii Dominus[b] Iesus Christus, multa constipatus angelorum militia, in obuiam tibi[c] adueniet.' **60** His auditis, fratres concussis singultibus nimium fecerunt[a] planctum. Ingens exoritur tristitia. Fletibus ciuitas redundat[b], dicens, 'Sancte ⌐Dauid,⌐ episcope, aufer tristitiam nostram'. Ille autem demulcens eos blandisque consolationibus sustollens, aiebat, 'Fratres, constantes estote. Iugum, quod accepistis ⌐unanimes⌐ ad finem perducite, ⌐et quecunque mecum uidistis et audistis, custodite et implete⌐.' Ab illa ergo hora usque ad diem obitus sui in ecclesia remanens, ⌐omnibus⌐ predicabat.

61 FAMA itaque[a] illa per uniuersam[b] Brittanniam [c]⌐Hiberniamque uelocissime in una die portata est ab angelo, dicens,⌐ 'Scitis quia in sequenti ebdomada [d]⌐dominus uester, Dauid agius, de hac luce migrabit ad Dominum'⌐. **62** Tunc [a]concursus sanctorum undique[b] ueluti apes procella imminente [c]alueario accedunt[c], ad sanctum

§ 59
a   profatus VND] profatur N⁵D³⁴⁷; *cf. § 5.*
b   Dominus noster ND, *more likely an accidental addition than an inadvertent omission in* V.
c   tibi VN] tui D
§ 60
a   fecerunt VN] egerunt D
b   redundat V] resultat ND
§ 61
a   itaque V] autem ND
b   uniuersam V] totam ND
c   atque Hiberniam ab angelo portata discurrit. Sic enim aiebat ND
d   sanctus episcopus Dewi migrabit in celum ND
§ 62
a   concursus sanctorum V] sanctorum concursus ND
b   undique V] utrimque ND
c   alueario accedunt V] alueario procedunt ND *The point is surely that the bees hasten home to the hive when storm threatens. The reading of* ND *appears to take* alueario *as ablative, 'as bees proceed from the hive', but that is the opposite of the sense. Perhaps the archetype read* alueariū *(accusative* aluearium; *cf.* alueariis *in § 43), and the* ū *was mistaken for* o.

every man, and no one is above him, for he is head and leader and prince of all the Welsh.[107] And all the holy men established that everyone who did not observe that decree concerning the sanctuary of Saint David should be anathema and cursed. § 58. So it was that, having been brought to old age, he was extolled as the head of all the British nation, and the honour of that country, and he completed this old age to the measure of 147 years.[108]

§ 59. When the day was approaching on which he would be repaid with the sacred reward of his merits, 22 February, as the brethren were celebrating Matins, an angel spoke to him, talking with a clear voice: "The day that has long been desired," he said, "is now accounted near." The holy bishop, recognizing the friendly voice, said to him with a joyful spirit, "Lord, now let your servant depart in peace."[109] But the brethren, only catching the sound in their ears but not discerning the separation of the words – for they had also heard them talking – were terrified and fell to the ground. Then the whole monastery was filled with the music of angels and the sweet-smelling fragrance of perfume. And the holy bishop, calling out in a loud voice, his mind lifted to heaven, said, "Lord Jesus Christ, receive my spirit."[110] Again the angel said with an audible voice, the brethren understanding him, "Make ready and gird yourself. On 1 March the Lord Jesus Christ, accompanied by a great host of angels, will come to meet you." § 60. Having heard these things, the brethren, with distraught sobbing, raised a great lamentation. A remarkable sorrow arose. The monastery overflowed with weeping, saying, "O holy Bishop David! Take away our sorrow!" And calming them with kind words of comfort, and supporting them, he said, "Brethren, be steadfast. Bear to the end the yoke that you have unanimously accepted; and whatever you have seen and heard with me, keep it and fulfil it." From that hour, therefore, to the day of his death, he remained in the church, preaching to everyone.

§ 61. And so the news was carried very quickly, in one day, throughout the whole of Wales and Ireland, by an angel saying, "Know that next week, your lord, the holy David, will depart from this light to the Lord." § 62. Then crowds of holy men came from all sides – just as bees hasten home to the hive when a storm threatens – and quickly made haste to visit the holy father. The monastery overflowed with tears, wailing resounded to the stars; young men grieved for him as their father, and old men as their son; and on the intervening Sunday, a great multitude heard him preach a most excellent sermon; he consecrated the Lord's Body with untrembling hands,

---

107 \i. *princeps omnibus Brittonibus/*, a gloss on the word *bragmaticus*, for which see previous note.
108 Jacob's age: Gen. 47.28.
109 Lk. 2.29.
110 Acts 7.58.

patrem uisitandum uelociter festinant[d]. Lacrimis ciuitas exundat. Vlulatus ad sidera resonat. Iuuenes ut patrem, senes ut filium lugent. Die autem interueniente dominica, audiente maxima multitudine, nobilissimam faciens predicationem, intemeratis manibus dominicum sacrabat corpus. Participato autem corpore et sanguine Domini, mox dolore correptus infirmabatur. Finito officio benedictoque populo, alloquitur omnes dicens, 'Fratres mei, perseuerate in his quę a me didicistis et mecum uidistis. Ego tertia feria in kalendis Martii patrum uiam ingrediar. Vos [e]ualete in Domino. Ego autem proficiscar. ⌜In hac terra nunquam nos amplius uisuri sumus.' Tunc omnium fidelium uox erecta est in luctum et in lamentationes, dicens, 'O utinam absorberet nos terra, combureret nos ignis, cooperiret nos mare. O utinam subita irruptione mors corriperet nos. Vtinam montes irruerent super nos'. Omnes pene succumbebant morti.⌝ A nocte uero dominica usque ad quartam post eius obitum feriam, flebiles, ieiuni, uigiles, omnes permansere aduenientes. **63** Veniente itaque tertia feria, ad pullorum cantus angelicis ciuitas impletur choris, celicis modulata cantibus, odore referta suauissimo. Matutina uero hora, clero psalmorum hymnos ad cantica reddente, Dominus Iesus sui presentiam ad patris consolationem impertiri[a], ceu per angelum promiserat, dignatus est. Eo uiso, totus in spiritu exultans, 'Tolle me,' inquit, 'post te.' Cum his uerbis, Christo comite, uitam Deo reddidit[b], atque angelica comitatus caterua, celestia petiit[c] limina.

64 ⌜O QUIS tunc posset ferre sanctorum fletus, ęgra suspiria anachoritarum, gemitum sacerdotum, rugitus discipulorum dicentium, 'A quo docebimur?', planctum peregrinorum dicentium, 'A quo adiuuabimur?', desperationem regum dicentium, 'A quo ordinabimur, corrigemur, instituemur? Quis clementissimus pater sicut Dauid? Quis interpellet pro nobis ad Dominum?', lamentationes populorum, ululatum pauperum, uociferationes infirmorum, clamorem monachorum, lacrimas uirginum, coniugatorum, penitentium, iuuenum, iuuencularum, puerorum, puellarum, infantium sugentium mamillas? Quid moror? Omnium uox una plangentium erat, reges enim ut arbitrum lugebant, seniores ut fratrem plangebant, adolescentes ut patrem illum honorabant, immo quem omnes ut Deum uenerabantur.⌝ **65** Corpus itaque eius, sanctorum fratrum ulnis apportatum, magno constipatum comitatu, honorifice terrę mandatum, in sua sepelitur ciuitate. Anima uero eius sine ullo decidui ęui termino per infinita coronatur secula seculorum. [a]<Ipse[b] nos suis[c] intercessionibus coniungat angelorum ciuibus, cuius deuote celebramus sollempnitatem in terris, prestante [d]Deo et Domino nostro Iesu Christo, cui est honor et gloria per infinita seculorum secula.> Amen.[e]

---

d   festinant VN[123689]D[47]] festinat N[45]D[128] *The manuscript evidence suggests that the archetype read festinant, showing that* concursus *was intended as a plural; several scribes have chosen to take it as singular.*

e   ualete in Domino V] in Domino ualete ND

§ 63

a   impertiri V] impertire ND
b   reddidit V] reddit ND
c   petiit V] petit ND

§ 65

a   *habet* VN[123]] *om. cett.*
b   ipse V] ille N[123]
c   suis <sanctis> N[12]
d   Deo et V] eodem N[12]
e   *Several later manuscripts conclude,* per infinita coronatur secula seculorum. Amen. *Those that continue are* V N[12345]D[12347].

and having partaken of the Body and Blood of the Lord, he was seized with pain, and became weak. Having finished the office and blessed the people, he addressed them all, saying, "My brothers, persevere in those things that you have learned from me, and have seen with me; on Tuesday, 1 March, I shall enter the way of the fathers;[111] farewell in the Lord, for I shall go away; we shall not see each other any more in this world." Then the voice of all the faithful was raised in mourning and lamentation, saying, "O we wish that the earth would swallow us, that fire would consume us, that the sea would cover us. O we wish that death would seize us with an instant stroke; we wish that the mountains would rush violently upon us," and they were almost all giving themselves up to death. From the Sunday night to the Wednesday after his death, all who came remained weeping, fasting, and watching. § 63. And so, when the Tuesday arrived, the monastery was filled at the time of cock-crowing with angelic choirs singing heavenly songs, and was full of the sweetest fragrance. At the hour of Matins, when the clergy had sung their psalms and hymns, the Lord Jesus saw fit to bestow his presence for the consolation of the father, as he had promised by the angel. When he saw him, his whole being rejoiced in the spirit, and said, "Take me with you." Upon these words, with Christ as his companion, he gave back his life to God, and accompanied by an angelic escort, he sought the heavenly gates.

§ 64. O who could then endure the weeping of the holy men, the deep sighing of the hermits, the moaning of the priests, and the wailing of the disciples, saying, "By whom shall we be taught?"; the lamentation of pilgrims, saying, "By whom shall we be assisted?"; the desperation of kings, saying, "By whom shall we be ordained, corrected, appointed? Who is so merciful a father as David? Who will intercede for us to the Lord?" The lamentations of the people, the wailing of the poor, the crying of the sick, the clamour of the monks, the tears of the virgins, of married people, of penitents, of young men, of young women, of boys, of girls, and of infants sucking the breast? Need I go on? The voice of all the mourners was but one, for kings mourned him as a judge, the older people mourned him as a brother, the younger honoured him as a father, indeed all venerated him as they did God. § 65. And so his body, borne in the arms of the holy brethren, accompanied by a great retinue, and committed to the earth with honour, was laid to rest within his monastery. But his soul, released from the limits of this fleeting life, is crowned throughout the endless ages of eternity. May he whose festival we devoutly celebrate on earth unite us by his intercessions to the angelic citizens, with almighty God and our Lord Jesus Christ, to whom be honour and glory throughout the endless ages of eternity. Amen

---

[111] The mention of the day of the week naturally invites attempts to work out the year in which Rhygyfarch would have placed David's death; A.D. 589 or 601 are the usual choices (Dumville, *Saint David*, 3).

66 HEC et alia plura, dum corruptibile et aggrauans animam gerebat habitaculum, sanctus operatus est pater ⌐Dauid⌐. Sed ex pluribus pauca ad restringendam ardentium sitim uili sermonis uasculo ministrauimus. Veluti cum quisque ᵃangusto castioris fialę gremio emanantem perpetuo fonte fluuium ad siccum haurireᵇ nequit, ita cuncta miraculorum signa ac deuotissimam uirtutum operationem preceptorumque obseruantiam nullus, quamuis stilo ferreo, cartis mandare poterit. Sed hęc, ut diximus, ex plurimis pauca omnibus ad exemplum et patris gloriam in unum collegimusᶜ, quę in uetustissimis patrię, maxime ipsius ciuitatis, sparsim inuenta scriptis, quę assidua tinearum edacitate ac annosis ęui terebraminibus per orasᵈ et cardines corrosa, ac ex antiquo seniorum stilo conscripta, nunc usque supersunt. In unum cumulata, ueluti ex florigero diuersarum herbarum horto, quasi subtilissimę apis rostro sugens, ad tanti patris gloriam et aliorum utilitatem, ne pereant, collegi. Ea uero, quę continuis temporum interuallis, deposita carnis sarcina, ac contemplata facie ad faciem deitate, tantum uerius agit et operatus est quantum Deo coniunctius inherescit, ex multorum relationeᵉ, qui uoluerit, agnoscere poterit. **67** Michi autem, qui Ricemarchus nominor, quique ingenioli mei capacitatem his, quamuis temerarius, subdidi, quicunque hęc deuota perlegerint mente, precibus deferant iuuamen, ut, quia patris, ueluti uerni, clementia ad pauxillum intelligentię florem ęstiuo carnis ardore prouexit, tandem me ante mei cursus terminum, exsiccatis concupiscenti uaporibus, ad frugem bonę messis maturis perducat operibus, ut cum messores, separata inimici zizania, horrea cęlestis patrię purgatissimis impleuerint manipulis, me, ueluti nouissimę messis fasciculum, intra cęlestis portę atrium, conspecto sine fine Deo, collocent, qui est benedictus super omnia Deus in secula seculorum. Amen.

---

68 ᵃDE GENEALOGIA SANCTI DAVID. INCIPIT genealogia sancti Dauid, archiepiscopi tocius Brittannie Dei gratia et predestinatione. Dauid fuit filius Sant, Sant filius Cheritic, Cheretic filius Cuneda, Cuneda filius Etern, Etern filius Patern, Patern filius Peisrud, Peisrud filius Doeil, Doeil filius Gurdeis, Gurdeil filius Dumn, Dumn

§ 66
ᵃ   angusto castioris ND] angustioris V
ᵇ   haurire V] exhaurire ND
ᶜ   collegimus V] conduximus ND
ᵈ   oras ND] horas V
ᵉ   relatione V] reuelatione ND
§ 68
ᵃ   *The genealogical passage is peculiar to* V *and should not be considered a part of Rhygyfarch's work. After the explicit,* V *also adds the collect, secretum, and postcommunion from the mass for St David's feast.*

§ 66. The holy father David performed these and many other works while a perishable and troublesome habitation held his soul.[112] But out of his many works we have provided just a few examples in the feeble vessel of my narrative in order to quench the thirst of those who are eager. In the same way that no one with the shallow bowl of a frugal drinking cup[113] can drain dry a river that flows from a perpetual spring, so no one, however strong his pen, can commit to writing all his signs and miracles, his most devout practice of virtuous powers, and his observance of the commandments. But, as we have said, we have collected these few works out of the many into one place to be an example for everyone, and to the glory of the father. They have been found scattered in the most ancient writings of our country, and especially of his own monastery; and although the books were eaten away along the edges and the spines by the constant devouring of grubs and the ravages of the passing years, and written in the handwriting of our forefathers, they have survived until now. For fear that they should perish, I have collected and gathered them together – as the bee delicately sucks with its mouth in a flowery garden of diverse plants[114] – to the glory of so great a father and for the benefit of others. Anyone who wants will be able from the testimony of many people to acknowledge those things which David, over the passage of time since he laid down the burden of the flesh and has contemplated the Godhead face to face, does and performs all the more truly for being so much closer to God. § 67. And as for me, Rhygyfarch by name,[115] I have applied the ability of my modest intellect to each of these matters, however imprudent I may be, so that whoever may have read these things with a devout mind may assist me with their prayers; and that, since the Father's mercy, like that of a spring, has carried me through the summer heat of the flesh to the tiny flower of my understanding, it may finally, when the vapours of desire have dried up and before the end of my course, bring me the fruit of a good harvest through timely works. So when the tares of the enemy are separated and the reapers have filled heaven's garners with unsullied sheaves,[116] they may find a place for me within the entrance of the heavenly gates, as a little sheaf of the latest harvest, endlessly to behold God, who is blessed above all things, God for ever and ever.[117] Amen

----

§ 68. CONCERNING THE GENEALOGY OF SAINT DAVID

Here begins the genealogy of Saint David, archbishop of the whole of Wales, by the grace and predestination of God. David was the son of Sant, Sant the son of Ceredig, Ceredig the son of Cunedda, Cunedda the son of Edern, Edern the son of Padern, Padern the son of Peisrudd, Peisrudd the son of Doeil, Doeil the son of

[112] Wis. 9.15: *Corpus enim quod corrumpitur aggrauat animam.*

[113] Strictly, *angusto castioris fialę gremio* 'from the narrow bosom of a rather chaste cup'; compare § 3, *castioris prandii parcitate* 'by the frugality of purer food'. *Angustus*, like *parcitas*, in conjunction with *castior* may suggest monastic frugality.

[114] cf. Ieuan ap Sulien, *Carmen Iohannis de uita et familia Sulgeni*, line 108: *iam subtilis apes degustat flore sapores* (ed. Lapidge, 'The Welsh-Latin poetry', 86).

[115] This spelling is confirmed by the author's brother, Ieuan ap Sulien, in *Carmen Iohannis de uita familia Sulgeni*, line 129, where he writes, *Rycymarch* (ed. Lapidge, 'The Welsh Latin Poetry', 86); also by the spelling of the name, *s.a.* 1099, in *Annales Cambriae* and *Brut y Tywysogion*, where <e> and <y> appear, which would be impossible if it were an /i/ sound (Jackson, *Language and History*, 668).

[116] cf. the parable of the tares, Mt. 13.24–30, 36–43.

[117] Rom. 9.5.

filius Guordumn, Guordumn filius Amguoil, Amguoil filius Amguerit, Amguerit filius Omid, Omid filius Perum, Perum filius Dobun, Dobun filius Iouguen, Iouguen filius Abalach, Abalach filius Eugen, Eugen filius Eudolen, Eudolen filius Eugen, Eugen filius sororis Marie.

EXPLICIT VITA SANCTI DAUID EPISCOPI ET CONFESSORIS.

MISSA DE EODEM

DEUS, qui beatum confessorum tuum Dauid atque pontificem angelo nuntiante Patricio prophetante triginta annis antequam nasceretur predixisti, quesumus ut, cuius memoriam recolimus, eius intercessione ad eterna gaudia perueniamus, per <Dominum nostrum, Iesum Christum, Filium tuum, qui tecum uiuit et regnat in unitate Spiritus Sancti, Deus per omnia secula seculorum>. <Amen>.

SECRETA

HOSTIAS laudis et preces deuotionis, quas tibi in honore beati confessoris tui Dauid atque pontificis, omnipotens Deus, deferimus, placatus intende; et quod nostrum non optinet meritum, tua clementia et illius pro nobis frequens intercessio efficiat per <Dominum nostrum, etc. Amen>.

POSTCOMMVNIO

REPLETI, Domine, participatione sacramenti, quesumus ut sancti Dauid confessoris tui atque pontificis meritis, cuius gloriosam celebramus festiuitatem, ineffabilis misericordie tue patrocinia sentiamus, per <Dominum nostrum, etc. Amen>.

Gwrddeil, Gwrddeil the son of Dwfn, Dwfn the son of Gworddwfn, Gworddwfn the son of Afwyl, Afwyl the son of Afweryd, Afweryd the son of Ofydd, Ofydd the son of Perwm, Perwm the son of Dobwn, Dobwn the son of Ywein, Ywein the son of Afalach, Afalach the son of Ieuan, Ieuan the son of Euddolen, Euddolen the son of Ieuan, Ieuan the son of the sister of Mary.

HERE ENDS THE LIFE OF SAINT DAVID BISHOP AND CONFESSOR.

THE MASS OF THE SAME

O God, who foretold your blessed confessor and bishop, David, by the message of an angel to Patrick, prophesying thirty years before he was born; we pray that by the intercession of him whose memory we celebrate, we may attain eternal joys, for ever and ever. Amen.

SECRET

Almighty God, being appeased, accept the sacrifices of praise and the prayers of devotion that we offer to you in honour of your blessed confessor and bishop; and what our merit may not obtain, may your mercy and his frequent intercession for us effect, through our Lord, etc. Amen.

POST-COMMUNION

O Lord, being satisfied by the partaking of the sacrament, we pray that by the merits of your confessor and bishop, Saint David, whose glorious festival we celebrate, we may be mindful of the patronage of your inexpressible mercy, through our Lord, etc. Amen.

7

SOME OBSERVATIONS ON THE 'NERO', 'DIGBY', AND 'VESPASIAN' RECENSIONS OF *VITA S. DAVID*

John Reuben Davies

Richard Sharpe has made the case for the primacy of the 'Vespasian' (V) recension of Rhygyfarch's *Vita S. Dauid* over the 'Nero' (N) and 'Digby' (D) versions, on editorial grounds.[1] Here, I shall offer some observations on the Latin style of V compared with ND, and the content of the different recensions, in order to reinforce the case for V's primacy; I shall also suggest a date for the composition of the *Life*.

Style, vocabulary, and content

One of the most notable features of V, which is the basis for our edition, is that it contains features of the pretentious 'hermeneutic' style of Latin. The 'hermeneutic' style is a legacy of Aldhelm and Alcuin, and one might expect to find it in an eleventh-century work – *Vita S. Neoti* is a good example of this type of composition from eleventh-century England – rather than a composition of the mid-twelfth century, as James argued that V was.[2] Such distinctive features of V are the author's fondness for Graecisms and obscure words, such as *agius* (Gk *hagios*), *cephal* (Gk *kephalos*), *bragminatio* (a very obscure word), and *fanum* (Gk *phanon*), which are all absent from ND.

Patrick Sims-Williams has argued that Rhygyfarch's text was expanded with numerous additional passages, 'easily recognisable from the trick of calling the saint *agius* rather than *sanctus*', and that V must date *ca* 1130×1200, 'later than Caradog of Llancarfan's *Vita S. Gildae*, which it quotes'.[3] But it is exactly the kind of Greek usage to which Sims-Williams drew attention that leads one to suspect that V was not written in an Anglo-Norman context, let alone as late as the reign of King John.

To deal with Sims-Williams's two points: first, the occurrences of *agius* are not restricted to the passages peculiar to V; *Dauid agius*, on its own, appears as a variant reading in two other places (§§ 32, 46). The use of the Greek title does not, therefore, necessarily identify passages peculiar to V. Secondly, the close parallels

---

1 Sharpe, 'Which text', above, Ch. 5.
2 Dumville and Lapidge (ed.), *The Annals of St Neots*, and review by Wright. Michael Lapidge ('The hermeneutic style') has given an account of this literary fashion as it affected Anglo-Saxon England. For the poetic works of Sulien's family, however, Lapidge says, 'Nor has it any of the features – particularly the predilection for hermeneutic vocabulary – which characterize the Anglo-Latin poetry of pre-Norman southern England' (p. 75).
3 Review of Evans, *Welsh Life of St David*, 469.

between Caradog's *Vita S. Gildae* (§ 4) and V (§ 5) beg the question of who was borrowing from whom. The 'Vespasian' extract uses the very obscure word, *bragminatio* (glossed *principatus uel dignitas*); this kind of pretentious vocabulary, as I have said, is unlikely to have been employed by a writer in a mid-twelfth-century Anglo-Norman context: it is not Caradog's style of writing, and it is unlikely that an author borrowing from him in the late twelfth century would have added such a word. It is surely more probable that the usage was borrowed by Caradog from Rhygyfarch.

We also find some florid, self-indulgent passages in V, which are absent from ND: in particular, there is a lament on the death of St David (§ 64), the kind of passage one might expect from Rhygyfarch, the author of *Planctus*, a 'lament' on the Norman invasion of west Wales.[4] One may note the series of rhetorical questions with which the lament for David begins, and compare it with the series of rhetorical questions which opens Rhygyfarch's *Planctus*.

There are some further clues to suggest that ND are derived from an earlier recension which V has followed/copied much more closely. ND have some telling, and apparently careless, abridgements. In § 4, by abridging the first sentence, ND fail to say that it was David who was conceived by Nonnita; moreover, there is no mention of David in the rest of this chapter. This also goes against the apparent convention that the saint's name is mentioned in each chapter. Something similar happens in § 15: the reading of V is clear, 'David and the three disciples meet', but ND's reading, 'to him three disciples come together', is less clear, and again, David's name is omitted. In § 16 (the story of Baia), the phrase, *in insaniam uersa*, 'having turned angry', is omitted by ND; but two chapters later, at § 18, where ND paraphrase V, this same phrase appears to have been borrowed from V's § 16 to fill out ND's shortened text. Stories about Patrick and Gildas in V have been omitted or toned down in ND. In ND § 3, Patrick is made to appear less jealous, and the suggestion that he was prepared to forsake Christ is removed. In ND § 5, the name of Gildas is removed from the story of the preacher who is silenced in the presence of the unborn David in his mother's womb. These editorial changes may have been intended to make the work more accessible to a wider audience.

There is a number of other paraphrases too: §§ 7, 8, and 14 are paraphrased by ND. In § 15, ND omit the details of the topographical setting of David's career; and § 18 is tastefully reduced to one sentence by ND.

Rhygyfarch seems to have favoured adjectives in *-fer*: *mortifer* (§§ 13, 38),[5] *saporifer* (§ 59), *fructifer* (§ 33);[6] this may be compared with Ieuan ap Sulien's writing in the poem, *de familia Sulgeni*, where he uses the adjective *dulcifer* at line 100 (*dulciferoque*).[7] The rare adjective, *lucifluus* (V, § 18), found (perhaps significantly) in the work of Aldhelm, and not present in ND, is another one used by Ieuan ap Sulien in *de familia Sulgeni*.[8]

One of the more distinctive features of V is that the author has a taste for beginning his sentences and clauses with an indicative verb coupled with the enclitic *-que*. Every incidence of this authorial feature has been removed from ND. There are 30 occurrences in 67 chapters, as follows.

---

4 For an edition and translation of this composition see Lapidge, 'The Welsh-Latin poetry'.
5 *mortifer* used by Gildas, Alcuin, and Anselm (*DMLBS*).
6 *fructifer* used by Aldhelm, Bede, and Orderic Vitalis (*DMLBS*).
7 Lapidge, 'The Welsh-Latin poetry', 84, 101; also used by Alcuin (*DMLBS*).
8 Lapidge, 'The Welsh-Latin poetry', 84, 100. See above for the significance of Aldhelm.

§ 3 *elegitque ... Parauitque ... misitque ... Nauigauitque*; § 4 *Inuenitque*; § 5 *Venitque*; § 7 *sparsitque*; § 8 *crescebatque*; § 11 *Vocauitque ... feceruntque ... Responditque ... benedixitque*; § 14 *Ostenditque*; § 15 *ueneruntque ... Dedidque ... Inuenitque*; § 18 *amputauitque*; § 38 *Accepitque ... stupueruntque ... Misitque ... comeditque ... inspexeruntque ... Nuntiauitque ... surrexeruntque ... maledixeruntque ... dampnaueruntque*; § 42 *Misitque*; § 43 *Secutaque sunt*; § 51 *orauitque*; § 57 *Dederuntque*

This feature is found elsewhere in the Latin hagiography of Wales. In Lifris's *Vita S. Cadoci*, it is fairly common, occurring 23 times in 70 chapters.[9] In *Vita S. Paterni* it happens six times in 31 chapters.[10] In *Vita S. Iltuti* there are six occurrences in 26 chapters, but never at the very beginning of a sentence.[11] There are no occurrences in *Vita S. Gundleii*. In *Vita S. Tathei* it happens only twice, in § 16, and in neither case at the beginning of a sentence. In the short *Vita S. Carantoci* there are two occurrences, in §§ 1 and 4, out of the four sections. *Vita S. Kebii* has thirteen occurrences in 20 chapters.[12] There are only two occurrences of this feature in the Book of Llandaf, one in *De primo statu Landauensis ecclesie*, and the other in *Vita S. Elgari*.[13] The only occurrence in Caradog of Llancarfan's signed works is in *Vita S. Cadoci*, § 14, where he is closely following Lifris's text (§ 21). In *Vita S. Maedoci*, a *Life* originating in Ireland but copied (and possibly modified) in Wales, there are ten examples in 57 chapters.[14] (*Vita S. Maedoci* shares some material with Rhygyfarch's *Vita S. Dauid*, Lifris's *Vita S. Cadoci*, and *Vita S. Teiloi*: all three *uitae* appear in MS. Cotton Vespasian A.xiv.)[15] So Rhygyfarch and his contemporary, Lifris, are far more prolific in their use of this construction than any of the other authors: it seems to go out of favour in the works that can be placed towards the middle of the twelfth century – the Book of Llandaf and the works of Caradog of Llancarfan.[16] Perhaps it is less likely, therefore, that this kind of feature would have appeared in the writing of someone working towards the end of the twelfth century.

If we were to suppose (as seems most likely from the wide dissemination of those recensions) that ND represent versions of the *Life* written for wider circulation – that is, beyond Wales – at the direction of Bishop Bernard in his campaign for the metropolitan status of St Davids, then the editorial actions of the reviser might be understood. First, all obscure, pretentious, or Greek vocabulary and expressions have been expunged. Secondly, all passages with syntax that does not conform to what the editor considered to be sound Latin style have been excluded or paraphrased. Thirdly, all derogatory or critical references to other saints have been removed (in

---

9   §§ 14 (× 2), 15, 17 (× 2), 21 (× 2), 23, 25 (× 2), 27, 28 (× 3), 35, 44, 53, 54, 58, 69 (× 4).

10   §§ 21, 22 (× 2), 25, 28, 31.

11   §§ 12, 15, 19, 23, 25 (× 2).

12   §§ 5, 7, 11, 12 (× 2), 13 (× 3), 16 (× 3), 18, 20.

13   *Book of Llan Dâv*, ed. by J.G. Evans, 3.

14   §§ 10, 12 [× 4], 19, 22, 30, 36, 56.

15   *Vita S. Dauid*, § 35 (the story of St Aidan/Maedóc, the book, and the oxen); cf. *Vita S. Aidiui siue Maidoc*, § 12 (ed. Plummer, *Vitae*, II), Lifris, *Vita S. Cadoci*, § 12 (*VSBG*), *Vita S. Teiliaui* (ed. J.G. Evans, *Book of Llan Dâv*, 101–2); the same story is also found in *Vita S. Cainnici*, § 4 (ed. Plummer, *Vitae*, I), Caradog of Llancarfan, *Vita S. Cadoci*, §§ 11, 26 (ed. Grosjean, 'Vie de saint Cadoc'), *Betha Fhindein*, § 6 (ed. Stokes, *Lives*), and *Vita S. Carthagi*, § 25 (ed. Plummer, *Vitae*, I).

16   The signed works of Caradog are *Vita S. Cadoci* and *Vita S. Gildae*, but I should also include *Vita S. Cungari*, *Vita S. Iltuti*, *Vita S. Gundleii*, and *Vita S. Tathei*; the Book of Llandaf may also have been written, in the main, by Caradog (for all this, see Davies, *The Book of Llandaf*, ch. 8). *Vita S. Iltuti*, in its present form, may be based on an earlier text. *Vita S. Paterni*, is most likely a product of Sulien's sons. *Vita S. Maedoci* is probably a product of the late eleventh or early twelfth century (cf. Sharpe, *Medieval Irish Saints' Lives*, 395).

particular, those about Patrick and Gildas), probably from the desire to remove ines-sential proper nouns. Peculiar names get in the way when a work is being addressed to a wider audience. This is very conspicuous in the O-versions of Lives of Irish saints (which were probably edited in an English context, and for more general edifying reading), replacing names with *quidam rex* and the like; a saint's associa-tions with particular places, people, or events were not considered important, and efforts were made to improve the Latin style of the archetypes.[17] In a similar way, the editor responsible for the archetype of ND seems to have objected to the use of indicative verbs with *-que*; he did not like even slightly adventurous vocabulary, such as *buccina* (§§ 5, 52, 'trumpet', a word found in the Bible), *sanctimonialis* (§§ 4, 5, 6, 'nun'), *lucifluus* (§ 18, 'clear'), *sinaxis* (§ 8, 'eucharistic prayer'), or even the inoffensive phrase, *in hac luce* (§§ 3, 61, 'in this light'); he certainly had no time for the more outlandish words, like *bragminatio* (§§ 5, 57), *bragmaticus* (§ 57), *cephal* (§ 57), or *agius* (*passim*), nor for the excessive rhetoric of a lament (§ 64).

The date of Rhygyfarch's Vita S. Dauid

If V most nearly represents Rhygyfarch's own words, can we work out from the evidence of this text when the work was composed? The date of the composition of *Vita S. Dauid* is not agreed on. Nora Chadwick argued that the *Life* (and she, of course, meant Wade-Evans's text of V, since James had not then muddied the waters) was written for the visit of William the Conqueror to St Davids in 1081.[18] More recent scholarship has tended to follow J.W. James's date of 1095.[19]

Some clues to the date of the composition of Rhygyfarch's *Vita S. Dauid* may lie in the text of V. In the lament for David (§ 64), one might see the saint acting as a surrogate for the author's father, Bishop Sulien, the teacher and adviser of kings. Sulien seems to have taken part in negotiations between Rhys ap Tewdwr and Gruf-fudd ap Cynan in 1081, and he would have met William the Conqueror in the same year.[20]

> § 64 O who could then endure the weeping of the holy men, the deep sighing of the hermits, the wailing of the priests, and the moaning of the disciples, saying, 'By whom shall we be taught?'; the lamentation of pilgrims, saying, 'By whom shall we be assisted?'; the desperation of kings, saying, 'By whom shall we be ordained, corrected, appointed? Who is so merciful a father as David? Who will intercede for us to the Lord?' ... The voice of the mourners was but one, for kings mourned him as a judge, the older people mourned him as a brother, the younger honoured him as a father, indeed all venerated him as they did God.

Like any saint's *Life*, the primary purpose of *Vita S. Dauid* is to promote and augment the cult; it publishes a rule of St David (§§ 21–31), written for use at St Davids; and possibly commemorates Bishop Sulien. The *Life* also connects David with the ruling dynasty of Ceredigion: first, by making Sanctus (king of Ceredi-gion), David's father (§ 2); and then recording the genealogy of David (§ 68), which

---

17 Cf. Sharpe, *Medieval Irish Saints' Lives*, 369–71.

18 Chadwick, 'Intellectual life', 174–6.

19 *Rhigyfarch's Life*, xi. James, however, thought he had edited a 'basic mid-twelfth-century text', and that it was impossible to get nearer to Rhygyfarch's words, so the date is applied to a lost version.

20 *AC* (B) 1082; *ByT* (Pen. 20) 1079; *ByT* (RB) [1081]; *ByS* 1079.

links him to the line of Cunedda, the progenitor of the second dynasty of Gwynedd, from whom Rhys ap Tewdwr was descended. It is therefore likely to have been written while Rhys ap Tewdwr was still in power.[21] ND lack the genealogy. Then, V makes some connections with places in Ceredigion: Sanctus finds the three gifts prophesying David's birth, 'next to the river Teifi … in a place called Llyn Henllan' (§ 2) – probably the village of Henllan, on the Teifi, in Ceredigion. V also has David educated at, and returning to *Vetus Rubus* (§§ 8, 14), probably Hen Fynyw, near Aberaeron, Ceredigion.[22] Furthermore, whereas Rhygyfarch showed, in his *Planctus*, or 'Lament', that he was quite capable of being explicitly anti-Norman, *Vita S. Dauid* appears to show no signs of anti-Norman sentiments.[23] Of the key chronological indicators – the connection with the royal line of Ceredigion, the connection with places in Ceredigion, and the apparent lament for Sulien – Bishop Bernard's reviser has played down the first (deleting the connection with the line of Rhodri Mawr), and removed the latter two. We might therefore assign the original composition to a date in the range 1091×1093: that is, between the death of Sulien and the defeat of Rhys ap Tewdwr at the hands of 'the Frenchmen' who were inhabiting Brycheiniog.[24]

---

[21] Maund, *Ireland, Wales, and England*, 33–8, for the career and lineage of Rhys ap Tewdwr. The southern branch of the line of Rhodri Mawr, to which Rhys belonged, was descended from Cadell ap Rhodri Mawr, who ruled in Ceredigion. Compare the genealogy of David, § 68, with Harley Genealogies nos 26 and 1 (ed. Bartrum, *EWGT*, 12, 9); cf. Mostyn MS 117, no. 2 (ed. Bartrum, 39) and Jesus College MS 20, no. 24 (ed. Bartrum, 47).
[22] See Sharpe, 'Which text', above, 98–9.
[23] Cf. *Planctus*, lines 16–20, 45–9 (Lapidge, 'The Welsh-Latin poetry', 90).
[24] *AC* (B) 1094; (C) 1091; *ByT* (Pen. 20) 1091.

8

ARMES PRYDAIN FAWR AND ST DAVID

G.R. Isaac

Armes Prydain Fawr 'The Great Prophecy of Britain' (*APF* henceforth), dated to the second quarter of the tenth century,[1] is a vaticinatory poem of 199 lines, preserved in NLW Peniarth MS 2,[2] known informally as 'The Book of Taliesin'. An edition, a translation and an analysis of the thematic structure of the poem will all be presented below. The poem expresses, in the form of prophecy, dissatisfaction with the interference of the English king Aethelstan (apparently)[3] in Welsh affairs, principally by means of a tax. This implies simultaneously protest against the policies of Welsh rulers, most prominently Hywel Dda, to accept that tax and interference in return for being left alone to pursue their own dynastic agendas. The poet places these protests in the context of a scathing attack on the nature of English rule in Britain in general, how they treacherously came to power and ousted the Britons, and how they will ultimately be driven back to where they came from in a glorious rebellion led secularly by the legendary saviour-heroes Cynan and Cadwaladr, and spiritually by St David.

It is correct to state that *APF* contains the earliest references to St David in (extant) Welsh literature. What earlier references there are to him at all are found in chronicles, a catalogue of saints, martyrologies and calendars, with various passing references to him in lives of other saints, and Asser's references to him in the *Life of King Alfred*.[4] All these references may be said to 'refer' in various ways to the historical, canonised man who was Saint David. They give us (precious little in fact) information about what was known or thought to be know about that man in the

---

[1] Ifor Williams, *Armes Prydein o Lyfr Taliesin*, Introduction, dated the poem to *ca* 930, in fact defining the period more narrowly as 927×937 (also see Williams and Bromwich, *Armes Prydein*). Dumville, 'Brittany and "Armes Prydein Vawr"', revised this to *ca* 942; Breeze, '*Armes Prydein*, Hywel Dda', to *ca* 940. Insofar as these revisions remain within the same quarter century, I do not feel a need to discuss them here. I am aware of attempts to justify even later dates, but only through the medium of oral information, both formally and informally presented, so I do not feel I can comment on these here. I hope these views will be made the subject of published discourse in time. Linguistically, my analysis of *dychyfroy*, line 38, note 20, is consistent with a tenth-century date. But neither this, nor anything else in the poem is really diagnostic. Much of the syntax has a distinctly pre-Middle-Welsh appearance. Cf. the contrasting mutation patterns in the verbal complex, e.g. line 113 *Dychyrch6ynt gyfarth* vs. line 83 *Lleith anoleith rydygyrchassant*: these patterns are, to the best of our understanding of the language of the period, accurately maintained throughout the poem (this is incidentally a tribute to the care of the copyists in transmission). But further research is still required before we can confidently rely on such features for dating purposes.

[2] Dated to the first half of the fourteenth century, Denholm-Young, *Handwriting*, 44, 78; Haycock, 'Llyfr Taliesin', 362; Huws, *Medieval Welsh Manuscripts*, 59. The poem is found on pages 13–18 of the manuscript.

[3] Aethelstan is not named, but he is understood to lie behind the references to *mechteyrn* 'the great king, the High King' in the poem.

[4] These references are conveniently summarised by Evans, *The Welsh Life of St David*, xv–xviii.

centuries from the seventh to the tenth, and about the way that knowledge of the man was integrated into the observances and chronologies of the times. In *APF*, on the other hand, St David is given the role of a powerful symbol. These references tell us nothing about any historical figure, but rather about the importance attached to a certain symbolic figure at the time of the poem, and in the place and context in which it was written. The fact that we know St David to have been a man of flesh and blood is of no more significance than the fact that we know that Myrddin, cited as an authority for the content of the poem in line 17, was not. They are both symbols, utilised by the poet in his political rhetoric to bolster and propagate his case.

APF is literature, and in important respects, it is fiction. But it is fiction which represents a particular view of a society and its governance, as well as its destiny. As such it is literary fiction with a strong political agenda, overt not covert (the latter may be thought to be true of all literature). What do the references to St David in the poem mean? Meaning, in one type of analysis, may be thought of as referentiality + context. But we would face difficulties applying this type of analysis to the case of St David in *APF*. In the first place, since we are inquiring after the content of the symbolic references to St David in the poem, it would seem that part of what we are looking for is that to which they refer. I think this leads to infinite regress; the symbol refers to what it refers to what it refers to what it refers to … Secondly, part of the context that has been agreed for the poem, that it is the work of a cleric of Dyfed, in political terms, or of the *parochia* of St David, in ecclesiastical terms,[5] depends on the interpretation of the references to St David. Obviously, if the references to St David are used to argue for a particular context for the poem, then the context of the poem cannot be used without circularity to illuminate the meaning of the references to St David. In the light of both these points, I conclude that, in the case of the references to St David in *APF* at least, the model of meaning that would make it referentiality + context is poorly applicable.

I therefore think that the question, 'What is the meaning of the references to St David in *APF*?', is rather to be be considered as synonymous with the question, 'How is the symbol "St David" used in *APF*?' In these terms, I think that there is, in fact, a little more to be said about St David in *APF* than has been said in the past. In what follows I shall not attempt a grand new analysis of early Welsh ecclesiastical history, if any such thing were meaningful at all. I shall simply show 'how the symbol St David is used' in the poem. This will inevitably result in what is more an appreciation of *APF*, than a study of St David.

I take this opportunity to present and analyse the whole poem. The justification for this in a volume on St David comes from the fact that *APF* is a formal and conceptual whole, and St David is integral to that whole. No understanding of that whole and of St David's role in it can be expected from an atomistic approach which sees the poem as a sequence of unconnected episodes. I stress here that *APF* is a single poem, with a quite symphonic form. It has an exposition, a development, a climax and a triumphant coda. It has not been subjected to processes of transmissional accretion. It has unity of form, theme, diction, topoi and ethos. There is always a danger that the extraction of a particular poem or series of poems from a manuscript context for separate editorial and analytical treatment can lead to a false impression of literary independence. But there is no justification in the case of *APF* for the view that Ifor Williams' edition is responsible for giving the poem

---

5   Evans, *The Welsh Life of St David*, xix.

a semblance of monolithic uniqueness. That uniqueness, I am sure, is given by the character of the extant text itself.

Full text and translation are given in the Appendix. Here follows an analysis of the form and thematic plan of the poem, according to the nine individual *awdlau* (*tirades* with internally consistent end-rhyme).

	awdlau
Exposition	I II
Development	III IV V VI VII
Climax	VIII
Coda	IX

I

lines 1–23: Sets up ambition of Britons (Welsh) to reconquer the island of Britain, establishes that this will be done with help of allies from other parts of the British Isles: there will be an alliance (*kymot*) between the Welsh (*Kymry*) and the 'men of Dublin' (*gwyr Dulyn*, Norsemen), the 'Irish of Ireland, Anglesey and Pictland' (*Gwydyl Iwerdon, Mon a Phrydyn*), the Cornish (*Cornyw*) and the men of Strathclyde (*a Chludwys*). Establishes that one of the main bones of contention is an unjust tax levied on the Welsh and administered by the 'officers of the high king' *meiryon mechteyrn*.

(line 24: Probably a gloss, or a stray line from another poem; breaks rhyme scheme.)

II

lines 25–44: Establishes illegitimacy of English sovereignty in Britain; their ignoble origins and dishonest strategies, the poem insists on the depiction of the English as little more than a disreputable band of seafaring heathen pirates who got lucky once. Hints of a particular strategy on their part to stamp out British resistance once and for all; Welsh reject this, and the Trinity should also; there is a hint of ethnic cleansing as we would understand it and resistance to it in these lines: 'The Trinity shall refuse the blow which is being planned, to devastate the land of the Britons, and set up settlements of the English.'

III

lines 45–63: Starts to detail the images of the English flight before the vengeful Britons.

IV

lines 69–86: Adds some detail about the tax and its collectors: the officers connected with the 'high king' before are here said to be based in Cirencester, *meiryon Kaer Geri*. Emphasises that any attempt to take the tax by force will be unsuccessful, mentions one of the (legendary) resistance leaders, Cadwaladr.

V

lines 87–106: Introduces the other resistance leader, Cynan. Together their forces will drive the English into Winchester (and presumably besiege them there). Saint David and other British saints will support the Welsh action.

VI

lines 107–26: Graphic images of the horrors of the battle, but with obvious fascinated delight in that horror, as suffered by the English. The enemy is specified as not simply generically English, but *Iwys* (line 108, also line 181), 'the men of Wessex' (cf. Bede, *HE* 3.7 *gens occidentalium Saxonum qui antiquitus Geuissae uocabantur*; *Geguuis* in Asser, *Giuoys* in the Annales Cambriae).

VII

lines 127–46: Interwoven with elaboration of the theme of the illegitimacy of English rule, emphasis on the support of Saints David and Garmon, and also support from Ireland, from the Irish, *G6ydyl*, and the 'heathens of Dublin', *gynhon Dulyn*, who will be united under the 'holy banner of David', *lluman glan Dewi*. (Note that the English are also called 'heathens', *gynhon*, lines 176, 183, although they, of course, had been Christians for centuries, unlike the Norsemen, who were seen as allies.)

VIII

lines 147–70: More details are given of the allies who will assist the Welsh; 'excellent, long-haired men from Ireland', and further support from 'Lego', from Dumbarton and from Brittany. Then there is what is effectively a curse on the English, followed by a climactic paean of praise to the two resistance leaders, Cynan and Cadwaladr.

IX

lines 171–99: Celebration of the predicted re-establishment of Welsh sovereignty over the whole island, and the shambolic and desperate retreat of the English back to where they came from: 'The foreigners will be on their way into exile, one after the other, on their way back to their comrades. The English will lie at anchor every day on the sea, the venerable Welsh will be victorious forever.' Final imprecation to St David to lead the rebellion, and praise of St David and God in heaven.

I now present the passages from the poem which mention St David.

A.

51 Y Ddu6 a Dewi yd ymorchymynynt,
52 talet, g6rthodet flet y allmyn.
53 G6naent 6y aneireu eisseu trefdyn.
54 Kymry a Saesson kyferuydyn,
55 y am lan ymtreula6 ac ym6rthryn,
56 o dirua6r vydina6r pan ymprofyn.

51 (They commend themselves to God and David,
52 that He may pay the foreigners back, that he may reject their treachery.
53 They commit shameful deeds for their lack of living space.
54 The Welsh and the English will meet,
55 they will charge and attack each other on the river bank,
56 with enormous armies, when they measure themselves up against each other.)

So St David can be invoked second only to God as a source of divine assistance in the battle against the usurpers. Insofar as line 52 contains third person *singular* imperatives, *talet, g6rthodet*, I assume we must understand these as referring to God alone, as supreme commander, St David fulfilling an auxiliary role. This is no doubt theologically correct in the context, though it is clear from the other references that St David can be conceived as playing a leading role in the campaign himself.[6]

B.

100 Nys g6naho mola6t meiryon mechteyrn,
101 na chynhoryon Saesson, keffyn ebryn,
102 nys g6naho medut medda6t genhyn,
103 heb talet o dynget meint a geffyn
104 o ymdifeit veibon ac ereill ryn.
105 Tr6y eirya6l Dewi a seint Prydyn,
106 hyt ffr6t ar Lego ffoha6r allmyn.

100 (The officers of the high king will do nothing praiseworthy in his name,
101 nor the heroes of the English, however fierce they might be;
102 drunkenness at our expense will not bring them any profit,
103 without paying back what they are fated to, however many
104 orphans and other wretches they have to suffer as a result.
105 Through the prayer of David and the saints of Britain,[7]
106 the foreigners will be put to flight to the channel of Legio.)[8]

Here St David is explicitly made the superior of all other saints of Britain, by the symbolic means of mentioning him alone by name, all the others generically only. This is one of the factors which point to the provenance of the poem in the St Davids area itself. If that argument is accepted, then there can be no justification

---

6 One could always suggest that suspension marks have been lost in transmission, so, originally, *talēt, *g6rthodēt*, third person *plural* imperatives. But the text is quite comprehensible as it stands, and the immediate scribe obviously felt no need for plural imperatives. So, critically, we have no reason to assume any scribe previous in the transmission felt such a need.

7 It is true that *Prydyn* is generally used to denote 'Pictland', rather than 'Britain', which is usually *Prydein*. I cannot justify the alternative usage here (also in line 62), except by following the arguments of I. Williams, *Armes Prydein o Lyfr Taliesin*, 14 and Williams and Bromwich, *Armes Prydein*, 21–2.

8 I suggest that *Lego* of the poem can be thought of as an orthographical variant (in this generally yod-less manuscript) of *Legio*, i.e. the Latin word taken as standing for one of the places called *Cair Legion* in the *Historia Brittonum* ch. 66a (with orthographic variants); so either Caerleon or Chester. The former identification allows us to think of the present line as indicating that the English will be driven into the Bristol Channel. Identfication with Chester would allow us to think of the English as being driven into the Irish Sea, but that does not seem to me quite as satisfactory as having them driven into the open ocean through the Bristol Channel. Also, while it is not clear to me in precisely what sense line 149, 'A fervent fleet will come from Legio', should be understood, Caerleon, as part of Welsh territory, can, at least, be conceived of as playing an important role in the rebellion against the English. I cannot imagine why a fleet from Chester could have such a role.

for arguing that *APF* is evidence of the expansion of the cult of St David to make him a saint of all Wales. Under this interpretation, the poet invokes St David first because he is the saint to whom he owes immediate allegiance, not because St David has anything like the status of spiritual figurehead of all the Welsh. The reference to Garmon discussed below, as I interpret it, similarly indicates the local character of St David.

C.

127 Dygorfu Kymry y peri kat,
128 a ll6yth llia6s g6lat a gynnullant,
129 a lluman glan Dewi a drychafant,
130 y tywyssa6 G6ydyl tr6y lieingant.
131 A gynhon Dulyn, genhyn y safant.
132 Pan dyffont yr gat, nyt ymwadant.

127 (The Welsh [ever] triumphed in giving battle,
128 and they will muster the peoples of many countries,
129 and they will raise the holy banner of David,
130 to lead the Irish by its linen.
131 And the heathens of Dublin will stand with us.
132 When they come to battle, they will not shirk.)

This is strictly not a reference to St David at all, but to 'St David's holy banner'. Whether there is any particular significance in the fact that St David's banner is explicitly called upon to lead the Irish contingent I am not qualified to say. I simply draw attention to the point, and invite comment from those who may better be able to comment on the relationship between the cult of St David and the Irish.

D.

133 Gofynnant yr Saesson py geissysant,
134 p6y meint eu dylyet or wlat a dalyant,
135 c6 mae eu her6 pan seilyassant,
136 c6 mae eu kenedloed, py vro pan doethant.
137 (Yr amser G6rtheyrn genhyn y sathrant:
138 ny cheffir o wir rantir an karant.)
139 Neu vreint an seint, pyr y saghyssant,
140 neu reitheu Dewi, pyr y torrassant.
141 Ymgetwynt Gymry, pan ymwelant,
142 nyt ahont allmyn or nen y safant,
143 hyt pan talhont seithweith g6erth digonsant
144 ac agheu diheu yg werth eu cam.
145 Ef talha6r o ana6r Garma6n garant
146 y pedeir blyned ar petwar cant.

133 (They will demand of the English what it was they were looking for,
134 what the strength of their claim on the land they hold is,
135 where the land they stem from is,
136 where their kinsmen are, from what land they came;
137 since Vortigern's time they trample around in our land:
138 our kin's plot cannot be taken by rightful means.

166

139   or the privilege of our saints, why did they disregard it,
140   or the rights of David, why did they offend against them.
141   The Welsh will ensure, when they are looking each other in the eye,
142   that the foreigners will not budge from the spot they are standing on
143   until they pay back sevenfold the damage they have done,
144   and their death will be certain for their misdeeds.
145   With the help of the kinsmen of Garmon,
146   the four years and the four hundred will be paid for.)

This is perhaps the densest reference to St David in the poem, and the meaning is the more indeterminate for that, I think. As a first approximation, we can certainly accept the reference to the English offending against the 'rights of St David' as a generic statement of English hostility to a Welsh way of life, as expressed from the point of view of a Dyfed cleric. But I wonder whether the poet may not be thinking of some more specific crime. The 'rights of St David' plausibly refer to some specific set of ecclesiastical privileges or regulations, even to a specific document,[9] of which the actions or policies of Aethelstan may have been in direct violation. It seems likely that such a set of privileges or a document will have existed, though I am not aware that we have any extant evidence for it in a St Davids context.

This passage also contains the only other specific hagiographical reference in *APF*, to *Garmawn*. I have previously suggested that this is a reference to St. Garmon as regional saint of Powys.[10] If so, then the juxtaposition of the saint of another region with St David would be consistent with the latter's character at this time still as a more or less regional saint of south-west Wales, rather than as a saint who could be connected widely with the whole of Wales.

E.

191   Saesson 6rth agor ar vor peunyd,
192   Kymry g6enera6l hyt Vra6t goruyd.
193   Na cheiss6ynt lyfra6r nac aga6r brydyd,
194   arymes yr ynys hon namyn hyn ny byd.
195   Iol6n i ri a gre6ys nef ac eluyd.
196   poet tywyssa6c Dewi yr kynifwyr,
197   yr yg Celi[11] Kaer am Du6 yssyd.
198   Ny threinc, ny dieinc, nyt ardispyd,
199   ny 6y6, ny wellyg, ny phlyg, ny chryd.

191   (The English will lie at anchor every day on the sea,
192   the venerable Welsh will be victorious forever.
193   They should not seek out the librarian[12] or the avaricious poet,

---

9 Comparable to the *Breint Teilaw* preserved in the Book of Llan Daf and edited in Wendy Davies, 'Braint Teilo'.

10 Isaac, '*Trawsganu Cynan Garwyn mab Brochfael*', 176, cf. Dumville, 'Sub-Roman Britain', 186. In the same place I have interpreted the 'four years and the four hundred' as an expression for the English usurpation of power from the Britons, with reference to the chronology in ch. 66 of the *Historia Brittonum*, where it is stated that the English (*Saxones*) came to Britain in the fourth year of Vortigern's reign and four hundred years since the Incarnation (*quadringentesimo primo anno*). Cf. Dumville, 'Some aspects of the chronology', 441 on this passage.

11 Ms. *yn yr yg gelli*.

12 While accepting Thomas Jones's observation (Jones, '*llyfrawr* < *librarius*') that Lat. *librarius*, probable source of the word *llyfra6r*, was *also* used to denote 'magician', I choose not to adopt the latter

194 there is no prophecy of this island except this one.
195 We pray to the Lord who created heaven and earth,
196 may David be a leader for the warriors,
197 for those who are in the Kingdom of Heaven with my God.[13]
198 He does not die, he does not flee, he does not tire,
199 he does not perish, he does not fail, he does not bend, he does not wither.)

This is the most explicit statement in the whole poem of the principle that St David should play a leading role in the prophesied coming uprising against the English. Since this passage obviously presents him precisely as a leader for the whole Welsh nation, this may be thought of conceptually as the kernel of his later role as saint of all Wales. But we should not conclude that this reflects any political, ideological reality of the time, since it would be natural for a cleric of the St Davids region to assume that his interests were the interests of all Wales and that it would therefore be appropriate for St David himself to lead the revolt spiritually, just as the cleric-poet himself presumably sees his ecclesiastical context as the context in which the ideas of revolt (through himself) are born and nurtured. The call for St David to lead the revolt as depicted symbolically in the poem reflects, in fact, iconically the ideological lead St Davids, through this particular cleric-poet, gives to the idea of revolt. So, at least, it may be thought to have been conceived by the poet. My reading of the conclusion of the poem has St David as the subject of the seven verbs in the last two lines.[14] If this is correct, then the fact that the poem ends with a paean of praise to St David significantly deepens his importance for the interpretation of the piece as a whole. The whole poem could then be thought of as setting out a political agenda (however unrealistic), entirely in the name of St David. It is, after all, in precisely such a context, the identification of the interests of 'St David' with the interests of the Welsh as a whole, that his later status as patron saint of all Wales must, in a suitably conducive secular political context, be thought of as having been established. While *APF* can therefore by no account be regarded as evidence for a David cult representing the whole of Wales in the tenth century, it does, by its very message and ambition, argue an ideological position from which just such a generalisation at some point must really have been made.

---

as the translation of the Welsh word in this context. I interpret the reference here as being to the 'librarian', the implication being that the reader of the poem should look no further for the true prophecy concerning the political future of Britain (hence also he should not look to the greedy professional poet either). In any case, I prefer this analysis of the word to the other suggestion, that it may be the plural in *-awr* of *llyfyr* (Williams, *Armes Prydein o Lyfr Taliesin*, 67; Williams and Bromwich, *Armes Prydein*, 70–1). There is no other instance of this plural of the word; it is otherwise consistently *llyfreu*, and trivial orthographic variants thereof, and that would have been metrically practicable as well, e.g. *na cheiss6ynt lyfreu na geu brydyd*. So it is difficult to motivate such deviant morphology as *llyfr* + *-awr*.

[13] Reading, modernised, *er yng Ngheli Gaer â'm Duw ysydd* (poetically free order for more conventional *er ysydd yng Ngheli Gaer â'm Duw*), a reference to all the saints and angels of heaven, who must certainly approve the return of the island to the sovereignty of the true Britons, and, perhaps, also, to the ancestors of the contemporary Welsh, in whose honour also the island should be cleared of the invaders.

[14] Not God as in the reading of Williams and Bromwich, *Armes Prydein*, 15.

Appendix:
Text and translation

Text

I

Dygogan awen dygobryssyn
maraned a meued a hed genhyn,
a phennaeth ehelaeth a ffraeth vnbyn,
a g6edy dyhed, anhed ym pob mehyn.
5   G6yr g6ychyr yn trydar, kasnar degyn,
escut yg gofut, ryhyt diffyn.
G6aethylg6yr hyt Gaer Weir g6asgara6t allmyn,
g6naha6nt goruoled g6edy g6ehyn,
a chymot Kymry a g6yr Dulyn,
10   G6ydyl Iwerdon, Mon a Phrydyn,
Corny6 a Chlud6ys; eu kynn6ys genhyn.
Atporyon uyd Brython pan dyorfyn.
Pell dygoganher amser dybydyn
teyrned a bonhed eu gorescyn,
15   g6yr Gogled yg kynted yn eu kylchyn,
ym perued eu racwed y diskynnyn.
Dysgogan Myrdin kyueruydyn[15]
yn Aber Perydon meiryon mechteyrn.
A chyny bei vn reith, lleith a g6ynyn.
20   O vn ewyllis bryt yd ym6rthuynnyn
meiryon, eu tretheu dychynnullyn,
yg ketoed Kymry nat oed a telhyn.
Yssyd 6r dylyeda6c a lefeir hyn.
(Ny dyffei a talei yg keithiwet.)

II

25   Mab Meir ma6r a eir, pryt na tharder[16]
rac pennaeth Saesson ac eu hoffed!
Pell b6ynt kychmyn G6rtheyrn[17] G6yned.
Ef gyrha6t allmyn y alltuded.
Nys arhaed6y neb, nys dioes dayar.
30   Ny wydynt py treiglynt ym pop aber.
Pan prynassant Danet tr6y fflet called,
gan Hors a Hegys oed yng eu ryssed.
Eu kynnyd bu y 6rthym yn anuonhed.
g6edy rin dilein, keith y mynuer.

---

[15] Ms. *kyueruyd hyn*. Note that the manuscript gives a capital to the initial of this line, as if it were the beginning of a section. But the rhyme continues, indication that there is no new *awdl*. The next *awdl* (change of rhyme) starts at line 25, which is not, however, marked with a capital.

[16] Ms. *thardet*.

[17] Ms. *y6rtheyrn*, but the syntax of this is unclear to me at this time; palaeographically speaking, *y* could arise by scribal error from *g*.

Translation

I

    The muse foretells that there shall rush
to our part wealth and property and peace,
and extensive domination and speedy nobles,
and after the troubles, communities in every place.
5   Excellent men in the tumult of battle, wild and steadfast,
quick under pressure, stubborn in defense.
Fighters will drive the foreigners as far as Caer Wair,[1]
they will celebrate after the difficulties,
and there will be an alliance between the Welsh and the men of Dublin,
10   the Irish of Ireland, Anglesey and Pictland,
the men of Cornwall and Strathclyde; they will all be welcomed by us.
The Britons will be remnants when they are victorious.
It has been foretold for a long time when there will come
rulers with the legitimacy of nobility for their conquest,
15   the men of the North in the front of the hall around them,
they attack at the forefront of battle.
Myrddin foretells that there will be a meeting
at Aber Peryddon of the officers of the high king.
And although no one has the right to do so – they will bemoan death –
20   the officers will fight with one will,
they will try to collect their taxes,
that no one in the treasuries of the Welsh would ever pay.
Whoever is a free man will say this.
(There would come no one who would pay taxes in captivity.)[2]

II

25   Son of Mary, of the great Word! For shame! that they are not broken,
the domination of the English and their arrogance.
May the slaves of Vortigern be far away!
He will drive the foreigners into exile.[3]
No one will receive them, they have no place on the earth.
30   They will not know where they are wandering in every estuary.
When they bought Thanet by mendacious guile,
Horsa and Hengist were in dire straits.
Their subsequent success at our expense was ignoble.
After a secret murder plot, the slaves wore the crown.

---

[1] Williams's identification of this with Durham on the River *Wear* remains plausible, but entirely without foundation beyond the linguistic identity (Williams, *Armes Prydein o Lyfr Taliesin* 12; Williams and Bromwich, *Armes Prydein*, 20). Perhaps there is a reference here to Lundy or the Isle of Wight, both of which appear to have been called *Ynys Weir* in early Welsh tradition, though the transmission of the name is not clear, cf. Bromwich, *Trioedd Ynys Prydein* No. 52, 231–2.

[2] Apparently a gloss.

[3] Williams, *Armes Prydein o Lyfr Taliesin* 22 and Williams and Bromwich, *Armes Prydein*, 29, emend the text to *gyrha6r* here, to make impersonal syntax, 'The foreigners will be driven into exile.' This seems unnecessary to me, and despite Williams' doubts, I regard *Mab Meir* as the subject of the 3sg. future form *gyrha6t*.

35 Dechymyd medda6t[18] ma6r wira6t o ved,
dechymyd aghen agheu llawer,
decymyd[19] anaeleu dagreu g6raged,
dychyfroy[20] etgyllaeth pennaeth lletfer,
dechymyd tristit byt a reher,[21]
40 pan uyd kechmyn Danet an teyrned.
G6rthottit trinda6t dyrna6t a b6yller,
y dilein g6lat Vrython, a Saesson yn anhed.
Poet kynt eu reges yn alltuded
no mynet Kymry yn diffroed.

III

45 Mab Meir ma6r a eir, pryt nas terdyn
Kymry rac goeir breyr ac vnbyn!
Kyneircheit, kyneilweit, vn reith c6ynnyn,
vn gor, vn gyghor, vn eissor ynt.
Nyt oed yr ma6red nas lleferynt,
50 namyn yr hebcor goeir nas kymodynt.
Y Ddu6 a Dewi yd ymorchymynynt;
talet, g6rthodet flet y allmyn.
G6naent 6y aneireu eisseu trefdyn.
Kymry a Saesson kyferuydyn,
55 y am lan ymtreula6 ac ym6rthryn,
o dirua6r vydina6r pan ymprofyn.
Ac am allt lafna6r a ga6r a gryn,
ac am G6y, geir kyfyrgeir, y am beurllyn,
a lluman ada6, agar6 disgyn,
60 a mal b6yt[22] balaon Saesson syrthyn.
Kymry kynyrcheit kyfun dullyn,
blaen 6rth von granwynyon, kyfyng oedyn.
Meiryon yg werth eu geu yng kreu[23] creinhyn,
eu bydin yg 6aetlin yn eu kylchyn.
65 Ereill ar eu traet tr6y goet kilhyn,
tr6y u6rch y dinas ffoxas ffohyn
ryfel heb dychwel y tir Prydyn,
attor tr6y la6 gyghor, mal mor llithryn.

---

18 Ms. *medda6*.
19 Sic ms.
20 I understand this as *dychyfro-* + -*oi*, 3sg. pres. subjunctive, with the Old Welsh ending -*oi*, here contracted in the verb with vocalic stem-auslaut. Cf. OW *boi* 3sg. pres. subjunctive of *bot*, examples in Falileyev, *An Etymological* Glossary, 159. And on the history of this ending, Isaac, *The Verb in the Book of Aneirin*, 365–8.
21 Ms. *ryher*.
22 Ms. om. *b6yt*.
23 Ms. *yn eu*.

35   Drunkenness accompanies a great drink of mead,
          crisis accompanies the deaths of many,
          sorrow accompanies the tears of women,
          – may cruel domination engender complaint –
          sadness accompanies a world in turmoil,
40   when the slaves from Thanet are our rulers.
          The Trinity shall refuse the blow which is being planned,
          to devastate the land of the Britons, and to set up communities of the English.
          May their retreat into exile be quicker
          than the Welsh lose all their land.

III

45   Son of Mary, of the great Word! For shame! that the Welsh do not break through,
          shame on the nobles and leaders!
          Both supplicants and sponsors complain with the same right,
          in one chorus, with one counsel, of one nature they are.
          It would not be out of pride that they would not countenance it,
50   but rather in order to shake off the shame, that they would not advocate peace.
          They commend themselves to God and David,
          that He may pay the foreigners back, that he may reject their treachery.
          They commit shameful deeds for their lack of living space.
          The Welsh and the English will meet,
55   they will charge and attack each other on the river bank,
          with enormous armies, when they measure themselves up against each other.
          And on the slope, blades and cries and attack,
          and on the Wye, cry after cry on the shining water,
          and the banner left behind, fearsome offensive,
60   and like wild cat's fodder, the English fall.
          The followers of the Welsh move united into battle,
          in close ranks were the pale-cheeks ranged.
          As for the officers, for their treachery they will wallow in their own blood,
          their army swimming in their blood around them.
65   Others flee on foot through the forest,
          through the fortress of the town the foxes will flee,
          war will be banished for ever from the land of Britain,[4]
          in their mean counsels, they will slip away like the sea.

---

4   See note 7.

IV

Meiryon Kaer Geri difri c6ynant,
70 rei y dyffryn a bryn nys dirwadant,
y Aber Perydon ny mat doethant.
Anaeleu tretheu dychynullant.
Na6 vgein canh6r y discynnant.
Ma6r watwar! namyn petwar nyt atcorant.
75 Dyhed y eu g6raged a dywedant.
Eu crysseu yn lla6n creu a orolchant.
Kymry gyneircheit eneit dichwant.
G6yr Deheu eu tretheu a amygant.
Llym llifeit llafna6r ll6yr y lladant.
80 Ny byd y vedyc m6yn or a wnaant.
Bydinoed Katwaladyr, kadyr y deuant,
rydrychaf6ynt Kymry, kat a wnaant.[24]
Lleith anoleith rydygyrchassant.
Yg gorffen eu tretheu agheu a 6dant.
85 Ereill arosceill ryplanhassant.
Oes oesseu eu tretheu nys escorant.

V

Yg koet, y maes, ym bro,[25] ym bryn,
canh6yll yn tywyll a gerd genhyn.
Kynan yn racwan ym pop discyn,
90 Saesson rac Brython g6ae a genyn.
Katwaladyr yn baladyr gan y unbyn,
tr6y synh6yr yn ll6yr yn eu dichlyn.
Pan syrth6ynt eu clas dros eu herchwyn,
yg custud a chreu rud ar rud allmyn,
95 yg gorffen pop agreith, anreith degyn,
Seis ar hynt hyt Gaer Wynt kynt p6y kynt techyn.
G6yn eu byt 6y, Kymry, pan adrodynt,
'Ryn g6ara6t y trinda6t or tralla6t gynt!
Na chrynet Dyfet na Gly6yssyg.'
100 Nys g6naho mola6t meiryon mechteyrn,
na chynhoryon Saesson, keffyn ebryn,
nys g6naho medut medda6t genhyn,
heb talet o dynget meint a geffyn
o ymdifeit veibon ac ereill ryn.
105 Tr6y eirya6l Dewi a seint Prydyn,[26]
hyt ffr6t ar Lego ffoha6r allmyn.[27]

---

[24] Ms. *wnant.*
[25] Ms. om. *ym bro.*
[26] Ms. *Prydeyn.*
[27] Ms. *allan.*

IV

The officers of Cirencester will lament bitterly,
70 some in the valley, some in the hills, they will not deny it,
that they did not come fortunately to the Mouth of Peryddon.
The taxes that they try to raise are a source of great trouble.
They attack with 18,000 men.
Such a great tragedy! Apart from four, none return.
75 They report unrest to their wives.
They wash their tunics full of blood.
The supplicants of the Welsh are not concerned for their lives.
The men of the South will fight for their taxes.
Sharp, slicing blades will cut decisively.
80 No doctor will be able to earn a living from what they do!
The armies of Cadwaladr, gloriously will they come,
the Welsh will arise, they will do battle.
They have sought out inevitable death.
At the end of their taxes they will know death.
85 Others, who were wise enough to bide their time, have struck.
For ever and ever, they will not raise their taxes.

V

In the forest, in the field, in the vale, on the hill,
a candle in the darkness walks with us.
Cynan is at the head of the troop in every attack,
90 The English sing a song of woe before the Britons.
Cadawaladr is a spear at the side of his men,
having picked them with complete wisdom.
When their troops fall into bed,
after hard work – red gore on the cheeks of the foreigners –
95 after every attack, persistent plundering,
the English will be on the way back to Winchester, fleeing the one faster than
the other.
Blessed the Welsh when they report,
'The Trinity has delivered us from the former troubles!
Neither Dyfed nor Glywysyng need tremble any more.'
100 The officers of the high king will do nothing praiseworthy in his name,
nor the heroes of the English, however fierce they might be;
drunkenness at our expense will not bring them any profit,
without paying back what they are fated to, however many
orphans and other wretches they have to suffer as a result.
105 Through the prayer of David and the saints of Britain,
the foreigners will be put to flight as far as the channel of Legio.[5]

---

[5] See note 8.

VI

Dysgogan awen dyda6 y dyd
pan dyffo Iwys y vn g6ssyl,
vn cor, vn gyghor, a Lloegyr lloscit,
110   yr gobeith anneira6 ar yn pryda6 luyd,
a cherd ar allfro a ffo beunyd.
Ny 6yr kud ymda, c6d a, c6d vyd.
Dychyrch6ynt gyfarth mal arth o vynyd,
y talu g6ynyeith g6aet eu heÌnyd.
115   Atvi peleitral, dyfal dillyd,
nyt arbett6y car corff y gilyd.
Atui pen gafla6 heb emennyd.
Atui g6raged g6ed6 a meirch g6eilyd.
Atui ubein[28] vthyr rac ruthyr ketwyr,
120   a llia6s lla6amhar kyn g6ascar lluyd.
Kennadeu agheu dychyferwyd
pan safh6ynt galaned 6rth eu hennyd.
Ef diala6r ar g6erth y treth beunyd,
ar mynych gennadeu ar geu luyd.
125   Dygorfu[29] Kymry tr6y kyfergyr,
yn gyweir gyteir gytson gytffyd.

VII

Dygorfu[30] Kymry y peri kat,
a ll6yth llia6s g6lat a gynnullant,
a lluman glan Dewi a drychafant,
130   y tywyssa6 G6ydyl tr6y lieingant.
A gynhon Dulyn, genhyn y safant.
Pan dyffont yr gat, nyt ymwadant.
Gofynnant yr Saesson py geissysant,
p6y meint eu dylyet or wlat a dalyant,
135   c6 mae eu her6 pan seilyassant,
c6 mae eu kenedloed, py vro pan doethant.
(Yr amser G6rtheyrn genhyn y sathrant:
ny cheffir o wir rantir an karant.)
Neu vreint an seint, pyr y saghyssant,
140   neu reitheu Dewi, pyr y torrassant.
Ymgetwynt Gymry, pan ymwelant,
nyt ahont allmyn or nen y safant,
hyt pan talhont seithweith g6erth digonsant

---

[28] Ms. *obein.*

[29] The minim misreading for putative *dygorui* (future) in this line and line 127, as argued for by Williams, *Armes Prydein o Lyfr Taliesin*, 50, and Williams and Bromwich, *Armes Prydein*, 55, is entirely possible, but the immediate scribe had no difficulty identifying and accurately copying other future forms in the poem, so I choose instead to interpret the *lectiones difficiliores* with the preterite as actually transmitted.

[30] See previous note.

VI

The muse foretells that the day will come,
when the men of Wessex meet for counsel,
in one chorus, with one counsel, and England will burn,
110   in the hope that our beautiful hosts will be put to shame;
but the foreigners will have to set out into daily flight.
They do not know where they are wandering, where they are going, where
                      they will be.
They will attack in battle like the bear from the mountain,
to avenge the blood of their comrades.
115   There will be a blow from a spear, continuous bloodletting;
the kinsman [of ours] will not spare his opponent's body.
There will be heads split open, emptied of brain.
There will be widowed wives and riderless horses.
There will be terrible crying before the onslaught of the attackers,
120   and many severed hands, before the armies separate.
Messengers will meet death
when the corpses stand so tightly that they stand up against each other,
The tax will be avenged with equal worth every day,
also the many embassies and false troops.
125   The Welsh [ever] triumphed[6] through assault,
ready for battle, united, unanimous, with one faith.

VII

The Welsh [ever] triumphed by giving battle,[7]
and they will muster the peoples of many countries,
and they will raise the holy banner of David,
130   to lead the Irish by its linen.
And the heathens of Dublin will stand with us.
When they come to battle, they will not shirk.
They will demand of the English what they were looking for,
what the strength of their claim on the land they hold is,
135   where the land they stem from is,
where their kinsmen are, from what land they came;
(since Vortigern's time they trample around in our land:
our kin's plot cannot be taken by rightful means.)[8]
or the privilege of our saints, why did they disregard it,
140   or the rights of David, why did they offend against them.
The Welsh will ensure, when they are looking each other in the eye,
that the foreigners will not budge from the spot they are standing on
until they pay back sevenfold the damage they have done,

---

6   See note 29.
7   See note 29
8   I.e. it is only by illegitimate means that the English have occupied the country.

177

ac agheu diheu yg werth eu cam.
145   Ef talha6r o ana6r Garma6n garant
y pedeir blyned ar petwar cant.

VIII

G6yr g6ychyr g6allt hiryon, ergyrdofyd,
y[31] dihol Saesson o Iwerdon dybyd.
Dybi o Lego lyghes rewyd,
150   rewinya6t y gat, r6ycca6t lluyd.
Dybi o Alclut g6yr drut, diweir,
y dihol o Prydein, virein luyd.
Dybi o Lyda6 pryda6 gyweithyd,
ketwyr y ar katueirch, ny pheirch eu hennyd.
155   Saesson o pop parth, y g6arth ae deubyd.
Rytreghis eu hoes, nys dioes eluyd.
Dyderpi agheu yr du gyweithyd,
clefyt a dyllid ac ang6eryt.
G6edy eur ac aryant a chanh6ynyd,
160   boet perth eu disserth yg werth eu drycffyd,
boet mor, boed agor eu kussulwyr,
boet creu, boet agheu eu kyweithyd.
Kynan a Chatwaladyr, kadyr yn lluyd,
etmycca6r hyt Vra6t ffa6t ae deubyd.
165   Deu vnben degyn, d6ys eu kussyl.
Deu orsegyn Saesson o pleit Dofyd.
Deu hael, deu geda6l g6latwarthegyd.
Deu diarchar bara6t vnffa6t, vnffyd.
Deu erchwynna6c Prydein, mirein luyd.
170   Deu arth nys g6na g6arth kyfarth beunyd.

IX

Dysgogan derwydon meint a deruyd.
O Vyna6 hyt Lyda6 yn eu lla6 yt vyd.
O Dyuet hyd Danet 6y bieiuyd.
O Wa6l hyd Weryt, hyt eu hebyr,
175   lletta6t[32] eu pennaeth tros Yrech6yd.
Attor ar gynhon Saesson ny byd.
Atchwel6ynt 6ydyl ar eu hennyd.
Rydrychaf6ynt Gymry kadyr gyweithyd,

---

[31] Ms. *o*.
[32] Ms. *llettata6t*.

and their death will be certain for their misdeeds.
145   With the help of the kinsmen of Garmon,
the four years and the four hundred will be paid for.[9]

VIII

Splendid, long-haired men, skilful in assault,
will come from Ireland to drive out the English.
A fervent fleet will come from Legio,[10]
150   it will annihilate the troop, it will tear the hosts.
Brave, faithful men will come from Dumbarton,
to drive them out of Britain, fine hosts.
A handsome troop will come from Brittany,
warriors on warhorses, they afford their enemy no respect.
155   The English will be shamed on every quarter.
Their time is over, they have no place in the world.
Death will come to the black troop,
sickness and pursuit and contempt.
After they have had gold and silver and other treasure,
160   may they find shelter in the bushes, because of their falsehood,
may the sea and the anchor be their counsellors,
may gore, may death be their comrades.
As for Cynan and Cadwaladr, glorious in their armies,
the fate which is destined for their part will be celebrated forever.
165   Two steadfast rulers, whose counsel is wise.
Two tramplers on the English in God's name.
Two generous men, two gift-giving cattle-raiders.
Two brave, ready men, of one fate, of one faith.
Two guardians of Britain, splendid armies.
170   Two bears, daily battle does not put them to shame.

IX

Prophets foretell all that will happen.
From Mynaw to Brittany, it will all be in their hands.[11]
From Dyfed to Thanet they will own it.
From the Wall to the Forth, throughout its estuaries,
175   their rule will spread across Erechwydd.[12]
No return will be possible for the heathens.
The Irish will return to their comrades.
Let the Welsh raise a shining host,

---

[9] See note 10.
[10] See note 8
[11] I leave open here whether Mynaw refers here to the region of south-east Scotland known as *Manau Guotodin* in *Historia Brittonum* ch. 62 or to the Isle of Man, as more usually in Welsh. Both references seem plausible to me. If south-east Scotland, the expression delimits rightfully Brittonic *lands*; if the Isle of Man, it delimits (roughly) rightfully Brittonic *seaboards*.
[12] I am not sure that the accepted analysis of *Erechwydd* is correct (Williams, *Armes Prydein o Lyfr Taliesin*, 62–5; Williams and Bromwich, *Armes Prydein*, 67–8), but have no alternative to offer at this time, so place no weight on the term or its interpretation.

bydinoed am g6r6f a th6r6f milwyr,
180   a theyrned De6s, rygedwis[33] eu ffyd.
Iwis y pop llyghes, tres a deruyd,
a chymot Kynan gan y gilyd.
Ny alwa6r gynhon yn gynifwyr,
namyn kechmyn Kadwaladyr ae gyfnewitwyr.
185   Eil Kymro llawen, llafar a uyd,
am ynys gym6yeit, heit a deruyd,
pan safh6ynt galaned 6rth eu hennyd,
hyt yn Aber Santwic, s6ynedic vyd.
Allmyn ar gychwyn y alltudyd,
190   ol 6rth ol, attor ar eu hennyd.
Saesson 6rth agor ar vor peunyd,
Kymry g6enera6l hyt Vra6t goruyd.
Na cheiss6ynt lyfra6r nac aga6r brydyd,
arymes yr ynys hon namyn hyn ny byd.
195   Iol6n i ri a gre6ys nef ac eluyd,
poet tywyssa6c Dewi yr kynifwyr,
yr yg Celi Kaer am Du6 yssyd.[34]
Ny threinc, ny dieinc, nyt ardispyd,
ny 6y6, ny wellyg, ny phlyg, ny chryd.

---

[33] Ms. *ryged6ys.*
[34] See note 11.

armies around beer and the tumult of soldiers,
180 and the rulers of God, who have kept their faith.
The men of Wessex in every fleet; there will be conflict,
and an alliance of Cynan with his comrades.
The heathens will not be called warriors,
but rather the slaves of Cadwaladr and his traders.
185 The descendents of the Welsh will be joyful, they will be talkative,
about the tormentors of the island, the swarm will have disappeared,
when the corpses stand so tightly that they stand up against each other,
as far as Sandwich, it will be blissful.
The foreigners will be on their way into exile,
190 one after the other, on their way back to their comrades.
The English will lie at anchor every day on the sea,
the venerable Welsh will be victorious forever.
They should not seek out the librarian or the avaricious poet,[13]
there is no prophecy of this island except this one.
195 We pray to the Lord who created heaven and earth,
may David be a leader for the warriors,
for the sake of those who are in the Kingdom of Heaven with my God.
He does not die, he does not flee, he does not tire,
he does not perish, he does not fail, he does not bend, he does not wither.

---

[13] See note 12.

9

THE CULT OF ST NON: RAPE, SANCTITY AND MOTHERHOOD IN WELSH AND BRETON HAGIOGRAPHY

Jane Cartwright

St David's mother, Non, the daughter of Cynyr of Caer Gawch, is a somewhat unusual saint, since, unlike the vast majority of the Welsh female saints, her popularity was not confined to one particular locality. She was commemorated at several different locations in south Wales, and her cult was also transferred to Brittany, Ireland, Cornwall and Devon. In Wales her feast was celebrated on 3 March and it is listed in most medieval Welsh calendars.[1] In Brittany Non's principal pardon is celebrated on the Sunday following the octave of Corpus Christi and a minor pardon is held in her honour at Dirinon on the second Sunday after Easter.[2]

Non is also unusual in the context of European hagiography in that she is a rare example of a raped female saint. The menaced virgin is a common topos in hagiography, and numerous female saints are threatened with rape or physical abuse. They frequently have to flee arranged marriages and are abducted, beaten, burned and tortured (occasionally having their breasts torn off) before eventually being decapitated. However, at no point during their torturous ordeals is their virginity violated, since virginity is almost a prerequisite for feminine sanctity, and the image of the female saint as the bride of Christ, a veiled consecrated nun, is inextricably linked with her physical purity. In the Middle Welsh *Life* of Gwenfrewy (St Winifred), for example, Gwenfrewy's tormentor rather ironically announces that: *oni byddi di vn a mi oth vodd, y lleddir dy benn a'r cleddyf hwnn* ('if you will not become one with me [i.e. have intercourse with me] *willingly* I'll cut off your head with this sword').[3] Gwenfrewy chooses martyrdom rather than defilement, yet is resurrected by St Beuno and later becomes abbess of a community of women at Gwytherin.

In an extensive study, Corinne Saunders confirms that in medieval English hagiography 'in no instance is the virgin actually raped'.[4] And Kathleen Coyne Kelly states categorically that there are no rape narratives in hagiography:

> *Virginity* always outlasts the *virgin* … I have never read a narrative which describes rape, or says that rape was committed, or even creates a 'before and after' scenario … It is possible to argue that rape is 'represented' in hagiography through a rhetoric

---

1   For example BL MS Cotton Vespasian A. xiv, fol. 2r (Latin) and NLW MS Peniarth 60, 54 (Welsh).
2   William Worcestre records that the feast of St Non was celebrated at Launceston in Cornwall on 3 July and it appears to have been celebrated at Altarnun on 15 June. Worcestre, *Itineraries*, ed. Harvey, 83.
3   Jones, 'Golygiad o Fuchedd Gwenfrewy', 154. All English translations are my own unless otherwise stated. I have added emphasis here. On the female saints of Wales see Cartwright, 'Dead virgins' and *Feminine Sanctity*.
4   Saunders, *Rape and Ravishment*, 125.

of silence, if not displacement and substitution, but the fact remains that there are no direct narratives of rape in hagiography.[5]

Although Non's case is unusual and deviates from the standard pattern found in the biographies of most candidates for feminine sanctity, as we shall see in this article she is not the only example of a raped female saint. Whilst the Catholic Church continues to canonize women for defending their virginity and choosing martyrdom rather than rape, in medieval hagiography there are instances when the violation of a pure, devout virgin was deemed not only appropriate, but necessary, in order to explain the conception of certain, powerful male saints – notably, although not necessarily exclusively, in the Celtic regions. Maria Goretti of Ancona, who was stabbed to death whilst resisting rape in 1902, was canonized by Pope Pius XII in 1950 for the heroic defence of her virginity and for forgiving her oppressor. She is the patron saint of rape victims.

Most of what is known of St Non is derived from the various versions of the *Life* of St David. Other sources include Middle Welsh poetry, local folklore, oral traditions, pictorial narratives and the impact of Non and David's cults on the ritual landscape. One particular manuscript copy of Giraldus Cambrensis's *Life* of St David, which has attracted little attention to date, contains an appendix including various miracles associated with David (performed up to the year 1388) and five short readings for the feast of St Non. British Library, MS Royal 13 C1 appears to be a compilation collected by William Worcestre in the fifteenth century. Folio 180v summarizes the rape of St Non, the story of the conception of David, Non's encounter with Gildas who is struck dumb in the presence of the pregnant mother and the tale which parallels the massacre of the innocents. The readings associated with Non's pregnancy were obviously intended to be read aloud on Non's feast-day and were meant specifically to celebrate the life of David's mother, here referred to as 'our mother':

De sancta Nonita leccio prima. Diem festi beate Nonita selebremus hunc psalmum resonent inde concrepent lecciones hinc populorum turbe letentur unde pauperes Christi sublevuentur. Igitur et nos gratulemur in domino et de vita ipsius matris nostre ad laudem et honorem dei aliqua perstringamus ad gloriam quippe laudis eius credimus impensum quicquid sanctis suis fuerit solempniter exhibitum.

(First reading about St Non. Let us celebrate the feast of the blessed Non. Let them shout out this psalm, then let them call forth the readings, hence let the crowds of people be happy, whereby the poor of Christ may be uplifted. Therefore, let us too rejoice in the Lord and narrate some things about the life of our mother herself to the praise and honour of God. Indeed, we believe that whatever has been performed solemnly for his saints is supplied to the glory of his praise.)[6]

The readings, which appear to be incomplete, break off before the birth of St David. They presumably once formed part of a service designed to celebrate the feast of St Non.

Although there is no Welsh prose *Life* of St Non, there is a late medieval Breton miracle play, *Buez Santez Nonn hac ez map Deuy*, extant in a unique fifteenth-century manuscript (Paris, Bibliothèque Nationale de France, fonds celtique 5)

<hr />

5   Kelly, *Performing Virginity*, 42–3.
6   BL MS Royal 13 Ci, fol. 180v. I am indebted to my colleague Janet Burton for her transcription and translation of this text. Thanks also to David Noy for checking the translation. See also Curley, 'Five *lecciones*', 59–75.

Plate 2. St Non and St David (left), stained glass, Llansanffraid parish church, Ceredigion.
(Photo by Jane Cartwright)

which elaborates upon the life of Non and embellishes the brief account of Non's experiences given in the Latin and Welsh *Lives* of David.[7] The *Buez* relocates the majority of the tale to Brittany and provides a dramatic and detailed account of the rape of Non – 'before, during and after'.

Having briefly outlined the principal sources for the cult of Non, the aim of this article is to shed light on much of the extant evidence available for her cult in Wales and Brittany, before analysing in more detail the significance of Non's role as a raped female saint. Although Non's popularity spread to Ireland and Cornwall, a detailed study of these regions is beyond the scope of the present paper.[8] This article, therefore, will focus primarily on the Welsh and Breton sources.

Ceredigion

The strong links between the cult of St David and Ceredigion have frequently been emphasised. E.G. Bowen calculated that there were eleven dedications to David and his mother in Ceredigion and that they ceased abruptly along a line marked by the Upper Ystwyth and Wyre rivers.[9] Rhygyfarch's *Vita S. David* is generally assumed to have been composed at Llanbadarn Fawr in Ceredigion and the later Welsh *Life*, *Hystoria o Uuched Dewi*, is believed to have been composed by an anchorite at Llanddewibrefi *ca* 1346.

Llanddewibrefi is one of the few locations mentioned in David's *Life* which remains easy to identify in modern Wales: many of the others, such as *Vallis Rosina/Glyn Rhosyn* and *Hoddnant* (all used to describe the site of David's principal monastery) require interpretation. Rhygyfarch's *Vita S. David* states that David was educated at *Vetus Rubus*, whilst the Welsh *Life* refers to his education at *Henllwyn*.[10] The Cotton Vespasian version of Rhygyfarch's *Vita S. David*, as well as the *vita* by Giraldus Cambrensis, interpret *Vetus Rubus* as *Hen Vynyw/Hen-meneu* (Old Menevia) and this has traditionally been taken to refer to Henfynyw in Ceredigion.[11] Oral tradition and local folklore claim that David was born and brought up by his mother at Llanon in Ceredigion (formerly Llan-non) and that he began his education at Henfynyw. The tradition is commemorated and reinforced by a modern stained glass window in the parish church of Llansanffraid (see Plate 2): Non is depicted as a caring mother and her young son David holds a book, reminding the viewer that this is reputedly the area in which he received his early education. The windows which were given to the church by the Thomas family of Belmont, Llanon, also include an image of San Ffraid, the church's patron saint.

In 1912 three anonymous articles appeared in the *Welsh Gazette* which attempted to 'prove' that David was born in Ceredigion and that he only left for spiritual work in Pembrokeshire in later life:

> St Non, undoubtedly, spent the whole of her life-time in Llan-non. The whole evidence of present-day Non survivals points to this, and again, this mass of evidence points to

---

7   Ernault, 'La vie de sainte Nonne', 230–301, 405–91; *Buez Santez Nonn*, ed. Le Berre *et al.*

8   I intend to publish a separate study on Non's cult in Ireland and Cornwall at a future date.

9   Bowen, 'Celtic saints in Cardiganshire', 15. See also Map I.5.

10 *Vita S. David*, §7, ed. Sharpe and Davis, above 116–17. *Welsh Life*, ed. Evans 3.

11 Giraldi Cambrensis, *Opera* (ed. Brewer *et al.*, vol. 3, 384); Wade-Evans (transl.), *Life of St. David*, 9; see also the discussion on Henfynyw (83–6) and Thomas and Howlett, '*Vita Sancti Paterni*', 102. On these dedications see also James, 'The geography of the cult of St David', above 75–6.

the fact that Dewi himself was born here and educated here as a young man, but that towards late manhood he left for spiritual work in Pembrokeshire.[12]

The same author paints a rather romantic picture of Non preaching from a rostrum at Llwyn Non in Llanon and converting the local populace to Christianity. Interestingly this author happily accepts that Non was a historical character and that she played an active role as a missionary. Pádraig Ó Riain, on the other hand, states that Non is a fabrication: 'as with many mothers of saints, Non shows signs of having been invented with a view to fleshing out the story of Dewi's birth and youth in Ceredigion'.[13] This is certainly plausible; however, whilst not wishing to suggest that Non was a historical character, I wonder why this particular element in the *Life* of St David has been singled out as a piece of pure fabrication. Why not focus on other elements in the medieval narrative such as the episodes in which David heals the blind, raises the dead, or eats poisoned bread – all of which, along with his unusual conception and birth – 'flesh out' the story of St David and form important components in the biographical patterning of the saint?[14] Throughout the twentieth century and possibly into the twenty-first century there has been a tendency to assume that the male saints were much more likely to have been historical figures than were the female saints and I would challenge the assumption that the *vitae* of almost all male saints contain a core element of historical 'truth'.

Gerald of Wales noted in his *Itinerarium Kambriae* that the miraculous birth and conception of David were some of the most important and remarkable elements in the *Life* of the saint.[15] Later authors, however, appear to have been uncomfortable with the story of David's conception and this has led to the suggestion that Non and Sant were married or that Non became a nun in widowhood.[16] The assumption that Non was a nun, it has been suggested, is based on a confusion stemming from the fact that her name is similar to *nonna*, Latin for 'nun'. The fact that most female saints (regardless of their names) are nuns or abbesses seems to have been overlooked, not to mention the fact that the rape of Non appears consistently in all of the medieval accounts. G.H. Doble goes a step further and argues that St Non was originally a male saint – perhaps a companion to St David – who was later changed into a female saint and became known as his mother. This conjecture is partly based on the assumption that St Non is the same saint as St Nonna, the male patron of Penmarch in Brittany.[17] Doble also interprets the name Nonnita, which occurs on an inscribed stone at Tregony in Cornwall, as a male name, although, as Charles Thomas points out, since TRIS FILI can be interpreted as *tres filii* ('three children'), the name most probably refers to a daughter named Nonnita.[18] The principal reason, however, which motivated Doble's search for alternative origins for St Non appears to have been the fact that he found Rhygyfarch's account of the rape of Non distasteful:

---

12 Anon., 'Folk-lore of the Cardiganshire coast', *Welsh Gazette* 18 January 1912. See also *Welsh Gazette* 4 January and 11 January 1912.
13 Ó Riain, 'The saints', 394.
14 On the 'patterned life' see Henken, *The Welsh Saints*.
15 Trans. Thorpe, *The Journey Through Wales*, 161.
16 Baring-Gould and Fisher, *Lives*, 4, 22–3; de Guise, *The Story of St Non*, 5. Farmer, *Oxford Dictionary of Saints*, 358.
17 Doble, *Saint Nonna*. In the *Life* recorded by Albert Le Grand the patron of Penmarch is named Vouga. *Les vies des saints*, ed. de Kerdanet.
18 Charles Thomas pers. comm. See also Okasha, *Corpus*, 299–301.

One day she fell into the power of Sant, the King of Ceredigion, the country in which she lived, – a violent, brutal man, like so many of those old Celtic chieftains. By him she became the mother of S. David ... It is a sad story, but the great comfort is that it is probably not true. I suggest in all humility a different answer to the question.[19]

And thus he proposes that Non was originally a male figure.

Returning to Ceredigion we note that for many years a ruined building in Heol Non, Llanon, was believed to be the medieval chapel of St Non and it was identified as such largely on the basis that a holy water stoup was found on the site.[20] Ceredigion County Council even announced plans to give the historic chapel a facelift and open it up to the public in 1988.[21] However, in 1998 Richard Suggett of the Royal Commission on the Ancient and Historical Monuments of Wales visited the site and confirmed that the building, known locally as 'Neuadd' (Hall), was in fact not a chapel but a sixteenth-century house.[22] What had been claimed to be a tomb recess was quite simply a fireplace, and the stoup must have been moved there from elsewhere. The chapel of St Non appears to have been pulled down around 1906. An article in the *Welsh Gazette* in 1912 records that Homerton House was built on the old site of the chapel and that a statue of Non formerly stood outside the building above the entranceway. It recalls that young boys from the village used to throw stones at the statue and that in this way it probably became defaced.[23] Samuel Meyrick visited Non's chapel in 1808 and it was also described by George Eyre Evans in 1903 shortly before it was demolished:

> The ruins of the chapel of St. Non, – in the part of the village rightly called Llanon – are well worthy of a visit. The massive walls of unhewn stones, and one small, pointed arch, attest their former sacred use; whilst on the exterior wall, well protected by thatch of the roof immediately above it, is a stone, 14 inches tall, and 12 inches broad, on which is carved the face of a woman with a child in her arms, traditionally reputed to be that of St. Non with her boy. Certain is it the face of the mother is unlike any other known to me, as intended for the Virgin Mary.[24]

Various articles on the stone carving have appeared, some claiming that the statue is a representation of St David in his mother's arms and others proposing it is more likely to be the Virgin Mary and child.[25] The statue is now kept at the Ceredigion museum in Aberystwyth and the museum's curator, Michael Freeman, has proposed that it may in fact be a Sheela-na-gig: the size of the statue and its curved arms are reminiscent of other examples of Sheela-na-gigs.[26] Although statues of native saints are a rarity in Wales, there is a sixteenth-century statue – presumably of St Non – above the entranceway to her church at Dirinon in Brittany. Ritual abuse of saintly figures – including throwing stones at images of the saints – is quite commonplace

[19] Doble, *Saint Nonna*, 4–5.
[20] Hague, 'St Non's Chapel'.
[21] Anon., 'Ancient church'.
[22] R. Suggett, 'Neuadd', unpublished document in RCAHMW archive.
[23] *Welsh Gazette* 18 January, 1912.
[24] Evans, *Cardiganshire*, 176–7.
[25] Anon., 'Aberystwyth meeting report', 164–6; Anon., 'St David and Cardiganshire', which includes an imaginative sketch by Dora Jones; Argus, 'Correspondence', 36; Lewes, 'Image of St Non', 32–3.
[26] Cf. Anderson, *The Witch*. I am grateful to Michael Freeman for sharing with me his detailed knowledge of the Llanon site.

in folk tradition.[27] The Llanon stone, however, in my view, is in too poor a state of repair to say anything with certainty about the figure it represents.

As far as the place-name is concerned, whilst Iwan Wmffre supports the view that Llanon reflects the name of the saint, Pádraig Ó Riain suggests that the name consists of the elements *llan* and *on(n)* (church of the ash tree) and that the name may originally have had no connection with the saint.[28] Dirinon in Brittany has also been interpreted as reflecting the name of a tree, although in this instance it is the first element in the place-name which is of relevance, not the name of the saint – *diri* ('oak trees').[29] The dedication to Non at Llanerchaeron does appear to be relatively modern and perhaps stems from the association of her name with the second element in the name of the river -aeron. A similar confusion may have led to Non's association with Caron/Tregaron, for the fifteenth-century poet Ieuan Llwyd Brydydd refers to *Non Wen o Gaer Garon* ('Holy Non of Caer Garon') rather than the more usual Non of Caer Gawch in a poem to St Doged. He visits Doged's well in the hope that washing in the holy water will enable him to see clearly again and envokes Doged's Ceredigion ancestors (Cedig, Ceredig and Cunedda – ancestors he shares, incidentally, with St David) as well as other saints associated with Ceredigion (Curig and Cynddylig).[30] The church at Tregaron is traditionally associated with another saint, Caron, whose feast-day was celebrated two days after St Non's on 5 March.

Carmarthenshire

Llanon in Ceredigion is not the only place in Wales to lay claim to being St David's birthplace. Llan-non in Carmarthenshire is another contender. Once again no textual evidence supports this view or allows us to date these traditions, and none of the Middle Welsh poems which record the tale of David's birth and boyhood refer specifically to any of the places called Llan-non. In a poem praising Siôn ab Ieuan and his wife Margred on St David's Day Lewys Glyn Cothi refers to numerous miracles performed at Llan-non in Carmarthenshire and links the place with David's mother.[31] Unfortunately, however, he fails to elaborate upon these specific Carmarthenshire traditions. The parish church at Llan-non is still dedicated to Non and in the garden of a house named Ffynnon Non (Non's Well) at Beidr Non (Non's Lane) is a holy well associated with the saint. It is claimed that Non drew water from the well when she was thirsty and that thereafter the water had healing properties.[32] According to another Carmarthenshire tradition, Non was reputed to have had a vision in a field named Eisteddfa Non (Non's Seat) at Llan-non. An angel appeared to her and told her to found a nunnery on the site. Needless to say, there are no records that there

---

[27] On the destruction and disfigurement of Sheela-na-gigs see Anderson, *The Witch*, 27–31.

[28] Wmffre, 'Language and History', Part 2 Vol. II, 766; Ó Riain, 'The saints of Cardiganshire', 390.

[29] Falc'hun, *Dirinon*, 3; Le Berre *et al.*, *Buez Santez Nonn*, 11; Tanguy, 'The cults of SS. Nonne and Divi', below, 208.

[30] *Gwaith Ieuan*, ed. Bryant-Quinn, 109, 151 nn. 68 and 70. Possibly Curig is also mentioned here because he was renowned for curing blindness.

[31] *Gwaith Lewys Glyn Cothi*, ed. Johnston, 72

[32] Davies, *Folk-Lore*, 303.

was ever a nunnery at Llan-non. Although the farmhouse at Eisteddfa still exists, the field is now hidden by a housing estate.[33]

Pembrokeshire

In all of the medieval Latin *Lives* of David the place of David's birth is preordained and an evil ruler who hears the prophecy vows to kill anyone who rests on the said spot. There are obvious parallels here with the biblical Herod (Matthew 2.1–19), and Thomas O'Loughlin has demonstrated that not only do the events in the *Vita S. David* mirror the scriptures, but the phraseology of scripture also permeates Rhygyfarch's narrative.[34] Non gives birth in a terrific thunderstorm which apparently prevents the evil king from venturing outside, thus ensuring that David remains unharmed:

> but the place where the labouring mother was groaning was lit with such serene light that it shone as if God were present, though the sun was obscured by clouds. The mother, in her labour, had a stone near her on which she had leaned with her hands when pressed by her pains, which is why to those who look the rock shows the mark impressed as on wax. It broke in half in sympathy with the mother in her agony; the other part of it jumped over the head of the nun as far as her feet when the mother gave birth. A church has been built in that place, and this stone lies hidden in the base of its altar.[35]

Although the *Life* does not specify the location of the church, it is traditionally believed to be in a field near St Non's well in Pembrokeshire, above St Non's Bay. The stone which bears Non's fingerprints has been eagerly sought in Pembrokeshire and, apparently, its location is often enquired of the parish priest of Saint-Divy in Brittany.[36] In 1898 Sabine Baring-Gould visited the remains of the medieval chapel in Pembrokeshire expecting to find an Ogham stone there, the indents on which could have been mistaken for Non's fingerprints. He was, however, disappointed.[37] Wade-Evans suggested that the stone was more likely to have been incorporated into a church at nearby Llan-non in the parish of Llanrhian.[38] No church or chapel is extant at the Pembrokeshire Llan-non.

An early Christian monument with a simple incised cross, thought to date from the late sixth, seventh or eighth century, currently stands in the ruins of Non's chapel, above St Non's Bay.[39] Although it is possible that this cross-incised stone was moved here from elsewhere, it is interesting to note that the fifteenth-century poet Ieuan ap Rhydderch refers to the tradition that David was born at *eglwys y groes* (the church of the cross). On the other hand, a more plausible interpretation of these lines could be simply that David was born into the Christian church:

---

[33] I collected various oral traditions associated with the female saints of Wales by means of a questionnaire sent out to vicars in Wales in 1992. I am grateful to J.H. Gravell, the former vicar of Llan-non, for this information.

[34] O'Loughlin, 'Rhygyfarch's *Vita Dauidis*', 179–88.

[35] *Vita S. David* § 6 (ed. and transl. Sharpe, above, 116–17).

[36] Pers. comm.. I am grateful to the Pantyfedwen fund of the University of Wales, Lampeter, for funding field work in Brittany.

[37] Baring-Gould, 'Exploration of St. Non's chapel', 347.

[38] Wade-Evans, 'Rhygyfarch's Life of Saint David', 37–8.

[39] Edwards, 'Monuments', 56–8.

Yn eglwys y groes, oesir	At the church of the cross, long life
Y ganed hwn, ganiad hir.	he was born, long stanza.
Pan esgores y pennaeth,	When the chief was born,
Y llech yn ddwylech ydd aeth.[40]	the stone became two stones.

The events mentioned in the poem mirror the condensed Middle Welsh *Life* which omits the episode involving the evil king altogether. Both sources refer only to the fact that the stone miraculously split in two in sympathy with Non and make no reference to her pressing on the stone to relieve the agony of her labour pains. The Breton *Buez* is unique in that it provides additional detail and has three tyrants flee in terror from the storm as Non kneels on the stone and presses her hands into the rock as though it were made from wax.[41] The additional detail in the Breton *Buez* is likely to have been added at the time of the *Buez*'s compilation or it may stem from oral tradition.

Whilst the Latin, Welsh and Breton narratives associate David's baptism with the appearance of a holy well, none of the written accounts refer to a holy well which appeared miraculously as he was born. Nevertheless, according to oral tradition St Non's well, near the ruins of the medieval chapel in Pembrokeshire, reputedly issued forth at the time of his birth, whilst another well at Capel-y-Pistyll in Porth Clais is claimed to be associated with his baptism. Although Capel-y-Pistyll (Well Chapel) no longer exists, remnants of the well can still be found in undergrowth near the car park at Porth Clais. Browne Willis records that the chapel took its name from the spring which ran under it into a cistern at the east end.[42] Laurence Butler has proposed that a similar system may originally have existed at Non's well above St Non's Bay. Since the orientation of the building currently believed to be the chapel is unusual in that it faces north–south, rather than east–west, it has been suggested that the medieval chapel may originally have stood nearer the well where there are now loose stones in a field, and that the water from the well may have flowed through the chapel as at Capel-y-Pistyll.[43] The ruins now believed to be Non's chapel could in fact have been a dwelling – perhaps the priest's or the well keeper's house. Alternatively, as Richard Fenton suggested in 1811, the well keeper's house may have stood where the loose stones are found in a field and another building appears to have once surrounded the holy water.[44] Although the orientation of the 'chapel' is unusual, it does have particularly large foundation stones and appears to consist of different phases of building.[45]

The only extant medieval description of the chapel and holy well are found in the work of Lewys Glyn Cothi. In his fifteenth-century *cywydd* to Edudful ferch Gadwgon and her sons he provides a valuable description of Edudful's pilgrimage to St Davids. She visits Non's chapel and washes her head in the holy water, worships an image (possibly of St Non) and leaves candles on the altar at St Non's before proceeding to St Davids where she leaves an offering. The description of the building is not detailed enough to substantiate Lawrence Butler's claims, but the juxtaposi-

---

[40] *Cywyddau Iolo Goch*, ed. Lewis, 242–3. The first line could also be translated as follows: 'At the church of the everlasting cross'. By the 1870s the stone had been set into the east face of the building.

[41] *Buez Santez Nonn*, ed. Le Berre *et al.*, 154–5.

[42] Willis, *Survey*, 53.

[43] J. Wyn Evans, pers. comm.

[44] Fenton, *Historical Tour*, 113.

[45] Baring-Gould, 'Exploration of St. Non's Chapel', 346.

tion of the church and the well water in the poem could suggest that the washing, worshiping and lighting of candles all take place at the same location. At any rate, the poem certainly provides us with a rare glimpse of late medieval pilgrimage to the site and stresses the importance of Non's well and chapel in association with the cathedral:

Edudful Dduwsul a ddaw	On Sunday Edudful comes
ar Dduw i wir weddïaw;	to pray sincerely to God;
bwrw ei phwys yn eglwys Non,	She visits Non's church,
bwrw ei phen lle bo'r ffynnon,	puts her head in the well
dyrchaf dwylaw yn llawen,	raises her hands merrily,
addoli oll i'r ddelw wen,	worships the holy image,
ennyn y cwyr melyn mawr,	lights the large, yellow candles,
a'i roi oll ar yr allawr;	and puts all of them on the altar;
oddyno heibio'dd â hi	From there she passes to
I glos da eglwys Dewi;	the good close of St David's church;
offrymu, cusanu'r sant,	makes an offering of crimson wax
iddo gŵyr rhudd ac ariant;[46]	and money and kisses the saint;

In the sixteenth century George Owen of Henllys described the well in his memoirs which were quoted by Browne Willis (1717): 'There is a fine Well beside it [the chapel], cover'd with a Stone-Roof, and inclos'd within a Wall, and Benches to sit upon round the Well.'[47] The well and its surrounding construction appear to have been more substantial than that which exists at the site today. The cowl-shaped hood over the present well may have been constructed in the late eighteenth century and it was restored in 1951. In his *Historical Tour Through Pembrokeshire* (1811) Fenton recalls being dipped in the well as a child:

> ... a most redundant spring arched over, and at one time inclosed with a wall. The fame this consecrated spring had obtained is incredible, and still is resorted to for many complaints. In my infancy, as was the general usage with respect to children at that time, I was often dipped in it, and offerings, however trifling, even of a farthing or a pin, were made after each ablution, and the bottom of the well shone with votive brass.[48]

As with many of the wells associated with St David, it was believed that the water was particularly beneficial for those suffering from eye complaints. Non's holy well at Altarnun, nevertheless, appears to have been associated with quite a different affliction – insanity or possibly epilepsy. In 1601 Carew provided a colourful description of what took place at the well:

> The water running from S. Nunn's well fell into a square and close-walled plot, which might be filled at what depth they listed. Upon this well was the frantic person set to stand, his back turned toward the pool, and from thence, with a sudden blow in the breast, tumbled headlong into the pond; where a strong fellow, provided for the nonce, took him, and tossed him up and down, alongst and athwart the water, until the patient, by foregoing his strength, had somewhat forgot his fury. Then was he conveyed to the church, and certain masses sung over him; upon which handling, if his right wits

---

[46] *Gwaith Lewys Glyn Cothi*, ed. Johnston, 371. On pilgrim routes in Wales see John and Rees, *Pilgrimage*.

[47] Charles, *George Owen of Henllys*, 184–5. Willis, *Survey*, 52–3.

[48] Fenton, *Historical Tour*, 112–13.

returned, S. Nun had the thanks; but if there appeared small amendment, he was bows-sened again and again, while there appeared in him any hope of life, or recovery.[49]

The modern chapel which now stands nearby the well in Pembrokeshire was built in 1934 from stones recycled from old cottages and possibly monastic buildings at Whitehall. Mr Morgan-Griffiths, a solicitor from Carmarthen, had the Chapel of Our Lady and St Non erected near his house for his wife, since she had converted to Catholicism.[50] The chapel contains a number of stained glass windows which depict native Welsh saints and above the altar is a representation of St Non in stained glass of the William Morris School. Clad in a blue gown, she clutches a book and her modern well can be seen in the background. According to the sisters of Mercy who now manage the house as a religious retreat, this window was originally located in the house and later moved to the chapel.[51] In the detail at the base of the window, Non is depicted arriving in Brittany in a boat accompanied by her son, David – here depicted as a young boy. The artist responsible for the windows seems to have been aware of the tradition that Non travelled to Brittany following the birth of St David, and the window, therefore, attempts to link both the Breton and the Welsh traditions.

Brittany

A similar window in Non's church at Dirinon, Finistère, depicts Non and David's arrival in Brittany – again in a boat (see Plate 3). The Breton *Buez*, which provides considerably more detail than the episodes involving Non in the Welsh *Lives*, suggests in its prologue that Non was raped in Ireland and that because of this shameful event she travelled to Brittany.[52] It is not clear whether the artist respon-sible for the windows at Dirinon, intended to depict Non leaving Ireland or Wales. The four scenes depicted in the nineteenth-century windows appear to be based on local oral tradition at Dirinon, rather than on specific events found in the Latin and Welsh *Lives* of David or the Breton *Life* of Non. Non, for example, is depicted baptising her own son in the presence of angels (see Plate 4). This links the church and the legend of St Non with other topographical features at Dirinon: for instance, the holy spring where she prayed for water to baptise the infant which later became known as Non's well. In Rhygyfarch's *Vita S. David* the saint is baptised by Ailbe and a blind man who holds David as he is baptised miraculously gains his sight. Neither the Vespasian nor the Welsh *Life* name this character, but in the Nero E. i version he is called Movi.[53] The Breton *Buez* goes a step further and has David cure two blind men, including one who was born without a nose or eyes.[54]

In the next scene in the stained glass cycle Non is depicted with the infant Divy resting on a rock (see Plate 5). This is presumably the stone known locally as St David's cradle (see Plate 6), for it is claimed that when David's mother placed him on a nearby rock it melted like wax under the baby's body and formed a natural

[49] Doble, *Saint Nonna*, 8.
[50] See Morgan-Guy, 'Shrine and counter-shrine', below, 286–95.
[51] Pers. comm.
[52] *Yues* has been interpreted by the editors of the *Buez* as *yuerdon* (Ireland), *Buez Santez Nonn*, ed. Le Berre *et al.*, 115.
[53] On the Breton ceiling paintings discussed below he is referred to as 'Mobvs'.
[54] *Buez Santez Nonn*, ed. Le Berre *et al.*, 156–9.

Plate 3. Non and David arrive in Brittany, stained glass, Church of St Non, Dirinon, Brittany. (Photo by Jane Cartwright)

Plate 4. Non baptises David, stained glass, Church of St Non, Dirinon.
(Photo by Jane Cartwright)

Plate 5. St David seated, detail of stained glass, Church of St Non,
Dirinon. (Photo by Jane Cartwright)

cradle.[55] Although *Vita S. David* and *Buez Santez Nonn* mention the stone which 'melted' under the pressure of Non's hands, neither refer to a similar miracle providing a cradle for her infant son. Non then hands over David to a group of monks so that he can receive a monastic education and, in the background of the scene, the church and chapel at Dirinon can be clearly seen. In the tracery lights Non is depicted ascending into heaven holding a book, mirroring the image of Non found on a fifteenth-century carved tomb in the sepulchral chapel at Dirinon, just a few feet south of the parish church.

Although the rather confusing prologue to the *Buez* suggests that Non returned to Brittany only after she was raped, all of the events in the play appear to take place in Brittany. The author of the *Buez* demonstrates a lack of awareness of certain locations, particularly those derived from Wales. Kereticus is described as both king of *Keretic* and *Demetri* (Ceredigion and Dyfed), whereas the Latin and Welsh *Lives* mention only that he is king of Ceredigion. Although Non leaves the place where she is raped (*Demetri*), no mention is made in the *Buez* of a lengthy maritime

---

55 Non has also become associated with another stone at Dirinon which, it is claimed, bears the imprints of her knees. See the photograph in Le Berre *et al.*, *Buez*, 4 and compare Abgrall, 'Les pierres', 66–7.

Plate 6. St David's cradle, Dirinon. (Photo by Jane Cartwright)

journey to Brittany. It is claimed that Non descended from good Breton stock: *tut fier a britonery / a noblanc a tj piuizic*[56] ('powerful people from Brittany, nobles of a rich house'), that she lived and died at Dirinon and her bones were interred in a tomb there: *he corff so hep gaou entre landerneau ha daoulas*[57] ('her body is to be found, without doubt, between Landerneau and Daoulas'). Interestingly, the *Buez*, which obviously postdates the elaborate tomb, also states that her body was buried in a brand new tomb at Dirinon where there was both a chapel and a church and where it had been preordained that her body would rest.[58] Thus, the Breton *Life* was composed shortly after the tomb was commissioned and its primary purpose appears to have been to elevate the status of Dirinon and emphasize the importance of the tomb and its sponsors. One post mortem miracle is recorded in which a perjurer suddenly drops dead in a nearby field having sworn a false oath at the tomb of St Non.

When the monument in question was taken apart it was found to contain merely a few bones belonging to an adolescent. R. Perrot visited the tomb and wrote an account of his adventures at Dirinon in *Archaeologia Cambrensis* in 1857. He was under the impression that the original tomb had been destroyed during the French Revolution and that only the recumbent figure of St Non had survived. This was based largely on information he was given locally over a glass of wine:

[56] *Buez Santez Nonn*, ed. Le Berre *et al.*, 132.
[57] *Buez Santez Nonn*, ed. Le Berre *et al.*, 115.
[58] *Buez Santez Nonn*, ed. Le Berre *et al.*, 172–3.

On adjourning to the contiguous cabaret for our usual demi-chopine de vin, and to obtain some information respecting the 'personality' of the statue, our suspicions as to the originality of the sarcophagus were confirmed. The grandmother of the house, and an octogenarian who was sipping his 'modicum', informed us that, during the great Revolution, the tomb was pulled down, the statue only escaping. In more tranquil times the tomb was re-erected, and then, probably, the remains of some other sarcophogus were collected for the purpose.[59]

The tomb has certainly been taken apart and reconstructed in a rather bizarre manner, which has led to one of the apostles being jammed in the middle of the tomb rather than positioned at the end, but the angels which hold Non's pillow (on the carving on top of the tomb) are far too similar to the angels bearing the heraldic shields (on the base of the tomb) to be part of a separate monument. As Yves-Pascal Castel suggests, only the coats of arms appear to have been defaced during the Revolution. It is, nevertheless, possible to make out some of the heraldry and Castel concludes that the tomb was commissioned in the fifteenth century by Simon de Kerbringal and Maufuric de Lézuzan, Abbot of Daoulas, who died in 1468.[60] In 1218 the Acts of the Abbey of Daoulas mention an *ecclesia sanctae Nonnitae* amongst the abbey's possessions and Bernard Tanguy has proposed that the Breton *Life* of Non was probably composed at the Abbey.[61] It has been claimed that the manuscript containing the Breton *Buez Santez Nonn* was discovered inside her tomb; in fact, it was found at the presbytery at Dirinon.

In the parish church at Dirinon there is also a silver reliquary which is reputed to contain some of the relics of St Non. Inside the reliquary, wrapped in silk, are two fragments of bone – probably a tibia – and a note from the bishop of Quimper (1805–23) authenticating the relics. The reliquary box is thought to have been made in Morlaix *ca* 1450 and on top of the reliquary is a small image of St David (see Plate 7).[62] In the Welsh *Lives* of St David Non disappears from the narrative when David begins his formal education, whereas the Breton *Buez* has a lengthy episode in which Non prepares for her death, makes her final confession and prays to the Virgin Mary for forgiveness. No references to Non's relics are extant in Welsh sources, and although the relics at St Davids Cathedral have attracted a great deal of attention, it does not appear to have been claimed that any of Non's relics were kept at the cathedral.[63] Around 1480 William Worcestre noted in his *Itineraries* that Non's body lay at Altarnun in Cornwall, six miles from Launceston where St David was born.[64] In 1281 the Commisary of the Dean and Chapter of Exeter carried out a visitation at Altarnun and recorded that there was a *Life* of St Non in a service book kept there, but unfortunately this is no longer extant.[65] In Brittany there are numerous chapels and churches dedicated to St David (St

---

59 Perrott, 'The tomb of Ste. Nonne', 250.
60 Peyron, *L'abbaye de Daoulas*, 20; Le Berre *et al.*, *Buez*, 12 and 37.
61 Le Berre *et al.*, *Buez*, 11, 14. See also Tanguy, 'The cults of SS. Nonne and Divi', below, 209.
62 When I asked the parish priest of Dirinon if he thought the reliquary contained the bones of St Non or St David, he replied that it contained both. The reliquary is labelled as both 'le reliquaire de sainte Nonne' and 'le reliquaire de saint Divy' in Le Berre *et al.*, *Buez*, 39 and 96. Cozan *et al.*, *La Bretagne au temps des Ducs*, 147–8, includes examples of other reliquaries of a very similar style made at Morlaix.
63 There is, however, an intriguing reference to a book relating the translation of SS. Andrew, David and Non in the *Liber Communis*: Jones and Freeman, *History and Antiquities*, 380.
64 Worcestre, *Itineraries*, ed. Harvey, 62.
65 Exeter Cathedral Library MS 3672A. Curley, 'Five *Lecciones*', 66, n. 29. There is a medieval image believed to represent St Non in stained glass at her church at Altarnun.

Plate 7. The reliquary of St Non, Dirinon. (Photo by Jane Cartwright)

Divy), particularly in Basse-Bretagne, although Non's cult appears to have centred on Dirinon. Near Dirinon one also finds the place-names Lannon and Lesnon, although there are no extant chapels or holy wells in these villages. Bernard Tanguy, who has provided a detailed study of Divy dedications in Brittany, proposes that many of the chapels now dedicated to Divy were originally associated with another Breton saint, St Ivy.[66] One location in Brittany which has firm associations with St David is the church at Saint-Divy, several miles from Dirinon.

Welsh traditions relating to St David have become firmly rooted at Saint-Divy thanks to a seventeenth-century visual narrative (dated 1676) painted on wooden panelling on the vaulted ceiling.[67] The visual narrative depicts several scenes from the *Life* of St David and appears to be based on a version of Rhygyfarch's *Life* of St David rather than the Breton *Life* of Non. In 1668, shortly before the paintings were conceived, two *epitomae* of Rhygyfarch's *Life* of St David were made widely available by the Bollandists,[68] and it is certainly plausible that these early printed versions of the *Life* may have been the source of inspiration for the artist. At any rate, the images and the fragments of texts and labelling interspersed in the images give the impression of drawing on a written source rather than local oral tradition, unlike the nineteenth-century stained glass cycle at Dirinon. Included in the painting are a number of Welsh place-names, such as *Portvs Mavgan* (Porth Maugan/Mawr) and *Brevy* (Llanddewibrefi), which are not mentioned in the Breton miracle play. David, for example, is depicted at the synod of Brefi with the earth miraculously rising beneath his feet. In the Breton *Buez* he is made archbishop at Lyons and there

---

[66] Le Berre *et al.*, *Buez*, 21–31; Tanguy, 'The cults of SS. Nonne and Divi', below, 213–19.

[67] The paintings were restored in 1961 and again 1998. See the images in Le Berre *et al.*, *Buez*, 49–70.

[68] The two *epitomae* (BHL 2108 and parts of BHL 2109) were published in Bollandus *et al.* (edd.), *Acta Sanctorum*, March vol. 1.

is no mention of the miracle which allowed the adoring crowd to hear his every word. Non is raped by Xanctvs/Sant (as in *Vita S. Dauid*), rather than Kereticus/Ceredig (as in *Buez Santez Nonn*). In Welsh tradition Ceredig, the eponymous ruler of Ceredigion, is St David's grandfather, but the Breton *Buez* omits a generation, referring to his father as Kereticus.

The paintings at Saint-Divy illustrate various scenes from the *Vita* including (i) St Patrick's angelic visitation when he is instructed that he must leave Vallis Rosina and go to Ireland, since God has assigned the valley to the unborn David. En route he resurrects Crvnither (usually known as Crumither); (ii) Sant's dream in which the king is warned of the coming of St David and told that he must go hunting near the river Teifi and collect three gifts for David. Depicted in the background of the scene is the Monastery of the Deposit mentioned in the *Vita*, not the nunnery visited by St Non in the *Buez*;[69] (iii) Sant's encounter with St Non in a rural landscape (see Plate 8). He is depicted in regal hunting garb on horseback, whereas Non is clad in a nun's habit with a rosary tied around her waist and a glowing aureola. The two rocks which rose to hide Non's shame as she was raped are suggestive of the event which is about to take place; (iv) the birth of St David (see Plate 9). Non kneels in an attitude of prayer with the newborn baby at her knees and the inscription records the miracle which caused the rock to split in two. (v) David's baptism by Belve (usually Ailbe), (vi) the synod of Brefi mentioned above and (vii) David's death at the ripe old age of 107 (usually 147). The sixth-century characters in the paintings are dressed in seventeenth-century costume, most notably in the hunting scene where Sant and his men seek the three gifts in preparation for the coming of St David.

Whilst it is generally assumed that the cults of St Non and her son David were transferred from Wales to Brittany at an unknown date during the middle ages, it is extremely difficult (if not impossible) to provide an accurate chronology for these cults in their entirety. Which came first: saints, place-names or cults? Did the proximity of the place-names Saint-Divy and Dirinon give rise to their association with these related saints, or did well-rooted traditions associated with David and Non influence the choice of place-names?[70] The frequency of recurrent adjacency in the Brittonic world has been highlighted by Olson and Padel who point out that two saints with adjacent dedications in one country often recur near each other in other Celtic-speaking regions: the cult of one reinforcing and strengthening the other.[71] Frequent contacts between Wales and Brittany throughout the middle ages, as well as common cultural inheritance – often including hagiographical sources – meant that the legendary material associated with Non and David was easily transferred between the two regions.[72] Whilst Rhygyfarch's *Vita S. David* seems to have been the predominant source, regional variations have given rise to different versions of the legend which appear to have happily co-existed: as we have seen, these are attested in oral tradition and visual depictions, as well as written sources such as the Breton *Buez*. Non's predominance in the title of the *Buez Santes Nonn hac ez map Deuy*, along with the central role she plays in the first three quarters of the play, has given rise to the impression that Non was possibly more popular than David in

69 Cf. Le Berre *et al.*, *Buez*, 54.
70 Cf. Davidstow and Altarnun in Cornwall.
71 Olson and Padel, 'A tenth-century list', 67.
72 See the discussion on the Welsh and Breton traditions associated with SS. Cadfan and Tysilio in Jones and Owen, 'Twelfth-century Welsh hagiography', 47–8, 66–8.

Plate 8. Non meets Sant, ceiling painting, Church of St Divy, Saint-Divy, Brittany.
(Photo by Jane Cartwright)

Brittany and that the cult of the mother figure appears to have overshadowed that of her son. Nevertheless, there are in fact more dedications to David than Non in Brittany and there is some uncertainty regarding the appropriation of relics at Dirinon, since the reliquary features a statuette of David.

Rape, sanctity and motherhood

Only in the Breton *Buez* is the rape of Non fully dramatized and Non's reaction to the rape voiced. There is a lengthy scene building up to the event in which Non calls at a nunnery and asks the abbess if she can join the convent and take a vow of virginity. She enters the chapter house and is accepted by the other sisters who all consider her to be a wise, pure virgin. On her way to mass, hurrying through an area of lonely woodland she meets Kereticus and is raped against her will.[73] In the Welsh *Lives* there is no moral condemnation of the incident, since David's birth has been foretold thirty years in advance and Sant is merely enacting part of the divine plan:

> When the foresaid thirty years had passed, divine providence sent Sanctus, king of the territory of Ceredig, as far as the kingdom of the people of Dyfed. And the king

---

[73] *Buez Santez Nonn*, ed. Le Berre *et al.*, 123–36.

Plate 9. Non gives birth to St David, ceiling painting, Church of St Divy, Saint-Divy, Brittany. (Photo by Jane Cartwright)

came across a nun named Nonnita, who was a virgin, an exceedingly beautiful girl, and modest. Lusting after her, he raped her, and she conceived his son, the holy David. Neither before nor after did she know a man, but continuing steadfastly in chastity of mind and body, she led her life most devoutly; for, from the very time she conceived, she lived only on bread and water.[74]

The Breton play, on the other hand, describes Non as being mortified by the attack:

Ach Autrou Doe so guir roe bet // me so oppre(ss)et an pret man digracc voar an placc discascun // ha me hoaz voar un ma hunan. Ne gorreif ma drem a breman // gant mez ha souzan voar an bet guerch voann ha glan ha leanes // me cret bout certes brasset. E nebeut spacc dre digracdet // ezof forzet violet tenn gant vn tirant hep consantj // ne gallenn muy ma mem difenn. Me ia sider da offerenn // hac ahannenn a mem tenno.[75]

(Oh Lord God, who is the true king of the world, I have just been abused. Hatefully in a moment, disgracefully, when I was alone and still fasting. I am now overwhelmed with shame and sadness. I was a virgin – pure and religious: I am almost certain that I'm pregnant. In an instant I have been forced and violated with brutality by a tyrant, against my will, without being able to defend myself. I will go to mass and then leave this place.)

---

74 *Vita S. David*, § 4 (ed. Sharpe and Davies, above, 112–13).
75 *Buez Santez Nonn*, ed. Le Berre *et al.*, 136

Ceredig's followers chastise the king for his loathsome conduct. He immediately repents and dashes off to confession.

For the virgin bride of Christ rape is a fate worse than death, and in medieval hagiography the female saint, obsessed by the preservation of her virginity, usually welcomes martyrdom. For only in death is the virgin saint released from her worldly prison of sensuality ascending to the spiritual world where she will join her heavenly bridegroom. Virginity is a virtue extolled by the Church Fathers as the most admirable physical state: the only physical state that bears resemblance to the *vita angelica*, the asexual angelic life enjoyed before the Fall. A number of early treatises on virginity persuade religious men and women to avoid marriage and opt for virginal maintenance. Jerome suggests that only when one's chastity is jeopardized should you contemplate suicide: thus, putting forward the idea that the consecrated virgin should welcome death rather than allow her virginity to be violated. Augustine, on the other hand, states that:

> the consecrated body is the instrument of the consecrated will; and if that will continues unshaken and steadfast, whatever anyone else does with the body or to the body, provided that it cannot be avoided without committing sin, involves no blame to the sufferer.[76]

In the Breton *Buez* Non tells Ceredig that she would prefer to suffer a cruel death than allow her virginity to be violated: *guell ve dif meruell hep dellit / eguet dren sceurt lit acuitaff*[77] ('I would prefer to die cruelly than to submit myself to such an embrace'). It is also worth recalling that both the *Vita S. Dauid* and *Hystoria o Uuched Dewi* emphasize that Non is chaste of mind and body – *diwair oedd hi o feddwl a gweithred*. More significantly, the five readings designed to celebrate the feast of St Non also add, in words which echo St Augustine's, that the body is not stained without the consent of the mind, and if a woman who is in love with Christ is violated against her will, her chastity is still 'woven into a crown'.[78] Virginity then, as depicted by the both the Early Church and medieval hagiography, is a mental as well as a physical attribute. Non is described as *dinam* – blameless or faultless – in a medieval Welsh *cywydd* of uncertain authorship and Dafydd Llwyd of Mathafarn refers to her as *diwair – feichiog* (chastely – pregnant).[79] Thus, Non is a kind of honorary virgin for, as Jocelyn Wogan-Browne points out, in the medieval period virginity was both gradable and negotiable.[80] Non's devotion to the ascetic life is confirmed not only by her decision never to have intercourse with any man, but also by her appropriate choice of food: 'for from the very time of her conceiving she lived on bread and water alone'. Interestingly, the Irish Penitentials also suggest that virginity may be restored through penance. According to the Penitential of Finnian, a nun who becomes pregnant should undertake penance for seven years living on bread and water alone. After this time her crown may be restored and she may don a white robe and be pronounced a virgin.[81]

Rather than taint St David's character in any way his unusual conception highlights his greatness and makes him an object of wonder. His importance, even whilst

[76] Augustine, *City of God*, ed. and transl. Knowles and Bettenson, 26.
[77] *Buez Santez Nonn*, ed. Le Berre *et al.*, 134.
[78] BL, MS Royal 13 C.i, fol. 180v.
[79] *Gwaith Dafydd Llwyd*, ed. Richards, 47.
[80] Wogan-Browne, 'The virgin's tale', 165–94.
[81] *Penitentialis Vinniani* § 21 (ed. Bieler, *The Irish Penitentials*, 81).

still in the womb, is made evident when Gildas is struck dumb in the presence of the pregnant Non. Although the episode is also recounted in the twelfth-century *Life* of Gildas, thought to have been composed by Caradog of Llancarfan, it is not mentioned in the earlier Breton *Life* of Gildas.[82] This seems to suggest either that the traditions about St Non were not known in Brittany by the ninth century, or that the anonymous Breton hagiographer was reluctant to include an episode which made St David appear to be more powerful than Gildas. Non's encounter with the preacher is referred to by a number of medieval Welsh poets including Dafydd Llwyd of Mathafarn:

> Non a ddôi i'r deml yn ddiwair – feichiog
> > O Dywysog dewisair,
> A'r Prelad aeth o'r gadair
> Heb allu pregethu gair.[83]

> (Non was coming to the temple chastely – pregnant/ with a splendid Prince, and the Prelate went from the chair without being able to preach a word.)

Dafydd Llwyd's reference to Non as being *diwair* ('chaste') and *beichiog* ('pregnant') is echoed in the work of Iorwerth Fynglwyd who describes the Virgin Mary as *beichiog heb ddim afiechyd*[84] (pregnant without taint – literally without disease). Unable to claim a virgin birth for David, Rhygyfarch resorts to the next best thing – his mother is a professed nun and remains a virgin up until the time of his conception. David's genealogy, found at the end of the Vespasian version and the beginning of the Welsh *Life*, links David to the Virgin Mary and claims that he is related to Eugen or Euddolau the son of the Virgin Mary's sister.[85] Other Welsh genealogies link the saints to Mary and it is frequently claimed that the saints' parents only have intercourse on one occasion. One senses, perhaps, a certain unease on the part of the hagiographer when dealing with the sexual conception of the saints. Since it was inappropriate – even blasphemous – to suggest sexless generation, the medieval hagiographer usually opted for the symbolic, miraculous or unusual conception. *Hystoria o Uuched Beuno* recounts how the saint's parents, who have been sleeping in the same bed for twelve years, do not have intercourse until ordered to do so by an angel: *Ac val y gorchynnawd yr angel vdunt, wynt ae gwnaethant. A beichiogi a gauas Beren y nos honno.*[86] ('They did it just as the angel had instructed them and Beren became pregnant that night'). *Buchedd Collen* describes St Collen's conception in symbolic terms, thus avoiding any mention of intercourse. In a dream Ethinen sees a dove carry her womb to heaven, return with it in her beak and place it back in her body. The next day she discovers that she is pregnant.[87]

In this context we can more easily understand why Non is raped: in order for her to conceive without experiencing sexual pleasure. Nor is Non unique – for she is not the only example of a raped female saint. According to a fragmentary, twelfth-century *Life* of St Kentigern, Thaney, Kentigern's mother, wished to imitate the Virgin Mary and give birth to a son whilst still a virgin. Her wish, however, was not granted since she was brutally raped against her will by Ewen son of Erwegende

---

82 Transl. Williams, *Two Lives of Gildas*, 88–91.
83 *Gwaith Dafydd Llwyd*, ed. Richards, 46; Henken, *Traditions*, 36.
84 *Gwaith Iorwerth Fynglwyd*, ed. Jones and Rowlands, 96.
85 *Vita S. David*, ed. Sharpe and Davies, above, 152–5. *Welsh Life*, ed. Evans, 1.
86 *VSBG*, ed. Wade-Evans, 16.
87 *Rhyddiaith Gymraeg*, ed. Parry-Williams, 37.

(Owain ab Urien). Beardless and dressed in female attire Ewen manages to convince her that she is still a virgin, even though she becomes pregnant. When her father discovered that she was pregnant he had her thrown off a cliff in a cart, and, since she survived the fall, he had her cast adrift in a boat. Again Thaney miraculously survived and gave birth to Kentigern, founder and patron of Glasgow cathedral. This anonymous *Life* is incomplete and breaks off after Kentigern's birth.[88] There is, however, another complete *Life* of Kentigern which was written by Jocelin of Furness towards the end of the twelfth century.[89] Interestingly, in this *Life* the rape of Thaney is omitted. Jocelin instead has a rather ambiguous account which avoids naming the father and suggests that Thaney may have had some sort of encounter with a soothsayer. In his prologue he criticises his source which he feels is contrary to the Catholic faith. Alan Macquarrie interprets this as a refererence to another *Life* (now lost) which must have claimed a virgin birth for Kentigern.[90] My own reading, however, leads me to believe that Jocelin is referring to the fragmentary *Life* and what he considers to be – in his words – 'tainted' and 'perverse' is the rape of Thaney. In the prologue he states: 'I deem it absurd that so precious a treasure should be swathed in vile wrappings, and therefore I have endeavoured to clothe it if not in gold tissue and silk, at least in clean linen.' Kentigern, he claims, was sanctified in the womb, 'so that he might prove that the special gift of the holy spirit is not constrained by the chain of original sin.'[91]

Neither Thaney nor Non, however, are free from original sin, and, unlike the Virgin Mary, both bring forth their progeny in pain. As we have seen, Non in her agony grasps a nearby rock and presses it so hard that the imprints of her hands are left on the rock as if it she had sunk her hands into wax. The Breton *Buez* places particular emphasis on Non's anguish during her labour: *quen sempl ezaff na gallaf quen // gant guentl hac anquen em bener ma na vezaf mam e berr amser // ez rentif sider ma speret*[92] ('I feel so ill; I can no longer be tortured by these labour pains. If I do not become a mother soon, I will surely give up the ghost.') She prays to the Virgin Mary for assistance and laments the fact that no wise or married woman is present to assist with the birth. This reminds the viewer of the birth of Christ who, according to the apocryphal gospels of Mary, was born without the presence of a midwife, since the two women, Selome and Zelomy, arrived after the birth had taken place. The fundamental difference here is that whilst Non is afflicted with pain, Mary uniquely shows no signs of pain or afterbirth.[93]

Thus, it seems that the virginity of the female saint is rendered violable when the maternity of an important male saint is at stake. Numerous scholars have stressed the importance of saintly genealogies in the Celtic regions, and Pádraig Ó Riain has proposed that the importance of familial relationships which often creates a network of saints is 'by and large an exclusively Celtic phenomenon'.[94] St David, through his paternal line, is linked with Cunedda Wledig whose family, according to the Welsh triads, is one of the three saintly lineages of the island of Britain. His grandmother, Meleri, was one of the twenty-four daughters of Brychan Brycheiniog – all of whom

[88] *Lives of S. Ninian and S. Kentigern*, ed. Forbes, 123–33.
[89] *Lives of S. Ninian and S. Kentigern*, ed. Forbes, 33–119; [Forbes], *Two Celtic Saints*, 29–119.
[90] Macquarrie, *Saints of Scotland*, 119.
[91] [Forbes], *Two Celtic Saints*, 30–1.
[92] *Buez Santez Nonn*, ed. Le Berre *et al.*, 155.
[93] On the Middle Welsh version see Williams, 'Buched Meir Wyry', 207–38.
[94] Ó Riain, 'Irish saints' genealogies', 23.

were Welsh saints and many of whom were mothers of male saints.[95] Thus, the two most prominent holy families of Wales were united and St David was born into a vast network of saints.

Whilst not wishing to state categorically that this is a specifically Celtic phenomenon,[96] I would like to stress that there are a significant number of mother saints in Welsh hagiography and that within a European context, this is somewhat unusual. There are indeed saintly mothers such as Monica (the mother of St Augustine) and Ida of Boulogne (the mother of the leaders of the First Crusade) who, like St Non, are accorded sanctity because of their relationship with their holy sons. However, as Anneke Mulder-Bakker points out:

> The usual corpus of 'sacred biographies' contains almost no mother saints, that is, saints whose sanctity is based on motherhood … There were, of course, saints who were mothers, but they were honored at the altar despite rather than because of their children.[97]

The vast majority of female saints venerated in medieval hagiography are virgins. Even the patron saint of childbirth – St Margaret of Antioch – was a virgin who had never experienced childbirth.[98] Although most female saints are threatened with rape, it is usually prevented by divine intervention. In the *Life* of St Lucy of Syracuse, for example, Lucy's pagan tormentor announces that she is to be sent to a brothel where she will be repeatedly raped until she dies. However, Lucy miraculously roots to the spot and a thousand strong men with ropes fail to remove her to the brothel.[99] Whereas in the majority of the *vitae* the inviolate virgin functions as a metonym for the institution of the Church,[100] and her inviolate body can therefore under no circumstance be polluted, this is not the case with St Non. Her legend is not meant to be read allegorically and her body does not stand for the Church. She merely imitates the holy family, and is accorded sanctity purely on the basis of her association with her holy progeny, in much the same way that St Anne is accorded sanctity because of her importance within the holy kinship. In Wales Non is a second Anne, and in Brittany also Non appears to have become associated with St Anne.[101] At Dirnon and Saint-Divy images of Anne teaching the virgin to read accompany images of Non and St David. In Wales, although St Non is not accredited with David's education she has become associated with his youth and formative years in Ceredigion and in this capacity performs a pedagogical function.

Perhaps because of her role as a maternal saint Non made a more relevant role model for medieval Welsh women than some of the virgin martyrs. In the poetry of the *Cywyddwyr* married noblewomen are more frequently compared to Non than to any other single female saint (with the obvious exception of the Virgin Mary). Lewys Glyn Cothi alone invokes Non forty-four times in his poetry. In one particular poem, an elegy to Gwenllian ferch Rhys, he refers to Gwenllian's ascent *i'r nef*

---

95   *Trioedd Ynys Prydein*, ed. Bromwich, 201; *Early Welsh Genealogical Tracts*, ed. Bartrum, 16, 20.

96   This would require a thorough, international survey which is beyond the scope of this paper.

97   Mulder-Bakker, *Sanctity and Motherhood*, 4.

98   Her *Life* was translated into Middle Welsh sometime before the middle of the fourteenth century. See Richards, 'Buchedd Fargred', 65–71.

99   de Voragine, *Golden Legend*, transl. Ryan, vol. 1, 27–9.

100   See the discussion on the *topos* of the menaced virgin in Kelly, *Performing Virginity*, 42–62.

101   In Brittany the cult of St Anne is particularly strong: indeed it is even claimed that Anne was a Breton.

ac i gôr Non ac i radd y gweryddon[102] ('to heaven and to Non's choir and to the rank of virgins'). Gwenllian, like Non, was not a virgin, since she was married to Dafydd ap Tomas and had a son called Rhys. It is possible, but by no means certain, that she retired to a nunnery following the death of her husband, and (like Non) she appears to have been accorded the status of honorary virgin by the poet.[103] Thus, Non's maternity appears not only to form the origin of her sanctity, but also to be the root of her relevance and appeal. It remains possible, yet ultimately inconclusive, that the rape element in Non's story is due to a Celtic bias towards the sanctity of familial ties and the legitimising cult of lineage.

---

[102] *Gwaith Lewys Glyn Cothi*, ed. Johnston, 108.
[103] See the discussion on Welsh poetry to pious wives in Cartwright, *Y Forwyn Fair*, 158–68.

10

THE CULTS OF SS. NONNE AND DIVI IN BRITTANY[1]

Bernard Tanguy

In Brittany there are relatively few saints who are only honoured in a single location. St Nonne is one of these, inasmuch as her cult is only attested at Dirinon, in a parish which also honours her son Divi. St Nonne is the patron saint of a chapel and a fountain located just over a kilometre to the south of the market town. Although the cult of Divi was introduced in a number of other locations, there was not a similar veneration for his mother in Brittany.[2]

It has been suggested that the saint should be seen as the eponym of the parish of Lennon; it cannot be established, however, whether the second element of the place-name is *-non* or *-on*. The church of Lennon is, at least since the sixteenth century, dedicated to the Holy Trinity. If in the case of the village of Lannon in Bannalec the possibility of an eponym in *Nonn*, associated with the Old Breton *lan* ('hermitage, monastery') is excluded by the fact of the form *Langoezen* in 1491,[3] it is, by contrast, indicated for the village of Lannon, in Kersaint-Plabennec, by the existence of the village of Lesnon, just over a kilometre to the south-west; the latter toponym is formed with the Old Breton *les*, 'court, castle'.

The cult of St Nonne (Non) is better attested across the Channel. In Wales, where she is the eponym of three place-names in Llan-non, she had five chapels altogether.[4] The principal site of her cult, however, is Altarnun ('altar of St Non'), in Cornwall. A tradition entered in the calendar of the abbey of St Michael's Mount in Cornwall, and recorded by William of Worcester in 1478, claimed that she was buried at Altarnun and that her son was born there.[5] The neighbouring parish is named Davidstow (OE: 'place of St David').

Although the saint figures on 3 March in a Welsh calendar from the twelfth century,[6] the church of Altarnun, like the abbey of Tavistock in Devon, honoured her on 15 June; the priory of Launceston, in Cornwall, included her on 3 July.[7] At Dirinon, the great pardon is celebrated on the Sunday after the Octave of Corpus Christi, and the lesser pardon on the second Sunday after Easter.

---

[1] Originally published as 'Les cultes de sainte Nonne et de saint Divi en Bretagne', in Yves Le Berre, Bernard Tanguy, and Yves-Pascal Castel (edd.), *Buez santez Nonn. Vie de sainte Nonne. Mystère breton* (np, 1999), 10–31; translated by Karen Jankulak.

[2] Cassard points out the presence, in Bordeaux in 1307–1308, of a ship named *Saincte Nonne*, having as its home port Le Conquet ('Les marins', 378). A document of 1495 refers to *Sainct Nonne* of Groix.

[3] Deshayes, *Dictionnaire*, 315.

[4] Llan-non, parish of Carmarthenshire, the village of Llansanffraid in Cardiganshire, and the farm of Llanrhian in Pembrokeshire. In the parishes of Cregrina (Radnorshire), Ilston (Glamorgan), Llansanffraid and Penbre (Carmarthenshire), and St Davids (Pembrokeshire).

[5] Orme, *Nicholas Roscarrock's Lives*, 162.

[6] Duine, *Saints*, 44.

[7] Orme, *Nicholas Roscarrock's Lives*, 162.

The cult of St Nonne at Dirinon

To what can we attribute the presence of the cult of St Nonne and that of her son at Dirinon? If we assume that one is the result of the other, this raises the question of anteriority. The cult of the mother is clearly the earlier. The Breton mystery play which was discovered in the nineteenth century in the presbytery of Dirinon, despite being a plagiarism of several passages of the Cambro-Latin *Life* of St David, is entitled not *Buez sant Divi*, but indeed *Buez santez Nonn*. We can assume that it was the very name of Dirinon which attracted this patronage. The presence of the saint may have been discerned from the toponym, perhaps as a counter to the pagan associations of its first element, *diri* ('oaks').

When did this happen? Nonne's name does not appear, it would seem, in any of the oldest Breton litanies. Those of the abbey of Saint-Martial of Limoges, known from a manuscript of the eleventh century – and which Duine believed were 'empruntées à quelque psautier péninsulaire du Xe siècle' – mention a saint called *Nonnice*; but, rather than seeing in this *Nonnita*, the name of the saint in the Welsh *Life* and in the Breton mystery play, it seems more likely that we have instead a 'distraction pour *Ninnoca*' – a saint who appears, for her part, in other ancient litanies.[8] In the absence of any evidence which might precisely date the cult at Dirinon, a deed of the abbey of Daoulas of 1218 gives at least an indication: the document mentions, in fact, amongst the possessions of the abbey *ecclesia Sanctae Nonnitae*, 'church of St Nonnite'.[9] *Nonnita* is the name given to the saint in the *Vita sancti Dauid siue Dewi epsicopi et confessoris*, written by the Welsh monk Rhygyfarch at the end of the eleventh century.[10] This is to the exclusion of the form *Nonn* found in other texts, such as the *Life* of the saint in Welsh compiled in the fourteenth century,[11] or the Welsh genealogy *Bonedd y saint* ('descent of the saints'), which indicates that 'Dewi was the son of Sant, son of Keretic, son of Cuneda wletic, and Nonn, daughter of Kenyr of Caer Gawch, in Mynyw, was his mother'.[12] Although it is entitled *Buez santez Nonn*, the Breton mystery play solely, and consistently, uses the form *Nonita*.[13]

A tradition, recorded by Nicholas Roscarrock in the first half of the seventeenth century, knows the saint by an additional name: *Melaria*:

> Sct Nonna or Nonita was in truth named Melaria and the sister of Gwen (the mother of Sct Cubie or Kebie and of Sct Cyfgine), both being daughters of Gyner of Caer <gowch> in Menes which some think was Meneva, after called Sct Davides, and hath bene surnamed Nunnita for that she was … a Christian Nunne who hauinge violence offred her by Zantus, a prince of Cardiganshire and the sonne of Sct Melary or Elery

---

8 Duine, 'Inventaire', 60.

9 Peyron, *L'abbaye*, 20.

10 Wade-Evans, 'Rhygyfarch's Life'. D. Simon Evans (*The Welsh Life*, xxxiii) dates the redaction between 1081 and 1085; J.W. James (*Rhigyfarch's Life*, xi) dates it *ca* 1095. See Davies, 'Some observations', below, 159–60.

11 Evans, *The Welsh Life*, liv.

12 Bartrum, *Early Welsh Genealogical Tracts*, 54: *Dewi m. Sant, M. Keredic, m. Cuneda wletic, o Nonn verch Kenyr o Caer Gawch y Mynyw y mam*. The form *Nonna* is also used by the *Vita* found in a Utrecht manuscript published in the *Acta Sanctorum* on the date of 1 March.

13 Although it announces that 'here begins the life of St Nonn and of her son Deuy' (*Aman ez desraou buez santez Nonn hac ez map Deuy*, vv. 1–2), the introduction states that 'we shall tell the legend of Nonita' (*ez fez dezo legent Nonita*, v. 6): ed. and transl. Le Berre, 115.

by Carticus the sonne of Cunedagus, was by him rauished, deflowred and gotten with child …[14]

The name Meleri appears in the earliest Welsh genealogies as that of the grandmother of the saint. *Cognatio Brychan* says, in fact, that 'Meleri, daughter of Brachan, was the wife of Keredic and the mother of Sant, the father of St David'.[15] The confusion was no doubt due to an erroneous interpretation of the same sort of formulation found in the Life of St Keyne: *Melari mater Sancti patris David*,[16] which could be interpreted as 'Melari, mother of the holy father David'.

From the Cambro-Latin Life *of St David to the* Buez Santez Nonn

The use of the form *sancta Nonnita* in 1218 in the abovementioned deed of the abbey of Daoulas, a letter from the bishop of Quimper, suggests that a version of the *Vita* by Rhygyfarch was known by the Augustinian canons. The use in the same deed of *ecclesia Sancti Monnae* to designate the church of Logonna-Daoulas, whose eponym is most certainly Onna, shows that in this case as well the canons had in mind insular sources, doubtless to augment the otherwise insignificant reputation of a Breton saint. *Munna*, for **Mo-unna*, is, in fact, another, hypocoristic, name of the Irish saint Fintan, founder of the Irish monastery of *Tech Munna* (Taghmon), who died in 635, and whose name figures in the litanies of Saint-Vougay, which are three series of Breton litanies of the tenth and eleventh centuries.[17] By contrast, at Logonna-Quimerch the eponym of the place continued to be honoured; he is today known as St Nonna, the result of an erroneous division of the Breton *San(d)onna*. Here he is celebrated the second Sunday of July, whereas at Logonna-Daoulas St Monna was honoured on 21 October.[18] The Augustinian canons chose, likewise, an insular saint as the patron of the priories of Bénodet, Camaret and Landerneau: this was the Anglo-Norman St Thomas Becket, the archbishop of Canterbury assassinated in 1170 and canonised since 1173. This cult is attested at Landerneau in 1218 and at Bénodet in 1233. It seems likely that between 1173, the date of the foundation of the abbey of Daoulas, and 1218, the monks of Daoulas made their mark on the patronages of their possessions. Can we go further and argue that the *Buez santez Nonn* was composed by a monk of the abbey? The hypothesis seems to have much merit.

The Breton text is in part a copy of the version of the *Life* written by Rhygyfarch; only a cleric would be in a position to accomplish such a procedure. The fact that the stage directions are given in Latin suggests that the rendering into Breton was, moreover, done from a Latin original. Before the death of the saint occurs, an extract in Latin from his *Legenda* was inserted, which explained that he died in the *civitas* of Menevia, in the abbey founded by St Patrick, and that he was buried on the order of *Malgon,* king of the Venedotes. The author claims to have borrowed these details, and the majority of the others concerning this saint from a book *de gestis regum*

---

14 Orme, *Nicholas Roscarrock's Lives*, 97.
15 Bartrum, *Early Welsh Genealogical Tracts*, 15: *Meleri filia Brachan, uxor Keredic et mater Sant, Sant pater S. David.*
16 *Acta sanctorum*, October, vol. IV, 276–7.
17 Loth, 'Les anciennes litanies', 137.
18 There is a village of Kerona in the territory of Saint-Ségal, to the east of Logonna.

britanorum, the very popular history written by Geoffrey of Monmouth in 1135.[19] This does not prevent the author from affirming subsequently that the saint died 'in Lower Brittany',[20] as did his mother, whose body, he says, rests at Dirinon, 'in the territory of Rivelen'.[21] This confusion is all of a piece with his treatment of insular names of people and places in the *Vita*.

The Breton text reproduces, at times slavishly, the Latin forms of names. Apart from the use of *Nonita*, the author also borrowed from Rhygyfarch's Life the unusual form *Davidagius*, which he seems not to have understood: it is clearly composed of *David agius*, the equivalent of Welsh *Dewi sant*, 'St David', but on several occasions he places the term *sanctus* before it, in a clearly tautological formation.[22] In similar fashion, the name of *Runuiter/Rumiter* is the result of an error in reading *Criumther* in Rhygyfarch's *Vita*: the initial C had disappeared, and the six minims following *r* were incorrectly interpreted by our author. In addition, the name of the island on which Paulinus lived was only partly made out, giving rise to a transcription that was imaginative in the extreme: behind *enesen languen vvmendi e jmmy* lurks, in fact, *insula wincdilantquendi*.[23] This form is found in two manuscripts held in Oxford, in the Bodleian Library,[24] but it is impossible to establish that one or the other might be the source of our text, or at least of its Latin version.

Although remaining faithful in the borrowed passages to the framework of the Cambro-Latin *Life*, our author nevertheless on a number of occasions took liberties with the text. He departs from it with respect to the number of years having passed since the death of *Runuiter*, fifteen rather than the twelve of the *Vita*, and locates in Ireland the 'island of *Rosina*', which the *Vita* gives as a valley in Dyfed. He substitutes for *Sanctus*, the father of David, the king *Kereticus/Keretic*, and describes him as reigning not only over the province of *Keretic*, but also, in contradiction of the *Vita*, over *Demetri*, that is, Dyfed. In similar fashion he introduces as an active character the king *Trisin* – confusing the letters *s* and *f* – while the *Vita* merely notes that St Gildas[25] was accustomed to preach in the time of the king *Triphunus* and his sons. Although he keeps the episode of the revival of the dead livestock, he makes their owners into a couple of worthy peasants, while in the *Vita* the matter concerns an Irish chieftain, described as *magus*, that is to say, 'druid', and his wife, who form a diabolical couple.

Contrary to what one might have expected, the captions of the paintings of the church of Saint-Divy, painted in 1676, do not take their inspiration from the *Buez santez Nonn*, but rather take their substance from a version of the *Vita* of Rhygyfarch, reproducing its phrasing at times word for word. They include names which

---

19 *Buez santez Nonn* (ed. and transl. Le Berre, p. 191). Although the citation is accurate, aside from the replacement of *confratres* with *2 fratres*, he could not have borrowed from Geoffrey the 'other' details, as they are not found in Geoffrey's work.

20 *Buez santez Nonn*, 2051 (ed. and transl. Le Berre, 193).

21 *Buez santez Nonn*, 1506, 1512 (ed. and transl. Le Berre, 172).

22 Cf. *Buez santez Nonn* (ed. and transl. Le Berre, 182, 189).

23 Charles Thomas (*And Shall these Mute Stones*, 100–101) suggests that *wincdi* is 'a descriptive noun-phrase rather than a true place-name', with *Lantquendi* presenting an archaic form of the word *lann*, 'enclosure with a monastic establishment, monastery' or 'enclosed cemetery', followed by the name of a person of Irish origin. I would like to thank Heather James for bringing this reference to my attention.

24 These are Oxford, Bodleian Digby 112, of the twelfth century, and Bodley 793 of the twelfth century (cf. Wade-Evans, 'Rhygyfarch's Life', 39–40, n. 5; and James, *Rhigyfarch's Life*, xix, 7).

25 Curiously, the author does not use the Breton form *Gweltaz*.

are not found in the *Buez*, such as *Teraeus, Port Maugan, Belve, Mobus, Brevy*.[26] The father of the saint is not *Kereticus* but rather *Xantus*. Where did the author of these captions encounter the Latin *Vita* of the saint? It is unfortunately impossible to say.

Forty years earlier, Albert Le Grand, at the end of the alphabetical table of his *Vies des saints*, cited among those saints for whom he claimed not to have 'encore trouvé les vies': 'saincte Noun. Patronne de la paroisse de Dire-Noun, Diocese de Cornoüaille'.[27] However, among the sources which he claimed to have consulted in composing his *Life* of St Gildas, we find 'le manuscrit de la vie de Sainte Nonnite, gardé en l'Eglise Parrochiale de Dirinon au Diocèse de Cornoüaille'.[28] The fact that he borrowed nothing from it, given the importance that the *Buez* gives to the relations between Nonnite and Gildas, is perplexing. Do the fortunes of the manuscript of the *Buez* explain not only the lacuna of the Dominican Le Grand, but also the content of the text of the paintings upon wood?

If we rely on an annotation found on folio 65r of the manuscript, it belonged in 1673 to Master Olivier Cloarec, who lived 'au lieu de la villeneuffve treflaouesnan' in the parish of Dirinon. This information is written over another annotation specifying that the manuscript belonged to 'Mr. Vergoz pretre'. According to Annie Le Men, notwithstanding that 'de 1647 à 1671, un Jean Vergoz était prêtre à Dirinon', 'la famille Vergoz était alliée à celle des Cloarec depuis 1642'.[29] It was therefore by this avenue that the *Buez* must have become the property of the Cloarec family. At the death of Olivier Cloarec, it passed into the hands of Jean Cloarec, as attested by an annotation on folio 66r of the manuscript: 'Ce present livre app(partient) a moy Jean Cloarec d(u village) de K/en cloarec en la paroisse de dirinon le 15è aoust mil six cent nonante sept 1697'.

St Nonne, avatar of St Nonna?

In a study of 1928 devoted to St Nonna, Canon Doble, after having concerned himself with the patronage of St Nonna at Penmarch, expressed serious doubts about the existence of St Nonne:

> It is not unreasonable to suppose that the real patron of the parishes of Altarnun, Pelynt, and Bradstone, in Cornwall and Devon, is a monk and missionary, perhaps even a bishop who was a companion of St Devi or David. When the story of his life was forgotten, the resemblance between his name and the word *nonna* (nun – religious) inspired the creation of the story of a violated nun, and the relation between St Nonna and St David was changed from 'companions' to 'mother and son'.[30]

---

[26] The form of some of these names differ from those of the version published by Wade-Evans, in which we find *Theibi* in the place of *Teraeus*, *Portus Magnus* in the place of *Port Maugan*, *Helve* in the place of *Belve*, *Monus* in the place of *Mobus*. On the other hand, we find *Crunither* rather than *Runither*.

[27] Le Grand, *Vies*, 1637 edition.

[28] Le Grand, *Vies* (1901), 25. I would like to thank André-Yves Bourgès for bringing this reference to my attention.

[29] I would like to thank Madame Annie Le Men for relaying this interesting information to me.

[30] Doble, *Saint Nonna*, 6. In fact Pelynt, 'parish of Nennyd' according to O.J. Padel (*A Popular Dictionary*, 132), has as its eponym a saint known in Wales as Nynnid.

Doble also noted that *Nonnita* appeared as a masculine name on an engraved stone in the cemetery of Tregony in Cornwall.[31] Even the name of Altarnun, 'altar of Nonn', suggesting that the altar of the saint was kept in this place as a precious relic, seems to support this theory.[32]

Having been misled by a note of the editors of the 1901 edition of Albert Le Grand's *Vies des saints*, which misguidedly identified St Vouga or Vio, celebrated on 15 June, with St Nonna,[33] Doble offered as proof the fact that the feast day of St Nonn at Altarnun, known also from calendar of Tavistock, coincided with this date. He noted that Garaby, in his *Vie des saints de Bretagne* published in 1837, claimed that the feast of St Nonna was celebrated in Penmarch on the first Sunday in July, but observed that the feast of St Nonn was also celebrated at Launceston on 3 July.[34]

Although the *Life* of St Vouga or Vio does indeed have its hero land at Penmarch and attributes to him a hermitage at this location, it never mentions the name Nonna. The church of Penmarch honoured its patron saint from at least the fifteenth century:[35] we find at Bordeaux in 1468 a caravel named 'le Sainct Nona de Penmarch'.[36] As a name for a boat this name appears several times subsequently, in various forms: in 1471 *Sent-Nonna* and *Sainct Nonne*, in 1476, *Saint-None*, etc.[37] The consistency of these forms, apart from the accidental feminisation *Saincte-Nonne* in 1505,[38] strongly argues that the original form is truly *Nonna* and not *Onna*, as at Logonna-Quimperch. The Breton pronunciation *Enez-Nonna* for the Island of Nona also reinforces this presumption, even if we cannot establish an early date for the place-name.[39]

We are however not able to completely exclude the possibility that the form *Nonna* might have been the result of a mis-division of the Breton pronunciation *Sanonna*[40] of *Sand Onna*.[41] The coincidental celebration of the feast of St Nonna of Logonna on the second Sunday of July and the celebration of that of Penmarch the first Sunday of July undermines the argument that we have here a St *Onna*, seeing that there is, to the south of the port of Brigneau, in Moëlan, a rocky plateau called Logonna.[42] This would seem to suggest that the cult of St Onna is not as localised as we might have thought.

Doble's argument did not convince his compatriot Charles Henderson. Concluding that 'there was much to be said for his contention',[43] he agued, nevertheless, in a long note appended to Doble's study, that the feminine sex of St Nonn was well-

[31] Henderson gives the text of the inscription (in Doble, *Saint Nonna*, 16): *Nonnita Ercilini Rigati tres filii Ercilini*, 'in memory of Nonnita, Ercilinus, and Rigatus, three sons of Ercilinus'.

[32] Doble, *Saint Nonna*, 9.

[33] Le Grand, *Vies* (1901), 223, n. 2.

[34] Doble, *Saint Nonna*, 6.

[35] It has an eighteenth-century statue of the saint.

[36] Cf. Delafosse, 'Marins', 54. We find in 1520 a mention of a 'paroissien de mon(seigneur) sainct nonne autrement en breton treoutre' (cf. Montfort, *Penmarc'h*, 262).

[37] Cf. Bernard, *Navires*, vol. III, 14, 22ff.

[38] Bernard, *Navires*, vol. III, 182.

[39] Le Berre, *Toponymie ... Deuxième Partie*, 62. In 1693, the *Neptune françois* calls it *I. Nonan* (*ibid.*); Cassini's map calls it *I. Nona*.

[40] We find a mention, in the customs register of the port of Royan in 1467 of 'la Sanonne de Puymarc'.

[41] Apart from the spelling *Senonne* appearing in the aforementioned registers in 1504, these mention with respect to Penmarch caravels named *Saint-Driagat* in 1500, *Sanctdriagat* in 1501, in which we can see the eponym St Riagat, patron saint of Treffiagat.

[42] Cf. Le Berre, *Toponymie ... Première Partie*, 36.

[43] Doble, *Saint Nonna*, 11.

established since the thirteenth century, and that numerous documents supported this: the church of Altarnun, notably, possessed since 1281 an 'Ordinale cum Vita sancte Nonnite [et] Sancti David'.[44] With respect to SS. Nonne, Nennyd (eponym of Pelynt) and Naunter (honoured at Grampound), all different hagionyms,[45] he showed, however, the limits of his approach and illustrated the difficulties which beset us over several centuries of unravelling a web, tangled, almost wantonly, by successive generations. The case of St Divi is in this respect particularly illuminating.

A number of Breton hagionyms were changed in form by the phenomenon of erroneous divisions followed by agglutinations or deglutinations. This phenomenon manifests itself above all when a hagionym beginning with a vowel is preceded by the term *saint*, in Breton, *sant*. Although, in Breton, the continuation, or the establishment (in -*d*), in the pronunciation, of the final -*t* of the word *sant* allows us to detect the existence, or absence, of a consonant at the beginning of a hagionym, in French it is not, by contrast, always easy to determine the radical form. This phenomenon enables confusion between two or even more saints: in the case at hand this involves Divi and Ivi, David and Avit, Davi and Avie, Divi/Ivi and Tevi, even Davi and Tëi. Disentangling this imbroglio is a challenge when one is confronted with churches for which the buildings have disappeared and, what is more, where one has access neither to early forms nor to a local pronunciation.

St Divi in Breton hagionomastic tradition

Of the abovementioned saints, St Divi is the first to be mentioned in texts from the Breton peninsula. In 884, the *Life* of St Paul Aurélien makes him one of the four most eminent disciples of St Iltud, after Paul, but before Samson and Gildas. According to Wrmonoc, *sanctus Devius* was surnamed *Aquaticus*, because he led, 'with bread and water, a very austere life in Christ'.[46] A variant of the epithet, *Aquilentus* is found two centuries later from the pen of Rhygyfarch.[47] As a good hagiographer, the Welsh monk claims to have found the substance of his text scattered amongst ancient texts from his country and principally from St Davids. His word must have greatly contributed to the increasing fame of the saint, whose cult was sufficiently prominent that the pope agreed to canonise him between 1119 and 1124, a unique distinction for a Celtic saint.[48] He even 'ordained that two pilgrimages to St David's would equal one to Rome and that three visits would be equivalent to one to Jerusalem itself'.[49]

Written for a political purpose, replete with fables according to Duine,[50] the *Life* of the saint does not mention Brittany at all. In order to accomplish, in the company of Teliau and Patern, his pilgrimage to Jerusalem, Dewi crossed *mare Britannicum* and travelled via Gaul, without any further detail. Unlike Lifris of Llancarfan, who

---

[44] Doble, *Saint Nonna*, 12. This is also the opinion of Elissa Henken (*Traditions*, 160), who estimated that 'the traditions concerning the mother of St David are ... well established'.

[45] Cf. Orme, *Nicholas Roscarrock's Lives*, 162.

[46] *Vita Pauli* (ed. Cuissard, 421).

[47] *Vita Davidis*, XLII (ed. Wade-Evans, 19). For *Aquilentus* and *Aquaticus* cf. Wade-Evans, 'Rhigyfarch's Life', 57, n. 1.

[48] See Sharpe, 'Which text is Rhygyfarch's *Life* of St David?', above, 102.

[49] Bowen, *Dewi Sant*, 91. On the canonisation, see also Grosjean, Review, 211, and James, 'The Cult', 105.

[50] *Memento*, no. 107.

located an episode of his *Life* of St Cadog on the Island of Cado in Belz,[51] Rhygy-farch pays no attention to the peninsula at all.

Even before his *Life* was written, the cult of the Welsh saint, or of a homonym, was not unknown in Brittany. Although the name *David* appears in the litanies of a tenth-century manuscript psalter conserved at Salisbury, litanies which have, as Duine noted, 'un caractère franco-breton',[52] it is a toponym that provides evidence of the existence of the hagionym Dewi in Brittany since the eleventh century. According to a charter of the Cartulary of the abbey of Quimperlé, the duke Hoel made, in 1069, a donation to the monks of the place of *Loc Deugui* or *Loc Deui* in Quiberon.[53] In 1146, Duke Conan III confirmed as possessions of the monks *Locus Sancti Deuui*.[54] Thus was born the priory of Lotivy, in Breton *Lotëwi*, situated in the territory of Saint-Pierre-Quiberon, in the north of the peninsula, near Portivy, 'the port of (Saint) Divi'. Dedicated today to the Virgin Mary, the chapel of Lotivy possesses a statue, not of St Divi, but of St Ivi as a deacon, a fact which renders uncertain the identification of this saint with the Welsh saint.

The problem is also raised with respect to Brandivy (Morbihan). In Breton *Berdëwi*, this ancient sub-parish of Grandchamp had, according to a document of 1634, as its patron saint Davi.[55] In 1748, in his manuscript register of the diocese,[56] the Abbot Cillart notes a double dedication: 'St Ivi Evêque (inconnu) St Laurent'.[57] For his part, Abbot Guilloux noted in 1890 that 'le nom de saint Ivy était écrit en gros caractères sur la croix paroissiale'.[58] This patronage can only be explained by an erroneous division, *Sand Divi* having been understood as being *sand Ivi*. The later choice of St Aubin as patron saint is very certainly due to the liturgical calendar, as his feast shares the same date as St David, 1 March. This does not prove, however, that the Welsh saint is the eponym of the place – a secular eponym cannot be ruled out, keeping in mind the meaning of the Old Breton place-name element *bran, bren*, 'hill'.

Although Lotivy, the earliest name of Sainte-Marguerite in Riec and a formation perhaps dating from as early as the eleventh century, contains a hagionym which may well be Divi, the identification of this person with the Welsh saint is nevertheless problematical. St Marguerite was already by the end of the seventeenth century the patron saint of the chapel. The building has no statue of St Divy. With St Divi honoured at Dirinon the last Sunday in July and St Marguerite honoured on 20 July, can we assume that the choice of the latter might have been dictated for liturgical reasons? The argument, as slender as it might be, cannot be entirely rejected.

A more thorny question is posed by the existence of the festival of Lotivy at Plunéret, the ferial chapel being dedicated, at least since the sixteenth century,[59] to

---

[51] Cf. Tanguy, 'De la Vie', 160–7.

[52] 'Inventaire', 47.

[53] Ed. Maître and Berthou, 188–9.

[54] Le Duc, *Histoire*, 598.

[55] Guilloux, 'Etudes', 430. Four kilometres to the south-east of the market town of Brandivy there is a village of Ménétavy.

[56] I would like to thank M. G. Le Duc for having sent a copy of this document, conserved in the Departmental Achives of Morbihan, shelf-mark D 1118.

[57] St Laurent was in fact the dedicatee of a ferial chapel of the sub-parochial district.

[58] Guilloux, 'Etudes', 431.

[59] On the lower purloin of the choir is this inscription: *Le jour de la Croix, en septembre 1554, fut assise la première pierre de cette chapelle Madame sainte Avoye ...*

St Avoie, in Breton *santez Avi*, one of the 11,000 virgins.[60] Very popular in Paris after the transfer of her relics to the abbey of Saint-Antoine, her cult was spread over a vast area, but remained relatively localised in Brittany. Apart from Plunéret, she is particularly honoured at Forges-La-Forêt (Ille-et-Vilaine), to the south of La Guerche, where she possesses a lateral chapel in the church;[61] at Plouray (Morbihan), a fountain is dedicated to her in the village of Saint-Avé, in Breton *Zan Awac'h*. At Plunéret, her great pardon, very well attended, is held on 6 May, and the lesser pardon is held the third Sunday of September. She is invoked, by analogy with her name, for children with birthmarks, in Breton *iviet*, who were sent to her chapel as a pilgrimage. Young children were seated on her boat, a clock of quartz, lightly hollowed in the middle, kept in the building, so that they might walk earlier.[62] One of the two neighbouring fountains also had the power to strengthen children, the water of the other being used to wash their eyes.[63] From all accounts, St Avoie replaced an eponymous saint, whom we might suppose to have been *sant Davi,* who later became by an erroneous division *sant Avi* and then feminised into *santez Avi*; this might have been Divi, who is invoked by the name Lotivy.

Another possibility is, however, suggested by the name of Saint-Avé. In Breton *Sentevi*, and given as *Senteve* in 1338, this name retains the memory of a small monastery mentioned in two charters of the Cartulary of Redon in 854, under the forms *Sent Thoui* or *Sint Toui*.[64] This same hagionym might explain, as well, the name of the village of Saint-Evy in Saint-Jean-Trolimon (Finistère), in Breton *Santevi*,[65] whose chapel contains a statue of St Ewy as a bishop.

As Joseph Loth suggested, the hagionym corresponds to that of the Welsh saint Tyfei,[66] the eponym of Lamphey (ancient *Lantefei*), in Pembrokeshire, and Llandyfeisant, in Carmarthenshire. According to the *Book of Llan Dâv*, in which appears a place-name *Lantiivei*, he was the son of Budic,[67] the king of Breton Cornouaille, and Anauued, the sister of St Teilo. When he was a child, wishing to protect a swineherd from a vindictive rich landowner, he was accidentally killed by him by a lance blow at Penally, in Pembrokeshire.[68] He was buried in this place. Honoured 27 March, he owed, suggested Baring-Gould, his appearance in the calendar to his membership in a noble and holy family. His brother was St Ismael, one of the favourite disciples of St David. Shortly after his death, his father regained the peninsula. He then had a son, St Oudoc, who then became bishop of Llandaf.[69]

---

60 A cousin of St Ursula, this saint escaped the massacre by the Huns beneath the walls of Cologne and took refuge in the environs of Boulogne where she was imprisoned in a tower by a barbarian chieftain. Each week, the Virgin caused an angel to bring her three loaves of bread. She was nevertheless martyred. Having been flogged, her breasts were mutilated, her eyes gouged out, and she was finally beheaded (cf. de Corson, *Les pardons*, 116).

61 Her legend is represented there in bas-relief.

62 Cf. *Bulletin de la Société polymathique du Morbihan* (1923), 55.

63 Cf. *Acta sanctorum*, October, vol. IX, 323.

64 Courson, *Cartulaire*, 369, 371.

65 M. Gilles Goyat, whom I would like to thank profoundly for this information, confirmed to me that the local pronunciation is indeed *san'te:vi*, with an open *e*.

66 Loth, *Les noms*, 119.

67 It is worth noting that the exile of a Budic in Wales is also invoked by a comital list from Cornouaille: 'Budic and Maxenri were two brothers. The first of them, in returning from *Alamannia* (for *Albania*), killed Marchell and recovered his patrimony' (ed. Maître and Berthou, 90).

68 Ed. Evans, 127, 130.

69 Baring-Gould, *The Lives*, vol. 16, 202.

From St David to St Teï, via St Avit

In parallel with the vernacular form *Divi*, we also find the forms *David*, *Davi*, found only in the charters of Redon in the ninth century,[70] excluding the form *Devi*, which is used by Wrmonoc. In place-names, the form *Davi* is twice associated with the Breton place-name element *lok*. The seat of an ancient chaplainry of the Hospitallers of St John of Jerusalem, the village of Lotavy in Priziac, had a chapel, but it was dedicated to the Virgin Mary. The village of Lotavy in Saint-Guen tells us nothing about him. By contrast, chapels of Saint-David, all disappeared, are mentioned at Lanmeur, Plouaret, Plouguernével, Scaër, and Tonquédec. Only those of Saint-David at Quimperlé and of Saint-Martin-des-Prés remain. Apart from the chapel of St David at Saint-Père-Marc-en-Poulet, a chapel which, it seems, honours King David – at least the building contains a statue of him – and from that of Saint-Martin-des-Prés, a parish which however lies on the linguistic frontier, all these cult sites are found in Lower Brittany.[71] In at least two cases the patronage of the Welsh saint is the result of a substitution: the chapels of St David in Plouaret and of Tonquédec are, in fact, situated in villages named Loguivy.

It is also St Ivi who lurks behind the name of the village of Saint-Avit at Plélo, if we judge by the mentions of a chapel of *Saint-Yvy* in 1482 and of the *capellania Sancti Yvi* in 1516. The patronage of St Avit is also attributed to a disappeared chapel at Plouhinec (Morbihan), but in the absence of any information concerning it, we cannot choose between Avit, David or Ivi.

Sometimes pronounced *sant Daï*, as a Quimperlé, whose early land registry shows a field named Parc-Saint-Dail, or at Scaër, a parish in which there is mention of a disappeared chapel of St Tay, but where also there exists a village of Miné-Sant-David, St David at times enters into competition with St Teï. Thus the chapel of St They of Plouhinec (Finistère), which possesses a statue of its patron saint as a monk, with a crosier, was in 1455 described as that of *Saint Dey* or of *Saint Davy*;[72] his pardon was celebrated the second Sunday of July. At Poullan, the chapel of St They, called also St Avi, whose pardon was celebrated the third Sunday in May, possessed a statue of St Evy.[73] The pardon of St Evy at Saint-Jean-Trolimon was celebrated the third Sunday of August, a day on which was also celebrated the pardon of Lothey in the seventeenth century.

St Divi, substitute for St Ivi

The extension of the cult of St Divi, without a doubt was assisted by the homophony between his name and that of St Ivi. St Ivi, deacon and confessor, is considered the last of the Breton saints of the early period to have emigrated to the peninsula. According to the *Vita* compiled in the fourteenth century by the English hagiographer John of Tynemouth,[74] he was a disciple of St Cuthbert who left the monastery of Lindisfarne (today Holy Island, in Northumberland) at the end of the seventh

---

70 The anthroponym *David*, *Dauui*, *Daui* appears several times.
71 See the map in Tanguy, 'Les cultes', 22.
72 Bernard, 'Études', 159.
73 Doble, *Saint Day*, 8.
74 *Acta Sanctorum*, October, vol. IV, 404–5. There is a translation of this text into Breton and French in Irien, 'Piou eo sant Ywi (Ivy)?', 5–8.

century for Brittany. At the end of an exemplary life, he died on 6 October. Nevertheless, his body was kept in the abbey of Wilton, in Wiltshire. According to John of Tynemouth, he was greatly venerated at the time of writing.[75] Compiled near the end of the eleventh century, the *Life* of St Edith claims that his relics were brought there by Pictish clerics, who themselves came from Scotland.[76] While this claim contradicts the claims of his *Life*, some have doubted that the saint ever visited the peninsula.[77] It is nevertheless a fact that a saint of this name has left numerous traces in Brittany.[78]

Although, like Divi, he is not the eponym of names in *Plou-* or in *Lan-*,[79] he is the eponym of at least eight place-names in *Lok-*: in Tréguier, we find Loguivy-les-Lannion (a dependence of the diocese of Dol), Loguivy-Plougras, Loguivy in Plouaret, in Ploubazlanec and in Tonquédec; in Léon, we have Loguivy in Plouguerneau; in Cornouaille, we have Loguivy in Rosnoën as well as in Tréméven. As the Breton pronunciation *Sandivi* shows, he is also the eponym of Sant-Divy in Léon, a fact confirmed by the village of Lesivy, one kilometre to the north of the market town; in Cornouaille he is the eponym of Saint-Yvi, in Breton *Sandivi*; in Vannes he is the eponym of Pontivy, in Breton *Pondi*, where he has a chapel. Other chapels are or were dedicated to him, at Moréac, at Plabennec, at Plélauff, at Plélo, and at Plounéour-Ménez.[80] Several others might be added to this list, such as those, now ruined, of Saint-Divy at Brennilis,[81] and at Scrignac, in Breton *Sandivi*, or even those, now disappeared, of Saint-Divy in Moustoir,[82] and at Plounéour-Trez. The existence, in some cases, of statues of St Divi, such as at Brennilis, Plounéour-Ménez, and Scrignac, or of St David, at Bodivit in Plomelin, a village which cannot commemorate St David, is not sufficient evidence to attribute the original dedications of these to the Welsh saint.

The expansion of the Welsh St David was accomplished, from all evidence, to the disadvantage of St Ivi. The notable fact that it was David's legend, and not that of Ivi (who was, as we have seen, the eponym of numerous names in *Lok-* in Tréguier) which we find in the Trégorrois Legendary of the fifteenth century,[83] is symptomatic of this process.

He is or was honoured as a substitute for St Ivi in several buildings, as in the church of Saint-Divy (Finistère), in the chapels of Saint-Divy at Brennilis, Plounéour-Ménez, and Scrignac, and in that of Saint-David at Loguivy in Plouaret. At Loguivy-les-Lannion, whose church possessed an silver arm-shaped reliquary of St Divy, dated to 1690, statues of the sixteenth century present the patron saint with a mitre and crosier. This is also how he is represented at Loguivy-Plougras, at Loguivy-de-la-Mer, at Loguivy in Tonquédec, at Pontivy, at Saint-Yvy in Moréac, at Loc-Ivy in Tréméven (Finistère). Curiously, as we have noted, it is, by contrast, a

---

[75] *Acta Sanctorum*, October, vol. IV, 405: *Apud Wiltoniam diebus nostris corpus ejus sanctum conservens in magna veneratione habetur.*

[76] *Acta Sanctorum*, September, vol. V, 371.

[77] Cf. *Revue de Bretagne*, 39 (1908), 206–8.

[78] See the map in Tanguy, 'Les cultes', p. 27.

[79] A place-name Lantivy was recorded at Saint-Nolff, Morbihan (Smith, *De la toponymie*, 43), but the first element, as is clear from the replacement of -d- by -t-, must be Breton *nant*, 'valley'.

[80] We should also note the presence at Sizun of a village of Bodivy, a compound made up of the Old Breton *bot*, 'domicile', and an eponym *Ivi*.

[81] Cassini's map spells the name *Saint Ivy*.

[82] No doubt it is from this chapel that the eighteenth-century statue of St Avite, kept in the parish church, has come.

[83] Cf. Duine, 'Bréviaires', 176.

statue of St Ivi as a deacon which is found in the chapel of Notre-Dame of Lotivy in Saint-Pierre-Quiberon. The same representation is found in the church of Trégon, but as St Davy, the dedicatee of a fountain near the market town.[84]

A victim of the development of the cult of St Divi, did St Ivi also fall victim to that of St Yves? The only certain attestation of St Yves that I have found strongly suggests that this is unlikely. The Breton forms of the name of St Yves (*Eozen, Erwan, Youenn*) do not submit easily to this process. However, the chapel, already in ruins in 1780, of Saint-Yves in Mendy, at Plabennec, appears several times in 1541, in an avowal of Louis Barbier, lord of Tronjoly in Plougar, as *chapelle monseigneur sainct Yvy* or *chapelle Sainct Yvy*.[85] Less certain is the case of the chapel, also destroyed, of Saint-Yves in Bourg-Blanc. The Abbot Le Guen believed that it dated to the foundation in 1328 by a certain Grallon le Fèvre of a hospital[86] placed under the protection of St Ivi.[87] However, in 1363 the will of Hervé of Léon speaks of a 'hospital in honour of God and St Yves'.[88] There is no doubt that the name Divi[89] appears in connection with Breton *koat* in the nearby village of Coativy, cradle of the noble family of that name;[90] but the form *Sancti Yvonis* employed in the document is unambiguous. This is not, moreover, the only example of a hospice placed under the protection of St Yves: there was also one at Saint-Renan by 1388, at Rennes by 1462, and at Brest by 1506, etc.

A relatively incoherent festive calendar

The cults of St Divi and Ivi are not without their serious problems regarding feast days. As noted above, St Divi is celebrated on 1 March,[91] his translations on 16 August and 26 September; St Ivi is celebrated on 6 October. As regards St Divi, these dates are observed at cult sites only very rarely: at Saint-Divy, the patronal feast is fixed at the first Sunday in March;[92] at Brandivy 1 March is the day of the patronal feast (today that of St Aubin). In contrast, St Divi is or was celebrated the last Sunday of July at Dirinon, at Moréac, and perhaps at Riec, where the pardon of St Marguerite is found on the same date; the same applies at Saint-David in Quimperlé.

As regards St Ivi, the distance from the official calendar is even more striking, as the date of 6 October is completely ignored, in preference for 1 March, at Pontivy, 9 April, at Tréméven (9 April) and above all the first Sunday of May at Loguivy-

---

[84] The saint is invoked to make young children walk.

[85] Nourry, 'Les manoirs', 238.

[86] Situated at the beginning of the road to Plouvien, this hospice existed until the Revolution.

[87] Le Guen, 'Antiquités', 147–8. Abbot Le Guen specified that 'on ne trouve plus en ce lieu que la statue de saint Yves'. He does not mention the fountain.

[88] Morice, *Mémoires*, vol. I, col. 1562: *Item do, lego, et concedo hospitali ad honorem Dei et sancti Yvonis ordinato in hospitio Grallonis Fabri apud Burgum Album.*

[89] The chapel of the ancient motte of Coativy-Bihan, whose existence is recalled by the plots of land of Jardin- and Parc-ar-Chapel, might have been dedicated to him; the neighbouring fountain still bears the name of *Feunteun Sant Yvi* (cf. Irien, 'Piou eo sant Ywi (Ivy)?', 12).

[90] The first known member of this family seems to have been Prigent of *Quoetivi,* cited in a charter of 1288 (Morice, *Mémoires*, vol. I, col. 1086).

[91] This date is found as early as the Martyrology of Óengus, compiled in Ireland *ca* 800, which gives for 1 March: *David Cille Muni* (ed. Stokes, 80).

[92] One other pardon is celebrated the first Sunday after Ascension, another the second Sunday of September.

les-Lannion, Loguivy-Plougras, Loguivy in Ploubazlanec at Loguivy in Tonquédec. Published in 1709, the Martyrology of Chastelain, which subsumes St Ivi under St Divi, gives for Loguivy-Plougras a date of 1 May: 'A Loguivy (*Locus Davidagii*) … sur la paroisse de Plougroas (*Plebs Crucis*) au Diocêse de Tréguier …, S. Divy (*Davidagius*),[93] Evêque régionnaire, patron de ce lieu'.[94] Although this date does not accord with that of St Divi, it is, notably, very close to that of 2 May to which the feast of *Santez Avi* is assigned at Plunéret by the Proper of Vannes of 1652.[95]

In one case, as in the other, we find ourselves faced with a festive calendar on this matter so different from the insular feasts that we are entitled to ask whether SS. Divi and Ivi of the Breton peninsula are not otherwise obscure homonyms of those known to us from insular sources. The reputation of the Welsh bishop at any rate eventually eclipsed St Ivi, whose cult had been, however, relatively widespread, even if it was nevertheless confined to Lower Brittany.[96] Although the *Buez santez Nonn* might have contributed to this eclipse, it did not inspire, however, the spread of the cult of its subject, St Nonne.

---

93 As noted above, this form should be read *David agius*.
94 Cf. Vallérie, 'Les références', 156.
95 The saint baffled the Bollandists: *Nihil aliud de dicta Avia potuimus scire* (*Acta Sanctorum*, May, vol. I, 169).
96 Although it is today in Upper Brittany, Plélo lies nevertheless on the linguistic border.

11

ST DAVID IN THE LITURGY: A REVIEW OF SOURCES

Daniel Huws

Coming across an article, an excellent recent article, on 'The cult of St David in the middle ages', and unaware that the author was an archaeologist, some readers might be disappointed to find in it nothing about liturgy.[1] Its one passing reference to liturgy is however a precious one, from the letter written to Thomas Cromwell by Bishop Barlow in 1538. William Barlow, the radical Reformer, complained that 'the people' (meaning no doubt the good folk of his chapter) wilfully solemnized the feast of St David and 'set forth relics in defiance of his admonition and the King's injunctions'. The relics consisted of 'two heads of silver plate enclosing two rotten skulls' and 'a worm-eaten book covered with silver plate'.[2] Barlow was not to appreciate that by way of recompense to us for the destruction of the relics which he no doubt managed to achieve soon afterwards he was providing the most precise reference we have to a Welsh metal-covered binding. Such a binding, we can safely say, would have been no later in date than the twelfth century, and was probably on a gospel-book. Had Barlow been a Matthew Parker and not a William Barlow, this book, 'the St Davids Gospels', might, who knows, have become Wales's answer to the Book of Kells.

My subject is not the archaeological monuments of the cult of St David but an incorporeal element of the cult of St David in the middle ages, its liturgy. What survives of liturgy is at best something that might be regarded as its libretto, together, sometimes, with something by way of a score. The performance is of course lost. The medium for what survives is books. The title of this paper is borrowed from and is a tribute to that admirable small volume by Silas Harris, *Saint David in the Liturgy*, published in 1940.[3] Harris observantly covers the ground and offers a framework which remains definitive. My offering is merely an up-to-date view of the relevant sources now available, some of them unknown in Harris's time.

Silas Harris, in default of Welsh sources, made good use of non-Welsh ones, English, Irish, Scottish – turning to survivors in the colonies, as it were, to discover about the obliterated homeland. Owain Edwards in his work on the Penpont Antiphonal, drawing on the expert help of the late Christopher Hohler, further extended the range of evidence from non-Welsh sources. I have not combed manuscript catalogues in the hope of making further additions; rather, I have confined myself to the evidence from Wales.

The rite of a saint can enter the liturgy via a martyrology, a calendar, a litany, or as a collect. Eventually perhaps, it might emerge with a full mass or office; first probably as an addendum in a service book, later by incorporation, and, finally,

---

1 James, 'The cult of St David'.
2 See *Calendar of State Papers, Domestic*, 31 March 1538.
3 Harris, *Saint David*.

late in the middle ages, stabilized in print. As Harris showed, David appears in early Irish martyrologies, in English calendars before A.D. 1100, notably the pre-1000 calendar, probably compiled at Canterbury, in the Leofric Missal (Bodleian Library, Bodley 579).[4] There is no reason to suppose that Wales lacked early martyrologies, calendars and litanies. But none survive. The earliest Welsh calendar is in BL, Cotton Vesp. A. xiv, of about 1200, probably written at Monmouth priory. It is a key document, earlier than any Welsh service book, but not a liturgical one.[5]

Service books fall into two main groups. On the one hand, those for use with the mass, the service of eucharist, said, or sung, by a priest, at an altar. The essential book is the *missal*, which may or may not have associated musical notation (a *noted missal*); the corresponding music for a choir would be in a *gradual*. On the other hand, those books for use with the office for daily hours (or 'set of offices', the term 'office' is fluid), the most familiar hours being those of matins, lauds and vespers. At the heart of the office is the reading, or singing, of the psalms; the psalms are accompanied by prayers and by other readings, from scripture or perhaps from *vitae*. The reading of the office could be private, by a priest (or a monk or even a layman) from a *breviary*, probably a small pocket breviary, or, if the office hours were celebrated communally they would normally be sung. For communal celebration the priest would use a large lectern breviary, and this, if it contained musical notation, would be a *noted breviary*. The text and notation for a choir would be in an *antiphonal* (*antiphonary*).

So what medieval service books survive? We know that, by royal injunction in 1549, they were all meant to be destroyed. Nevertheless, scores survived not only the destruction of 1549 but also later purges. And the Welsh survivors? Echoing down the years, since this question was first asked, come cries of dismay at the realization that hardly any Welsh books survive at all. Harris set out the evidence. Was the initial destruction more effective, we wonder, than in England, Scotland or Ireland? This is hard to believe. Was post-Reformation adherence to Rome less firm? Not so, or, at least, not before 1678. Was the neglect met with by survivors greater? Perhaps.[6]

The count of known Welsh medieval survivors of the books needed by a priest for the central acts of worship, celebration of mass and of the office, totals four missals and not one breviary. Two missals are manuscripts, neither of them of Welsh origin, adapted for Welsh use, Hereford Cathedral MS p.iii.4 (a manual/missal) and Oxford, All Souls MS 11, and two are printed missals with manuscript additions adapting them for local use, one from Conwy and one from Llanbadarn Fawr, both now in the National Library of Wales.[7] Then there are fragments. A list which I have compiled over the years of medieval manuscript fragments which were found in a 'Welsh' context (used as wrappers for sixteenth century Welsh manuscripts or

---

4 Dumville, *Liturgy*, 39–65. Harris reflects the prevailing view of his time, that the calendar was of Glastonbury origin.

5 On the calendar in Cotton Vesp. A. xiv, see Harris, 'A kalendar' and Hughes, *Celtic Britain*, 53–66.

6 One example of a Welsh medieval missal which survived at least until the 1660s was from Erbistock. It is mentioned in a note by John Salusbury in NLW MS 732, p. 45: 'To this Erbyn the parish church of Erbistock is dedicated whose feast is on the 13th day of January and the ould Masse Book of the parish saith he was an Abbot and I conceive he was an Abbot.'

7 On the Hereford manual/missal, see below, 226–7; on All Souls 11, see Watson, *Descriptive Catalogue*; on the Conwy missal, see Huws, *Medieval Welsh Manuscripts*, 269–86; on the Llanbadarn Fawr missal, see Harris, 'A Llanbadarn Fawr calendar'.

archives, or in sixteenth century Welsh bindings) runs to over sixty.[8] Of these, over half are liturgical manuscripts, over a third missals. None of these fragments, let it be said, happens to contain liturgy for a Welsh saint.

Before looking at the liturgy of St David in Wales and its sources we need to ask a question: how early was the feast of St David celebrated throughout Wales? By a decree in 1398 and by convocation in 1415 the feast was to be celebrated throughout the province of Canterbury, as a *simplex* with nine lections. Slowly, such a decree would have become operative; slowly, service books would have come to make provision for it. But well before 1398, as Harris shows, the feast had been celebrated in the dioceses of Exeter and Hereford. That it was similarly celebrated in the three Welsh dioceses other than St Davids might be taken for granted, but the evidence is equivocal.

There are ancient dedications to St David in the dioceses of Llandaf and Hereford, but none in north Wales. But David already by the time of the composition of *Armes Prydain* in the mid-tenth century, a poem in which he is invoked to rally the Irish and Welsh against the English, was a political symbol. By the twelfth century, the evidence both literary and historical shows that the primacy of St Davids had come to be acknowledged throughout Wales, even in the north, and St Davids had found fame as a place of pilgrimage. One would expect this supremacy to be reflected in such liturgical evidence as we possess, but this is not the case. The surviving liturgical books, as we have noticed, are very few. Such witnesses as we have, mainly service books and calendars, are listed, by diocese, in Appendix 1. To summarize: in three dioceses there is, as one would expect, one local fixture, the patron saint of the diocese; in St Asaph, there is none. Again, in St Davids, Llandaf and Bangor, there is sufficient consistency in calendars to indicate what would have been the diocesan model; in St Asaph, there is not. The answer to our question about Welsh celebration of St David outside his own diocese before 1398 is that liturgical evidence from Bangor and St Asaph is lacking while that from Llandaf is negative.

The absence of service books leads us to cast around for other sources of evidence of observance of saints' days or of devotion to saints. Poetry is one. The circumstances which prompted professional Welsh bards to compose the numerous surviving poems to saints have escaped record; some poems were perhaps motivated by personal devotion to a local saint, others were no doubt commissioned by lay or ecclesiastical patrons. All medieval Welsh poetry was probably sung: reason suggests that the occasion of singing poems to saints would have been on the feast or vigil of the saint, but, again, evidence is lacking. On the eve of the Reformation we meet one reference to singing vernacular poetry in a chapel during a vigil.[9] Whatever the motivation of the bards, the surviving poetry to St David might be expected to reflect the extent of his cult. The indications are that devotion to St David was still confined to the south. From the twelfth-century *awdl* by Gwynfardd Brycheiniog to the *cywyddau* of the fourteenth and fifteenth centuries, all poems apart from a *cywydd* by Iolo Goch are by poets whose associations are with south Wales; and Iolo Goch's bardic circuit is known to have encompassed the diocese of St Davids.

While the few illuminations in surviving medieval Welsh manuscripts do not help us, other iconographical evidence occasionally can do so. By about 1500, we learn

---

8 It is a list I have compiled which ought to be tidied up and published.
9 Williams and Jones, *Gramadegau'r Penceirddiaid*, 223. The reference is by Richard Longford, referring to Poulton, near Trefalun, between Chester and Wrexham, in the 1530s or 1540s.

from stained glass windows that St David was at home in the dioceses of Bangor and St Asaph and that St Asaf, as patron, was given dignity in Llandyrnog, in his own diocese (earlier than any known liturgical commemoration).[10]

Calendars were needed by lawyers, whether of the law of Hywel (calendars occur in some fifteenth-century Welsh lawbooks) or of the law of England. Fixed points in the lawyers' year were determined by the ecclesiastical calendar; and documents needed to be dated, and frequently were by giving the saint's day. In the absence of calendars, evidence on which they might be reconstructed lies in surviving deeds and documents which are dated by feast-days, and these may include feast-days of saints not included in the Sarum calendar. But recovering such evidence calls for patience. Even when medieval documents have been well catalogued, lists and catalogues may fail to note references to feast-days in dating clauses (silently converting to day and month); recovering the full evidence demands a daunting search. Nevertheless, something can be offered, by way of indication. Hywel Emanuel noticed the value of such datings and published a number of examples he had encountered:[11] they include David in the dioceses of Hereford, St Davids and St Asaph, thirteenth to fifteenth centuries; Deiniol, Bangor, fourteenth century; Teilo, Llandaf, fifteenth century. The thirteenth- and fourteenth-century letters and documents edited in *Littere Wallie* and calendared in *Ancient Correspondence* include only two dated by feasts of a Welsh saint, David on each occasion, one a letter from Carmarthen in 1278 the other a charter of Gruffudd ap Gwenwynwyn in (probably) 1271.[12] Interesting evidence is thrown up by the published edition of the court rolls of Caernarfon for 1361–1400.[13] The feasts of five Welsh saints are used for dating: Beuno, David, Dwynwen, Peblig and Trillo. Apart from the addition of Trillo, these saints correspond exactly to those given prominence in the contemporary Llanbeblig Books of Hours. In Wynnstay MS 36, an early-fifteenth-century Welsh law manuscript written in the Llandeilo Fawr area, the specimen *cwynion* include dating by the feasts of David and Teilo.

Lastly, invocations and oaths. As early as about 1090 in Cambridge, Corpus Christi College MS 199, the copy of St Augustine's *De Trinitate* written at Llanbadarn Fawr by Ieuan ap Sulien, we meet the scribe's invocations of saints David and Padarn. Later, in the fifteenth century, in two law manuscripts from the Teifi valley written by the same hand, we meet, in BL Add. 22356, invocations of David, Gwenog and Lawrence (*Dewi Brefi ora*, *Dewi Brefi yn ganhorthwy*, *Gwenoc helpa*, etc.), and, in Llanstephan 116, invocations of Gwenog and Gwnnen.[14] We have the nice example of St Thomas of Hereford, no lover of the Welsh, whose only oath is said to have been 'by Seynt Dewy'. Charming evidence, but anecdotal to a fault. There is however a field which might lend itself to statistical research: oaths in Welsh poetry. The poetry of the *cywyddwyr*, satire and love poetry included, is littered with invocations of the saints, 'myn Dewi', 'myn Derfel', etc. The choice of saint may as often as not be determined by the needs of *cynghanedd*; even so, the padding-words called forth by *cynghanedd* needed to be familiar to the ears of listeners, not to distract from the main thrust of the poem.

[10] Lewis, *Stained Glass*, 72, 56; Gray, *Images of piety*, 34–6.
[11] Emanuel, 'Notes'.
[12] Edwards, *Littere Wallie*, the two examples on 86 and 132, and J.G. Edwards, *Calendar*.
[13] Jones and Owen, *Caernarvon Court Rolls*.
[14] James, 'Llyfr cyfraith', 394–5. There is similar invocation of 'Dewi Brefi' by the scribe of a fifteenth-century collection of prophecies in Welsh, BL, Add. 19710, fol. 38.

223

The mass

For all the losses, let us count our blessings. Among the detritus we find *a* mass for St David and *an* office. The mass is in Hereford Cathedral MS P.iii.4. It was first published by Henderson in his edition of the York Missal[15] (Henderson mistakenly deduced that it came from the diocese of St Asaph). It was then published by Harris. It includes the full proper, with a sequence, *Dauid celi clarum sidus*, and with provision for weekly commemoration. Harris suggests that the composition of the sequence was not earlier than about 1400.[16] It is a fair assumption that the mass was written for use in the diocese of St Davids; on this point, and on the manuscript itself, a noted manual to which the mass of St David is an addition, without music, see below, 226–7.

Harris made good use of non-Welsh surviving liturgical books to compensate for the scarcity of Welsh ones. He presents early evidence from the dioceses of Exeter and Hereford and evidence from Sarum books after 1415. By way of a proper for a mass, the least to be expected was a collect. Harris notices and prints forms of three collects: one, *Deus qui beatus confessorem tuum David*, which is first met in the proper prayers at the close of Rhygyfarch's *Vita*, was, to judge by the surviving evidence, the form invariably used in Wales (and in a few Sarum books in the fifteenth century);[17] a second, *Deus qui ecclesie tue beatum David pontificem tuum*, which derives from the *vita* compiled by Gerald of Wales, was adopted for use in the diocese of Hereford;[18] and a third, *Omnipotens sempiterne Deus qui beato David confessori tuo*, first appears in Sarum books later than 1415.[19] The first and second also occur, as alternatives, in the office for St David in the Penpont Antiphonal. Harris makes the point that there is good reason to suppose that the collects recorded by Rhigyfarch and Gerald were existing ones; their origin might be much earlier than the *vitae*. Nine lections for the office of St David, are, as Harris shows, found by 1340 in Exeter and a closely related set appears in the printed 1531 Sarum breviary.[20]

Two sources unknown to Harris provide additional texts of the sequence he knew only from a single copy, *David celi clarum sidus*. The first is a fifteenth-century sequentiary/hymnal at St Asaph cathedral, a manuscript which has escaped attention except for a passing reference by John Fisher.[21] The manuscript is recorded in the

---

[15] Henderson, *Missale*, II, xiv–xvii.

[16] Harris, *Saint David*, 38.

[17] Harris, *Saint David*, 13–14, 28–9, 34, 46; Edwards, *Matins*, 115–16. Edwards, n. 8, lists many additional manuscript service books in which this collect occurs. To these may be added NLW MS 22253A, a fifteenth-century breviary which belonged to the parish of Lanteglos by Fowey, Cornwall, see Hague, *Handlist of Manuscripts*, VIII, s.n., and Orme, 'A fifteenth-century prayer-book'.

[18] Harris, *Saint David*, 17–19, 48; Edwards, *Matins*, 116–17.

[19] Harris, *Saint David*, 26–7; Edwards, *Matins*, 117, with list of additional manuscripts containing the collect in n. 12.

[20] The nine lections from the Sarum breviary, Paris, BN MS lat. 17294, are now printed below, pp. 242–5.

[21] Fisher, 'MSS.' The sequentiary/hymnal is now listed in the addenda of Ker, *Medieval Manuscripts*, V.25. The manuscript is of parchment of poor quality, contains 44 leaves (collation 1–2⁸, 3⁸ wants 1, 4⁸, 5⁸ wants 8, 6⁸ wants 1 and 8), one of the wanting leaves, following fol. 16, containing the end of the sequence for St David. It measures *ca* 185×140 mm (written space 140 × 110 mm), written 24 lines to the page by a single hand. There are plain 2- or 3-line red initials. The binding is of blind-tooled calf of the eighteenth century.

St Asaph cathedral library in 1878. Its earlier history is unknown; there is no obviously helpful internal evidence. The manuscript contains 63 sequences, arranged according to *temporale, sanctorale* and *commune*, followed by 75 hymns. All except two of the sequences are to be found in contemporary Sarum books. The two exceptions are St Anne, whose sequence only appears among *nova festa* in Sarum printed supplements from 1496, long after her feast had come to be celebrated, and St David (on fol. 16v). The presence of this sequence, the Welsh provenance (late though it is) and the unrefined script and production of the manuscript concur to suggest a Welsh origin. This manuscript could indeed stake a claim to be not only the sole surviving medieval Welsh hymnal but also the sole surviving medieval service book produced in Wales. The presence of the sequence might suggest the diocese of St Davids as first candidate, but by the fifteenth century it cannot exclude a possible origin elsewhere in Wales, even perhaps in the diocese of St Asaph.

The second new source of *Dauid celi clarum sidus* is Peniarth 356. This is a composite book of teaching texts, mostly Latin grammar, put together about 1470, perhaps in the abbey of Valle Crucis, by Thomas Pennant, later abbot of Basingwerk.[22] Among miscellaneous material which occurs sporadically throughout the book is, on fol. 61, the sequence for St David (with collect *Deus qui beatus confessorem tuum* on fol. 61v).

The office

No medieval breviary from Wales survives. Harris had to glean. But in 1969 the National Library of Wales bought at Sotheby's a fourteenth-century manuscript antiphonal, 'the Property of a Lady', a book still in medieval wooden boards, but lacking several quires, and about a quarter of its text. This manuscript, now NLW 20541E, has no tracable history after about 1600. Its most notable feature is a full sung office for the feast of St David. After its acquisition the National Library came to know that the home of 'the lady' was Penpont, in the parish of Llansbyddyd, Breconshire. Penpont is a house built about 1666 by Daniel Williams, the head of a cadet branch of the Williams family of Abercamlais. The house and contents were sold in 1991.[23] Until then it had been in the unbroken possession of the Williams family. A member of the family, Dr Penry Williams, the historian, who had not known of the existence of the antiphonal, later confirmed that a lady of the house had not been above selling heirlooms. The Penpont Antiphonal, as it is now called, is one which Owain Edwards has made his own, by a series of articles, by his study, *Matins, Lauds and Vespers for St David's Day*, and by his facsimile edition.[24] While there is no comparative material from Wales, Professor Edwards by an exhaustive search for parallels elsewhere has thrown great light on both text and chant of the office of St David, and on the affiliations. He suggests as the likeliest dates of composition of the office either soon after 1224 or about 1285.[25]

Another liturgical source unknown to Harris offers a fragment of a processional

22 On the manuscript, see Thomson, *Descriptive Catalogue*, 114–31.
23 On the house, see Haslam, *Powys*, 367–8; *Country Life*, 186, no. 25 (18 June 1992), 78–81. The contents were sold by Sotheby's on 22 October 1991. I am grateful to Mr Walford Jones for letting me see his marked copy of the sale catalogue.
24 Edwards, *Matins*; Edwards, *National Library of Wales MS. 20541E*.
25 Edwards, *Matins*, 159–68.

hymn to St David written by Thomas Saint, archdeacon of St Davids in the years 1500–13. This fragment survives in the extracts made by James Ussher from a lost manuscript of Thomas Saint.[26] Ussher also preserved extracts from the Lives which Saint composed in Latin verse of five saints associated with the diocese: David, Justinian, Caradog, Non and Teilo, together with extracts from lections for the feast of St Teilo.

When Reform arrived the Hereford manual belonged to the parish church of Crickadarn; the Penpont antiphonal eventually found refuge at Penpont. Beyond that, their histories have not been clarified. The remainder of this paper attempts to place these two manuscripts, the two primary sources of our knowledge of the liturgy of St David in medieval Wales, in a more exact historical setting.

Hereford Cathedral P.iii.4

In Hereford Cathedral P.iii.4 Silas Harris recognised in the inscriptions 'llanvair keric kadarn church' (upper pastedown) and 'the church of llanvair y keric kadarn' (fol. 120) what Henderson had failed to recognize, the old name of the parish of Crickadarn. These inscriptions are by a hand of mid-sixteenth century. The manuscript is a noted manual of the use of Sarum written in the first half of the fifteenth century. It also includes, as do many manuals, elements of a missal: in this case, the proper of major feasts of the ecclesiastical year, including those of a few saints (Stephen, John the Baptist, Peter and Paul, Leonard, Edmund [Rich], Blaise and Catherine). The production is professional. We could look for an atelier in some major centre of production of service books such as Oxford or London.

In the fifteenth century the book was either still unbound or had suffered through being poorly bound in the first place. Two quires were already lost. In this imperfect condition the manual was bound (or rebound) with one small added quire (fols 54–6), containing the Mass of the Holy Name (one of the *nova festa*) and with part of another manuscript, of separate origin, including the penitential psalms and a litany (fols 109–19). This fifteenth-century binding, on six bands, is that which still survives (with the cathedral library chain still attached). The pastedowns and flyleaves of this binding offer precious evidence: they are recycled fragments of court rolls of the Welshry of the lordship of Hay, partly of mid-fourteenth-century, partly of fourteenth/fifteenth-century date. Perhaps already present when the manual was bound (or rebound), or perhaps added soon after, in a crude hand, on six blank leaves of the last quire of the original book, are the masses for St David, for the Dedication of a Church and for Candlemas (fols 102–8).

In its description of P.iii.4, the recent catalogue of the Hereford Cathedral manuscripts makes some new points.[27] Firstly, that Saint Osburga in the litany provides a firm link with Coventry. This does not however bear on our present concerns: the litany is in the added section at the end of the manual, of different origin. Secondly, that there is a reference on the end flyleaf (fol. 120v, one of the fragmentary court rolls) to John the vicar of 'Laneygan', for which identification with Llanigon, near Hay, is suggested. The identification is doubtless correct: Llanigon was in the Welshry of the lordship of Hay. Then, on fol. 120, written before use of the fragment as a pastedown, in a fifteenth-century hand, is the draft of the opening

---

[26] Thomas, 'A lost manuscript'. See comment by Edwards, *Matins*, 141–2.
[27] Mynors and Thomson, *Descriptive Catalogue*.

of the will of one Thomas ab Ieuan who desired to be buried 'in ecclesia beate Marie et sancti Kined[ ]'. The dedication is probably that of Llangynidr, also known as 'Eglwys Fair a Chynidr'; Aberysgir and Llan-y-wern, churches originally dedicated to Cynidr, later, like Llangynidr, having joint dedications, are unlikelier possibilities. On the same page, not noted in the catalogue, in poor early-sixteenth-century script, is a note of the debts, both in kind and in money, of one David John: among them is that of a sow to *Lewys ap Rychert lantheuayloc tre yr grayge*. Hay, Llanigon, Crickadarn, Llangynidr and now Llandyfaelog Tre'rgraig. We are drawn into a triangle to the east of Brecon, its sides no more than 15 miles long, whose corners are at Crickadarn, Hay and Llangynidr. Somewhere here, in the archdeaconry of Brecon, the Hereford manual evidently spent the last hundred years or so of its working life, serving among other things for the celebration of the feast-day of the patron of the diocese. It no doubt survived the destructive early years of Protestantism in the hands of someone of complicit or tacit recusant sympathy.

NLW 20541E

It is simplest to trace the history of the Penpont Antiphonal backwards. The numerous marginal notes and scribbles cease around the year 1600. Thereafter there is nothing to reveal its history until 1969. Its good condition shows that it was kept dry, protected from dirt, perhaps not even an object of curiosity. It was a sleeper. Knowing that the Williams family was at Abercamlais and Penpont during all these years, that the family was a markedly clerical one (descended from Thomas Williams of Abercamlais, vicar of Llansbyddyd from 1572, who died in 1613), and having regard to the sixteenth-century inscriptions, there is every reason to guess that for over three hundred years it was a sleeper at Penpont.[28] Let us look at some of the inscribed names (all given in Appendix 2), and first, those associated with named places, all of them dating from the middle or later years of the sixteenth century. Three names are of persons from Talgarth, one from Tal-y-llyn, and one, John Wylyam, is named 'organ player of Tal[ ]'. Several other names may be associated with Talgarth. Roland Hughes (with his inkling of Greek in 'Hugonides') is probably the vicar of Talgarth of that name who resigned in 1560 (which suggests that he was an adherent of Rome, and a person likely to have preserved the antiphonal from destruction); his successor was William Thomas, vicar from 1560 to 1583, a good Protestant no doubt, but a tolerant one, if he is the William Thomas whose name is inscribed twice (in script less educated than one would expect of a vicar);[29] William Goch is probably the William Goch, gentleman, who by grant of the patron presented William Prosser as vicar in 1583;[30] Gunter and Prosser were prominent Talgarth families. On fol. 119 in a hand probably earlier than 1550 is a draft opening of a letter addressed to 'Master William Wachan'. Could he be Sir William Vaughan of Porthaml, Talgarth (who died not later than 1553)? Another possible candidate is

---

28 For a pedigree of the family and some particulars, see Jones, *A History*, IV.149–51, and IV.165–6. Blanch, the first wife of Daniel Williams, builder of Penpont, was a daughter of Hoo Games of Newton (d. 1657) whose family had been at the heart of Breconshire affairs during Elizabethan times. Blanch after the death of her brother John in 1675 was one of four co-heiresses of the Games property. A number of portraits in the Penpont sale were of likely Newton provenance.

29 For the appointment of William Thomas on the resignation of Roland Hughes, see NLW, St Davids Diocesan Records, BR/ 2, p. 34.

30 Theophilus Jones, *A History*, III.57

William Vaughan, a canon of St Davids, *fl.* 1512–39. Names which, to judge by their script, might be a little later, include John Dillwyn of Brecon (the Dillwyn family was from the parish of Llan-gors) and the alien-sounding William Bowringe, who could write a good italic hand and quote Plato in English. Something of the ambience of a school is suggested by scraps of Greek and of Latin grammar which occur in a few margins (e.g., fols 101, 112v, 115v, 144v); and could Bowringe have been a writing-master? In these years after the Reformation, we find ourselves, by an odd chance, in the same triangle as that to which the Hereford manual led us, and close to Penpont, three miles to the west of Brecon.

One of the earlier names inscribed in the manuscript is that of Geoffrey Thomas, *clericus*, who might be Master Geoffrey Thomas, *fl.* 1486–1512, for some of these years perpetual vicar of St John the Evangelist, Brecon.[31] Another Geoffrey ap Thomas of the same parish was ordained deacon by the bishop of Hereford in 1521. The antiphonal appears therefore to have been in the Brecon area, perhaps in Brecon itself, by about 1500. It was still in liturgical use in the sixteenth century, witness, for example, the hand of the marginal notes on fols 131v and 132. But there was a century and a half or so of history before 1500.

The Penpont antiphonal does not have the ostentation of illumination, but it is thoroughly professional work. The script is excellent (that of the psalter less so) and the distinctive penwork decoration of initials is of high quality. This decoration may well lead some future researcher studying the decoration of fourteenth-century manuscripts to identify its place of production. Again, perhaps, Oxford or London. But surely, one might ask, there must be other liturgical pointers, apart from St David. They are disappointingly few. One is another full but irregular office (irregular in Sarum terms): that of St Leonard. The staves were drawn, but for this additional office, unlike that for St David, the necessary musical notation was evidently not to hand. The staves were left blank. A second indicator is a memorial for St Ethelbert, no office, merely a memorial. Thirdly, in one of the two litanies there is (though there is no St David) a mysterious saint 'Sustinian'. Owain Edwards proposed an answer to this puzzle: we have here a miscopied 'Justinian', associate of David, whose relics were also at St Davids and whose dedications are in the vicinity.[32] Justinian occurs in several St Davids's calendars. Lastly, there is the addition by a fifteenth-century hand on fol. 283 of a memorial for St Winifred which could, but by this date need not, be taken as evidence of Welshness.

So we come to face the question: for which church was the antiphonal written? Who would have commissioned an antiphonal with these particular features? The calendar, alas, is gone. Before concluding that the Proper for St David necessarily indicates the diocese of St Davids, we need to eliminate Exeter and Hereford, two dioceses which adopted the cult of St David early, earlier it appears than the other Welsh dioceses. Of Exeter it can be said that there are no other indicators. Of Hereford, that the only indicator is the memorial for St Ethelbert; there is no full proper for the patron saint, no Dedication, no feast of St Thomas of Hereford. But the memorial for St Ethelbert alerts us to looking for some sort of Hereford connection. The diocese of St Davids, the obvious option, appears to have the best claim, unambiguously so if we accept Edwards's emendation of 'Sustinian'. And we must account for St Leonard. The cult of St Leonard was widespread in England, with

[31] *Episcopal Registers of St David's*, ed. Isaacson – see index *s.n.* Geoffrey ap Thomas, Geoffrey Thomas.
[32] Edwards, *Matins*, 27.

over 170 dedications, many of them associated with the Benedictines, especially numerous in Yorkshire and in the west Midlands of England.[33] But Leonard did not find a place in the Sarum calendar. In the Hereford Breviary his office is given nine lections. In Wales, he had only one dedication, a chapel in Spittal, Pembrokeshire, hardly a destination for an antiphonal.

To this discordant set of clues we must add one more. On fol. 161, in a fifteenth-century hand, is the teasing inscription 'of yᵉ freres Augustyns [   ] / *aut quid aut venio*'. To the person who wrote it, to anyone he expected to read it, the inscription implies a knowingness about the Austin friars; they impinged in some way on the lives of the keepers of the antiphonal. The only house of Austin friars in Wales was in Newport, Gwent.

To conclude, a suggestion (other equally speculative ones might perhaps be conjured up).[34] Could the original *destinaire* have been a bishop of St Davids, the antiphonal intended for use by his clergy when he was at Ludlow? The quality of production is worthy of a bishop; the Proper for St David would have been the one necessary addition to the basic Sarum model; Ludlow, the seat of the Council in the Marches, was an important town in Welsh public life, not only to members of the Council (we have record of attendance by bishops of St Davids in 1398, 1483, 1493);[35] Ludlow was in the diocese of Hereford; there was in Ludlow a chapel of St Leonard (maintained by the Hospitallers at Dinmore);[36] and there was in Ludlow an Augustinian friary. From Ludlow to Brecon was no great step.

Appendix 1

Welsh dioceses: Liturgical manuscripts and calendars

The manuscripts listed are those which provide evidence of liturgical observation of saints' feast-days within dioceses. Manuscripts marked by asterisks are secular manuscripts with graded calendars, calendars probably never intended for liturgical or even religious use.

St Davids

NLW 20541E. Sarum Antiphonal (Penpont Antiphonal). s.xiv med.
> Proper of the office of St David. See O.T. Edwards *Matins, Lauds and Vespers* and O.T. Edwards, *National Library of Wales MS. 20541E*

Hereford Cathedral P.iii. 4. Sarum Manual. s.xv¹.
> Proper of mass of St David added. Printed in Harris, *Saint David in the Liturgy*. Crickadarn.

Cambridge, Trinity College B.10.13 (224). NT, *sermones*. s.xiii. Hasguard.
> Added in calendar, s.xv–xvi: David, Dedication of St Davids and Dedication of Hasguard.

---

33 Arnold-Foster, *Studies*, 111–13.
34 For other suggestions, see Harper, *Music in Welsh Culture*, 217–26, where the presence of an office of St Leonard is given its full due.
35 Isaacson (ed.), *Episcopal Registers of St. David's 1397–1518*, see index.
36 *VCH, A History of Shropshire*, II.93.

BL, Add. 22720. *Horae.* s.xv.

In calendar: David (red), Non, Dedication of Haroldston. Added: Teilo, 'Gistilianus', Ciaran, Rhian, Patrick.

NLW, printed Sarum Missal (1531). Llanbadarn Fawr.

Manuscript additions in calendar: 'Vestilianus', Non, Ciaran, Rhian, Caradog, Padarn (also, his Translation). See Harris, 'A Llanbadarn Fawr calendar'.

Bodley, Laud 667. Sarum *Ordinale.* s.xv. St Johns priory, Brecon.

In Calendar: David (red, ix l', 'dup' added), Non.

Dublin, Trinity College 783. Extracts made by Ussher in 1645–6 from the lost MS of Thomas Saint, archdeacon of St Davids, 1500×1513.

Hymn to David; lections for Teilo; Lives of David, Non, Justinian, Teilo, Caradog. See G.C.G. Thomas, 'A lost manuscript'.

*BL, Add. 14912. Medicine, in Welsh. s.xiv/xv

In calendar: David, Curig (red); Padarn.

*NLW, Wynnstay 36. Welsh law. s.xv[1]

In calendar: David, Non, Teilo (red); Caron, Curig, Cewydd.

*NLW, Peniarth 40. Welsh law. *ca* 1480

In calendar: David, Teilo (red); Ilar, Ffraid, Curig and Julita, Cewydd.

Llandaf

NLW 17110E. *Liber Landavensis.*

Vitae of SS Teilo, Dyfrig, Euddogwy, s.xii. Divided into lections for Teilo (s.xii–xv), for Dyfrig and Euddogwy (s.xv only). See Huws, *Medieval Welsh Manuscripts*, p. 152.

*Paris, Bibliothèque Nationale, N. a. line 693. Astrology, etc. s.xiii/xiv

In calendar: Teilo (red); David. See Avril and Stirnemann, *Manuscrits enluminés, s.n.*

Bodley, Hatton 106. Psalter. s.xiv[2].

In calendar: Teilo (red). In litany: Teilo, Dyfrig, Euddogwy.

Oxford, All Souls 11. Sarum Missal. *ca* 1490. Tregaer (Tregare).

Sarum calendar includes David, Chad, etc. Added: Dedication of Tregaer, Translation of Teilo, Dyfrig and Euddogwy on 4 October, Derfel (his chapel nearby in Llanfihangel Llantarnam). See Watson, *Descriptive Catalogue.*

Bangor

For St Deiniol, see Harris, 'Liturgical commemorations: I'. The Bangor Pontifical, produced in England and not adapted for local use, is irrelevant.

NLW, printed Sarum Missal (1494). Conwy.

Added in calendar: Deiniol. Added on flyleaves: Proper for Deiniol and Dwynwen. See Huws, *Medieval Welsh Manuscripts*, pp. 269–86.

NLW 17520. *Horae* (Llanbeblig Hours). s.xiv/xv. Llanbeblig.

In calendar: David, Deiniol, Peblig and Dedication of St Peblig (red). In litany: Dwynwen. See Huws, *Medieval Welsh Manuscripts*, p. 278.

Stonyhurst College 61. *Horae* (fragmentary). s.xv. Llanbeblig.

In calendar: Deiniol, Peblig (red), Beuno. In litany: Dwynwen and many other north Wales saints. Memorial for Peblig. See Ker, *Medieval Manuscripts*, IV, pp. 449–51; Huws, *Medieval Welsh Manuscripts*, p. 278.

NLW, Peniarth 225. Miscellanea of Thomas Wiliems.

Includes the only known text of 9 lections for St Deiniol. Printed in Harris, 'Liturgical commemorations: I'.

St Asaph

St Asaf is absent from the liturgy and from all Welsh calendars before s.xvi[2]; only after his promotion in Scotland, after 1500, did his cult become widely recognised. See Harris, 'Liturgical commemorations: II'.

NLW, Peniarth 191. *Gwasanaeth Mair* (Hours of BVM in Welsh), etc. s.xv med. Pennant Melangell.
    In calendar (incomplete): David, Melangell (red), Teilo (blue), Non, Caron, Padarn, Mael and Sulien. See Huws, 'Llyfr Melangell', 23–4.

NLW, Peniarth 356. Latin grammar, etc, written *ca* 1470 by Thomas Pennant, later abbot of Basingwerk. See D. Thomson, *Descriptive Catalogue*, pp. 114–31.
    Includes (fol. 61r–v) sequence and collect for St David.

*Oxford, Jesus 22. Medicine, in Welsh. s.xv[2]
    Calendar: Gwenfrewi (red).

*NLW 3026 (Mostyn 88). Medicine, etc. Written by Gutun Owain. 1488–9.
    Calendar: many local Welsh saints, none in red (see M.E. Owen, 'Prolegomena i astudiaeth').

*Peniarth 27i. Calendar. Written by Gutun Owain. Similar to NLW 3026.

*Peniarth 186. Calendar. Written by Gutun Owain. Similar to NLW 3026.

*Oxford, Jesus 141. Historical texts. Written by Gutun Owain. 1499.
    Calendar: many local Welsh saints, none in red.

*BL, Add. 12193. *Fasciculus temporum*, in Welsh. 1508.
    Calendar: David, Erbin, Cynbryd, Curig, Gwenfrewi (red). Many other local saints.

*Llanstephan 117. Miscellany, religious and secular. 1542–54. Ruabon.
    Calendar: David (red). Many local Welsh saints.

Unlocated

BL, Cotton Vesp. A xiv. *Vitae*, etc. s.xii/xiii. ?Monmouth priory (but not diocesan). Antiquarian rather than liturgical in purpose. Relevant to St Davids and Llandaf. See Harris, 'The Kalendar', and K. Hughes, *Celtic Britain*, pp. 53–66.

St Asaph Cathedral. Sarum sequentiary/hymnal. s.xv.
    Includes the sequence for St David.

Appendix 2

Names inscribed in the Penpont Antiphonal

(All sixteenth-century in date unless otherwise indicated.)

'Powell / ap John ap Thomas' (fol. 2)
Roland Hughes ('Rolande Hugonides [ ]ster de swyf de Lester', fol. 2)
Wyllyam Gozt [Goch] (fol. 24v, 'Thys ys Wyllyam Gozthe booke and Ryhard ap Holl', fols 129v, 130)
John ap Thomas (fol. 72v)
John Dillwyn 'de villa Brecon' (fol. 114)
Jhon ap W (fol. 117)
Wyllyam ap John (fol 117v)

Wyllyam Wachan (fol. 119: 'Master Wyllm' Wachan I becheke yow ...', fol. 176v, Wyllyam Wachan)

Willyam ap Thomas (fol. 126 and fol. 186v, Wyllyam Thomas)

William Bowringe (fol. 127v, displaying his three scripts: writing an English couplet in secretary, a quotation, in English, from Plato, in italic, his name in textura; his hand also on fol. 142)

Ryhard ap Ho[we]ll (fol. 129v)

John Wylyam 'organ player off Tall[ ]' (fol. 135v)

Gwenllian verch Tomas (fol. 165) (date s.xv/xvi)

[ ] Watkin 'de Talgarth' (fol. 172, note of a bond to Watkyn [ ] Thomas 'de Talellyn')

William Watkyn (fol. 185v, 'iste liber pertinet ad me Willm Watkyn')

Galfridus Thomas, clericus (fol. 224, 'per me Galfridum Thomam clericum')

Meredith Prosser (fols 226v, 270v, 271)

John Thomas Gunter, Watkyn Thomas Vaghan, Res Thom[ ] (fol. 247)

Thomas ap John (Thomas ap John ys the tru yonor of this boke', fol. 252)

Thomas ap Hoel Res 'deTalgarth', yeoman (fol. 258, note of a bond to Ris Thomas ap Res 'de Talgarth')

Jenkyn Davys (fol. 301)

12

THE OFFICE OF ST DAVID IN PARIS, BIBLIOTHÈQUE NATIONALE, MS LAT. 17294

Owain Tudor Edwards

Bibliothèque nationale, Paris, shelf mark MS lat. 17294 is a remarkably beautiful book. It is an early fifteenth-century breviary, and it happens to contain liturgical material for the celebration of St David's Day. The most obvious characteristic of the book is that it is richly decorated on every folio. Art historians have naturally examined it and Victor Leroquais and Eleanor Spencer have written about it, but other than that it has been recognized as being of Sarum use, its liturgical features continue to require further investigation.[1] As observance of the feast of St David on 1 March was made obligatory in the province of Canterbury in 1398, service books of British origin produced after this time normally contain a reference in the *Kalendar* along with instructions in the *Sanctorale* as to how it was to be celebrated. This particular breviary being no exception, it became one of many witnesses to St David's Day celebrations during the period of a hundred and forty-five years before King Henry VIII's injunction suppressing the worship of non-scriptural saints.[2]

My aim in this essay is to draw attention to the Parisian source and to make observations on noteworthy features. Matters that arise in this kind of investigation will be touched upon, in order to be able to view the manuscript in context. These include referring to material for celebrating St David in a typical book of hours, regulations for the feast of St David, in particular with regard to the matter of *ruling*, and I refer to statutes concerning liturgical books in general. Let us turn first to service books.

Liturgical material for mass and the divine office tended, especially from the thirteenth century, to be provided in separate books, for economic reasons.[3] Medieval service books were produced to meet the specific needs of the people performing different functions. The bishop, for example, had his own pontifical containing the texts and chants he had to perform in the few services in which he had an essential role. The deacon might only have the texts that it was his task to read from his gospel-book, while the subdeacon had his own set of texts in his epistle-book. The

---

1 Leroquais, *Les bréviaires*, iii, 271–348; Spenser, 'The master', 607–12.
2 *Concilia magnae Britannicae et Hiberniae*, ed. Wilkins, III, 863. Thomas Cranmer, primate of England and Wales, presented his bishops in Convocation in 1543 with the injunction that, 'all mass books, antiphoners, portuises in the Church of England, should be newly examined, corrected, reformed and castigated from all manner of mention of the bishop of Rome's name, from all apocryphas, feigned legends, superstitious orations, collects, versicles, and responses; that the names and memories of all saints, which be not mentioned in the Scripture, or authentical doctors, should be abolished and put out of the same books and calendars; and that the services should be made out of the Scriptures, and other authentic doctors'.
3 Hughes, *Medieval Manuscripts for Mass and Office*, is a helpful survey of the kinds of service books that were compiled during the middle ages.

celebrant had the texts he would chant at mass in his sacramentary and missal while the choir had the music in the gradual and possibly also in a troper. The texts and rubrics of the divine office were in the collectar, lectionary and breviary while the chants to be sung were in the antiphonal or antiphoner. Noted missals and noted breviaries were produced, but the musical notation and literary texts of these books, in more cases than not, were not mixed. When they were, it might be evidence of affluence, or of a desire to obtain as high a degree of accuracy in the regulation of services as possible.[4] Instructions as to who was to do what, when, where and how in the conduct of mass and office were in the ordinal, and in the consuetudinary or customary of the prevailing rite. A short version of these came in the rubrics in the *Temporale* in both missal and breviary in connection with the first Sunday of Advent. Other regulations were given at the beginning of the Psalter. Common practices might not be referred to at all, being taken for granted, with the result that it is not easy to obtain an impression of how services were conducted. If one were to prepare a performance of the medieval liturgy today an intimate familiarity with the execution of *all* the elements concerned would be required, along with intuition and a certain adventurousness of spirit. The educational theoretician John Dewey's expression, 'learning by doing', might be apt in this context![5]

It need hardly be said that medieval service books were costly treasures. Music books were especially so, because they were often large-sized, which meant that a sheep had to be expended for each bifolium of parchment.[6] Service books were not normally provided for lay people attending church in the middle ages. They would have been of little practical use to the greater proportion of lay churchgoers. Especially outside large towns, most people were illiterate. Literacy was not, however, necessarily associated with the richest people, but initially with clerics and, later, the merchant classes.[7] As late as 1547, a law was passed (I Ed. VI, c. 12 § 14), by which peers of the English parliament were granted a privilege equivalent to benefit of clergy, 'although they cannot read'.[8]

One particular kind of book may even have derived some of its popularity from its appeal to illiterate readers. Books of hours were traditionally illustrated with miniatures representing biblical situations and scenes from the life of saints. The central and original text was a shortened version of the Office of the Blessed Virgin, provided as an instrument of piety for lay people to use in private contemplation, in imitation of the life of prayer of the religious.[9] Gradually, from the tenth century, books of hours increased in scope to include, amongst other items, selected offices

---

4   As exhibited, notably, in the service books of the Dominicans, for example. For the background to this tradition, see Bonniwell, *A History*.
5   Dewey rejected the tenet that knowledge was something a teacher simply could pass on to the pupil. He argued that it was acquired through the pupil's experiencing relevant activity: the educational process had two sides, one psychological and one sociological, neither of which should be neglected. The child's upbringing, including the acquisition of knowledge, provided a continual reconstruction of the child's view of the world in the light of experience. (Dewey: *Democracy and Education*; *Education Today*; *Art as Experience*.)
6   Since some leaves of manuscripts appear to be rougher or more easily recognizable as the outside of a skin than others, one might assume that medieval tanners had found a way of splitting hides to produce two bifolia from each sheep. I am indebted to Dr Patricia Stirnemann, Institut de recherche et d'histoire des textes, Paris, however, for kindly ascertaining that the technique of splitting larger skins was not apparently developed until the nineteenth century. See Bat-Yehouda and Sirat, 'La description', 333–53.
7   Ackerman, *Backgrounds*, 35ff.
8   Feilden, *A Short Constitutional History*, 82.
9   Brown, *Understanding Illuminated Manuscripts*, 23–4.

and memorials of saints in the form of an antiphon text and a collect. These richly illustrated books were very popular from the thirteenth century to the Reformation, particularly in France and Flanders. British saints feature in some of them. As an example of a memorial in a book of hours, here is a transcription of the material given for St David in London, BL MS Add. 54, 782. St David is depicted as a royal saint, in reference either to his descent from King Sant of Ceredigion or his supposed connexion with King Arthur.[10]

> *Antiphona*: Iste est qui ante deum magnas uirtutes operatus est et omnis terra doctrina eius repleta est. Ipse intercedat pro peccatis omnium populorum.[11]
>
> *Versiculus*: Ora pro nobis sancte Dauid. *Responsio*: Ut digni efficiamur promissionibus Christi.
>
> *Oratio*: Deus qui beatum Dauid confessorem tuum atque pontificem angelo nunciante triginta annis antequem nasceretur predixisti concede quesumus, ut eius festiuitatem colimus eius intercessione ad eterna gaudia perueniamus per Christum dominum nostrum. Amen.[12]

There is a common misconception that books were very rare objects in medieval times. Perhaps, it would be more accurate to say that not many people have any conception at all as to the number of books to be found. There were fewer by far than today, certainly, but the impression, based on the number of medieval service books surviving, that there were very few, is not right. It cannot be. British episcopal statutes repeatedly insist that churches were required to have the appropriate service books. The Church provided intricate details about how services were to be carried out. They were not improvised. It might reasonably be asked whether chant books were compulsory for parish churches, or whether they were only required in the largest cathedral and collegiate foundations where a choir of men and boys performed the services? The answer is clearly in the affirmative. All churches were supposed to have the appropriate books 'for singing and reading'.[13] This was because all services, even in parish churches, should ideally be sung. Everything, including prayers and lessons, was sung to one or other of a number of forms of Gregorian chant. After the very influential *Canons of Oxford* (1222) had been circulated, the matter of books and church ornaments was being given serious attention throughout England and Wales. Parish priests could be confronted with the long arm of ecclesiastical law in the person of the diocesan archdeacons who 'visited' or inspected their churches to check that regulations were carried out correctly.[14]

Some of the omissions reported after churches had been inspected are revealing in so far as they indicate times of economic decline. At the end of the thirteenth century, for example, a prior of Brecon, who was accused of allowing books from the library to remain in pawn with the Jews, denied the charge, although he admitted

---

10 The manuscript is reproduced in *The Hastings Hours*, ed. Turner. The material under discussion is at 39–40.

11 This antiphon – no music is provided in the manuscript – is the antiphon to the Magnificat at Second Vespers of a confessor in the Common of Saints. See the modern edition of the medieval Sarum Breviary, *Breviarium ad usum insignis ecclesiae Sarum*, ed. Procter and Wordsworth, ii, 422.

12 See Harris, *Saint David in the Liturgy*, 13–14, and Edwards, *Matins, Lauds*, 115–16.

13 *Ad hec precipimus ut quelibet ecclesia habeat ... libros ad psallendum et legendum ydoneos ...* (ed. Powicke and Cheney, *Councils*, 29 § 18).

14 The archdeacon's rounds will have been carried out on the lines described by Bishop Peter Quinel of Exeter's statutes of 1287, *de visitationibus et procurationibus archidiaconorum et modo visitandi* (ed. Powicke and Cheney, *Councils*, 1034 § 40).

that a burgess of Ludlow had them in safe keeping for the use of the house. In 1401, Carmarthen Priory was found to have loaned out many of its essential books, the monastery Bible included.[15]

Clergy were admonished to see to it that their churches were *decenter ornate tam in libris quam in sacris vasis et vestimentis*. In many mid-thirteenth century episcopal statutes, this phrase reoccurs and the proper books were specified as *missale, breviarium, antiphonarium, gradale, tropharium, ordinale, et psalterium*.[16] In larger churches, these were supposed to be duplicated. The stipulation reminds us that choir and clergy performing services at night during winter will of necessity have had to commit the liturgy to memory.[17] It is quite possible that in a poor church the vicar only had a missal and a breviary. He could have loaned the other books if he heard that the archdeacon was going to come on an inspection, but he would probably have been found out sooner or later and forced to comply with the regulations. These appear to have been strictly carried out, to judge by the number of shortcomings reported.

In an attempt at estimating the number of Sarum antiphonals that would have existed in England and Wales on the eve of the Reformation, I calculated a figure in excess of twenty thousand.[18] Many missals and breviaries were smaller than choir books. They were of a convenient size to fit into a pouch or a pocket. Others, but fewer, were larger being intended for reading at the lectern. Special skills in music notation were not required in their production. They will have been cheaper and more readily available than antiphonals and graduals. The number of Sarum breviaries, therefore, may reasonably have been higher than that of the antiphonals in use before the destruction of Latin service books began in 1550.[19] The total was arguably well over thirty thousand. It is against this background we shall shortly turn to a particular breviary in the Bibliothèque nationale, Paris. Before that, however, a word of explanation about what I have referred to as 'Sarum use' is advisable.

Before the *Book of Common Prayer* was introduced in 1549 and enforced by the Act of Uniformity, no single order of service had been followed in England and Wales. In Britain as on the Continent, regional variants of a common Roman rite existed side by side. Local traditions governed the choice of saints included in the annual cycle of feasts, the names and order of the saints invoked in the Litany, as well as detailed matters like the selection of texts and chants for all the services. Episcopal statutes show how bishops attempted to achieve a degree of uniformity in their dioceses, and it might be expected that archbishops tried to do the same. This was certainly the motive behind the publication of the only printed edition in 1519 of the breviary for the Norwegian province of Nidaros, according to Archbishop Erik Valkendorf's foreword to the publication.[20] A desire for national uniformity is similarly expressed in the colophon, *pars estiualis*, of Bishop William Elphinstone's

---

[15] Cowley, *The Monastic Order*, 146.

[16] At Lincoln in 1239, Norwich (1240–43), Winchester (1247), Ely (1239–56), London (1249–59), and other places subsequently (ed. Powicke and Cheney, *Councils*, 273 § 34, 351 §36, 410 § 47, 519 § 22 and 647 § 62).

[17] Ed. Powicke and Cheney, *Councils*, 599 § 15.

[18] Edwards, 'How many Sarum antiphonals', 155–80.

[19] The injunction was signed on Christmas Day 1549 so there was hardly time to begin the destruction before the New Year.

[20] Edwards, 'Musical source material', 59–83. For the facsimile edition of the Nidaros breviary see, *Breuiaria ad usum ritumque sacrosanctem Nidrosiensem*. The content is discussed in, *Ordo Nidrosiensis Ecclesiae*, ed. Lilli Gjerløw, and *Antifonarium Nidrosiensis ecclesiae*, ed. Gjerløw, *passim*.

adaptation of the Sarum breviary for Scotland that was printed in 1509–10 ... *non solum ad ecclesie sue Abirdonensis verumetiam ad totius ecclesie scoticane usum percelebrem.*[21]

Then as now, the primate of England's see was Canterbury. However advantageous such uniformity might have been considered in England, it was simply not possible – nor likely to be achieved, considering the deeply entrenched independence of spirit of archbishops of York.[22] The archbishop of Canterbury's cathedral, Christ Church, was in a monastery, however, so it could not provide a norm for the daily services of the office in non-monastic churches – cathedrals, collegiate foundations and parish churches, whose services were in general shorter than monastic services. In Britain, by the late middle ages, the most highly respected services of the international Latin liturgy were performed in accordance with regulations laid down at Salisbury. Clergy found that the Salisbury Cathedral Ordinal provided solutions to most liturgical problems, and the 'use of Sarum,' as it was known, came to have a standardizing influence.[23] One of the natural consequences of its widespread popularity was that when additions were made to the Sarum *Kalendar*, these were copied into new books and disseminated, while old books were amended as required with additions written into margins.

The feast of St David will have been commemorated locally, in all probability since the seventh century. Irish and English references to the feast indicate liturgical observance, but as the records are very incomplete, especially in pre-Conquest times, the form this took is not known. The significance of the Sarum connexion was that because of it, the feast came to be celebrated throughout England and Wales, as well as in those parts of Scotland and Ireland that had adopted Sarum use.[24] The proper office of St David, which is arguably a thirteenth-century composition, confirms that it will have been celebrated as a feast of the highest grade in churches dedicated to St David in the diocese of St Davids itself.[25] It was one of the eight occasions classed as Principal Double feasts: Christmas, Epiphany, Easter, Ascension Day, Whitsunday, the Assumption of the Blessed Virgin Mary, the feast of the patron saint, and the feast commemorating the dedication of the church.[26]

Given enough local veneration, it is possible that St David's Day was also celebrated as a *Festum duplex principale* in churches dedicated to St David in the other Welsh dioceses, as well as in the nearby dioceses of Hereford and Exeter, from which

---

21 The Aberdeen Breviary, *Breuiarij Aberdonensis*, ed. Blew.

22 Welsh tradition maintained that St Davids was also an archbishopric, as asserted by Rhygyfarch who relates that when David and his companions Teilo and Padarn were visiting the patriarch in Jerusalem: *Deinde diuina fultus electione, ad archiepiscopatum Dauid agium prouehit: Vita S. Dauid* § 46 (ed. Sharpe and Davies, above, 140–1).

23 An extensive literature on the Sarum use is given in Sandon, 'Salisbury ['Sarum'], use of', 158–63. The central work is Frere, *The Use of Sarum*.

24 In 1172, a council of the Irish bishops summoned by Henry II decreed that the liturgical use of England was to be observed in Ireland. Harrison takes this to mean Sarum use (Harrison, *Music in Medieval Britain*, 16). In the preface to the breviary of Aberdeen referred to in note 21 above, David Laing gives evidence showing that some of the Scottish dioceses also adopted Sarum use in the twelfth century (*Pars estiualis*, viii–xx).

25 Edwards, *Matins, Lauds*, ch. v.

26 For the Sarum classification of feasts, see *Breviarium ad usum insignis ecclesiae Sarum* (ed. Procter and Wordsworth, iii, p. xli). According to the *Kalendar* of St Davids in a manuscript in Cambridge, Trinity College Library (MS 224, [B. 10. 13]), the dedication of the cathedral appears to have been 15 June. The entry of *Kal. Ded. ecclesie Meneu.* begins by the date *17 Kal.* but continues by *16 Kal.*

early evidence exists of devotion to the saint.[27] The initiative for celebrating the feast as more than a purely local solemnity came with Archbishop Roger Walden's decree of 1398.[28] The feast was to be observed throughout the province of Canterbury on 1 March, with nine lessons, and the rest according to the Common of Saints. This meant that the longest of the continuous series of services comprising the divine office, the night service of matins, was to follow the longer of two possible structures. One consisted of a single nocturn, while the other had three. In non-monastic services, each nocturn included three lessons. Many feasts were celebrated with matins of a single nocturn of three lessons, the same order of service as in matins on a non-festal weekday. A greater number of feasts, however, had three nocturns, as in liturgical matters length was often a means of emphasizing solemnity. Because of Archbishop Walden's directive, the matins of St David was to have nine lessons and, consequently, a responsory following each of these, as well as nine antiphons with psalms, and everything else which was to be included in matins according to the conventions adhered to by churches following Sarum use. The instruction meant that everything for the celebration of the feast was to be taken from the Common, not only the material for matins, but also for the other services during the day. The cycle of services began the evening before with first vespers, and continued through to second vespers on the evening of the day itself.

The mandate that there should be nine lessons made the form matins would take clear enough to any clergyman. Both the texts and chants to be sung for the various items were those of the Common of Saints for the class of saint of which David was a representative, namely a confessor bishop. The instruction frequently occurs in the ordinal for the precentor to look in the Common of Saints for all the remaining liturgical material for the performance of services (*et caeteris omnibus ad officium sanctorum*). While some saints were celebrated with proper offices, others were treated to a more general appreciation of their sanctity with set texts and chants from the Common, their names being substituted for N. in the collect. As they were repeated from time to time, these chants from the Common of Saints will have become particularly familiar with the clergy and vicars choral who performed the canonical hours.[29] The performance of the lessons, the responsories, antiphons and hymns on St David's Day will thus have been enriched by connotations with similar celebrations for a number of other saints.

The extent to which clergy throughout Britain followed the decree to include the feast of St David in their annual cycle of liturgical events is unknown. The new directive in 1415, following the translation of Bishop Henry Chichele of St Davids to the archbishopric of Canterbury the previous year, might have been a measure in an attempt to ensure that the observance was actually carried out. On the other hand, it might also have arisen from a desire to classify the feast more precisely. Chichele, or his bishops in Convocation, felt the need to define the solemnity more specifically than Walden had done, although in practice there will have been no difference in the manner in which the commemorative services were carried out in most churches.

---

[27] On the churches dedicated to St David, of which there were forty-two in the diocese of St Davids alone, see Baring-Gould and Fisher, *The Lives*, II.316–22.

[28] *Concilia magnae Britannicae et Hiberniae*, ed. Wilkins, III.234: *cum ix lectionibus, et caeteris omnibus ad officium sanctorum.*

[29] For aspects of musical symbolism, specifically associations derived from repetition with particular reference to the Office of St David, see the present author's, 'Musical symbolism', 271–90.

The new prescription was *cum regimine chori*.[30] This term recurs frequently in the Sarum ordinal, particularly in connexion with feasts classed as Simples of Nine Lessons, the classification St David's has. The canons of Salisbury regulated their services in detail, and their classification of solemnities is treated with great thoroughness.[31] As the regulation *cum regimine chori* is not self-evident, a word clarifying the matter of 'ruling' may be timely. The alert listener in the middle ages might have heard distinctions between different kinds of services because of the ruling. He or she may also have *seen* differences. The result was partly a practical detail, partly a visual one. The visual aspect would not have been apparent in all cathedrals. It depended on how much of a view the people in the nave had of what took place in the choir. On the other hand, it would, of course, have made a difference for the clergy and singing men who were performing the service as much for their own benefit as for any possible onlookers.

The canons of non-monastic cathedral foundations were priests from whose number the senior dignitaries who had responsibility for the daily running of the cathedral services were chosen. Apart from the dignitaries whose duties compelled them to reside permanently close to the cathedral, the dean, precentor, chancellor and treasurer, the canons also had care of parish churches elsewhere, from which they received part of their income.[32] Cathedrals worked out various systems whereby they ensured that there would always be enough canons in residence to be able to carry out their main task, the continuous daily round of worship. Each canon paid a deputy[33] to carry out his duties in his own church, and another deputy to sing for him in the cathedral choir. Deputies were permanent; the intention being that the choir should always up to strength. On special feasts, most of the canons also attended the cathedral, and the total number of clergy and vicars choral increased. For the congregation, the appearance of a long procession of men and boys in their vestments going up to the choir stalls was in itself a means of confirming the significance of the occasion.

The responsibility for organising the performance of the liturgy in each of the secular cathedrals, a task which in the middle ages was synonymous with leading the choir in the music and singing certain solo parts himself, had to be undertaken by a man of musical ability. This was the precentor, but he could delegate responsibility for 'ruling' the choir. Every canon in residence had to take his turn as the 'hebdomadary canon', or canon of the week, when he ministered as celebrant at the high altar, apart from on the most important feasts when the dean or otherwise most senior dignitary did so. The precentor also appointed two canons as rulers of the choir for a fortnight at a time. They sat on either side of the aisle and led their side of the choir, the clergy and choristers on the south side, on which the dean sat, being known as *decani,* while those on the precentor's side were *cantoris.* As principal ruler, or *rector*, the canon or possibly his vicar choral, began a number of the chants by giving the note or singing the opening phrase. On feasts of nine lessons, both of

---

30 *Concilia magnae Britannicae et Hiberniae*, ed. Wilkins, III.376: *cum regimine chori et ix lectionibus perpetuis futuris temporibus etiam celebrentur* ('It shall be celebrated with ruling (or "conducting") of the choir and with nine readings even for all times in the future').

31 *Breviarium ad usum insignis ecclesiae Sarum*, ed. Procter and Wordsworth, II.462–75; III.xl–xliv.

32 At St Davids, there was no dean, the bishop took the role of the dean as chairman of the chapter, as he also did at the colleges in Abergwili and Llanddewibrefi. On canons' emoluments generally, see Edwards, *The English Secular Cathedrals*, 39–49.

33 Lat, *vicarius*, hence 'the Vicar'. For the organisation of these duties, see Edwards, *The English Secular Cathedrals,* 257–91, and Harrison, *Music*, 4–9.

the canons on duty ruled the singing together in silk copes.[34] For the most solemn occasions, double feasts, the number of rulers increased to four, the canons, not their vicars choral, in their distinctive copes occupying small desks on either side of the aisle at the end furthest from the choir steps. The precentor himself joined them on the feasts of highest grade, like St David's Day in St Davids cathedral, making five rulers in all. The number of men singing the opening 'solo' section of the invitatory psalm, and other similar solo sections, thus clarified the liturgical grading of the feast. In cathedral choirs following the Sarum direction that St David's feast was to be celebrated *cum reg.*, the invitatory would have been sung by the two rulers together, while at St Davids, five of the canons including the precentor sang it.

These details about the number of men that ruled the choir on different occasions would not have been relevant apart from in churches which were meant to have enough singers to observe such niceties. Clergy were expected to keep the canonical hours of prayer. If alone, they could have recited them but the aim was that these services were to be sung. The feasts of saints as well as the feasts prescribed in the *Temporale* consisted of music from beginning to end. It would be erroneous, consequently, to think that Chichele, by decreeing that the St David services were to be sung with a ruled choir, was *necessarily* increasing the solemnity of the occasion. They should have been sung anyway, and the form of matins to be followed had already been defined in Walden's decree.

It was conventional when celebrating the matins of saints, to include short episodes from the legend of the saint in some or all of the nine lessons intoned, instead of chanting those provided in the Common of Saints.[35] This was a way of giving the occasion a more individual character by reviving memory of the saint's achievements or suffering. Considerable variation occurred with regard to content and length of the nine lessons that were intoned at matins. It has yet to be ascertained how stable the tradition represented by the selection in the Sarum Breviary published in Paris by Chevallon and Regnault in 1531 was.[36] The lessons in this breviary are longer than those found in most manuscript breviaries. Sets of lessons for the matins of St David normally take their point of departure from Rhygyfarch's *Vita*, or the Giraldus version of it. The versions by these two authors are both so long that they are impractical for liturgical purposes. A selection of short incidents from the legend was made for breviary readings and these are often distinctive. Additions and glosses not found in the basic legend frequently occur, naturally providing food for thought.

Dependence on the legend may also be seen in the breviary readings for St David's Day to which we now turn, in Bibliothèque nationale, Paris, MS lat. 17, 294. The manuscript is known as 'The Salisbury Breviary'. This is not a happy choice of title since it is only one of thousands of breviaries representing the use of the cathedral of Salisbury, and because in one respect, this is decidedly an untypical Sarum book. In contrast with the great majority of service books, this one was

---

[34] Edwards, *The English Secular Cathedrals,* 58–59, 166, 270. Sandon, *The Use of Salisbury, The Ordinary of the Mass,* ix.

[35] As Silas M. Harris has observed (Harris, *The Liturgy of St David,* 49), two breviaries, from Hereford and Worcester, provide six readings from the legend and three from the homily on the gospel *Homo quidam peregre* for the feast of a confessor bishop.

[36] Procter and Wordsworth's edition includes details of the printed editions of Sarum breviaries, xli–lii. Pfaff maintains that the forms of the Sarum mass and office were standardized by the time the printed service books were introduced: Pfaff, *New Liturgical Feasts,* 33. Most of the manuscript sources are earlier than the printed books, and they show much variety.

profusely decorated. Its appearance has more in common with a book of hours than most breviaries; there are so many small pictures and forms of marginal embellishment. It is a luxurious production, and it looks as if it has hardly been used at all. It is a small thick book containing some 830 folios of the thinnest vellum imaginable. The Psalter is missing, and it has been suggested that originally the material was intended for two volumes.[37]

John Lancaster, duke of Bedford and regent of France, ordered its production between 1420 and 1424, probably from a workshop in Paris. The breviary was still unfinished when he died in 1435. Two scribes copied the text, while many illuminators were involved in the decoration. This is lavishly applied to each folio; four pictorial scenes are in the margins on the *recto* and *verso* of most of the folios, and in addition, a large inhabited letter marks the beginning of different sections – for example, in the *Sanctorale*, of material for each new feast. Between the scenes depicted, garlands of flowers, fruit, fleurons and ivy fill a quadratic space within a clear border. Leroquais estimated that the breviary contains some 4,300 pictorial units, and with admirable diligence, he attempted to identify the subjects depicted. In her description of the breviary, Spencer notes that there are forty-six large miniatures and some thirty smaller ones, and she suggests that if the book had been completed, it would have contained some 6,750 pictorial units not counting the very many historiated capitals and heads framed within smaller capitals.[38]

The texts and illustrations for the feast of St David are on folios 426v, 427r and 427v. The text amounts to one hundred and seventy-one lines, with about four words to a line over six columns. The scenes in the margin are related to the legend, and as elsewhere throughout the breviary, the plan seems to be to illustrate part of the subject matter in the adjoining column of text. Anyone, even if illiterate, perusing this book will have had much to think about, and much to enjoy admiring.

The liturgical material for St David's Day in Paris, Bibliothèque nationale, MS lat. 17,294 occurs in the correct place in sequence in the body of the book, after Mathias, the thirteenth apostle (24 February), and before Chad (2 March). Feasts are not dated in the text but indicated exactly in the *Kalendar*. A long rubric precedes the St David material. This is concerned with delaying the feast of St Mathias by a day on leap years.[39] A proper collect for St David is then given, and the nine lessons follow.[40] The material concludes with a rubric advising that all the rest, i.e. the texts and chants of the antiphons and responsories to be sung, should be taken from the Common of a Confessor.

A collation of breviary lessons for St David, from an exhaustive range of medieval sources is a task awaiting a patriotic philologist. In anticipation of such a study,

---

[37] These observations on the physical characteristics of the breviary and its history are indebted to Spencer's article: 'The master'. She does not comment on the material concerning St David.

[38] Incorporation of heads or faces in large capital letters is not a typical characteristic of French manuscripts, according to Spencer. It is, however, found in British manuscripts, as readers will know who have looked at the Penpont Antiphonal, NLW MS 20541 E. This book is available in a facsimile edition: Edwards (ed.), *National Library of Wales MS 20541 E*.

[39] *Cum bissextus fuerit festum beati Mathie apostoli fiat in quarta die a cathedra sancti petri et f littera bis numereter. Si hoc festum in sabbato proximo post diem cinerum contigerit ibi celebretur et secunde vespere de ipso festo erunt et solennis memoria de dominica. Completorium uero quadragesimale non mutatur [mutetur]*. This is identical with the rubric in Procter and Wordsworth, *Breviarium ad usum insignis ecclesiae Sarum*, iii, 186.

[40] The prayer (*Oratio*) is the one commonly found in Sarum books, though not in the proper office. It begins, *Omnipotens sempiterne Deus* ... See Edwards, *Matins, Lauds*, 117, and Harris, 26.

my transcription of the lessons for the matins of St David in this Parisian manuscript can show the value of this kind of source material. Colleagues might feel inclined to continue with exertions in that direction.[41]

SANCTI DAUID EPISCOPI ET CONFESSORIS NOUEM LECTIONES[42]

Lectio i Cum sanctus Germanus predicaret in Britannia contra hereseum Pelagiam, iam[43] beatum Patricium sibi ad familiare contubernium sociauit. Qui cum occiduos partes Wallie pertransiret, tandem ad locum amenum et sibi gratum, qui Wallis Rosina[44] nuncupatur, peruenit,[45] ubi proposuit habitare et soli Deo ibidem deseruire. Cui angelus apparens dixit, 'Hanc eternum sedem, o periuste, modo prouidit Deus uni uiro nondum nato sed triginta annis post hec nascituro. Dominus autem misit me ad te, ut ostendam tibi totam Hibernie insulam de sede quadam, qui est in Rhosina Ualle et nunc Sedes Patricii nominatur.

Lectio ii Et adiecit insula quatenus per tuam predicationem ad fidem ecclesie conuertetur.' Quod et factum est. Cumque sanctus Patricius destinaretur in Hiberniam a Celestino papa anno domine incarnationis quadringentesimo tricesimo tertio, sic igitur Uallis Rosina dimittitur electo Dauid nondum nato, sicut fuerat prius ab angelis nuntiatum, in qua nunc sedes episcopalis est posita et Meneuensis ecclesia est constructa.

Lectio iii Beatus uero Dauid nondum natus sed in utero materno conclusus egregius predicator futurus diuinitus est ostensus. Cum enim magister quidam Gildas nomine uirtute pariter et opinione opereque preclarus populum predicando informaret et mater beati Dauid adhuc pregnans ad ecclesiam intraret, Gildas subito obmutuit[46] et ultra predicare non presumpsit, donec ipsa ad fores ecclesie ad eius rogatum exiret, et tunc iterum predicauit.[47]

Lectio iv Interrogatus autem a populo cur interrupta predicatione obmutuerat. Respondit, 'Ego communi loquela uos alloqui potui predicare autem non potui, quia mulier, que iam rogata, exiuit ecclesiam. Ad demonstrandam sue prolis excellentiam, dum uobis

---

[41] Breviary lessons have received little attention in studies of the Welsh saints, but a recent exception, to which Dr Jonathan Wooding kindly drew my attention, is Curley, 'Five *lecciones*', 59–75.

[42] I include the most obvious references here to sentences that are identical or similar in the lessons for the matins of St David that I have at hand, in modern publications of medieval breviaries. These are abbreviated as follows:

AB, *Breuiarij Aberdonensis*, ed. Blew.

EB, the Exeter breviary: *Ordinale Exon*, ed. Dalton, III, 213–15;

HB, *The Hereford Breviary*, ed. Frere and Brown, 120–2;

SB (the Sarum breviary published in Paris by Chevallon and Regnault in 1531), ed. Procter and Wordsworth, III, 187–94;

WB, a fifteenth-century Worcester breviary referred to in HB, 120–1.

Rhygyfarch, *Vita S. David* (ed. Sharpe and Davies, above, 107–55).

Giraldus, in *Opera*, ed. Brewer *et al.*, III.377–404.

Detailed punctuation and capitalization of names occur rarely in the Latin of breviary readings. This source is no exception. I have capitalized names and added some punctuation to help make the meaning clearer, and retained the original 'u' for 'v' and 'e' for 'æ' and 'œ'. The word *nondum* is invariably written as two words in the manuscript.

[43] In codice: *nam*.

[44] In codice: *walli rosina*.

[45] SB, *lectio* i.

[46] In codice: *obmituit*.

[47] AB, *lectio iii*; SB, *lectio ii*; Rhygyfarch, *Vita S. Dauid* § 5 (ed. Sharpe and Davies, above, 112–15).

uerbum dei proponerem, monita celitus superuenit. Puerum paritura est, qui maiorem gratiam et potestatem habebit quam ego, qui etiam honoris priuilegio sapientia fulgore et sermonis facundia cunctos Britannie doctores incomparabiliter excello.' Et ex sancti uiri uita sequenti ueritas declarabit.[48]

Lectio v Cum autem compleatur dies natiuitatis eius secundum quod angelus predixerat, beatus Dauid ingenuis natalibus ortus Carentine prouincie principis filius fuit. Ipso igitur nato in lucem emisso diuina miracula minime defecerunt. Et iam ut baptizari deberet ab Elieo Meneuense episcopo redeunte de Hibernia ac nunc applicante in portu, qui dicitur Gleis, ad baptizandi ipsius ministerium fons limpidissime aque subito emanauit, qui nunquam antea ibi uisus fuit.[49]

Lectio vi Uir autem quidam gracia diuina cecus a puericia defectum etiam habens in naso, qui eius faciem non modicum deturpabat, puerum de fonte leuauit, quem cum adhuc in sinu suo teneret, intelligens infantis sanctitatem accepit aquam, in qua puer ter mersus fuerat. Aspersit que exita[50] faciem suam tribus uicibus et statim lumen oculorem et faciei integritatem mirabiliter est adeptus.[51]

Lectio vii Puer uero crescebat plenus spiritu sancto litterarumque adductus studiis super omnes coetaneos perspicatis ingenii uelocitate proficiebat. Adeo namque desuper gracia perfusus erat ut discipuli eius uiuam columbam cum rostro aureo tanquam eum docentem se uidisse multociens testarentur. Uinum et siceram[52] et omne, quod inebriare potest, respuens Christi precursorem laudabili emulatione in hoc, sicut in aliis multis imitare studens acceptabilem Deo uitam in pane et aqua perduxit unde et lingua sua indigne Britannica sed in latinum translata ipsum dei seruum Dauid Aquaticus nuncupabat.[53]

Lectio viii Crescentibus in eo uirtutum meritis uir sanctus carnem suam ab omni inmundicia seruans immunem ad sacros ordinem graduum prouectus tandem sacerdotali dignitate est sublimatus. Exinde ergo perrexit ad sanctum Paulinum quondam sancti Germani discipulum, uirum Deo deuotum et excellenter in sacris litteris eruditum. Cui diuinis taliter mancipatus officiis est associatus et tam doctrinis eius instructus quam exemplis informatus deuotioni et lectionibus intentus mansit apud eum et deferens multis annis.[54]

Lectio ix Eo tempore contigit, quod magister eius Paulinus tam in etatis et ingruencia quam lacrimarum, quibus habundabat affluencia dolore oculorum grauiter affligeretur ita, ut uisu penitus priuaretur. Uocauit igitur seruos suos singillatim et de eorum sanctitate confisus, ut oculos eius tangerent et benedicerent rogauit sperans se uisum innocentum meritis adipisci. Quod cum factum fuisset et nullum releuamen sentiret, Dauid tandem discipulum suum uirum Deo carum ad se uocauit et dixit illi, 'Dauid, considera oculos meos. Multum enim cruciant me.' Qui respondens ait, 'Pater mi, ne precipias michi uultum tuum respicere. Nam decem anni ex quo tecum scripture operam dedi et adhuc faciem tuam non aspexi.' Paulinus uerecondiam serui Dei admirans, 'Extende,' inquit, 'manum tuam et tange oculos meos et sanabor.' Quod cum factum fuisset, continuo

---

48 EB, *lectio i*; SB *lectio ii* 2nd part; Rhygyfarch, *Vita S. Dauid* § 5 (ed. Sharpe and Davies, above, 112–15). See also *lectiones iii* and *iv* of the St Nonita material, in Curley.
49 EB, *lectio ii*; SB *lectio iii*.
50 Meaning uncertain.
51 EB, *lectio ii*.
52 In codice: *ciseram.*
53 AB, *lectio viii*; EB, *lectio iii*; SB, *lectio iii*; WB, *lectio iii*; Giraldus, 384.
54 AB, *lectio ix*; EB, *lectio iv*.

uisum recepit et oculorum suorum plenam sanitatem adeptus est.[55] Cetera omnis de communis unius confessoris & pontificius.[56]

Translation

ST DAVID, BISHOP AND CONFESSOR: NINE LESSONS

Lesson 1 While St Germanus was preaching in Britain against the Pelagian heresy he admitted St Patrick into his fellowship. Passing through the western part of Wales, he arrived at length at a pleasant and for him acceptable place called Rose Valley, where he proposed to live and do service there to God alone. An angel appearing to him (Patrick) said, 'Oh most just! God has now consigned this habitation for evermore to one man alone, a man not yet born but to be born in thirty years time. The Lord, however, has sent me to you that I may show you the whole island of Ireland from this abode in Rose Valley, which now is to be called Patrick's Seat.'

Lesson 2 Moreover, the Lord added, 'The island will be converted to the faith of the church through your preaching.' Which has been done. And when St Patrick was appointed to Ireland by Pope Celestine in the four hundred and thirty-third year of the incarnation of the Lord, Rose Valley was consigned in this way to David, the elect, not yet born, as predicted by the angel, where the episcopal seat is now placed and the church of Menevia has been built.

Lesson 3 The blessed David, not yet born but confined in his mother's womb, showed divinely in this manner that he should be an excellent preacher in the future. For, when a certain teacher by the name of Gildas, distinguished equally in thought and deed, was instructing the people by preaching, and the blessed David's pregnant mother entered the church, Gildas suddenly became speechless and could not preach before she at his request had gone to the church door and had gone out, and then he preached again.

Lesson 4 Asked by the people why he cut short his sermon, he became silent and replied, 'I could converse with you as normal but I could not preach, because the woman appeared that was asked just now and left the church. While I propounded to you the word of God, she was directed by divine power to show her progeny's excellent qualities. She shall give birth to a son who will have greater grace and power even than me, I who am without comparison and excel all the learned of Britain through the privilege of my dignity, the brilliance of my wisdom, the richness of my eloquence.' And the truth of this was confirmed subsequently in the life of the holy man.

Lesson 5 When moreover the time of his delivery had been fulfilled as the angel had predicted, blessed David was born, of noble birth, a native of the area, son of the prince of the province of Carentine [Ceredigion]. Sent out into the world then, divine wonders did not fail to appear. When he was to be baptized by Elieus, the bishop of Menevia, who had returned from Ireland and was now at the harbour that is called Porth Gleis, a spring of the clearest water appeared for the office of baptism, which had never been seen before.

Lesson 6 A certain man, however, by divine will blind since childhood and lacking also his nose, which disfigured his face not a little, had borne the boy held to his breast to the font. Understanding the holiness of the child, he took the water in which the boy

---

[55] EB, *lectio iv*; SB, *lectio iv*; WB, *lectio iv*.
[56] I am grateful to Dr Espen Karlsen for his comments on my reading of the text and translation.

had thrice been immersed and three times sprinkled his face and at once marvellously gained the light of his eyes and his face was made whole.

Lesson 7 The boy grew up full of the Holy Spirit and eagerly bent upon letters made quicker progress than all his contemporaries through his natural ability. Indeed, to such a degree that grace was imbued from above, the pupils could testify to having seen many times a live dove with a golden beak teaching him, as it were. Rejecting wine and fermented liquor and all that could intoxicate, with praiseworthy emulation in this as in much, this forerunner of Christ led a mode of life acceptable to God on bread and water, from which in his native Britannic tongue, the same translated into Latin, the servant of God was called 'David the Waterman.'

Lesson 8 The holy man, while the merits of virtue were growing in him, protecting himself, his body immune to all foulness, advanced to take holy orders and at last was raised to priestly dignity. After that, therefore, he went on to St Paulinus, formerly a pupil of St Germanus, [or alternatively, perhaps, a pupil of the late St Germanus] a learned man devoted to God and in excellent fashion erudite in the Holy Scriptures. In such a way, he joined with him, and immersed himself in the divine office, just as much concerned with his teaching as with his example. He concentrated on his devotions and reading, and remained with him staying for many years.

Lesson 9 It so happened at that time that his teacher Paulinus, who both in advancing years and with tears flowing in abundance, had pain in his eyes that might deprive him of his sight. He summoned therefore his servants one by one, relying on their sanctity, and asked them to bless and touch his eyes, hoping his sight would be cured by the merits of the innocents. This was done and no relief was felt. At last, he called David his student, a man dear to God, and said, 'Consider my eyes, David, they torment me much indeed!' Answering, he said, 'Father, do not order me to look at your face, for it is ten years since I devoted myself to the Holy Scriptures with you and I have not looked at your face yet.' Paulinus, admiring the modesty of God's servant said, 'Reach out your hand and touch my eyes and I will be cured.' This was done, and he immediately received his sight and his eyes were made completely healthy.

Observations on the readings

These are readings of the length normally found in manuscript breviaries, which is to say that each is about half the length, or even shorter, than that of the readings in the printed Sarum Breviary to which reference has been made. Some sentences correspond exactly to the wording found in the printed Sarum breviary or to other sources, while others are unlike them. In common with the legend, as written by Rhygyfarch and Giraldus, names are important, and there are many of them, being included to give credible points of reference to the story. The first reading begins by mentioning St Germanus, St Patrick and the Pelagian heresy. There is no reference after this to the heresy, but it would immediately have sparked off associations for anyone that knew the legend, with St David, who was accredited with having stamped it out. Actual places that existed are mentioned, to prove the assertions true: Vallis Rosina, St Patrick's Seat,[57] Ireland, Menevia with its cathedral and bishop's

---

[57] D. Simon Evans points out (*The Welsh Life*, 26), that there is no such place in St Davids now, but that from the top of Carn Llidi the coast of Ireland is visible on a clear day.

palace, and Porthclais. The region from which David hailed is called Carentine, derived from, or intended to refer to, Ceredigion.

The editor of the lessons attempts to get the historical David to fit in with dates that they thought they knew, of the other people mentioned in the legend. In particular, he makes use of the politically bold assertion in the legend that Patrick was sent away to Ireland so that the unborn David could convert Wales. Uncertainty surrounds the facts about the one or more men who carried out the work with which St Patrick is accredited, but the person who wrote this version of the breviary lessons appears to know from the legend that Patrick was supposed to have been called to Rome where he was consecrated bishop by Pope Celestine.[58] He dates this as in the year 432, the year in which the pope died. We have, from this information, the reason for the unexpected exactness of the assertion that Patrick received his marching orders in the 433rd year of the incarnation of the Lord. Celestine I was pope 422–32, and clerics may well have known that he attempted to root out the Pelagian heresy by sending St Germanus of Auxerre to Britain in 429 (and Germanus was to go there again later in the year 447). By naming Germanus's campaign in Britain and Patrick's being sent away from Wales to convert the Irish instead – which were accepted legendary 'facts' – the narrator may have hoped to make the prophesy of David's birth more credible.[59] Given the date of St Patrick's dispatch to Ireland in A.D. 432, and St David's birth thirty years later in 462, Gildas (b. 421) would have been at the height of his power at an age of forty-one when he became dumb in Non's presence. The weakness with this calculation is, nonetheless, that after living for 147 years, St David's death in 609 occurred on a Saturday, not on a Tuesday as required in the legend. 1 March was a Tuesday in 606 and 617.[60]

The editor of this set of lessons gives a twist to the part of the story that is about how Gildas could not preach. While some sources of the legend do not even name the preacher who was unable to preach in the presence of an unborn boy who was going to be his superior, or alternatively, in some versions, a priest could not preach in the presence of a bishop without his permission, Gildas here becomes the subject of the eulogy himself. It is he, not the future archbishop and saint, who is without equal and excels over all the learned of Britain because of the privilege of his rank, wisdom and eloquence. This, however, by no means weakens the point of the story, because this great man had to keep silent in the presence of an even greater, though unborn, dignitary.[61]

There is no attempt to give a chronologically complete *vita*. Emphasis is, however, given to miracles: the miracle of his birth as prophesised, the miracle of Gildas not being able to preach in David's presence though not yet born, the miraculous appearance of the spring of clear water for his baptism, and two miracles about blindness. In the first, the water from the font in which David was baptized cures Elieus,[62] in

---

[58] Questions that scholars have long debated about the Irish patron saint, not least about person, time, place and achievements, are dealt with in Binchy's skilful demolition of scholarly myth and misunderstanding in, 'Patrick and his biographers', 7–173.

[59] Narrative techniques used in the legend are illustrated in the present author's, 'Symbolism', 143–58.

[60] For a discussion of the many uncertain dates in the calculation see, Miller, 'Date-guessing', 33–61; Bowen, *Saints, Seaways*, ch. 5.

[61] Rhygyfarch, *Vita S. Dauid* § 5 (ed. Sharpe and Davies, above, 112–15); also see Evans, *The Welsh Life of St David*, 28–31, for different readings of this incident.

[62] Sources differ on the matter of where Ailbe, Elue or Eilvyw was bishop. Some refer to his being bishop of *Muninentium/Muneuensium*, of the Munstermen in Ireland, others of *Meneuense* or St Davids (see Henken, *Traditions*, 38–40). Here it is the latter choice.

the second, David restores his sight to his teacher Paulinus. The character sketch drawn in these readings is of an ascetic literary person of quick intelligence and much learning. He is metaphorically said to be *Christi percursorem,* the forerunner of Christ, a John the Baptist figure. I have argued elsewhere that the figure emerging in the legend is, rather, an imitation of Christ himself.[63]

Appendix on Miniatures in Plates 10–12

Plate 10

In fol. 426v, the uppermost miniature in the left margin belongs to the material for the feast of St Mathias and depicts a canon speaking to a group of people, telling them when to celebrate the feast on leap years. '*Cum bissextus fuerit festum ...*'

Twelve scenes are depicted in the miniatures and, in addition, there are five letters encapsulating heads, one of a woman and the other four of men.[64] Five letters are richly decorated with pattern work and the spaces in the margins not occupied by the miniatures, as well as between the two columns of text on each folio, are filled with garlands of leaves and flowers.

In fol. 426v the second miniature down is a large, seven-line high, inhabited initial embedded in the left-central text as the letter 's' of *Sancti David.* The letter 's' viewed side-on is strongly drawn and is vigorously three-dimensional as the pink and red inner surfaces of the letter change direction. Standing in the letter, a mitred bishop with his crosier in his left hand, presumably St David, gives a benediction with his right. He has a finely patterned blue chasuble with decorative trim.

The third miniature down, in the left margin, shows a group of five people in church, three canons and two laymen. One of the religious, wearing an alb, is kneeling at the lectern reading the collect that is written alongside in the central text; '*Omnipotens sempiterne* [deus]'. The beginning of this text is shown in a didascalar caption above the tonsured head of the reader. Two men standing to the left are also tonsured. The one that is in the foreground has a surplice over a grey cassock, and over this, a grey almuce trimmed with little tassels. Observing them from the right are a man and women in the congregation.

The miniature in the left lower corner shows a bishop, defined as a saint by the halo visible behind his mitre, preaching from a pulpit to a group of four people, one a saintly cleric with a halo, the other three, two men and a woman, laypeople. From the phylactery scroll, the bishop is identified as St Germanus of Auxerre, opponent of the free-will Pelagian heretics, so the priest at the side of the pulpit must be his companion St Patrick. The bearded man sitting in the centre before the pulpit, wearing a flowing white robe with gold edging, and on his head a hat that looks rather like a crown, could be a royal personage. This being so, it might be implied that it was St David's father, Prince or King Sant of Ceredigion. A matronly figure in a red dress and a bearded man in a green cloak accompany him, both with hats. The artist has achieved an effect of depth by diminishing the size of the floor tiles towards the back of the picture.

---

[63] Edwards, 'Symbolism', 156–8.
[64] The content was identified very briefly by Leroquais: *Les bréviaires,* 319.

Plate 10. Miniatures illustrating the Office of St David in Bibliothèque nationale, Paris, MS lat. 17294, fol. 426v. (Photo courtesy of the Bibliothèque nationale)

Plate 11. Miniatures illustrating the Office of St David in Bibliothèque nationale, Paris, MS lat. 17294, fol. 427r. (Photo courtesy of the Bibliothèque nationale)

Plate 12. Miniatures illustrating the Office of St David in Bibliothèque nationale, Paris, MS lat. 17294, fol. 427v. (Photo courtesy of the Bibliothèque nationale)

The scene in the lower right corner shows an angel appearing to St Germain and St Patrick in blue cassocks in a walled garden in fertile countryside. It is Rose Valley. Each is holding his open book as a mark of learning, and identification is given in the labels over their tonsured head. The angel's message shown in the phylactery scroll, '*Hanc etenim sedem*' refers to the text stating that, indeed, the location was henceforth to be known as Patrick's seat.

Plate 11

The fifth miniature, fol. 427r, in the left lower margin, depicts the consecration of St Patrick. Clad in an alb with a blue yoke, he kneels before Pope Celestine who sits on a finely ornamented throne. A cardinal robed in red says, '*Cumque sanctus*'.

In the picture at the uppermost right corner of fol. 427r, we see St Gildas preaching in church. A caption 'Magnus Gildas' identifies him. Behind a narrow pillar, sits a rather large lady with three other people standing besides her. This might have been taken to be Non, David's pregnant mother, if the following scene had not been there. The woman in blue looks older than expected.

The miniature in the right margin, centrally positioned, shows a group of six people in church. The text shown is 'Cur interrupta – Ego communi,' and refers to the questioning of Gildas in the fourth lesson, as to why he had stopped preaching. The elegant young lady on the left is obviously with child, and since Non was supposed to be 'exceedingly beautiful,' it was surely meant to be her. But, for her to turn up in church with the man who raped her – Leroquais sees it as a fulfilment of the prediction, confirmed by the arrival of St David's parents – is somewhat fanciful.

The miniature at the lower right of fol. 427r depicts a scene from the baptism of St David. A spring has miraculously appeared and water is seen running to the right of the scene. The inscription is '*Ipso igitur nato ...*' ('*Ipso igitur nato in lucem emissio diuina miracula minime defecerunt*', from the fifth lesson.) The family group, with St David half the size of the others, stand before a mitred bishop amongst trees in the same fertile landscape of Rose Valley.

Plate 12

The caption on the next miniature, in the upper left corner of fol. 427v, is '*Puer vero ...*' It refers to the beginning of lesson 7, about David growing up, full of the Holy Spirit and making quicker progress at school than all his contemporaries because of his natural abilities. It depicts a class where a priest in a blue cope with red hood teaches three adult students wearing hats. The artist has refrained from including the dove with the golden beak, or expressed more poetically, the refined voice, that taught David.

In the centre of the left margin, the miniature depicts David being ordained a priest by a mitred bishop sitting on his throne in all his splendour. David, now tonsured and wearing an alb, kneels before him. The priest assisting the bishop has a red dalmatica with a golden stole over an alb. He holds a phylactery scroll with the caption referring to the first word of the eighth lesson, 'Crescentibus.' The direction of the beams in the roof and walls, and the scaling of the floor tiles again show the artist's interest in perspective.

In the lower left corner, the miniature shows two bearded men in conversation. Possibly, indeed probably, in view of the text referred to, the two men are St David and St Paulinus, as Leroquais suggests. The caption held by a third person in a red cassock with blue hood reads, '*Cui divinis*' and refers to the second half of the eighth lesson.

The last of the series of miniatures is in the lower right corner of fol. 427v. It depicts the final scene in the ninth lesson in which St David cures St Paulinus of his blindness. The texts given are '*Considera oculos meos*', spoken by Paulinus, and '*Pater mi, ne precipias michi*', by David.

In view of the fact that the size of the pages is small, this series of miniatures includes surprisingly realistic representations of ecclesiastical vestments and church interiors. The choice of episodes included in breviary lessons is often distinctive. The miniatures that accompany the lessons in this manuscript make it one of the most fascinating sources known.

13

A TRIAD OF TEXTS ABOUT SAINT DAVID

David Howlett

In honour of the patron saint of Wales, who is also my namesake, let us consider three texts about Saint David, first the *Vita S. Dauid* published by Rhygyfarch ap Sulien in A.D. 1081, second *Trucidare Saxones*, a Cambro-Latin martial poem published perhaps on Saint David's Day, 1 March 1200, third the Office for Saint David's Day, composed after 1220 and extant in a manuscript written during the period 1320–1390.

1. *Rhygyfarch's* Vita S. David

Sulgenus Sapiens, Sulien the Wise, twice Bishop of Saint David's, once 1072/3–1078 and again 1080–1085, had four sons, Rhygyfarch, Arthgen, Deiniol, and Ieuan.[1] From the family home at Llanbadarn Fawr in Ceredigion literary works of the father and the oldest and youngest sons survive.[2] Sulien may be responsible for introduction of the *Vita S. Maedoc* into Wales, if he did not himself compose it. The oldest son Rhygyfarch composed the prose *Vita S. Dauid* and three poems, *De Psalterio* 'On the Psalter', *De Messe Infelici* 'On an Unhappy Harvest', and *Planctus Rice-march*, 'Rhygyfarch's Lament' for the Norman Conquest of Wales. The youngest son Ieuan composed the prose *Vita S. Paterni* and three poems, *Inuocatio Iohannis* 'Ieuan's Invocation', *Carmen de Vita et Familia Sulgeni* 'Song about the Life and Family of Sulien', *Disticha Iohannis* 'Ieuan's Distichs', and an Old Welsh englyn on the episcopal staff of Saint Padarn.

A hallmark of works that issued from the house of Sulien the Wise is apparent limpid simplicity that proves on analysis to hide astonishing complexity. Though each of the features is simple, together they comprise a tightly woven text that one might describe in painter's diction as intensely polychromatic and in musician's diction as densely polyphonic. Rhygyfarch practised this compositional technique to such a degree that one might describe him, if he had been a circus performer, as juggling many balls while breathing fire and riding a unicycle.

The text on pp. 264–8, below, is based upon my collation of London, British

---

[1] *Sulgenus* 'begotten' or 'born on a Sunday' seems to have named his sons systematically, the first *Rhygyfarch* meaning 'Praise of the King', the second *Arthgen* combining the element *arth* 'bear' or 'Arcturus' or 'Arthur' with the element *-gen* from the father's name, the third *Deiniol* 'Daniel' after the fourth of the major prophets, the fourth *Ieuan* 'Iohannes' after the fourth of the evangelists.

[2] For primary texts see *Vitae Sanctorum Hiberniae*, II, 141–63; *VSBG* (ed. and trans. Wade-Evans, 150–70, 252–69); Lapidge, 'The Welsh-Latin poetry', 68–106; I. Williams, *The Beginnings*, 181–9; Howlett, *The Celtic Latin Tradition*, 233–42, 338–42; Howlett, *Cambro-Latin Compositions*, 103–18; Howlett, 'A miracle'; Thomas and Howlett, '*Vita Sancti Paterni*', for which see 65–77 for evidence of the date 1081. For secondary literature see Lapidge and Sharpe, *BCLL*, nos 31–3, 14–15; no. 103, 36; no. 475, 125.

Library, MS Cotton Vespasian A.XIV, which was written in south-eastern Wales after the Norman Conquest, perhaps at Brecon Priory about A.D. 1200. I have slightly altered the orthography of this manuscript to make it consistent with the orthography of manuscripts from the scriptorium at Llanbadarn Fawr, notably Dublin, Trinity College, MS 50 (A.4.20), which contains the autograph of Rhygyfarch, and Cambridge, Corpus Christi College, MS 199, which contains the autograph of Ieuan, silently restoring the Classical diphthongs *ae* and *oe* for the flattened *e* of the Vespasian manuscript and *t* before *e* and *i* for the occasional *c* of the Vespasian manuscript. All other changes are marked in the apparatus that follows the text. Capital letters and punctuation marks in boldface represent features of the Vespasian manuscript. I have arranged the text *per cola et commata* 'by clauses and phrases', marked clausular rhythms with macrons and breves, and cursus rhythms with acute and grave accents, and numbered sentences to the left of the text and lines to the right of the text, noting numbers of words, syllables, and letters. The traditional chapter numbers of Wade-Evans's edition are preceded by §.

Rhygyfarch suggests immediately to readers and hearers alike his intention to compose Latin of a high literary register by making all the lines of his prologue end with faultless Ciceronian metrical clausulae of alternating long and short syllables: a molossus-trochee in *mūndī dīlēxīt*, a cretic-trochee in *ātquĕ praēscĭuīt*, a trochaic metron in *praenūntĭāuĭt*, a molossus-trochee in *Dēuuī clāmāuīt*, a cretic-iamb in *patrēm quĭdēm prĭus*, a cretic-double trochee in *nōn sŏlūm prōphĕtātŭs*, and a double cretic in *inditātŭs īnnōtŭīt*. The lines of the prologue end simultaneously with faultless cursus rhythms of alternating stressed and unstressed syllables.[3] Thereafter the lines of his chapters end with faultless cursus rhythms.

The six lines of the prologue exhibit *duplus*, duple ratio 2:1, two lines for the first sentence and four lines for the second sentence. The rhymes also exhibit duple ratio, four of *a* and two of *b*. In chapter I note, as well as the lines that rhyme with adjacent and alternate lines, the rhymes placed chiastically *a-b-c–d-e-d'-c'-b'-a'* round the central line 12, *clamat* 11 with *sonat* 13, *praenuntiant* 10 with *duxit* 14, *uocatur* 9 with *cognominatur* 15, and *monasterium* 8 with *dominium* 16.

Rhygyfarch fixed the text incrementally by making numbers of elements in one part the key to numbers of elements in the next.[4] The three words of the title afford a key to the three parts of incipit, prologue, and introductory chapter I. The six syllables of the title afford a key to the six lines of the prologue and the six sentences of chapter I; they may represent also the six days of the Hexaemeron. The twenty-three syllables of the incipit afford a key to the twenty-three lines of chapter I. The fifty-two letters of the incipit afford a key to the fifty-two words of the prologue, which may represent also the fifty-two weeks of a solar year, and the 365 letters, which may represent the 365 days of an ordinary solar year.

According to § 58 of Rhygyfarch's *Life*

---

3   For the tradition of such composition in Insular Latin literature see Howlett, *Celtic Latin Tradition*, 21–8; Howlett, *British Books*, 22–30; Howlett, 'Insular Latin writers' rhythms', 53–116; Howlett, *Cambro-Latin Compositions*; Howlett, *Caledonian Craftsmanship*; Thomas and Howlett, '*Vita Sancti Paterni*', passim.

4   For other examples of this in Medieval Latin literature see Howlett, 'Arithmetic rhythms', 209; 'Insular acrostics', 32–3; Howlett, '*Synodus Prima Sancti Patricii*', 252–3; Howlett, 'The structure', 268; Howlett, 'Enigma variations', xi–xii; Howlett, 'Sixes and sevens', 60–1; Howlett, *Caledonian Craftsmanship*, 4, 51, 85, 89, 96, 102, 115, 141, 150, 152, 155, 186–7; Thomas and Howlett, '*Vita Sancti Paterni*', 46.

Sicque ad senium perductus omnis Brittannicae gentis caput et patriae honor canebatur quod senium centum quadraginta septem admodum annis compleuit

(And so, led through to old age, the head of the entire Brittonic race and the honour of the fatherland was sung because he fulfilled altogether the old age of 147 years.)

The patriarch Jacob, whose other name was Israel, died, according to Genesis 47.28, at the age of 147. As Gildas in *De Excidio Britanniae* 22.1 described his fellow Britons as *praesentem Israelem* 'present Israel',[5] Rhygyfarch equated the age of David, *omnis Brittannicae gentis* [i.e. *praesentis Israel*] *caput et patriae honor*, with the age of Israel at death. In this sentence the number of syllables is 49, the square of 7, a sabbath of sabbaths, the number of years that precede a Hebrew jubilee,[6] and the number of letters and spaces between words is 147. As in chapter 58 the 147 letters and spaces between words so in the prologue the 147 syllables represent the 147 years of the life of David.

Rhygyfarch made numerical words exhibit their values. In the prologue from | *ueriloquis* the thirtieth syllable is the first of *terdenis* 'three times ten', 'thirty'. In chapter I sentence 2 there are three words before | *tribus*. From the beginning of chapter I to the space before this six-lettered word there are sixty words, which divide by *hemiolus* or sesquialter ratio 1½:1 or 3:2 at 36 and 24, at *tria* |.

Consider the diction about the deposit of gifts. From | *deposita* 3 to *Depositi* | 9 there are sixty-six words, which divide by *epogdous* or sesquioctave ratio 1⅛:1 or 9:8 at 35 and 31, at | *positum* 6. The sixty-six words from | *deposita* to *Depositi* | divide by sesquialter ratio 3:2 at 40 and 26, in the twenty-six words from | *tria* to *tribus* |. The remaining forty words divide by sesquioctave ratio at 21 and 19, there being nineteen words from | *deposita* to | *tria* and twenty-one words from *tribus* | to *Depositi* |.

In chapter II the first sentence contains sixty-three words, which divide by duple ratio 2:1 at 42 and 21, so that the second two-thirds begin at | *geminae* 'doubled'. These numbers in the first sentence also fix incrementally the structure of the chapter, 42 the number of lines and 21 the number of sentences.

In chapter II between *nec nisi peractis prius triginta annis nascetur* | 12 and | *sed neque ante triginta annos nascetur* 15 there are thirty-one words. In *neque ante triginta annos nascetur* there are thirty letters. After *Patricius* | 13 the thirtieth word is *triginta* | 15.

In Antiquity a tradition of gematria, common to Hebrew and Greek and Latin, reckoned the numerical values of names and words. As in both Hebrew and Greek every letter of the alphabet bears numerical value, so in Latin there is a dual system of number, in one of which I = 1, V = 5, X = 10, L = 50, C = 100, D = 500, M = 1000,[7] in the other of which A = 1, B = 2, C = 3 ... T = 18, V = 19, X = 20, and later, including K = 10, X = 21, Y = 22, Z = 23. Rhygyfarch's brother Ieuan states explicitly in the acrostic poem that names him that he used this latter system.[8] In such a system every word bears both a semantic meaning and a numerical value, as in Hebrew הבל 'Abel' = 5+2+30 or 37, כלב 'Caleb' = 20+30+2 or 52, in Greek AΔAM 'Adam' = 1+4+1+40 or 46 and MAPIA 'Maria' = 40+1+100+10+1 or 152 and IHCOYC 'Iesus' = 10+8+200+70+400+200 or 888, in Latin BRITTANNIA

---

5   Howlett, 'The prophecy', 156–60.
6   For another example of this see Thomas and Howlett, '*Vita Sancti Paterni*', 59.
7   For an account of this system see Walsh and Ó Cróinín, *Cummian's Letter*, 122–3. For an account of the Greek system see Bede, *De temporum ratione* (ed. Jones, 272–3).
8   Howlett, *Celtic Latin Tradition*, 235.

= 2+17+9+19+19+1+13+13+9+1 or 103, HIBERNIA = 8+9+2+5+17+13+9+1 or 64, BRIGITA = 2+17+9+7+9+19 +1 or 64, and ULTÁN = 20+11+19+1+13 or 64. There are clear examples of the value in Greek alphabetical notation of AΔAM 'Adam' as 46,[9] MAPIA 'Maria' as 152,[10] and IHCOYC 'Iesus' as 888.[11] For an example of multilingual gematria consider the Greek Apocalypse 13.18, in which the number of the beast, εξακοσιοι εξηκοντα εξ, 666, exhibits descending value of the Roman numerals DCLXVI. This number is the sum of the letters of the Latin name NERO CAESAR, spelled in Hebrew letters נרון קסר, 50+200+6+50+100+60+200 or 666. The example best known in a Latin literary text is Martianus Capella *De Nuptiis Philologiae et Mercurii*, in which at the beginning of book II Philologia reckons multilingual gematria on her name and that of Mercury to determine their compatibility. For evidence of the transmission of this remarkable work to Insular scholars four hundred years before Rhygyfarch see Ogilvy, Gneuss, Reynolds, and Bischoff and Löfstedt.[12]

I have published elsewhere an analysis of the Hebrew text of the Book of Judges 3.7–11,[13] a passage in which the fifty-second word is the name כלב 'Caleb', the numerical value of which is 52, and an analysis of an Anglo-Norman poem that refers to gematria while practising it.[14]

In the system used by Ieuan and Rhygyfarch the Christian name DAVID bears a numerical value of 4+1+20+9+4 or 38. From the beginning of prologue sentence 2 line 3 | *Iste itaque sanctus* [*i.e.* David] to *Dauid* | inclusive there are thirty-eight letters and spaces.

The name DEUUI bears a numerical value of 4+5+20+20+9 or 58. From the beginning of prologue sentence 2 line 3 | *Iste* to the space after *Deuui* | inclusive there are fifty-eight letters and spaces.

Again in chapter II Rhygyfarch wrote in line 38 DAVID, the *I* of DAVI being the fifty-eighth letter of the line.

Patrick's name in the accusative form PATRICIVM bears a numerical value of 15+1+19+17+9+3+9+20+12 or 105. From the cross (for monosyllabic *crux*) at the beginning of the prologue to *Patricium* | inclusive there are 105 syllables. The name in the nominative form PATRICIVS bears a numerical value of 15+1+19+17 +9+3+9+20+18 or 111. In chapter II after *Patricius* | 1 the 105th word is *Patricius* | 13. Between *Patricius* | 13 and | *Patrici* 26 there are 111 words.

The name SANCTVS bears a numerical value of 18+1+13+3+19+20+18 or 92. Between *Deuui* | and | *Sanctus* there are ninety-two syllables.

The place-name CERETICA bears a numerical value of 3+5+17+5+19+9+3 +1 or 62. From the beginning of the prologue *Cereticae* | is the sixty-second word.

The river-name AMNEM THEIBI bears a numerical value of 1+12+13+5+12 +19+8+5+9+2+9 or 43+52 or 95. From the beginning of the prologue | + (for *crux*)

9 Howlett, 'Five experiments', 67; Howlett, *British Books*, 238–40; Howlett, 'Hellenic learning', 73–4; Howlett, 'Arithmetic rhythms', 201; *Caledonian Craftsmanship*, 156–75.

10 Howlett, 'Five experiments', 30; Howlett, 'The Brigitine hymn', 82; 'Hellenic learning', 72–6; Howlett, *Cambro-Latin Compositions*, 82; Howlett, *Sealed*, 41.

11 Howlett, 'Five experiments', 30; *British Books*, 119–23, 538–40; 'Hellenic learning', 74–6; 'Arithmetic rhythms', 200; *Cambro-Latin Compositions*, 82; *Sealed from Within*, 89–91; *Caledonian Craftsmanship*, 1–9, 156–60.

12 Ogilvy, *Books Known to the English*, 199–200. Gneuss, 'A preliminary list', 1–60, nos 48, 67, 95–6, 129, 438; Reynolds, *Texts and Transmission*, 245–6; *Anonymus ad Cuimnanum Expossitio Latinitatis* (ed. Bischoff and Löfstedt, *Index grammaticorum* 168–9).

13 Howlett, *Celtic Latin Tradition*, 29–32; *British Books*, 34–7.

14 Howlett, 'Gematria', 90–2.

to *amnem Theibi* | inclusive there are ninety-five words. From the beginning of the angelic speech | *Crastina* to *amnem Theibi* | inclusive there are ninety-five letters.

The place-name LINHENLAN bears a numerical value of 11+9+13+8+5+13 +11+1+13 or 84. From the beginning of chapter I to *Depositi monasterium uocatur* |, the place to which the gifts found at *Linhenlan* must be taken, there are eighty-four words.

The Christian name MAUCANNUS bears a numerical value of 12+1+20+3 +1+13+13+20+18 or 101. The place-name MAUCANNI MONASTERIUM bears a numerical value of 12+1+20+3+1+13+13+9+12+14+13+1+18+19+5+17+9+20+12 or 72+140 or 212. The place-name DEPOSITI MONASTERIUM bears a numerical value of 4+5+15+14+18+9+19+9+12+14+13+1+18+19+5+17+9+20+12 or 93+140 or 233. From *amnem Theibi* | to *Depositi* | there are ninety-three syllables. From *amnem Theibi* | to *Depositi monasterium uocatur* | there are 101 syllables. From *amnem Theibi* | to *Maucanni monasterium* | there are 212 letters. From *amnem Theibi* | to *Depositi* | *monasterium* there are 233 letters.

As David's rule of monastic life allowed no one to own anything, Rhygyfarch's story of the *tria munera* is a form of narrative charter that confers on David thirty years before his birth through *ceruum piscem apumque examen* the right to use the products of forest, stream, and field.[15] Rhygyfarch names the three gifts three times: *ceruum piscem apumque examen*, then in reversed order, *fauum scilicet partemque piscis et cerui*, then separately but still in reversed order, *fauus enim, piscis uero, ceruus autem*.

The word FAVUS bears a numerical value of 6+1+20+20+18 or 65. From *fauum scilicet* | to | *fauus* there are sixty-five syllables.

The word PISCIS bears a numerical value of 15+9+18+3+9+18 or 72. From the first mention of the word, from | *piscem*, to the last *piscis aqua uiuit* |, there are seventy-two words.

The word CERVUS bears a numerical value of 3+5+17+20+20+18 or 83. Before the first mention, | *ceso prope fluuium ceruo* 5, there are eighty-three words. Between *cerui* | 7 and | *sicut enim ceruus* 16 there are eighty-three words.

Rhygyfarch presses the gifts into service as explanations of David's character, the *fauus* like *mel in cera* representing David's ability to perceive the spiritual sense within the literal historical sense of Scripture, the fish that lives in water representing David's drinking of water as distinct from wine or beer or mead, the stag that triumphs over the ancient serpent and desires the spring of water representing David's triumph over demons and his fountains of tears. But there is a further connection. The description of David in Welsh as *dyfrwr* 'water man' represents Rhygyfarch's reference to *aquaticam eius uitam – aqua – et aqua – Dauid aquaticae uitae*. The word AQUA bears a numerical value of 1+16+20+1 or 38, identical with the numerical value of the name DAVID. From | *aquaticam* to | *aqua* there are thirty-eight letters. Between *aqua* | and | *et aqua* there are thirty-eight syllables. From the space before | *aqua* to *aquaticae* | inclusive there are thirty-eight letters and spaces between words.

The numerical value of the three gifts combined, FAVUS 65 and PISCIS 72 and CERVUS 83 is 220. From | *Nam* to *tria ibi* | *munera* there are 221 letters.

The Christian name CRVIMTHER bears a numerical value of 3+17+20+9+12+19+8 +5+17 or 110. The name is Irish, derived from *presbyter* 'priest'. Between the name

---

15 For another example see Howlett, *Cambro-Latin Compositions*, 116, n. 18.

Cruimther | 'priest' and | *episcopus* 'bishop', which he became, there are 110 letters and punctuation points.

Rhygyfarch began as he intended to continue throughout the text of this wonderfully composed Life.[16] To a post-romantic sensibility the interweaving of these arithmetic coincidences within what appears to be a simple straightforward narrative may seem a *tour de force*. But many examples of Cambro-Latin texts, literary and diplomatic and epigraphic alike, demonstrate with clarity that admits no shadow of doubt that Rhygyfarch's compatriots had been writing like this since at least the fifth century, and they continued to write like this until at least the fifteenth century. None of the forms of artifice we have been considering, clausular and cursus rhythms, rhymes, and multiple overlapping of word-, syllable-, and letter-counts infixed in smooth prose, can be tacked like decoration on to a nearly completed work, much less inserted into someone else's already completed work. They belong to the earliest stages of conception and execution of a composition, which they fix in the form intended by the author to be absolutely irreformable.[17] This analysis, by no means complete, is yet complete enough to demonstrate that the version of *Vita S. Dauid* preserved in MS Cotton Vespasian A.XIV represents more nearly than any other Rhygyfarch's authorial text.

2. Trucidare Saxones: *A Cambro-Latin martial poem*

A Cambro-Latin poem, *Trucidare Saxones soliti Cambrenses*, survives in two manuscripts.[18] One is Leiden, Universiteitsbibliotheek, MS Vossianus. lat. F.77, folio 144ra–vb (L), written during the thirteenth century according to du Méril, in Normandy in 1282 according to Lapidge and Sharpe, during the early part of the fourteenth century according to M.R. James. The other is closely related, Cambridge, Corpus Christi College, MS 181, p. 277 (C), from Saint Mary's, York, written during the earlier part of the fourteenth century according to Lapidge and Sharpe, during the fifteenth century according to M.R. James. In both manuscripts the stanzas are preceded on the left by paraphs. In the Cambridge manuscript the stanzas are enclosed by brackets on the right. I have marked rhyme and assonance with italics and alliteration within lines with underline.

The poet arranged many of his words in chiastic and parallel patterns that confirm the word order of the narrative and help to fix the text. First in the former part of the poem.

1	1a	trucidare
2	1b	cognatos
4	2	Saxonienses
5	3	uenite iam strenue loricis armati
6	2'	Saxonum
7	1'a	trucidati
8	1'b	nati

---

[16] I hope to demonstrate this soon in an edition, translation, and analysis of the complete Life.

[17] James, *Rhigyfarch's Life*, presents the abbreviated Nero Recension as Rhygyfarch's original work, an opinion the present writer cannot endorse.

[18] Lapidge and Sharpe, *BCLL*, no. 82, 30–1. Wright, *The Political Songs*, 56–8. Du Méril *Poésies Populaires*, vol. 2, 275–7. James, *A Descriptive Catalogue*, vol. 1, 424. I owe thanks to the Librarian and Fellows of Corpus Christi College for permission to consult the Cambridge manuscript and to Professor David Dumville for loan of a microfilm of the Leiden manuscript.

The central parts of this smaller chiasmus consider the English. Then in the latter part of the poem.

22 1a	Anglum		
25 1b		uirtuosos	
27 2a			strenuo
28 2b			Arthurus
28 2c			uictores
29 3			regnabat Parisius potestas Romana
30 2'a			strenuus
31 2'b			Arthurus
36 2'c			uictoriosos
42 1'a	Anglia		
44 1'b		uirtutem	

The central part of this smaller chiasmus considers the French. Then in a pattern that connects the former part with the latter.

13 1	rex		
13 2		Arthurus	
19 3			Britonibus
21 4a			Arthuri
24 4b			Britones
25 5			uirtuosos filii patres imitantur
26 4'a			Arthurum
26 4'b			Britones
33 3'			Britones
38 2'		Arthurus	
46 1'	reges		

The central part of this larger chiasmus considers the British.

The poem consists of twelve quatrains, in each of which the first three lines exhibit thirteen-syllable goliardic metre and the fourth line exhibits a dactylic hexameter. The poet may have known hexameters as the principal medium of Latin verse in inscriptions on stones and mosaics and in manuscript from Romano-British times to the high middle ages in Wales.[19] He may also have known the earliest extant example of goliardic metre in the inscription for Audiua at Trescawen House, Llang-wyllog Parish, Llantrisant in Anglesey. In that sixth-century text of thirteen lines each couplet contains thirteen syllables, the last line containing thirteen letters.[20] If our poet knew that poem or others that succeeded it, his choice of metres might be understood as a patriotic statement, deeply rooted in the Cambro-Latin tradition.

The two halves of the poem end at the sixth stanza and the twelfth, which share the same rhyme. In the concluding hexameters six of twelve stanzas exhibit rhyme or assonance between the caesura and the end. Though in each stanza all four lines end identically, rhymes further from the end divide the stanzas into four forms, three of each – A, abab, I, II, VI; B, abba, III, V, VIII; C, abbb or abaa, IIII, VII, XII; D, aabb, VIIII, X, XI.[21]

Reckoning A=1, B=2, C=3 … X=21, Y=22, Z=23, the numerical value of the

---

19 Howlett, *Cambro-Latin Compositions*, 17–32, 39, 96–100, 103–8, 122–3, 131, 135–7, 156–64.

20 Howlett, *Cambro-Latin Compositions*, 26–7. Howlett, *Insular Inscriptions*, 42–5.

21 For play with internal vowel rhymes in sixth- and seventh-century verse see Howlett, *Cambro-Latin Compositions*, 19, 22–6, 159–60, and 'Hiberno-Latin poems in the Book of Cerne', 1–21.

name BRITONES is 2+17+9+19+14+13+5+18 or 97. From | *Britones* 2 to *sibi* | [*i.e.* *Britonibus*] 20 inclusive there are ninety-seven words.

The numerical value of the name SAXONIENSES is 18+1+21+14+13+9+5 +13+18+5 +18 or 135. From the beginning of the poem to the space before *Saxonienses* 4 inclusive there are 135 letters and spaces between words.

The numerical value of the name ARTHURUS is 1+17+19+8+20+17+20+18 or 120. From the *A* of *Arthurus* 13 to the space after *durus* 16 at the end of stanza IIII there are 120 letters and spaces between words.

The numerical value of the name DAVID is 4+1+20+9+4 or 38. In the last stanza of the first half of the poem there are before *Daui* in *hoc Arthuri patruus uelit impetrare sanctus* thirty-eight letters. After *Daui* there are thirty-eight syllables to the end of the stanza. In *festum Martis in* | *kalendis instare ad natale solum Britones studeat reuocare* from the upright bar to the end of the stanza there are fifty-nine letters and spaces between words, coincident with the fifty-nine days in an ordinary year before Saint David's Day on the kalends of March.[22] *Arthuri patruus* is David, who like the patriarch Jacob lived according to § 58 of the *Vita S. Dauid* by Rhygyfarch ap Sulien 147 years.[23] The 147th word from the end of the poem is *patruus*.

The numerical value of the name RICARDUS is 17+9+3+1+17+4+20+18 or 89. From *Ricardum* | 42 to the end of stanza XI there are eighty-nine syllables.

The numerical value of the name ANGLIA is 1+13+7+11+9+1 or 42. In the middle of line 42 is *Anglia*, before which there are forty-two letters in stanza XI.

The last quarter of the twelve stanzas begins at stanza X, the fourth stanza of the second half, in which the fourth word is *quatuor*. The fortieth syllable of the stanza is the first of line 40, *hii monarchiam tenuerunt ut probiores.*, which from the space before *hii* to the space after *probiores.* inclusive contains forty letters and punctuation mark and spaces between words. In line 44 the fourth word is *quadrupla*. In *uirtutem regis quia quadrupla gloria mactat.* there are forty-four letters and punctuation point and spaces between words. In the last quarter of the poem the sixty-one words divide by the ratio 5:4 at 34 and 27, at | *quatuor* and *quadrupla* |.

The central words of the entire poem are the central words at the caesura of a central line 24, *ad natale solum* | *Britones studeat reuocare*. The 648 syllables of the poem divide by symmetry at 324 and 324, at *reuoc* | *are*. The 1837 letters and spaces between words divide by symmetry at 919, at *reuoc*| *a* |*re*.

The poet may have known the *Planctus Ricemarch*, a lament for the Norman Conquest of Wales composed by Rhygyfarch ap Sulien between 1093 and 1099,[24] to which this work may be seen as a response. The poet certainly knew the work of Geoffrey of Monmouth, specifically the *Prophetie Merlini* and the account of Arthur and Frollo in *Historia Regum Britannie* VII iii–iv §§ 112–17 and IX xi § 155, published between January and March 1136.[25] He must have written after the accession of Richard I in 1189 and before the copying of the Leiden manuscript in 1282, according to *A Bibliography of Celtic-Latin Literature* 'c. 1200'. If one supposed, after noting the play in stanzas X and XI on 4 and 40 and 44, that our poet followed the reckoning of the *Annales Cambriae*, in which *Annus I* is A.D. 444,[26] and added to that one year for every letter of the poem from | *trucidare* to

---

[22] For many examples of a tradition of calendrical composition in Insular literatures from the fifth century to the fifteenth see the works mentioned in notes 3, 4 and 10 above.

[23] See above, 254–5.

[24] Howlett, *Cambro-Latin Compositions*, 108–13.

[25] Howlett, *The English Origins*, 57–9.

[26] Howlett, *Cambro-Latin Compositions*, 153–5.

the end of the dating clause *scimus festum Martis in kalendis instare* |, 444 and 756 would equal 1200. One might suggest tentatively Saint David's Day, 1 March 1200, as the date of publication.

According to a widespread convention by which authors refer to their subjects and to themselves in places determined by *epogdous*, sesquioctave ratio, 1⅛:1 or 9:8,[27] this text of forty-eight lines divides at lines 23 and 25. The 256 words divide at 136 and 120, at *scimus festum | Martis in kalendis instare* in line 23 and after line 25, at *sic Arthurum | Britones uirtute sequantur* 26. Certainly the poet used the name and day of the national patron, Saint David, to celebrate the 'historical' Arthur, perhaps because his name was David or Arthur or Dewi map Arthur or something similar. Or perhaps he was thinking of a contemporary Arthur who would lead a campaign against the English considered at the centre of the first chiasmus and the French considered at the centre of the second chiasmus, specifically against the kings of the English and the French disparaged in stanzas XI and XII. In the *Annales Cambriae* we read[28]

> Annus MCCII. Arthurus dux Armoricanorum Britonum a rege Iohanne in belli conflictu cum multis baronibus et militibus Philippo regi Francorum fauentibus captus est et Alienor soror eius cum ipso. ...
> Annus MCCIIII. Arthurus dux Armoricanorum Britonum in carcere regis Iohannis obiit uel ut alii uolunt occisus est.

> (Year 1202. Arthur Duke of the Armorican Britons was captured by King John in the conflict of battle with many barons and soldiers aiding Philip King of the French and Eleanor his sister with him. ...
> Year 1204. Arthur Duke of the Armorican Britons died in a prison of King John or, as others want, he was killed.)

The poet has provided means for readers to determine the exact text and structure of his composition, a likely date, and a possible purpose. What remains to be discovered is more certain evidence of his name and the place in which he composed this remarkable poem.

3. *The Office for Saint David's Day*

See pp. 270–3ff below. By arranging the text thus we can see the parallelism between *antiphona* and *uersus*, between *psalmi* and *hymnus*, between *capitulum* and *uersiculus*, between *responsorium* and *responsio*, and note that the last couplet of the *responsorium* at the end of the first part is repeated at the end of the beginning of the second part. The *antiphona, responsorium*, and *uersus* are in syllabic metres and rhyme schemes devised by Insular Celts, in the *antiphona* heptasyllables, in

---

[27] For other examples of authorial self-reference at places determined by sesquioctave ratio and one-ninth and eight-ninths see Howlett, 'Some criteria', 198–9; 'Aldhelm', 70; 'Miscouplings', 271–6 and 277–80; 'Arithmetic rhythms', 193–225; 'Two works of Saint Columban', 29; 'Numerical play', 63–4; 'Sixes and sevens', 49–70; 'Busnois' motet *In hydraulis*', 189–90; 'Five experiments', 5, 15–17, 28–30; 'The polyphonic colophon', 83; 'Seven studies', 36, 46; '*Rubisca*', 89; 'Insular Latin writers' rhythms', 83, 87; 'Insular acrostics', 30, 33–4, 43; *The Book of Letters*, 46; *Celtic Latin Tradition*, 84, 115, 119, 129, 132, 181, 215, 222, 227–8, 259, 267, 272, 354, 371–2, 378, 384, 394; *English Origins*, 25, 45, 61, 66, 73, 88–90, 95, 98, 104, 109, 117–18, 122–3, 127, 142, 145–6; *British Books*, 240, 246, 540, 611–12; *Cambro-Latin Compositions*, 42–3, 62–3, 67, 74, 107, 112–13, 137, 140, 152; *Caledonian Craftsmanship*, 22, 90, 95, 106, 160, 184.

[28] *Annales Cambriae* (ed. Williams ab Ithel, 63).

the parallel *uersus* hexasyllables, in the *responsorium* alternating octosyllables and heptasyllables, the last couplet of which is reformed as a hendecasyllabic verse at the end of the *uersus*. The latter *antiphona* is also in alternating octosyllables and heptasyllables. In this office, as in *Trucidare Saxones*, we see use by a Cambro-Latin poet of verse-forms devised within his own tradition, exported to the whole of Latin Christendom, here reappropriated for a domestic purpose, the honour of the national patron saint. In his first address, *O desiderabilis*, he plays upon knowledge of the Hebrew etymology that underlies the name דוד *Dauid* 'beloved', and as he begins, so he continues.

In the first *antiphona* the seventeen words divide by sesquialter ratio 3:2 at 10 and 7, at *forma* | and | *reformatus*, between which there are seven words. The ten words from the beginning to *forma* | and from | *reformatus* to the end divide again by the same ratio at 6 and 4, there being four words from the beginning and six words to the end.

In the *uersus* the poet plays on the neuter noun *locum* and the verb *locare*, the former in the accusative plural *loca*, the latter in the imperative singular *loca*, on the name of Saint David as *pastor*, shared with King David, who was also *pastor* 'a shepherd', and perhaps on *pascua* 'pasture-land' and *pascha* 'Easter'.

Proof that our author understood the ancient conventions of his own tradition appears most clearly in the *oratio*. Compare it with what Rhygyfarch wrote:

> Deus qui beatum confessorem tuum Dauid atque pontificem angelo nuntiante Patricio prophetante triginta annis antequam nasceretur praedixisti quaesumus ut cuius memoriam recolimus eius intercessione ad aeterna gaudia perueniamus per Dominum nostrum Iesum Xpistum Filium tuum qui tecum uiuit et regnat in unitate Spiritus Sancti Deus per omnia saecula saeculorum Amen.

As Rhygyfarch composed and spelled this prayer there are forty-nine words, the square of 7, a sabbath of sabbaths that precedes a Hebrew jubilee. Including the *Amen* there are exactly fifty words and 365 letters and spaces between words, one for every day of a solar year. As our author adapted the prayer the thirtieth syllable is the last of *triginta* |. After *triginta annis antequam nasceretur* 'thirty years before he would be born' there are thirty-eight letters and spaces to the first letter of *cuius* 'his', 38 being the numerical value of the name *Dauid*. Another fine example of our author's punctilio is *cuius festiuitatem* | *colimus* 'whose festival we celebrate', in which the last syllable of *festiuitatem* is the fifty-ninth. The thirty-one days of January and the twenty-eight days of February comprise fifty-nine days before the first day of March. As this text belongs to the office of vespers, the evening *before* Saint David's Day, the present tense of *cuius festiuitatem colimus* is perfectly appropriate. In the text as revised for this office there are still forty-nine words, fifty including *Amen*, but instead of Rhygyfarch's 365 letters and spaces between words, one for every day of a solar year, there are 354, one for every day of a lunar year.

In five books, *The Celtic Latin Tradition of Biblical Style, Cambro-Latin Compositions: Their Competence and Craftsmanship, Sealed from Within: Self-Authenticating Insular Charters, 'Vita Sancti Paterni', The Life of Saint Padarn and the Original 'Miniu'*, and *Insular Inscriptions*, I have tried to demonstrate the high craftsmanship, indeed the high art, exhibiting a unique sense of continuous self-possession, in the literary, diplomatic, and epigraphic monuments of the Cambro-Latin tradition. The texts considered here add a triad of compositions to that illustrious list, three compositions that relate directly to the patron saint of people and nation, *desiderabilis uultu forma presulum*.

Gematria

Alphanumeric values of names and words

HEBREW

הבל 'Abel'	5+2+30 = 37
כלב 'Caleb'	20+30+2 = 52
נרון קסר 'Nero Caesar'	50+200+6+50+100+60+200 = 666.

GREEK

AΔAM 'Adam'	1+4+1+40 = 46
MAPIA 'Maria'	40+1+100+10+1 = 152
IHCOYC 'Iesus'	10+8+200+70+400+200 = 888

LATIN

BRITTANNIA 'Britain'	2+17+9+19+19+1+13+13+9+1 = 103
HIBERNIA 'Ireland'	8+9+2+5+17+13+9+1 = 64
BRIGITA 'Brigit'	2+17+9+7+9+19+1 = 64
ULTÁN 'Ultán	20+11+19+1+13 = 64

RHYGYFARCH *Vita Sancti Dauid*
Personal Names

CRVIMTHER 'Cruimther'	3+17+20+9+12+19+8+5+17 = 110
DAVID 'David'	4+1+20+9+4 = 38
DEUUI 'David'	4+5+20+20+9 = 58
MAUCANNUS 'Maugan'	12+1+20+3+1+13+13+20+18 = 101
PATRICIVM 'Patrick'	15+1+19+17+9+3+9+20+12 = 105
PATRICIVS 'Patrick'	15+1+19+17+9+3+9+20+18 = 111
SANCTVS 'Sant'	18+1+13+3+19+20+18 = 92

Place-Names

AMNEM THEIBI 'river Teifi'
    1+12+13+5+12+19+8+5+9+2+9 = 43+52 = 95
CERETICA 'of Ceredigion'
    3+5+17+5+19+9+3+1 = 62
LINHENLAN 'pool by the old church'
    11+9+13+8+5+13+11+1+13 = 84
DEPOSITI MONASTERIUM 'Monastery of the Deposit'
    4+5+15+14+18+9+19+9+12+14+13+1+18+19+5+17+9+20+12 = 93 + 140 =233
MAUCANNI MONASTERIUM 'Maugan's Monastery'
    12+1+20+3+1+13+13+9+12+14+13+1+18+19+5+17+9+20+12 = 72+140 = 212

Gifts

FAVUS 'honeycomb'	6+1+20+20+18 = 65
PISCIS 'fish'	5+9+18+3+9+18 = 72
CERVUS 'stag'	3+5+17+20+20+18 = 83
AQUA 'water'	1+16+20+1 = 38
FAVUS + PISCIS+ CERVUS	65+72+83 = 220

Trucidare Saxones
ANGLIA 'England'   1+13+7+11+9+1 = 42
ARTHURUS 'Arthur'   1+17+19+8+20+17+20+18 = 120
BRITONES 'Britons'   2+17+9+19+14+13+5+18 = 97
DAVID 'David'   4+1+20+9+4 = 38
RICARDUS 'Richard'   17+9+3+1+17+4+20+18 = 89
SAXONIENSES 'Saxons'   18+1+21+14+13+9+5+13+18+5+18 = 135

1. *Rhygyfarch's* Vita S. David

VITA SANCTI DAVID

          3 6 15

INCIPIT VITA BEATI DAVID QUI ET DEUUI EPISCOPI ET CONFESSORIS .

§ 1   10 23 52

1 + **DOMINUS** noster quamuis omnes suos ante constitutionem múndi diléxit .
    átque praescí*uit* :   a
    nonnullos tamen multis reuelationum ostensionibus praénunti*áuit* .   a
2 Iste itaque sanctus quem tinctio **DAVID** uulgus autem **DÉUUI** clam*áuit* :   a
    ueriloquis angelorum oraculis ad pátrem quidem prí*us* .   b
    deinde ad Sanctum Patricium terdenis annis priusquam nasceretur nón solum
        pròphetá*tus* :   b
    uerum etiam misticis donationum muneribus inditátus innótu*it* .   a   6
§ 2   52 147 365
I1 Nam quodam tempore pater eius meritis et nómine Sánc*tus* .
    Cereticae gentis regali poténtia fré*tus* :
    qua tandem deposita caeleste regnum comparans angelica in somnis monitus uóce
        audí*uit* .
    Crastina die expergefactus uenátum itú*rus* .
    ceso prope fluuium ceruo : tria ibi munera reperies iúxta amnem Theí*bi* :   5
    ceruum scilicet quem persequeris . piscem . apumque examen . in arbore positum
        in loco qui dícitur Línhenlan .
2 Ex his itaque tribus reserues fauum scilicet partemque píscis et cér*ui* :

    quae custodienda filio ex te nascituro transmitte ad Maucanni mónasté*rium* .

    quod nunc usque Depositi monastérium uoc*átur* .
3 Quae quidem munera huius uítam praenúntia*nt* .   10
4 Fauus enim mellis : eius sapiéntiam clám*at* .
    sicut enim mel in cera : ita spiritalem sensum historico cépit instruménto .

5 Piscis uero aquaticam eíus uitam són*at* .
    sicut enim piscis aqua uiuit : ita iste uinum et siceram . et omne quod inebriare
        potest respuens . beatam Deo uitam in pane tántum et àqua dúx*it* .
    inde etiam **DAVID** aquaticae uitae cógnomin*átur* .   15
6 Ceruus autem in antiquo serpente sígnat domín*ium* .
    sicut enim ceruus expoliatis serpéntibus pás*tus* .
    fontem aquae desiderans acceptis uiribus uelut iuuentúte renou*átur* :
    sic iste quasi ceruorum pedibus super excélsa státu*tus*
    antiquum humani generis serpentem uiribus nocendi contra semetípsum expóli*ans* .   20
    fontem uitae assiduis lacrimarum cúrsibus adópt*ans* .
    de die in diem renouátus proféc*it* :

THE LIFE OF HOLY DAVID

THE LIFE BEGINS OF BLESSED DAVID WHO [IS] ALSO DEUUI BISHOP AND CONFESSOR

+ Our Lord, although He loved and foreknew all His own before the constituting of the
world,
yet announced beforehand many [lit. 'not none'] by many showings of revelations.
This holy man, therefore, whom baptism called David but the people Deuui,
first, indeed, by truth-uttering oracles of angels to the father,
then to holy Patrick three times ten years before he would be born not only
prophesied,
but even became known, marked out by mystic gifts of donations.

For at a certain time his father, in merits and name Sant [*i.e.* 'Holy']
strengthened by royal power of the people of Ceredigion,
which finally laid down, preparing for the celestial realm, he heard warned in sleep by an
angelic voice,
'On tomorrow's day, wakened, about to go hunting,
with a stag slain near a river, you will find there three gifts by the river Teifi,
a stag, understand, which you will pursue, a fish, and a swarm of bees placed in a tree in
the place that is called Linhenlan [Welsh 'pool by the old church'].
From these three therefore you should reserve the honeycomb, understand, and part of the
fish and of the stag,
which send across to be guarded for the son who is going to be born from you to Maugan's
monastery,'
which until now is called the monastery of the Deposit.
'Which gifts, indeed, announce beforehand his life.
For honeycomb of honey proclaims his wisdom,'
for just as honey in wax, so he took the spiritual sense from the historical instrument [*i.e.*
the literal sense of Scripture].
'The fish, in truth, sounds his watery life,'
for just as a fish lives in water, so this man, spitting out wine and beer and all that can
inebriate, led a blessed life for God on bread and water alone;
thence also is David surnamed 'of the watery life'.
'The stag, however, signifies dominion over the ancient serpent,'
for just as the stag, fed on despoiled serpents,
desiring a fountain of water, with powers received as he is renewed in youth,
so this man, as if stood above lofty regions on the feet of stags,
despoiling the human race's ancient serpent of the powers of doing harm against himself,
taking for his use a fountain of life with assiduous flowings of tears,
from day to day renewed he progressed,

265

ut in nomine Sanctae Trinitatis salutarem scientiam castioris prandii parcitate
dominandi in daemones habere potestátem incíper*et* .   23

§ 3

II1 **DEINDE** Patricius Romanis eruditus disciplinis . comitantibus uirtutum turmis pontifex
effectus : gentem a qua exuláuerat petíu*it* .
*i*n qua fructuosi operis lucernam oleo geminae caritatis infatigabili refíciens labór*e* :

non sub modio sed super candelabrum impónere uól*ens* .
ut cunctos glorificato omnium Pátre rorár*et* :
Cereticae gentis regiónem ádi*it* .   5
*i*n qua per aliquantulum témporis cònuersát*us* .

Demética ìntrat rúra :
ibique perlustrans tandem ad locum qui Vallis Rosina nominabátur peruén*it* .

2   Et gratum agnoscens locum : deuouit Deo ibi fidéliter dèseruír*e* .

3   Sed cum haec secum meditando reuolueret : apparuit ei ángelus Dómin*i* .   10

4   Tibi inquit non istum locum Déus dispósu*it* .
sed filio qui nondum est natus . nec nisi peractis prius triginta ánnis nascé*tur* .

5   Audiens autem haec sanctus Patricius : moerens et stupens irátusque díx*it* .

6   Cur Dominus despexit seruum suum ab infantia sua sibi seruientem cum timóre et
amór*e* .
elegitque alium nondum in hac luce natum . sed neque ante triginta ánnos nascé*tur* ? 15

7   Parauitque fugere et Dominum suum Iesum Xpistum desérere díc*ens* .

8   Cum ante Domini mei conspectum incassum labor méus redíg*itur* .
et mihi qui nondum est nátus praepón*itur* :
uadam et tali labori amodo nón subiáce*am* .

9   Sed Dominus multum diligébat Patríci*um* :   20
misitque ad eum ángelum sú*um* .
ut illum uerbis familiáribus blàndir*étur* .

10 Cui ait . Patríci laetár*e* .

11 Dominus enim misit me ad te ut ostendam tibi totam Hibérniam ínsul*am* :
de sede quae est in Rosina Valle . quae modo Sedes Patrícii nòminá*tur* .   25

12 Aitque ángelus é*i* .

13 Exulta Patrici : tu enim eris apostolus illius totius ínsulae quam cérn*is* .

14 Multaque propter nomen Domini Dei tui ín ea pàtiér*is* :
sed Dominus erit tecum in omnibus quáe factúrus s*is* .

15 Nondum enim uerbum uítae accép*it* .   30

16 Ibique prodesse debes . ibi parauit tibi Dominus sedem : ibi signis et uirtútibus
ràdi*ábis* .
totamque gentem Déo subiug*ábis* .

17 Sít tibi hòc in sígn*um* .

18 Totam tibi ínsulam osténd*am* .

19 Curuentur montes . humiliábitur pélag*us* .   35
oculus trans omnia euectus . ex loco prospectans uidébit promíss*um* .

20 His dictis erectisque oculis ex loco in quo stabat qui modo Sedes Patricii dicitur : totam
prospéxit ínsul*am* .

21 Tandem animus Patricii sedatus . libenter dimisit locum sanctum . **DÁVID** ági*o* .   38
*p*aransque náuem in Pòrtu Mágn*o* .

so that in the name of the Holy Trinity he would begin to have salutary understanding, by the sparseness of a more chaste diet, the power of holding dominion against demons.

Then Patrick, learned in Roman disciplines, made a bishop with throngs of virtues accompanying, sought the people with which he had lived in exile,

among which, restoring with indefatigable labour the lamp of fruitful work with the oil of twinned charity [*i.e.* love of God and love of man],

wishing to place [the lamp] not under a measuring basket but upon a candelabrum,

so that, with the Father of all glorified, it might enlighten all with its moisture,

he approached the region of the people of Ceredigion,

in which having consorted [lit. 'having turned his mind together'] through a little space of time,

he enters the fields of Demetia,

and there wandering along he came through at last to a place which was named the Valley of the Moor [Welsh *rhos* 'headland', 'moor', 'heath' + Latin adjectival suffix *-ina*].

And acknowledging the pleasing place [Welsh *Hodnant*, *hod* or *haut* 'pleasant' + *nant* 'valley'], he vowed to serve God there faithfully.

But while he was turning these things over by meditating with himself there appeared to him an angel of the Lord.

'For you,' he says, 'God has not disposed this place,

but for a son who has not yet been born and will not be born unless thirty years have been run through first.'

Hearing these things, however, holy Patrick, grieving and being astounded and enraged, said,

'Why has the Lord despised His own servant serving Him from infancy with fear and love,

and chosen another not yet born in this light, but nor will he be born before thirty years?'

And he prepared to flee and to desert his own Lord Jesus Christ, saying,

'Since before the sight of my Lord my labour is reduced to no purpose,

and one who has not yet been born is placed before me,

I shall go and from now I shall not lie subject to such labour.'

But the Lord loved Patrick much,

and He sent to him His own angel,

so that he might blandish him with familiar words.

To whom he says, 'Patrick, rejoice.

For the Lord has sent me to you that I might show to you the whole island of Ireland,

from the seat which is in the Valley of the Moor', which now is named the Seat of Patrick.

And the angel says to him,

'Patrick, exult, for you will be the apostle of the whole of that island which you behold.

Many things on account of the name of the Lord your God you will suffer in it,

but the Lord will be with you in all the things that you are going to do.

For it has not yet received the word of life.

And there you ought to go forth, there the Lord has prepared for you a seat, there you will radiate with signs and virtues,

and you will subjugate the whole people to God.

This may be as a sign for you.

The whole island I will show to you.

Mountains may be bent low, the sea will be lowered,

the eye lifted across all things looking forth from [this] place will see what is promised.'

With these things said and the eyes raised from the place in which he was standing, which now is called the Seat of Patrick he foresaw the whole island.

Finally the calmed spirit of Patrick willingly left the holy place to holy David,

and preparing a ship in the great port [Welsh *Porth Mawr*],

suscitauit quendam senem nomine Cruimther . per duodecim annos iuxta litus íllud
    sepúl*tum* .   40
nauigauitque Patricius in Hiberniam . habens secum núper suscitá*tum* :
qui postea epíscopus fáctus es*t* .   42

Manuscript readings: incipit kal martii deleui; prologus 1 + suppleui; prol. 3 clamat; prol. 6 ditatus. I 5 repperies. I 6 linhenlanú . I 14 dixit. I 7 expoliatus. .xxx^ta. II 2 karitatis. II 15 .xxx.^ta. II 40 criumther. (.xii.)

2. Trucidare Saxones: *A Cambro-Latin martial poem*

I	¶ Truci*d*are **S**ax*ones* *s*oliti Cambr*enses*	a	A
	Ad *c*og*n*atos Brit*ones* *e*t *C*ornu*b*i*enses*	b	
	*Re*qui*r*u*nt* *ut* *ue*n*iant* per *a*cutos *e*nses	a	
	Ad *d*ebellando*s* *i*nimico*s* Saxon*ienses* .	b	
II	5 ¶ Ven*ite* iam strenu*e* loricis arm*ati*.	c	A
	*S*unt *m*agna Saxonum *m*utuo *necati* .	d	
	*E*rit *p*ar*s* residu*a* p*er* uos trucid*ati* .	c	
	Nunc *d*ocumen*ta* *d*at*e* qua sitis origin*e* *n*ati .	d	
III	¶ **M**erl*in*us ueri*d*ic*us* *n*unquam dixit u*anum*.	e	B
	10 *E*xpellendum popul*um* *p*redixit ue*x*anum	f	
	*E*t uos hoc cons*il*ium *n*on *s*eruat*is* *s*anum .	f	
	*Cer*nite fallaces *q*uo*r*um genus omne profa*num* .	e	
IIII	¶ *P*redeces*s*or u*a*lidus *r*ex noster Arth*urus*	g	C
	*S*i uix*is*set hodi*e* fu*i*ssem *s*ecu*r*us	h	
	15 *N*ullus *e*i *S*axonum rest*it*isset m*urus* .	h	
	*E*sset *e*is sicut meruerunt *i*n prece d*urus*.	h	
V	¶ Procur*et* Omnipot*ens* *s*ibi *s*uccess*orem*	i	B
	*S*altem *s*ibi *s*imi*lem* nol*lem* melior*em*	j	
	Qui tolla*t* Britonibu*s* antiquum dol*orem*	j	
	20 Et sibi restituat patri*am* *p*atri*e*que dec*orem* .	i	
VI	¶ Hoc *A*rthuri patru*us* uelit *i*mpetr*are*	k	A
	*S*anct*us* Daui *m*axim*us*: *A*nglum *u*ltra *m*ar*e* .	l	
	*S*cim*us* festum Martis *i*n kalend*is* *i*n*s*tare.	k	
	Ad natale *s*olum Britones *s*tudeat reuoc*are* .	l	
VII	25 ¶ Virt*u*osos *f*ilii pat*r*es imit*antur*.	m	C
	*S*ic Arthurum Br*itones* uirtute sequ*antur*.	n	
	*Q*uam *p*robo *q*uam strenu*o* monstrant *p*roc*r*e*antur*.	n	
	*U*t fu*it* *A*rthurus sic u*i*ct*ores* hab*eantur*.	n	
VIII	¶ *R*egnabat *P*arisius *p*otestas *R*om*ana*	o	B
	30 Frollo gig*as* strenu*us* cuius mens ur*s*ana .	p	
	Hunc Arthurus perim*it* cred*it* fides *sana*	p	
	*T*estis *t*entorium *s*i*t* *e*t *i*nsula Parisi*ana* .	o	
VIIII	¶ *I*nsan*it* *qui* Britones nec*at* gene*rosos*.	q	D
	*V*idetur *quo*d habeat sic *e*os *e*xosos .		q

he raised up a certain old man, by name Cruimther [Irish *cruimther* 'priest' < Latin *presbyter*], buried through twelve years next that shore,
and Patrick sailed into Ireland, having with him the man recently raised up,
who afterward was made a bishop.

I   Cambrians accustomed to massacre Saxons look to [or 'demand of'] related [lit. 'together-born'] Bretons and Cornishmen that they come with sharp swords for warring against Saxon enemies.

II   Come already armed vigorously with corselets. A great part of the Saxons have been slaughtered reciprocally. The residual part will be massacred through you. Now give evidences of what origin you have been born from.

III   Truth-uttering Merlin never said a vain thing. He predicted an insane people to be expelled, and you do not keep this sane counsel. Behold deceitful men, the whole race of them profane.

IIII   The powerful predecessor, our king Arthur, if he were alive today, I would be sure, no wall of the Saxons would resist him. He would be to them, just as they deserved, harsh in [their] entreaty.

V   May the Omnipotent procure for him a successor, at least similar to him – I would not wish a better – who would bear away ancient grief from the Britons and restore to them the fatherland and the fatherland's beauty.

VI   The paternal uncle of Arthur, the greatest saint, David, wishes to obtain this by entreaty: the Englishman beyond the sea. We know the feast to be imminent on the kalends of March. Let him be eager to recall Britons to the natal ground.

VII   Sons imitate virtuous fathers. So let Britons follow Arthur in virtue. They show by how upright, by how vigorous a man they are begotten. As Arthur was, so let them be held victors.

VIII   Roman power ruled at Paris, Frollo the vigorous giant, his mind bearlike. Him Arthur kills, sane faith believes; let the tent and the Parisian island be witness.

VIIII He is insane who slaughters well-born Britons. It is seen that he holds them thus

	35	Namque per *inu*idiam clam*at* <u>o</u>diosos	r	
		Semper <u>et</u> <u>a</u>ssidue qu*os* <u>au</u>dit uic*toriosos*.	r	

			s	D
X		¶ <u>Ex</u> hac gente quatuor sunt imp*eratores* :	s	
		Arthurus <u>Broin</u>*sius* <u>for</u>*te*s <u>bel</u>*latores*	t	
		Constantinus Bre*nnius* <u>fere</u> <u>for</u>*tiores*.	t	
	40	Hii monarchiam tenuerunt ut pro*biores* .		

			u	D
XI		¶ Solum s*uum* <u>K</u>arol*um* <u>F</u>rancia pre*iactat*	u	
		Et R*icardum* <u>A</u>nglia pro*bitate iactat*.	v	
		Pauc*itatem* numer*us* m*aior* l*abefactat*	v	
		Virtutem regis q*u*ia q*u*adrupla gloria m*actat*.		

			k	C
XII	45	¶ *Istis suis* fin*ibus* contig*it* regn*are* .	l	
		Illis duces presid*es* reges tr*iumphare*	k	
		Qu*ibus* n*ullo* merito se poss*int* equare .	k	
	48	Est quam regn*are* longe plus indup*erare* .		

3 requiraunt C. accutos LC. 7 nos L. 9 Mellinus ueredicus LC. 12 Scernite L. 13 arturus L archurus C. 16 ei LC. 22 dam L. 23 in deest LC. 25 imutantur. 26 arturum LC. 26 arturus L. 30 gygas L. 37 .iiii.^{or} L. impetratores L. 38 Arturus L. broynsius C. 41 preiectat L. 42 lactat L. 44 q3 ea *with* ea *interlined* L. 46 ¶ llis L. ¶ Illis C. 47 mito L.

The etymologically correct reading *Merlinus ueridicus* 9 is confirmed by rhyme of *Merlinus* with *Cernite* and of *ueridicus* with *consilium*. Supply of *in* 23 satisfies requirements of grammar, syntax, prosody, and alliteration.

3. *The Office for Saint David's Day*

IN FESTO SANCTI DAVID[29]

AD PRIMAS VESPERAS

antiphona	O desid*erabilis*	*uersus*	Qui c*o*lis pasc*ue*
	uultu forma pre*sulum*		non marcentis *loca*
	fac ut m*iserabilis*		pastor precip*ue*
	iste cetus e*xulum*		gregem tuum *loca*
	reformatus h*abilis*		ubi Regem contempletur gracie
	fit ad uite tit*ulum*		Gloria Patri et Filio et Spiritui Sancto
	Euouae		ubi Regem contempletur gracie

psalmi	*Feriales*	*hymnus*	Iste confessor Domini

capitulum	Ecce sacerdos magnus	*uersiculus* Amauit eum Dominus et ornauit eum

responsorium Pastor D*auid* quem sic p*auit responsio* Stola glorie induit eum
        parca lanx modest*ie*
   ut det*rita* carn*e* u*ita*
      foue*retur gracie*
   mina g*regem* ubi *Regem*
      contempl*etur gracie*

[29] Ed. Edwards, *Matins, Lauds*, 101–2.

hateful, for through envy he calls them odious whom he hears of as always and assiduously victorious.

X   From this race are four emperors: Arthur, Broinsius, strong warriors, Constantine, Brennius, almost stronger. They kept the monarchy as more upright men.

XI   France boasts only of [lit. 'hurls before'] its own Charles, and England boasts of Richard in uprightness. A greater number destroys [such] paucity, as a fourfold glory endows the virtue of [our] king.

XII   It has befallen to these latter to reign as king in their own bounds, to the former to triumph over dukes, presidents, kings, to whom they could by no merit make themselves equal. It is by a long way more to command as emperor than to reign as king.

ON THE FEAST OF HOLY DAVID

AT FIRST VESPERS

antiphon	O form [*i.e.* model] of bishops, desirable in countenance [or 'appearance'], grant that this miserable throng of exiles, reformed, may be made fit for the title of life.
verse	You who inhabit the places of a pasture-land that does not waste away, excellent shepherd, place your flock where it may contemplate the King of grace. Glory to the Father and to the Son and to the Holy Ghost, where it may contemplate the King of grace.
psalms	for liturgical use on ordinary days
hymn	This confessor of the Lord
chapter	Behold the great bishop
versicle	The Lord loved him and adorned him
responsory	Pastor David, whom the restrained balance of modesty so pastured that with the flesh trodden down the life of grace might be encouraged, drive the flock where it may contemplate the King of grace.
response	The stole of glory put on him

****

antiphona	Dominum magnific*auit*
	sanc*ti* patri*s* an*ima*
	qui n*il* pe*ne* reput*auit*
	mun*di* probatiss*ima*
	Iesu bo*ne* *s*et prob*auit*
	quod *t*u sis par*s* opt*ima*
psalmus	Magnificauit

oratio   Deus qui beatum Dauid confessorem tuum atque pontificem angelo nunciante triginta annis antequam nasceretur predixisti tribue nobis quesumus ut cuius festiuitatem colimus eius intercessione ad eterna gaudia perueniamus Per Dominum nostrum Iesum Xpistum Filium tuum qui tecum uiuit et regnat in unitate Spiritus Sancti Deus per omnia secula seculorum Amen

alia oratio   Deus qui ecclesie tue beatum Dauid confessorem tuum atque pontificem mirabilem tribuisti doctorem concede propicius ut ipsum apud te pium semper habere mereamur intercessorem Per Dominum nostrum Iesum Xpistum Filium tuum qui tecum uiuit et regnat in unitate Spiritus Sancti Deus per omnia secula seculorum Amen

****

antiphon   The soul of the holy father magnified the Lord, he who reckoned as almost nothing the things most approved by the world, but, good Jesu, he proved that you may be the best part.

psalm   He has magnified

prayer   God, Who with an angel announcing foretold blessed David Your confessor and pontiff thirty years before he would be born, grant to us, we ask, that we who cultivate his festival by his intercession may come through to eternal joys, through Our Lord Jesus Christ Your Son, Who with You lives and reigns in the unity of the Holy Spirit, God, through all ages of ages. Amen.

another prayer God, Who to Your Church have given blessed David Your confessor and wondrous pontiff, grant, Gracious One, that we may merit always to have the same with You as holy intercessor, through Our Lord Jesus Christ Your Son, Who with You lives and reigns in the unity of the Holy Spirit, God, through all ages of ages. Amen.

14

THE RELICS OF ST DAVID: THE HISTORICAL EVIDENCE

F.G. Cowley

The appointment of Bernard as bishop of St Davids in 1115 brought to an end one of the most disruptive and destructive periods in the history of the see. The entries in the *Annales Cambriae* and the associated versions of the *Brut y Tywysogion* present a catalogue of the calamities in which the cathedral and see were involved in the last quarter of the eleventh century: a succession of Norse raids, the virtual destruction of the cathedral on three occasions (1071–1073, 1078 [1080] and 1090), a dynastic conflict involving Norse, Irish and Welsh which culminated in the battle of Mynydd Carn in 1081, the visit of the Conqueror to St Davids in the same year and the advent of the Normans into Dyfed in great force in 1093. It is during this period of upheaval that the first reference to the relics of St David appears in the historical record. The *Annales Cambriae* contains the entry: 'The reliquary of St David was stolen from his church and it was despoiled of the gold and silver with which it was covered';[1] and the *Brut y Tywysogion*: 'A year after that, the shrine of David was taken by stealth from the church, and close to the city it was completely destroyed.'[2] These entries have not been securely dated. They have been assigned to the period 1088–91 but probably belong to the year 1090. Significantly perhaps the annalist does not mention the fate of the relics. Had they been stolen, the St Davids annalist would probably have been loath to acknowledge it; had they been saved, he would surely have mentioned it. The Norse raids, through their very intensity, remained in the collective memory of the clergy of the see, and over a century later Gerald of Wales, in his digest of the Life of the hermit Caradog, records

> that when the city of Menevia through frequent attacks by pirates borne on long ships from the Isles of Orkney had been left desolate for a period of seven years through the sins of the inhabitants, a certain devout priest after rooting out the thorns and brambles scarcely reached the tomb of the confessor David on the seventh day.[3]

Gerald was even more specific when asked by Pope Innocent III if St Davids had any privileges dealing with its claims to metropolitan status. The church, he replied, was often plundered by pirates

> coming thither in summer in their long ships … and was often left desolate and almost in ruins, its books, privileges, its vestments, its phylacteries and treasures being carried away also and its canons and clergy sometimes slain.[4]

---

1   *AC* (ed. Lloyd, 178–9; ed. Williams Ab Ithel, 28–9).
2   *ByT* (Pen. 20) (ed. and transl. Jones, 18, 156).
3   *De sancto Caradoco heremita* (ed. Horstman, *Nova Legenda Anglie*, I, 174).
4   Giraldus Cambrensis, *De iure et statu Menevensis ecclesiae* (ed. Butler, *Autobiography*, 183–4).

The desolate state of the cathedral and its precinct, the violence of the Normans who had appropriated property belonging to the church, and the success with which Archbishop Anselm of Canterbury had exercised metropolitan rights over St Davids by suspending Wilfred (1085–1115),[5] the last Welsh bishop of the see, prompted Rhygyfarch, son of the late Bishop Sulien, to write a Life of the founder saint. It was essentially a public relations exercise. Written 1093×95, it emphasised the sanctity and power of the saint, his appointment as archbishop by the Patriarch of Jerusalem and the extensive rights once enjoyed by his church. The *Life* gave tremendous impetus to the diffusion of the cultus of St David during the twelfth century but, significantly, it is silent about any shrine of the saint or of miracles performed at his tomb. It merely states that when he died 'his body, borne in the arms of the holy brethren, accompanied by a great retinue, and committed to the earth with honour, was laid to rest within his monastery'.[6] Rhygyfarch had to be content with publicising the secondary relics which the Patriarch of Jerusalem had given him: an altar covered with skins and veils, a bell renowned for its miracles, a pastoral staff 'lustrous with glorious miracles' and a 'coat woven from gold'.[7]

Even from this admittedly scanty evidence one could assume that the bodily remains of St David had been lost by the end of the eleventh century. Such an assumption is placed beyond any doubt by what we know of Bishop Bernard's episcopate.

Bernard was the first Norman bishop of St Davids. He had been a courtier, a chaplain and later chancellor to King Henry I's wife, Matilda. He was intruded into the see, as the *Brut* makes clear, 'in contempt of the clerics of the Britons'. Yet, once installed, he eagerly embraced the traditions of the cathedral and see passed on to him by members of the *clas*. His episcopate was one of great achievement. He built a new cathedral, he reorganised the *clas* into a cathedral chapter, he secured an extensive territorial diocese for his see after a prolonged dispute with Llandaf, he introduced orders of monks new to Wales: the older Benedictines, the Augustinian canons and the new reformed orders of Tiron and Citeaux, he attempted to obtain metropolitan status for his see but died before the final hearing could be held at the Council of Reims in 1148.

Bernard's cathedral was completed and dedicated in 1131 and the occasion was probably used to secure the translation of the body of a local holy man, the hermit Caradog, to his final resting place. The acquisition of Caradog's body in 1124 had been a stroke of good fortune for Bernard, for here was a man of heroic sanctity who had performed a number of miracles during his lifetime and had gained the affection and devotion of Welsh, Flemish and Anglo-Normans. When his coffin was opened at the translation ceremony, his body was found incorrupt. William of Malmesbury, the monk-historian, was present on this occasion and when he tried, out of devotion, to cut off one of his fingers and take it away with him, the saint, as though feeling the cutting, clenched his fingers into the palm of his hand, and withdrew his hand into his cloak. His body was buried, Gerald of Wales tells us, in the left aisle of the church of St Andrew and St David, beside the altar of St Stephen, the protomartyr.[8]

5   Davies, *Episcopal Acts*, I, 235, D16.
6   Rhygyfarch, *Vita S. David* § 65, ed. Sharpe and Davies, above, 150–51.
7   Rhygyfarch, *Vita S. David* § 48, ed. Sharpe and Davies, above, 140–41.
8   *De sancto Caradoco heremita* (ed. Horstman, *Nova Legenda Anglie*, I, 176); Giraldus Cambrensis, *Itinerarium Kambriae* I §2, transl. and ed. Thorpe, 144–5 and notes.

The presence of William of Malmesbury at St Davids is of crucial importance because it gives weight to what is said of the body of St David in an interpolated passage of his *Gesta Regum Anglorum*:

> Concerning this famous and incomparable man, I find no certainty whether he died at Glastonbury, or ended his life in his own see. They say he lies with St Patrick, [that is, at Glastonbury] and the Welsh, by their habit of praying to him, and often in conversation, definitely confirm this, telling how Bishop Bernard more than once looked for his body, and in face of many protests, could not find it.[9]

The cautious tone of this passage, so typical of William, suggests that it represents his own words, probably passed to a later revisor and editor of his work.

Bishop Bernard never secured the canonisation of David, as is so frequently stated even by modern writers. He did, however, obtain from Pope Calixtus II what was probably a written privilege or indulgence which accorded to English pilgrims who journeyed twice to St Davids the same blessings as those who journeyed once to Rome. Again the authority for this statement is William of Malmesbury.[10]

Although no one knew where his relics were, the cultus of St David, thanks to Rhygyfarch and Bernard, grew in popularity in the twelfth century. Welsh bards like Gwynfardd Brycheiniog sang his praises and his cultus was even taken up by the Anglo-Normans and Flemings who used his name as a battle-cry in their wars against the Irish.[11] The cultus was reinforced too by the writing of a new life of St David. Gerald of Wales wrote his life 1192×94 and it is, for the most part, a polished version of Rhygyfarch's. It makes no mention of the bodily remains of David – they were still missing, but Gerald, in addition to mentioning the secondary relics recorded by Rhygyfarch, records for the first time another secondary relic: the Imperfect Gospel. David was engaged in copying the gospel of St John. On the ringing of the bell he jumped up and hastened to the church without either closing the book or completing the page. When he returned to the scriptorium he found the column which he had begun, already completed in gold letters by the work of an angel. 'He closed the book and removed it from the sight of human eyes, making no addition to it whatsoever. Whence it is that even to this day', writes Gerald,

> the inside of the book, which was closed and bound into a volume becomingly adorned with silver and gold, is not shown to the eyes of men. No one is said to have dared to look inside the book or to open its seal from the time of St David almost to modern times. But in these last days some men presumed to essay that ... but being grievously and suddenly smitten by the anger of heaven, they were recalled from their rash daring. That text moreover is called by the inhabitants of this district the Imperfect Gospel, and even to this day it is renowned for its miracles and virtues, and is not undeservedly held in the highest reverence by all.[12]

---

9   William of Malmesbury, *Gesta*, *Additamenta* Bk I § 25, ed. Mynors, 810–11. There is a similar account, also interpolated, in his *De Antiquitate Glastonie Ecclesie* which gives David a death date of A.D. 546 and records that his relics were translated to Glastonbury in A.D. 962 in the reign of King Edgar by a lady named Aelswitha: see Scott, *The Early History of Glastonbury*, 63–7.

10 Harris, 'Was St. David ever canonized?', 30–2; William of Malmesbury, *Gesta* Bk V § 45, ed. Mynors, 778–81.

11 Owen, 'Prolegomena', 51–79; *Song of Dermot and the Earl* (ed. Orpen, lines 987, 1938, 3442–55, cited in Lloyd, *History of Wales*, II.541 and n. 25).

12 I have used the text and translation of Bowen Jones, 'The Life of St. David', 241–3, 293–5.

Over three quarters of a century now pass and the scene moves from St Davids to the priory of St Michael's, Ewenni in the diocese of Llandaf. Ewenni was a small priory of Benedictine monks dependent on the great abbey of Gloucester and in the 1260s and 70s was ruled by John de Gamages, a monk of noble birth who went on to be prior of St Guthlac's, Hereford (another dependency of Gloucester) before being elected abbot of Gloucester in 1284. We know much about John de Gamages because a Gloucester monk wrote an obituary of him when he died in 1306. Suffice to say here that he was a man of conventional piety, an astute administrator and public relations man of the calibre of Abbot Samson of Bury rather than like the other-worldly visionary, Ailred of Rievaulx. The obituarist records that while John was prior of Ewenni:

> The Lord revealed to him in a vision the body of St David, bishop of St Davids, whose place of burial had been unknown to the clergy of the same church and to the inhabitants of that land for ages past. After the vision his body was found whole, outside the southern door, at the fixed measure of paces shown to him in the vision, by measuring from the said door, up to the place in which it was buried, as easily and as certainly as though the said prior had been present at his burial.[13]

The obituary of John de Gamages is the only source known to me which mentions this memorable discovery. All the versions of the Welsh *Brut* are silent on the issue, but the discovery does receive some confirmation from an entry in the *Annales Cambriae*. The entry relates that in 1275 'work was begun on the shrine of St David in the church of Menevia'. The shrine is almost certainly the stone base which spans the third northern bay from the east end of Peter de Leia's church. This would have been surmounted in medieval times by a wooden portable feretory.[14]

It would not be difficult even for a medieval devil's advocate to challenge the authenticity of John de Gamages' discovery. Even if one discounts Glastonbury's claim that David's relics were acquired and taken to Glastonbury abbey in 962 by Aelswitha, a relative of the bishop of St Davids, there are still two charters, one by Cadwgan, bishop of Bangor, another by Gervase, bishop of St Davids, which attest that Leominster priory possessed an arm of St David well before John's alleged discovery of the whole body.[15]

What made John de Gamages so preoccupied with the relics of St David at this time? What made the need to discover the body so urgent or, to put it in other words, what made the discovery so propitious? The early part of Richard of Carew's episcopate from 1256 to the Treaty of Montgomery in 1267 was a period of great disorder and devastation within the diocese, for it was constantly traversed by warring armies. Llywelyn ap Gruffydd had organised a series of successful campaigns into Meirionnydd, Builth, Deheubarth and Powys and had raided deeply into Pembroke and Glamorgan. During the ensuing conflict, as the bishop complained to the king in 1259, the clergy were exposed to violence, injury and sometimes death, their churches and houses burned so that if the king did not apply a remedy they would have to leave their churches and go into exile. Such was the breakdown in law and order that in 1265 the king vetoed a plan to build a bridge across the Teifi

---

13 *Historia et cartularium monasterii Sancti Petri Gloucestrie*, ed. Hart, I, 39–40; cf. Cowley, 'A note', 47–8.
14 *AC*, ed. Williams ab Ithel, 104; Coldstream, 'English decorated shrine bases', 15, and esp. 20–1. Each side of the base is illustrated in Evans and Worsley, *Eglwys Gadeiriol Tyddewi*, 121 and in Rees, *The Medieval Shrines*, 4–5.
15 Morgan, 'An edition of the cartulary of Leominster Priory', fols 72–3, nos. 71–2.

linking Newcastle Emlyn with the episcopal estate at Adpar because it would ease the way of thieves and malefactors. Wagons carrying money and food from the episcopal estates and money, food and wax renders from innumerable churches were waylaid and robbed. Equally damaging to the cathedral finances was that warfare and the conditions it promoted discouraged pilgrims. As the tide of warfare receded northwards after the Treaty of Montgomery, the cathedral administration needed to recoup its losses, to enhance the status of the cathedral as a pilgrimage centre, and give a new stimulus to the practice of pilgrimage. What better way to achieve these ends than by recovering, the founder-saint's mortal remains.[16]

But what of John de Gamages? Why should a prior of a small cell of monks in another diocese be preoccupied with the burial place of St David? It may of course be that he was just very interested in saints' lives, for he left a volume entitled *Legendum Sanctorum* to his abbey on his death. But there is another explanation. Gloucester abbey had been in financial difficulties throughout the third and fourth quarters of the thirteenth century, partly through over-ambitious building programmes and partly, one suspects, through mismanagement. A crisis was reached in 1273 when the Crown appointed a custodian, the equivalent of a general receiver, to restore order and stability to the abbey finances. It seems almost certain that it was about this critical time that John de Gamages had his vision. Might not the discovery of David's body be a means of obtaining the assistance of the bishop and chapter of St Davids in recovering two properties in the diocese of St Davids which Gloucester abbey had lost in the twelfth century: the property administered by Chertsey abbey monks at Cardigan and the far richer property of the former *clas* church of Llanbadarn Fawr? This was one of the richest churches in Wales and from 1245 in the patronage of the Crown. Despite repeated efforts Gloucester never recovered these properties but that object may have been one of the motives in the mind of John de Gamages.[17]

In the decades after the discovery, the body was dismembered and parts acquired by individuals and other churches. Among the first to profit was the king himself. Edward I made a triumphal progress through Wales after its conquest, and came on pilgrimage to St Davids on 26 November 1284. Edward was a devout pilgrim. He and his father had, by the frequency of their visits, virtually put Walsingham on the map as a Marian shrine. He was also a collector of relics and always took some with him on his campaigns.[18] But there were political overtones to this visit. He had already obtained in north Wales part of the regalia of the princes of Gwynedd: the Croes Nawdd (a relic of the true cross) and the alleged crown of King Arthur. At St Davids he acquired the head and other parts of the skeleton of St David and in the following year the Bury St Edmunds chronicler records that 'the King led a solemn procession from the tower of London to Westminster bearing the head of St David … and other relics which he had brought from Wales'. These were potent symbols of Welsh pride and identity and the ceremony was a demonstration, as another chronicler recorded, that the glory of the Welsh had been transferred to the English.[19] A

---

16 Davies, *Episcopal Acts* I, 395, D 641; I, 405, D 667; There is a useful map of the episcopal estates in Evans and Turner, *St Davids Bishop's Palace*, 13.

17 Graham, 'The abbey', 55–6; Malden, 'The possession', 141–56 and Lewis, *A Short History.*

18 *AC*, ed. Williams ab Ithel, 108. For Edward's particular brand of piety, see Prestwich, 'The piety of Edward I', 120–8; Dickinson, *The Shrine*, 19–21, 39–40; for Edward's lavish benefactions to Bishop Thomas Bek, see Williams, *The Welsh Church*, 2nd edn, 44–5.

19 *Chronicle of Bury St Edmunds*, ed. Gransden, 85 and no. 2; *Waverley Annals, s.a.* 1283, ed. Luard, *Annales Monastici*, vol. 2, 401.

little later, Edward placed a relic of St David on the high altar of the church of Great St Helen at Bishopsgate and an arm of St David was among the many relics found among the king's effects when he died.[20] These latter relics may have been slivers of bone rather than whole limbs. Among the churches that shared in the discovery were Salisbury cathedral, which possessed 'a relik of St Davyd' and Reading abbey which possessed an arm bone. A thorough search of relic lists would perhaps bring to light further examples.[21]

It is unfortunate we do not have a representative spread of accounts recording receipts of offerings made at St Davids shrine in the last two centuries of the middle ages. It would have enabled us to gauge the periods when the shrine was most popular as a focus of pilgrimage and allow a comparison to be made with other great pilgrimage centres such as Canterbury, Walsingham and Durham. Apart from offerings made at St Davids itself, there were frequent, if not annual, tours with the relics to different parts of the diocese in the early fourteenth century, for the duties of tenants and burgesses in this connection are noted in the *Black Book of St Davids*. The only money receipts noted, however, are the two sets of entries in the *Liber Communis* for the year 1490 when a perambulation of the relics brought in 28s. 4d. from southern parts of the diocese, 26s. 8d. from parts of Gower and £3 from parts of Brecon; and for the year 1492 when 17s. 2d. accrued from a perambulation of Ystrad Tywi, 33s. 8d. from parts of Gower and £3 from parts of Brecon. Despite the lack of documentation it is possible that the reigns of the first three Edwards may have witnessed the period of the shrine's greatest popularity, attested by the frequency of finds of Edwardian coins in the vicinity of the cathedral, and the building by Bishop Henry de Gower (1328–47) of the great hall in the episcopal palace for the accommodation and entertainment of distinguished pilgrims. Since Henry de Gower was not a man of great private means, the financing of the building of the great hall must have come largely from pilgrim's offerings.[22]

William Barlow's appointment to St Davids in 1536 brought to the see a radical Protestant who used his fiery eloquence in the pulpit and in letters to Thomas Cromwell to denounce the superstitious practices he found in his diocese, among them those of pilgrimage and the veneration of relics. It is unnecessary here to enter into the details of his career; they are dealt with in another paper.[23] Suffice it to say that Barlow provides us with a description of the relics as they existed in his day. In a letter to Thomas Cromwell dated 31 March 1538, he relates how he had admonished the canons of St Davids not 'to set forth feigned reliques for to allure the people to supersticion' and goes on to say that on St David's day:

> certen reliques were set forth which I caused to be sequestrered and taken awaye, detaynyne them in my custody until I maye be advertised of your lordships pleasour. The parcels of the reliques are these: two heedes of sylver plate enclosinge two rotten skulls stuffed with putrified clowtes; item, two arme bones, and a worme eaten booke covered with sylver plate.[24]

---

20 Cowley, 'A note', 47–8.
21 Wordsworth, *Ceremonies and Processions*, 39; Hurry, *Reading Abbey*, 129.
22 *The Black Book of St Davids*, ed. Willis-Bund, 37, 81, 89, 95, 123, 125, 153, 161. The *Liber Communis*, itself an incomplete transcript, has been printed in Jones and Freeman, *The History and Antiquities*, 369–89, esp. 376 and 378. King, *Handbook to the Cathedrals of Wales*, 165, Evans and Turner, *St Davids Palace*, 18; Evans and Worsley, *Eglwys Gadeiriol Tyddewi*, 27.
23 See also the details given in Williams, *Welsh Reformation Essays*, 111–24.
24 Wright, *Three Chapters*, 184.

Since Edward I had taken St David's skull, the two heads were probably those of St Justinian, David's confessor and of the hermit Caradog. The worm-eaten book was certainly the Imperfect Gospel mentioned by Gerald of Wales.

What happened next is matter for speculation. Barlow could have done one of three things. He could have despatched the relics to London to be dealt with there. This happened to a number of Welsh relics such as the statue of Our Lady of Penrhys and the image of Derfel Gadarn. He could have burnt the relics: this apparently was the action taken with the relics of St Thomas of Canterbury. He could have mingled the relics with other human bones to prevent their future identification and given them a common burial. It is extremely unlikely that he returned them to the cathedral.

Apart from Privy Council letters ordering a search for jewels embezzled from the shrine in the 1540s, Barlow's letter is the last reference we have to the relics. But the story does not end there. In 1866, during the Victorian repair and restoration of the cathedral, Mr Clear, clerk of the works to the architect Sir Gilbert Scott, uncovered a niche/hagioscope in the east wall of the cathedral built by Bishop de Leia (1176–98) which had been partly filled with a heap of bones embedded in mortar. They were removed, placed in an oak chest and buried under the pavement in front of the niche. There they were to remain for the next fifty-four years. Meanwhile, writers on the cathedral began to speculate on the bones: whose bones were they and why were they walled up in the niche? Some were of the opinion that they were the bones of St David and of one or more other saints, either St Justinian or St Caradog or both. They based their claim on very slender evidence: one set of bones belonged to a tall man and St David according to Rhygyfarch was a tall man, and the bones had been set in mortar to prevent their desecration at the Reformation. These ideas were eagerly taken up by William Williams, the new dean appointed in 1919. Williams was an Anglo-Catholic and the first dean of a Welsh cathedral to restore the use of eucharistic vestments. He was appointed at a critical time in the history of the Welsh church. The Act of Disestablishment came into force in June 1920 and there were genuine fears that the finances of the church would be seriously affected. As dean, Williams was conscious of the need of funds for the continuing restoration of the cathedral. The restoration of a shrine as a focus for renewed pilgrimage would go some way to meet this need. In 1920 Dean Williams had the oak chest dug up and the bones put in a new reliquary which was then displayed in the old recess behind an iron grill. Formal pilgrimages to St Davids were now resumed after a period of nearly four hundred years. The organisation primarily responsible for this was the Society of St David, Lampeter College, whose members made the first pilgrimage, encouraged by Dean Williams. In 1924 the Revd Arthur Baring-Gould published a pilgrim's manual which became 'the basic guide and service book for such journeys to St Davids'.[25]

The decision to give the bones found in 1866 a place of honour in the cathedral and the publicity which ensued caused bitter controversy in the 1920s and 1930s. Some were seriously concerned that the bones were assumed to be those of St David and St Justinian without any serious historical or anatomical investigation being made. The controversy spilled over into the local and national press and the *Church Times* gave it substantial coverage, allowing ample space for letters, some

---

25 See the references in Evans, 'The Reformation', 5; letter from Dean T.E. Jenkins, 13 March 1961; Barnwell, 'The lately discovered crosses', 67–9; Morgan-Guy, 'The society of St. David'. I am also greatly indebted to Mrs Nona Rees for photocopies of material in St Davids Cathedral Library.

of which were significantly signed with a pseudonym. The controversy came to a head in 1929 or soon after when a member of the chapter, Canon W. G. Spurrell published a short pamphlet entitled *In Re The Bone Relics* which amounted to an all-out attack on the authenticity of the relics. The pamphlet was a scholarly one and the evidence produced unanswerable. Pressure was now brought to bear on Canon Spurrell to withdraw the pamphlet and this he reluctantly did. When it was proposed to raise the matter of the relics again during the deanery of David Watkyn Morgan (1931–40), he declared that he would not allow the subject to be discussed and that if an attempt were made to do so, he would dissolve the chapter meeting.[26]

Thus matters remained until 1996 when Dean Wyn Evans called a chapter meeting to raise the whole question again and to seek if possible a definitive decision on whether the bones could include those of St David. The examinations subsequently undertaken under the direction of Professor Bernard Knight at the Royal Infirmary, Cardiff and of Professor Robert Hedges at the Radio Carbon Accelerator Unit at Oxford, are discussed elsewhere in these conference proceedings. The investigations prove conclusively that the bones could not have been those of sixth-century saints and belonged rather to persons living in the period from the eleventh to the thirteenth centuries. The tests also showed that the bones were set in mortar and sealed up in the niche within the same time scale. They could therefore include the bones of Caradog who died in 1124 but are more likely to be those of churchmen buried in ground outside the east end of Peter de Leia's church which were sealed in the niche when extensions were made to the cathedral. Further speculation would not be profitable.

---

[26] Letters to me from the late Reverend Silas M. Harris dated 8 December 1967, 2 January 1968; 16 January 1968; 26 February 1968. A copy of the pamphlet has survived in the reference collections of Haverfordwest Public Library; I am indebted to the Librarian for a photocopy.

15

AMS RADIOCARBON DATING OF BONES FROM ST DAVIDS CATHEDRAL

T.F.G Higham, C. Bronk Ramsey and L.D.M Nokes

Introduction

In 1866, during restoration work at St David's Cathedral overseen by Sir Gilbert Scott, a number of bones were discovered in a niche behind a wall behind the High Altar in the Holy Trinity Chapel.[1] Some cathedral authorities suggested that the remains might be associated with St David, or perhaps St Justinian, both of whom are said to have been enshrined on the northern side of the Presbytery in A.D. 1275.[2] St David is thought to have died in the late sixth century A.D. An oak casket was constructed in 1921 to house the bones and this was placed in the niche during further restoration work and has remained on display in the cathedral ever since.

In 1997, the casket was opened and bones from it examined at the Forensic Medicine department at Cardiff Royal Infirmary. The results of the analysis are outlined by Nokes *et al.*[3] Briefly, around 50 bone fragments were found, some of which were very small pieces of bone (<1 cm long) and others include parts of femora and tibiae. There were also some cranial bones. The lower limb bones appeared to belong to perhaps three individuals.[4]

Samples from seven of the bones were submitted for radiocarbon analysis using AMS (Accelerator Mass Spectrometry) to the Oxford Radiocarbon Accelerator Unit (ORAU) in 1996 by one of us (LDMN). Care was made to submit different pieces of bone to exclude the possibility that one individual was dated more than once. The bone samples included three femoral heads (denoted 'FH' in Table 2), two femora and two ulna. In addition, a sample of charcoal recovered from mortar within the cathedral wall which sealed the casket within which the bones were discovered was submitted.

Method

Since AMS radiocarbon dating enables the analysis of bone samples in the milligram range, it is crucial that samples are pretreated with care prior to dating, so that potential contaminants are removed. Bone is one of the more challenging sample types dated using radiocarbon. About 20% of bone comprises organic compounds; 90–95% of which is collagen. The remaining organic fraction consists of non-collagenous proteins. The bulk of the bone is hydroxyapatite, an inorganic cement. Early radiocarbon work on this material demonstrated its unreliability because of

---

[1] Nokes *et al.*, 'Observation', 66–70.
[2] Nokes *et al.*, 'Observation', 66–70.
[3] Nokes *et al.*, 'Observation', 66–70.
[4] Nokes *et al.*, 'Observation', 66–70.

Table 2. AMS radiocarbon determinations for the bones recovered from St Davids. OxA-6609 and 6610 were found placed in glass tubes which had been put into the casket in the 1920s. All femoral heads were interpreted to be male.

OxA-number	Sample code	$d^{13}C$	Radiocarbon age B.P.	Calibrated age A.D.	
				68% prob. range	95.4% prob. range
6606	SD (reconstructed femur)	−18.6	760 ± 45	1220–1235 (8.0%) 1240–1290 (60.2%)	1185–1305 (94.2%) 1370–1380 (1.2%)
6607	S1 (femoral shaft)	−19.0	865 ± 45	1060–1090 (11.1%) 1120–1140 7.7% 1155–1225 (45.6%) 1230–1245 (3.8%)	1035–1145 (35.7%) 1150–1265 (59.7%)
6608	FH 2 (femoral head left side)	−19.4	950 ± 40	1020–1065 (26.8%) 1080–1125 (27.8%) 1135–1160 (13.6%)	1015–1190 (95.4%)
6609	Tube 2 (ulna)	−19.3	860 ± 45	1065–1085 (7.3%) 1120–1140 (6.1%) 1155–1245 (54.8%)	1035–1145 (31.8%) 1150–1270 (63.6%)
6610	Tube 1 (ulna)	−19.2	925 ± 40	1035–1145(63.7%) 1150–1160 (4.5%)	1020–1195 (93.2%) 1200–1210 (2.2%)
6611	FH 1 (femoral head right side)	−18.4	695 ± 40	1275–1305 (45.5%) 1365–1390 (22.7%)	1255–1330 (61.1%) 1340–1395 (34.3%)
6612	FH 3 (femoral head right side)	−19.4	870 ± 40	1060–1090 (12.3%) 1120–1140 (8.5%) 1155–1225 (47.5%)	1035–1145 (36.6%)

its propensity for post-depositional exchange. The fibrous nature of the collagen gives bone strength and flexibility. Collagen molecules consist of three polypeptides each made up of about 1,000 amino acids per chain. These molecules are arranged in fibrils, themselves arranged into a right handed coil (fibre) weighing between 95,000 and 102,000 Daltons. Radiocarbon laboratories use established techniques to decalcify the bone, removing the hydroxyapatite and isolating the collagen fraction for radiocarbon analysis. Various techniques exist for purifying the resulting collagen and removing humic and fulvic contaminants. At ORAU, ultrafilters are used to select only the >30,000 Dalton molecular weight fraction, which includes undegraded collagen. This method was not used in 1997 when the St David's material was dated however, instead, ion exchange techniques were used.

Around 0.9 g of bone was sampled from each of the St David's bones for AMS dating. The bone was first powdered using a mortar and pestle and then decalcified using dilute acid. Further purification of this fraction involved a NaOH wash, designed to mobilise humic contaminants, a further acid wash and gelatinisation of the collagen using a weakly acidic water (pH=3) in a constant incubation temperature (65° C) for 20 hours. The gelatin was then purified using ion exchange columns and the extracted amino acids were freeze-dried. Each sample was combusted, graphitised and AMS dated.[5]

---

[5] See for current method: Bronk Ramsey and Hedges, 'Hybrid ion sources', 539–45; Bronk Ramsey *et al.*, 'Radiocarbon dates', 459–79.

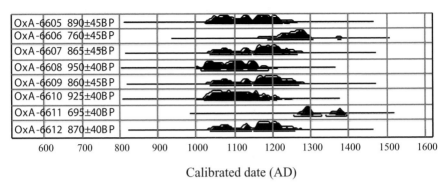

Calibrated date (AD)

Figure 2. AMS radiocarbon determination for the charcoal sample dated from St Davids

Table 3. AMS radiocarbon determination for the charcoal sample dated from St Davids. The charcoal was interpreted as being placed in the cement used to seal the niche in which the bones were discovered in the 1860s.

OxA-number	Sample code	$d^{13}C$	Radiocarbon age B.P.	Calibrated age A.D.	
				68% prob. range	95.4% prob. range
6605	–	−24.2	890 ± 45	1040–1095 (25.3%)	1025–1225 (94.0%)
				1120–1140 (10.7%)	1230–1245 (1.4%)
				1155–1215 (32.2%)	

Conventional radiocarbon ages B.P. were calculated with reference to the conventions outlined by Stuiver and Polach.[6]

Results

The radiocarbon results are shown in Table 2. It is immediately apparent that the radiocarbon ages are much younger than would be expected had the bone belonged to human beings living in the sixth century A.D.

Because the production of ^{14}C in the upper atmosphere is not constant, determining calendrical or solar ages requires conversion of the radiocarbon ages using a 'calibration curve'. The calibration curve is constructed from high precision radiocarbon measurements obtained from dendrochronologically dated tree rings, that presently extend back to *ca* 11,800 years before present. The INTCAL98 calibration curve (Fig. 2);[7] and the OxCal 3.6 calibration software programme was used to convert radiocarbon dates to calendar time.[8] Our calibrated results are consistent with a Late Medieval date and again clearly post-date the time of St David. The calibrated radiocarbon results span the eleventh to fourteenth centuries A.D. but the majority cluster within the eleventh to twelfth centuries.

6   Stuiver and Polach, 'Discussion: reporting of 14C data', 355–63.
7   Stuiver, 'INTCAL98', 1041–83.
8   Bronk Ramsey, 'Development'.

The date obtained from the charcoal sample discovered in the mortar wall which sealed the casket (OxA-6605) is similar to the majority of the bone dates. The radiocarbon date of 890 ± 45 BP overlaps with the calendar ages calculated for the majority of the bones themselves, with the exception of OxA-6611 which is significantly younger. Archaeologically, the age of the charcoal ought not to be older than the date of the bone samples which it seals. There are two possible explanations. First, since the species of the charcoal which was dated is not known there is a possibility that 'inbuilt age' has affected the radiocarbon result. Inbuilt age is defined as the difference in age between the death of the sample and the archaeological event which is to be dated. In the case of wood, it is the combination of *growth age* (the age of old wood in a tree) and *storage age* (the time the tree was lying around before it was used).[9] Inbuilt age produces non-systematic offsets causing the radiocarbon determination to be too old compared with the dated event. It could be that in this case the charcoal is one or two centuries too old because of inbuilt age. Second, two of the bone determinations might be contaminated with more modern carbon which was not completely removed by the pre-treatment applied. Neither explanation is able to be excluded with confidence. It is possible that both are operating in tandem, skewing the charcoal date to the old and the bone date to the young. In general, however, we conclude that the radiocarbon dates show the deposition of bones occurred within the *ca* A.D. 1000–1200 period, with greater precision than this hampered by the possibilities described above and the 'wiggles' inherent in the radiocarbon calibration curve.

Conclusion

The suite of AMS radiocarbon determinations from the casket found at St Davids produced results which were inconsistent with a sixth-century date. The bones found in the casket may have been the remains of important figures in the history of the cathedral, but St David himself can be excluded with confidence.[10]

---

[9] McFadgen, 'Dating', 379–92.
[10] Thanks are due to the staff at the Oxford Radiocarbon Accelerator Unit for AMS dating the samples described here. We are grateful to Dr J.M. Wooding (Dept of Theology and Religious Studies, University of Wales Lampeter) for organising the conference and the subsequent opportunity to compile this brief report.

16

SHRINE AND COUNTER-SHRINE
IN 1920s AND 1930s DEWISLAND?

John Morgan-Guy

C.H. Morgan-Griffiths, the wealthy Carmarthen solicitor and diocesan registrar, by his own account first conceived the idea of building a Roman Catholic chapel in the vicinity of St Davids around 1928, about the time that work began on the construction of St Non's House.[1] The original intention was to build at Whitewell Field, the site of one of the medieval chapels closely associated with the cathedral and the cult of St David, but as work advanced on the building of St Non's House as the Morgan-Griffiths' summer residence in 1929, it was decided to relocate the chapel on an adjacent site. Here it would overlook both the ruins of the medieval chapel, reputed birthplace of St David, and the site of St Non's Well. Morgan-Griffiths' wife was herself a Roman Catholic,[2] and it was this fact which seems to have provided the initial impetus for the building of the Roman Catholic chapel at St Non's.[3]

The publicity surrounding the construction of the chapel made much of the claim that St Non's was the first Roman Catholic place of worship opened at or near St Davids since the disruptions of the Reformation. Morgan-Griffiths made this claim himself,[4] and it was echoed in the *West Wales Guardian* of 10 August 1934,[5] in *The Universe* on the same date,[6] and in *The Tablet* of the following day.[7] By contrast, neither Bishop Francis Vaughan of Menevia, who laid the foundation stone on St David's Day 1934, nor Archbishop Francis Mostyn of Cardiff, who preached at the celebration of the first Mass in the completed building on the following 2nd August, made reference to this in their respective addresses.[8] It was not, in fact, the case. There had been an earlier attempt to re-establish a Roman Catholic presence in St Davids, but it had ended in failure. Archbishop Mostyn in particular would have known of it, as he was vicar-apostolic (1895–1898) and bishop of Menevia (1898–1921) at the time.

Between St Non's and St Davids stands the house known variously as Bryn-y-garn, Dewiscourt and Warpool Court. From 1880 this had belonged to a Charles Morgan, whose wife, Claudine Isabel Winifred, became a Roman Catholic after his death. Mrs Morgan had built a chapel in the grounds of the house, which, as it is estimated it could seat 120, was clearly intended to serve more than her own

---

[1] Morgan-Griffiths, *Chapel*, 5. Reference will be made frequently in this paper to this now rare but invaluable source for the history of the conception and construction of St Non's.
[2] Morgan-Griffiths himself was not.
[3] de Guise, *The Story of Non(ne)*, 7.
[4] Morgan-Griffiths, *Chapel*, 5.
[5] Quoted Morgan-Griffiths, *Chapel*, 30, 32.
[6] Morgan-Griffiths, *Chapel*, 46.
[7] Morgan-Griffiths, *Chapel*, 53.
[8] The addresses are quoted *verbatim* in Morgan-Griffiths, *Chapel*, 11 and 17–26.

household. Mrs Morgan maintained a priest at her own expense, and the chapel was opened, with a Sung Mass celebrated by Fr Dudley Cummings, on 31 July 1898. The initiative was, however, short-lived. In 1899 Mrs Morgan was declared bankrupt, and the property sold. Services in the chapel ceased. The purchaser, Mrs Ada Miller-Williams of Aberystwyth, was an artist, who converted the building into a studio.[9]

The parallels with the 1934 initiative are striking; a private chapel, built at the expense of an individual patron, but available to the wider community. However, reference to this 'false start' in the ceremonies of 1934 would have struck the wrong note. The emphasis was upon the reclamation of the tradition, the restoration of Catholic worship to St Davids. Archbishop Mostyn, nonetheless, may have been making an indirect reference to the failed initiative of 1898 when during his sermon on 2 August 1934 he prayed of St Non's Chapel 'Long may this little Church stand here to carry on its Holy purpose ...'[10]

There could be no more striking a contrast between two strands of the 'Celtic Revival' than those illustrated at Warpool Court and St Non's Chapel. The artist Ada Miller-Williams and her son Basil, owners of Warpool Court 'relished the romance of their Celtic heritage'.[11] The medium in which they chose to express it was painted ceramic tiles, heraldic and genealogical, tracing their family's Welsh and Irish antecedents. The tiles, still *in situ* on the walls of the public rooms at Warpool Court and well restored, are in many cases lavishly decorated in 'Celtic' designs deriving in the main from the Books of Durrow and of Kells. In the years following 1899, when she purchased the property, Ada Miller-Williams was working towards an artistic celebration of the 1000th anniversary of the accession of Hywel Dda (1909), but that celebration as she conceived it was wholly secular in tone. The designs from the books of Durrow and of Kells are entirely decontextualized, and emptied of their religious meaning and significance.

By contrast, the Morgan-Griffiths' work at St Non's, undertaken within a year of Ada Miller-Williams' death, struck a different note. The architect chosen was a local man, David Thomas, and the emphasis was strongly on an assertion of historic Christian continuity. The stone used for the foundations was from a group of ruined cottages at Whitewell, themselves, it was believed, built in their turn from pre-Reformation ecclesiastical buildings on that site.[12] The piscina and the holy water stoup both came from the ruins of local, pre-Reformation chapels, the former at Caerforiog, the latter at Gwrhyd, between St Davids and Llanrhian.[13]

The five windows, four of them specially commissioned, took up the theme of continuity, but this time not so much with the pre-Reformation church of the high middle ages as with the earlier age of the Celtic saints. The figures are of Winifred, Brynach, David and Bride. The principal, east, window, brought from St Non's House, and executed by the firm established by William Morris, depicts the patron saint, Non, the nearby St Non's Well, and one scene from her life, the arrival with

9   Information derived from 'A History of Warpool Court and its Owners', an illustrated typescript kept at Warpool Court. The house is now a hotel, and this document is available to patrons on request. Earlier owners of the house had included the Green family, one of whom, Charles Alfred Howell Green, was to become archbishop of Wales in November 1934, only three months after St Non's Chapel was opened.
10 Morgan-Griffiths, *Chapel*, 22.
11 'A History of Warpool Court'.
12 Morgan-Griffiths, *Chapel*, 6.
13 Morgan-Griffiths, *Chapel*, 6, 7.

her infant son in Brittany.[14] These images were carefully chosen. The cult of St Winifred, centred at Holywell (Flints.), in the middle ages had been by far the most prominent in north Wales, and the well itself remained a focus for pilgrimage and devotion even after the depredations of the Reformation, being much visited by Catholic recusants. Indeed, so deep-seated and influential was the cult of Winifred that her very name became generic for a Welsh woman.[15]

St Bride or Bridget of Kildare was another obvious choice, not only because of her Irish associations, or because St Non's chapel is built as close as is feasible to the shores of St Bride's Bay. Welsh and Irish interrelationships had been close from earliest times, but it is probable that the inclusion of Bride among the saints in the chapel windows was a conscious recollection of the tradition that Bride herself had been involved in Christian missionary work here in south-west Wales.[16]

In the third window David, as so often in the iconography of the Gothic Revival, is depicted in the robes of a medieval archbishop – the inspiration clearly the vociferous assertions of Welsh ecclesial autonomy in Geoffrey of Monmouth and particularly Giraldus Cambrensis in the twelfth century. The richly-robed David contrasts with the figure of Brynach in the fourth window, dressed as a hermit.[17]

Overall, the completed chapel, with its rough and unrelieved stone exterior and interior, as *The West Wales Guardian* for 10 August 1934, reported, was one where 'great care has been taken to make [it] a replica of the Chapels which at one time existed in the neighbourhood'.[18] The message conveyed by the building, then, was entirely consistent. The Catholic church in Wales was here asserting its direct historic continuity with the church of the age of St David, and with that of pre-Reformation days in this place. It was a theme which was taken up in their addresses by both Bishop Francis Vaughan of Menevia at the laying of the foundation stone on St David's Day 1934, and by Archbishop Francis Mostyn of Cardiff, at the opening of the completed building on the following 2 August.

Francis Mostyn came of impeccable Welsh lineage. He was the fourth son of the eighth baronet of Talacre, Flintshire, and his family was a cadet branch of that of Lord Mostyn of Mostyn Hall in the same county. The Mostyns could trace their connections with north Wales back at least to the fourteenth century. Francis Mostyn himself, as vicar-apostolic, bishop of Menevia and, finally, as archbishop of Cardiff until his death in 1939, strongly sought to identify the Catholic church with the land and people of Wales. He was an advocate of the cause of the Welsh martyrs of the sixteenth and seventeenth centuries,[19] and a supporter of the Converts' Aid Society, which sought to assist converts to Catholicism in Wales from the Anglican church and from nonconformity.[20] He was energetic, presiding both in Menevia

---

[14] Morgan-Griffiths, *Chapel*, 13, 15.

[15] Lord, *Words with Pictures*, 51.

[16] The tradition is mentioned, for example, in Wight, *The Pilgrim's Guide*, 13.

[17] Morgan-Griffiths, *Chapel*, 13–14. During the twentieth century, the depiction of St David changed, the emphasis being placed more upon his austerity and simplicity of life than on medieval ideas of archiepiscopal or metropolitical authority. Thus, for example, the images of the saint in the parish church at Llanddewi Brefi and the ante-chapel at Trinity College, Carmarthen, are more akin to the vision of the saint as 'God's gypsy' in Gwenallt's poem, than they are to the Victorian revival of medieval precedents. Jones, *Eples*, 63–4. The poem is briefly discussed by Allchin, *Praise Above All*, 61–2, where it is quoted in translation. The figure of Brynach is here depicted with the high cross from Nevern (Pembs.), a church closely associated with him.

[18] Quoted in Morgan-Griffiths, *Chapel*, 32.

[19] Hughes, *Winds of Change*, 103–4.

[20] Hughes, *Winds of Change*, 41.

and at Cardiff over an unprecedented growth in the numbers of Catholics in those dioceses.[21] He was most definitely 'missionary minded'. Catholic schools, he believed, were 'cradle[s] of mission'[22] and he advocated the building of modest and inexpensive churches to serve the spiritual needs of the scattered, and often numerically small, groups of Catholics throughout south Wales.[23] Mostyn would have seen immediately the value and importance of the building of St Non's Chapel, not just to serve the needs of Catholics in this far corner of the widespread parish of Haverfordwest, but as symbolic for a church growing in numbers and confidence of a renewed Catholic presence at Tyddewi. All of these notes, historic continuity, renewed presence, mission, were struck in the forthright and uncompromising sermon that he preached from the door of St Non's.[24]

By contrast, Francis Vaughan, the diocesan bishop who had succeeded Mostyn in Menevia, was a more eirenic figure. Of equally distinguished Welsh ancestry – his family, always staunchly catholic, had been settled at Courtfield on the Herefordshire – Monmouthshire border since the sixteenth century – he was more fluent in Welsh than his predecessor, and more accommodating in his attitude towards non-Catholics. He had, for example, been widely respected by Christians of all persuasions during his ministry as parish priest at Barry in Glamorgan.[25] His family had given long and distinguished service to the Catholic church. Six of his uncles were priests and bishops, including Cardinal Vaughan of Westminster and Roger Vaughan, Archbishop of Sydney[26]. His own brother, Herbert, was also a priest. Vaughan did not share Mostyn's ebullient confidence over the conversion of Wales to catholicism; he was more cautious – perhaps realistic – and occasionally gloomy, as to the prospect.[27] Less inclined to 'missionary activity', he saw rather the religious orders, particularly the contemplatives, as 'power-houses of prayer', in the laying of firm foundations for a gradual spiritual growth, and a deepening of commitment.[28] It was probably through Vaughan's influence that the Passionists bought St Non's when Morgan-Griffiths died, little more than a year after the chapel opened. Otherwise, it might have met the same fate as its short-lived predecessor at Warpool Court.

Vaughan's short address on St David's Day contrasted sharply with that of Mostyn five months later. The sermon included words like 'quietly'and 'gradually', it emphasized prayer, and the strength of faith that would come through the renewed Presence of Christ in that part of the country.[29] Ultimately, it was this vision of

---

[21] Hughes, *Winds of Change*, 7–10.

[22] Hughes, *Winds of Change*, 30.

[23] Hughes, *Winds of Change*, 26.

[24] The full text of the sermon, preached on Mark 14, verse 14, 'The Master saith, where is my Refectory, where I may eat the Pasch with my disciples?', is printed in Morgan-Griffiths, *Chapel*, 17–26.

[25] Hughes, *Winds of Change*, 103, 162.

[26] It was Bishop Vaughan's uncle, the Cardinal, who had welcomed in 1898 the setting up of the diocese of Menevia, with Mostyn as its first bishop, with the words : 'The idea of a Welsh diocese, a Welsh bishop, and a bilingual clergy would not only make a special appeal to Welsh Catholics, but would break down prejudice and encourage a sympathy in the non-Catholic Welsh, and so open the way to conversions,' Wilson, *The Life of Bishop Hedley*, 130. Mostyn himself was Welsh-speaking, but never fluent. He did, however, enthusiastically foster the Welsh language and identify himself with Welsh culture in his diocese. Hughes, '"No longer"', 344.

[27] Hughes, '"No longer"', 10, 11, 37.

[28] Hughes, '"No longer"', 47.

[29] 'With prayer – silent persevering prayer – the Church is coming into her own again … Earth's greatest treasure, Our Lord in the Blessed Sacrament, will reside here; and may He dominate and make His divine influence felt throughout this part of Pembrokeshire': Morgan-Griffiths, *Chapel*, 11. In these words, one is inescapably reminded of those of the Jesuit Gerard Manley Hopkins, in his poem 'God's

Vaughan's, rather than that of his more sanguine and uncompromising archbishop, which was to prevail. St Non's House, with the chapel, became, what it remains, a Retreat and Conference centre, in the late twentieth and early twenty-first century with an increasingly ecumenical emphasis.

Nonetheless, Mostyn's shadow did fall over the ceremonies attendant upon the laying of the foundation stone. During the service two hymns were sung. One was – perhaps inevitably – F.W. Faber's celebrated 'Faith of our Fathers'.[30] The composition of one who was himself a convert, the hymn is an inspiring evocation of the post-Reformation days of Catholic recusancy, of persecution and of the sufferings of the small English and Welsh catholic community in the days of the penal laws. The hymn was as much a badge of 'belonging' for the catholic – though with considerably more religious significance – as is the singing by Welsh supporters of Pantycelyn's 'Guide me, O thou great Redeemer' at international rugby matches.

The second hymn sung had been composed for the occasion by Mostyn himself. It encapsulates in its four verses and refrain the archbishop's own religious outlook and hopes for the people of Wales, and deserves to be quoted in full:

> O Great Saint David, still we hear thee call us
> Unto a life that knows no fear of death;
> Yea, down the ages, will thy words enthral us,
> Strong, happy words : 'Be joyful, keep the Faith'
>
> On Cambria's sons stretch out thy hands in blessing,
> For our dear land thy help we now implore.
> Lead us to God, with humble hearts confessing
> Jesus, Lord and King for evermore.
>
> Christ was the centre rock of all thy teaching,
> God's holy Will – the splendour of its theme.
> His grace informed, His love inflamed thy preaching,
> Christ's sway on earth, the substance of thy dream.
>
> On Cambria's sons …
>
> In early childhood, choosing Jesus only,
> Thy fervour showed His yoke was light and sweet !
> And thus for thee, life's journey was not lonely –
> The path made plain by prints of wounded feet.
>
> On Cambria's sons …
>
> O Glorious Saint, we wander in the dark;
> With thee we seek our trusted guide in Rome.
> Help him to steer Saint Peter's saving barque,
> That we may safely reach our heavenly home.
>
> On Cambria's sons …[31]

Grandeur', and particularly the last lines: 'Oh, morning, at the brown brink eastward, springs – / Because the Holy Ghost over the bent / World broods with warm breast and with ah! bright wings': Gardner and MacKenzie, *The Poems*, 66.

30 Appropriately, and perhaps significantly, the hymn was sung in a Welsh translation.

31 There is no record of the tune to which this hymn was sung. However, the Organist and Master of the Choristers at St Woolos' Cathedral, Newport, has pointed out to me that the unusual metre of the hymn restricts the possibilities. One is the Londonderry Air ('Danny Boy'). If the hymn was sung to this traditional Irish melody – a distinct possibility given the number of expatriate Irish catholics in Wales – then a further strand of significance is woven into the story. 'Danny Boy' is perhaps,

The hymn, otherwise unexceptionable, has a sting in its tail. As the final verse shows clearly, for Mostyn, the religious future for Wales could only be defined in terms of a renewed submission to Rome. In his hymn, and in his sermon at the opening of the chapel in August 1934, the archbishop of Cardiff forthrightly distanced himself, and by implication his church, from what had been happening at the nearby cathedral over the previous decade.

II

Trystan Owain Hughes has succinctly discussed the concept of a 'national' church in early twentieth century Wales, and Anglican attitudes towards it.[32] As the storm-clouds of disestablishment gathered, and its possible implications began to sink in, the need for the Church of England in Wales to find its roots and gain a cultural iden-tity became ever more pressing. 'The Church was encouraged, not only to present itself as being in the descent of the Welsh saints, but also to show itself to value the culture which they had nurtured. Tainted by the charge of Anglicization, it now had to reinvent itself as the national Church in Wales'.[33] As Hughes points out, few people expressed this more emphatically than Lord Sankey, who in the aftermath of disestablishment asserted : 'the Church in Wales is a Catholic and National Church … As a national church we are the old Christian Church in these islands. The saints of the Church of God are sons of the race. They sleep in Welsh soil, hard by the shrines they loved and served so well. The self-same prayers which moved their lips move ours. Today we are the heirs of their beliefs and of their traditions.'[34] These words were uttered in 1922, little more than a decade before Mostyn's hymn and sermon at St Non's. The stage was being set for what Hughes described as the 'bitter war of words' between the Anglican and Roman Catholic churches in Wales, which was to last for more than forty years.[35]

Lord Sankey's positioning of the Church in Wales as the true, lineal descendant of the church of David and the other Celtic saints may be construed as the opening shots of the war, but the battle-ground had been carefully prepared. Hymns (as we have already seen) were not merely expressions of popular piety, but could also be useful propaganda. Three prominent Welsh Anglican hymnwriters in particular had made contributions in this respect in the previous decades, William Morgan, Eben-ezer Josiah Newell and Timothy Rees.[36] Morgan, better known by his bardic name 'Penfro', and rector of Manafon in Montgomeryshire at the time of his death in 1918, had composed in Welsh and English a hymn for St David's Day.[37] In it, alongside

---

par excellence, the unofficial national anthem of expatriate Irish the world over, expressive of what the Welsh would call *hiraeth*. Such a melody would certainly heavily underline the sentiments of Mostyn's fourth verse.

[32] Hughes, 'Continuity', 123–38; Hughes, ' "No longer" ', 336–65.

[33] Hughes, 'Continuity', 124.

[34] Quoted in Hughes, 'Continuity', 125.

[35] Hughes, 'Continuity', 129.

[36] By contrast, the earlier, nineteenth century, Tractarian hymnwriters in Wales had tended to emphasize the church's Catholic heritage in doctrine and sacrament. See for example, Freeman, 'The contribu-tion of some Tractarians', 73–93.

[37] Manafon seems to attract poets and nationalists. Walter Davies (Gwallter Mechain) was rector here from 1807 to 1837, and, more recently, R.S. Thomas. The Welsh text of Penfro's hymn, *Molwyn di, O Dduw ein tadau*, is no. 205 in *Emynau'r Eglwys*. The English version is less easily found. It was, however, printed in the January 1941 edition of the Welsh Church Quarterly, *The Faith in Wales*,

references to David's refutation of the Pelagians, Wales itself figures prominently as the 'Fatherland', with David as its protector, and (implicitly) the Anglican church as the guardian of the true faith and guide for its people.

Wales as the 'Fatherland' was also the vision of Timothy Rees, from 1931 to 1939 bishop of Llandaf. In the hymn 'Lord, Who in Thy perfect wisdom', David (Dewi) is linked with Dyfrig, Deiniol and Teilo and 'all the gallant saintly band' whose 'prayer and labour Hallowed all our fatherland'. For Rees, God formed 'our ancient nation In remote barbaric days, To unfold in it [His] purpose To [His] glory and [His] praise'. The land and the people of Wales had, then, to say the least, a special place in the purposes of God. The Anglican church in Wales, in continuity with the church of David and the other saints ('Still Thy ancient Church remaineth – Witness to Thy changeless love') was the instrument for the working out of those purposes.[38]

How the purposes of God would be worked out in the land of Wales had been the theme of another hymn for St David, that composed by Ebenezer Josiah Newell, 'We praise thy name, all holy Lord'.[39] Inspired by 'all the saintly band whose prayers Still gird our land about', by zeal, faith, charity and fortitude, the churchpeople of Wales were called to witness to the gospel. It was through such hymns as these, 'popular' theology, that the churchpeople of Wales were imbued with a sense of their 'place' and of their mission.

III

The activities of William Williams, dean of St Davids in the 1920s, have to be seen against this background and in this context. Williams, as Trystan Hughes pointed out, was 'particularly zealous in his espousal of Celtic-Anglican continuity'.[40] This he combined with an aversion to Roman Catholicism. In the immediate aftermath of disestablishment, indeed, within months of the Act taking effect, in August 1920 Williams – conveniently – 're-discovered' what he believed to be, or simply maintained were, relics of Wales' patron saint.[41] There was absolutely no concrete

---

alongside the Welsh. Interestingly, several of the sentiments expressed in this hymn are echoed, especially in verses two and three, in Mostyn's.

38 The hymn, whether sung in English or Welsh, still remains popular in the Church in Wales. For the full text, see Rees, *Sermons and Hymns by Timothy Rees*, 121–2. Rees's importance for the Church in Wales in the testing years of the 1930s has been largely forgotten. However, recently Densil Morgan has drawn attention to it: Morgan, *The Span*, esp. 88–91. Morgan says of Rees that his premature death 'deprived the Church in Wales of one of its most humble, endearing and impressive sons. The loss of Rees, compounded by the onset of war, led to the failure to materialize of the "new epoch" in the Church's history' (91). The 'new epoch' would have been that in which the implications of what Morgan described as Rees's 'radical incarnationalism' were worked out. As Rees himself expressed it, 'There is nothing secular but sin' (quoted by Morgan, *The Span*, 90). There is a need for a new biography of Rees, to replace the very short study by J.L. Rees, *Timothy Rees*.

39 The hymn is that appointed for St David's Day in *English Hymnal* (no. 211). As this hymn-book was first published in 1906, it was probably composed between 1891 and 1900, when Newell was serving as a curate in Porthcawl. The Church in Wales in the twentieth century unfortunately tended to regard scholar-clergy with a blend of puzzlement, embarrassment and hostility. Newell, a modest and self-effacing man, like his contemporaries Hartwell Jones and Wade-Evans, ended his days as a parish priest in England. The historical outlook of Newell is perhaps best exemplified in his *A Popular History of the Ancient British Church*, published in 1887.

40 Hughes, 'Continuity', 130.

41 Re-discovered, for, in fact, the bones which Williams exhumed and placed in a reliquary, had been first uncovered by workmen at the cathedral in 1866. That they were those of David and Justinian

evidence that they were; even circumstantial evidence was against the claim. The principal relic of David was known to have been confiscated by Edward I in the late thirteenth century, and the others destroyed when the shrine was at least partly dismantled during the episcopate of William Barlow in the sixteenth.[42] However, to Williams, and, arguably, the fledgling Church in Wales desperate to secure its claim to continuity, they were a godsend.

The reliquary was placed in an arched recess in the west wall of the Trinity Chapel, behind the high altar, and the whole enclosed with an ornamental iron screen, through which it could be seen and touched. Dean Williams had, in effect, recreated, in a more modest form than its medieval predecessor, a shrine for St David. By 1922 the respected journal of the Cambrian Archaeological Association, *Archaeologia Cambrensis*, was maintaining 'there is no reason whatever why they [the bones] should not be a portion of the actual relics of St David'.[43] In 1925, Edward Foord went further : 'In the recess is the oaken iron-bound chest containing the bones of St David and his legendary preceptor, Justinianus ... They have been examined by competent authorities,[44] who came to the conclusion that the bones were those of a very tall man and a short man. One of the skulls is said to indicate great brain capacity. So far as the literary evidence has any weight, it does state that St David was a man of great stature, and it may be concluded that there is considerable probability that the chest really encloses the mortal remains of the patron saint of Wales.'[45] This was wishful thinking, if not romantic nonsense, but it was a considerable propaganda coup for the Church in Wales.[46]

With the 'relics' of David safely back in a place of honour in the cathedral, Williams cemented the Church in Wales' claim to historic continuity with the age of the saints still further in July 1925, with an ecumenical service to commemorate the 1600th anniversary of the Council of Nicaea. The service, was, however, much more than that. As well as Anglicans and nonconformists, representatives of the eastern Orthodox churches were present, including the patriarch of Jerusalem. It was, of course, the claim in Rhygyfarch's *Life of St David* that David had journeyed to the Holy City, and had there been consecrated to the episcopate that was uppermost in the minds of the organizers.[47] It was to commemorate this event that the patriarchs present at the 1925 service presented a reliquary casket to the cathedral.[48]

In his sermon, the first archbishop of Wales, Alfred George Edwards, so long an outspoken and hostile critic of disestablishment and of notions of a distinctively Welsh church, now took the opportunity to assert its identity and continuity, but because of David's consecration, a continuity with the ancient churches of the east

---

was then, it seems, wholly discounted, for they were simply re-interred. As Wyn Evans remarked, it would be fair to suggest that they were 'bones disturbed when the ground level [of the Trinity Chapel] was lowered ... and that they were placed out of reverence in the recess which was blocked up in the 1520s ...' Evans and Worsley, *St Davids Cathedral 1181–1981*, 137.

42 See Cowley, above.

43 *Archaeologia Cambrensis*, 7th series, 2 (1922), Report of the Haverfordwest Meeting, 445.

44 Unnamed.

45 Foord, *St Davids, Llandaff and Brecon*, 82.

46 For example, unless one believed in bilocation, it was hard to credit the claim regarding one of the skulls. It was the skull of David which had been confiscated by Edward I and taken to London. Recent scientific analysis has finally laid the myth to rest. The bones have been shown to date from considerably later than the time of David and Justinian. See Higham *et al.* above.

47 'Then, secured by divine election, he promoted holy David to the archiepiscopate', *Vita S. David*, ed. Sharpe and Davies, above, 140–1.

48 Evans and Worsley, *St Davids Cathedral*, 137,

and not with the Latin west. The whole 'ecumenical' service was a calculated snub to the Roman Catholic church. Representatives of the Roman Catholic church were not present,[49] and at the service the Nicene Creed was recited in English, Welsh, Greek and Russian, but – deliberately – not in Latin. A.W. Wade-Evans understood the significance of the whole event. It was, he said, 'but an anti-Roman gesture'.[50] It was also, sadly, yet another instance of shameless and unscrupulous behaviour on the part of A.G. Edwards. It was quite in character for one whose earlier vehement opposition to disestablishment and ruthless attempts to quash the pro-disestablishment movement in the Anglican church in Wales have been described as going 'a long way to ... alienating a nation, harming the spiritual mission of the church and virtually destroying the spiritual life of nonconformity ...'[51]

Finally, Dean Williams in June 1926 was at least in part responsible for the revival of organized pilgrimages to the cathedral, and now to the restored shrine.[52] In this he was energetically aided and abetted by Arthur Baring-Gould, the saintly, but naïve and eccentric vicar of St Martin's, Haverfordwest, from 1908 to 1955.[53] Baring-Gould was a rather undiscriminating enthusiast for all things 'catholic' and his Haverfordwest church speedily became the meeting point for St Davids pilgrims. It was here that the 'Itinerarium or Service of Departure' was held, each pilgrim receiving as badge a blessed cockle-shell threaded with a ribbon in the diocesan colours of black and gold.[54] At the cathedral there were services, including an 'Itinerary of the altars' in which the pilgrims perambulated the building *en route* to devotions before the reliquary in the Trinity chapel, singing between each station verses of the hymn 'Jerusalem, my happy home, When shall I come to thee?' attributed to St Augustine. Ironically, this great doctor of the church, whose thought and writings so influenced the pre- and post-Reformation churches of the Latin west, was now being (implicitly) invoked in this way to recall St David's debt to the east. It was to Jerusalem, and not to Rome, that the Welsh church was to look for its roots.[55]

IV

When these developments at the cathedral in the 1920s are understood, then the anxiety on the part of the Roman Catholic hierarchy in Wales, Mostyn and Vaughan, is more easily appreciated. The opportunity to establish a focus for devotion at the

---

[49] It is not clear whether they were invited but declined, or simply ignored. The latter is more likely.

[50] *The Welsh Outlook* (January 1926), 9–10. Quoted by Hughes, 'Continuity', 129. Hughes briefly discusses the service, on 128–9.

[51] Brown, 'Traitors', 49.

[52] Initial strong support came from members of the Society of St David, originally a devotional society at St David's College, Lampeter, which traced its origins to 1884, but which in 1914 had been re-launched as a national society. Dean Williams and Arthur Baring-Gould were early supporters. (Williams had himself been a student at the college). For the history of the society, see Morgan-Guy, 'The Society of St David'.

[53] Arthur Baring-Gould was the half-brother of the more famous Sabine Baring-Gould, the squire-parson of Lew Trenchard in Devon, and prolific author and hymnwriter. His most famous composition was 'Onward, Christian soldiers'. Both were great romantics, much influenced by the Anglo-Catholic Revival, and Arthur had begun his ministry as his brother's curate. Baring-Gould's long ministry in Haverfordwest is described in David Smith, *'They Did it their Way'*, 58–89.

[54] The pattern of these early pilgrimages, which lasted over three days, is recorded in Wight, *The Pilgrim's Guide*, 48. As late as 1960, when the writer first went to St Davids, even more modest parochial pilgrimages began in the same way at St Martin's.

[55] My friend Canon T.H.J. Palmer, who was a Minor Canon at the cathedral in the early 1960s, has reminded me that the hymn was still being sung during the perambulation of the altars even then.

site generally believed to have been the birthplace of St David was one eagerly to be grasped. St Non's Chapel would not house any relics of the saint, but rather a greater Presence, as Bishop Vaughan made clear on St David's Day 1934, that of Christ in the Blessed Sacrament. 'Earth's greatest treasure, Our Lord in the Blessed Sacrament, will reside here.'[56] In August, Mostyn returned to the same theme, albeit more bluntly. He contrasted the new chapel, 'where the faithful can receive the Sacraments instituted by our Divine Saviour and listen to the Gospel and the teaching which He taught to His disciples'[57] with the cathedral, where until the sixteenth century 'the Holy Sacrifice of the Mass was offered up, and where the Blessed Sacrament of the Holy Eucharist was reserved' but not thereafter. 'Although used for the worship of God ... no longer the [home] of Jesus in the Sacrament of the Blessed Eucharist' was his verdict upon St Davids and the other Anglican cathedrals and churches in Wales.[58]

In a very real sense, St Davids Cathedral and St Non's Chapel can in the 1920s and 1930s be seen as 'shrine and counter-shrine', and, in microcosm, witnesses to the acrid hostility between the Anglican and Roman Catholic churches in Wales, as, both with a renewed sense of their 'Celtic' roots and heritage, sought to claim continuity with the age of the saints, and make good their further claim to being the true spiritual home of the people of Wales.[59]

In the sanctuary of St Non's Chapel there still stands, as there has since 1934, a large, rather out-of-scale, white marble statue, carved by R. and L. Boulton of Cheltenham. It is a copy of the statue of Notre Dame des Victoires, in the Parisian church of that name. The feast of Our Lady of Victories, celebrated on the fourth Sunday of October, was inaugurated to give thanks for the victory of Louis XIII and Cardinal Richelieu over the French protestants at the siege of La Rochelle in 1628. The placing of the statue here was symbolic of the confidence of Mostyn and others in 1934 as to which church's claim to being the true Catholic church in Wales, and its people's true spiritual home, would ultimately be vindicated.

---

[56] Morgan-Griffiths, *Chapel*, 11.

[57] Morgan-Griffiths, *Chapel*, 21.

[58] Morgan-Griffiths, *Chapel*, 20–1. This was a favourite theme of Mostyn's. Only five years before he had claimed that the cathedrals 'stood as cold and empty shells awaiting the time when new life would be infused into them, and they would be once more used for the purpose for which they were erected'. *Western Mail*, 15 October 1929. Quoted by Hughes, 'Continuity', 131. Perhaps significantly, the strongest rebuttal of Mostyn's assertion came in the same newspaper three days later from Dean Williams of St Davids.

[59] The full sad story of the hostility is ably described in Hughes, *Winds of Change*.

17

THE ARCHBISHOPRIC OF ST DAVIDS AND THE BISHOPS OF *CLAS CYNIDR*

John Reuben Davies

In the last decade of the eleventh century, Rhygyfarch ap Sulien of Llanbadarn Fawr described in his *Vita S. Dauid* how the Patriarch of Jerusalem advanced David to the 'archbishopric'; later, at the synod of Brefi, David's *ciuitas* is 'declared the metropolis of the whole country, so that whoever might rule it should be regarded as archbishop'.[1] Rhygyfarch's literary efforts to promote the cult of St David and the dignity and privileges of the bishopric were a prelude to the sustained, and ultimately unsuccessful, campaign for metropolitan status begun in the 1130s by Bishop Bernard and continued into the thirteenth century by Gerald of Wales.[2] The historical reality of an archbishopric of St Davids in the early middle ages, to which Rhygyfarch, Bernard, and Gerald all appealed, has in fact a fairly solid grounding in the sources. There may be no evidence of metropolitan status, but the nature of the bishopric's former archiepiscopal rank can be illustrated by reference to the native Welsh law-codes.

In six versions of *Cyfraith Hywel*, there is a section on the seven bishop-houses of Dyfed. Here we seem to have evidence for the nature of ecclesiastical organisation in Dyfed before the end of the ninth century.[3] Thomas Charles-Edwards has shown that we may infer from this tract that each constituent *cantref* of Dyfed (which represented territories once ruled by local petty kings) had its own bishop.[4] Comparison with Irish ecclesiastical organisation, moreover, should lead us to expect that in the fifth and sixth centuries – the period of significant Irish settlement and influence in Dyfed – there would have been seven bishops in Dyfed, corresponding to the petty kingdoms, 'even if there were no specific evidence to suggest it'.[5]

From the meagre near-contemporary historical sources, we can only discern the name of one bishop who was operating in South Wales in the fifth or early sixth century: that is, St Dyfrig (he is mentioned in the earliest *Life* of St Samson).[6] We do not know where his see was based – Caerwent seems a good guess – but the implication of the *Life* of St Samson is that his jurisdiction extended throughout South

---

[1] *Vita S. Dauid*, §§ 46, 53; for text and translation, see above, 107–55.
[2] The standard account of the controversy over the metropolitan status of St Davids remains Davies, *Episcopal Acts*, I.190–232.
[3] For all this, see Charles-Edwards, 'The seven bishop-houses'; but compare Etchingham, 'Bishoprics in Ireland', at 22–25.
[4] Charles-Edwards, 'The seven bishop-houses', 251–2.
[5] *Ibid.*, 251.
[6] *Vita I S. Samsonis*, I.3, 15, 33, 34 (ed. Flobert, *La Vie ancienne*; transl. Taylor, *The Life of St Samson*). I take this earliest *Life* of St Samson to be a work of the Merovingian period, on account of its corrupt Latinity. See Davies, 'The saints of south Wales', 370–1.

Wales.[7] At the very beginning of the eighth century, however, we can see that the old Romano-British and sub-Roman *ciuitas*-based bishoprics are beginning to mutate. Aldhelm, the abbot of Malmesbury, in a letter to King Geraint of Dumnonia, makes reference to the '*sacerdotes* of the Demetae [Dyfed]' who glory in the currency of their worldly possessions.[8] *Sacerdos* in this context seems to mean 'bishop'.[9] We therefore have contemporary evidence for a multiplicity of bishops operating in the early medieval kingdom of Dyfed. In this context, the law-tract on the 'Seven Bishop-Houses of Dyfed' would appear to be a later reflection of the multiplication of bishops in early eighth-century Dyfed, implied in Aldhelm's letter.

Thomas Charles-Edwards has argued that the bishops – or archbishops – at St Davids (*Mynyw*) exercised a kind of episcopal over-lordship from the latter part of the ninth century.[10] The existence of a hierarchy among Welsh bishops in the eighth and ninth centuries is implied in the obit of Elfoddw, 'archiepiscopus in Guenedote regione'.[11] This tells us that the authority of Elfoddw was territorial (covering the kingdom of Gwynedd). It also suggests that, in the same way that the kings of Gwynedd were over-lords of smaller kingdoms, so the jurisdiction of the ecclesiastical rulers, the archbishops of Gwynedd, would have encompassed areas subject to other bishops. Likewise, we find Asser, towards the end of the century, describing his kinsman, Nyfys (*Nobis*), as *archiepiscopus* at St Davids;[12] and from the latter half of the ninth century until about the end of the tenth, political developments in Wales could have meant that the over-lordship of the bishop of St Davids might have extended as far as that of the over-lordship of the king of Deheubarth.[13]

So we can see that an archbishopric, if not an archbishopric of strict metropolitan status – an archbishopric in practice we could say – probably existed for some time during the latter stages of the early middle ages. At first, an 'archbishop' of St Davids may have exercised his jurisdiction over bishops in the petty-kingdoms of Dyfed (the bishops to whom Aldhelm was probably referring); by the later ninth century, the 'archbishops' of St Davids had probably extended their sphere of control across a number of minor bishoprics throughout Deheubarth. Can we, however, put any flesh on this bare skeleton of a thesis? Can we at least catch a glimpse of this 'archbishopric' or episcopal over-lordship in operation? I hope that I may be able to provide a few morsels that can be attached to the skeleton.

---

7 Caerwent, the Roman *Venta Silurum*, was the *ciuitas* capital for what is now south-eastern Wales; cf. Knight, 'The early Church in Gwent'. Dyfrig had jurisdiction as far west as the monastery of Piro on Caldey Island, near Tenby (if we accept the identification of Piro's island with Caldey, which I do).

8 *Demetarum sacerdotes* (ed. Ehwald, *Aldhelmi Opera*, 484).

9 *Sacerdos* could mean 'bishop' or 'priest': the opening of the letter makes reference to a recently held council of *episcopi* which drew together an innumerable crowd of the *sacerdotes* of God from nearly all of Britain: Aldhelm's employment of *sacerdos* seems therefore to be a stylistic device rather than a term of differentiation.

10 Charles-Edwards, 'The seven bishop-houses', 257–61.

11 *AC*(A) 345 [= A.D. 809].

12 For all this, see Charles-Edwards, 'The seven bishop-houses', 257.

13 Charles-Edwards, 'The seven bishop-houses', 260–1. The over-kingdom of Deheubarth developed out of Dyfed and across the whole of south-west Wales, taking in Ceredigion and Ystrad Tywi.

John R. Davies

The episcopal succession at St Davids in the early middle ages

In his account of a tour of Wales, *Itinerarium Kambriae*, Gerald of Wales listed the episcopal succession to the see of St Davids:[14]

> Sederunt autem a tempore Dauid, successiuis temporum curriculis, archiepiscopi ibidem uiginti quinque, quorum haec nomina: Dauid, Eliud qui et Theliau uocatur, Keneu, Morwal, Haernueu, Elwaid, Gurnueu, Leudiwit, Gorwiust, Gogaun, Cledauc, Aman, Eludged, Elduuen, Elaue, Mailswid, Sadurnue, Catulus, Sulhaithuai, Nouis, Sadurnueu, Doithwal, Asser, Archuail, Sampson.
>
> Tempore Sampsonis huius, pallium in hunc modum est translatum ... Sederunt autem a Sampsonis ibidem tempore, usque ad praedicti Henrici primi tempora, nouemdecim, quorum haec nomina; Kuielm, Retherth, Eluin, Lunuerc, Nergu, Sulidir, Eneuris, Morgeneu; qui primus inter episcopos Meneuiae carnes comedit ... Nathan, Iewan, hic Iewan una sola nocte uixit episcopus, Arwistel, Morgenennith, Eruin, Tramerin, Ioseth, Bleidhud, Sulghein, Abraham, Wilfre. Post hos uero, subacta iam Wallia, usque hodie tres: tempore regis Henrici primi Bernardus, tempore regis Stephani Dauid secundus, tempore regis Henrici secundus Petrus Cluniacensis monachus.

(Now, from the time of St David, twenty five archbishops presided [at Mynyw] in their successive turns; these are their names: David, Eliud (also called Teilo), Cyneu, Morwal, Haernfyw, Elwedd, Gwrnfyw, Llywdywyd, Gorwywst, Gwgon, Clydog, Amon, Eiludiedd, Eldufyn, Eilaf, Maelswydd, Sadyrnfyw, Catulus, Sullaethfe, Nyfys, Sadyrnfyw, Doethwal, Asser, Arthfael and Samson.

In the time of this Samson, the pallium was taken away in this way ... Likewise, from the time of the same Samson, until the time of the aforementioned Henry I, nineteen bishops presided, whose names are these: Kuielm, Rhydderch, Elfyn, Llyn-ferth, Nergu, Sulidir, Eneurys, and Morgeneu, who was the first among the bishops of Mynyw to eat meat ... Nathan, Ieuan (this Ieuan was bishop for one night only), Arwy-styl, Morgynnydd, Erfyn, Tryferyn, Joseph, Bleddudd, Sulien, Abraham and Wilfred. And after these, since the subjugation of Wales, to the present day, there have been three: Bernard in the time of Henry I, David II in the time of King Stephen, and Peter, the Cluniac monk, in the time of Henry II.)

By comparison with Gerald's list of the bishops of St Davids down the centuries, the report of the episcopal succession at St Davids (*Meneuia* or *Mynyw*) that we receive from *Annales Cambriae*, the *Brutiau*, and other sources is as follows.

David, the founder of the see, died in 601.[15] There is no reference to Teilo. Cynog (probably Gerald's *Keneu*) died in 606, although no see is attributed to him.[16] There is then a gap in the record until Sadyrnfyw 'the Generous', who died in 831.[17] This Sadyrnfyw appears in a witness-list of ostensible ninth-century origin, which was copied out by John Leland in the sixteenth century, but is now lost.[18] Nyfys appears to have been translated from the episcopal church of Llandeilo Fawr to the 'arch-bishopric' of St Davids in 840.[19] He was related to Asser, the biographer of King Alfred;[20] Nyfys was expelled from his see by Hyfaidd ap Bleddri, king of Deheu-

[14] *Itinerarium Kambriae*, II, i (ed. Brewer *et al.*, *Giraldi Cambrensis Opera*, VI.102–4).
[15] *AC* (A) 157 [= A.D. 601] *Dauid episcopus Moni iudeorum*.
[16] *AC* (A) 162 [= A.D. 606] *Dispositio Cinnauc episcopi*; (B) *Depositio Kenauc*.
[17] *AC* (A) 387 [= A.D. 831] *Satur<n>biu Hail Miniu moritur*. The Sadyrnfyw of the 'Chad' memoranda (nos. 5, 8) is unlikely to have been the same person as the bishop of Mynyw.
[18] *Suturn[b]ius episcopus Meneuensis* (ed. Smith, *The Itinerary*, IV.168).
[19] *AC* (A) 396 [=A.D. 840] *Nobis episcopus in Miniu regnauit*.
[20] Asser, *Life of King Alfred*, § 79: *Nobis archiepiscopum, propinquum meum* (ed. Stevenson, *Asser's Life*, 65–6).

298

barth, and died in 873.[21] Llynferth was consecrated in 874/5,[22] but we are not given a death-date.

Asser, if he held the see of Mynyw, must have done so after Llynferth (who appears to have succeeded Nyfys), in the period around 885, when he was called to Alfred's court. There is no explicit evidence that Asser was bishop of St Davids, but he implies it in his *Life* of King Alfred, where he tells us about king Hyfaidd:[23]

qui saepe depraedabatur illud monasterium et parochiam Sancti Degui, aliquando expulsione illorum antistitum qui in eo praeessent, sicut et Nobis archiepiscopum, propinquum meum, et me expulit aliquando sub ipsis.

(who often assaulted that monastery [St Davids] and the jurisdiction of St David, sometimes by expelling those bishops who were in charge of it, as happened to my kinsman Archbishop Nobis; *he even expelled me on occasion during this period.*)

When Asser died, in 909 or 910, he was bishop of Sherborne (Dorset),[24] but was remembered in the Welsh chronicles as a Welsh bishop or archbishop.[25]

As we move into the tenth century, we come across a bishop called Gorchywyl, who died in 907;[26] but the location of his see is not recorded in the annals, and Gerald did not include him in his list. Llynferth II died in 944.[27] This Llynferth must be the *episcop[us] Dauid Lunberth nomine* found in a charter in the Book of Llandaf (237b *Villa Tref Ceriau*).[28] A list of Canterbury consecrations, drawn up in the twelfth century, has *Lunuerd* consecrated in 929.[29] Eneurys, who died in 946, seems to have succeeded Llynferth.[30] He appears, in an earlier guise in the Book of Llandaf, as a priest attesting the same charter as Bishop Llynferth II. Perhaps he was his chaplain.

Rhydderch, who died in 955, is not given a see in the annals.[31] The text of *Brenhinedd y Saesson* in the Black Book of Basingwerk erroneously makes Rhydderch a bishop of Llandaf: he does not appear in any other episcopal list in this capacity. (Either the copyist was utterly ignorant, or it was by no means established that Rhydderch had been a bishop of St Davids.) Morgeneu was killed by vikings in 999.[32] He is the bishop whom Gerald says was the first to eat meat.

Another bishop, Morgynnydd, died in 1025;[33] but none of the annalistic sources attributes a see to him. Gerald placed a further three bishops between him and his predecessor, Morgeneu.[34] Morgynnydd's successor, Erfyn died in 1040.[35] Joseph is

---

[21] *AC* (A) 429 [= A.D. 873] *Nobis et Mouric moriuntur.*

[22] *AC* (B) [873]: *Llanwerth episcopus consecratur.* The *Brutiau* give the date as A.D. 875.

[23] Ed. Stevenson, *Asser's Life*, 65–6; trans. Keynes and Lapidge, *Alfred the Great*, 94–6. See further, Lloyd, *A History*, II.215, 226 (n. 159); Keynes and Lapidge, *Alfred the Great*, 52.

[24] ASC (A, B) 909 (C, D) 910.

[25] *AC* (A) 444 [=A.D. 909] *Asser defunctus est*; *AC* (B) *Asser episcopus*; *AC* (C) *Asser episcopus Britannie*; *ByT* (RB) *Asser, archesgob ynys Brydein*; *ByS Asser, archescop y Brutannyeit.*

[26] *AC* (A) 443 [=A.D. 907] *Guorchiguil moritur*; *AC* (B) *Gorchewil episcopus moritur.*

[27] *AC* (A) 500 [=A.D. 944] *Lunberth episcopus in Miniu obiit.*

[28] *Book of Llan Dâv* (ed. Evans, 238, 239).

[29] Canterbury, Cathedral Chapter, *Chartae Antiquae*, C. 117v.

[30] *AC* (A) 502 [= A.D. 946] *Eneuris episcopus Miniu obiit.*

[31] *AC* (B) [964] *Riderch episcopus obiit*; *ByT* (Pen. 20) [964]. Cf. Dumville, *Saint David*, 24, n. 104.

[32] *AC* (B) [999] *Meneuia uastata est a gentilibus, et Morganeu episcopus ab eis occisus est.*

[33] *AC* (B) [1025] *Morgannuc episcopus obiit*; not in *AC* (C). *ByT* (Pen. 20), *Morgynnyd*, altered by a later scribe to *Morgeneu*; *ByT* (RB) *Morgeneu*; *ByS Morgynnyd.*

[34] Nathan, Ieuan, Arwystyl.

[35] *AC* (B) [1040] *Erwyn episcopus Meneuiae obiit*; *AC* (C) *Heruin*; *ByT* (Pen. 20) 1038 [= 1040] *Heruini*; *ByT* (RB) *Hennin*; *ByS Hermini*. The name is most likely ModW *Erfyn*.

the next bishop of St Davids in the chronicles; he died in 1063.[36] Gerald placed an extra bishop, named Tryferyn, before Joseph; Tryferyn also appears in the Canterbury list of Professions, but as a bishop consecrated in 963.

The Canterbury list, which is in any case unreliable, becomes particularly corrupt at this point. The entry is based on a source common to the compilers of the Book of Llandaf, where the parallel text (which does not include the information about the St Davids bishops) has the date as 983.[37] In both cases, the date is anachronistic, for it refers to consecrations by Archbishop Ælfric, who held the primatial see from 995 to 1005. The Canterbury list also reports that Ælfric consecrated Tryferyn's nephew, *Elnod* (a miscopying of *Eluod*=Elfodd, perhaps), as his successor at St Davids. *Elnod* is otherwise unattested. William Stubbs gave Tryferyn's dates as 995–1005, based on the dates of Archbishop Ælfric.[38] Gerald made no mention of *Elnod*, although he does make Tryferyn a bishop of St Davids; but the position of Tryferyn in his list equates him chronologically with the bishop of that name known from John of Worcester's Chronicle, and the Anglo-Saxon Chronicle, who died in 1055.

From Bleddudd (who died in 1073) onward,[39] Gerald's list agrees with our other sources: Sulien (1073–1078, resigned),[40] Abraham (1078–1080),[41] Sulien again (1080–1085, resigned),[42] Wilfred (1085–1115), Bernard (1115–1148), David fitz Gerald (1148–1176), Peter de Leia (1176–1198).[43]

The bishops of Clas Cynidr/Glasbury

A list of bishops of *Clas Cynidr* at Glasbury (Y Clas-ar-Wy, Brycheiniog), found in a fourteenth-century manuscript, but whose orthography suggests an eleventh-century exemplar, reads as follows:[44]

---

36 *AC* (B) [1064] *Ioseph Meneuiae episcopus obiit*; *AC* (C), *ByT*, *ByS* [1063].

37 *Book of Llan Dâv* (ed. Evans, 252).

38 Stubbs, *Registrum Sacrum Anglicanum*.

39 *AC* (B) [1071] *Bleiduth episcopus Meneuiae obiit*; *ByT* (Pen. 20), *ByS* 1071 [= 1073]; *ByT* (RB) [1073]. The Canterbury list anachronistically says, *et ab eodem archiepiscopo* [viz. Æthelnoth] *Bledud episcopus Sancti Dauid Cantuariae consecratus est* (ed. Woodruff, 'Some early professions', 163): if Bleddudd succeeded Joseph in 1063, the archbishop of Canterbury would have been the notorious Stigand.

40 *AC* (B) [1071] *Sulgen illi episcoptui successit*; *ByT*, *ByS* [1073]. AC (C) [1076] *Sulgenus episcoptum deserit*; *ByT*, *ByS* [1078].

41 *AC* (C) [1076] *Abraham accepit*; *ByT*, *ByS* [1078]. *AC* (C) [1078] *Abraham a gentilibus occiditur*; *ByT*, *ByS* [1080] *ac y bu varw Abraham, escob Mynyw*.

42 *AC* (C) [1078] *Sulgenus iterum episcopatum accepit*; *ByT*, *ByS* [1080]; *AC* (B) [1085] Sulgenius episcopatum reliquit cui [Wil]fre successit. Gerald does not refer to Sulien's second term, though.

43 The last four are well attested: see *St Davids Episcopal Acta* §§ 1–47 (ed. Barrow, 33–74).

44 Fleuriot, 'Les évêques de la Clas Kenedyr'. Douai MS 322, in which the list is found, is a book of presumed English provenance, whose small size (170 × 110 mm) would suggest that it was written for personal use (the manuscript is described in Cassard, *Catalogue général*, VI.171–2; it otherwise contains extracts from the works of Isidore of Seville, Gregory the Great, Ambrose of Milan, Anselm of Bec, and Bernard of Clairvaux). The episcopal list is on fol. 2, and is followed by a canon concerning the penance to be imposed for violating the *refugium* of the church, which is adapted, almost verbatim, from the first of the so-called 'Three Irish Canons' found uniquely in Cambridge, Corpus Christi College, MS 265, a late eleventh-century manuscript of Worcester provenance (ed. Bieler, *The Irish Penitentials*, 182; I am grateful to J. Wyn Evans for drawing my attention to this connection).

Hec sunt nomina episcoporum Clas Chenedre: Brecchert, Keneder, Gueman, Gurbrit, Meilic, Morgennic, Rederch, Dauit, Wilfret, Hithail, Heruuit, Albri, Tremerin, et inde discessit ad Herefordiam.

(These are the names of the bishops of Clas Cynidr: *Brecchert*, Cynidr, Gwyfan [?Gwrfan], Gwrfryd, Meilyg, Morgynnydd, Rhydderch, David, Wilfred, Ithel, Erwyd [?Erfyn], Ælfric, Tryferyn, and from there he left for Hereford.)

One name in particular stands out: that of Tryferyn (*Tremerin*) who corresponds with Gerald's *Tramerin*. As I have already observed, a bishop of this name is also known from John of Worcester's Chronicle as a pious Welsh bishop who died in 1055 and had been acting on behalf of Æthelstan, bishop of Hereford, who, through blindness, was incapable of performing his episcopal duties.[45]

Another of the bishops of Clas Cynidr who may coincide with one of the bishops of St Davids is Morgynnydd: a bishop of this name appears in Gerald's list. In the annals, this bishop's see is not recorded. If these two are the same bishop, then he seems to be placed rather early in the Glasbury list. If, for the sake of argument, Morgynnydd had been translated from Glasbury to St Davids in 999, to succeed Morgeneu, then there would have been six bishops between him and Tryferyn, who died in 1055. If, however, the *Morgennic* of the Glasbury list were to be identified with the Morgeneu of Gerald's list and the annals, then the dates become more workable. If Morgeneu, as the annals suggest, became bishop of St Davids in the middle of the tenth century, then we have a more likely span of around a hundred years in which to fit his seven successors at Glasbury.[46]

Morgennic's successor at Glasbury was Rhydderch. Again, there is a bishop of this name in Gerald's list and in the annals. The annals do not give Rhydderch a see; but if he is the same Rhydderch that Gerald has recorded, then Gerald placed him too early in the succession, before Llynferth and Eneurys. In the annals, Rhydderch comes between Eneurys and Morgeneu. It is difficult to see how the Glasbury Rhydderch could have been a bishop of St Davids: it is only the unreliable Gerald who puts him in the St Davids succession (and then in the wrong place). If Rhydderch had simply been bishop at Clas Cynidr, then he could have succeeded Morgeneu when (and if) the latter bishop moved to St Davids, their episcopates running concurrently, Rhydderch predeceasing Morgeneu.[47] When Rhydderch died, in 955, his death (as a bishop known at, or associated with, St Davids) was recorded by the annalist.

A third bishop, *Heruuit* may be a miscopying for *Heruin*, which would correspond to Gerald's Erfyn and the Bishop Erfyn in *Annales Cambriae* who died in 1040.[48]

The Welsh annals, from Bishop Nyfys (840–73) onwards, appear to provide something approaching a full account of the bishops of Mynyw. Gerald's list, on the other hand, is inherently untrustworthy. 'Archbishop' Samson, whom he clearly equates with St Samson of Dol (the bishop who attended a council at Paris in the third quarter of the sixth century [556×573]), is placed later than Nyfys and Asser,

---

[45] John of Worcester, *Chronicle, s.a.* 1055 (ed. Darlington, *et al., The Chronicle of John of Worcester*, II.578). The Anglo-Saxon Chronicle (C and D) also records the death of *Tremerig*, Bishop Æthelstan's deputy during his unspecified infirmity.

[46] He may have succeeded Eneurys in 946, or Rhydderch in 964/5.

[47] The Glasbury Rhydderch may also, of course, have been a completely different person.

[48] *Heruuit*, however, is properly the ModW name Erwyd, and may therefore be correct as it stands, bearing no relation to the episcopal succession of St Davids.

both historical figures of the mid- to late ninth century. Gerald had no doubt been reading Asser's *Life* of King Alfred, where Nyfys is styled 'archbishop'; Samson would have to have succeeded Nyfys and Asser for Gerald's theory of the transference of the pallium to Dol to hold water. Gerald's *Tramerin*, from his place in the list, must be the bishop of the same name who was bishop at Glasbury and assistant to Æthelstan of Hereford.

This apparent connection between the annals, Gerald's list, and the Glasbury list requires an explanation. Whatever the status of *Morgennic*, Rhydderch, and *Heruuit*, it nevertheless appears that the *Tremerin* of the Glasbury list is the same person spoken of by John of Worcester and the Anglo-Saxon Chronicle, and the *Tramerin* (bishop of St Davids from 1040) in Gerald's episcopal list and the corrupt Canterbury document.[49] (It seems unlikely that there were two bishops with this otherwise unattested name in south Wales at the same time). One explanation for the apparent overlap in the episcopal lists is that bishops of Glasbury moved on to become bishops of St Davids. In a similar way, Nyfys (*Nobis*), who was Teilo's bishop at Llandeilo Fawr, appears to be the same Nyfys who became bishop – or archbishop – of St Davids in 840 – a bishop who was also claimed by Llandaf in the early twelfth century.[50]

We should also note the significance of Bishop Llynferth of St Davids' appearance in charter 237b of the Book of Llandaf. The charter describes how Llynferth, *episcopus Dauid*, intervened in a dispute between Llifio (the bishop of 'Llandaf') and the king of Brycheiniog, concerning Llanfihangel Tal-y-llyn, a property about seven miles north-west of Llangynidr (a church presumably dependent on Glasbury) and eight miles south-west of Glasbury. The appearance of Llynferth in this context seems genuine enough: Llandaf would have had no reason to interpolate the presence of a bishop of St Davids in a witness-list. We may interpret this situation in two ways (apart from taking the text at face value). Llifio may, in reality, have been a bishop of Glasbury, with Llynferth intervening in an archiepiscopal capacity – at this time, Hywel Dda would have had over-lordship of Brycheiniog – but Llifio is not mentioned in the Glasbury list. Alternatively, Llifio may be an interpolated figure, the grant really having been made to the bishop of St Davids.[51] In support of either of these theories, we may observe that the same property was originally granted to a bishop called *Guruan* in charter 167 (the only charter of this bishop); the third bishop of Glasbury is *Gueman* – the same person, perhaps?[52] Llandaf charter 237b seems to show that the bishops of St Davids had some jurisdiction in property-transactions associated with the bishops of Glasbury.[53]

49 Bishop Erfyn, *Tramerin*'s predecessor in Gerald's list, died in 1040 (see n. 35, above).

50 See nn. 21–3, above. Nyfys is the nineteenth bishop of Llandaf in the Book of Llandaf, but does not receive any grants (*Book of Llan Dâv*, ed. Evans, 217). Nyfys was included in the Llandaf succession as a bishop of Teilo. His name may be derived from an episcopal list rather than the Lichfield Gospels, otherwise we should expect to find versions of the 'Chad memoranda' among the Llandaf charters.

51 The one other grant to Llifio in the Book of Llandaf is of a property in Gŵyr (*Penn i Bei in Rosulgen*, Rhosili, charter 239); his appearance is therefore probably interpolated in one or other of the texts.

52 The forms *Guruan* and *Gueman* are close enough for confusion in copying: a miscopying of a notional form, *Guman*, could have produced *Guruan* in the Book of Llandaf; or, more likely, *Gueman* could have been produced from a miscopying of *Gueruan*, *Gurman*, or *Guorman*, in the case of the Glasbury list (cf. 'Guorman' for 'Guruan', *Book of Llan Dâv*, ed. Evans, 77).

53 Charter 237b may (with 146 and 167) originate from a Llan-gors archive: Llan-gors (which lies between Glasbury and Llangynidr, about 1½ miles south-east of Llanfihangel Tal-y-llyn, and about three miles to the east of Brecon) is described in the charter as Bishop Llifio's *monasterium*. In charter 146, Llan-gors is linked – as in 237b – with the ruling dynasty of Brycheiniog, and is granted

There appears, therefore, to be a link between a pre-Conquest episcopal church at Glasbury and the see of St Davids, from at least the middle of the tenth century, in the person of *Gueman*/Gwrfan to the first half of the eleventh, with Tryferyn. I should like to suggest that the bishopric of Cynidr/Glasbury was, in some way, suffragan to an 'archbishopric' of St Davids, which, as we have seen, is an historical entity, attested as late as the end of the ninth century, but whose significance is otherwise unclear.[54] Moreover, like the episcopal community of St Teilo at Llandeilo Fawr in the mid-ninth century, Clas Cynidr appears to have been a source of the successors of St David before the Norman Conquest.

Here then, may be some glimpses of the archbishopric of St Davids in operation – the morsels of flesh that I mentioned earlier, which can be attached to the skeletal frame of an archbishopric otherwise only known from the survival of archiepiscopal terminology. We appear to have an archiepiscopal see, based at St Davids, that extended its jurisdiction over bishoprics as far east as the Wye, possibly as late as the middle of the eleventh century; moreover, an archiepiscopal see that drew on its suffragan bishops for its own archiepiscopal succession.

Table 4. The Episcopal Succession at St Davids and Clas Cynidr Represented in the Sources

GERALD	AC/BRUTIAU	CLAS CYNIDR
Dauid	Dauid (d. 601)	
Eliud/Theliau		
Keneu		
Morwal		
Haernueu		
Elwaid		
Gurnueu		
Leudiwit		
Gorwiust		
Gogaun		
Cledauc		
Aman		
Eludged		
Elduuen		
Elaue		
Mailswid		
Sadurnue	Sadyrnfyw (d. 831)	
Nouis	Nobis (840–73)	
Sadurnueu		
	Llanwerth (after 874/5)	

---

as the royal burial site. (For Llan-gors, see, Sims-Williams, 'The provenance of the Llywarch Hen poems', esp. 61–2.)

[54] It was attested by Asser in the late ninth century, and comparable to the 'archbishopric' of Gwynedd: *AC* (A) 345 [=A.D. 809]: *Elbod<u>g archiepiscopus Guenedote regione migrauit ad dominum* (see above, 297).

GERALD	*AC/BRUTIAU*	CLAS CYNIDR
Doithwal		
Asser	Asser (*c.* 885)	
Archuail	= ? Guorchiguil (d. 907)	
Samson		
Kuielm		
Retherth		
Eluin		
Lunuerc	Lunberth (d. 944)	
Nergu		
Sulidir		
Eneuris	Eneuris (d. 946)	
	? Riderch (d. 955)	
Morgeneu	Morganeu (d. 999)	Morgennic (either here)
Nathan		
Iewan		
Arwistel		
Morgenennith	Morgannuc (d. 1025)	(or here) Morgennic
		[Rederch]
		[Dauit]
		[Wilfret]
		[Hithail]
Eruin	Erwyn (d. 1040)	Heruuit
		[Albri]
Tramerin		Tremerin
Joseth	Joseph (d. 1063)	
Bleidhud	Bleiduth (d. 1073)	
Sulghein	Sulien (1073–78)	
Abraham	Abraham (1078–80)	
	Sulien (*again* 1080–85)	
Wilfred	Wilfred (1085–1115)	
Bernard	Bernard (1115–48)	
David	David (1148–76)	
Peter	Peter (1176–98)	

18

THE DYNASTY OF DEHEUBARTH
AND THE CHURCH OF ST DAVIDS

Huw Pryce

The Norman conquest of Dyfed that followed the killing of Rhys ap Tewdwr, king of Deheubarth, in 1093 had profound consequences for the church of St Davids. There are hints that Rhys's relations with St Davids had been close: *Historia Gruffudd ap Cynan* describes him as taking refuge at the church before the battle of Mynydd Carn in 1081,[1] while a note added to the C-text of *Annales Cambriae* or the Annals of St Davids in British Library, MS Cotton Domitian A.i states that Rhys gave Pebidiog, the cantref in which St Davids is situated, to the church the following year.[2] Gerald of Wales similarly claimed that it was the native princes of south Wales who had endowed St Davids with Pebidiog.[3] From the late eleventh century, however, the bishopric was subjected both to the influence of the English crown and marcher lords and to the authority of Canterbury. True, the dynasty of Deheubarth survived and staged a major territorial recovery under Gruffudd ap Rhys (ob. 1137) and his sons, most notably Rhys ap Gruffudd or the Lord Rhys (ob. 1197).[4] Yet the context of its relations with St Davids had changed significantly. Valuable light is shed on those relations by agreements that Bishop Iorwerth of St Davids made in 1222×1223 with two sons of the Lord Rhys, Maelgwn (ob. 1230×1231) and Rhys Gryg (ob. 1233), in which the parties settled disputes concerning various lands claimed by the bishop.[5] The following discussion will look in detail at these documents in order to assess what they imply about the landholding of St Davids and its relations with secular power in an era of conflict in south-west Wales. First, though, it is necessary to sketch in some background from the late eleventh century onwards.

Relations between the dynasty of Deheubarth and the see of St Davids during the long twelfth century between Rhys ap Tewdwr's death in 1093 and the election of Iorwerth as bishop in 1215 were mainly distant. The lack of authority or even influence enjoyed by the dynasty stands in instructive contrast to the position in Gwynedd, where, despite the subordination of Bangor to Canterbury, the native rulers remained the dominant secular power, exercising regalian right during vacan-

---

[1] *Historia Gruffud vab Kenan*, ed. Evans, 13; see also *Vita Griffini*, ed. Russell, 68–9. Cf. Jones, 'The Mynydd Carn "Prophecy"', 78, which suggests that the meeting of Gruffudd ap Cynan and Rhys ap Tewdwr at St Davids before the battle was an invention, modelled on Rhys's submission to William I.

[2] Lloyd, 'Wales and the coming', 177, n. 1.

[3] Giraldus Cambrensis, *De Jure et Statu Menevensis Ecclesiae*, II (ed. Brewer *et al.*, *Opera*, III.154). The church's close relations with Rhys may also be implicit in the connection made by Rhygyfarch in his *Vita S. Dauid* between St David and the dynasty of Ceredigion: *Vita S. David* § 4 (ed. Sharpe and Davies, above, 112–13); cf. Davies, 'The saints', 389–90.

[4] Davies, *Conquest*, 45–6, 50–5; Smith, 'Treftadaeth'.

[5] *St Davids Episcopal Acta*, ed. Barrow, 122–3, 176–7 (no. 107, App., no. IV) = *AWR*, nos. 43, 52.

cies and sometimes influencing episcopal appointments.[6] At St Davids, not only did bishops make professions of obedience to the archbishop of Canterbury from 1115 onwards, but the crown claimed regalian right from at least Henry II's reign and the native dynasty had little if any control over the church or the choice of bishops.[7] This is not surprising: on the ground, it was the marcher families which exercised effective power. Moreover, these families quickly came to identify themselves with St David and his cathedral church. A telling indication of this identification is provided by Gerald of Wales in the preface to the version of his *Expugnatio Hibernica* dedicated to King John *ca* 1209, where he stresses that the first invaders of Ireland in the later twelfth century had been the men of the diocese of St Davids.[8] This is of a piece with the testimony of the Anglo-French poem on the invasion that the marchers invoked St David in their battles in Ireland from 1169 onwards.[9]

The importance of royal and marcher influence is further illustrated by the personnel appointed as bishops.[10] In 1115 the Welsh members of the cathedral clergy failed to secure the consecration of a compatriot, and Bernard, Norman chaplain of Matilda, Henry I's queen, was consecrated, a reflection of the English king's authority in Wales.[11] Canterbury and the crown also played a crucial part in the appointments of Peter de Leia, prior of Wenlock, in 1176 and of Geoffrey of Henlow, prior of Llanthony, in 1203. The only local appointment before 1215 was that of David fitz Gerald (1148–76), member of a prominent marcher family and half-Welsh and half-Norman by descent, though his nephew Gerald of Wales was twice an unsuccessful candidate for the bishopric.[12] Likewise Bishop Bernard made Henry, son of King David I of Scotland, steward of the lands of the bishopric, an office subsequently transferred by David fitz Gerald to his brother Maurice fitz Gerald (ob. 1176), whence it passed to Maurice's son and grandson.[13]

Yet if the church of St Davids slipped from the grasp of the descendants of Rhys ap Tewdwr, the process of disengagement was by no means complete. The B-text of the *Annales Cambriae* rejoiced at Anarawd ap Gruffudd's killing in 1137 of the Fleming Letard Litelking, described as 'an enemy of God and St David', an act that won Anarawd the support of all the people and clergy of St Davids.[14] Anarawd's half-brother and eventual successor, the Lord Rhys, was buried in the cathedral in 1197 and Latin verses were inscribed on his tomb.[15] True, according to the Annals of Winchester, the funeral arrangements were delayed by the awkward fact that Rhys had died under a sentence of excommunication promulgated by Bishop Peter de Leia, indignant at the way he had been captured and dragged half-naked through a

---

6 Pryce, 'Esgobaeth Bangor', esp. 42–50; *Episcopal Acts*, ed. Davies, II.415–37; Howell, 'Regalian right', 274–5.

7 *Canterbury Professions*, ed. Richter, 37–8, 46, 52–3, 61, 64 (nos. 64, 93, 112a, 112b, 144, 153); Howell, 'Regalian right', 277–82.

8 Giraldus Cambrensis, *Expugnatio Hibernica* (ed. Scott and Martin, 262); for the date, see *ibid.*, lxxi.

9 *The Deeds*, ed. Mullally, 72, 78, 102, 141 (lines 744–5, 753, 987, 1935–6, 3400–3, 3450–3); cf. Rowlands, 'The making', 156.

10 For a recent survey, see Evans, 'Bishops'. See also *St Davids Episcopal Acta*, ed. J. Barrow, 2–11.

11 *Episcopal Acts*, ed. Davies, I.133–5.

12 Richter, *Giraldus*, 54–6, 88–126. Marcher interests were also represented in the thirteenth century by Anselm le Gros (1231–47), a cousin of William Marshal II, earl of Pembroke, and Richard de Carew (1256–80): *St Davids Episcopal Acta*, ed. Barrow, 11, 13.

13 *Ibid.*, 5–6, 59–60 (no. 33 and note).

14 *AC* (B) 1137: *pro quo facto Anaraut omnium Menevensium cleri et populi habuit* [*sic*].

15 *ByT* (Pen. 20) 1197.

wood by the prince's sons, acting on their father's orders, until men of William de Braose had come to the rescue. However, the sentence was lifted after penance had been administered on the prince's corpse, allowing it to be buried in consecrated ground.[16] The episode highlights two sides to Rhys's relations with the church. On the one hand, we have a devotion to St David, who was also patron of the church at the prince's stronghold of Dinefwr as well as of Llanddewibrefi, of which Rhys is portrayed as the protector in Gwynfardd Brycheiniog's poem to the saint, possibly performed in the prince's presence in the 1170s.[17] In addition, a passing reference in Gerald's *Descriptio Kambriae* shows Rhys on pilgrimage at St Davids, though his devotion did not extend to acceding to the canons' request in 1188 to prevent Archbishop Baldwin from visiting the cathedral on his preaching tour round Wales (lest the visit should prejudice the see's claim to metropolitan status), despite effective lobbying by the canons among members of the prince's court.[18] On the other hand, devotion to the saint did not guarantee wholehearted respect for his apostolic successor. Admittedly, Rhys co-operated with the bishop on at least one occasion, when they expelled libidinous monks from Great Malvern's cell at Llandovery.[19] But the bishop's position as a marcher lord was a potential source of conflict, and Peter de Leia became a target in Rhys's expansionist campaigns following Henry II's death in July 1189. Five years before the kidnap already mentioned, the prince's son Gruffudd ap Rhys had captured the bishop's castle at Llawhaden.[20]

I shall return to some of the history of St Davids from the late eleventh century onwards when assessing the significance of the lands mentioned in Bishop Iorwerth's agreements with two of the Lord Rhys's sons in 1222×1223. Next, however, let us pause to consider the political situation in the early thirteenth century together with the circumstances of Iorwerth's appointment as bishop in 1215. After the Lord Rhys's death in 1197 Deheubarth fragmented as his sons and grandsons fought over the succession: as J.E. Lloyd put it, perhaps too harshly, 'After the giant came the pygmies.'[21] In 1215, in a series of campaigns led by Llywelyn ap Iorwerth, prince of Gwynedd, by then the most powerful Welsh ruler, some of these so-called pygmies reconquered substantial areas from the crown and the marchers, including Emlyn, Cemais, Cilgerran, Cardigan and Carmarthen. The following year Llywelyn stabilized control of these territories at Aberdyfi by imposing a partition of Deheubarth between two of the Lord Rhys's surviving sons, the eldest, Maelgwn, and a younger half-brother, Rhys Gryg, together with their nephews, Rhys Ieuanc and Owain, sons of Gruffudd ap Rhys, who had died in 1201.[22]

Despite some adjustments, and despite Llywelyn's undertaking at Worcester in March 1218 to ensure the restoration of lands and castles belonging to the king's

16 *Annales Monastici*, ed. Luard, II.66.
17 *AWR*, no. 90; Owen, 'Prolegomena', 61–3; Jones and Owen, 'Twelfth-century Welsh hagiography', 52–4, 61–5.
18 Giraldus Cambrensis, *Itinerarium Kambriae*, I.1 and *Descriptio Kambriae* II.14 (ed. Brewer *et al.*, *Opera*, VI.15–16, 191).
19 Giraldus Cambrensis, *Speculum Ecclesiae*, II.32 (ed. Brewer *et al.*, *Opera*, IV.100–1).
20 *AC* (B) 1192. The castle was demolished by Hywel Sais and Maelgwn ap Rhys the following year: *AC* (B) 1193. Cf. *ByT* (Pen. 20) 1192, 1193; *ByT* (RB) 1192, 1193; *ByS* 1192, 1193; 'Cronica de Wallia', ed. Thomas Jones 1193.
21 Lloyd, *The Story*, 79. For these succession struggles, see Smith, 'Dynastic succession', 212–13; Smith, 'The "Cronica de Wallia"', 262–5.
22 *ByT* (Pen. 20) 1216; *ByT* (RB) [1216]; *ByS* 1216; 'Cronica de Wallia', ed. Thomas Jones 1215 [=1216]. For a map of the division, see Davies, *Conquest*, 228.

adherents in south Wales,[23] the broad pattern of this partition continued some six years later when Maelgwn and Rhys Gryg made their agreements with the bishop: the lands named in each agreement all lay in the areas assigned to them in 1216, apart from the commote of Caerwedros, presumably acquired by Maelgwn following the death of his nephew Rhys Ieuanc in August 1222.[24] The rest of Maelgwn's share consisted of Cemais, Emlyn and Cantref Gwarthaf in Dyfed, Gwynionydd in Ceredigion, Hirfryn (including Llandovery) in Cantref Bychan and Malláen in Cantref Mawr, while Rhys held the remaining commotes of Cantref Bychan and Cantref Mawr. (On 29 August 1220 Llywelyn had forced Rhys Gryg to surrender further conquests made in 1217, namely, Cydweli, Carnwyllion, Gwidigada and Gower, although Rhys appears to have been soon restored to Cydweli and still held it in 1222.)[25]

Iorwerth's election to the see of St Davids took place precisely at the time of the conquests that redounded to the benefit of the Deheubarth dynasty. This surely helps to explain why it bucked the trend of a century that had witnessed the appointment of a series of non-Welsh bishops. In January 1215 King John had urged the election of an English candidate, Hugh Foliot, a member of the Hereford cathedral chapter and archdeacon of Shropshire who eventually became bishop of Hereford (1219–34).[26] However, despite knowing that the king and archbishop of Canterbury wanted another Englishman (like the previous bishop, Geoffrey of Henlow), the canons of St Davids elected Iorwerth, whom Gerald of Wales called 'a pure Welshman' and 'a good and straightforward man'.[27] Royal assent was given on 18 June 1215 and Iorwerth was consecrated three days later at Staines.[28] His consecration – together with that of Cadwgan, abbot of Whitland, as bishop of Bangor – delighted the author of the *Cronica de Wallia*, who made a point of noting that two Welshmen had been appointed to the sees.[29] What made John change his mind and accept Iorwerth is not stated in any of the sources. J.E. Lloyd assumed that the king had to bow to pressure from Llywelyn ap Iorwerth in the critical period leading up to Magna Carta, accepted by John three days before he assented to Iorwerth's election.[30] However, this view has been questioned by J. Beverley Smith, who attributes the decisive intervention to William Marshal, earl of Pembroke, the most powerful lord in the diocese and the man to whom John had entrusted the temporalities on 11 January 1215 following Geoffrey's death the previous year.[31] These interpreta-

---

23 *AWR*, no. 241. Cf. Pryce, 'Negotiating', 16–17 and references given there.
24 Cf. Lloyd, 'The age', 173, 175. The precise distribution of lands in Ceredigion between Rhys Ieuanc and Owain is unknown, other than that it excluded the commotes of Mebwynion and Gwynionydd, which formed part of Maelgwn's share, and that Rhys had the commote of Anhuniog, where he granted Rhandir Llan-non to St Davids in 1215×1222; he also seems to have held Llanbadarn Fawr in the commote of Perfedd by the end of his life: Lloyd, *The Story*, 89; *AWR*, no. 57; 'Gwaith Phylip Brydydd', ed. M.E. Owen, no. 14 (esp. 195–6). Nor are details recorded of Llywelyn ap Iorwerth's division of the lands of Rhys Ieuanc between Maelgwn and Owain ap Gruffudd, Rhys Ieuanc's brother: *ByT* (Pen. 20) 1222; *ByT* (RB) 1222; *ByS* 1222.
25 *Royal and Other Historical Letters*, ed. Shirley, I.176–7 = *AWR*, no. 248; Smith and Pugh, 'The lordship', 222–3; Walker, 'Hubert de Burgh', 470–1; Carpenter, *The Minority*, 217–19.
26 *English Episcopal Acta*, VII, ed. Barrow, xlviii–l.
27 Giraldus Cambrensis, *De Jure et Statu Menevensis Ecclesiae*, VII (ed. Brewer *et al.*, *Opera*, III.361).
28 J.B. Smith, 'Magna Carta', 357.
29 'Cronica de Wallia', ed. Thomas Jones 1214 [=1215].
30 Lloyd, *A History*, II.688, followed by Howell, 'Regalian right', 280, and *St Davids Episcopal Acta*, ed. Barrow, 10.
31 Smith, 'Magna Carta', 357–8. Cf. Howell, 'Regalian right', 282.

tions need not be mutually incompatible: given Llywelyn's dominance in Wales at a time of crisis for the king, the Marshal may have persuaded John that it would be impolitic to inflame Welsh sentiment by blocking the election of a Welsh candidate. Had the balance of power been different, so too might have been the outcome at St Davids.

Be that as it may, the important point to emphasize is that not only was Iorwerth Welsh but he had also been abbot of the Premonstratensian house of Talley (Talyl-lychau), an *Eigenkloster* of the Deheubarth dynasty founded by the Lord Rhys about seven miles north-east of Dinefwr.[32] Irrespective of the precise influences that secured assent for his election, Iorwerth thus had closer connections with the dynasty than any previous bishop since Wilfrid. It does not follow, of course, that he would put the interests of the dynasty above those of his church; but his background at Talley might at least have made it easier for him to cultivate good relations with his erstwhile patrons. That this was so is suggested by the presence of his successor as abbot of Talley as a witness to both of Iorwerth's agreements with members of the dynasty and also to a charter recording Rhys Ieuanc's gift to the bishop of Rhandir Llan-non in Ceredigion, a document discussed further below.[33]

A further potential channel of communication was provided by one of Iorwerth's senior clergy, Maredudd ap Rhys, archdeacon of Cardigan, as Maredudd was another son of the Lord Rhys and thus brother to Rhys Gryg and Maelgwn.[34] After his death and burial in St Davids cathedral in 1227, Maredudd was succeeded as archdeacon by his son Gruffudd ap Maredudd, who died in 1242.[35] (It is worth adding that Rhys Gryg was also buried in the cathedral in 1233, six years after Maredudd, despite having granted his body for burial to Strata Florida abbey thirty-five years previously.)[36] If, as seems very likely, Maredudd is identifiable with the Archdeacon Maurice of Cardigan whose consent was required by Gerald of Wales before the latter would agree to the election of Geoffrey of Henlow in 1203, he had presumably been appointed to the office during the pontificate of Peter de Leia and thus quite possibly during the lifetime of the Lord Rhys.[37] In any event, Maredudd's tenure of the office – together with the thirteen mother-churches which, with five townships, made up his inheritance according to a late thirteenth-century list of Rhys's sons – reflects Rhys's determination to embed his dynasty's hold on Ceredigion, which after its definitive annexation in 1165 became a cornerstone of the restored principality of Deheubarth.[38]

In assessing the significance of Bishop Iorwerth's relations with the lay members of the Deheubarth dynasty let us turn first to the charter in which Rhys Ieuanc gave Rhandir Llan-non 'in its ancient bounds and limits to God and St David and Bishop Iorwerth of St Davids and his successors', a document datable to June 1215

---

[32] *ByT* (Pen. 20) 1215; *ByT* (RB) 1215; *ByS* 1215; 'Cronica de Wallia', ed. Thomas Jones 1214 [= 1215]. Rhys probably founded the abbey between 1184 and 1189: Smith and O'Neil, *Talley*, 5–6; Smith, 'Treftadaeth', 46, n. 39.

[33] See above, n. 5; *AWR*, no. 57.

[34] Maredudd witnessed a charter in favour of Strata Florida issued in 1198×1227 by Maelgwn's son Maelgwn Fychan: *AWR*, no. 63.

[35] *ByT* (Pen. 20) 1227, 1242; *ByT* (RB) 1227, 1242; *ByS* 1227, 1242; 'Cronica de Wallia', ed. Thomas Jones 1242. See also Pearson, *Fasti*, 57.

[36] *ByT* (Pen. 20) 1233; *ByT* (RB) 1233; *ByS* 1233; 'Cronica de Wallia', ed. Thomas Jones 1234 [=1233]; *AWR*, no. 50.

[37] Giraldus Cambrensis, *De Jure et Statu Menevensis Ecclesiae*, III (ed. Brewer *et al.*, *Opera*, III.323).

[38] 'Cronica de Wallia', ed. Thomas Jones, 41. On the importance of Ceredigion to Rhys's reconstituted kingdom of Deheubarth, see, for example, Turvey, *The Welsh Princes*, 106–7.

× August 1222.[39] This differs from the agreements of his two uncles with the bishop in that it records what appears to be a new gift, rather than the outcome of a dispute involving the restoration of what was adjudged to be rightful property of the church. Indeed, it is the only extant charter recording a gift to the church of St Davids by a Deheubarth ruler: the dynasty's other charters for ecclesiastical beneficiaries – both surviving texts and those known only from mentions in other sources – are in favour of monasteries and other religious houses. We can only guess how far Rhys Ieuanc was motivated by a belief that land associated with Non, mother of St David, should be held by her son's successors.[40] What is certain is that the bishops held on to the land, which lay just south of Llansanffraid in the commote of Anhuniog in Ceredigion, as Llan-non appears as an episcopal township in 1326 in the extent known as the *Black Book of St Davids*.[41]

The agreements with Maelgwn and Rhys Gryg both bear a time-date of 1222 (presumably 25 March 1222 × 24 March 1223 by modern reckoning), and, to judge by their differing witness lists, were issued on different occasions. However, both have important similarities to each other, being records of settlements of disputes between the bishop and the Welsh rulers pronounced by the dean, chancellor and treasurer of Hereford cathedral acting as papal judges delegate. Moreover, in each case the settlement involved a recognition of the church's title to the lands in dispute, while allowing the rulers to retain most of them for a nominal rent, with only a few being restored to the bishop at once. The agreements therefore witness to Bishop Iorwerth's readiness to seek the remedies of canon law in defence of his church's rights. At the same time, both the immediate and, to judge by later evidence, the longer-term material gain to the church was limited.

The bishop's claim against Maelgwn concerned lands in Cantref Bychan (namely, Llandovery), Ceredigion and Dyfed.[42] Maelgwn and his son Maelgwn Fychan (ob. 1257) recognized the bishop's right to all the lands claimed but the specific provisions varied. With regard to Llandovery, Maelgwn Fychan was to give homage to the bishop and provide him with safe conduct whenever he travelled through the land and a procuration in the castle of Llandovery at least once a year; the men of the land would give military service like the other men of St David. The agreement in respect of Cenarth Mawr (now known simply as Cenarth) in Emlyn was more complex: the land, with its mill, fish-trap and other appurtenances, was restored to the bishop, who then granted half of the mill and fish-trap, together with the service of the men of the adjacent township of Dol-y-bryn, to Maelgwn Fychan for his lifetime. The other lands in the bishop's claim were likewise restored to him, but these were granted in their entirety to Maelgwn Fychan for his lifetime in return for the annual render of one sparrowhawk. The lands listed are numerous and the identification of some is uncertain. Like Cenarth, several were located in Emlyn, namely, Maenordeifi, Pen-boyr, Cilgerran and Clydai; at least three in Ceredigion, namely, Llannerch Aeron,[43] Gartheli and *Lanechren* in Gwynionydd; and at least two in Cemais, namely, Moylgrove and Monington.

---

[39] *AWR*, no. 57.
[40] Cf. Baring-Gould and Fisher, *Lives*, IV.22–5; Dumville, *Saint David*, 27–9.
[41] *The Black Book*, ed. Willis-Bund, 210–11. Cf. Lloyd, *The Story*, 89–90. The dating of the extent to 1326 is vindicated in Davies, 'The Black Book', 158–60.
[42] *St Davids Episcopal Acta*, ed. Barrow, 122–3 (no. 107); *AWR*, no. 43.
[43] I am grateful to Gerald Morgan for pointing out that *Lanarthayron* probably represents Llannerch Aeron (Allt Llannerch Aeron in the vicinity of SN 485 595) rather than Llannarth (SN 423 578) in the commote of Caerwedros, as the latter place is some distance from the Aeron. Although of course not

The settlement with Rhys Gryg, lord of most of Ystrad Tywi, lists fewer lands than that with Maelgwn ap Rhys and poses fewer problems of interpretation.[44] Rhys and his sons recognized the bishop's right in the lands he claimed, all of which were located in Cantref Mawr, specified as the whole commote of Llandeilo (that is, Maenordeilo) with its appurtenances, namely, an area north-west of Llandeilo Fawr to the west of Afon Dulais as well as the *maenor* of Llanddarog, the township of Llangynnwr and the lands of Abergwili which certain Welshmen had unjustly held. (It is notable that Rhys is presented as having authority over Abergwili by virtue of its being a detached appurtenance of Maenordeilo, despite its location in Gwidigada, a commote that Rhys had surrendered in August 1220.)[45] The land west of the Dulais was restored up to the border with the commote of Cetheiniog apart from various named lands granted by Rhys or his men to the church of Llandeilo Fawr and Talley abbey, as were all the lands of Abergwili, which Rhys and his sons agreed to warrant against the Welshmen who had held them. Rhys and his sons were allowed to retain the other lands in return for homage, an oath on relics that they would faithfully support the bishop and his church, men, land and possessions, and an annual render of a goshawk; they would also ensure that the men of the lands would serve in the bishop's army when summoned.

How had the various lands named in the agreements fallen into the hands of the dynasty of Deheubarth? The short answer is simple: through military conquest and the subsequent partition of Deheubarth in 1215–16. It does not follow, however, that Maelgwn and Rhys Gryg had themselves first been responsible for depriving the bishop of St Davids of all of the lands in question. Admittedly the detailed provisions in the settlement with Rhys Gryg concerning Gwgan Sais, Cedifor ab Ynyr and other nobles may indicate that these men had seized the bishop's lands in Abergwili recently, during Rhys Gryg's tenure of the commote of Gwidigada prior to August 1220. Gerald of Wales's assertion that negligence by Iorwerth's predecessor, Bishop Geoffrey, had led to lands of St Davids in Ystrad Tywi being 'almost irrevocably occupied by the powerful men of the country' likewise points to fairly recent losses.[46] However, there is a strong case for supposing that many of the lands had originally been lost earlier, in at least some instances to marcher lords rather than Welsh rulers: Llandovery and Cilgerran are likely candidates, as their earliest castles were built by marchers, and in the former lordship Richard fitz Pons made extensive grants, including the castle church and all the tithes from his demesnes, to the priory of Great Malvern by 1127.[47] Archbishop Anselm clearly believed that possessions of St Davids had fallen victim to Norman conquerors during the pontificate of Bishop Wilfrid, as he ordered Robert, earl of Shrewsbury, his brother Arnulf of Montgomery, Ralph Mortimer, Philip de Braose, Bernard de Neufmarché and others to restore any lands, tithes or churches that belonged to Wilfrid's church.[48] Nor had the threat abated two decades later, to judge by a privilege Bishop Bernard

---

proof of the identification, it is worth noting that Maelgwn died at Llannerch Aeron in 1230×1231: *ByT* (Pen. 20) 1231; *ByT* (RB) 1231; *ByS* 1231; Lloyd, *A History*, II.674, n. 110.

[44] *St Davids Episcopal Acta*, ed. Barrow, 176–7 (App., no. IV); *AWR*, no. 52.

[45] Llangynnwr was another detached portion, although in this case Rhys had apparently recovered the commote of Cydweli in which it was located shortly after surrendering it in 1220 and still held the commote in 1222. See above, 308.

[46] Giraldus Cambrensis, *De Jure et Statu Menevensis Ecclesiae*, VII (ed. Brewer *et al.*, *Opera*, III.350).

[47] Lloyd, *A History*, II.429, 519; *Episcopal Acts*, ed. Davies, I.246 (D. 65). For the later expulsion of the Malvern monks from their cell at Llandovery, see above, n. 19.

[48] *Episcopal Acts*, ed. J. Conway Davies, I.236 (D.24). Gerald of Windsor, Arnulf's officer at Pembroke

obtained from Pope Calixtus II in 1123 confirming and protecting the possessions of St Davids, and ordering the restitution of any possessions seized by violence.[49] As we shall see, a similar picture emerges from the writings of Gerald of Wales, although he laid part of the blame for the losses of lands at the door of the bishops. It appears, then, that in the late eleventh and early twelfth centuries the church of St Davids suffered from the same combination of 'lay power and invasion of monks' which Bishop Urban (1107–34) blamed for the losses of the church of Llandaf.[50] In contrast to Llandaf, however, the continuing volatility of the political situation in much of the diocese of St Davids meant that later in the twelfth century former episcopal estates changed hands between settlers and the Welsh and possibly also led to further losses.

This is certainly the impression given by Gerald of Wales, who complained in his *De Jure et Statu Menevensis Ecclesiae* that all the bishops from Wilfrid to Geoffrey had been responsible for impoverishing the church of St Davids through alienating lands. As Gerald was well-informed about St Davids, there seems no good reason to dismiss the substance of these allegations, which provide the most detailed evidence for the church's losses of property in the twelfth century.[51] Indeed, a few of the places he names turn up in the agreement between Bishop Iorwerth and Maelgwn ap Rhys. Thus Cenarth was listed among the lands that Bishop Wilfrid had been forced to alienate by the Norman settlers in Dyfed during the reign of Henry I.[52] If, as seems likely, *Aberguemi* is a corrupt reading of *Abergweun* (Fishguard), this may be a further example, as Fishguard is said by Gerald to have been abjured by Bishop Bernard, thereby being removed from Pebidiog – in whose rural deanery it nevertheless remained – and attached to the fitz Martin lordship of Cemais.[53] The church's loss of Moylgrove and Monington, likewise located in Cemais, may also have resulted from conquest by the fitz Martins rather than from the reconquests of Cemais by the Lord Rhys in 1191 or by Llywelyn and his Deheubarth allies in 1215.[54]

Similarly, Julia Barrow's tentative identification of the commote of *Estriat* with Ystlwyf (usually rendered in Latin texts as *Oysterlath* or variants thereof) is reinforced by Gerald's assertion that Ystlwyf was lost by the church of St Davids during David fitz Gerald's pontificate (1148–76) as the result of its occupation by 'great men and magnates' – possibly a reference to its conquest by the Lord Rhys, confirmed by Henry II in 1171 – and had not been recovered at the time of the *De Jure*'s composition *ca* 1218.[55] True, the agreement with Rhys Gryg suggests that the bishop had held on to, or already recovered, some demesne lands in the commote,

---

castle, ravaged the bounds of St Davids in 1097: *AC* (BC) 1097; *ByT* (Pen. 20) 1095 [=1097]; *ByT* (RB) 1093 [=1097]; *ByS* 1095 [=1097].

[49] *Councils*, ed. Haddan and Stubbs, I.315–16. Jones and Freeman, *The History*, 311, n. (y), suggest that the papal confirmation was requested in response to wholesale alienations under Bishop Wilfrid.

[50] *The Text*, ed. Evans with Rhys, 88; cf. J.R. Davies, 'The Book', 39–43; *idem*, *The Book*, 46–53.

[51] For the poverty of the bishops of St Davids in this period, cf. *St Davids Episcopal Acta*, ed. J. Barrow, 10.

[52] Giraldus Cambrensis, *De Jure et Statu Menevensis Ecclesiae*, II (ed. Brewer *et al.*, *Opera*, III.152). Gerald added that Wilfrid also alienated some lands through friendship.

[53] *Ibid.* (ed. Brewer *et al.*, *Opera*, III.154); cf. *Taxatio*, ed. Ayscough and Caley, 274–5. For the use of this Welsh place-name in another thirteenth-century St Davids source, see *AC* (C) 1210: *Fissegard, id est, Abergweun*.

[54] For the fitz Martins and Cemais, see Lloyd, *A History*, II.425; Walker, 'The lordships', 151–2.

[55] Giraldus Cambrensis, *Symbolum Electorum, Ep.* XXXI; *De Jure et Statu Menevensis Ecclesiae*, II (ed. Brewer *et al.*, *Opera*, I.309; III.155). Cf. *ByT* (Pen. 20) 1171; *ByT* (RB) 1171.

quite possibly at Meidrum, where the bishops of St Davids possessed a manor by the early fourteenth century.[56] However, Bishop Iorwerth established his church's rights over the whole commote. One complicating factor here was that some of its lands were held by Whitland abbey, to which the Lord Rhys had granted at least part of Ystlwyf, including Llanfihangel Abercywyn, where the abbey possessed a grange down to the Dissolution.[57] That the church of St Davids continued to claim rights in this area is suggested by an agreement in 1352 by which the parson of Llanfihangel Abercywyn, who was also archdeacon of St Davids, renounced, with the assent of the bishop and chapter of St Davids, all right he claimed against Whitland regarding land in Ystlwyf and Abercywyn in return for an annual rent of 60s. from the monks' lands in the same area.[58] If, as J. Wyn Evans has suggested, Meidrum was the mother-church of the commote, and Llanfihangel Abercywyn originally its daughter-church, then Iorwerth was in effect claiming all the land subject to the mother-church,[59] just as the claim to Maenordeilo and its appurtenances from Rhys Gryg seems to have been based on the *parochia* of the mother-church of Llandeilo Fawr, whose ownership had been successfully vindicated against Llandaf by Bishop Bernard.[60] With respect to Maenordeilo, however, the bishop and chapter are explicitly said to have consented to various grants to Llandeilo Fawr and Talley, so that these were excluded from the lands restored to St Davids.

It is likely that Bishop Iorwerth based his claim to many if not all the lands named in both agreements on a written text, known as the *graphium* of St David, that set out the possessions of his church. This is certainly so with respect to the agreement with Maelgwn, which states that Maelgwn and his son recognized the bishop's right in all the disputed lands 'according to the bounds assigned in the *graphium* of St David'. This must be the same as 'the book of possessions which is called the *graffium*' taken, with the chapter seal, from their custodians by David fitz Gerald according to the anonymous account of that bishop composed shortly after his death in 1176.[61]

Both the term *graphium* and the reference to bounds suggest that the book contained charters or at least summaries of grants that included boundary clauses.[62] Perhaps the *graphium* of St David resembled, in purpose if not in form, the *Liber*

56 *The Black Book*, ed. Willis-Bund, 234–41. At least some of the demesne lands of the manor had been held by either Bishop Thomas Wallensis (1248–55) or Bishop Thomas Bek (1280–93): *ibid.*, 234–5; cf. J. Conway Davies, 'The Black Book', 159.

57 Dugdale, *Monasticon*, V.591 = *AWR*, no. 29 (lost charter datable to Christmas 1189×1195); Williams, *Atlas*, 66, 91 (map 12).

58 *CPR 1350–4*, 316; cf. E. Phillimore *apud Description*, ed. Owen, I.213–14, which suggests that these were perhaps the same lands in Ystlwyf as those mentioned by Gerald. The prebend of Meidrum was attached to the stall of the archdeacon of St Davids in the fourteenth century: Evans, 'Meidrum', 17; Pearson, *Fasti*, 53.

59 Evans, 'Meidrum', esp. 13–15. Cf. the suggestion that the boundaries of Ystlwyf were coextensive with those of the parish of Meidrum: Lloyd, 'Boundaries', 12.

60 Cf. *ibid.*, 7–8; for the oldest description of the boundaries of Llandeilo Fawr, see *The Text*, ed. Evans with Rhys, 78. For Bishop Urban of Llandaf's unsuccessful claim to Llandeilo Fawr, see *Episcopal Acts*, ed. Davies, I.152, 168, 180; Davies, *The Book*, 17, 71–2, 89.

61 Richter, 'A new edition', 248.

62 Cf. Davies, 'Charter-writing', 103–4. There is evidence that charters recording gifts of land to St Davids had been issued at least as early as the ninth century, though whether copies of these or other pre-Norman charters were included in the *graffium* can only be a matter for speculation: cf. E. Phillimore *apud Description*, ed. H. Owen, IV.428; Davies, 'The Latin charter-tradition', 261 and n. 19; Brett, 'John Leland', 179–80.

Landauensis, referred to by the late middle ages as the *graphus* of St Teilo.[63] More-over, already by the early twelfth century, quite possibly before *Liber Landauensis* began to be written, the church of Llandaf appears to have possessed a document referred to as the *cirografum* (or, in Welsh, the *gref*) of St Teilo which set out the history, privileges and bounds claimed by the church. Thus in October 1119 Bishop Urban appealed to the authority of the *cyrografum sancti patroni nostri Teiliaui* in a letter to Pope Calixtus II, and a similar reference (*ut in cirografo demonstratur*) is found in the record of a privilege purportedly issued in favour of Llandaf by Gruffudd ap Llywelyn (ob. 1063).[64] This *cirografum* was possibly the same as the *gref Teliau* cited in an addition to *Liber Landauensis* made in the first half of the thirteenth century – namely, a text including an account of the cantrefs of Morgannwg contained in a judgement allegedly made by King Edgar preserved in an ancient *carta* that had almost rotted away.[65] Furthermore, the bishopric of Bangor may have possessed a similar record of its possessions, to judge by a reference to the *graffia* of the church in a highly suspect list of royal benefactors of Bangor copied by the antiquary Henry Rowlands (1655–1723).[66] As these examples from Llandaf and Bangor show, not all the claims to lands and rights contained in such records of possessions can be taken at face value. Nevertheless, irrespective of whether the church's title to the lands described in it was as well founded as it purported to be, 'the *graphium* of St David' provided Bishop Iorwerth with evidence that seems to have been accepted both by the judges delegate and by Maelgwn ap Rhys.

Finally, why did Bishop Iorwerth decide to take action about the disputed lands when he did, and how successful was he in recovering them for St Davids? It should be stressed that we know nothing about the immediate background to his claims, and thus whether he had already begun negotiating with Maelgwn and Rhys before the matter went before judges delegate. One possibility, however, is that Iorwerth sought to take advantage of the opportunity presented by the resurgence of native power in Deheubarth, and thought that he stood a better chance of gaining accept-ance of his church's right to the disputed lands from native rulers than he would have from the marcher lords. His connections with the dynasty of Deheubarth by virtue of his previous office as abbot of Talley may have been an advantage here. An addi-tional consideration, especially relevant with respect to Maelgwn, may have been the

---

63 *The Text*, ed. Evans with Rhys, 340: *ut in hoc sacro sancti Teliai graffo sparsim intuentibus patebit.* For the date, see Huws, *Medieval Welsh Manuscripts*, 150–1. See also Huws, above, 314.

64 *The Text*, ed. J.G. Evans with Rhys, 87, 270. Both texts were copied by Hand A and rubricated by Hand B in 1119×1134: Huws, *Medieval Welsh Manuscripts*, 129, 135, 142; J.R. Davies, '*Liber Landavensis*'. Although the text of Gruffudd's privilege probably derives from an authentic document datable to *ca* 1060 (as argued in Davies, *The Llandaff Charters*, 129), the reference to the *cirografum* may nevertheless be a later interpolation.

65 *The Text*, ed. J.G. Evans with Rhys, 248; cf. *ibid.*, 247; Huws, *Medieval Welsh Manuscripts*, 129, 143. The judgement is spurious as it anachronistically synchronizes Edgar (959–73) with Hywel Dda (ob. 950): J.R. Davies, *The Book*, 66–7 and n. 28. The context of the references to the *cirografum* and the *gref* of St Teilo suggests that it consisted of, or contained, the text *De primo statu Landauensis ecclesie* that opens the main part of *Liber Landauensis* copied by Hand A: cf. *The Text*, ed. Evans with Rhys, 68–71; Davies, *The Book of Llandaf*, 77–9, 110–11. If so, it was not identical with the document *Braint Teilo*, although the latter text was one of the sources of *De primo statu*: cf. *ibid.*, 64.

66 Willis, *A Survey*, 183. Compare also the testimony of witnesses in 1537 to the existence of a book called *Graphus Sancti Bewnoi* belonging to the church of Clynnog Fawr in Arfon: Owen, 'An episode', 179, 183. This may have been identical with the 'Book of St Beuno' and contained records of donations to the church: Sims-Williams, 'Edward IV's confirmation charter', 231–2, 235; *idem*, 'The uses', 22.

threat to the rulers' hold on their conquests in Dyfed posed by Llywelyn's agreement with the crown at Worcester in March 1218 that lands occupied in 1215 should be restored to the king's barons and adherents in south Wales; indeed, this had already led to Rhys Gryg's being deprived of some of his gains in 1220.[67] Maelgwn argu- ably had much to gain from recognizing that he and his son would henceforth hold the disputed lands in Emlyn and Cemais from the bishop: if the lands belonged to St Davids, this would undermine the entitlement of William Marshal II and the fitz Martins respectively to recover them under the terms of the Worcester agreement. The same applied to Rhys's tenure of Llangynnwr in Cydweli.[68] Nor were Maelgwn and Rhys necessarily concerned solely with the prospects of a marcher recovery: they may also have reckoned that submission to the bishop would weaken claims by their powerful ally Llywelyn to overlordship over their lands, including those in Ceredigion and Ystrad Tywi that the prince of Gwynedd had apportioned among them in 1216.[69]

Whatever the precise calculations that motivated the bishop and the Deheubarth rulers in 1222×1223, the political situation reflected in the territorial dispositions of the agreements proved short-lived. As the result of a campaign by William Marshal II in south-west Wales, Maelgwn and Rhys Gryg submitted – along with Llywelyn – to Henry III at Shrewsbury on 7 October 1223 and surrendered most of their conquests.[70] The estates claimed by Bishop Iorwerth in Dyfed were now restored to marcher control, and there is no evidence that they were subsequently recovered by the church of St Davids. Furthermore, in the longer term the church appears to have gained only limited additions to its demesne lands even within the patrimonial lands retained by Maelgwn and Rhys and their descendants in Ceredigion and Ystrad Tywi.[71] Apart, possibly, from Meidrum in Ystlwyf, the only other lands named in the agreements that appear as episcopal manors in the early fourteenth-century *Black Book of St Davids* are Gartheli in the commote of Mebwynion in Ceredigion and Abergwili and Llandeilo Fawr together with its *patria* in Cantref Mawr.[72] In addi- tion, Bishop Iorwerth had received Llan-non from Rhys Ieuanc.[73] Both Maelgwn and Rhys continued to assert rights over the lands of St Davids since, after Iorwerth's death in 1229, they took over the custody of the church's temporalities in their lands, and Rhys Gryg's heirs similarly sought to exercise regalian right in 1247.[74]

The main significance of the agreements considered in this paper, then, is not their consequences for the future, but rather the light they shed on a particular moment in

---

[67] Although Iorwerth was not present at Llywelyn's agreements at Worcester in March 1218, he may have learned of their terms from William Marshal II, earl of Pembroke, who was: *AWR*, nos. 240–2. On 1220, see above, 308.

[68] Cf. *AWR*, no. 241; above, 308.

[69] Cf. above, 307.

[70] Lloyd, *A History*, II.663 and n. 46; Carpenter, *The Minority*, 313–14. Among the lands surrendered by Maelgwn were the lordships of Cemais, Cilgerran and Emlyn, while Rhys was finally deprived of Cydweli.

[71] For the later history of Maelgwn, Rhys Gryg and their descendants in Deheubarth, see Lloyd, *The Story*, 91–105; *idem*, 'The age', 173–200. The distribution of territory between Maelgwn and Rhys had changed in one important respect by 1227, as the latter, rather than Maelgwn, is recorded as holding the castle of Llandovery in that year: *ibid.*, 177.

[72] The commote of Ystlwyf remained in the hands of the Deheubarth dynasty, being held in 1261 by Rhys Gryg's son Maredudd ap Rhys (ob. 1271): *Littere Wallie*, ed. Edwards, 104–5 (no. 199) = *AWR*, no. 347, c. ii.

[73] *The Black Book*, ed. Willis-Bund, 204–5, 210–11, 240–51, 262–75.

[74] Howell, 'Regalian right', 277–9. Cf. also *St Davids Episcopal Acta*, ed. Barrow, 13.

relations between the church of St Davids and the dynasty of Deheubarth, a moment created in large part by extensive Welsh reconquests. This in turn has important implications for an understanding of the troubled history of that church's land-holding over the preceding century and more.

19

THE STATUTES OF ST DAVIDS CATHEDRAL 1224–1259

Julia Barrow

In the thirteenth century the bishops of St Davids began to issue statutes for their cathedral chapter. In doing so they were taking part in a wider European trend, as bishops of the late twelfth and thirteenth centuries started to issue statutes for their cathedral chapters, and, quite often, cathedral chapters themselves made compilations of their regulations for future canons to observe. The thirteenth century was a legislative age, not least in the church, and part of the aim of this paper will be to show how wider European patterns, especially in the wake of the Fourth Lateran Council, made themselves felt in Wales. More particularly however the aim is to set St Davids in the context of the province of Canterbury in the thirteenth century, to see how it compared with larger and richer establishments. First, the forms of thirteenth-century cathedral legislation will be set within the general framework of ecclesiastical statute making, taking note of how cathedral statutes were issued, compiled and preserved, and then attention will be paid to its principal aims, which overwhelmingly concentrated on the regulation of residence, the division of the chapter finances, the disciplining of the minor clergy and the organisation of the liturgy.

To begin with we should devote some attention to St Davids cathedral chapter in the thirteenth century. It appears to have begun to shift away from the old *clas* system towards the pattern of a northern French cathedral chapter (the type of model favoured in post-Conquest England) under Bishop Bernard 1115–1148:[1] although no charters of Bernard for the chapter survive, some assumptions about his activities can be made from the names of St Davids canons occurring in witness lists to his charters. Moreover it is possible to guess at what happened in Bernard's pontificate from what we know about the chapter in the time of his successor, David fitzGerald. Bernard introduced some canons of Anglo-Norman descent,[2] he set up the four archdeaconries,[3] he altered the dedication of the cathedral to include St Andrew as well as St David,[4] and it may have been he who encouraged the chapter to have its own seal (mentioned in the *Vita Davidis Secundi* as existing in David

---

[1] *Fasti Ecclesiae Anglicanae 1066–1300*, IX, *The Welsh Cathedrals*, ed. Pearson, xxi [*Fasti Ecclesiae Anglicanae* hereafter *FEA*].

[2] Jordan, archdeacon of Brecon; William, archdeacon of Carmarthen; perhaps also Simon, canon; David fitzGerald, archdeacon of Cardigan, was of Cambro-Norman descent: *FEA 1066–1300*, IX, *The Welsh Cathedrals*, ed. Pearson, 54, 57, 58, 69.

[3] *FEA 1066–1300*, IX, *The Welsh Cathedrals*, ed. Pearson, xxi and 53, 54, 57, 58; the earliest occurrence of an archdeacon of St Davids is more secure than Pearson (*ibid.*, 53) states, since the charter of Gilbert earl of Pembroke in which he appears is not the deed (in fact a missing charter purportedly issued by Wizo the Fleming) stated to be inauthentic in *St Davids Episcopal Acta*, ed. Barrow, 34, no. 2.

[4] *St Davids Episcopal Acta*, ed. Barrow, 3.

fitzGerald's pontificate).[5] Llandaf, by comparison, underwent similar changes in the early thirteenth century under Bishop Henry (1193–1218),[6] while the development of the cathedral chapter at Bangor occurred between 1177 and 1215.[7] No charters of bishops of St Davids for their chapter survive before the pontificate of Iorwerth, however, which makes the evolution of that body obscure.[8] Until the 1220s the only dignitaries were the four archdeacons; only in 1224 did Iorwerth establish the precentorship.[9] No other dignity appeared until 1259 when Bishop Richard de Carew set up the treasurership.[10] The earliest occurrence of a chancellor is in 1287.[11] The medieval chapter of St Davids had no dean to take charge of the canons.

Numbers of canons were small by the standards of English and French cathedrals. Whereas the largest English cathedral chapters had numbers in the fifties by the thirteenth century, and the largest French chapters, such as Chartres, rather more,[12] St Davids, after reaching a peak of 18 in 1253, had 16 canons, including all the dignitaries, from the late 1250s onwards.[13] The total of 16 first occurs in 1259, when the number can be calculated from the names of canons listed as present or absent in Bishop Richard's statutes of that year, and adding in the archdeaconry of Cardigan, which is not mentioned and which may perhaps at that point have been vacant. St Davids was thus smaller than any English secular cathedral chapter – Lichfield, the smallest, had 21 prebends, and Exeter and Hereford were somewhat bigger with 24 and 28 respectively. St Davids is more closely comparable with Llandaf, which had fifteen canons in the thirteenth century but only 14 in the fourteenth century.[14] Figures in Scottish cathedrals varied, but could be much lower.[15]

The range of canons at St Davids during the thirteenth century was fairly mixed in terms of background. Some were members of Anglo-Norman families in Pembrokeshire,[16] some bore Welsh toponyms (all in South Wales),[17] several bore English

---

5 Richter, 'A new edition', 248–9.

6 *Llandaff Episcopal Acta 1140–1287*, ed. Crouch, xxx–xxxii; *FEA 1066–1300*, IX, *The Welsh Cathedrals*, ed. Pearson, xxi.

7 Pearson, 'The creation of the Bangor cathedral chapter', 167–81; *FEA 1066–1300*, IX, *The Welsh Cathedrals*, ed. Pearson, xxii. The equivalent process at St Asaph probably happened over the same period: Pearson, 'The creation and development', 35–56; *FEA 1066–1300*, IX, *The Welsh Cathedrals*, ed. Pearson, xxiii.

8 *St Davids Episcopal Acta*, ed. Barrow, nos. 85–6.

9 *St Davids Episcopal Acta*, ed. Barrow, no. 85, of 1224; in fact the earliest precentor occurs about a decade before the post was endowed: *FEA 1066–1300*, IX, *The Welsh Cathedrals*, ed. Pearson, 50.

10 *St Davids Episcopal Acta*, ed. Barrow, nos. 130–1; *FEA 1066–1300*, IX, *The Welsh Cathedrals*, ed. Pearson, 51.

11 There was no dean at St Davids until the nineteenth century. For the earliest chancellor of St Davids, see *FEA 1066–1300*, IX, *The Welsh Cathedrals*, ed. Pearson, 51.

12 K. Edwards, *The English Secular Cathedrals* (2nd edn), 33; for more detail on specific cathedral chapters see individual volumes in the series: John Le Neve, *Fasti Ecclesiae Anglicanae 1066–1300*, new ed. Greenway *et al.* in progress; Le Neve, *Fasti Ecclesiae Anglicanae 1300–1541*, new ed. by Horn *et al.*; and *Fasti Ecclesiae Gallicanae*, ed. H. Millet *et al.*, in progress.

13 *St Davids Episcopal Acta*, ed. Barrow, no. 122 of 1253 (18 canons) and no. 131 of 1259 (16 canons); for the later middle ages, see *FEA 1300–1541*, XI, ed. Jones, 65–73. St Davids also had six cursal prebendaries, who were of somewhat lowlier status than the canons: *ibid.*, 73–9; Browne Willis, *A Survey*, 6–7, 30–1.

14 *Llandaff Episcopal Acta 1140–1287*, ed. Crouch, xxxi.

15 Brechin had 'at least six prebends by 1274'; Moray (Elgin Cathedral) had 18 in 1226 and 23 by 1242: *Fasti Ecclesiae Scoticanae Medii Aevi ad Annum 1638*, ed. Watt *et al.* (revised version), 57, 283.

16 For example, four members of the de Barri family, Richard de Knovill and Tancard de Roche: *FEA 1066–1300*, IX, *The Welsh Cathedrals*, ed. Pearson, 52, 54, 55, 59.

17 For example, Master John de Sweynese (Swansea), Roger of Pembroke, Thomas of Swansea, and

toponyms (particularly those of Herefordshire and Shropshire),[18] a declining number had Welsh forenames, and some had Welsh patronymics.[19] Of the one hundred and six members of the chapter who occur in the thirteenth century, 44 were *magistri*.[20] In another sense, however, the intake was more limited: hardly any St Davids canons before the Edwardian conquest of Wales belonged to other cathedral chapters: those who did were mostly canons of Hereford, the English see with the closest links to the diocese of St Davids.[21] Bishops Anselm and Thomas Wallensis had been canons of English cathedrals, Exeter and Lincoln respectively, before their appointment as bishop,[22] but they apparently did not build up contacts between these chapters and that of St Davids. By contrast, all the English secular cathedral chapters, and especially the four richest, Lincoln, York, Salisbury and Wells, were linked together by a network of high-flying pluralists with prebends in three or four cathedrals simultaneously.[23] These were never, of course, the majority, but were a very noticeable and quite sizeable minority. They tended to be royal clerks or otherwise in royal favour, which might explain why St Davids was only very slightly involved in this network before Edward's Welsh wars. Kings up to and including Henry III had preferred to leave St Davids chapter under the patronage of Anglo-Norman families in Wales, provided that royal influence could be exercised over the choice of bishops.[24] During Edward I's reign, however, it became politically necessary to link St Davids cathedral chapter into royal patronage networks and the number of St Davids canons who simultaneously held prebends in English cathedrals rose.[25] Until the late thirteenth century St Davids thus was rather deficient in one source of influence, for although the English pluralists referred to above were, in the main,

---

Master Simon of Radnor, while John of Ystlwyf came from Carmarthen (*FEA 1066–1300*, IX, *The Welsh Cathedrals*, ed. Pearson, 51, 69, 70 and 65).

[18] For example, Master Thomas of Bosbury, William of Ledbury, Master Hugh of Clun and Master John of Whitchurch (*FEA 1066–1300*, IX, *The Welsh Cathedrals*, ed. Pearson, 53, 64, 70, 71).

[19] Most of the archdeacons of Cardigan had Welsh names (*FEA 1066–1300*, IX, *The Welsh Cathedrals*, ed. Pearson, 57–8); so too did a thirteenth-century archdeacon of Carmarthen (*FEA 1066–1300*, IX, *The Welsh Cathedrals*, ed. Pearson, 59) and canons Asser and Elidir ab Elidir (*FEA 1066–1300*, IX, *The Welsh Cathedrals*, ed. Pearson, 62), but this represented a steep decline in Welsh names among the chapter from the situation in the twelfth century. David, acceptable in both linguistic camps, remained popular, however (cf. *FEA 1066–1300*, IX, *The Welsh Cathedrals*, ed. Pearson, 62). For examples of Welsh patronymics, cf. John son of Asser, Nicholas Meilyr, Master Walter ab Eynon (*FEA 1066–1300*, IX, *The Welsh Cathedrals*, ed. Pearson, 64, 66, 71).

[20] Calculated from the entries *FEA 1066–1300*, IX, *The Welsh Cathedrals*, ed. Pearson, 50–72.

[21] Canons of St Davids with prebends in other cathedrals before the Edwardian conquest were Master Gerald of Wales (Hereford), Master Edward de la Cnolle (Wells), Master Simon of Radnor (Hereford and Llandaf), Master Thomas of Bosbury (Hereford), and, in 1276, on the eve of Edward's campaign of 1277, Master Peter de Quivel (Exeter) (*FEA 1066–1300*, IX, *The Welsh Cathedrals*, ed. Pearson, 54, 55, 62, 70).

[22] For Bishops Anselm and Thomas, see *ibid.*, 48 and *St Davids Episcopal Acta*, ed. Barrow, 11–13; in the twelfth century Bishop Bernard of St Davids had perhaps been a canon of Hereford (*ibid.*, 2–3; *FEA 1066–1300*, IX, *The Welsh Cathedrals*, ed. Pearson, 46).

[23] Cf. the careers of, e.g., Master Walter Map, Hugh of Wells, Master Elias of Dereham and John Maunsell the elder in the following volumes (all ed. Greenway), of *FEA 1066–1300*: I, *St Paul's, London*, 26, 48, 60; III, *Lincoln*, 3, 13, 16, 36, 73, 75, 102, 129, 163; IV, *Salisbury*, 89–90; V, *Chichester*, 30; VI, *York*, 25; VII, *Bath and Wells*, 33, 61–2; also *FEA 1066–1300*, VIII, *Hereford*, ed. Barrow, 93.

[24] English royal influence can be assumed in most episcopal appointments at St Davids from the election of Bernard in 1115 onwards, save in the cases of Iorwerth (1215–29) and Richard de Carew (1256–80): *St Davids Episcopal Acta*, ed. Barrow, 2–14.

[25] Master John of Dalderby (Lincoln), Master John Lovel (Lichfield, Lincoln, Wells), Master Reginald de Brandon (St Pauls), Master William Burnel (Wells, Exeter, Lichfield, Salisbury, York, and also Llandaf): *FEA 1066–1300*, IX, *The Welsh Cathedrals*, ed. Pearson, 59, 64, 67, 71.

absentees, they did visit the cathedrals to which they were attached,[26] and would have informed their colleagues about practices elsewhere.

At St Davids this external influence seems to have been limited largely to the bishops, who almost alone had extensive experience, through their earlier careers and their frequent journeys to ecclesiastical councils and royal meetings, of other places and other ways of doing things. Iorwerth, who issued the earliest set of St Davids statutes in 1224, was a former Premonstratensian abbot and would thus have brought to his role the outlook of a member of a Europe-wide religious order;[27] Thomas Wallensis, who issued a longer set of statutes in 1253, had been a Paris scholar, a protégé of Bishop Robert Grosseteste and a canon of Lincoln.[28] By contrast, Richard de Carew's experiences were concentrated within south-west Wales, but in his statutes of 1259 he was able to make important additions to Thomas's legislation.[29] St Davids was not slow off the mark in drafting statutes, and we may guess that its clergy maintained correspondence with clerics at Salisbury and elsewhere.

The thirteenth century saw a quite unparalleled quantity of ecclesiastical legislation, and it is necessary to sketch out some of this to show where cathedral statutes fit in. One of the chief examples of the legislative boom, the Fourth Lateran Council of 1215, was also one of the main sources of inspiration.[30] The Fourth Lateran overwhelmingly had the greatest impact in making bishops and their subordinates think about the need to tighten up regulations on clerical behaviour, but it was not the origin of the process, since it grew out of moves towards greater regulation of ecclesiastical affairs in the twelfth century. This process had not chiefly been led by the papacy, but rather had been driven by diocesans who eagerly asked popes, especially Alexander III, for rulings on contentious issues.[31] Several bishops, moreover, felt the need to lay down diocesan statutes in the period immediately before this whole area of operations was given extra impulse by the Fourth Lateran. Bishop Odo de Sully of Paris (1196–1208), Bishop William Tournebu of Coutances (1185–99) and Archbishop Stephen Langton of Canterbury (1207–28) all issued diocesan statutes.[32]

Nonetheless it is the period after 1215 which is richest in diocesan statutes. For England, their framework has been mapped out by Christopher Cheney, who identified 34 separate texts for thirteenth century England and was able to group them into three main families. The first of these descended from Bishop Richard Poore's statutes for Salisbury 1217×1219, the second from Worcester statutes issued by Walter de Cantilupe in 1240, and the third from Bishop Robert Grosseteste's

[26] For some examples of ordinarily non-resident canons visiting their cathedral see a list of payments made to members of the chapter of Hereford in 1273: *Charters and Records of Hereford Cathedral*, ed. Capes, 130–2, with comment in *FEA 1066–1300*, VIII, ed. Barrow, xxviii.
[27] *St Davids Episcopal Acta*, ed. Barrow, 10–11 and no. 85.
[28] *St Davids Episcopal Acta*, ed. Barrow, 12–13 and no. 122.
[29] *St Davids Episcopal Acta*, ed. Barrow, 13–14 and no. 131.
[30] Cheney, *English Synodalia* (2nd edn), 34–5; at 36–7 he argues that the Fourth Lateran did not itself cause the increase in diocesan legislation in the thirteenth century but that both sprang from the same roots; see also Dobiache-Rojdestvensky, *La vie paroissiale*, 72, stressing the importance of twelfth-century sources for thirteenth-century French diocesan statutes.
[31] E.g. (among many other examples) Bishop Roger of Worcester, 1164–79: see Cheney, *Roger*, 166–212.
[32] Bishop Odo's were the most influential: see Cheney, C.R. *English Synodalia*, 34, 55–6, and also Johanek, 'Die Pariser Statuten', 327–47; for the dating of Stephen's statutes, 1213×1214, see Cheney, *English Synodalia*, viii.

statutes for Lincoln.[33] Salisbury was the single most influential diocese in England where diocesan statutes were concerned, because of the sequence of statutes issued by Richard Poore and his successors Robert of Bingham and Giles of Bridport, which were exported to Durham (when Richard Poore became bishop there 1228), to Canterbury when Edmund of Abingdon, previously treasurer of Salisbury, became archbishop, and to several other churches. This influence is also noticeable when we look at internal cathedral organisation: Salisbury's *Nova Constitutio* of 1214[34] and, above all, its liturgical practices (the Use of Sarum),[35] became the benchmarks by which many other English cathedrals, and St Davids cathedral, measured themselves in the thirteenth century and later.

It is worth pausing a moment to think about Richard Poore, his achievements and the circumstances which led him to issue so much documentation – the *Nova Constitutio* which he issued as dean of Salisbury with his chapter in 1214, the diocesan statutes of Salisbury of 1217×1219, the *Consuetudinarium* for Salisbury cathedral of 1217×1220, probably the 'Old Ordinal' of Salisbury, and in addition a series of charters for Salisbury cathedral, some of which clearly had the force of statutes, and one of which was an inspeximus of a charter later inserted into his *Nova Constitutio*.[36] Richard Poore was a highly gifted administrator working in a period of unusual legal activity and would thus have been likely to issue statutes in any case, but he was also prompted by a local motive. This was the removal of the cathedral from the Old Sarum hill-top site to the flat land below, a move sanctioned by Honorius III in 1218, but one which the Salisbury clergy had clearly been mulling over for some time before. The move, which allowed the rebuilding of the cathedral on a much larger scale, necessitated fund-raising, and a noticeable feature of Poore's legislation both for diocese and chapter was the stress on raising money from laity and clergy both within the see and beyond its limits.[37]

The main aim of diocesan statutes of the thirteenth century, as Christopher Cheney pointed out, was the regulation of the life, behaviour and duties of the parish clergy, and of relations between them and their parishioners.[38] This was a response to the large number of appropriations of parish churches by monasteries in the twelfth century and beyond, which led to fears about insufficient provision of pastoral care as monasteries failed to ensure sufficient income for vicars and even tried to employ chaplains whom they could sack at will. Diocesan statutes thus paid relatively little attention to monasteries or cathedrals, but many of the topics which they dealt with have echoes in cathedral statutes. The topics which crop up in both types of statute

---

[33] Cheney, *English Synodalia*, viii.

[34] *FEA 1066–1300*, IV, ed. Greenway, xxvii.

[35] On Salisbury's liturgical influence, see Morgan, 'The introduction of the Sarum Calendar', 179–206.

[36] *Nova Constitutio* (*The Register of St Osmund*, ed. Jones, I, 374–80; diocesan statutes 1217×1219 (*Councils and Synods with Other Documents Relating to the English Church*, II, *1205–1313*, ed. Powicke and Cheney, I, 57–96); *Consuetudinarium* 1217×1220 (*Register of St Osmund*, ed. Jones, I, 1–185); 'Old Ordinal' (cf. *The Use of Sarum*, ed. Frere, I, xi–xiii; II, vii–xi); and, in addition, a series of charters for Salisbury cathedral, some of which clearly had the force of statutes and one of which was an inspeximus of a charter later inserted into Poore's *Nova Constitutio* (*English Episcopal Acta*, XIX, *Salisbury 1217–1228*, ed. Kemp, nos. 356–8, 364–5, 376–7, of which the last, no. 377, is the inspeximus). [*English Episcopal Acta* hereafter *EEA*]

[37] *FEA 1066–1300*, IV, ed. Greenway, xxvii–xxviii; for Poore's organisation of fund-raising in his cathedral statutes, see *Register of St Osmund*, ed. Jones, II, 11–12; see also the comments in his diocesan statutes about how to guard money raised in churches after sermons by visiting preachers: *Councils and Synods*, II, *1205–1313*, ed. Powicke and Cheney, i, 85, paragraph 76.

[38] Cheney, *English Synodalia*, 52.

are the education, behaviour and dress of clergy, the correct administration of the sacraments, the upkeep of the fabric and equipment of churches, the need for due decorum in graveyards, and the making of wills. Clearly, there was opportunity for the two types of document to influence each other.

There also seem to be parallels in the way the texts were compiled.[39] Diocesan statutes usually give no clear guidance as to author. Clearly, they had to be issued by a bishop, sometimes but not necessarily in consultation with his synod, but actual authorship is less certain. Bishops may have relied on the senior clerics in their household.[40] There was much reuse of existing texts, though this was done selectively; for example, as Christopher Cheney showed, Walter de Cantilupe, bishop of Worcester, made use of Richard Poore's text but put the material into an order which would allow him to comment in a homiletic fashion on the duties of a priest;[41] similarly, as Donald Watt has shown in his study of Scottish church councils, David de Bernham bishop of St Andrews was aware of Richard Poore's statutes but made hardly any use them in his 1242 statutes, whereas some contemporaneous statutes, probably from the diocese of Aberdeen, made quite full use of them.[42] Promulgation of the statutes may sometimes have been an informal affair, though bishops might expect parish clergy to keep copies of the texts together with their service books.[43] Diocesan synods do not necessarily bear the name of a bishop,[44] and, where they do, this is not necessarily integral to the text but has sometimes been added as a rubric;[45] they also do not necessarily bear dates, and do not list the names of those in attendance when the document was issued. Circulation and survival might also be rather haphazard, though clearly these texts were valued, and were eagerly used in other dioceses as sources of ideas and phrasing.

Turning now to cathedral statutes, we should note that they are hard to pin down as a genre. It is difficult, for one thing, to say how far they were legally binding.[46] Their phrasing and the fact that they normally lack validation suggest that they were chiefly intended as an aid to memory. It may be helpful to break down the materials into four separate types of text, though the reader should note that there is some overlap between the four groups:

- compilations of 'customs and statutes', the best-known and most comprehensive type, frequently though not always lacking the name of the issuer or issuing body, and the date of compilation.[47] They also lack validation, save in many instances for being copied into codices kept by the relevant cathedral chapter for the purpose of recording such matters. Often the texts were built up by accretions

---

[39] Suggested, but not expanded upon, by Cheney, *English Synodalia*, 145.

[40] Cheney, *English Synodalia*, 49, discussing Richard Poore's use of Thomas de Chobham's *Summa de casibus penitentie*; in more general terms on the authorship of cathedral statutes, see K. Edwards, *English Secular Cathedrals*, 115–19.

[41] Cheney, *English Synodalia*, 90.

[42] Watt, *Medieval Church Councils in Scotland*, 56–7, 59.

[43] Cheney, *English Synodalia*, 45–6.

[44] E.g. 'Constitutiones cuiusdam episcopi', *Councils and Synods*, II, *1205–1313*, ed. Powicke and Cheney, i, 181; see also Watt, *Medieval Church Councils in Scotland*, 58–9.

[45] *Councils and Synods* II, *1205–1313*, ed. Powicke and Cheney, i, 169–81, William of Blois for Worcester 1229.

[46] Edwards, *English Secular Cathedrals* (2nd edn), 26–7.

[47] *Statutes of Lincoln Cathedral*, ed. Bradshaw and Wordsworth, II, 11–25 (Lichfield), 44–85 (Hereford), 91–104 (York).

over a long period, as at Lichfield.[48] Occasionally, however, the precise circumstances of composition can be traced, as in the document drawn up by Lincoln cathedral chapter in 1214 to set out guidelines for Bishop Brice of Moray's new foundation of canons at Spynie (the nucleus of what became the chapter of Elgin cathedral).[49]

- letters, written from one church to another, giving advice.[50] This was never gratuitously done: the church receiving the advice had in all cases sought it. Survival of such letters tends to be informal – not as original sealed documents, as they surely originally were, but copied into letter collections or cartularies. Dating is rare and since these documents often lack personal names, setting them in a precise context can be hard.
- charters issued by, usually, the bishop or the bishop and chapter acting together.[51] These texts quite often survive in the original and were validated in a perfectly normal fashion, by sealing.
- dated documents usually in the third person referring to promulgation on a particular day in a particular place by the bishop, sometimes with the dean and chapter, or by the dean and chapter alone.[52] The three sets of statutes issued for St Davids by Iorwerth, Thomas Wallensis and Richard de Carew are of this type.[53]

Let us go back to each of these groups in turn:

Customs and statutes are intended to be timeless, or at least to be ancient, like the *Institutio Osmundi* of Salisbury, purportedly issued by Osmund in 1091, but in fact, as Diana Greenway has shown, begun *ca* 1150 and compiled in stages down to the time when Richard Poore was dean (up to 1214).[54] They usually open *Hec sunt* – 'These are' – 'These are the dignities and customs' (*Institutio Osmundi*),[55] 'These are the dignities and customs and liberties' (Lincoln 1214),[56] 'These are in part the customs and observations of the church of Lincoln' (Lincoln for Spynie, Moray version),[57] 'These are the customs and observations of the church of Hereford' (the mid-thirteenth century Hereford statutes).[58] The earliest Lichfield statutes, more consciously trying to impress, open with a quotation from the Psalms and then say that the work sets out the 'constitutions and customs of the church of Lichfield'.[59] The joining together of ancient customs and of statutes, by which are clearly meant regulations made at a particular point in time, is deliberate. These texts are compilations, uniting customs, usually liturgical, which had probably never previously been

---

[48] *Statutes of Lincoln Cathedral*, ed. Bradshaw and Wordsworth, II, 11–25 (the statutes open with an arenga (*ibid.*, II, 11–12) and then the words *Est ergo in ecclesia Lich' consuetum antiquitus et statutum* (*ibid.*, II, 12).

[49] *Statutes of Lincoln Cathedral*, ed. Bradshaw and Wordsworth, II, 137–42 (opening, p. 137, *Hec sunt dignitates et consuetudines et libertates ecclesie Linc'*). See also a different version of Lincoln's instructions for Moray in the following note.

[50] For example, *Registrum Episcopatus Moraviensis*, ed. Innes, 44–8, no. 48 (letter of Dean Roger and the chapter of Lincoln describing their customs to the clergy at Spynie).

[51] See literature cited in nn. 73–82 below.

[52] *Nova Constitutio* (*Register of St Osmund*, ed. Jones, I, 374–80); *EEA*, XI, *Exeter 1046–1184*, ed. Barlow, 73, no. 84 (statutes of Bishop Bartholomew and Exeter cathedral chapter of 1161).

[53] *St Davids Episcopal Acta*, ed. Barrow, nos. 85, 122, 131.

[54] Greenway, 'The false *Institutio*', 77–101.

[55] *Register of St Osmund*, ed. Jones, I, 212–15.

[56] *Statutes of Lincoln Cathedral*, ed. Bradshaw and Wordsworth, II, 137.

[57] Anon. *Registrum Episcopatus Moraviensis*, ed. Innes, 44, no. 48.

[58] *Statutes of Lincoln Cathedral*, ed. Bradshaw and Wordsworth, II, 44.

[59] *Statutes of Lincoln Cathedral*, ed. Bradshaw and Wordsworth, II, 11–12.

written down, and details of the duties of dignitaries, drawn probably from one of the many treatises on ecclesiastical offices, with legislation about residence or about the organisation of chapter finances which had often originated in the form of charters. For example, the Hereford customs include provisions about residence and absence which had been laid down in bulls of Innocent IV.[60] The point of putting customs and statutes together was to create a more logically worked out text which could in its most developed form cover a wide range of aspects of chapter activities and which could be read aloud in chapter. The Hereford text begins with a long section on the customs of the church, concerning the installation of canons, residence and absence, and finances, followed by a section on the customs of the choir, dealing with the duties of dignitaries, behaviour in choir and the minor clergy.[61]

Letters of advice written by one chapter to another tend to be much shorter, usually concentrating on only a few points. (Lincoln's advice for the Moray canons based at Spynie was, more unusually, in two versions, a long letter and a set of regulations.)[62] The emergence of some churches as better-equipped to give advice than others deserves some thought: across Europe there was a noticeable, though rather informal, hierarchy of authority. On the continent, where such letters were quite common in the twelfth and thirteenth centuries, an ecclesiastical province might provide the framework within which advice was sought: hence Utrecht asked for advice from its metropolitan cathedral, Cologne,[63] and from the cathedrals of Liège, Münster and Minden, all within the province of Cologne;[64] Würzburg cathedral chapter supplied information to its metropolitan cathedral chapter, Mainz, about an internal chapter dispute being heard by the latter as an appeal court.[65] However, some cathedrals and one major collegiate church, St Martin's of Tours, corresponded over a much wider range. St Martin's of Tours advised Mainz cathedral (the two churches shared a common dedication),[66] and also Archbishop Philip of Cologne,[67] while Le Mans cathedral advised Paderborn cathedral (the two churches shared a patron saint, Liborius),[68] and Hildesheim was in correspondence with Bamberg, Merseburg and Liège, as well as with Verden in the province of Mainz to which Hildesheim belonged.[69] Such long-distance correspondence might be principally intended to beg for relics or to set up confraternity arrangements, but interest in how things were done elsewhere was strong.

As far as England and Wales were concerned, within the province of Canterbury the cathedral of the metropolitan see was monastic and could not set standards for secular cathedrals. By the second decade of the thirteenth century, Salisbury seems

---

60 Barrow, 'Appendix I: The Constitution of Hereford Cathedral', 634.
61 *Statutes of Lincoln Cathedral*, ed. Bradshaw and Wordsworth, II, 44–85.
62 *Statutes of Lincoln Cathedral*, ed. Bradshaw and Wordsworth, II, 137–42.
63 *Het oudste cartularium van het Sticht Utrecht*, ed. Muller, no. 80; *Oorkondenboek van het Sticht Utrecht tot 1300*, ed. Muller, Bouman, Heeringa and Ketner, I, no. 297.
64 *Oorkondenboek van het Sticht Utrecht*, ed. Muller *et al.*, I, nos. 265–7.
65 Johanek, 'Ein Brief zur Geschichte', 25.
66 Würzburg, Staatsarchiv, Mainzer Bücher verschiedenen Inhalts, 17, fols 101v, 102v.
67 Farmer, *Communities*, 268. The letter is datable 1180×1181.
68 *Chartularium insignis ecclesiae Cenomannensis quod dicitur Liber Albus capituli*, ed. Lottin, no. 198; Paderborn sent a copy of the *Vita* of St Liborius to Le Mans, *Westfälisches Urkundenbuch*, IV, ed. Wilmans, no. 17.
69 *Urkundenbuch des Hochstifts Hildesheim*, ed. Janicke and Hoogeweg, I, nos. 136, 575 (according to the latter document, Hildesheim was also in confraternity with Rheims cathedral and the collegiate church of St Gereon in Cologne), and 755; *Cartulaire de l'Eglise Saint-Lambert*, ed. Bormans and Schoolmeesters, I, nos. 88–90.

to have taken over this position, certainly so by 1224 when Iorwerth said in his St Davids statutes that the canons of St Davids should follow the ordinal of Salisbury for the offices of the Virgin and of the dead and that the precentor should have the same customs as the precentor of Salisbury.[70] However, in the period up to about 1214 there was no clear-cut hierarchy. We find Salisbury cathedral asking St Paul's cathedral in 1209 for advice about services during the Interdict,[71] and it was Lincoln and not Salisbury which was approached, from outside the province of Canterbury, by the clergy of Bishop Brice of Moray.[72] Probably it was Richard Poore's hard work at Salisbury, both as dean and as bishop, which gave his cathedral the edge, and perhaps it was Salisbury's extensive fund-raising campaigns across England in and after 1218 which made Poore's work more widely known and enhanced Salisbury's reputation.

Charters containing statute material for cathedral chapters were usually issued for specific purposes – to found a chantry arrangement, or to increase (and at the same time regulate) the common fund or to endow a new prebend, for example. They conform to the normal models of episcopal or clerical charters of the twelfth and thirteenth centuries, in both external and internal features. One diplomatic development which can be traced in several dioceses, however, is the growing use of vocabulary suggestive of legislation. Bishops of Salisbury and bishops of Bath, for example, were using the verb *statuere* in some of their charters for Sarum Cathedral and Wells Cathedral respectively from the middle of the twelfth century, beginning with Bishop Jocelin de Bohun's establishment of the multiple prebend of Heytesbury for Sarum chapter between 1142 and 1149.[73] Robert of Lewes, bishop of Bath (1136–66), used the verb *statuere*.[74] His successors, Reginald de Bohun (1174–91) and Savaric (1192–1205), used more developed formulae – *statuimus et confirmamus* in nine out of twenty-six charters of Reginald for the chapter,[75] and *provida deliberatione statuimus* under Savaric, the latter phrase referring to consultation with the chapter of Wells in documents dealing with the common fund, setting up prebends or ordaining anniversary services.[76] At Salisbury, use of *statuere* intensified after 1217 under Richard Poore.[77] At York, Archbishop Roger of Pont-l'Evêque used the verbs *decernimus* and *statuimus* in a foundation charter for a chapel within York Minster *ca* 1180.[78] At Exeter, use of *statuere* began under Bishop Henry Marshal (1194–1206).[79] Yet not all episcopal chanceries were keen to adopt this phrasing. Bishops of Lincoln and Chichester showed little interest in it. Only one bishop of Hereford used it (and only once) before 1234, though it became more popular under Ralph de Maidstone and Peter of Aigueblanche in the mid-thirteenth

---

70 *St Davids Episcopal Acta*, ed. Barrow, no. 85: *Servitium etiam de Sancta Maria et servitium pro defunctis fiant secundum ordinale ecclesie Sar'.*
71 *The Later Letters of Peter of Blois*, ed. Revell, 109–11, no. 20.
72 See literature cited in nn. 49–50 above.
73 *EEA*, XVIII, *Salisbury 1078–1217*, ed. Kemp, no. 120.
74 *EEA*, X, *Bath and Wells 1061–1205*, ed. Ramsey, nos. 49, 50, 53 and cf. 55, which was addressed to the townspeople of Wells but which was issued on behalf of the chapter.
75 *EEA*, X, *Bath and Wells 1061–1205*, nos. 149, 162–6, 168–9, 171, and note use of the verb *statuere* in nos. 155, 157–8, 160–1, 167, 172, 174.
76 *EEA*, X, *Bath and Wells 1061–1205*, nos. 244, 246, 249–53, 258, 261.
77 *EEA*, XIX, *Salisbury 1217–1228*, ed. Kemp, nos. 357–8, 364–5, 376–7.
78 *EEA*, XX, *York 1154–1181*, ed. Lovatt, no. 129 of 1173/4×1181, perhaps 1177×1181.
79 *EEA*, XII, *Exeter 1186–1257*, ed. Barlow, nos. 191–2, 198 and cf. no. 189 ('*decrevimus*').

century.[80] *Acta* of the bishops of St Davids for the chapter barely use it either.[81] Wells and Salisbury, wealthy and with a strong interest in internal organisation, were quick to adopt language of regulation. Other chapters turned to it only as it became necessary to tighten up financial arrangements in the thirteenth century.

Dated third-person statutes go back to the middle of the twelfth century at least. Bishop Bartholomew of Exeter and his chapter issued a set of statutes concerning arrangements for the farming of chapter estates in 1161.[82] Unlike charters, a text of this sort might allow coverage of a wider range of regulations, and, like compilations of customs and statutes, texts of this sort might be read aloud. Bishop Thomas's 1253 statutes say the text should be read in chapter at least once a week, and that canons should use it as a mirror to examine their own behaviour.[83] Nevertheless, dated statutes are usually responses to particular circumstances – Iorwerth was legislating to establish the precentory, the principal aim behind Thomas's statutes was probably to arrange for short-term control of the treasury before a proper dignity could be established, and Richard's statutes finally set up a treasury.[84] Quite often, financial circumstances impelled legislation. It is not surprising that Exeter was the earliest English cathedral chapter to receive such statutes, for its chapter ran its estates communally rather than splitting them into separate prebends.[85] Other cathedrals only began to need statutes once they had built up significant sources of joint income – the common fund or commons, created at most cathedrals for the use of resident canons only.

Although the statutes issued by Iorwerth, Thomas and Richard are essentially responses to particular crises rather than attempts to cover the whole range of the activities of canons and vicars, nevertheless they touch on most of the topics which normally feature in thirteenth century cathedral statutes. The most crucial issues were those of residence and the management of chapter affairs. It was not regarded as necessary, indeed it was probably not regarded as desirable, to enjoin residence on all canons. In both Iorwerth and Thomas's statutes the object was to encourage some canons to reside by increasing the value of the common fund, and by restricting the payment of commons to residents (Thomas specified that they would need to perform residence for ¾ of the year, a higher proportion of time than, for example, the ¼ year term at Salisbury).[86] Residence was only actually enforced for vicars and,

---

[80] *English Episcopal Acta*, VII, *Hereford 1079–1234*, ed. Barrow, no. 150; Ralph de Maidstone, bishop of Hereford 1234–9, used the verb *statuere* in two charters concerning the funding of vicarages in the cathedral (*Charters and Records of Hereford Cathedral*, ed. Capes, 73–4, 74–5; for use of the verb by his successor, Peter of Aigueblanche, bishop of Hereford 1240–68, see Oxford, Bodleian MS Rawlinson B329, fol. 7v of 2 December 1261 and London, British Library, Egerton Charter 2212 of January 1262; for Lincoln and Chichester *acta*, see *English Episcopal Acta*, I, *Lincoln 1067–1185*, ed. Smith, *English Episcopal Acta*, IV, *Lincoln 1186–1206*, ed. Smith, *The Acta of Hugh of Wells*, ed. Smith, *The Acta of the Bishops of Chichester, 1075–1207*, ed. Mayr-Harting, *English Episcopal Acta*, 22, *Chichester 1215–1253*, and 23, *Chichester 1254–1305*, both ed. Hoskin.

[81] Bishops of St Davids used the verb *statuere* in chapter statutes (*St Davids Episcopal Acta*, ed. J. Barrow, nos. 85, 122, 131), but not in other documents for the chapter, where they preferred the verb *ordinare* (cf. no. 143).

[82] *EEA*, XI, *Exeter 1046–1184*, ed. Barlow, no. 84

[83] *St Davids Episcopal Acta*, ed. Barrow, no. 122: *Ut igitur in libello hoc tamquam in speculo possitis perspicere, ne per oblivionem aliquid negligatis, sepius ante vos saltem in ebdomada semel legatur* (p. 140).

[84] *St Davids Episcopal Acta*, ed. Barrow, nos. 85, 122, 131.

[85] Blake, 'The development', 5. See also *FEA 1066–1300*, X, ed. Greenway, xvii.

[86] *St Davids Episcopal Acta*, ed. Barrow, nos. 85, 122: cf., in latter, Thomas's arrangement for payments to residentiaries: *concessimus canonicis in posterum in ecclesia nostra ad minus per tres quartas*

in 1259, for the treasurer. Bishop Thomas laid down that vicars who failed to attend should be punished by their *prepositus*;[87] Bishop Richard was more specific, laying down that all vicars should attend matins, prime, high mass and vespers each day. He also enjoined strict residence on the newly established treasurer.[88]

Control of residence was closely linked to finances and all three bishops laid down strict rules about the latter. Iorwerth's statutes established the equivalent of an annual general meeting for the chapter at which (and only at which) leases of chapter property could be agreed, with the use of the chapter seal, not to be used for this purpose at other times. (There are clear echoes of the Salisbury *Nova Constitutio* here.) Iorwerth also set up two proctors to look after the chapter's property, that is the commons, to keep receipts and to represent the other canons in lawsuits.[89] Thomas replaced the proctors with a single steward and made tighter regulations about the farming out of chapter lands: no longer should these pass from tenant to tenant by a hereditary system termed *esta* in the statutes (Welsh *estyn*, bestowal or gift).[90] He also created a fabric fund which he put under the control of three canons, each to have a separate key, who would make weekly statements about receipts and expenditure.[91] Richard established proctors to deal with cathedral property in Ireland, and legislated for fund-raising for the fabric fund throughout the diocese – a point at which his cathedral statutes start to look rather like diocesan statutes; indeed, another issue raised in his text, the punishment of violators of immunities within the diocese, is in a similar vein.[92]

During the thirteenth century bishops in their diocesan statutes developed rules concerning the testamentary powers of clergy, which in fact built in part on customs going back at least to the twelfth century in some cathedrals laying down that a year's payment of prebendal revenues should be made to the estates of deceased canons to allow the payment of debts and the provision of charitable bequests and anniversaries. Bishop Richard's statutes pick this up, laying down the payment of a year's prebendal income to executors of dead canons, provided that a silk cope was given to the chapter unless it had already been granted by the canon while alive.[93]

Occupying nearly as important a role in the statutes as the topics of residence and finance was the topic of the choir. Regulations for the liturgy and for behaviour in choir are not systematically dealt with in the St Davids statutes. The reason for this seems to have been that the chapter had a copy of some of the Salisbury material, probably Richard Poore's *Consuetudinarium* of 1217×1220, since Iorwerth says that the service of the Virgin Mary and the service of the dead should be said according to the use of Sarum, while Thomas says that entry into and egress from the choir should be done according to the manner and rule of Sarum.[94] Richard's regulations about the duties of the treasurer, in which he goes into detail about the lighting arrangements for particular feasts, echo Poore's *Consuetudinarium*.[95] Iorwerth,

---

anni continue, vel, necessitate cogente, interpollatim residentibus, ecclesiam Sancti Dogmaelis in Pebidiauk.

[87] *St Davids Episcopal Acta*, ed. Barrow, no. 122.
[88] *St Davids Episcopal Acta*, ed. Barrow, no. 131.
[89] *St Davids Episcopal Acta*, ed. Barrow, no. 85.
[90] *St Davids Episcopal Acta*, ed. Barrow, no. 122.
[91] *St Davids Episcopal Acta*, ed. Barrow, no. 122.
[92] *St Davids Episcopal Acta*, ed. Barrow, no. 131.
[93] *St Davids Episcopal Acta*, ed. Barrow, no. 131.
[94] *St Davids Episcopal Acta*, ed. Barrow, nos. 85, 122.
[95] *St Davids Episcopal Acta*, ed. Barrow, no. 131; for the *Consuetudinarium*, see *Register of St Osmund*, ed. Jones, I, 8–11.

following Richard Poore, set up a system for saying obits for deceased canons and bishops, with their names being recorded in the cathedral's martyrology.[96] Here St Davids was imitating not only Salisbury but many other cathedrals, notably Lincoln and Hereford, which had both been doing this for much longer.[97] Unluckily the martyrology of St Davids does not survive.

An important part of the regulation of the liturgy was the regulation of the behaviour of the minor clergy, not only in choir but also outside the cathedral. They had to enter the choir before the *Gloria patri* of the first psalm of each canonical hour, and their dress in choir was carefully regulated by Bishop Richard along lines similar to those elsewhere, for example at Glasgow according to a charter of 1201/2: black copes and surplices in winter and surplices in summer.[98] Demarcation from the canons was ensured by making the latter wear amices. Since vicars were, because of their occupation, highly visible to the local community, their behaviour when, so to speak, off duty, was regulated too, in a way which never applied to canons. Richard ruled that they should avoid fornication and visits to taverns, and laid down that their concubines should be beaten through the city of St Davids (it must have been lucky for the vicars' womenfolk that the city of St Davids, the enclosed area round the cathedral, was so small). Richard also laid down that the vicars should live 'in the city' 'because there are sirens in the sanctuary (Isaiah 13, 22) and often Dagon next to the Ark of the Lord (1 Sm. 5, 3–4)'.[99] Here we see some influence creeping in from a trend sweeping English cathedrals from the mid-thirteenth century onwards, beginning at York and Lincoln, to make vicars live communally in colleges, with their own communal buildings protected from the outside world, at least at night, by a gate.[100] St Davids did not yet have the financial resources to follow suit in 1259, but it was anxious to make sure that the vicars lived close at hand to the cathedral.[101]

A final point to note, one raised by both Thomas and Richard, is the state of the cathedral graveyard, which had houses built on it (a not at all uncommon procedure in the middle ages – graveyards, being sacred spaces, gave a measure of protection from acts of violence). The regulation of human activities in graveyards was a common topic in thirteenth-century diocesan statutes. Thomas ordered the houses to be removed by the following Michaelmas, but it is obvious from Richard's statutes, which order the houses to be moved by the following Whitsun, that Thomas's order

---

[96] *St Davids Episcopal Acta*, ed. Barrow, no. 85.

[97] A twelfth-century obit list was copied into Lincoln's Great Bible, fols 204v–206v; it is published in *Giraldi Cambrensis Opera* (ed. Brewer, *et al.* VII.153–64); it is also published, with subsequent Lincoln obit lists, in *Statutes of Lincoln Cathedral* (ed. Bradshaw and Wordsworth, II, i, ccxxxv–ccxlvii), and the compilations are discussed by Greenway, *FEA 1066–1300*, III, *Lincoln*, xvi; for Hereford's obit book, a manuscript of the fourteenth century but copying a compilation made in the late thirteenth century which contained much eleventh- and twelfth-century material, see *FEA 1066–1300*, VIII, Appendix I, 99–158.

[98] *St Davids Episcopal Acta*, ed. J. Barrow, no. 131; a charter of William the Lion for Glasgow cathedral of 1201 or 1202 says that vicars should wear surplices and black copes according to the statutes of the cathedral: *Regesta Regum Scottorum* II, *The Acts of William I King of Scots 1165–1214*, ed. G.W.S. Barrow with Scott, 402–3, no. 426; at Salisbury, black copes were worn for most of the year: see *Register of St Osmund*, ed. Jones, I, 34–7.

[99] *St Davids Episcopal Acta*, ed. Barrow, no. 131.

[100] See *Vicars Choral at English Cathedrals*, ed. Hall and Stocker.

[101] Later in the middle ages communal accommodation was provided for the 8 vicars choral and 4 choristers at St Davids: Browne Willis, *A Survey*, 29–30, 32–3.

had had no effect. Richard seems also to have wanted to appease the local residents by asking the local elders to fix the limits of the graveyard.[102]

In conclusion, Iorwerth, Thomas and Richard's statutes between them form a valuable source, not merely for the internal workings of the cathedral of St Davids in the thirteenth century, but also for the way in which ideas were transmitted in the thirteenth century through the ecclesiastical network. St Davids, though operating on a much smaller budget than the great English cathedrals, was quick to find out about developments elsewhere: one sign of its awareness of current developments was its early adoption of Salisbury as a suitable model to follow. It was almost certainly the bishops of St Davids themselves who took the lead in introducing new trends to their cathedral, since they travelled more extensively than the members of their chapter.

---

[102] *St Davids Episcopal Acta*, ed. Barrow, nos. 122, 131.

20

THE CRISIS OF THE SIXTEENTH CENTURY

Glanmor Williams†

Throughout the middle ages there existed a close and lively connection between Rome and St Davids. In the written and oral traditions of the saint himself, much was always made of that unforgettable pilgrimage to the Eternal City reputedly undertaken by David, Teilo and Padarn, in the course of which the bells of Rome were claimed to have rung of their own accord to greet Dewi Sant.[1] Centuries later, some time between the years 1119 and 1124, Pope Calixtus II was formally to recognize the cult of Dewi, the only Welsh saint ever to achieve such distinction at the hands of the pope; a dignity which was vastly to enhance his status and prestige.[2] So much so that it became widely accepted that two journeys by a pilgrim to St Davids was the equivalent of one to Rome. The outcome was that his church at St Davids became one of the most popular and best-known pilgrim resorts to exist anywhere in Wales.

In the light of the towering reputation which St Davids enjoyed in the medieval church and, in particular, its unique association with Rome and the papacy, it was to be expected that such a major change of direction in religion as that unloosed by the Protestant Reformation should have a profound effect on the tradition of both Saint David and his church. It first made itself abruptly apparent in the reign of Henry VIII; emanating not from anyone within the church of St Davids but from an Englishman who was installed as prior of the house of Augustinian Canons at Haverfordwest. The man in question, William Barlow,[3] later to be bishop of the diocese, came to the priory as a result of the patronage of a lady who had already been the cause of tumultuous upheaval in the Church and in the kingdom at large. Anne Boleyn, now King Henry's second queen, and marchioness of Pembroke, in 1534 dispatched her servant and protégé, William Barlow, to become prior of the house of Augustinian Canons at Haverfordwest, the biggest and most important town within the lordship of Pembroke. It was not a specially large or wealthy house, being valued at only £133 per annum in 1536 and having no more than six canons at that time, though that put it among the bigger Welsh houses of the period.[4] It also occupied a strategic position on Milford Haven and had the potential to become the focus for the whole area of new reformed teaching. Barlow arrived there in July 1534 just in time to take the oath of loyalty to the Crown required of all clerics under the newly passed Act of Supremacy.[5] It would seem that what was envisaged as his

---

† Sir Glanmor Williams died on 4 February 2005.
[1] Baring-Gould and Fisher, *The Lives*; Dumville, *Saint David*; Henken, *Traditions*; Glanmor Williams, 'The tradition', 109–26
[2] Williams, 'The tradition', 115. [Though see Sharpe, 'Which text', above, 102.]
[3] For the Barlows, see Charles, 'The Barlows', 179–98; Rupp, *English Protestant Tradition*, ch. 4.
[4] Williams, *The Welsh Church*, 563; cf. Cowley, 'The regular clergy, 1093–1540'.
[5] *Letters and Papers, Foreign and Domestic, of the Rei Henry VIII ...*, VII.1024, 19.

special role was to carry out at Haverfordwest the same task of vigorous, new-style evangelizing that another of Anne Boleyn's agents, Hugh Latimer, had just been sent to fulfil at Bristol.[6] Bristol, by the way, was the trading metropolis of the west and the chief commercial centre with which Haverfordwest and other Bristol Channel ports were in contact.

The newcomer was a descendant of the Essex–Hertfordshire branch of the landed family of Barlow and the son of John and Christian Barlow, who had been deprived of their possessions after being involved in Perkin Warbeck's rebellion of 1497.[7] William Barlow was one of four brothers, two of whom became clerics like himself. William entered the Order of Austin Canons and studied at Oxford, where he graduated D.D. Between 1509 and 1528 he was prior of three small Augustinian houses in succession, the last of which, Bromehill, was dissolved by Cardinal Wolsey in 1528.[8] Barlow was already one of those strongly attracted to Protestant teaching. Although his career from 1528 to 1534 is somewhat obscure, he probably served as a diplomat engaged in negotiations over Henry VIII's troubled marital affairs. The eldest of his brothers, Roger, an intelligent and successful merchant, was in close contact with Sir Thomas Boleyn, Anne's father, and another brother, John, was also a member of Anne's household.[9] These contacts with Boleyn, father and daughter, were doubtless what accounted for William's being sent to Haverfordwest in 1534.[10] He arrived there without ever having previously set foot in Wales, as far as is known, and with no knowledge of its language, cultural history or tradition.

St Davids was an unpromising diocese for a zealot of William Barlow's persuasions. The cathedral church, not to mention many lesser shrines, including that of the holy taper at Haverfordwest, was one of the most highly-esteemed places of medieval pilgrimage in Wales. It was regarded by Barlow as a hotbed of what he deemed to be 'superstition' and 'idolatry'. The bishop at this time was Richard Rawlins (1523–36),[11] and he and nearly all his clergy' were strongly conservative in their bent. They had already given an indication of their sympathies by choosing as their proctor for the Lower House of Convocation in 1531 none other than the leading opponent of the Crown – Peter Ligham, Dean of the Arches.[12] Nor were the laity any better in Barlow's view. According to his judgement, they were 'miserably ordered under the clergy'.[13] Those novel anti-papal doctrines so enthusiastically promoted by Barlow found few supporters in Pembroke lordship; so to strengthen what he described as his endeavours 'against Anti-Christ (i.e., the pope) and all his confederate adherents', he brought his three brothers, Roger, John and Thomas, with him to his new abode.[14]

Nevertheless, it is worth noting that there were, on the other hand, some aspects of life in south-west Wales which offered Barlow prospects of a possibly more favourable response. South Pembrokeshire was one of the few parts of Wales where conditions were not wholly unpropitious for the reception of changes in religion. In and around its little sea-ports there flourished a small but active merchant class, in

6   Williams, *Wales and the Reformation*, 62.
7   Rupp, *English Protestant Tradition*, ch. 4.
8   *ODNB*, III.938.
9   *ODNB*, III.939; Yardley, *Menevia Sacra*, 88–91.
10 Ives, *Anne Boleyn*.
11 Yardley, *Menevia Sacra*, 86–7.
12 Lehmberg, *The Reformation Parliament*, 12.
13 Wright, *Three Chapters,* 77.
14 Charles, 'The Barlows', 179–98.

regular touch with Bristol and other trading centres, which were often the seedbeds of new ideas. The people of the area may also have been susceptible to some extent to anti-clericalism and heresy. At all events, the only cases of heresy to be found in the pages of the medieval registers of St Davids diocese relate to this area.[15] Even more important, perhaps, there existed a sizeable community of English-speaking people, some of whom might be influenced by the anti-papal and pro-reforming literature of Henry VIII's reign and by Barlow's fiery preaching, to both of which propaganda media, the rest of the population of the diocese was largely immune. As early as 1535 – possibly earlier – at least one of Barlow's servants possessed a copy of the New Testament in English and other similar books. Barlow himself, by virtue of being prior of Haverfordwest, enjoyed control of three out of four pulpits to be found in the town,[16] and he seems to have taken full advantage of this for delivering himself of torrid anti-papal sermons.

Even while newly arrived as prior, Barlow's enthusiasm for innovation and his appetite for power led him to meddle in the affairs of the diocese in a way which was almost bound to give offence to Bishop Rawlins and his clergy. He opened his campaign with a series of orations which violently attacked the institution of the papacy and some of its doctrines. St David and his church must surely have figured prominently in these tirades. These proceedings aroused the enmity not only of the secular clergy but of the Dominican Friars of Haverfordwest as well. They may perhaps have felt their professional status as preachers affronted by the eloquence as well as the heresy of this brash interloper. Certainly, it was one of their number who was Barlow's chief antagonist in public and who, at Bishop Rawlins's instigation, presented a series of articles against him to the King's Council.[17] Barlow himself probably stood too high in the favour of Anne Boleyn and Cromwell to be seriously damaged by these attacks, but his opponents had been able to take vengeance on his servant by accusing him of heresy. Barlow complained that they had ransacked this man's house at Tenby and confiscated the New Testament in English and other books belonging to him. They had seized these volumes amid 'vehement reproaches and clamorous exclamations against heresies, he protested, 'as if to have the Testament in English were horrible heresy'.[18] He ended his catalogue of complaints with the accusation that his servant's enemies had caused him to be imprisoned by the mayor of Tenby.

Barlow denounced in unmeasured terms the hostility of the clergy: 'there is not one', he thundered, 'that sincerely preacheth God's word, nor scarce one that heartily favoureth it, but all utter enemies thereagainst'. Nor was he any less scathing about what he perceived to be the backwardness of the diocese 'with its enormous vices, fraudulent exactions, misordered living and heathen idolatry'. He knew of no diocese, he asserted, 'more corrupted, nor none so far out of frame, without hope of reformation, unless your mastership (i.e. Cromwell) shall see a redress'.[19] The redress which Barlow badly wanted was his own appointment as suffragan bishop within the diocese, something which he managed to obtain by letters to that effect from Cromwell, only to complain on 19 March 1535 that those self-same missives were being studiously opposed or ignores by the bishop and his officers. Barlow's

[15] Williams, *The Welsh Church,* 530–1.
[16] Phillips, *The History of Pembrokeshire*, 416.
[17] Williams, *Welsh Reformation Essays*, 112–13.
[18] Wright, *Three Chapters*, 77–80.
[19] Wright, *Three Chapters*, 79.

own complaints were being seconded by those of his brother, John, who wrote to inform Queen Anne's chamberlain that Bishop Rawlins and his minions were stirring up the opposition not only of the clergy but also most of the laity, gentry and commons alike.[20]

It may very well have been the brothers Barlow who, about this time, tried to discredit Bishop Rawlins still further by reporting to Cromwell the bishop's erroneous views concerning the nature of purgatory and the validity of prayers for the dead. Rawlins's reply to such charges survives in the State Papers of 1535. He was undoubtedly somewhat conservative in his views on purgatory, admitting that he thought it proper to pray for the souls of the departed but without mention of any special place or any name. But he firmly denied any intention of reviving the popish purgatory, or any notion that expiatory acts such as offering candles, purchasing grants or pardons, or saying any paternosters before some designated altar could release any souls from purgatory.[21]

At this stage, however, Barlow was clearly making little or no headway in carrying out his designs for the diocese and its bishop. So disappointing was his progress that, in the early summer of 1535, he was, at his own request, removed from Haverfordwest to become prior of the Augustinian house at Bisham in Berkshire. Shortly afterwards, he was back on the diplomatic trail, accompanying Lord Robert Howard on an important mission to Scotland, intended to induce its king, James V, to abandon the pope. In January of the following year he was promoted to be bishop of St Asaph.[22] About the same time, the Barlow cause in St Davids was being trumpeted by his brother, John, who wrote to Cromwell to warn him of the conservative instincts of the Welsh, especially those of the diocese of St Davids. He alleged that the bishop and his clergy were persuading the gentry there to stick with them in their old ways. They had recently given assistance to the Irish rebels and they unashamedly voiced the hope of seeing the world alter and change again. Cromwell may well have taken these warnings seriously, for when Bishop Rawlins died on 22 February 1536 he wasted no time in translating William Barlow from St Asaph to St Davids.[23]

It was as well for the Barlow brothers that they stood so high in Cromwell's estimation in view of the disgrace and execution of Anne Boleyn so soon afterwards, in May 1536. The downfall of their powerful patroness had made them very apprehensive at first. Dangerous rumours had been flying around in Pembroke about how heavily the Barlows depended on the treasonable Boleyn connection and warnings issued that they might attempt to escape by sea from Milford Haven. But, thanks to Cromwell's protecting wing, both brothers escaped unscathed from this crisis.

William Barlow probably arrived back in England from Scotland about the end of June or the beginning of July 1536.[24] His return to St Davids diocese rather later that autumn soon shattered the uneasy peace which had prevailed since his departure in 1535. Any hopes that his opponents may have cherished that Anne Boleyn's fall had weakened her favourite's position were soon dispelled. Before the end of the year, in an important letter to Cromwell, Barlow made plain yet again his intentions in respect of the diocese.[25] Once more he struck the familiar note

---

[20] *Letters and Papers*, VIII.412.
[21] *Letters and Papers*, X.225.
[22] Thomas, *The History of the Diocese* of *St Asaph*, I.22–3.
[23] *Letters and Papers*, XI.1427.
[24] Williams, *Welsh Reformation Essays*, 124–35.
[25] *Letters and Papers*, XI.1427.

about what he believed to be the inveterate 'superstition' which characterized the veneration afforded to the relics of St David, together with what he condemned as the 'horrible blasphemy of God and his verity which made St Davids to Wales what Bethel and Dan were to Israel'. In this letter and also in an accompanying document headed 'instructions for the bishop of St Davids suits' we are given what might be dubbed 'the Barlow plan for the diocese'. Its two most important features were: first, a proposal to remove the see from St Davids – dismissed by Barlow as the 'most barren angle in the diocese' – to St Peter's, Carmarthen; and second, to endow grammar schools and Protestant preaching, funded mainly from the proceeds of suppressed colleges or friaries.[26]

What Barlow did not tell Cromwell in his correspondence, however, was that he was also trying to force upon the cathedral chapter an unconstitutional enlargement of his own authority over it. His attempt to do so precipitated an immediate trial of strength between himself and his canons. It is at this point that we can begin to see that this was something more complex than a straightforward wrangle between a Protestant bishop and his old-fashioned clergy. For it quickly became plain that his canons were not simply resisting Barlow's proselytizing tendencies but also, and possibly more important in their eyes, his attempts to make himself complete master of the chapter. If he could succeed in so doing, then there was every reason to suppose that his bolder and more revolutionary plans to eliminate the name and influence of Dewi Sant; remove his cathedral; and change the complexion of religious beliefs and practices might be achieved. of Barlow's protege and successor, Robert Ferrar, was later to show that a *Protestant* bishop could meet with even fiercer opposition from *Protestant* canons who believed their established rights were being infringed.[27]

What was at stake here? Throughout the middle ages and, indeed, until as late as the beginning of the nineteenth century, St Davids was in the unusual position of having no dean. In the absence of a dean, the precentor had established a prescriptive right to be regarded as the head of the chapter.

To complicate matters, however, there was considerable uncertainty concerning the degree of authority enjoyed by the bishop over the chapter. William Barlow, for his part, was not content with the wide powers which the chapter ordinarily accorded to the bishop and was pressing to the utmost his claim to the powers which would have been exercised by the dean if there had been one. When it had become unmistakably Barlow's intention to go much further than any of his predecessors had done in subordinating the chapter to episcopal control, the canons naturally resisted with some spirit. If their bishop was seeking to get his way by denouncing their shortcomings to Cromwell they would reply in kind. In January 1537 Cromwell received from the hands of Rowland Lee, President of the Council of the Marches, a schedule of accusations against Barlow, drawn up on behalf of the canons by one Roger Lewes, LL.B. It accused him of having said that in earlier times no one had preached the Word of God truly; confession was inexpedient; reverence of the saints pure idolatry – so much for Dewi Sant! –; and purgatory was an invention of the bishop of Rome for lucre. He was also alleged to have declared that where two or three simple persons such as cobblers and weavers were assembled in the name of God, *there* was the true church, and that the king could make any learned layman

26 *Letters and Papers*, XI.1427, 1428.
27 Williams, *Welsh Reformation* Essays, 224–35.

a bishop.[28] Even allowing for a considerable degree of exaggeration on the part of the canons in the heat of a controversy with their bishop, it can nevertheless be well understood what consternation the expression of such views must have caused in a conservatively minded diocese.

A month or two later, the conflict took a new and more envenomed twist when Barlow accused the leader of St Davids chapter, its precentor, Thomas Lloyd of complicity with pirates, imprisoned him, and seized his possessions.[29] This violent and unheralded attack on the precentor was distinctly revealing. It seemed to indicate that Barlow was willing to jump at any opportunity of disgracing the head of the party opposed to him. In so doing, however, he over-reached himself. Lloyd was a well-liked figure at St Davids and in the diocese generally. He and his friends among the canons were not disposed to submit without a struggle. Lloyd brought an action against Barlow in the Court of Star Chamber,[30] and although the surviving documents relating to it are slight and unsatisfactory they do at least make it clear that the real issue at stake was a clash of jurisdiction between bishop and precentor, and not Lloyd's complicity with pirates, as Barlow had alleged.

Thomas Lloyd and his friends among the canons could also count on the sympathy and support of powerful laymen within the diocese against Barlow. In particular, they had enlisted the backing of Richard Devereux, deputy-justice of South Wales and son and heir of Lord Ferrers, the most significant lay figure in west Wales. Close as William Barlow was to Thomas Cromwell, the latter was obviously keen to keep down the political temperature in the strategically vital area of south-west Wales at a time when the Pilgrimage of Grace, the most dangerous armed rebellion of the sixteenth century, was raging in the North of England and discontent was seething in Ireland. It would appear that Cromwell was distinctly disinclined to encourage his hot-headed lieutenant in St Davids; and the documents fall silent for the best part of a year until March of 1538.

The year 1538 opened up ideal opportunities for Barlow to embark on fresh onslaughts against the chapter and the cathedral. This was a time of dramatic changes in many cathedrals and houses of religion, when sacred relics associated with them which, for centuries, had been subject to the devotions of pilgrims and other worshippers were brutally removed, when friaries were suppressed, and larger monasteries which had escaped the dissolution of 1536 were induced to surrender. Proposals were also put forward for creating a number of new cathedrals and for moving some of the existing ones (including St Asaph) to new sites. In these circumstances. Barlow, as might be imagined, was more vociferous than ever in pressing his programme for what he believed to be the reform of his diocese. Writing from Carmarthen on 31 March 1538, he denounced the canons for having set forth what he called 'feigned relics' 'for to allure the people to superstition on St David's Day'.[31] In this letter and several others in the course of the year, he repeated his favourite projects for the removal of the see and the establishment of grammar schools. In fairness to him it might be admitted that, Carmarthen, the largest town in Wales and the hub of many radiating roads, would have made a more convenient centre for the administration of his large and sprawling diocese than the out-of-the-way St Davids; but the root cause of his objection was that the cathedral was far too inti-

---

28 *Letters and Papers*, XII.i. 93.
29 *Letters and Papers*, Addenda, 1.I, 1225.
30 PRO, Star Chamber, Henry VIII, 23/177.
31 *Letters and Papers*, XIII.i, 634; Wright, *Three Chapters*, 183–6.

mately associated with medieval religion for Barlow's taste. He condemned it out of hand for always having been 'esteemed a delicate daughter of Rome, naturally resembling her mother in shameless confusion and like qualified with other perverse properties of execrable malignity, as ungodly image service, abominable idolatry, and licentious liberty, of dishonest living, popish pilgrimages, deceitful pardons, and feigned indulgences'. These 'memorial monuments of Rome's puppetry' could not be extirpated unless the see were translated.[32] Those ancient relics believed to be those of St David and other lesser saints, Barlow contemptuously dismissed as 'two heads of silver plate, enclosing rotten skulls stuffed with putrified clouts; two arm bones and a worm-eaten book covered with silver plate'.[33] There can be no doubt that moving the cathedral church from St Davids to Carmarthen led Barlow to hope that it would thereby become possible to exert his authority over the canons more effectively.

The canons, for their part, were no less determined that the cathedral should remain at St Davids. They were, it was reported, prepared to spend to their shirts in the quarrel'.[34] There is no reason to doubt that there was a deep corporate pride in the ancient link of the patron saint with the cathedral that bore his name. I hope it would not be thought too cynical of me to suggest that the canons were also mindful of the very large sums of money that accrued every year from the offerings of the devout who flocked to St Davids. They were also, no doubt, keenly aware that a move to Carmarthen was bound to bring them in closer and longer contact with their troublesome bishop every year. As a visible token of their deep hostility to Barlow and their unmistakable affection for the patrimony of Saint David and his church and as a symbol of their hopes for the future, they embarked on an ambitious building programme which seems to have overstrained their resources and got them into serious financial difficulties. Nothing could have exasperated their bishop more. He denounced their proceedings as being quite intolerable: to think that they 'should consume utterly the small residue of the church treasure remaining in their custody, without any profitable effect, saving to nourish chattering conventicles of barbarous and rural persons, the deformed habitations of the poor collegians in such beggarly vein and so wretchedly that honesty will abhor to behold them'.[35] All Barlow's protests and threats were entirely in vain. A last despairing appeal to Cromwell by brother John Barlow went unanswered. The canons had successfully defied their bishop.

The outcome of the trial of strength between William Barlow and his chapter and the ultimate fate of St David's cathedral was settled, as it happened, by an unexpected turn of events from outside. Earlier, in the spring of 1538, it might well have seemed as if Barlow, the royal servant and one of Cromwell's favourites, would surely carry the day against the chapter. In August of the same year, however, the Dominican friary of Carmarthen was dissolved. Within its walls lay buried Edmund Tudor, earl of Richmond, grandfather of King Henry VIII. The friary church, although well-known as a burial-place for Welsh notabilities such as Sir Rhys ap Thomas, or that great poet, Tudur Aled,[36] had no particular significance for the Tudor family, still less for the royalty of England. But it was a church near to where Edmund

---

[32] *Letters and Papers*, XIII.ii, 614; Wright, *Three Chapters*, 206–10.

[33] Wright, *Three Chapters*, 184–5.

[34] *Letters and Papers*, XIII.ii, 1132.

[35] Wright, *Suppression*, 184–5.

[36] Williams, *Wales and the Reformation*, 50–1.

Tudor had died, and so he had been buried there. When his son, Henry Tudor, had founded the Tudor royal dynasty as Henry VII, king of England, that had given his father's tomb greatly enhanced status. So, when the friary where he lay was extinguished, the decision was taken to remove his tomb and his remains to a fitting final resting-place. There seemed to be no other choice but St Davids, site of the greatest church in west Wales. This transference was almost certainly the deciding factor in ensuring that the cathedral church remained on its traditional site.[37] Moreover, if further confirmation were needed, Cromwell and other Reformers lost much of their influence as Henry VIII pursued a markedly more conservative line in religion.

In 1540, the execution of Thomas Cromwell deprived Barlow of his most powerful patron, and there are no longer to be found any appeals for the reorganization of the cathedral and diocese like those which had been pressed so importunately during the years from 1535 to 1538. Yet this did not mean the abandonment by Barlow of all hope of fulfilling some, at least, of his plans. In 1541, less than a year after Cromwell's execution, he obtained permission for the college of Abergwili to be transferred to Brecon.[38] There he established a new collegiate foundation and grammar school. There again, he gradually weakened the resistance of his chapter by introducing his own nominees to its midst as opportunities presented themselves.

Although Barlow had failed in his campaign to move the cathedral, it was during his episcopate that the famous shrine of Saint David himself had been destroyed. Barlow, as has already been seen, took a very critical view of what he contemptuously referred to as the 'feigned relics' of Saint David, yet it may not have been he who was responsible for demolishing it, but some of his canons. A letter written in 1540–1 to the Privy Council charged the President of the Council in the Marches with finding out what jewels had been embezzled from the shrine and who had been responsible.[39] Not until 1544 was the Court of Augmentations informed that the price obtained for the shrine was £66 13s. 4d. In August 1546, a warrant was issued to the Treasurer of that court to pay a reward of £40 to one James Leach for his expenses incurred in recovering 'plate and jewels which did belong to St Davids shrine in Wales'.[40] Still later, in Edward VI's reign Bishop Ferrar was to accuse some of his canons of despoiling the cathedral of crosses to the value of four to five hundred marks.[41]

The remains and the reputation of the great patron saint himself may have suffered to such an extent at this time that we may well wonder how he ever managed to recover so much lost ground. Without going into excessive detail, two main reasons may be suggested for this. First, that the celebration of St David's Day during the middle ages had never been of an exclusively religious nature. There is good evidence that the commemoration had always included feasting and jollification of an essentially secular kind. This highly popular practice would appear to have continued in subsequent centuries.[42] Secondly, and as least as important in my view, there was the rehabilitation of the Celtic Church by Protestant Reformers. By a stroke of poetic justice, the man chiefly responsible for this was Richard Davies, bishop of St Davids from 1561 to 1581. He argued very persuasively, if not too historically, that

---

37 Evans, 'The Reformation and St Davids, 1–16.
38 Williams, *Wales and the Reformation*, 143–4.
39 Evans, 'The Reformation and St Davids', 7, 5.
40 Evans, 'The Reformation and St Davids'.
41 Williams, 'The tradition of St David'.
42 Williams, *Wales and the Reformation*, 244–6.

Christianity had been introduced into Britain in apostolic times, centuries before the tainted papal brand had been introduced by Augustine of Canterbury. The Celtic Church had maintained its faith in all its gospel purity. Who represented that Church more authentically than St David? This revamping of British Church History, whatever it may have lacked in historicity, wanted nothing in fervour and popularity. In Wales it was to count for infinitely more than Barlow's ferocious attacks.

One brief postscript. Although Barlow's iconoclastic onslaughts have usually been thought to have derived their inspiration from his total lack of sympathy with David, his church and people, the odd thing is that it is rarely remembered that in the second half of the seventeenth century schemes not dissimilar to some of those of Barlow were propounded for the removal of the cathedral to Carmarthen – this time not by a benighted Englishman and outsider but, remarkably enough, by a cleric born of Carmarthen parentage and one who cherished a deep concern for the religion and language of the Welsh. He was William Thomas, bishop from 1677 to 1683, and an ardent member of the Welsh Trust and bosom friend of Stephen Hughes.[43] Soon after coming to St Davids he advocated the move on the grounds that 'he knew St David's to be generally apprehended of as an useless place', whereas he believed 'Carmarthen to be a rich populous town'.[44] But Thomas met with no better success than Barlow had done. This time again, the greatest obstacle was a dramatic twist in high politics: the discovery of an alleged Catholic plot by the infamous Titus Oates designed to kill the king. It was this supposed conspiracy which, in the words of an old St Davids historian, Edward Yardley, raised 'so much more than ordinary ferment in the nation' and 'took ifs up most men's thoughts'.[45] Thomas remained as bishop until 1683, but never again mooted the proposal to move his see.

---

[43] Yardley, *Menevia Sacra*, 114–16.
[44] Yardley, *Menevia Sacra*, 115.
[45] Yardley, *Menevia Sacra*, 116.

21

THE DIOCESE OF ST DAVIDS
IN THE EARLY NINETEENTH CENTURY: A REAPPRAISAL

W.N. Yates

In a sermon preached in 1879, and subsequently published under the title 'Why are the Welsh people alienated from the Church?' Dean Edwards of Bangor put the blame firmly on the actions of the British government during the eighteenth and nineteenth centuries and the appointment by them of non-Welsh bishops:

> In 1715, with the exception of thirty-five separatists' congregations, the entire people of Wales adhered to the Church. But after that date, for more than a hundred and fifty years, the rulers of the state, in pursuit of a worldly policy, sent into Wales chief pastors ignorant of its language and traditions, and aliens in sympathy, to the people. During that long period, the followers of the apostles came into Wales, not to accomplish the spiritual work of saving souls, but as Government agents, to destroy the language and quench the national spirit. The fruits of this policy are known to you. The thirty-five meeting houses of 1715 have become, in 1879, nearly three thousand.[1]

It was an appealing but simplistic analysis of Welsh religious history which by the last quarter of the nineteenth century had been adopted, not just by Welsh nonconformists but by the leaders of its established church, and it is an analysis which has dominated, albeit with some modifications in recent years, Welsh religious historiography for the century and a quarter which has elapsed since Dean Edwards preached his sermon.

As far as the diocese of St Davids is concerned the views of Dean Edwards have been compounded by depressing accounts of its condition since Erasmus Saunders put pen to paper in the early eighteenth century and described parishes without services and others held by pluralists who 'having so little time, and so many places to attend upon, how precipitately and as if out of breath are they obliged to read the prayers, or to shorten or abridge them … and like hasty itinerants to hurry from place to place'.[2] Within the last decade the view has been expressed that before the middle years of the nineteenth century, within the diocese of St Davids, 'many of the churches were dilapidated, the services conducted in them slovenly, and those officiating at them worldly and corrupt'.[3] The ecclesiastical revival in the diocese was seen as having been inaugurated by Connop Thirlwall, who became bishop in 1840, though even this has been challenged recently and the modernisation of the diocese attributed to his successor, Basil Jones (1874–97).[4] Recent work on English dioceses has, however, shown that, far from being an 'age of negligence', the late eighteenth

---

1 Edwards, *Wales and the Welsh Church*, 313–14.
2 Quoted by O.W. Jones, 'The Welsh church in the eighteenth century', 104.
3 Cragoe, *An Anglican Aristocracy*, 195.
4 Cragoe, *An Anglican Aristocracy*, 208–10.

and early nineteenth centuries were in fact a period of substantial ecclesiastical reform directed by energetic bishops determined to improve standards of pastoral care. Is it really the case that somehow Wales failed to participate in a movement that was so marked in England, or is it rather the case that so much that has been written about the Welsh church in this period has simply failed to notice what was actually going on at diocesan and parochial level? It is my intention to show that the second of these analyses is more accurate than the first, by a reappraisal of the condition of the diocese of St Davids between the consecration of Samuel Horsley as bishop in 1788 and the death of John Banks Jenkinson in 1840. It is a reappraisal based not on the acceptance of statements made by those with an axe to grind but on an examination of episcopal charges, visitation returns and other diocesan records.

We should begin by looking at the five men who occupied the bishopric of St Davids between 1788 and 1840: Samuel Horsley, William Stuart, George Murray, Thomas Burgess and John Banks Jenkinson. Horsley, who has been the subject of an impressive modern biography,[5] was an acknowledged leader of the reformers in the episcopate in the late eighteenth century and was successively bishop of St Davids (1788–93), Rochester (1793–1802) and St Asaph (1802–6). His successor, Stuart, was another reformer, who was George III's personal choice for the vacant archbishopric of Armagh, to which he was translated in 1800. His tenure of the archbishopric was marked by his vociferous lobbying for the appointment of more committed reformers to the Irish episcopate, for increased government grants for the building of new churches and glebe houses, and for the more efficient administration of the body that administered these grants, the Irish Board of First Fruits.[6] Murray's episcopate was very short, little more than two years before his early death in 1803, but the few remaining documents from his episcopate show him to have been a competent administrator of the diocese. Burgess was one of the leading lights of his generation, a scholar who was also an effective administrator and a champion of ecclesiastical reform; his lasting contribution to both his diocese and the wider Welsh church was the university in which this conference is being held.[7] After Burgess his successor, Jenkinson, the nephew of the Hackney Phalanx prime minister, Lord Liverpool, was a much duller character; a stiff and inflexible high churchman who disliked Evangelicals, but who was nevertheless another competent administrator and a generous benefactor, maintaining a school for 150 poor children at Carmarthen at his own expense.[8]

It is important to state at the outset that the diocese of St Davids had two particular problems which, though not unique in England and Wales, presented its bishops with considerable difficulties. The first was the physical size of the diocese which, before minor modifications in the 1840s and far more draconian ones in 1923, covered the whole of the counties of Breconshire, Cardiganshire, Carmarthenshire and Pembrokeshire, most of the parishes in Radnorshire, the rural deanery of Gower in Glamorganshire and a small number of parishes in Herefordshire, Monmouth-

---

5 Mather, *High Church Prophet*.
6 There is no biography but some useful references in Akenson, *The Church of Ireland*, 14–15, 75–7, 116–17, 124–5; some of Stuart's papers are held in the Bedfordshire Record Office (WY 994–5) and his correspondence with Archbishop Brodrick of Cashel and Emly, mostly relating to the management of the Board of First Fruits, is in the National Library of Ireland, MS 8869.
7 Again there is no full modern biography but Price, *Bishop Burgess*, partly meets this need and reflects the fact that few original papers have survived.
8 *ODNB*, XXIX.981–2. There are entries for the four other bishops: VII.773–5 (Burgess), XXVIII.199–202 (Horsley), XXXIX.904–5 (Murray) and LIII.199 (Stuart).

shire and Montgomeryshire. The second was the overall poverty of the diocese, which affected not just its parochial benefices but the bishopric as well. The value of this was so low that the bishops could not meet the expenses of their office without holding other preferment *in commendam*. Horsley was also rector of Newington Butts in Surrey; Murray was archdeacon of Man and dean of Bocking; Burgess and Jenkinson both held prebends at Durham, and from 1827 Jenkinson was also dean of Durham. It is important to emphasise that pluralism in the late eighteenth and early nineteenth centuries was no bar to episcopal efficiency. Parochial livings could be served by curates and the residence qualifications attached to most cathedral dignities and prebends were fairly limited. Bishops were only expected to reside in their dioceses, and to carry out confirmations and visitations, during the summer months, since during the winter they had to be in London to carry out their parliamentary duties in the House of Lords. There is currently not a shred of evidence that the fact that the bishops of St Davids held other preferment *in commendam* contributed in any way to the neglect of their episcopal duties and responsibilities.

In addition to the two problems outlined above, the bishops of St Davids were by the 1780s faced with two other problems which they needed to resolve. The first was the disruption in the diocese caused by the Evangelical revival and the popularity of Calvinistic Methodism. The second was the fact that the poverty of parochial livings meant that, whereas in most other English and Welsh dioceses it was almost invariably the case that incumbents and curates were university graduates, the diocese of St Davids had great difficulty in recruiting graduate clergy. Its benefices were simply not sufficiently well-endowed to attract those whose families could afford to send them to universities, of which there were none in Wales, and many benefices were held by the sons of modest farmers who had been educated at either a local grammar school or one of the academies established for the training of nonconformist ministers. For a reforming bishop these were matters which demanded immediate and sustained attention.

Episcopal attitudes in both England and Wales to the Evangelical revival of the eighteenth century have been much criticised in both the nineteenth and the twentieth centuries for having contributed to the growth of nonconformity and there has been an assumption that, if matters had been handled more sensitively, far fewer people would have seceded from the established church. The difficulty of this response is that it fails to recognise the potential challenge of Evangelicalism, theologically, socially and politically to the nature of Anglicanism as it had emerged from the religious conflicts of the sixteenth and seventeenth centuries. Whilst the church in England and Wales was separated from Rome, apart from the brief hiatus of Mary I's reign, from the 1530s, Anglicanism as a distinct theological position did not really come into its own until the 1620s. The church that emerged from the Reformation process in England and Wales was a moderately Calvinist church in terms of both its theology and its liturgy, though retaining the administrative structure of the pre-Reformation church. It was the survival of this structure, and particularly of episcopacy, combined with a degree of theological ambiguity in its liturgical texts, which enabled the leadership of the church in England and Wales to begin its rejection of Calvinism in the first quarter of the seventeenth century, and to move towards a return to a more Catholic interpretation of its doctrinal formularies and its liturgy in the second quarter. This was in its turn disrupted by the Civil Wars and Interregnum of the 1640s and 1650s. Whilst one must be careful of interpreting the restoration of the monarchy and of Anglicanism in 1660 as an unqualified victory for high churchmen who had gone into exile over the previous decade, that was certainly the eventual outcome. The secession of the more advanced Puritans unwilling to accept the religious settlement and new *Book of Common Prayer* in 1662, secured the domination of the established church by those who were the successors of the men who had, in a sense, created 'Anglicanism' in the 1620s.[9] For Anglican churchmen, whose doctrinal standpoint in the eighteenth century was much influenced by a memory of the religious confusion of earlier years and a determination not to repeat the experience, the Evangelical revival seemed to threaten a return to an earlier age and doctrines which they regarded as fundamentally un-Anglican.

Orthodox Anglican churchmen, and the bishops of St Davids between Horsley and Jenkinson could all be described as such, had three main objections to Evangelicalism. The first was its enthusiasm, its appeal to the Spirit, its flirtation with religious radicalism, which orthodox churchmen, especially after the French revolution, saw as a likely precursor to political radicalism. Anglican political and religious philosophy had a very clear view of the value of an ordered and structured society based on a belief in the divine nature of monarchy, non-resistance to lawful authority and a close relationship between church and state.[10] The more radical Protestants had regarded such views as erastian and they had caused great difficulties in Scotland before the abolition of episcopacy in that country in 1690. Orthodox churchmen were concerned that if Evangelicalism was encouraged within the established churches of England, Ireland or Wales it might lead to the constitution being subverted or, at the very least, a modification of the ecclesiastical establishment on the Scottish model in which classic Anglicanism would be difficult, if not impossible, to maintain. The second objection to Evangelicalism was its perceived adoption of Calvinist doctrines which classic Anglicanism had rejected. In this respect, at least, orthodox Anglicans can be fairly accused of misrepresenting Evangelicalism. Some Evangelicals were certainly Calvinists, but by no means all. The followers of John and Charles Wesley were as Arminian in their theology as any orthodox Anglican and in England it was their followers, the Wesleyan Methodists, who formed a majority of the Evangelicals within the established church. In Wales, however, the bishops were on stronger ground. Wesleyan Methodism had relatively little impact, being largely confined to North Wales, and within the diocese of Bangor it was quickly weakened by the internal schism known as *Y Wesle Bach*.[11] Welsh Evangelicalism, especially in South Wales, was from its earliest manifestations in Howell Harris, Daniel Rowland and William Williams 'Pantycelyn', firmly identified with Calvinism.[12] The third, especially episcopal, objection to Evangelicalism was its perceived lack of respect for authority and its willingness to create a church within a church. Although the early Welsh Evangelicals regarded themselves as members of the established church and, if they were clergy, frequently held benefices within it, that did not prevent them establishing separate chapels for their own followers at which services of a character not authorised by the *Book of Common Prayer* might be held and in which they celebrated Holy Communion amidst scenes verging on

9   There is a substantial literature on this topic. For a brief overview see Yates, *Buildings*, 7–22. The more detailed studies include Tyacke, *Anti-Calvinists*; Spurr, *The Restoration Church*; Green, *The Re-Establishment*.
10 For the nature of the Anglican view of the church-state relationship between the late seventeenth and early nineteenth centuries see the major studies by Clark, *English Society*, 119–276, and Colley, *Britons*, 18–54.
11 See Watts, *The Dissenters*, 34.
12 On Harris see Tudur, *Howell Harris*, and on Rowland see E. Evans, *Daniel Rowland*. For an overview see Morgan, *The Great Awakening*.

emotional hysteria, as witnessed by Howell Harris' description of such a celebration by Daniel Rowland at Llangeitho, the Cardiganshire parish of which he was then curate, in 1743:

> I was last at the Ordinance with Brother Rowlands where I saw, felt and heard such things as I can't send on paper any Idea of ... Such Crying Out and Heart Breaking Groans, Silent Weeping and Holy Joy, and Shouts of Rejoicing I never saw. Their Amens and Cryings, Glory in the Highest &c would inflame your soul was you there. 'Tis very common when he preaches for Scores to fall down by the Power of the Word, pierced and wounded and overcom'd by the Love of God and Sights of Beauty and Excellency of Jesus, and lie on the Ground.[13]

Another serious breach of ecclesiastical discipline was the use by the Methodists, both Wesleyan and Calvinistic, of itinerant preachers, many of whom were merely laymen.

What many have considered to be the high-handed actions of the Anglican episcopate in the eighteenth and early nineteenth centuries have to be seen against this background. When Bishop Squire of St Davids revoked Daniel Rowland's licence as curate of Llangeitho and Nantcwnlle in 1763 it followed a period in which he had established chapels for his followers in the parishes of Cardigan, Henfynyw, Llanbadarn Odwyn, Llanbadarn Trefeglwys, Llanddewibrefi, Llandysul and Lledrod. One of the two chapels he established in the parish of Llanddewibrefi was within walking distance of his own parish church at Llangeitho.[14] Bishop Squire undoubtedly regarded Rowland's actions as potentially schismatic and it is difficult not to accept that he had justification in taking this view. Nevertheless, even in the diocese of St Davids, there were some variations in episcopal policy towards Evangelicals in the late eighteenth and early nineteenth centuries. Bishop Burgess, though not himself an Evangelical, had some sympathy for Evangelical enthusiasm and collaborated, unlike some of his high church contemporaries, in the establishment of both the, wholly Anglican, Church Missionary Society and the, non-denominational, British and Foreign Bible Society.[15] Bishops Horsley and Jenkinson were much more aggressively hostile towards Evangelicalism. Horsley took the view that

> the crime and folly of the Methodists consists, not so much in heterodoxy, as in fanaticism; not in perverse doctrine, but rather in a disorderly zeal for the propagation of the Truth.[16]

Nevertheless he sought to control their influence in his two Welsh dioceses, both at St Davids and later at St Asaph, by declining to license Evangelicals to curacies and, wherever possible, denying them preferment to benefices. Horsley's fear that Calvinistic Methodism would eventually result in schism was in fact fulfilled in 1811 when, faced with the fact that there were not enough sympathetic Anglican clergy to celebrate Holy Communion in their chapels, the Calvinistic Methodist Association meetings at both Bala and Llandeilo decided that they would in future ordain their own ministers. Whilst the schism only took place gradually over the first

---

13 Quoted in Campbell, *The Religion of the Heart*, 105.
14 Jenkins, 'The Established Church and Dissent in Eighteenth-Century Cardiganshire', 465.
15 Price, *Bishop Burgess*, 40–1.
16 Horsley, *The Charge*, 30.

half of the nineteenth century its impact on the established church was dramatic, probably more so in lack of confidence than in actual numerical decline.[17]

To some extent the drift of some clergy into Calvinistic Methodism may well have been linked with the other diocesan problem, the failure to recruit graduate clergy. Faced with an absence of graduates the bishops of St Davids had no alternative but to ordain men who had been educated only at a grammar school or at one of the academies that had been set up by the older dissenting bodies in Wales, the Presbyterians and the Independents, for the training of their own ministers. The academy at Carmarthen produced both orthodox clergy, such as Archdeacon Thomas Beynon of Cardigan, and some, such as Thomas Charles of Bala, who were prominent among the Calvinistic Methodists.[18] Bishop Horsley took the line that in future all candidates for ordination must have been to a 'reputable public school' and he also provided them with lists of books on which he would 'examine the candidates for Orders, and in which I shall expect to find them expert'. Burgess stipulated that he would only ordain non-graduates who had studied divinity at one of nine licensed grammar schools in the diocese: Brecon, Cardigan, Carmarthen, Haverfordwest, Lampeter, Rhayader, St Davids, Whitton (Rads.) and Ystrad Meurig (Cards.).[19] It was a similar line to that taken half a century earlier by Bishop Thomas Wilson of Sodor and Man, most of whose clergy were non-graduates. Wilson insisted that all candidates for orders must have attended one of the four grammar schools in the Isle of Man, and also have spent some time in the bishop's household and be licensed as lay assistants to elderly or infirm clergy, by 'reading the Lessons and Psalms, and now and then a homily'.[20] He also established post-ordination training for the clergy through issuing guidance on books to read and by establishing libraries for their use.[21]

Burgess decided that the existing arrangements for the education of the clergy were still inadequate. Post-ordination training was to be achieved through the establishment of clerical societies in each of the diocese's twenty rural deaneries, at which the clergy would meet 'to promote theological study and to support each other in their clerical work'.[22] Pre-ordination training was to be made more intensive and satisfactory through the establishment of a combination of a theological college and a proto-university, which is perhaps the best definition of the college eventually established at Lampeter in the 1820s. Burgess had announced his intention to establish such a college in 1804, shortly after his consecration as bishop. However, the difficulty of raising funds and finding a suitable location for the college, meant that the preparatory phase of the exercise lasted eighteen years. It was not until a site was offered in Lampeter that the foundation stone was eventually laid in 1822, and the first students were not admitted until 1827, two years after Burgess had been translated from the diocese of St Davids to that of Salisbury.[23] However, Bishop Jenkinson made clear his commitment to his predecessor's vision by stating that 'I

---

17 The schism has been dealt with, in detail, from a Calvinist Methodist perspective, in Jenkins, *The Life of Thomas Charles*, vol. 2, 237–333. A similar examination, from the perspective of the established church, remains to be undertaken.

18 *DWB*, 37.

19 Jones, 'The mountain clergyman', 170–83.

20 Keble, *The Life of Thomas Wilson*, 796–9.

21 Manx National Heritage Library, MD 436, folder 2/3; Keble, *The Life of Thomas Wilson*, 250–8; Ferguson, *The Parochial Libraries*.

22 Price, *Bishop Burgess*, 37.

23 Price, *Bishop Burgess*, 50–7; for a more detailed account of the college's foundation see Price, *History of St David's University College*.

shall in future look exclusively to St David's College, and to our Universities for a supply of candidates' for ordination.[24] The title of the new institution is also not without significance. In 1811 Burgess had carried out a visitation of the cathedral at St Davids and had read to the chapter a charge in which he had emphasised the importance of the cult of St David in the history of the Welsh church.[25] Burgess was a strong believer, along with much of the antiquarian lobby in Wales, 'in the notion of the Ancient British Church, independent of Rome until the Normans absorbed it into the Roman Catholic church in the twelfth century',[26] and collaborated with Iolo Morganwg in the establishment of a Cambrian Society in Dyfed in 1818, presiding at its first *eisteddfod*, generally regarded as the first of the series of modern national *eisteddfodau*, at Carmarthen in 1819.[27]

The college which Burgess had founded continued to provide the sort of education he had desired, almost exclusively to those seeking ordination, for more than a century. The original course lasted for four years: 2½ years of classics and 1½ of theology, together with Welsh and English composition. The first and second vice-principals became, respectively, bishops of Llandaf and of Ely and Winchester. The first Professor of Welsh, Rice Rees, was the most distinguished Welsh scholar of his generation. Of the students admitted between 1827 and 1849, the vast majority came from the diocese of St Davids, the constituency for which the college had been founded, and nearly half were the sons of farmers, the social group which had provided the diocese's clergy in previous years. Most were ordained by the bishops of St Davids and Llandaf, the two Welsh dioceses which had had problems attracting graduate clergy. A few of the 350 Lampeter-trained clergy ordained before 1851 were ordained by bishops in England. The college was, however, criticised for paying too much attention to the classics, and not enough to theology, which was not the case at St Bees, founded in 1816 by Bishop Law of Chester to train the non-graduate clergy who tended to serve parishes in the northern part of his diocese, or the early theological colleges founded at Chichester in 1839 and Wells in 1840. It was also criticised for failing to place enough emphasis on the Welsh language, especially the training of the clergy to preach in Welsh, which had always been one of the strengths of the nonconformist academies.[28] Nevertheless, whilst not wishing either to dismiss or ignore these criticisms, it is essential to set them in a broader context. Burgess and Jenkinson succeeded in establishing an institution that achieved its purpose of providing improved education and training for the non-graduate clergy of the diocese; an institution that laid the foundation for higher education in Wales; and an institution which, for an unbroken 175 years, has been in the forefront of the academic study of theology.

Apart from their contribution to clerical education, had the reforming bishops of St Davids from Horsley to Jenkinson succeeded in transforming the levels of pastoral care in their diocese between 1788 and 1840? We are fortunate that for the whole period from 1799 until the First World War there are, at regular intervals, surviving records of the visitations of the diocese carried out by its successive bishops. The most valuable of these are the questions addressed by bishops to their clergy and the replies made to them. Surprisingly, only one complete set of such

[24] Jenkinson, *A Charge*, 34.
[25] Burgess, *Bishops and Benefactors, passim.*
[26] See Burgess, *Tracts on the Ancient British Church, passim.*
[27] Price, *Bishop Burgess*, 42–9.
[28] Price, *Bishop Burgess*, 64–9.

returns, those for Bishop Jenkinson's visitation in 1828, have been analysed,[29] and although they provide a valuable snapshot of the diocese in that year they do not provide the basis for analysis over a longer period. Providing that sort of analysis for a diocese of more than four hundred parishes is a daunting exercise and I have confined myself to that of one archdeaconry, that of Carmarthen, which covered about a quarter of the parishes in the diocese, over a period of about forty years, by looking at the visitation returns for 1799, 1813, 1828 and 1842.[30] The archdeaconry of Carmarthen was, in many respects, a microcosm of the diocese as a whole. It comprised a majority of Welsh-speaking, but a significant minority of English-speaking, parishes; two administrative centres, at Carmarthen and Swansea; a cluster of small towns (Kidwelly, Laugharne, Llandeilo, Llandovery, Llanelli and St Clears); and a predominantly agricultural population but with growing centres of industry along its south-eastern fringes. The returns for the whole of this period show that in many respects the established church in this corner of Wales was far from decadent in the early nineteenth century, though there were some parishes in which there was room for improvement and on which the reforming agenda of its bishops had seemingly made little impact.

1. *Clergy and residence*

Although the archdeaconry of Carmarthen, as most other parts of England and Wales, had its fair share of non-resident clergy, it is clear from the returns that the overwhelming majority of parishes were being served by a clergyman who lived within either that parish or one immediately adjacent. Indeed the only cases in which a church was being served by a clergyman who lived at a considerable distance were Llanfynydd and Pencarreg in 1813. Where curates were being employed, either as assistants or to serve cures for non-resident incumbents, there was a significant rise in the value of stipends which, in many cases, doubled between 1813 and 1842. One reason frequently given by the clergy for not residing in their parishes was the lack of a glebe or parsonage house, or one that was inadequate. Returns were made at different dates of inadequate houses at Brechfa, Kidwelly, Laugharne, Llangynydd, Meidrim and Rhosili, but there were also reports of new or improved houses at Cynwyl Gaeo and Pembrey.

2. *Services and sacraments*

The service pattern within the archdeaconry was very clear. The norm was one Sunday service (single duty) and monthly communion. Double duty (two or more Sunday services) was confined to the churches of the towns and a few of the larger villages. For part of the period the churches at Abergwili, Carmarthen and Llandeilofawr also had two celebrations of Holy Communion each month. The large number of parishes with at least a monthly communion service was, by English and Welsh standards, exceedingly high, though it was paralleled by the situation in the archdeaconry of Cardigan, where in 1828 a total of 86 out of 104 churches, compared with 76 out of 103 in the archdeaconry of Carmarthen, had them. Walter Morgan endeavours to make a correlation between parishes that were English- rather than Welsh-

---

[29] Morgan, 'The diocese of St David's', Part One, 5–49, and Part Two, 12–48.
[30] National Library of Wales, SD/QA/62, 68, 70 and 73.

speaking and those that did not have a monthly communion service.[31] However, a detailed examination of these parishes in the archdeaconry of Carmarthen shows that the unifying factor was as much geography as it was language. All the parishes with communion services less than once a month were grouped in three areas of the archdeaconry: twenty were in the rural deanery of Gower and the vast majority were English-speaking; twelve were in the north-eastern part of Carmarthenshire, in an area bounded by the towns of Lampeter, Llandeilo and Llandovery, and all of these were Welsh-speaking; and eight were in the south-western part of Carmarthenshire adjacent to the towns of Laugharne and St Clears, of which three had services in English and five had bilingual or Welsh services. As far as language was concerned, apart from the rural deanery of Gower, most services remained in Welsh throughout the period though with a slight increase in the number of bilingual, rather than Welsh only, services during its second half. Some clergy noted in their returns that they held services at least partly in English for the benefit of visitors who did not understand Welsh.

Although most churches also held services, and frequently Holy Communion, on the major festivals and fasts, such as Christmas Day and Good Friday, few other weekdays were observed by a service in church. Those churches with regular weekday services were confined to the towns or the larger villages, with such services throughout the whole period at Carmarthen and Swansea. Some of the returns in 1828 and 1842 suggested that there was considerable Evangelical influence in a few parishes within the archdeaconry, notably at Llanddewi and Llangynydd, served by the same clergyman in 1828, and at Llanelli, Llanllwch, Llansamlet, Loughor and Oxwich in 1842. This was the year that Bishop Thirlwall asked a question about the use of hymn books, frequently a sign of Evangelical influence at this date as most high churchmen still disliked them. The replies indicate that about a third of the churches in the archdeaconry were using hymn books, particularly those in which the services were in Welsh and at which Rees's *Welsh Hymns* was generally used.

3. *The condition of church buildings*

In 1828 Bishop Jenkinson asked a question about the fabric and furnishings of churches. The vast majority of clergy reported that their churches were in 'decent', 'good' or 'tolerable' repair. Only seven out of 103 churches were reported as being in poor repair, and a further eleven reported that they were either 'under repair' or had recently been restored or refitted. One of the most substantial of these restorations had been at Llanelli, where the church had been both enlarged and refitted, and a slightly later plan of 1839 showing these improvements has been preserved.[32] Even so the return indicates that more church accommodation was still needed in Llanelli, and that also appears to have been the case at Llanllwch. Elsewhere, churches were generally large enough to accommodate those who wished to attend them and a major campaign of church extension in the archdeaconry did not begin until the 1850s.[33]

[31] Morgan, 'The diocese of St David's', Part Two, 35–6.
[32] National Library of Wales, SD/F/314.
[33] Cragoe, *An Anglican Aristocracy*, 220.

4. *Catechising and schools*

Most clergy endeavoured to preserve the traditional custom of catechising on Sundays but were finding it increasingly difficult to persuade parents to send their children to be catechised. Part of the solution to the problem was to transfer catechising to the Sunday schools where they had been established, and this transfer is recorded in some of the returns. There was, however, a vast shortage of both day and Sunday schools in the archdeaconry. Some parishes had fee-paying schools, frequently both transitory in nature and not very well administered. Endowed schools were few and far between and frequently relied on the generosity of landed families, such as the Talbots of Penrice Castle who funded schools at Oxwich, Penrice, Reynoldston and Rhosili; Lord Dynevor funded a school at Llandeilofawr and the Earl of Cawdor one at Llanfihangel Aberbythych. Many Sunday schools relied heavily on the parish clergyman or his family for their maintenance and operation. The circulating school movement, established by Griffith Jones of Llanddowror and continued after his death in 1761 by Bridget Bevan, had been discontinued after her own death in 1779, when her relatives contested the will in which she had left £10,000 for the continued support of the schools.[34] However, by the first decade of the nineteenth century the dispute had been resolved and the schools were once more operational, though on a much smaller scale, with the result that two parishes, Llanybydder and Myddfai, both reported in 1813 that they had unsuccessfully applied to Mrs Bevan's Charity for the establishment of circulating schools. A major effort to promote education was undertaken by the National Society, founded in 1811. Although the society provided grants to establish schools, such grants were dependent on enough financial support being raised locally, and this was not always forthcoming. By 1828 there were National Society schools at Carmarthen, Laugharne, Llandovery (Llandingad parish), Llanelli and Morriston (Llangyfelach parish). The National Society school established at Port Eynon in 1815 relied for its continued support on the generosity of the Talbot family of Penrice Castle.

5. *Other parochial charities*

Apart from small sums for poor relief, few parishes had other than educational charities and two of these, at Cilycwm and Llanfihangel Abercywyn, were charged with maladministration in 1799. The only parish with an endowed almshouse was Llanwrda; this had been established by the late Miss Letitia Cornwallis for four 'maiden gentlewomen', who each received an annual salary of forty pounds.

6. *The impact of dissent*

It is very clear from the returns that the full impact of dissent had been felt within most of the archdeaconry before the end of the eighteenth century. Although attendances at the parish churches were low, frequently less than a fifth of the population and the number of communicants even lower, there was not that much variation in the level of attendances and the number of communicants between 1799 and 1842 in the majority of parishes. In a few there was a further decline over the period but in others there was an increase in both the level of attendance and the number of communicants. The one exception to this general rule was the more rural, and

---

[34] Jones, 'The Welsh church in the eighteenth century', 107.

wholly English-speaking, western part of the rural deanery of Gower, where dissent had made relatively little impact in the eighteenth century and a number of new congregations were established in the first four decades of the nineteenth. Altogether 74 of the 107 parishes and chapelries in the archdeaconry appear to have had at least one dissenting meeting house and many had several. The body variously described as Independents or Presbyterians had established meetings in 41, the Baptists in 35, the Calvinistic Methodists in 50 and the Wesleyan Methodists in 20. Six parishes had Unitarian meetings, there was one Moravian one, and three Primitive Methodist meetings, the last all being established after 1820 in the rural deanery of Gower.

The replies rarely revealed the level of antipathy or otherwise between the established church and the dissenters, many of whom from time to time attended Anglican services, though evidence of collaboration is implied by those for Llangathen and Newchurch in 1799, Llanfallteg and Port Eynon in 1828, and Llanddeusant in 1842. The other side of the coin is, however, revealed by the replies to Bishop Thirlwall's question in 1842 about the payment of parish clerks. They should have been paid for by the church rates, but many dissenters objected to having to pay for the upkeep of the parish churches as well as that of their own meeting houses, and, where they were able to control the annual vestry, frequently refused to levy them. When they were levied some dissenters refused to pay them.[35] In 26 out of 98 parishes making returns the parish clerk, where there was one (which there mostly was), was not paid from the church rates. These included large urban parishes like Swansea, where the parish clerk received no salary compared with the £30 paid from the rates to the parish clerk at Carmarthen. In a few rural parishes the clerk still received payments levied on produce or agricultural equipment but in most they had to rely solely on fees, especially for digging graves if they also performed the duties of sexton, or were paid by the officiating clergyman. In at least ten parishes, mostly Welsh-speaking, the returns make it clear that no church rate has been levied, and it seems fair to conclude that the reason for the rate not being levied was the refusal of a dissenting majority at the annual vestry, summoned for this purpose, to levy a rate.

How can we summarise the situation in the archdeaconry of Carmarthen in the first forty years of the nineteenth century? The returns in respect of clerical residence and the frequency of services, and the prevalence of single duty in rural parishes, were replicated in most other parts of England and in Wales. On the other hand, the high proportion of rural parishes with monthly communion services was matched in few other parts of Britain or Ireland, where quarterly communion tended to be the norm. The reasons for this are extremely hard to explain. It was certainly not a new development as the majority of parishes with monthly communion services in 1799 also had them in 1755.[36] The condition of church buildings was also favourable and with clear evidence of building work in progress. This is an area on which more research needs to be done, though the poor survival of vestry minutes and churchwardens' accounts in many Welsh parishes, or the granting of faculties in the diocesan records, will make this a rather hazardous exercise, and it will need to rely heavily on such national records as those of the Incorporated Church Building Society now held in Lambeth Palace Library. The problems in relation to catechising were certainly not confined to the diocese of St Davids but were being experienced throughout England and Wales, and almost certainly reflect the profound economic

---

[35] See Machin, 'A Welsh church rates fracas', 462–8.
[36] National Library of Wales, SD/QA/61.

and social changes that were taking place in the late eighteenth and early nineteenth centuries in both town and countryside. The area in which there seem to have been particular local problems was in the provision of schooling and charitable support for the poor. The vast majority of the parishes in the archdeaconry of Carmarthen had either no, or at the very least inadequate, provision for the education of their children or the support of their poorer inhabitants. There is little doubt that the lack of such provision can be attributed to the fact that there were few parishes in which the principal landowners or the clergy were sufficiently wealthy to have been able to endow charities. At the other, and richer, end of the country, in the county of Kent, provision was very different. Here almost half the parishes in the county had an established school by the first decade of the nineteenth century; in the two decades following the establishment of the National Society for Education in 1811, more than twenty new schools were established funded by the Society and local benefactions. In addition some eighteen schools had been established by the 1840s by the British and Foreign School Society, founded in 1807, the nondenominational rival to the established church's National Society. The extent of other parochial charities in Kent is also impressive. In a survey conducted in 1786–8 only 127 out of 405 parishes in the county, and these mostly very small, had no parochial charities. The remaining 278 had a total of 980 charities covering not just educational provision, but the monetary relief of poverty; food, clothing, accommodation and fuel for the poor; apprenticeships; endowments for sermons; and funds for the repair of churches.[37] It was a vastly different picture from that in the majority of parishes (roughly the same in number) in the sprawling and mountainous diocese of St Davids.

The reasons for this vastly different picture, however, were not episcopal lethargy or clerical incompetence. They were related to poverty and geography, problems which the established church was, on its own, in no position to solve. Bearing in mind these difficulties, the state of the established church in the diocese of St Davids bore comparison with that of the established church in other parts of Britain and Ireland, a little worse in some areas and rather better in others. It is by no means clear that, except in the area of clerical education, the efforts of reforming bishops had done that much to improve the condition of the established church in the early nineteenth century from that in the late eighteenth century, but they had certainly ensured that it had got no worse. The government-inspired reform programmes of the 1830s and 1840s, which aimed to tackle the underlying problems of pluralism and non-residence through a redistribution of ecclesiastical endowments, were dealing with problems which dated from the pre-Reformation period and which successive generations of bishops had failed to persuade successive generations of governments to resolve. Within the limits of their powers the reforming bishops of St Davids from Horsley to Jenkinson, had, like their episcopal colleagues elsewhere, done their best to manage and improve a difficult situation. They should be given credit for that.

---

[37] Yates, Hume and Hastings, *Religion and Society*, 35–6, 94–6, 104.

BIBLIOGRAPHY

ABGRALL, J., 'Les pierres à empreintes—les pierres à bassins', *Bulletin de la société archéologique du Finistère*, 17 (1890) 62–72.

ACHESON, A., *A History of the Church of Ireland 1691–1996* (Dublin 1997).

ACKERMAN, R.W., *Backgrounds to Medieval English Literature* (New York 1966).

AKENSON, D.H., *The Church of Ireland: Ecclesiastical Reform and Revolution, 1800–1885* (New Haven 1971).

ALLCHIN, A.M., *Praise Above All. Discovering the Welsh Tradition* (Cardiff 1991).

ALLEN, J. Romilly, 'Catalogue of the early Christian monuments in Pembrokeshire', *Arch. Camb.* Third Series 13 (1896) 290–306.

ANDERSON, A.O and M.O. (edd.), *Adomnán's* Life *of Columba* (Oxford 1991).

ANDERSON, Jørgen, *The Witch on the Wall: Medieval Erotic Sculpture in the British Isles* (London 1977).

ANON., 'Aberystwyth meeting report', *Arch. Camb.* Fifth Series 14 (1897) 164–6.

———, 'Ancient church to be rescued from neglect', *Western Mail*, 12 July 1988.

——— (ed.), *Breuiaria ad usum ritumque sacrosanctem Nidrosiensem* (Oslo 1964).

———, Cardiff Public Library, *Catalogue of manuscripts, books, engravings, references, etc., relating to St David, St David's Day, St David in romance, and the cathedral church of St Davids, Pembrokeshire* (Cardiff 1927).

———, 'Folk-lore of the Cardiganshire coast', *Welsh Gazette* 4 January, 11 January, 18 January 1912.

———, 'A history of Warpool Court and its owners' (manuscript history of Warpool Court, n.d.).

———, 'St David and Cardiganshire', *Welsh Gazette*, 29 February 1912.

'ARGUS' 'Correspondence', *Transactions of the Cardiganshire Antiquarian Soc.* 1.3 (1913) 36.

ARMSTRONG, E.C.R., 'Irish bronze pins of the Christian period', *Archaeologia* 72 (1921–2) 71–86.

ARNOLD-FOSTER, F., *Studies in Church Dedications of England's Patron Saints* (London 1899).

AVRIL, F. and P.D. STIRNEMANN, *Manuscrits enluminés d'origine insulaire VIIe–XXe siècle* (Paris 1987).

AYLMER, G. and J. TILLER (edd.), *Hereford Cathedral: A History* (London 2000).

AYSCOUGH, S. and J. CALEY (edd.), *Taxatio ecclesiastica Angliae et Walliae auctoritate P. Nicolai IV circa A.D. 1291* (London 1802).

BACHELLÉRY, E., Nécrologie A. W. Wade-Evans, *Études celtiques* 11 (1964–5) 165–8.

BARING-GOULD, S. 'Exploration of St. Non's Chapel, near St. Davids', *Arch. Camb.* Fifth Series 15 (1898) 345–8.

———, *The Lives of the Saints,* 16 vols (London 1873–98).

——— and J. FISHER, *The Lives of the British saints. The saints of Wales and Cornwall and such Irish saints as have dedications in Britain*, 4 vols (London 1907–13).

BARLOW, F. (ed.), *English Episcopal Acta*, XI, *Exeter 1046–1184* (Oxford 1996).

——— (ed.), *English Episcopal Acta*, XII, *Exeter 1186–1257* (Oxford 1996).

BARNES, T. and N. YATES (edd.), *Carmarthenshire Studies: Essays presented to Major Francis Jones* (Carmarthen 1974).

BARNWELL, E.L., 'The lately discovered crosses at St. David's', *Arch. Camb.* Third Series 13 (1867) 67–9.

BARROW, G.W.S. with W.W. SCOTT (ed.) *Regesta Regum Scottorum* II, *The Acts of William I King of Scots 1165–1214* (Edinburgh 1971).

Bibliography

BARROW, J. (ed.), *English Episcopal Acta*, VII, *Hereford 1079–1234* (Oxford 1993).

—— (ed.), *St Davids Episcopal Acta 1085–1280*, South Wales Record Society 13 (Cardiff 1998).

——, 'Appendix I: The constitution of Hereford Cathedral in the thirteenth century', in Aylmer and J. Tiller (ed.), *Hereford Cathedral*, 633–6.

—— (ed.), *Fasti Ecclesiae Anglicanae 1066–1300*, VIII, *Hereford* (London 2002).

BARTLETT, R., *Gerald of Wales 1146–1223* (Oxford 1982).

BARTRUM, P.C. (ed.), *Early Welsh Genealogical Tracts* (Cardiff 1966).

BAT-YEHOUDA, M.Z. and C.S., 'La description des matériaux des manuscrits hébreux: vingt-cinq ans d'expérience', in Maniaci and Munafò (edd.), *Ancient and medieval book materials*, 333–53.

BERNARD, Daniel, 'Études sur le Cap-Sizun—III. À propos de la chapelle de Monsieur Sainct-They, en Cléden-Sap-Sizun', *Bulletin de la Société archéologique du Finistère* 37 (1910) 145–60.

BERNARD, J., *Navires et gens de mer à Bordeaux (vers 1400-vers 1550)* (Paris 1968).

BEST, R.I. and H.J. LAWLOR (edd.), *The Martyrology of Tallaght* (London 1931).

BETHELL, D., 'The Making of a twelfth century relic collection', in Cuming and Baker (edd.), *Popular Belief*, 61–65.

BEVAN, R.E., 'Notes on Llanarth and neighbourhood' *Trans. Cardiganshire Antiquarian. Soc.* 4 (1926) 60–70.

BIELER, L., '*Anecdotum Patricianum*', *Measgra i gCuimhne Mhichil Uí Chléirigh* (Dublin 1944) 220–37.

—— (ed.), *The Irish Penitentials*, Scriptores Latini Hiberniae 5 (Dublin 1963).

BINCHY, D.A., 'Patrick and his biographers: ancient and modern', *Studia Hibernica* 2 (1962) 7–173.

BISCHOFF, B. and B. LÖFSTEDT (edd.), '*Anonymus ad Cuimnanum*': *Expositio Latinitatis*, Corpus Christianorum Series Latina 133D (Turnhout 1992).

BLACKBURN, M.A.S. and M.J. BONSER, 'Single finds of Anglo-Saxon and Norman coins – 2', *British Numismatic Jnl* 55 (1985) 55–78.

BLAIR, J. and R. SHARPE (edd.), *Pastoral Care Before the Parish* (Leicester 1992).

BLAKE, David, 'The development of the chapter of the diocese of Exeter, 1050–1161', *Jnl of Medieval History* 8 (1982) 1–11.

BLEW, W. (ed.), *Breuiarij Aberdonensis ad percelebris ecclesie Scotorum potissimus usum et consuetudinem*. Facsimile edition published by the Bannatyne Club (London 1854).

BOAKE, E.J., 'Report on the excavation of the chapel at St Justinian, St David's', *Arch. Camb.* 81 (1926) 381–94.

BONNIWELL, William R., *A History of the Dominican Liturgy* (New York 1944).

BORMANS, S. and E. SCHOOLMEESTERS (edd.), *Cartulaire de l'Eglise Saint-Lambert de Liège*, 6 vols (Brussels 1893–1935).

BOWEN, E.G., 'Celtic saints in Cardiganshire', *Ceredigion*, 1 (1950–51) 3–17.

——, *Dewi Sant—Saint David* (Cardiff 1983).

——, *The St David of History—Dewi Sant: Our Founder Saint* (Abertystwyth 1981).

——, *Saints, Seaways and Settlement in the Celtic Lands* (Cardiff 1969); 2nd edn (Cardiff 1977).

——, *The Settlements of the Celtic Saints in Wales* (Cardiff 1954).

BOWEN JONES, T., 'The Life of St. David by Giraldus Cambrensis' (MA thesis, University of Wales Cardiff 1934).

BRADSHAW, H. and C. WORDSWORTH (edd.), *Statutes of Lincoln Cathedral*, 3 vols (Cambridge 1892–7).

BRAMLEY, K.A., *et al.* (edd.), *Gwaith Llywelyn Fardd I ac eraill o Feirdd y Ddeuddegfed Ganrif* (Cardiff 1994).

BREEZE, A., '*Armes Prydein*, Hywel Dda, and the reign of Edmund of Wessex', *Études celtiques* 33 (1997) 209–22.

BRETT, C., 'John Leland, Wales, and early British history', *WHR* 15 (1990–1) 169–82.

——, Review of Jankulak, *The Medieval Cult*, *CMCS* 44 (2002) 107–9.

BREWER, J.S., J.F. DIMOCK and G.F. WARNER (edd.), *Giraldi Cambrensis Opera*, 8 vols, Rolls Series XXI (1861–91).

BROMWICH, Rachel (ed. and transl.), *Trioedd Ynys Prydein. The Welsh Triads*, 2nd edn (Cardiff 1978).

BRONK RAMSEY, C., 'Development of the radiocarbon calibration program', *Radiocarbon* 43 (2001) 355–63.

———— and R.E.M. HEDGES, 'Hybrid ion sources: radiocarbon measurements from microgram to milligram', *Nuclear Instruments and Methods in Physics Research* B 123 (1999) 539–545.

————, P.B. PETTITT, R.E.M. HEDGES, G.W.L. HODGINS and D.C. OWEN, 'Radiocarbon dates from the Oxford AMS system: archaeometry datelist 30', *Archaeometry* 42 (2000) 459–479.

BROOKE, C.N.L., 'The archbishops of St Davids, Llandaff and Caerleon-on-Usk', in Chadwick (ed.), *Studies in the Early British Church*, 201–242.

————, 'The Canterbury forgeries and their author', *Downside Review* 68 (1950) 462–76; 69 (1951) 210–31.

BROWN, M.P., *Understanding Illuminated Manuscripts. A Guide to Technical Terms* (London 1994).

BROWN, R.A. (ed.), *Proceedings of the Battle Conference on Anglo-Norman Studies. III. 1980* (Woodbridge 1981).

BROWN, Roger L., 'Traitors and compromisers: the shadow side of the Church's fight against disestablishment', *Jnl of Welsh Religious History* 3 (1995) 35–50.

BRYANT-QUINN, M. Paul (ed.), *Gwaith Ieuan ap Llywelyn Fychan, Ieuan Llwyd Brydydd a Lewys Aled* (Aberystwyth 2003).

BURGESS, T. [Bishop], *Bishops and Benefactors of St David's Vindicated* (Carmarthen 1812).

————, *Tracts on the Origin and Independence of the Ancient British Church* (London 1815).

BUTLER, H.E. (ed.), *Autobiography of Giraldus Cambrensis* (London 1937).

Calendar of the Patent Rolls preserved in the Public Record Office (London 1891–).

CAMPBELL, E. and A. LANE, 'Excavations at Longbury Bank, Dyfed, an early medieval Settlement in South Wales', *Medieval Archaeology* 37 (1993) 15–77.

CAMPBELL, T.A., *The Religion of the Heart: A Study of European Religious Life in the Seventeenth and Eighteenth Centuries* (Columbia 1991).

CAPES, W.W. (ed.), *Charters and Records of Hereford Cathedral*, Cantilupe Society, vol. 3 (1908).

CARLEY, J.P. and D.R. TOWNSEND (edd.), *The Chonicle of Glastonbury Abbey* (Woodbridge 1985).

CARLISLE, N., *A Topographical Dictionary of the Dominion of Wales* (London 1811).

CARPENTER, D.A., *The Minority of Henry III* (London 1990).

CARTWRIGHT, Jane (ed.), *Celtic Hagiography and Saints' Cults* (Cardiff 2003).

————, 'Dead virgins: feminine sanctity in medieval Wales', *Medium Ævum* 71 (2002) 1–28.

————, *Feminine Sanctity and Spirituality in Medieval Wales* (Cardiff, forthcoming).

————, *Y Forwyn Fair, Santesau a Lleianod* (Cardiff 1999).

CARVER, M. (ed.), *In Search of Cult: Archaeological Investigations in honour of Philip Rahtz* (Woodbridge 1993).

CASSARD, J.C., 'Les marins bretons à Bordeaux au début du XIVe siècle', *Annales de Bretagne* 86 (1979) 379–97.

Catalogue général des manuscrits des Bibliotheques Publiques des Départements, vol. VI (Paris 1878).

CHADWICK, N.K., 'Early intellectual life in west Wales', in Chadwick (ed.), *Studies in the Early British Church*, 121–182.

———— (ed.), *Studies in the Early British Church* (Cambridge 1958).

———— (ed.), *Studies in Early British History* (Cambridge, 1959).

CHADWICK, O., 'The evidence of dedications in the early history of the Welsh church', in Chadwick (ed.), *Studies in Early British History*, 173–188.

CHARLES, B.G., 'The Barlows of Slebech', *NLWJ* 5 (1948) 179–98.

—— (ed.), *A Calendar of the Records of the Borough of Haverfordwest 1539–1669* (Cardiff 1967).

——, *George Owen of Henllys: A Welsh Elizabethan* (Aberystwyth 1973).

——, *The Place-Names of Pembrokeshire* (Aberystwyth 1992).

CHARLES-EDWARDS, T.M., *Bishops, Saints and Clasau: The Background to the History of the Diocese of St Asaph*, The Hellins Lectures on the History of the Diocese of St Asaph, 1 (St Asaph, 2003).

——, *Early Christian Ireland* (Cambridge 2000).

——, 'The seven bishop-houses of Dyfed', *BBCS* 24 (1970–2) 247–62.

CHENEY, C.R., *English Synodalia of the Thirteenth Century*, 2nd edn (Oxford 1968).

CHENEY, M.G., *Roger, Bishop of Worcester 1164–1179* (Oxford 1980).

CLANCY, T.O., 'The real St Ninian', *Innes Review* 52 (2001) 1–28.

CLARK, J.C.D., *English Society 1688–1832* (Cambridge 1985).

CLOVER, H. and M. GIBSON (edd.), *The Letters of Lanfranc archbishop of Canterbury* (Oxford 1979).

COHEN, M.R., *Under Crescent and Cross: The Jews in the Middle Ages* (Princeton NJ 1994).

COLDSTREAM, Nicola, 'English decorated shrine bases', *Jnl of the British Archaeological Association* 129 (1976) 15–34.

COLGAN, John, *Acta Sanctorum Hiberniae* (Louvain 1645).

COLLEY, L., *Britons: Forging the Nation 1707–1837* (New Haven 1992).

COLLINGWOOD, R.G., *The Idea of History* (Oxford 1946).

CORSON, Guillotin, de, *Les pardons et les pèlerinages du pays de Vannes* (Rennes 1898).

COSTIGAN, N.G. *et al.* (edd.), *Gwaith Dafydd Benfras ac Eraill o Feirdd Hanner Cyntaf y Drydedd Ganrif ar Ddeg*, Cyfres Beirdd y Tywysogion, 6 (Cardiff 1995).

COURSON, A. de, *Cartulaire de l'abbaye de Redon en Bretagne* (Paris 1863).

COWLEY, F.G., 'A note on the discovery of St. David's body', *BBCS* 19 (1960) 47–8.

——, *The Monastic Order in South Wales, 1066–1349* (Cardiff 1977).

——, 'The Regular Clergy, 1093–15401, *Pembrokeshire County History*, Vol. 2 (2002), chap. 23.

COZAN, Jean-Yves *et al.*, *La Bretagne au temps des Ducs* (Daoulas 1991).

CRAGOE, M., *An Anglican Aristocracy: the Moral Economy of the Landed Estate in Carmarthenshire, 1832–1895* (Oxford 1996).

CRAWFORD, O.G.S., *Said and Done* (London 1955).

——, 'Western seaways', in D. Buxton (ed.), *Custom is King: Studies in Honour of R.R. Marett* (London 1936), 181–200.

CROUCH, D. (ed.), *Llandaff Episcopal Acta 1140–1287*, South Wales Record Society, 5 (Cardiff 1988).

——, *William Marshal: Court, Career and Chivalry in the Angevin Empire 1147–1219* (London 1990).

CUISSARD, C. (ed.), 'Vie de saint Paul de Léon en Bretagne d'après un manuscrit de Fleury-sur-Loire conservé à la Bibliothèque publique d'Orléans', *Revue celtique* 5 (1881–3) 413–60.

CUMING, G.J. and D. BAKER (edd.), *Popular Belief and Practice* (Studies in Church History no. 8: Cambridge 1972).

CUNLIFFE, B., *Facing the Ocean: The Atlantic and its peoples 8000 BC–AD 1500* (Oxford 2001).

CUNNINGHAM, B. and R. GILLESPIE, 'The cult of St David in Ireland before 1700', in [Morgan] Guy and Neely (edd.), *Contrasts and Comparisons*, 26–42.

CURLEY, M.J., 'Five *lecciones* for the feast of St Nonita: a text and its context', *CMCS* 43 (2002) 59–75.

DAHL, S., 'The Norse settlement of the Faroe Islands', *Medieval Archaeology* 14 (1970) 60–73.

DALTON, J.N. (ed.), *Ordinale Exon* (London 1926).

DANIEL, I. *et al.* (edd.), *Cyfoeth y testun: ysgrifau ar lenyddiaeth Gymraeg y oesoedd canol* (Cardiff 2003).

DARK, K., *Britain and the End of the Roman Empire* (Stroud, 2000).

DARLINGTON, R.R. *et al.* (edd.), *The Chronicle of John of Worcester*, 3 vols (Oxford 1995)

DAVIDSON, A. (ed.), *The Coastal Archaeology of Wales*, CBA Research Report 131 (York 2002).

DAVIES, D.S. (ed.), *The Welsh Life of St David* (Cardiff 1988).

DAVIES, J.C., *Folk-Lore of West and Mid-Wales* (Aberystwyth 1911).

DAVIES, J. Conway, *Episcopal Acts and Cognate Documents Relating to Welsh Dioceses 1066–1272*, 2 vols (Cardiff 1944–6).

———, 'The Black Book of St. Davids', *NLWJ* 4 (1945–6) 158–76.

DAVIES, J.L. and D.P. KIRBY (edd.), *From Earliest times to the Coming of the Normans: Cardiganshire County History* Vol. I (Cardiff 1994).

DAVIES, J.R., 'The Book of Llandaf: a twelfth-century perspective', in Harper-Bill (ed.) *Anglo-Norman Studies XXI*, 31–46.

———, *The Book of Llandaf and the Norman Church in Wales* (Woodbridge, 2003).

———, '*Liber Landavensis*: its date and the identity of its editor', *CMCS* 35 (1998) 1–11.

———, 'The saints of south Wales and the Welsh church', in Thacker and Sharpe (edd.) *Local Saints*, 361–95.

DAVIES M., 'Field systems of South Wales; G: Cardiganshire' in A.R.H. Baker and R.A. Butlin (edd.), *Studies of Field Systems in the British Isles* (Cambridge 1973) 522–9.

DAVIES, R.R., *The Age of Conquest: Wales 1063–1415* [pbk reprint of *Conquest, Coexistence, and Change*] (Oxford 1991).

——— (ed.), *The British Isles 1100–1500 Comparisons, Contrasts* (Edinburgh 1988).

———, *Conquest, Coexistence, and Change: Wales 1063–1415* (Oxford 1987).

DAVIES, Wendy, 'Braint Teilo', *BBCS* 26 (1975) 123–37.

———, 'Charter-writing and its uses in early medieval Celtic societies', in Pryce (ed.) *Literacy*, 99–112.

———, 'The consecration of bishops of Llandaff in the tenth and eleventh centuries', *BBCS* 26 (1974–76) 53–73.

———, *An Early Welsh Microcosm. Studies in the Llandaff Charters* (London 1978)

———, 'The Latin charter-tradition in western Britain, Brittany and Ireland in the early mediaeval period', in Whitelock *et al.* (edd.), *Ireland in Early Mediaeval Europe*, 258–80.

———, *The Llandaff Charters* (Aberystwyth 1979).

———, *Patterns of Power in Early Wales* (Oxford 1990).

———, *Wales in the Early Middle Ages* (Leicester 1982).

DAVIES, W.S. (ed.), 'Giraldus Cambrensis: *De Invectionibus*', *Y Cymmrodor* 30 (1920).

DAWSON, M.L., 'The monastery of Rosnat or Tygwyn, Pembrokeshire', *Arch. Camb.* fifth series 15 (1898) 1–20.

DE CLERQ, C. (ed.), *Concilia Galliae A. 511–A. 695*, Corpus Christianorum, series Latina, 148A (Turnhout 1963).

DE GREGORIO, S., 'Texts, *topoi* and the self: a reading of Alfredian spirituality', *Early Medieval Europe* 13 (2005) 79–96.

DE GUISE, Elizabeth, *The Story of Non(ne). The Mother of St David* (St Non's Retreat n.d.).

DE KERDANET, D.-L. M. (ed.), *Les vies des saints de la Bretagne Armorique par Fr Albert Le Grand* (Brest 1837).

DE VORAGINE, Jacobus, *The Golden Legend*, transl. William Granger Ryan, 2 vols (Princeton 1993).

DELAFOSSE, M., 'Marins et marchands bretons à la Rochelle au Xve et XVIe siècles', *Mémoires de la Société d'Histoire et d'Archéologie de Bretagne* 33 (1953) 53–71.

DELEHAYE, H., *Cinq leçons sur la méthode hagiographique* (Brussels 1934).

———, *The Legends of the Saints*, trans. D. Attwater (London 1955).

DENHOLM-YOUNG, N., *Handwriting in England and Wales* (Cardiff 1954).

DESHAYES, A., *Dictionnaire des noms de lieux bretons* (Douarnenez 1999).

DEWEY, J., *Art as Experience* (New York 1958).

———, *Democracy and Education* ([1916]; New York 1944).

———, *Education Today* (New York 1940).

DICKINSON, J.C., *The Shrine of Our Lady of Walsingham* (Cambridge 1956).

DIMOCK, J. (ed.), *Giraldi Cambrensis Opera*—see BREWER, *et al.*.

DOBIACHE-ROJDESTVENSKY, Olga, *La vie paroissiale en France au XIIIe siècle d'après les actes épiscopaux* (Paris 1911).

DOBLE, G.H., 'The Leominster Relic List' *Trans. of the Woolhope Naturalist's Field Club* 31 (1942) 58–65.

———, *Lives of the Welsh Saints*, edited with an introduction by D. Simon Evans (Cardiff 1971).

———, *St Constantine, King and Monk, and St. Merryn,* Cornish Saints series 26 (Truro 1930).

———, *Saint Day, Monk and Confessor, Patron of St Day in Cornwall. With notes on the ancient chapel of Holy Trinity at St Day.* Cornish Saints Series no. 32 (Exeter 1933).

———, *Saint Nonna, patron of Altarnon and Pelynt. With an Essay on the Cult of St Nonna in Cornwall by Charles Henderson, MA.* Cornish Saints Series no. 16 (Liskeard 1928).

———, *The Saints of Cornwall*, ed. D. Attwater, 6 vols (Truro 1960–97).

DOBSZAY, László (ed.), *The Past in the Present. Papers Read at the IMS Intercongressional Symposium and the 10th Meeting of the CANTUS PLANUS, Budapest & Visegrád*, 2 vols (Budapest 2003).

DODGSHON, R., 'Early society and economy', in Davies and Kirby (edd.), *From Earliest Times*, I.343–364.

DODWELL, B. (ed.), *The Charters of Norwich Cathedral Priory*, Pipe Roll Society, new ser. 40, 46 (1974–85).

DRIVER T., 'The Road to Menapia after all?' *Archaeology in Wales* 42 (2002) 60–1.

DU MÉRIL, E. (ed.), *Poésies populaires latines du moyen age*, 2 vols (Paris, 1843 and 1847).

DUGDALE, W., *Monasticon Anglicanum*, ed. J. Caley, H. Ellis and B. Bandinel, 6 vols in 8 (London 1817–30).

DUINE, F., 'Bréviaires et Missels des églises et abbayes bretonnes de France antérieures au XVIIe siècle', *Bulletin et Mémoires de la Société archéologique d'Ille-et-Vilaine* 35 (1906) 1–219.

———, 'Inventaire liturgique de l'hagiographie bretonne', *Bulletin et Mémoires de la Société archéologique d'Ille-et-Vilaine* 49 (1922).

———, *Memento des sources hagiographiques de l'histoire de Bretagne. Première partie: les fondateurs et les primitifs (du Ve au Xe siècle)* (Rennes 1918).

———, *Saints de Domnonée* (Rennes, nd).

DUMVILLE, D.N. (ed. and transl.), *Annales Cambriae, A.D. 682–954: Texts A–C in Parallel*, Basic Texts for Brittonic History, I (Cambridge 2002).

———, 'Brittany and "Armes Prydein Vawr"', *Études celtiques* 20 (1983) 145–59.

———, '*Félire Óengusso*: problems of dating a monument of Old Irish', *Éigse* 33 (2003) 19–48.

———, *Liturgy and the Ecclesiastical History of Late Anglo-Saxon England* (Woodbridge 1992).

———, Review of D.S. Evans, *The Welsh Life*, *Jnl of Welsh Ecclesiastical History* 5 (1988) 99–101.

———, Review of A.P. Smyth, *Alfred the Great*, *CMCS* 31 (1996) 90–3.

——, *Saint David of Wales*, Kathleen Hughes Memorial Lectures on Mediaeval Welsh History 1 (Cambridge 2002).

——, 'Some aspects of the chronology of the *Historia Brittonum*', *BBCS* 24 (1974) 439–45.

——, 'Sub-Roman Britain: history and legend', *History* 62 (1977) 173–92.

—— and KEYNES, S. D. (gen. edd.), *The Anglo-Saxon Chronicle. A Collaborative Edition* 23 vols (Cambridge 1983—).

—— and LAPIDGE, M. (edd.), *The Annals of St Neots with Vita Prima Sancti Neoti* (Cambridge 1984).

DYBDAHL, A., O.K. LEDANG and N.H. PETERSEN (edd.), *Gregorian Chant and Medieval Music, Proceedings from The Nordic Festival and Conference of Gregorian Chant Trondheim, St. Olavs Wake 1997* (Trondheim 1998).

DYKES, D.W., 'Anglo-Saxon coins in the National Museum of Wales', *Amgueddfa, Bulletin of the National Museum of Wales* 24 (1976) 2–31.

EDWARDS, H.T., *Wales and the Welsh Church* (London 1889).

EDWARDS, J. (ed.), *Footprints of Faith* (Llanelli Borough Council *ca* 1989).

EDWARDS, J.G., *Calendar of Ancient Correspondence concerning Wales* (Cardiff 1935).

—— (ed.), *Littere Wallie preserved in Liber A in the Public Record Office* (Cardiff 1940).

EDWARDS, Kathleen, *The English Secular Cathedrals in the Middle Ages* (Manchester 1949), 2nd edn (1967).

EDWARDS, N., 'Celtic saints and early medieval archaeology' in Sharpe and Thacker (edd.), *Local Saints*, 225–265.

——, *Corpus of Early Medieval Inscribed Stones and Stone Sculpture in Wales,* Vol. 2, forthcoming.

—— (ed.), *Landscape and Settlement in Medieval Wales* (Oxford 1997).

——, 'Monuments in a landscape; the early medieval sculpture of St David's', in Hamerow and MacGregor (edd.), *Image and Power*, 53–77.

——, 'Stones and stone sculpture in Wales: context and function', *Medieval Archaeology* 45 (2001) 15–39.

—— and A. LANE (edd.), *The Early Church in Wales and the West* (Oxford 1992).

——, *Early Medieval Settlements in Wales AD 400–1100* (Cardiff 1988).

EDWARDS, Owain Tudor, 'How many Sarum antiphonals were there in England and Wales in the middle of the sixteenth century?' *Revue Bénédictine,* 99 (1989) 155–180.

——, *Matins, Lauds and Vespers for St David's Day. The Medieval Office of the Welsh Patron Saint in National Library of Wales MS 20541 E* (Cambridge 1990).

——, 'Musical source material for a study of the medieval use of Nidaros', in Dybdahl, *et al.* (edd.), *Gregorian Chant and Medieval Music*, 59–83.

——, 'Musical symbolism in two medieval liturgical celebrations', in Dobszay (ed.), *The Past in the Present*, II.271–290.

—— (ed.), *National Library of Wales MS 20541 E. The Penpont Antiphonal*, Ottawa, Canada 1997).

——, 'Symbolism in the legend of St. David', Gillingham and Merkley (edd.), *Chant and its Peripheries*, 143–158.

EHWALD, Rudolf (ed.), *Aldhelmi Opera* (Berlin 1919).

EMANUEL, H.D., 'An analysis of the composition of the Vita Cadoci', *NLWJ* 7 (1951–2), 217–27.

——, 'The Latin Life of St Cadoc: a textual and lexicographical study', unpublished MA dissertation (Aberystwyth 1950).

——, 'Notes on the use of Celtic Saints' festivals in dating', *NLWJ* 9 (1955–6) 110–2.

——, Review of J.W. James, *Rhigyfarch's Life, Jnl of the Historical Soc. of the Church in Wales* 22 (1967) 40–2.

ERNAULT, E. 'La vie de sainte Nonne', *Revue celtique*, 8 (1887) 230–301 and 405–91.

ETCHINGHAM, C., 'Bishoprics in Ireland and Wales in the early middle ages', in [Morgan-] Guy and Neely (edd.), *Contrasts and Comparisons*, 7–25.

EVANS, D. Simon, *A Grammar of Middle Welsh* (Dublin 1964).

EVANS, D.S. (ed.), *Buched Dewi o lawysgrif Llanstephan 27* (Cardiff 1959).

────── (ed.), *Historia Gruffud vab Kenan* (Cardiff 1977).

────── (ed.), *The Welsh Life of St David* (Cardiff 1988).

EVANS, E., *Daniel Rowland and the Great Evangelical Awakening in Wales* (Edinburgh 1985).

──────, 'Early medieval ecclesiastical sites in south-east Wales: rapid field survey of selected sites', unpublished Glamorgan-Gwent Archaeological Trust Report 2004/019.

EVANS, George Eyre, *Cardiganshire: A Personal Survey of Some of its Antiquities, Chapels, Churches, Fonts, Plate and Registers* (Aberystwyth 1903).

──────, *Lampeter* (Aberystwyth, 1905).

EVANS, H., *The Tŵr Y Felin Guide to St Davids*, 2nd edn (St Davids 1923).

EVANS, J.G. with RHYS, J. (edd.), *The Text of the Book of Llan Dâv* (Oxford 1893).

EVANS, J.Wyn, 'The Anglican church in Llanelli', in Edwards (ed.), *Footprints of Faith*, 1– 29.

──────, 'Anglicaniaeth', *Diwinyddiaeth* 32 (1981) 10–25.

──────, 'Aspects of the Early Church in Carmarthenshire', in James (ed.), *Sir Gâr*, 239– 253.

──────, 'Bishops of St Davids from Bernard to Bec', in R.F. Walker (ed.), *Pembrokeshire County History*, 270–311.

──────, 'The bishops of St Davids from Bernard to Bec' in R.F. Walker (ed.) *Medieval Pembrokeshire*, 273–275.

──────, 'The early church in Denbighshire', *Denbighshire Historical Soc. Transactions* 35 (1986) 61–82.

──────, 'Meidrum: some sidelights on the Church and Parish', *Carmarthenshire Antiquary* 29 (1993) 13–22.

──────, 'The Reformation and St Davids Cathedral', *JWEH* 7 (1991) 1–16.

──────, 'St David and St Davids: some observations on the cult, site and buildings' in Cartwright (ed.), *Celtic Hagiography*, 10–25.

──────, 'St Davids Cathedral, the lost centuries', *JWEH* 3 (1986) 73–92.

──────, 'The survival of the *clas* as an institution in mediaeval Wales: some observations on Llanbadarn Fawr', in Edwards and Lane, *The Early Church*, 33–40.

──────, 'St David and St Davids and the coming of the Normans', *Trans Honourable Soc. Cymmrodorion (new series)* 11 (2005) 5–18.

────── and R. TURNER, *St Davids Bishop's Palace. St Non's Chapel* (Cardiff rev. ed. 1999).

────── and R. WORSLEY, *Eglwys Gadeiriol Tyddewi 1181–1981: St Davids Cathedral* (St Davids 1981).

EVANS, R. and L. JOHNSON (edd.), *Feminist Readings in Middle English Literature: The Wife of Bath and All her Sect* (London 1994).

FALC'HUN, François, *Dirinon* (La Guerche-de-Bretagne 1986).

FALILEYEV, A., *An Etymological Glossary of Old Welsh* (Tübingen 2000).

FANNING, T., 'Some bronze ringed pins from the Irish midlands', *Jourrnal of the Old Athlone Soc.* 1 (1974–5) 211–15.

──────, *Viking Age Ringed Pins from Dublin*, Medieval Dublin Excavations 1962–81, Ser. B, vol. 4 (Dublin 1994).

FARMER, D.H., *Oxford Dictionary of Saints* (Oxford 1992).

FARMER, Sharon, *Communities of St Martin: Legend and Ritual in Medieval Tours* (Ithaca NY 1991).

FEILDEN, H.S.C., *A short constitutional history of England* (Oxford 1899).

FENTON, Richard, *A Historical Tour Through Pembrokeshire* (London 1811).

FERGUSON, J., *The Parochial Libraries of Bishop Wilson* (Douglas 1975).

FINBERG, H.P.R. (ed.), *The Agrarian History of England and Wales* (Cambridge 1972).

FISHER, John, 'MSS. in the St. Asaph Cathedral library', *BBCS* 1 (1921–3) 166–7

──────, 'Welsh church dedications', *Transactions of the Honourable Society of the Cyrmmrodorion* (1906–7) 76–108.

FLEURE, H.J. and J.E. ROBERTS, 'Archaeological problems of the west coast of Britain', *Archaeologia Cambrensis* 70 (1915) 405–20.

FLEURIOT, L. (ed.), 'Les évêques de la *Clas Kenedyr*, évêché disparu de la region de Hereford', *Études celtiques* 15 (1976–8) 225–6.

FLOBERT, P. (ed.), *La Vie ancienne de Saint Samson de Dol* (Paris 1997).

FOORD, E., *St Davids, Llandaff and Brecon* (London 1925).

FORBES, A.P. (ed.), *Lives of S. Ninian and S. Kentigern Compiled in the Twelfth Century* (Edinburgh 1874) 123–33.

[————], *Two Celtic Saints: The Lives of Ninian and Kentigern* (Felinfach 1989).

FOX, C., 'An Irish bronze pin from Anglesey', *Arch. Camb.* 95 (1940) 248.

FREEMAN, P., 'The contribution of some Tractarians in mid-nineteenth century Wales to Welsh poetry and hymnology', *NLWJ* 32 (2001) 73–93.

FRERE, W.H. (ed.), *The Use of Sarum*, 2 vols (Cambridge 1898–1901).

FRERE, W.H. and L.E.G. BROWN (edd.), *The Hereford Breviary* (London 1911).

FRIEDMAN, T., *The Georgian Parish Church, 'Monuments to Posterity'* (Reading 2004).

GALBRAITH, V.H., *An Introduction to the Study of History* (London 1964).

GARDNER, W.H. and N.H. MACKENZIE (edd.), *The Poems of Gerard Manley Hopkins*, 4th edn (Oxford 1970).

GILLINGHAM, B. and P. MERKLEY (edd.), *Chant and its Peripheries, Essays in honour of Terence Bailey* (Ottawa 1998).

GJERLØW, Lilli (ed.), *Antifonarium Nidrosiensis ecclesiae* (Oslo 1979).

———— (ed.), *Ordo Nidrosiensis Ecclesiae*, Oslo 1968)

GNEUSS, Helmut, 'A preliminary list of manuscripts written or owned in England up to 1100', *Anglo-Saxon England* 9 (1981) 1–60.

GRAHAM, Rose, 'The abbey of St Peter at Gloucester', *Victoria County History, Gloucestershire*, vol. 2 (1907), 53–61.

GRAHAM-CAMPBELL, J., 'The early Viking Age in the Irish Sea area', in H.B. Clarke *et al* (edd.), *Ireland and Scandinavia in the Early Viking Age* (Dublin 1998), 104–30.

GRANSDEN, A. (ed.), *The Chronicle of Bury St Edmunds 1212–1301* (London 1964).

GRAY, M., *Images of piety: the iconography of traditional religion in late medieval Wales*, BAR British Series 316 (Oxford 2000).

GREEN, C.A.H., *The Setting of the Constitution of the Church in Wales* (London 1937).

GREEN, I.M., *The Re-Establishment of the Church of England* (Oxford 1978).

GREENWAY, D.E., 'The false *Institutio* of St Osmund', in Greenway *et al.* (edd.), *Tradition and Change*, 77–101.

———— (ed.), *Fasti Ecclesiae Anglicanae 1066–1300*: I, *St Paul's, London* (London 1968).

———— (ed.), *Fasti Ecclesiae Anglicanae 1066–1300*: III, *Lincoln* (London 1977).

———— (ed.), *Fasti Ecclesiae Anglicanae 1066–1300*: IV, *Salisbury* (London 1991).

———— (ed.), *Fasti Ecclesiae Anglicanae 1066–1300*: V, *Chichester* (London 1996).

———— (ed.), *Fasti Ecclesiae Anglicanae 1066–1300*: VI, *York* (London 1999).

———— (ed.), *Fasti Ecclesiae Anglicanae 1066–1300*: VII, *Bath and Wells* (London 2001).

———— (ed.), *Fasti Ecclesiae Anglicanae 1066–1300*, X, *Exeter* (London, 2005).

GREENWAY, D., C. HOLDSWORTH and J. SAYERS (edd.), *Tradition and Change: Essays in Honour of Marjorie Chibnall* (Cambridge 1985).

GRIFFITH, W.P. (ed.) *'Ysbryd Dealltwrus ac Enaid Anfarwol': Ysgrifau ar Hanes Crefydd yng Ngwynedd* (Bangor 1999).

GRIMES, W.F., 'A leaden tablet of Scandinavian origin from South Pembrokeshire', *Arch. Camb.* 85 (1930) 416–17.

GROSJEAN, P., 'Édition et commentaire du commentaire du *Catalogus sanctorum Hiberniae secundum diversa tempora* ou *De tribus ordinibus sanctorum Hiberniae*', *Analecta Bollandiana* 73 (1955) 197–213, 289–322.

————, Review of Margaret R. Toynbee, *S. Louis of Toulouse and the Process of Canonisation in the Fourteenth Century*, *Analecta Bollandiana* 49 (1931) 210–16.

GRUFFYDD, G. and H.P. OWEN, 'The earliest mention of St David?: an addendum', *BBCS* 19 (1960–2) 231–2.

GUILLOUX, Abbé, 'Études sur une paroisse bretonne. Brandivy', *Revue historique de l'Ouest* 6 (1890) 427–74.

HADDAN, A.W. and W. STUBBS (edd.), *Councils and Ecclesiastical Documents relating to Great Britain and Ireland*, 3 vols (Oxford 1869–78).

HAGUE, D.S., 'St Non's Chapel, Llanon', unpublished document, SN 56 NW, RCAHMW.

Handlist of Manuscripts in the National Library of Wales (Aberystwyth 1940–).

HALL, R. and D. STOCKER (edd.), *Vicars Choral at English Cathedrals* (Oxford, 2005).

HAMEROW, H. and A. MACGREGOR (edd.), *Image and Power in the Archaeology of Early Medieval Britain: Essays in honour of Rosemary Cramp* (Oxford 2001).

HANDLEY, M.A., 'Isidore of Seville and "Hisperic Latin" in early medieval Wales: the epigraphic culture of Llanllyr and Llanddewi Brefi', in Higgitt, *et al.* (edd.), *Roman, Runes and Ogham*, 26–36.

HARPER, S., *Music in Welsh Culture before 1650* (Aldershot, 2007).

HARPER-BILL, C. (ed.), *Anglo-Norman Studies. XXI. 1998* (Woodbridge 1999).

HARRIS, Silas M., 'The Kalendar of the *Vitae Sanctorum Wallensium*', *Jnl of the Historical Soc. of the Church in Wales* 3 (1953) 3–53.

———, 'Liturgical commemorations of Welsh saints: I', *Jnl of the Historical Soc. of the Church in Wales* 5 (1955) 5–22; 6 (1956) 5–24

———, 'A Llanbadarn Fawr Calendar', *Ceredigion* 2 (1952–55) 18–26.

———, *Saint David in the Liturgy* (Cardiff 1940)

———, 'Was St. David ever canonized?', *Wales* 4 (1945) 30–2.

HARRISON, Frank Ll., *Music in Medieval Britain* (London 1958).

HART, W.H. (ed.), *Historia et cartularium manasterii Sancti Petri Gloucestria*, 3 vols, Roll Series XXXIII (London 1888).

HARVEY, J.H. (ed.), *William Worcestre: Itineraries* (Oxford 1969).

HASLAM, Richard, *Powys. The Buildings of Wales* (London 1979).

HAYCOCK, Marged, 'Llyfr Taliesin', *NLWJ* 25 (1988) 357–86.

HEAL, F., *Reformation in Britain and Ireland* (Oxford 2003).

HEDGES, R.E.M., I.A. LAW, C.R. BRONK, and R.A. HOUSLEY, 'The Oxford accelerator mass spectrometry facility: technical developments in routine dating', *Archaeometry* 31 (1989) 99–113.

HEIST, W.W., *Vitae Sanctorum Hiberniae* (Brussels 1965).

HENDERSON, W.G., *Missale ad usum insignis ecclesiae Eboracensis*, Surtees Society Vols 59–60 (1872).

HENKEN, E.R., *Traditions of the Welsh Saints* (Cambridge 1987).

———, *The Welsh Saints: A Study in Patterned Lives* (Cambridge 1991).

HIGGITT, J., K. FORSYTH and D.N. PARSONS (edd.), *Roman, Runes and Ogham. Medieval Inscriptions in the Insular World and on the Continent* (Donington 2001).

HILL, P., *Whithorn and St Ninian* (Stroud 1997).

HINES, J., A. LANE and M. REDKNAP (edd.), *Land, Sea and Home: Proceedings of a Conference on Viking-period Settlement*, Medieval Archaeology Society Monograph 20 (2004).

HOLMES, B.J., 'The synod of Llanddewi Brefi', *Jnl of Welsh Religious History* 3 (1995) 1–14.

HORSLEY, S., *The Charge ... to the Clergy of His Diocese delivered ... in the year 1790* (London 1792).

HORSTMANN, C. (ed.), *Nova Legenda Angliae* (Oxford 1901).

HOSKIN, P. (ed.), *English Episcopal Acta, 22, Chichester 1215–1253* (Oxford 2001).

——— (ed.), *English Episcopal Acta, 23, Chichester 1254–1305* (Oxford 2001).

HOWELL, M., 'Regalian right in Wales and the march: the relation of theory to practice', *WHR* 7 (1974–5) 269–88.

HOWLETT, D.R., 'Aldhelm and Irish learning', *Archivum Latinitatis Medii Aevi* 52 (1994) 37–75.

———, 'Arithmetic rhythms in Latin letters', *Archivum Latinitatis Medii Aevi* 56 (1998) 193–225.

360

————, *The Book of Letters of Saint Patrick the Bishop* (Dublin 1994).

————, 'The Brigitine hymn *Xpistus in nostra insula*', *Peritia* 12 (1998) 79–86.

————, *British Books in Biblical Style* (Dublin 1997).

————, 'Busnois' motet *In hydraulis*: an exercise in textual reconstruction and analysis', *Plainsong and Medieval Music* 4 (1995) 185–91.

————, *Caledonian Craftsmanship: The Scottish Latin Tradition* (Dublin: Four Courts, 2000).

————, *Cambro-Latin Compositions, Sealed from Within: Self-Authenticating Insular Charters* (Dublin 1999).

————, *Cambro-Latin Compositions: Their Competence and Craftsmanship* (Dublin 1998).

————, *The Celtic Latin Tradition of Biblical Style* (Dublin 1995).

————, *The English Origins of Old French Literature* (Dublin 1996).

————, 'Enigma variations', *Ad Familiares: The Jnl of Friends of the Classics* 16 (1999) xi–xii.

————, 'Five experiments in textual reconstruction and analysis', *Peritia* 9 (1995) 1–50.

————, 'Gematria, number and name in Anglo-Norman', *French Studies Bulletin* 60.4 (2006) 90–2.

————, 'Hellenic learning in Insular Latin: an essay on supported claims', *Peritia* 12 (1998) 54–78.

————, 'Hiberno-Latin poems in the Book of Cerne', *Peritia* 15 (2001) 1–21.

————, 'Insular acrostics, Celtic Latin colophons', *CMCS* 35 (1998) 27–44.

————, *Insular Inscriptions* (Dublin 2006).

————, 'Insular Latin writers' rhythms', *Peritia* 11 (1997) 53–116.

————, 'A miracle of Maedoc', *Peritia* 16 (2002), 85–93.

————, 'Miscouplings in couplets' and 'Singers' ratios in *Rauca Sonora*', *Archivum Latinitatis Medii Aevi* 55 (1997) 271–76 and 277–80.

————, 'Numerical play in Wulfstan's verse and prose', *Mittellateinisches Jahrbuch* 31 (1996) 61–67.

————, '*Orationes Moucani*: early Cambro-Latin prayers', *CMCS* 24 (1992) 55–74.

————, 'The polyphonic colophon to Cormac's Psalter', *Peritia* 9 (1995) 81–90.

————, 'The prophecy of Saxon occupation in Gildas *De Excidio Britanniae*', *Peritia* 16 (2002) 156–60.

————, '*Rubisca*: an edition, translation, and commentary', *Archivum Latinitatis Medii Aevi* 9 (1995) 71–90.

————, 'Seven Studies in seventh-century texts', *Peritia* 10 (1996) 1–70.

————, 'Sixes and sevens in Anglo-Latin prologues', *Mittellateinisches Jahrbuch* 35 (2000) 49–70.

————, 'Some criteria for editing Abaelard' *Archivum Latinitatis Medii Aevi* 51 (1993) 195–202.

————, 'The structure of the *Liber Angeli*', *Peritia* 12 (1998) 254–70.

————, '*Synodus Prima Sancti Patricii*: an exercise in textual reconstruction', *Peritia* 12 (1998) 238–53.

————, 'Two works of Saint Columban', *Mittellateinisches Jahrbuch* 28 (1994 for 1993) 27–46.

HUGHES, A., *Medieval Manuscripts for Mass and Office: a Guide to their Organization and Terminology* (Toronto 1982).

HUGHES, K., *Celtic Britain in the Early Middle Ages* (Woodbridge 1980).

HUGHES, T.O., 'Continuity and conversion: the concept of a national church in twentieth-century Wales and its relation to "the Celtic Church" ', in Pope (ed.), *Religion and National Identity*, 123–138.

————, ' "No longer will we call ourselves Catholics in Wales but Welsh Catholics": Roman Catholicism, the Welsh language and Welsh national identity in the Twentieth Century', *WHR* 20 (2000) 336–65.

————, *Winds of Change. The Roman Catholic Church and Society in Wales 1916–1962* (Cardiff 1999).

HURRY, J.B., *Reading Abbey* (London 1901).

HUWS, D., 'Llyfr Melangell: ail-greu llyfr defosiynol', *Llên Cymru* 25 (2002) 21–7.

———, *Medieval Welsh Manuscripts* (Cardiff 2000).

INNES, C. (ed.), *Registrum Episcopatus Moraviensis e pluribus codicibus consarcinatum circa A.D. MCCCC*, Bannatyne Club, 58 (Edinburgh, 1837).

IRIEN, J. an, 'Piou eo sant Ywi (Ivy)?', *Minihi Levenez* (Lent 1990) 5–8.

ISAAC, G.R., '*Trawsganu Cynan Garwyn mab Brochfael*: a tenth-century political poem', *Zeitschrift für celtische Philologie* 51 (1999) 173–85.

———, *The Verb in the Book of Aneirin: Studies in Syntax, Morphology and Etymology* (Tübingen 1996).

ISAACSON, R.F. (ed. and transl.), *Episcopal Registers of St. David's 1397–1518*, 3 vols (London 1917–20).

IVES, E.W., *Anne Boleyn* (Oxford 1986)

JACKSON, K.H., 'The Idnert Inscription: date, and significance of ID–', *BBCS* 19 (1962) 232–4.

———, *Language and History in Early Britain* (Edinburgh 1953).

JAMES, Christine, 'Llyfr cyfraith o Ddyffryn Teifi: disgrifiad o BL, Add. 22,356', *NLWJ* 27 (1991–2) 383–404.

JAMES, H., 'The Cult of St David in the Middle Ages', in Carver (ed.), *In Search of Cult*, 105–11; reprinted in *Jnl of the Pembrokeshire Historical Soc.* 7 (1996–7) 5–25.

——— (ed.), *Sir Gâr: Studies in Carmarthenshire History. Essays in memory of W.H. Morris and M.C.S. Evans* (Carmarthen 1991).

JAMES, J.W., 'A history of the origin and development of the Celtic Church in Wales between the years 450 AD and 630 AD', unpublished DD dissertation (Durham 1931).

——— (ed.), *Rhigyfarch's Life of Saint David* (Cardiff 1967).

———, 'The Welsh version of Rhigyfarch's Life of St David', *NLWJ* 9 (1955) 1–21.

JAMES, M.R., *A Descriptive Catalogue of the Manuscripts in the Library of Corpus Christi College Cambridge* (Cambridge 1912).

JAMES, T.A., 'Air photography of ecclesiastical sites in south Wales' in Edwards and Lane (edd.) *The Early Church*, 62–76.

———, 'The bishop's palace and collegiate church, Abergwili', *Carmarthenshire Antiquary* 16 (1980) 19–43.

———, 'Excavations at the Augustinian priory of St John and St Teulyddog, Carmarthen 1979', *Arch. Camb.* 134 (1985) 120–61.

JANICKE, K. and H. HOOGEWEG (ed.), *Urkundenbuch des Hochstifts Hildesheim und seiner Bischöfe*, 6 vols (Hanover 1896–1911).

JANKULAK, K., *The Medieval Cult of St Petroc* (Woodbridge 2000).

JENKINS, D.E., *The Life of Thomas Charles BA of Bala* (Denbigh 1908).

JENKINS, D. and M.E. OWEN, 'The Welsh marginalia in the Lichfield Gospels, Part I and Part II: The "Surexit" memorandum', *CMCS* 5 (1983) 37–66 and 7; (1984) 91–120.

JENKINS, G.H., 'The established church and dissent in eighteenth-century Cardiganshire', in Jenkins and Jones (edd.), *Cardiganshire County History,* Vol. 3, 453–77.

——— and I.G. JONES (edd.), *Cardiganshire in Modern Times, Cardiganshire County History,* Vol. III Cardiff 1998).

JENKINS, J.G., *Maritime Heritage: the Ships and Seamen of Southern Ceredigion* (Llandysul 1982).

JENKINS, R.T. (ed.), *Y Bywgraffiadur Cymreig (*London 1953).

JENKINSON, J.B., *A Charge delivered to the Clergy of the Diocese of St David's* (London 1828).

JOHANEK, P., 'Ein Brief zur Geschichte des Würzburger Domkapitels im 12. Jahrhundert', *Mainfränkisches Jahrbuch für Geschichte und Kunst* 26 (1974), 24–34.

———, 'Die Pariser Statuten des Bischofs Odo von Sully und die Anfänge der kirchlichen Statutengesetzgebung in Deutschland', in Linehan (ed.) *Proceedings of the Seventh International Congress of Medieval Canon Law*, 327–47.

JOHN, T. and N. REES, *Pilgrimage: A Welsh Perspective* (Llandysul 2002).

JOHNSTON, Dafydd (ed.), *Gwaith Lewys Glyn Cothi* (Cardiff 1995).

JONES, A.H.M., J.R. MARTINDALE and J. MORRIS, *Prosopography of the Later Roman Empire (260–641)*, 3 vols (Cambridge 1971–1992)

JONES, B. (ed.), *Fasti Ecclesiae Anglicanae 1300–1541, The Welsh Dioceses*, XI (London 1965).

JONES, C.W. (ed.), *Bedae Venerabilis Opera Pars VI Opera Didascalica II, Corpus Christianorum Series Latina* CXXIIIB (Turnholt 1977).

JONES, D. Gwenallt, *Eples* (Llandysul 1951).

JONES, G.R., 'Post-Roman Wales' in Finberg (ed.), *The Agrarian History*, 279–382.

JONES, Graham, 'Comparative research rewarded: religious dedications in England, Wales and Catalunya', in Jones (ed.), *Saints of Europe*, 210–260.

———, 'Diverse expressions, shared meanings: surveying saints in the context of 'European culture', in Jones (ed.), *Saints of Europe*, 1–28.

——— (ed.), *Saints of Europe: Studies towards a Survey of Cults and Culture* (Donington 2003).

JONES, G.P. and Hugh OWEN (edd.), *Caernarvon Court Rolls, 1361–1400* (Caernarfon 1951).

JONES, Howell Ll. and E.I. ROWLANDS (edd.) *Gwaith Iorwerth Fynglwyd* (Cardiff 1975).

JONES, Lisa Eryl, 'Golygiad o Fuchedd Gwenfrewy', unpublished MPhil. thesis (University of Wales Cardiff, 2000).

JONES, N.A., 'The Mynydd Carn "prophecy": a reassessment', *CMCS* 38 (1999) 73–92.

——— and M.E. OWEN, 'Twelfth-century Welsh hagiography: the *Gogynfeirdd* poems to saints', in Cartwright (ed.) *Celtic Hagiography*, 45–76.

——— and H. PRYCE (edd.), *Yr Arglwydd Rhys* (Cardiff 1996).

JONES, O.W., 'The mountain clergyman: his education and training', in Jones and Walker (edd.), *Links with the Past*, 165–84.

———, 'The Welsh church in the eighteenth century', in Walker (ed.), *A History*, 103–20.

——— and D. WALKER (edd.), *Links with the Past: Swansea and Brecon Historical Essays* (Llandybie 1974).

JONES, Theophilus, *A History of the County of Brecon*, enlarged edition, 4 vols (Brecknock 1909–30).

JONES, Thomas (ed. and transl.) *Brenhinedd y Saesson, or, The Kings of the Saxons. BM Cotton MS. Cleopatra B.v. and The Black Book of Basingwerk, NLW MS. 7006* (Cardiff 1971).

——— (ed.) *Brut y Tywysogyon, Peniarth MS. 20* (Cardiff 1941).

——— (ed. and transl.) *Brut y Tywysogyon, or, The Chronicle of the Princes. Red Book of Hergest Version* (Cardiff 1955, 2nd ed., Cardiff 1973).

——— (transl.) *Brut y Tywysogyon, or, The Chronicle of the Princes. Peniarth MS. 20 Version* (Cardiff 1952).

——— (ed.) ' "Cronica de Wallia" and other documents from Exeter Cathedral Library MS. 3514', *BBCS* 12 (1946–8) 27–44.

———, '*llyfrawr < librarius*', *BBCS* 11 (1944) 137–38.

———, Review of J.W. James, *Rhigyfarch's Life, Studia Celtica* 3 (1968) 156–7.

JONES W.B. and E.A. FREEMAN, *The History and Antiquities of St. David's* (London 1856).

JONES, W.H. Rich (ed.), *The Register of St Osmund*, 2 vols, Rolls Series XXVIII (London 1883–4).

KAIN, R.J.P. and R.R. OLIVER, *Historic Parishes of England and Wales: An Electronic Map of Boundaries before 1850 with a Gazetteer and Metadata* (Colchester 2001).

KEBLE, J., *The Life of Thomas Wilson* (Oxford 1863).

KELLY, K.C., *Performing Virginity and Testing Chastity in the Middle Ages* (London 2000).

KEMP, B.R. (ed.), *English Episcopal Acta*, 18, *Salisbury 1078–1217* (Oxford 1999).

——— (ed.), *English Episcopal Acta*, 19, *Salisbury 1217–1228* (Oxford 2000).

KER, N.R. (Vol. 4 with A.J. PIPER) *Medieval Manuscripts in British Libraries*, 5 vols (Oxford 1969—2002).

KERSHAW, P., 'Illness, power and prayer in Asser's *Life of King Alfred*', *Early Medieval Europe* 10 (2001) 201–24.

KEYNES, S.D., 'On the authenticity of Asser's Life of King Alfred', *Journal of Ecclesiastical History* 47 (1996) 529–51

———, and M. LAPIDGE. (transl.) *Alfred the Great. Asser's Life of King Alfred and other contemporary sources* (Harmondsworth 1983).

KING, R.J., *Handbook to the Cathedrals of Wales*, 2nd edn (London 1887).

KIRBY, D.P., 'Asser and his Life of King Alfred', *Studia Celtica* 6 (1971) 12–35.

KISSOCK, J., ' "God made nature and men made towns": post-Conquest and pre-Conquest villages in Pembrokeshire', in Edwards (ed.), *Landscape and Settlement*, 127–129.

KNIGHT, J.K., 'The early Church in Gwent, II: the early medieval Church', *Monmouthshire Antiquary*, 9 (1993) 1–17.

———, 'Late Roman and Post-Roman Caerwent; some evidence from metalwork', *Arch. Camb.* 145 (1996) 34–66.

KNOWLES, D. and H. Bettenson (edd. and transl.) *Augustine: City of God* (Harmondsworth 1972).

KRUSCH, B. and W. LEVISON (edd.), *Passiones Vitaeque Sanctorum aevi Merovingici, Monumenta Germaniae Historica: Scriptores Merovingicarum*, IV–VI (Hanover 1902–10).

LAPIDGE, M., 'The hermeneutic style in tenth-century Anglo-Latin literature', *Anglo-Saxon England* 4 (1975) 67–111; reprinted in Lapidge, *Anglo-Latin Literature*, 105–49.

———, 'The Welsh-Latin Poetry of Sulien's Family', *Studia Celtica* 8/9 (1973–74) 68–106.

——— and M. HERREN (transl.), *Aldhelm: The Prose Works* (Ipswich 1979).

——— and Richard SHARPE, *A Bibliography of Celtic-Latin Literature 400–1200*, Royal Irish Academy Dictionary of Medieval Latin from Celtic Sources, Ancillary Publications I (Dublin 1985).

———, *Anglo-Latin Literature* (London 1993)

LARGILLIÈRE, *Les saints et l'organisation chrétienne primitive dans l'Armorique bretonne* (Rennes 1925).

LAURENT, C. and H. DAVIS (edd.), *Irlande et Bretagne, vingt siècles d'histoire* (Rennes 1994).

LE BERRE, A., *Toponymie nautique de la côte sud du Finistère. Première partie: De Quimperlé à Beg-Meil* (Paris 1960).

———, *Toponymie nautique de la côte sud du Finistère. Deuxième partie: De Beg-Meil à Audierne* (Paris 1961).

LE BERRE, Yves (ed. and transl.), 'Buez santes nonn had ez map deuy', in Le Berre *et al.* (edd.), *Buez santez Nonn*, 113–94.

———, Bernard TANGUY and Yves-Pascal CASTEL, *Buez Santez Nonn. Vie de sainte Nonne. Mystère breton* (Minihi-Levenez 1999).

LE DUC, Dom P., *Histoire de l'abbaye de Sainte-Croix de Quimperlé* (Quimperlé n.d.).

LE GRAND, Albert, *Vies des saints de la Bretagne Armorique* (Nantes 1637).

———, *Vies des saints de la Bretagne Armorique*, rev. ed. (Quimper 1901).

LE GUEN, Abbé, 'Antiquités du Léon et plus spécialement du canton de Plabennec', *Bulletin de la Société archéologique du Finistère* 15 (1888) 125–68.

LE NEVE, John (ed.), *Fasti Ecclesiae Anglicanae 1300–1541*, new edn by J.M. Horn *et al.*, 12 vols (London 1962–7).

——— (ed.), *Fasti Ecclesiae Anglicanae 1066–1300*, new edn by D.E. Greenway *et al.*, 9 vols (London 1968–).

LEHMBERG, S.E., *The Reformation Parliament, 1529–36* (Cambridge 1970).

LEROQUAIS, V., *Les bréviaires manuscrits des bibliothèques publiques en France* (Paris 1934).

Letters and Papers, Foreign and Domestic, of the Reign of Henry VIII ..., 23 vols (London 1862–1932).

LETHBRIDGE, T.C. and H.E. DAVID, 'Excavation of a house-site on Gateholm, Pembrokeshire', *Arch. Camb.* 85 (1930) 366–74.

LEWES, E., 'Image of St Non, at Llanon, Cardiganshire', *Arch. Camb.* Sixth Series 19 (1919) 32–33.

LEWIS, F.R., *A Short History of the Church of Llanbadarn Fawr* (Aberystwyth 1937).

LEWIS, Henry (ed.) *Cywyddau Iolo Goch ac Eraill* (Cardiff 1937).

LEWIS, J.M., 'A survey of the early Christian monuments west of the Taf', in Boon and Lewis (edd.), *Welsh Antiquity* (Cardiff 1976), 177–92.

LEWIS, Mostyn, *Stained Glass in North Wales up to 1850* (Altrincham 1970).

LEWIS, Saunders, 'Damcaniaeth Eglwys Brotestannaidd', in *idem, Meistri'r Canrifoedd* (Cardiff 1973).

LINEHAN, P. (ed.), *Proceedings of the Seventh International Congress of Medieval Canon Law*, Monumenta Iuris Canonici, series C, Subsidia vol. 8 (Vatican City 1988).

LLOYD, J.E., 'The age of the native princes', in Lloyd (ed.), *A History of Carmarthenshire*, I.113–200.

———, 'Bishop Sulien and his family', *NLWJ* 2 (1941) 1–6.

———, 'Boundaries and local divisions', in Lloyd (ed.) *A History of Carmarthenshire*, I.5–15.

——— (ed.) *A History of Carmarthenshire*, 2 vols (Cardiff 1935–9).

———, *A History of Wales from the Earliest Times to the Edwardian Conquest* 2 vols (London 1911); 3rd edn (London 1939).

———, *The Story of Ceredigion* (Cardiff 1937).

———, 'Wales and the coming of the Normans (1039–1093)', *Transactions of the Honourable Soc. of Cymmrodorion* (1899–1900) 122–79.

LLOYD-MORGAN, G., 'The artefacts', in Ward *et al.*, *Excavations at Chester*, p. 27.

LORD, P., *Words with Pictures: Welsh Images and Images of Wales in the Popular Press* (Aberystwyth 1995).

LOT, F., *Mélanges d'histoire bretonne (VIe-XIe siècle)* (Paris 1907).

LOTH, J., 'Les anciennes litanies des saints de Bretagne', *Revue celtique* 11 (1890) 135–51.

———, *Les noms des saints bretons* (Paris 1910).

LOTTIN, R.J.F. (ed.), *Chartularium insignis ecclesiae Cenomannensis quod dicitur Liber Albus capituli* (Le Mans, 1869).

LOVATT, Marie (ed.), *English Episcopal Acta, 20, York 1154–1181* (Oxford 2000).

LOYN, H.R., *The Vikings in Wales* (London 1976).

LUARD, H.R. (ed.), *Annales Monastici,* 5 vols, Roll Series XXXVI (London 1864–69).

LUDLOW, N., 'Early medieval ecclesiastical sites project: 2. Pembrokeshire: gazetteer of sites', unpublished Cambria Archaeology Report 2003/39.

———, 'Early medieval ecclesiastical sites project stage 2: assessment and fieldwork in Ceredigion, Part 1: overview' unpublished Cambria Archaeology Report 2004/31.

———, 'St Cristiolus' churchyard, Eglwyswrw, Pembrokeshire: a post-Conquest cist cemetery', *Arch. Camb.* 149 (2000) 20–48.

———, 'Spiritual and temporal: church building in medieval and later Carmarthenshire', *Carmarthenshire Antiquary* 36 (2000) 71–86.

MAC AIRT, S. (ed.), *The Annals of Inisfallen* (Dublin 1951).

MAC MATHÚNA, S., 'Contributions to a study of the Voyages of Saint Brendan and Saint Malo', in Laurent and Davis (edd.), *Irlande et Bretagne*, 40–55.

MACHIN, G.I.T., 'A Welsh church rates fracas: Aberystwyth 1832–3', *WHR* 6 (1972–3) 462–8

MACQUARRIE, A., *The Saints of Scotland. Essays in Scottish Church History AD 450–1093* (Edinburgh 1997)

MAÎTRE, L., and P. DE BERTHOU (edd.), *Cartulaire de l'abbaye de Sainte-Croix de Quimperlé* (Rennes 1904).

MALDEN, H.E., 'The possession of Cardigan Priory by Chertsey Abbey', *Trans. Roy. Hist. Soc.* 5 (1911) 141–56.

MANIACI, M. and P.F. MUNAFÒ (edd.), *Ancient and medieval book materials and techniques* (Vatican City 1993).

MATHER, F.C., *High Church Prophet: Bishop Samuel Horsley (1733–1806) and the Caroline Tradition in the Late Georgian Church* (Oxford 1992).

MAUND, K.L., *Ireland, Wales, and England in the Eleventh Century* (Woodbridge 1991).

MAYR-HARTING, H. (ed.), *The Acta of the Bishops of Chichester, 1075–1207*, Canterbury and York Society 56 (Torquay 1964).

MCFADGEN, B.G., 'Dating New Zealand archaeology by radiocarbon', *New Zealand Jnl of Science* 25 (1982) 379–92.

MCKEE, H. and J., 'Counter arguments and numerical patterns in early Celtic inscriptions: a re-examination of *Christian Celts: Messages and Images*', *Medieval Archaeology* 46 (2002) 29–40.

METZGER, B. M., *The Text of the New Testament* (Oxford 1960); 3rd edn (Oxford 1992).

MILLER, M., 'Date-guessing and Dyfed', *Studia Celtica* 12/13 (1977/78) 33–61.

MILLET, H. (ed.), *Fasti Ecclesiae Gallicanae*, 6 vols to date (Turnhout 1996–).

MONTFORT, R., *Penmarc'h à travers ses historiens* (Penmarc'h 1985).

MOORE-COLYER, R., *Welsh Cattle Drovers* (Ashbourne 2002).

MORGAN, D. Densil, *The Span of the Cross. Christian Religion and Society in Wales 1914–2000* (Cardiff 1999).

MORGAN, D.L., *The Great Awakening in Wales* (London 1988).

MORGAN, Kathleen M., 'An edition of the cartulary of Leominster Priory up to the mid-thirteenth century' (MA thesis, University of Wales, Cardiff 1972).

MORGAN, N., 'The introduction of the Sarum Calendar into the dioceses of England in the thirteenth century', in Prestwich *et al.* (edd.), *Thirteenth Century England VIII*, 179–206.

MORGAN, R. and R.F. Peter POWELL, *A Study of Breconshire Place-Names* (Llanrwst 1999).

MORGAN, W.T., 'The diocese of St David's in the nineteenth century: the unreformed church', *Jnl of the Historical Soc. of the Church in Wales* 21 (1971) 5–49; 22 (1972) 12–48.

MORGAN-GRIFFITHS, C.H., *Chapel of Our Lady and St Non* (privately printed 1934).

MORGAN-GUY, J., 'The Society of St David. Some Reflections on its history', *Verbum. The Termly Magazine of the University Chapel of St David, University of Wales, Lampeter*, Easter Term 2000 (unpaginated).

———— and W.G. NEELY (edd.), *Contrasts and Comparisons: Studies in Irish and Welsh Church History* (Welshpool 1999).

MORRIS, J. (ed.), *Arthurian Sources* 6 vols (Chichester 1995).

————, 'The dates of the Celtic saints', *Journal of Theological Studies* 17 (1966) 342–91.

MORRIS, J.E., *The Welsh Wars of Edward I* (Oxford 1901 and 1968).

MORRIS, R., *Churches in the Landscape* (London 1989).

MULDER-BAKKER, A.B. (ed.), *Sanctity and Motherhood: Essays on Holy Mothers in the Middle Ages* (New York 1995).

MULLALLY, E. (ed.), *The Deeds of the Normans in Ireland. La Geste des Engleis en Yrlande. A New Edition of the Chronicle formerly known as The Song of Dermot and the Earl* (Dublin 2002).

MULLER, S. (ed.), *Het oudste cartularium van het Sticht Utrecht* (The Hague 1892).

————, A.C. BOUMAN, K. HEERINGA and F. KETNER (edd.), *Oorkondenboek van het Sticht Utrecht tot 1300*, 5 vols (Utrecht 1920–59).

MURPHY, K., 'Excavations at Llanychllwydog Church, Dyfed', *Arch. Camb.* 136 (1987) 77–93.

MYNORS, R.A.B. and R.M. THOMSON, *A Descriptive Catalogue of the Manuscripts of Hereford Cathedral Library*, 2 vols (Woodbridge 1993).

————, R.M. THOMSON, and M. WINTERBOTTOM (edd.), *William of Malmesbury, Gesta regum Anglorum* (Oxford 1998–9).

NASH-WILLIAMS, V.E., *The Early Christian Monuments of Wales* (Cardiff 1950).

NEWELL, *A Popular History of the Ancient British Church* (London 1887).

NOKES, L.D.M., W. EVANS, B.H. KNIGHT and C. DENT, 'Observation on the recent examination of bones from St David's Cathedral', *Medicine Science and the Law* 40.1 (2000) 66–70.

NOURRY, A., 'Les Manoirs des Xve et XVIe siècles au coeur du Léon' (Maîtrise d'Histoire, Brest, Université de Bretagne Occidentale 1997).

Ó CORRÁIN, D. (ed.), *Irish Antiquity: Studies Presented to Professor M.J. O'Kelly* (Cork 1981)

Ó RIAIN, P., 'Hagiography without frontiers: borrowing of saints across the Irish Sea', in Walz (ed.), *Scripturus Vitam*, 41–8.

———, 'The Irish element in Welsh hagiographical tradition', in Ó Corráin (ed.), *Irish Antiquity*, 291–303.

———, 'Irish saints' genealogies', *Nomina* 7 (1983) 23–29.

———, *The Making of a Saint: Finbarr of Cork 600–1200* (London 1997).

———, 'The Saints of Cardiganshire', in Davies and Kirby (edd.), *From Earliest Times*, I.378–96.

———, 'The Tallaght martyrologies, redated', *CMCS* 20 (1990) 21–38

———, 'Towards a methodology in early Irish hagiography', *Peritia* 1 (1982) 146–60.

O'BRIEN, E., 'Pagan and Christian burial in Ireland during the first millenium AD: continuity and change', in Edwards and Lane (edd.), *The Early Church*, 130–7.

O'LOUGHLIN, T., *Celtic Theology* (London 1999).

———, 'One island, one people, one nation: early Latin evidence for this motif in Ireland,' *Institute of Technology Blanchardstown Journal* 4 (2001) 4–13.

———, 'Rhygyfarch's *Vita Dauidis*: an *apparatus biblicus*', *Studia Celtica*, 32 (1998), 179–88.

OGILVY, J.D.A., *Books Known to the English, 597–1066* (Cambridge MA 1967).

OKASHA, E., 'A new inscription from Ramsey Island', *Arch. Camb.* 99 (1970) 68–72.

———, *Corpus of Early Christian Inscribed Stones of South-west Britain* (London 1993).

OLSON, B.L. and O.J. PADEL, 'A tenth-century list of Cornish parochial saints', *CMCS* 12 (1986) 33–71.

ORME, N., 'A fifteenth-century prayer-book from Cornwall: MS NLW 22253A', *Jnl of the Royal Institution of Cornwall* NS 2, 3.2 (1999) 69–73.

———, *Nicholas Roscarrock's Lives of the Saints: Cornwall and Devon* (Exeter 1992).

———, *The Saints of Cornwall* (Oxford 2000).

ORMROD, W.M. (ed.), *England in the Thirteenth Century* (Harlaxton 1985).

ORPEN, G.H. (ed.), *The Song of Dermot and the Earl* (Oxford 1892).

OWEN, E., 'An episode in the history of Clynnog church', *Y Cymmrodor* 19 (1906) 68–88.

OWEN, H. (ed.), *The Description of Penbrokshire by George Owen of Henllys, Lord of Kemes*, 2 vols (London 1892–1936).

———, *Gerald the Welshman* (London 1904).

OWEN, M.E., 'Canu i Ddewi', in Bramley (ed.), *Gwaith Llywelyn Fardd*, 435–478.

——— (ed.), 'Gwaith Phylip Brydydd', in Costigan *et al.* (edd.), *Gwaith Dafydd Benfras*, 159–233.

———, 'Prolegomena i astudiaeth lawn o lsgr. NLW 3026, Mostyn 88, a'i harwyddocâd', in Daniel *et al.* (edd.), *Cyforth y testun*, pp. 349–84.

———, 'Prolegomena to a study of the historical context of Gwynfardd Brycheiniog's Poem to Dewi', *Studia Celtica* 26/7 (1991–2) 51–79.

PADEL, O.J., 'Local saints and place-names in Cornwall', in Thacker and Sharpe (edd.) *Local Saints*, 303–60.

———, *A Popular Dictionary of Cornish Place-Names* (Penzance 1988).

PAGE, N.A. and R.P. SAMBROOK, 'Dinefwr historic settlements project: gazetteer', unpublished Cambria Archaeology Report 29799.

PARRY-WILLIAMS, T. H. (ed.) *Rhyddiaith Gymraeg: Y Gyfrol Gyntaf Detholion o Lawysgrifau 1488–1609* (Cardiff 1979).

PEARSON, M.J., 'The creation of the Bangor cathedral chapter', *WHR* 20 (2000) 167–81.

————, 'The creation and development of the St Asaph cathedral chapter, 1141–1293', *CMCS* 40 (2000) 35–56.

———— (ed.), *Fasti Ecclesiae Anglicanae 1066–1300*, IX, *The Welsh Cathedrals* (London 2003).

PERROTT, R. 'The tomb of Ste. Nonne, at Dirinon, in Britanny [sic.]', *Arch. Camb.* 8 (1857), 249–58.

PETERSEN, J., *British Antiquities of the Viking Period, found in Norway*, in H. Shetelig (ed.), *Viking Antiquities in Great Britain and Ireland*, Part V (Oslo 1940).

PEYRON, Chanoine P., *L'abbaye de Daoulas* (Quimper: no date).

PFAFF, R. W., *New Liturgical Feasts in Later Medieval England* (Oxford 1970).

PHILLIMORE, E. (ed.), 'The *Annales Cambriæ* and Old-Welsh genealogies from *Harleian MS.* 3859', *Y Cymmrodor*, 9 (1888), 141–83.

PHILLIPS, J., *The History of Pembrokeshire* (London 1909).

PLUMMER, Carolus (ed.), *Vitae Sanctorum Hiberniae*, 2 vols (Oxford 1910).

POPE, R. (ed.), *Religion and National Identity. Wales and Scotland c. 1700–2000* (Cardiff 2001).

POWICKE, F.M. and C.R. CHENEY (edd.), *Councils and Synods with Other Documents Relating to the English Church, II, 1205–1313*, 2 vols (Oxford 1964).

PRESTWICH, Michael, 'The piety of Edward I', in Ormrod (ed.), *England*, 120–8.

————, R. BRITNELL and R. FRAME (edd.), *Thirteenth Century England VIII* (Woodbridge 2001).

PRICE, D.T.W., *Bishop Burgess and Lampeter College* (Cardiff 1987).

————, *History of St David's University College, Lampeter: vol I to 1898* (Cardiff 1977).

PROCTER, F. and C. WORDSWORTH (edd.), *Breviarium ad usum insignis ecclesiae Sarum*, 3 vols (Cambridge 1879–86).

PRYCE, H., 'Church and society in Wales, 1150–1250: an Irish perspective', in Davies (ed.), *The British Isles*, 27–47.

————, 'Esgobaeth Bangor yn oes y tywysogion', in Griffith (ed.) *'Ysbryd Dealltwrus'*, 37–57.

———— (ed.), *Literacy in Medieval Celtic Societies* (Cambridge 1998).

————, *Native Law and the Church in Medieval Wales* (Oxford 1993).

————, 'Negotiating Anglo-Welsh relations: Llywelyn the Great and Henry III', in Weiler with Rowlands (edd.), *England and Europe*, 13–29.

————, 'Pastoral care in early medieval Wales' in Blair and Sharpe (edd.) *Pastoral Care*, 41–62.

———— with the assistance of INSLEY, C. (ed.), *The Acts of Welsh Rulers, 1120–1283* (Cardiff 2005).

PUGH, T.B. (ed.), *The Middle Ages*, Glamorgan County History Vol. III (Cardiff 1971).

RAMSEY, F.M.R. (ed.), *English Episcopal Acta*, X, *Bath and Wells 1061–1205* (Oxford 1995).

REDKNAP, M., 'An early medieval ringed pin and a medieval brooch from Swansea Bay', *Morgannwg* 44 (2000) 136–140.

————, *Vikings in Wales: an Archaeological Quest* (Cardiff 2000).

————, 'Viking-age settlement in Wales and the evidence from Llanbedrgoch on Anglesey', Hines, *et al.* (edd.), *Land, Sea and Home*, 139–75.

———— and A. LANE, 'Llangorse Crannog–interim excavation reports', *Medieval Archaeology* 33–37 (1989–93) and *Archaeology in Wales* 29–32 (1989–92).

REYNOLDS, L.D., *Texts and Transmission, A Survey of the Latin Classics* (Oxford 1983, corr. rept 1986).

REES, D., 'The Changing Borders of Iscennen', *Carmarthenshire Antiquary* 24 (1988) 15–21.

REES, John Lambert, *Sermons and Hymns by Timothy Rees, Bishop of Llandaff* (London 1946)

————, *Timothy Rees of Mirfield and Llandaff* (London 1945).

REES, Nona, *The Medieval Shrines of St David's Cathedral* (St Davids 1998).

REES, Rice, *An Essay on the Welsh Saints or the Primitive Christians usually considered to be the founders of churches in Wales* (London 1836).

REES, W., *South Wales and the Borders in the Fourteenth Century* (Ordnance Survey Maps 1932).

REES, W.J. (ed.), *Lives of the Cambro-British Saints* (Llandovery 1853).

REMFRY, P.M., 'Cadwallon ap Madog Rex de Delvain 1140–1179 and the reestablishment of local autonomy in Cynllibwg' *Radnorshire Soc. Transactions* 65 (1995) 11–32.

REVELL, Elizabeth (ed.), *The Later Letters of Peter of Blois*, Auctores Britannici Medii Aevi XIII (Oxford 1993).

RHYS, J., *Celtic Folklore: Welsh and Manx* (Oxford 1901).

RICHARDS, Leslie (ed.) *Gwaith Dafydd Llwyd o Fathafarn* (Cardiff 1964).

RICHARDS, M., 'Buchedd Fargred', *BBCS* 13 (1949) 65–71.

——, 'The Carmarthenshire possessions of Talyllychau', in Barnes and Yates (edd.), *Carmarthenshire Studies*, 110–21.

——, *Welsh Administrative and Territorial Units* (Cardiff 1969).

RICHMOND, C. and HARVEY, I. (edd.) *Recognitions: Essays presented to Edmund Fryde* (Aberystwyth 1996).

RICHTER, M. (ed.), *Canterbury Professions* (Canterbury and York Society, 67; Torquay 1973).

——, 'Canterbury's primacy in Wales and the first stage of Bishop Bernard's opposition', *Jnl of Ecclesiastical History* 22 (1971) 177–89.

——, *Giraldus Cambrensis: The Growth of the Welsh Nation* (Aberystwyth 1972); 2nd edn Aberystwyth, 1976).

——, 'The Life of St David by Giraldus Cambrensis', *WHR* 4 (1968–9) 381–6.

——, 'A new edition of the so-called *Vita Davidis secundi*', *BBCS* 22 (1966–8) 245–9.

ROBERTS, T., 'Welsh ecclesiastical place-names and archaeology', in Edwards and Lane (edd.), *The Early Church*, 41–4.

ROWLANDS, I.W., 'The making of the march: aspects of Norman settlement in Dyfed', in Brown (ed.), *Proceedings of the Battle Conference*, 142–57, 221–5.

RUPP, E.G., *English Protestant Tradition* (Cambridge 1949).

RUSSELL, P. (ed. and transl.), *Vita Griffini Filii Conani* (Cardiff 2005).

SADIE, S. (ed.), *The New Grove Dictionary of Music* (London 1980/2001).

SANDON, N., 'Salisbury ['Sarum'], Use of' in Sadie (ed.), *The New Grove Dictionary of Music, Second edition* (London 2001), vol. 22, 158–63.

—— (ed.), *The Use of Salisbury, The Ordinary of the Mass* (Lustleigh 1984).

SAUNDERS, C., *Rape and Ravishment in the Literature of Medieval England* (Cambridge 2001).

SCHARER, A., 'The writing of history at King Alfred's court', *Early Medieval Europe* 5 (1996) 177–206.

SCOTT, A.B. and F. X. MARTIN (edd.) *Expugnatio Hibernica, The Conquest of Ireland, by Giraldus Cambrensis* (Dublin 1978).

SCOTT, J. (ed.), *The Early History of Glastonbury: an edition, translation and study of William of Malmesbury's* De Antiquitate Glastonie Ecclesie (Woodbridge 1981).

SELMER, C., *Navigatio Sancti Brendani Abbatis from the Earliest Latin Manuscripts* (South Bend, IN 1959).

SHARPE, R., *Adomnán of Iona: Life of St Columba* (Harmondsworth 1995).

——, 'Gildas as a father of the church', in M. Lapidge and D. Dumville (edd.), *Gildas: New Approaches* (Woodbridge 1984), 193–205.

——, *A Handlist of the Latin Writers of Great Britain and Ireland before 1540* (Turnhout 1997).

——, *Medieval Irish Saints' Lives* (Oxford 1991).

—— *et al.*, *English Benedictine Libraries* (London 1996).

SHIRLEY, W.W. (ed.) *Royal and Other Historical Letters Illustrative of the Reign of Henry III from the Originals in the Public Record Office*, 2 vols (London 1862–6).

SIMPSON, W.D., *St Ninian and Christian Origins in Scotland* (Edinburgh 1940).

SIMS-WILLIAMS, P., *The Celtic Inscriptions of Britain: Phonology and Chronology, c.400–1200*, Publications of the Philological Society 37 (Oxford 2003).

———, 'Edward IV's confirmation charter for Clynnog Fawr', in Richmond and Harvey (edd.), *Recognitions*, 229–41.

———,'The five languages of Wales in the pre-Norman inscriptions', *CMCS* 44 (2002) 1–36.

———, 'The provenance of the Llywarch Hen poems: a case for Llan-gors, Brycheiniog', *CMCS* 26 (1993) 28–63.

———, Review of Davies, *The Llandaff Charters*, *Jnl of Ecclesiastical History* 33 (1982) 124–9.

———, Review of D.S. Evans, *The Welsh Life*, *Journal of Ecclesiastical History* 43 (1992) 468–70.

———, 'The uses of writing in early medieval Wales', in Pryce (ed.) *Literacy*, 15–38.

SMITH, David, *'They Did it their Way'. The story of St Martin of Tours, Haverfordwest* (Haverfordwest 1992).

SMITH, David M. (ed.), *The Acta of Hugh of Wells, Bishop of Lincoln 1209–1235*, Lincoln Record Society 88 (Woodbridge 2000).

——— (ed.), *English Episcopal Acta* I, *Lincoln 1067–1185* (Oxford 1980).

——— (ed.), *English Episcopal Acta* IV, *Lincoln 1186–1206* (Oxford 1986).

SMITH, J.B. 'The "Cronica de Wallia" and the dynasty of Dinefwr', *BBCS* 20 (1963–4) 261–82.

———, 'Dynastic succession in medieval Wales', *BBCS* 33 (1986) 199–232.

———, *Llywelyn ap Gruffudd, Prince of Wales* (Cardiff 1998).

———, 'Magna Carta and the charters of the Welsh princes', *English Historical Review* 99 (1984) 344–62.

———, 'Treftadaeth Deheubarth', in Jones and Pryce (edd.) *Yr Arglwydd Rhys*, 18–52.

———, and B.H. St. J. O'NEIL, *Talley Abbey, Carmarthenshire*, 2nd impression (London 1970).

——— and T.B. PUGH, 'The lordship of Gower and Kilvey in the middle ages', in Pugh (ed.), *Glamorgan County History*, 205–65.

SMITH, J.M.H, 'Oral and written: saints, miracles and relics in Brittany c. 850–1250', *Speculum* 65 (1990) 309–43.

SMITH, L.T. (ed.), *The Itinerary in Wales of John Leland in or about 1536–9*, 5 vols (London 1907–10)

SMITH, W.B.S., *De la toponymie bretonne. Dictionnaire étymologique.* Supplement to *Language* 16, no. 2 (April-June 1940).

SOUTHERN, R.W., 'The Canterbury forgeries', *EHR* 73 (1958) 193–226.

SPENSER, Eleanor P., 'The master of the Duke of Bedford: the Salisbury Breviary', *Burlington Magazine* (December 1966) 607–12.

SPURR, J., *The Restoration Church of England, 1646–1689* (New Haven 1991).

STACEY, R., Review of Jankulak, *The Medieval Cult*, *Albion* 34 (2002), 180.

STEVENSON, W.H. (ed.), *Asser's Life of King Alfred* (Oxford 1904).

STOKES, W. (ed. and transl.), *Félire Óengusso Céli Dé: The Martyrology of Oengus the Culdee* (London 1905).

——— (ed.), *Irish Glosses. A Mediaeval Tract on Latin Declension with examples explained in Irish* (Dublin 1860)

——— (ed. and transl.), *Lives of the Saints from the Book of Lismore* (Oxford 1890).

STONEMAN, W.P. (ed.), *Dover Priory*, Medieval Library Catalogues of Great Britain 5 (London 1999).

STRANGE, W.A., 'The rise and fall of a saint's community: Llandeilo Fawr, 600–1200', *Jnl of Welsh Religious History* 2 (2002) 1–18.

STUBBS, W., *Registrum Sacrum Anglicanum*, 2nd edn (London 1897).

STUIVER, M. and H.A. POLACH, 'Discussion: reporting of 14C data', *Radiocarbon* 19 (1977) 355–63.

————, P.J. REIMER, E. BARD, J.W. BECK, G.S. BURR, K.A. HUGHEN, B. KROMER, G. McCORMAC, J. VAN DER PLICHT and M. SPURK, 'INTCAL98 radiocarbon age calibration, 24,000–0 Cal AD', *Radiocarbon* 40 (1998) 1041–83.

TANGUY, Bernard, 'De la Vie de saint Cadoc à celle de saint Gurtiern', *Études celtiques* 26 (1989) 157–85.

————, 'Les cultes de sainte Nonne et de saint Divi en Bretagne', in Le Berre *et al.* (edd.), *Buez santez Nonn*, 10–31 (translated by K. Jankulak as Chapter 10 of this book, above 207–19).

TAYLOR, T. (transl.), *The Life of St Samson of Dol* (London 1925).

THACKER, A.T. and R. SHARPE (edd.), *Local Saints and Local Churches in the Early Medieval West* (Oxford 2002).

THOMAS, C., *And Shall These Mute Stones Speak?: Post-Roman Inscriptions in Western Britain* (Cardiff 1994).

————, *The Early Christian Archaeology of North Britain* (Oxford 1971).

————, 'The Llanddewi-Brefi Idnert Stone' *Peritia* 10 (1996) 136–83.

———— and David HOWLETT (ed. and transl.), '*Vita Sancti Paterni* The Life of Saint Padarn and the Original *Miniu*', *Trivium* 33 (2003), 1–129

THOMAS, D.R., *The History of the Diocese of St Asaph*, 3 vols (Oswestry 1909–13).

THOMAS, G.C.G., 'A lost manuscript of Thomas Saint, archdeacon of St. Davids, 1500–1513', *NLWJ* 24 (1985–6) 309–38.

THOMSON, D., *A Descriptive Catalogue of Middle English Grammatical Texts* (New York and London 1979).

THOMSON, R.M., *Catalogue of the Manuscripts of Lincoln Cathedral Chapter Library* (Woodbridge 1989).

THORPE, L. (transl. and ed.), *Gerald of Wales: The Journey through Wales and The Description of Wales* (London 1978).

TOORIANS, L., 'Wizo Flandrensis and the Flemish settlement in Pembrokeshire', *CMCS* 20 (1990) 99–118.

TOULMIN-SMITH, L. (ed.) *Leland's Itinerary in England and Wales* (London 1964).

TOYNBEE, M.R., *S. Louis of Toulouse and the Process of Canonization in the Fourteenth Century* (Manchester 1929).

TUDUR, G., *Howell Harris: From Conversion to Separation, 1735–1750* (Cardiff 2000).

TURNER, D.H. (ed.), *The Hastings Hours. A 15th-Century Flemish Book of Hours made for William, Lord Hastings now in the British Library* (London 1983).

TURNER, R., 'St Davids bishop's palace, Pembrokeshire', *The Antiquaries Jnl* 80 (2000) 87–194.

————, 'Fish weirs and fish traps' in Davidson (ed.), *The Coastal Archaeology*, 99–100.

TURVEY, R. *The Welsh Princes: The Native Rulers of Wales 1063–1283* (London 2002).

TYACKE, N.R.N., *Anti-Calvinists* (Oxford 1987).

USSHER, James, *Ecclesiarum Britannicarum Antiquitates* (Dublin, 1639).

VALLÉRIE, 'Les références bretonnes et celtiques dans le Martyrologe de l'abbé Chastelain', *Bulletin de la Socété archéologique du Finistère* 110 (1982) 147–70; 112 (1983) 177–224.

[VICTORIA COUNTY HISTORY] *A History of Shropshire*, vol. 2 (Oxford 1973).

WADE-EVANS, A.W., 'The death-years of Dewi Sant and Saint Dubricius', *Anglo-Welsh Review* 10.26 (1960) 63–4.

————, 'Parochiale Wallicanum', *Y Cymmrodor* 22 (1910) 22–124.

————, 'Rhygyvarch's Life of Saint David', *Y Cymmrodor*, 24 (1913) 1–73.

———— (transl.) *Life of St. David* (London 1923).

———— (ed.) *Vitae Sanctorum Britanniae et Genealogiae* (Cardiff 1944).

WAINWRIGHT, G.J., *Coygan Camp: a Prehistoric, Romano-British and Dark Age Settlement in Carmarthenshire,* Cambrian Archaeological Association (Cardiff 1967).

WALKER, D.G. (ed.), *A History of the Church in Wales* (Penarth 1976).

————, *Medieval Wales* (Cambridge 1990).

WALKER, G.S.M. (ed.), *Sancti Columbani Opera*, Scriptores Latini Hibernici 3 (Dublin 1959).

WALKER, R.F., 'Hubert de Burgh and Wales, 1218–1232', *English Historical Review* 87 (1972) 465–94.

———, 'The lordships of Pembrokeshire in the thirteenth and fourteenth centuries', in Walker (ed.), *Medieval Pembrokeshire*, 140–94.

——— (ed.), *Medieval Pembrokeshire: Pembrokeshire County History, Vol. II* (Haverfordwest 2002).

WALSH, Maura and Dáibhí Ó CRÓINÍN (ed. and trans), *Cummian's Letter* De Controuersia Paschali *together with a related Irish computistical tract* De Ratione Conputandi (Toronto 1988).

WALZ, D. (ed.), *Scripturus Vitam: Festgabe für Walter Berschin zum 65. Geburstag* (Heidelberg, 2002).

WARD, S. *et al.*, *Excavations at Chester: Saxon Occupation within the Roman Fortress, Sites excavated 1971–1981, Archaeological Service Excavation and Survey report No.7* (Chester 1991).

WATKINS, T. Arwyn, Review of Evans, *The Welsh Life*, *CMCS* 17 (1989) 89–92.

WATSON, A.G., *A Descriptive Catalogue of the Medieval Manuscripts of All Souls College, Oxford* (Oxford 1997).

WATT, D.E.R., *Medieval Church Councils in Scotland* (Edinburgh 2000).

——— *et al.* (edd.), *Fasti Ecclesiae Scoticanae Medii Aevi ad Annum 1638* revised version Scottish Rec Soc (2003).

WATTS, M.R., *The Dissenters: the Expansion of Evangelical Nonconformity* (Oxford 1995).

WEILER, B.K.U. with I.W. ROWLANDS (edd.) *England and Europe in the Reign of Henry III (1216– 1272)* (Aldershot 2002).

WESTWOOD, J.O., *Lapidarium Walliae: the early inscribed and sculptured stones of Wales* (Oxford 1876–9).

WHARTON, H., *Anglia Sacra,* 2 vols (London 1691).

WHITELOCK, D., *The Genuine Asser*, Stenton Lecture 1967 (Cambridge 1968).

———, R. McKITTERICK and D. DUMVILLE (edd.), *Ireland in Early Mediaeval Europe: Studies in Memory of Kathleen Hughes* (Cambridge 1982).

WIGHT, Marjory, *The Pilgrim's Guide to St David's and its Cathedral* (Gloucester, Crypt House Press, n.d. but pre–1930)

WILKINS, David (ed.), *Concilia magnae Britannicae et Hiberniae* (London 1737).

WILLIAMS, D.H., *Atlas of Cistercian Lands in Wales* (Cardiff 1990).

WILLIAMS, Glanmor, 'Henry de Gower', *Arch. Camb.* 80 (1981) 1–18.

———, *Religion, Language and Nationality in Wales* (Cardiff 1979).

———, 'The tradition of St David in Wales', in Williams, *Religion, Language and Nationality*, 109–26.

———, *Wales and the Reformation* (Cardiff 1997).

———, *The Welsh Church from Conquest to Reformation,* 2nd edn (Cardiff 1976).

———, *Welsh Reformation Essays* (Cardiff 1968).

WILLIAMS, G.J. and E.J. JONES, *Gramadegau'r Penceirddiaid* (Cardiff 1934).

WILLIAMS, Hugh (ed.), *De excidio Britanniae, fragmenta, liber de Paenitentia, accedit et lorica Gildae,* 2 vols (London 1899–1901).

——— (transl.), *Two Lives of Gildas by a Monk of Ruys and Caradoc of Llancarfan* (Felinfach 1990).

WILLIAMS, Ifor (ed.), *Armes Prydein o Lyfr Taliesin* (Cardiff 1955).

———, *The Beginnings of Welsh Poetry* (Cardiff 1980).

——— and Rachel BROMWICH (edd.), *Armes Prydein, The Prophecy of Britain, from the Book Of Taliesin* (Dublin 1982).

WILLIAMS (Ab Ithel), J. (ed. and transl.), *Annales Cambriae* (Rolls Series 20; London 1860).

WILLIAMS, J.E. Caerwyn, Review of J. W. James, *Rhigyfarch's Life*, *WHR* 4 (1968–9) 183–5.

WILLIAMS, Mary, 'Buched Meir Wyry', *Revue celtique*, 33 (1912), 207–38.

WILLIAMS, R., '*Vita Grifini filii Conani'*, *Arch. Camb.* Third Series 12 (1866) 28–45, 112–131.

WILLIS, Browne, *A Survey of the Cathedral Church of St David's and the Edifices Belonging to it, as they stood in the Year 1715* (London 1717).

———, *A Survey of the Cathedral Church of Bangor* (London 1721).

WILLIS-BUND, J.W. (ed.), *The Black Book of St. David's*, Cymmrodorion Record Series, 5 (London 1902).

WILMANS, R. (ed.), *Westfälisches Urkundenbuch*, IV (Münster 1874).

WILSON, Anselm, *The Life of Bishop Hedley* (London 1930).

WILSON, S.E., *The Life and After-life of St John of Beverley* (London 2006).

WINTERBOTTOM, M. (ed.), *Gildas: The* Ruin of Britain *and other Documents* (Chichester 1978).

WMFFRE, Iwan, 'Language and History in Cardiganshire Place-Names', unpublished PhD thesis (University of Wales, Swansea 1998).

WMFFRE, I., *The Place-Names of Cardiganshire* BAR British Series 379, 3 vols (Oxford 2004).

WOGAN-BROWNE, J., 'The virgin's tale', in Evans and Johnson (edd.), *Feminist Readings*, 165–94.

WOODING, J.M. *Communication and Commerce along the Western Sealanes AD 400–800*, BAR International Series 654 (Oxford 1996).

WOODRUFF, C.E., 'Some early professions of canonical obedience to the see of Canterbury', *Transactions of the St Paul's Ecclesiological Soc.*, 7 (1911–15) 161–76.

WORDSWORTH, C., *Ceremonies and Processions of the Cathedral of Salisbury* (Cambridge 1901).

WRIGHT, N., Review of Dumville and Lapidge, *The Annals of St Neots*, *CMCS* 10 (1985) 89–92.

WRIGHT, T. (ed. and transl.), *The Political Songs of England from the Reign of John to that of Edward II*, Camden Society (London 1839).

———, *Three Chapters of Letters relating to the Dissolution of the Monasteries*, Camden Society (London 1843).

YARDLEY, E., *Menevia Sacra*, ed. F. Green (Cardiff 1927).

YATES, W.N., 'The "Age of the Saints" in Carmarthenshire: a study of church dedications', *Carmarthenshire Antiquary* 9 (1973) 53–81.

———, *Buildings, Faith and Worship: the Liturgical Arrangement of Anglican Churches 1600–1900* (Oxford 1991).

———, R. HUME and P. HASTINGS, *Religion and Society in Kent, 1640–1914* (Woodbridge 1994).

INDEX

STUDIES IN CELTIC HISTORY